D1558586

アメリカ・カナダ大学連合日本研究センター
INTER-UNIVERSITY CENTER FOR JAPANESE LANGUAGE STUDIES

KANJI IN CONTEXT

中・上級学習者のための漢字と語彙 ［改訂新版］

[Revised Edition]

A STUDY SYSTEM FOR INTERMEDIATE AND ADVANCED LEARNERS

The Japan Times

Compiled by:	Inter-University Center for Japanese Language Studies
Editors:	Soichi Aoki
	Tamaki Kono
Contributors:	Tomotaro Akizawa
	Soichi Aoki
	Tamaki Kono
	Kiyomi Kushida
	Takashi Matsumoto
	Makiko Ohashi
	Hiroko Otake
	Ari Sato
	Tsukasa Sato
Previous Edition Editors and Contributors:	
	Koichi Nishiguchi
	Tamaki Kono
Translation and Proofreading:	
	James C. Baxter

First edition: December 2013
Second printing: June 2014

Layout design and typesetting: Asahi Media International
Cover design: Keiji Terai
Printing: Tosho Printing Co., Ltd.

Published by The Japan Times, Ltd.
5-4, Shibaura 4-chome, Minato-ku, Tokyo 108-0023, Japan
Phone: 03-3453-2013
http://bookclub.japantimes.co.jp/

ISBN978-4-7890-1529-5

Printed in Japan

はじめに

Kanji in Context —A Study System for Intermediate and Advanced Learners は、1994 年の初版発行以来、中・上級学習者が漢字力を高めるのに最適な教材として大変多くの方々にご好評いただきました。中・上級レベルの学習者にとって、漢字の習得が必要不可欠であることは言うまでもありませんが、特に非漢字圏の学習者にとって、漢字習得の難しさが日本語の上達の上で大きな障害となることが少なくありませんでした。この教材により、多くの中・上級学習者がこの「漢字の壁」を乗り越えることができ、上級レベルの日本語力を身につけたことは、著者としても大きな喜びです。

2010 年、それまでの 1,945 字から 2,136 字へと増補された改定常用漢字表が新たに発表されました。そこで、これに合わせ、新しい常用漢字すべてを盛り込んだ *Kanji in Context* 改訂新版の作成に着手しました。改訂にあたっては、例文、ふりがな、英訳の一つ一つに至るまで全内容を見直すと共に、これまで多くの方々にお使いいただいた中で生まれてきた様々なアイデアを加えました。「中・上級学習者に絞った常用漢字学習のための漢字教材」という従来の基本的なコンセプトを踏襲しつつ、より学習がしやすくなるような工夫を数多く取り入れています。旧版以上にこの教材を活用して、さらに多くの学習者が「漢字の壁」を乗り越えてくれることを願っています。

この教材は、旧版も含め、多くの教員が作成に関わることで初めて実現することができました。教材の完成を、完成に携わったすべての方々と共に喜びたいと思います。また、旧版を熱心に学習し、厳しくも有益なコメントを寄せてくれた多くの本校学生に感謝の意を表したいと思います。そして、今回の改訂版の作成を企画し、細かな注意と忍耐が必要な編集作業を常にバックアップしてくださったジャパンタイムズ日本語出版編集部の関戸千明さん、岡本江奈さんにお礼を申し上げたいと思います。

2013 年 11 月

アメリカ・カナダ大学連合日本研究センター

Preface

Since the publication of its first edition in 1994, *Kanji in Context—A Study System for Intermediate and Advanced Learners* has received high praise from a great many students and instructors of Japanese who regard it as the very best textbook for enhancing intermediate and advanced learners' skills in mastering *kanji*. It hardly needs saying that learning Chinese characters is absolutely essential for intermediate- and advanced-level students of Japanese. But for students who come from outside the cultural sphere where Chinese characters are used, the difficulty of acquiring mastery of these characters has often been a major hindrance to progress. The authors of *Kanji in Context* take great pleasure from the fact that many intermediate- and advanced-level students have been able, by using this textbook, to get over the "wall of Chinese characters" and to achieve highly advanced skills in Japanese.

We commenced work on this revised edition of *Kanji in Context* in 2010, when a revised table of *kanji* for everyday use (*Kaitei Jōyō Kanji Hyō*) was published by the Ministry of Education, Culture, Sports, Science and Technology of Japan, and the number of characters designated for common use was increased to 2,136 from 1,945. In the present edition we have incorporated the changes in the table of *kanji* for everyday use. In addition we carried out a complete, item-by-item review of the content of the first edition of *Kanji in Context*, including sample sentences, use of *furigana*, and English translations, and we implemented ideas that occurred to us after receiving feedback from users of the first edition. While we have inherited and remained faithful to the basic concept that won praise—the creation of a *kanji* textbook specifically for intermediate and advanced students, designed to facilitate learning all the everyday use characters—we have been able, in this new edition, to introduce many innovations that make learning easier than it has been up to now. We hope that this edition will help even more students to get over the "wall of Chinese characters" than the previous edition.

Kanji in Context is the product of the labor of many present and past instructors at the Inter-University Center for Japanese Language Studies, including those who contributed to the making of the first edition. All of us who have been involved in the creation of this textbook share in the joy of its completion. We wish to express our sincere gratitude to Chiaki Sekido and Ena Okamoto of The Japan Times Publications Department, who planned for this revised edition and constantly backed up our editorial work with patience and careful attention to detail.

November 2013

Inter-University Center for Japanese Language Studies

目 次
(Contents)

*　　　　*　　　　*

*　　　　*　　　　*

この教材の内容と使い方

Ⅰ．本教材の概要

Kanji in Context—A Study System for Intermediate and Advanced Learners は、初級のコースを終了した人および中・上級レベルで学習中の人が、それまでに身につけた漢字や語彙の基礎の上に、さらに多くの漢字と語彙を体系的かつ効率的に学び、最終的に常用漢字(2,136字)すべてを理解できるようにするための教材です。本教材は、**本冊**と**ワークブック**の2種類の教材からなっています。

本教材はいくつかの際立った特長を持っています。

☐ 中・上級の学習者に対象を絞り、目標を明確にした教材

本教材は、中・上級の学習者に対象を絞り、学習者が常用漢字すべてを理解できるようになるよう段階的に学習が進められる教材として作成されました。

中・上級に特化した教材のため、初級段階で必要となる基本漢字の字形の学習や日常語彙についてはあまり重視されていません。一方、初級段階で学習する漢字であっても、その読みや語例については、中・上級レベルのものを積極的に導入しています。

また、漠然と習得漢字を増やしていくのではなく、常用漢字すべての理解という到達目標を明確にし、その目標達成のための手順を具体的に提示しています。常用漢字というのは、文部科学省により制定された漢字表で、公文書、新聞、雑誌、書籍など現代日本語を書き表す時の基準とされているものです。日本語母語話者のための学校教育においても、常用漢字の習得が目標とされていることから分かるとおり、日本語母語話者と同等の漢字力と言えます。常用漢字がすべて理解できれば、日本語で書かれた文章に現れる漢字のほぼすべてについて、その読みや意味が推測できるということになります。本教材では、中・上級日本語学習者の漢字学習の最終的な達成目標として相応しいと考えられる「常用漢字すべてのマスター」を設定し、この目標を達成するためのプログラムを具体的に示すこととしました。

☐ 漢字を体系的に学ぶことができる

中級以上の段階では、学習者に要求される漢字と語彙が飛躍的に増加します。それを効率よく習得するためには、一つ一つバラバラに覚えるのではなく、漢字や漢字語彙の背後にある体系にも目を向けながら学習する必要があります。

一般に漢字には、形・音・意味の3つの体系があると言われています。形の体系というのは漢字の字形構成の一般規則のこと、音の体系というのは字形構成素に基づく漢字の読みの共通性や類似

性、そして、意味の体系というのは同じく字形構成素に基づく漢字の意味の成り立ちの体系のことです。

漢字はこれら３つの要素が有機的に絡み合ったものです。このような漢字の体系に関する知識を適切に習得すれば、新しい漢字や語彙の習得を飛躍的に促進すると同時に、知らない漢字や語彙が出てきた時にその意味や読み方を類推できる力がつきます。

漢字の使用頻度等に基づいて漢字学習をしていくと、それぞれの漢字を別々に学習することになります。そのため、漢字間のつながりが無視され、漢字体系の理解が難しくなります。本教材の**本冊**では、このような漢字の形・音・意味の体系に関する情報が自然に身につくよう、漢字の提出順が工夫されています。

□ 漢字の学習だけでなく、漢字語彙の習熟も大きな目標とする

中・上級の学習者にとっては、新しい漢字の習得もさることながら、漢字語彙を増やし、その正しい用法を身につけることも非常に重要です。しかし、もっぱら個々の漢字が学習の中心で、語彙についてはいくつかの例を示すだけであったり、学習者にはあまり重要でない語が提示されていたりして、語の習得には適さない教材も見られます。

本教材では、漢字の学習だけでなく、語彙の学習ももう一つの教育目標として明確に定めました。そのために、**本冊**では、日本語学習者に重要と思われる語彙を学習段階を加味しながら選び、提示しました。また、**本冊**で覚えた語彙は、**ワークブック**で関連語や例文を見ながら、コンテクストの中での使い方が学べるようになっています。

□ 段階的に学習することができる

これまでの漢字教材では多くの場合、一つの事項は一度だけ提示され、その時に必ず覚えるというアプローチをとってきました。しかし、漢字にしろ漢字語彙にしろ、一度の学習で100％確実に習得できるとは考えられません。

本教材では、ある段階で漢字を学習している時には、それ以前に学習した項目を積極的に提出することで記憶の定着を図り、同時に未習の項目はできる限り提出せず、提出が必要な場合でも学習者に負担ができるだけかからないように工夫されています。例えば、**ワークブック**におけるふりがなは、その段階で未習の語についてのみ、ふるようにしています。また、未習漢字を含む語については、原則として**ワークブック**の問題とならないようにしています。

また、基本的な語に限って一通り常用漢字全体の理解をし、次の段階でこれら基本語の復習をしながらさらに語彙を増やしていく等、段階を踏んで教材全体の学習を進めていくことができるようになっています。

次に、**本冊**と**ワークブック**について、各々具体的な内容について説明します。なお、詳しい説明を必要としない学習者は、Ⅳの「本教材の使い方」を読んで学習を始めてください。

Ⅱ．本冊の概要

1．本冊の主な内容

本冊では、主として次のような情報が提示されています。

1）常用漢字 2,136 字の漢字（以下、この 2,136 字を本教材の「学習漢字」と呼びます。）
2）学習漢字の読み
3）学習漢字の画数と書き順
4）学習漢字の語例とその読み方および英語訳

2．学習漢字の選定

1981 年に文部省は、現代日本語を書き表す場合の漢字使用の目安として 1,945 字の常用漢字表を発表しました。この常用漢字表は広く社会に受け入れられ、公文書、新聞、雑誌、書籍など現代日本語を書き表す時の基準となりました。

発表後およそ 30 年が経過し、その間の日本語の変化に合わせ、2010 年に大幅に改訂がなされました。それまでの 1,945 字に新たに 196 字を加え、5 字削除を行い、新たな音訓等を追加・変更・削除した改定常用漢字表です。今後は、この新しい常用漢字表が、日本社会における漢字使用の基準となっていくでしょう。

この常用漢字表は非常に重要なものです。例えば、新聞で用いられる漢字は、新聞社が決めた新聞常用漢字表に従って決められますが、本教材で扱う常用漢字 2,136 字は、この新聞常用漢字表の漢字のほぼすべてを含んでいます。ですから、本教材で常用漢字すべてをマスターすれば、新聞で使われる漢字のほぼ 100％が既知の漢字になるのです。新聞記事のどこを見ても、そこで使われているすべての漢字の読みや意味が分かるという状態を想像してみてください。もちろん、知らない語は出てくるかもしれません。しかし、その語の読みと意味は必ず推測できるので、記事全体の理解に大いに役立つでしょう。

また、この新しい常用漢字は、旧日本語能力試験 1 級で必要とされる漢字をすべて含むので、N1 合格のための学習にも最適だと言えます。

以上から、本教材では、この改定常用漢字表のすべて、2,136 字を学習漢字としています。

3．学習漢字の水準づけ

本教材では、2,136 字の学習漢字を、日本語の学習段階に対応して 7 つの水準に分けました。その概要は以下の表の通りです。

水　準	学習漢字数	解　　説
第1水準	250字	初級の日本語コースを終了した学習者であれば必ず学習した経験があると考えられる基礎的な漢字。
第2水準	100字 （累計350字）	中級の日本語コースで学習している学習者であれば必ず学習した経験があると考えられる漢字。
第3水準	850字 （累計1,200字）	中級の日本語コースで一般的に学習されると考えられる漢字。
第4水準	220字 （累計1,420字）	中級の日本語コースでしばしば現れるが一般的とは考えられない漢字、あるいは、上級の日本語コースで一般的に学習されると考えられる漢字。
第5水準	412字 （累計1,832字）	上級の日本語コースでしばしば現れるが一般的とは考えられない漢字。
第6水準	110字 （累計1,942字）	特別な領域や分野の特殊な語彙の中でしか使われない漢字。
第7水準	194字 （合計2,136字）	改定常用漢字表で新たに加えられた漢字。（「誰」と「略」については第1、第4水準で学習済み。）

　国立国語研究所が行った調査によると、最も使用頻度の高い500字だけで新聞で使われる漢字の約80％をカバーすることができ、1,000字知っていれば新聞漢字の94％をカバーできるということです。この調査の1,000字と本教材の第3水準までの漢字が正確に一致するわけではありませんが、本教材の第3水準（1,200字）まで勉強すれば、新聞に出てくる漢字の95％程度がすでに知っている漢字になると予想できます。

　ちなみに、この第3水準までを学習すれば、旧日本語能力試験2級までの漢字の90％以上をカバーし、第4水準まで学習すれば97％以上となります。N2合格のためには、第3〜4水準までの学習で十分だと言えるでしょう。

　本教材の到達目標はあくまで常用漢字すべてのマスターにありますが、そこに至る学習は、以上の理由で、第1水準から学習を始め、より頻度の少ない漢字へと学習を進めていくのが効果的だと考えます。また、第3水準までマスターすれば、多くの場合、読み物の大意を理解しながら読み進めることも十分可能になっていますので、第4水準以降の学習と並行して、様々な読み物を多く読む練習も効果的でしょう。

4．学習漢字の配列

　3のように7つの水準に分けた学習漢字は、漢字の重要度や難易度を基本に、字形や意味のつながり、語彙のつながりなど、様々な面に配慮して、水準ごとに方針を立てて配列しました。

第１水準と**第２水準**では、各学習漢字の語例のうち、一番初めに示した語の意味のつながりを中心に配列しました。

　第３水準と**第４水準**では、以下のような点を総合的に考慮して学習漢字を配列しました。

<基本的な方針>
・基本語例が学習者にとってなじみがあり、使用頻度も高いと思われる学習漢字から順に提示する。

<副次的な方針>
・重要な熟語を構成する漢字は隣接して提示する。
・共通の字形要素を持ち、字形がある程度類似している漢字は隣接して提示する。
・共通の字形要素を持つわけではないが、字形が類似していて紛らわしい漢字は隣接して提示する。
・基本語例が一定の語彙グループを形成している場合、そのような漢字はまとめて提示する。

　第５水準では、もっぱら字形要素の共通性に基づいて学習漢字を配列し、**第６水準**では、各々のグループごとに字形要素の共通性と学習漢字の語例の語彙体系を考慮して学習漢字を配列しました。最後の**第７水準**では、新たに常用漢字表に加えられた漢字について、その語例の語彙体系を基に配列されています。

　このような結果が巻末の「**学習漢字一覧表**」(p. 304) です。本書の学習漢字はこの表の配列順で提示されています。

５．語例の選定と配列

　語例には、漢字語彙能力の核となり、かつ成人学習者の興味と関心に対応した重要な語彙を精選しました。提示語彙数は約 9,500 語となっています。

　各学習漢字の語例のうち、赤字で示した語例は、その学習漢字の読みをマスターする上で必要不可欠であり、かつ基本的と考えられる**基本語例**です。この基本語例だけを学習していくことでも、全常用漢字の重要な読みのほとんどがマスターできるように構成されています。それ以外の語例は、漢字の意味や語構成の共通性、読みの共通性と類似性、語例の難易度などを考慮して配列しました。なお、重要と思われる語は、未習の漢字や本書の学習漢字以外の字を含むものでも提示しました（ただし、その場合には＊や▲などの印をつけました──「６．凡例」を参照）。

6. 凡　例

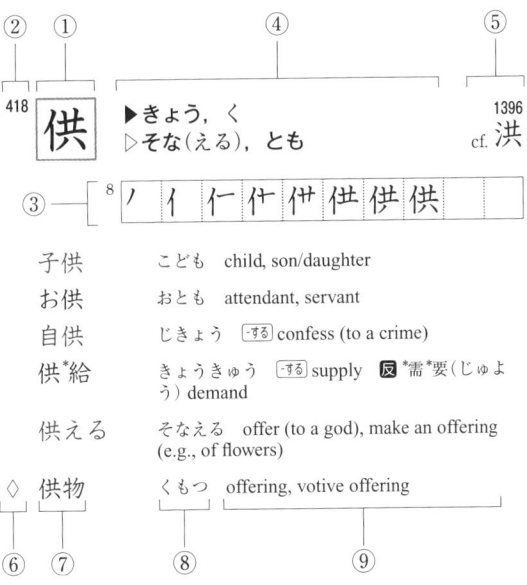

①見出し字／②漢字番号／③総画数と書き順

④漢字の読み

1）常用漢字表にあげられた漢字の読みをすべて提示しました。▶には音読みを、▷には訓読み
を示してあります。（　　）内は送りがなの部分です。

2）細字は、その読みが常用漢字表の「特別なものまたは用法のごく狭いもの」であることを示
します。

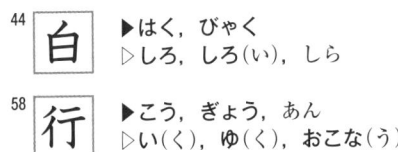

⑤形の似ている字に関する情報

　場合によっては、形が似ている漢字について注意を促すため、cf. として見出し字部分の一番右
に、類似字とその漢字番号を示してあります。

⑥難易度を示すマーク／⑦語例

学習の便宜のために、語例には難易度を示しています。

基本語（赤字）……その学習漢字の読みをマスターする上で必要不可欠であり、かつ基本的と考
えられる語。この基本語だけを学習すれば、全常用漢字の読みの大部分をマスターできるよ
うに構成されています。全部で約 3,700 語あります。

学校	がっこう　school
学生	がくせい　student

◇……語彙的に難易度が高く、学習の優先順位が他の語例に比べて低い語。

◇　火*影	ほかげ　light of a fire/flame（＊は未習漢字を表す。）
◇　木立	こだち　grove, cluster of trees

歴……歴史・文学に関する特殊な語、現在ではあまり使われない語

歴 大名	だいみょう　*daimyō*, feudal lord
歴 文	ふみ　a letter (to someone)

特……きわめてまれにしか使われない特殊な語、使用域が限られている語

特 緑青	ろくしょう　copper/green rust, patina
特 歩	ふ　pawn (in Japanese chess)

本教材では、まず赤字の基本語だけを学習します。基本語を身につけるだけで、常用漢字の読み
の大部分がマスターできます。基本語の学習が終わったら、黒字で印のついていない語を学習しま
す。これにより、よく使われる重要な語彙を増強することができます。最後に◇の語を学習し、必
要に応じて歴 特の語の学習に進みます。このように、基本語から始め、難易度をステップアップ
しながら常用漢字全体を繰り返し学習することで、記憶の定着と語彙の増強が合わせてできます。
語例の中に未習漢字や学習漢字以外の漢字が含まれる場合は、それらの漢字に以下の印をつけま
した。

＊……未習漢字（ただし、すぐ次に学習漢字として出てくる場合は無印。第1・第2水準の漢字
（1-350）はすべて既習漢字として扱った。）

*統一	とういつ　-する unify
三つ*角	みつかど　three-way junction

▲……常用漢字以外の漢字

茶▲碗	ちゃわん　(rice) bowl, teacup
▲淘汰	とうた　-する select, weed out, screen, sift

⑧語例の読み

特殊な読み方をする語例には、以下の印をつけました。

△……その語例が常用漢字表の「付表」の語彙であることを示す。これらは常用漢字表で認めら
れている当て字や熟字訓である。

一人	△ひとり　one person
二十*歳	△はたち　twenty years old

▲……常用漢字外の読み方であることを示す。

一寸　　　▲ちょっと　(just/for) a moment, slightly

歴 細雪　　▲ささめゆき　light snowfall

⑨語例の意味

する……熟語動詞（語例に「する」をつけて動詞として使えるもの）であることを示す。

出発　　　しゅっぱつ　する depart, leave
計算　　　けいさん　する calculate, compute

vt./vi.……英訳からだけでは他動詞／自動詞が判別できない場合に限り、*vt.* または *vi.* を表示した。

続ける　　つづける　*vt.* continue
続く　　　つづく　*vi.* continue

cf. ……漢字の使い方や関連語に関する情報を示した。

石けん　　せっけん　soap　cf. 石けん can be written as 石鹸, but 鹸 is not a *Jōyō Kanji*.

作家　　　さっか　novelist　cf. 筆者(ひっしゃ) writer, 著者(ちょしゃ) author

abbr. ……略語であることを示す。

日本銀行　にほんぎんこう　the Bank of Japan　cf. *abbr.* 日銀(にちぎん)

短*期大学　たんきだいがく　junior college　cf. *abbr.* 短大(たんだい)

反……反対語であることを示す。

主*観*的な　しゅかんてきな　subjective　cf. 反 客*観*的な(きゃっかんてきな) objective

本音　　　ほんね　real intentions　反*建前(たてまえ) formal principles/policies, a professed position

⑩異体字

　第7水準では、見出し字の隣に見出し字に似た形の漢字が（　）で示されていることがあります。これは異体字と呼ばれるもので、読みや意味が全く同じですが、字形が少し異なる漢字です。異体字も一般に使われることがありますので、注意してください。

1960 餌（餌）　▶じ
　　　　　　　▷えさ, え

⑪ワークブックとの対応

　ワークブックとの対応がすぐ分かるように、本冊では、ワークブックの回ごとに回数の数字と共に区切りがつけられています。

第 3 回

52 家　▶か, け
　　　▷いえ, や

⑫コラム

漢字と語彙の学習をいっそう促進するため、本書では２種類のコラムを設けました。

● 〈漢字の形に気をつけましょう〉のコラム

同じ構成素をもつ漢字や字形の似ている漢字をいくつかまとめて提示しました。

● 語彙に関するコラム

語彙の学習を促進するために、意味のつながりをもつ語彙をまとめて提示しました。

7．索引

漢字学習の便宜のために、本冊には３つの索引が載せてあります。①音訓索引、②字形索引、③語彙索引の３つです。以下、順に使い方を説明します。

①漢字の読み方が分かっている場合　→　音訓索引

漢字の読み方（音読みまたは訓読み）が分かっている時は、音訓索引で漢字を引きます。音訓索引では本書の学習漢字のすべての読み方があいうえお順（五十音順）で提示され、該当する学習漢字と漢字番号がその後ろに示されています。訓読みの場合は送りがなも示されています。

②漢字の読み方が分からない場合　→　字形索引

漢字の読み方が分からない場合は、字形索引で引きます。字形索引では、漢字の形を手がかりとして調べます。

漢字は、点と線の無秩序な図形ではありません。漢字には、いわば"部品"とも言える字形構成素が多数あり、ほとんどの漢字はそのような部品の組み合わせでできています。組み合わせ方には一定のパターンがあり、構成素の配置によって以下の９つのタイプに分けることができます。

1	▮	レフト（left）	伝	凝	提
2	▯	ライト（right）	別	敬	断
3	▬	トップ（top）	今	冠	声
4	▭	ボトム（bottom）	先	基	替
5	▛	トップ・レフト（top & left）	局	広	戻
6	▙	レフト・ボトム（left & bottom）	道	起	題
7	▜	トップ・ライト（top & right）	句	載	
8	▢▢▢▢	エンクロージャー（enclosure）	円	凶	区	国
9	■	ソリッド（solid）	弓	止	耳	長

字形索引では、このような字形構成素のパターンを使って、以下の手順で漢字を調べます。

１）まず、調べたい漢字を見て、字形構成素を見つけます。

２）巻末の字形構成素チャートでその構成素の番号を調べます。１〜８のどのタイプにも含まれない時は、９のソリッドから探してください。チャートでは構成素が上記の９つのタイプごとに画数順に並べられていますから、構成素の配置と画数をよく確認して調べてください。

3）構成素の番号をもとに、字形索引で漢字を調べます。それぞれの字形構成素の項では、画数順で漢字が提示され、その漢字番号が示されています。

　調べたい漢字に字形構成素が２つ認められることがよくありますが、そのような場合はどちらの構成素で調べてもかまいません。たとえば「休」の場合、左側の「イ」からでも、右側の「木」からでも引くことができます。あるいは「思」の場合、上の「田」からでも、下の「心」からでも引くことができます。また、たとえば「馬」は、単独の漢字としても、構成素（レフト）としてもよく使われますが、単独で使われる場合の「馬」もレフトに含めてあります。

③語彙を探したい場合　→　語彙索引
　本冊に収録されているすべての漢字語彙をあいうえお順（五十音順）に並べ、それが掲載されている漢字番号を示しました。この索引を使って掲載箇所を探せば語彙の意味を調べることができますから、本冊を学習辞典のように使うことができます。

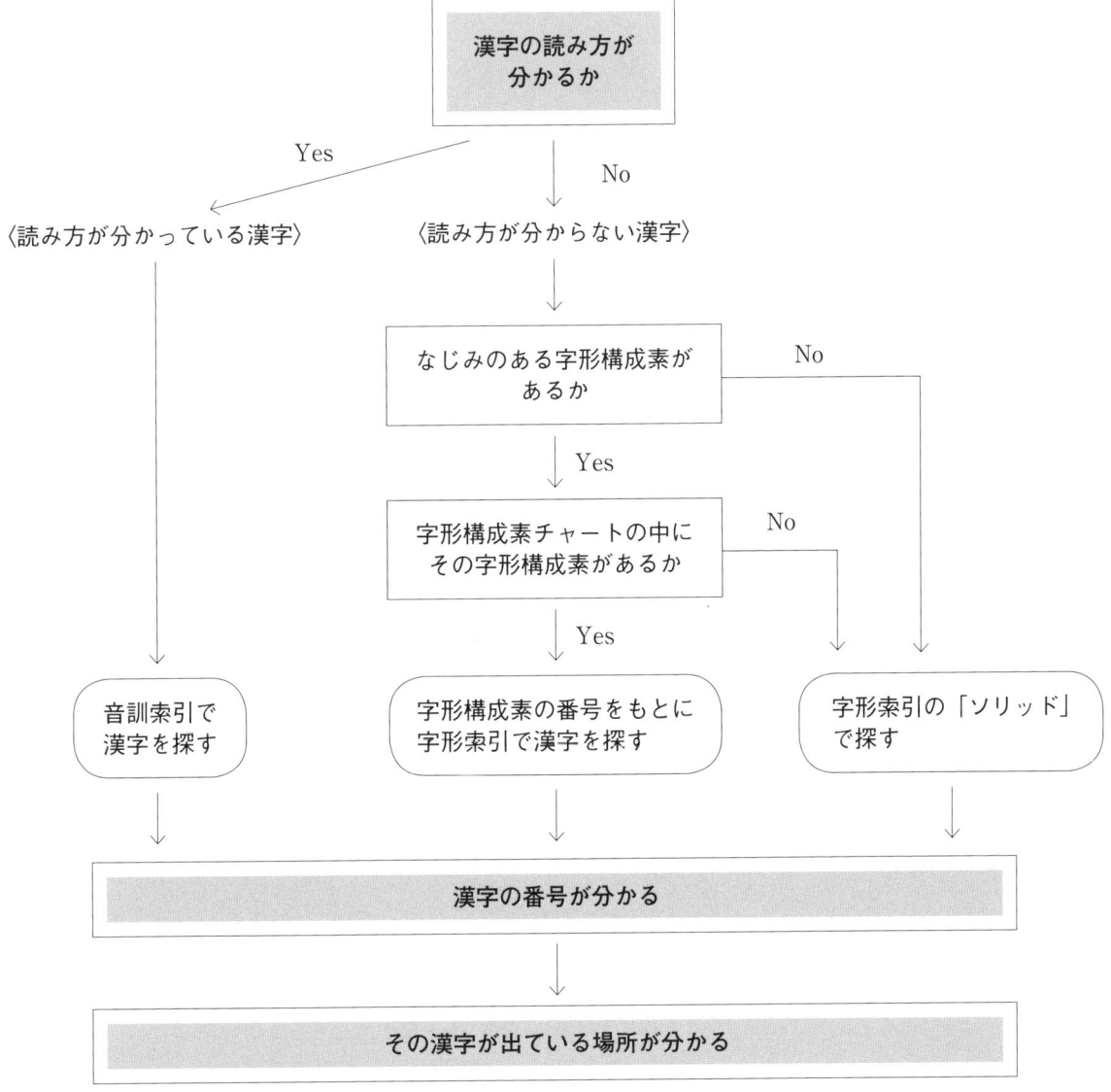

Ⅲ．ワークブックの概要

1．ワークブックの主な内容

　ワークブックでは、毎回、本冊に示された学習漢字を順番に 10 〜 15 字ずつ（第 1・第 2 水準では約 10 〜 30 字ずつ）取り上げ、語例の使い方に習熟し、漢字語彙を拡充するために役に立つと思われる学習材料を様々な形で提示しています。各回は大きく 3 つのセクションから成り立っています。各セクションの内容は以下の通りです。

　　Ⅰ．学習漢字の語例を含む複合熟語、慣用的な表現、文の構成など
　　Ⅱ．学習漢字の語例の関連及び関連語、表現の対比など
　　Ⅲ．学習漢字の語例を使った実際的な例文

　では、それぞれについて例をあげながら説明します。例の中の下線は本冊で提示された語例であることを示しています。

Ⅰ．学習漢字の語例を含む複合熟語、慣用的な表現、文の構成など

　このセクションでは、提示されている表現を勉強し、語の基本的な使い方を学習します。

　　1）学習漢字の語例を含む複合熟語
　　　　例）和平交渉　　団体旅行　　支持率　　技術移転

　　2）漢字の語例を含む広い意味での慣用的な表現
　　　　　例）平和を守る　　公平な態度　　家具付きの家　　質問に対する答え

　　3）学習漢字の語例を使った文の構成
　　　　例）男も女も同等の扱いをする　　議論が平行線をたどる
　　　　　　上体を大きく後ろに反らす　　手紙を封筒に入れて送る

Ⅱ．学習漢字の語例の関連及び関連語、表現の対比など

　このセクションでは、提示されている表現を勉強し、他の語彙との意味の関連を学習します。

　　1）学習漢字の語例の関連及び関連語
　　　　例）戦争　　平和
　　　　　　管理職　　平社員
　　　　　　足し算　　引き算　　掛け算　　割り算
　　　　　　電車 / バス の切符　　映画 / コンサート のチケット

　　2）表現の対比
　　　　　例）収入　←→　支出　（←→は、反意語であることを示す）
　　　　　　意見 / 提案 に反対する　←→　意見 / 提案 に賛成する
　　　　　　ビールを冷やす　―　ビールが冷える（―は、自動詞／他動詞関係であることを示す）

Ⅲ．学習漢字の語例を使った実際的な例文

このセクションでは、例文をよく読んで、下線で示した語の文中での使い方を学習します。

例文は、成人学習者が興味を持って学習を進めることができ、かつ、学習漢字の語例の用法を学習するのに最も適当と思われるものを提示しました。下線の語の読み方は別冊にまとめて示してあります。

2．ワークブックで扱う語例

ワークブックでは、本冊で提示された語彙のうち、すべての赤字の語（基本語）と、無印の語、および◇の語を扱っています（→「II-6．凡例」を参照）。また、基本語は太字で示し、基本語を含む文は、その項目番号を黒丸としています。基本語だけを先に学習する時は、ワークブックの黒丸の項目を選んで行ってください。

なお、未習漢字を含む語（＊印のついている語）については、原則としてワークブックの下線語としては取り上げていません。ただし、わずかですが、基本的な読みを含むという理由で、未習漢字を含むにもかかわらず基本語となっている語があります。これらについては、基本語としてワークブックで学習します。

歴特の語については、特殊で使用頻度が低いと思われるため、読みが重要だとして基本語になっているごく一部の例外を除き、ワークブックでは扱っていません。

3．ワークブックと学習水準

ワークブックの Vol. 1 では、本冊の第1水準から第3水準まで（1-1200）の漢字の語彙が、また Vol. 2 には第4水準から第7水準まで（1201-2136）の語彙が、それぞれ提示されています。

Ⅳ. 本教材の使い方

1. 対象レベル

　本教材の目標は、常用漢字すべてのマスターにありますので、常用漢字未習得の学習者であれば誰でも、本教材を使って学習を進めることができます。

　しかし、基本的な漢字さえも知らなければ、漢字の字形一つを覚えるのにも大変な労力がかかります。短期間で2,000を超える漢字を習得するには、すでに持っている漢字知識を有効に活用していくことが必要不可欠です。基本的漢字を身につけていれば、新しい漢字を基本漢字の組み合わせとして、あるいは類似した字形の漢字として、そして同一の音や類似した意味の漢字として、効率的に学ぶことができるのです。

　この意味で、本教材を使って効果的に学習するためには、最低限、通常の初級コースで学ぶ漢字約300〜500字程度を習得していることが必要です。具体的に言えば、本教材の学習漢字のうち、第1・第2水準（1-350）の学習漢字の大部分が理解できる程度の漢字力は必要となります。このレベル以上の学習者であれば、本教材の本冊とワークブックを並行して使用して、効率よく体系的に漢字と語彙を学べるでしょう。

　現在まだ初級段階で勉強している人は、本教材の本冊を使って、教科書で勉強した漢字の知識を整理し、熟語等の語彙を増やすことができます。その場合、ワークブックはある程度漢字と語彙の知識が増えた段階で使い始めればいいでしょう。

2. どこから学習を始めるか

　大まかに言うと、本教材の第1水準と第2水準は初級段階、第3水準は中級段階、第4・第5水準は上級段階、第6・第7水準は超上級段階となります。学習者は自分の知識・能力や勉強のしかたの好みによってどこから勉強を始めてもかまいませんが、本教材は、常用漢字すべてをマスターするための教材として構成されていますので、第1水準の初めから順に最後まで勉強することを薦めます。第1・第2水準では、学習漢字の大部分はすでに知っていることと思いますが、そこでも初級の語彙にとどまらず、中・上級学習者に必要な語彙を積極的に提示してあります。そのため、第1水準から学習することは、中・上級学習者にとっても、語彙の拡充に十分、役立つでしょう。

3. 本教材を使った漢字と漢字語彙の学習

　本教材を十分に活用していただくために、ここでは本教材の特長を生かした基本的な学習方法について解説します。

　本教材は、これまで漢字学習をしてきて、すでにある程度の漢字を習得している学習者を対象とし、このような学習者が常用漢字すべてを理解できるようになるための教材として作成されています。この目的のため、以下の三つの段階に分け、それぞれ4つのステップを踏んで学習を続けるようになっています。

─────〈学習者はワークブックを使って、以下のような要領で勉強を進めてください。〉─────

第一段階：基本語の学習（常用漢字の読みの習得）

ステップ1　学習漢字の基本的知識の形成
　本冊で学習漢字の字形、基本語（赤字）の意味と読み、及びそれを構成している漢字を確実に覚えてください。この知識が各学習漢字の知識の基本になります。

ステップ2　学習漢字の意味と用法の理解
　本冊で基本語以外の語例を勉強し、学習漢字の意味と用法を確認してください。なお、まず基本語（赤字）だけに絞って学習を進める場合は、覚える必要はありません。

ステップ3　語例の使い方と関連語の学習
　学習した漢字の語例の使い方や関連語をワークブックで勉強してください。基本語（赤字）だけに絞って学習をする場合は、ワークブックの項目番号が黒丸で表示されているものだけをしてください。太字で示されている語が基本語ですので、その意味と読みと使い方を確実に覚えてください。万が一分からない場合は、もう一度本冊に戻って勉強してください。

ステップ4　習得の確認
　基本語について、確実に習得しているかを確認してください。日本語の先生や友達に簡単なクイズを作ってもらう、フラッシュカードを作る等もいい練習になります。また、ワークブックに出ている文を自分で作れるかを試してみるのも役立ちます。

　以上、ステップ1〜4の仕方で学習を続け、基本の学習を第156回まで修了します。基本語はおよそ3,700語あります。これらすべてをマスターすることで、新聞や雑誌など、日常目にする日本語の読み物に現れる漢字のほとんどについて、その意味や読みが推測できるようになるでしょう。

第二段階：無印語の学習（常用漢字の読みの復習と語彙の拡充）

　第二段階では、習得した常用漢字すべてについて、語彙を増強していきます。第1回に戻り、基本語の復習と共に、◇や歴特以外の語（無印の語）について、基本語についてと同様の仕方で学習をしていきます。基本語学習ですでにすべての常用漢字は既習になっていますので、未習漢字を含む語例（＊を含むもの）についても学習をしてください。なお、無印の語については、そのすべてがワークブックで扱われているわけではなく、重要な語、使い方が難しい語に絞っていますので注意してください。基本語の学習時よりも覚えるべき語数は多くなりますが、基本語の学習で常用漢字の字形や読みをすでに習得しているので、基本語の学習時よりも学習は速く進むでしょう。この方法で第156回まで修了します。

第三段階：◇や歴特の語の学習（常用漢字の読みすべての習得と語彙の拡充）

　最後に、残った◇や歴特の語について、また第1回に戻って学習していきます。これらの語は、一般的には重要性が低い語と考えられる語で、ワークブックでも扱われていません（◇の語については、一部ワークブックでも扱っています）。本冊で確認をし、必要に応じて学習を進めればいいでしょう。ただし、常用漢字の読みを100％すべて完璧にできるようにしたい場合は、これらの語も含め、すべて読めるようにすることが必要となります。

Introduction

I. Overview of Text

Kanji in Context—A Study System for Intermediate and Advanced Learners has been designed to allow learners who have completed a beginning course or are currently studying at the intermediate or advanced level to systematically and efficiently build on the foundation of *kanji* and vocabulary that they have previously acquired, so that upon completion they will have an understanding all of the 2,136 *kanji* designated for common use by the Japanese Ministry of Education. This text is divided into two parts, a main book and a 2-volume workbook.

Kanji in Context has several distinctive features:

☐ The text is specifically designed for intermediate and advanced learners, with clearly stated objectives

Kanji in Context was written with the needs of intermediate and advanced learners of Japanese in mind, and the content is presented in a manner that facilitates progress in stages, enabling learners to understand all the everyday use *kanji*.

As a text specifically for intermediate and advanced students, *Kanji in Context* does not place the emphasis on learning the basic forms of *kanji*, as is necessary at the elementary stage of Japanese language study. Rather, it takes a proactive approach to introduction of intermediate- and advanced-level language, focusing on readings of *kanji* and examples of their usage, even when presenting characters that should have been learned at the elementary level.

Further, instead of proceeding by simply adding more and more characters to be learned, we make clear in this text that the ultimate objective is to understand all of the everyday use *kanji*, and we present specific sequential steps for the attainment of that goal. The term "everyday use *kanji*" refers to the table of characters that was established by the Ministry of Education, Culture, Sports, Science, and Technology, as revised in 2010; these are the characters that are considered standard for writing the Japanese language that is used today in official documents, newspapers, magazines, books, and other media that employ writing. Mastering these everyday use *kanji* is the goal of the education provided in schools for native speakers of Japanese, as well, and it can be said that achieving mastery is acquiring a power equivalent to that possessed by educated native speakers. If one has an understanding of all the everyday use *kanji*, one becomes able to infer the readings and the meanings of nearly all of the *kanji* that appear in Japanese writing. In *Kanji in Context*, we have set mastery of all the everyday use *kanji* as the final goal—a goal we believe is appropriate for intermediate- and advanced-level students—and we lay out a concrete program for achievement of that goal.

☐ *Kanji* can be learned in a systematic fashion

At the intermediate level and above, the number of *kanji* needed by learners rises sharply. In order to effectively meet this growing need, it is not adequate to learn each new character randomly; rather, it is also necessary to study the systematic connections that lie behind *kanji* and *kanji*-

based vocabulary. In general, there are three basic elements to *kanji*: form, sound, and meaning. Form refers to the principles behind the structure of *kanji* (the components and their positions within a character); sound to the shared connections and similarities in the readings of particular *kanji*, as based on their components; and meaning to the underlying system of meaning in *kanji*, as based on their components.

These three elements are organically intertwined within the *kanji*, and a proper knowledge of them will not only bring a dramatic increase in the speed at which new *kanji* and vocabulary are digested, but will also foster the ability to infer the meaning and reading of previously unencountered *kanji* vocabulary.

If one learns *kanji* simply by studying them one by one in the order of frequency with which they are used, it becomes an exercise in learning individual characters. Connections between *kanji* are ignored, and it is difficult to understand that *kanji* belong to a system. In this main volume of *Kanji in Context*, the order of presentation of characters has been arranged to facilitate learners' natural acquisition of information about the system of form, sound, and meaning of those characters.

☐ Focus of study is not on *kanji* only, but also on *kanji*-based vocabulary

In addition to the acquisition of new *kanji*, it is also important for intermediate and advanced learners to learn new vocabulary words that incorporate those *kanji* and the correct usage of those words. However, traditional *kanji* textbooks have focused excessively on the study of characters one by one, providing only a sprinkling of vocabulary words, which, more often than not, have little practical use for learners.

In contrast, this text goes beyond mere study of *kanji* to include the acquisition of vocabulary as one of its objectives. Thus the main book contains an abundant collection of essential vocabulary words, all of which have been selected with the different stages of learning in mind. Moreover, the usage of the vocabulary in the main book can be learned in context through the example sentences and related words in both volumes of the workbook.

☐ *Kanji* can be easily acquired by repeated exposure

In the majority of *kanji* textbooks, each *kanji* or word is presented only once, an approach based on the assumption that it will be fully mastered at the time it appears. However, a single presentation does not guarantee that the character or word will be effectively acquired by the learner. For this reason, the same target vocabulary and related words are repeatedly presented in *Kanji in Context*, and the frequent contact with a particular *kanji* or word reinforces its acquisition. At the same time, to the extent we could, we have limited the presentation of items that have not been previously studied, and in instances when it has been necessary to present such items, we have made an effort to keep the burden on the learner as light as possible. For example, in the workbook, we have added *furigana* to words and *kanji* that have not previously been studied. Also, in the exercises in the workbook, we have as a rule not included words that incorporate previously unstudied *kanji*.

Gaining an understanding of basic words and the system of everyday use *kanji*, and then at the next stage expanding vocabulary while reviewing the basic words, students will be able to make orderly progress through these textbooks, with each stage building upon the previous stage.

Now follows a description of the contents of the main book and the workbook. Learners who do not need to go over these details should at least read "IV. How to Use *Kanji in Context*" before commencing their study.

II. Overview of Main Book

1. Main Contents

The main book presents the following information:

1) 2,136 *kanji*: all 2,136 *Jōyō Kanji*
2) The readings of the *kanji*
3) The number of strokes and stroke order in the *kanji*
4) Vocabulary using the *kanji* and the corresponding *kana* readings and English equivalents

2. Selection of the *Kanji* in This Text

In 1981 the Japanese Ministry of Education published the *Jōyō Kanji Hyō*, a list standardizing the use of *kanji* in modern written Japanese. 1,945 characters were selected, and their *on* and *kun* readings (Chinese-derived and Japanese readings) were delimited. The authority of this list deeply permeated Japanese society to the point where it came to serve as the standard for modern *kanji* usage in official documents, newspapers, magazines, books, and the like.

Nearly three decades after publication of the *Jōyō Kanji Hyō*, in 2010, a wide-ranging revision was completed, taking into account changes that had occurred in the Japanese language. To the original list of 1,945 characters, 196 more characters were added, and 5 characters were deleted. Some new *on* and *kun* readings were authorized, some others changed, and some others eliminated. It is highly likely that the resulting new *Kaitei Jōyō Kanji Hyō* will become the standard for *kanji* usage in Japanese society from now on.

The revised Ministry of Education *Jōyō Kanji* list is extremely important, and in this text, we treat all 2,136 characters on the list. Although newspaper publishers and others have the right to establish their own lists of *kanji* that they will regularly use, in practice virtually all of the characters on their lists are included among these 2,136. Thus a student who masters the material presented in *Kanji in Context* will be familiar with nearly 100% of the *kanji* that are used in newspapers. If you are just beginning to use this book, please imagine being able to understand the readings and the meanings of practically all the *kanji* that appear in any article in a newspaper. To be sure, there may be some words that you are not familiar with. But if you have gained command of the material in this textbook, you will be able to infer the correct readings and meanings in almost all cases, and that will be enormously helpful in comprehending the meaning of the whole article.

It is also worth noting that all of the *kanji* that appeared in the Level 1 examination of the old Japanese Language Proficiency Test are included in the new table of characters for everyday use. Mastering *Kanji in Context* is one of the very best ways of preparing to pass the current N1-level proficiency test.

3. *Kanji* Levels

The 2,136 *kanji* appearing in the main book have been divided into seven levels corresponding to the following stages of learning:

Level	No. of *Kanji*	Stage
1	250	These are elementary *kanji* that a learner who has completed a beginning course is expected to have already studied.
2	100 (subtotal: 350)	These are *kanji* that an intermediate learner is expected to have already studied.
3	850 (subtotal: 1,200)	These are *kanji* that are generally taught in an intermediate course.
4	220 (subtotal: 1,420)	These are *kanji* that may be covered in certain intermediate courses but are not necessarily common to such courses, or *kanji* that are generally taught in advanced courses.
5	412 (subtotal: 1,832)	These are *kanji* that may be covered in certain advanced courses but are not necessarily common to such courses.
6	110 (subtotal: 1,942)	These are special *kanji* which appear only in the vocabulary or terminology of particular fields.
7	194 (total: 2,136)	These are *kanji* that were added to the list of *Jōyō Kanji* when the Ministry of Education revised the list in 2010. Note, however, that in *Kanji in Context* the character 誰 is presented in Level 1, and the character 賂 is presented in Level 4.

According to a study by the National Language Research Institute, the 500 most often used *kanji* represent roughly 80% of the *kanji* found in newspapers, and 94% of newspaper *kanji* can be covered by 1,000 characters. We should note that a few of the 1,000 characters on the National Language Research Institute list are not presented in Levels 1-3 of this textbook, but if you have learned the 1,200 characters in Levels 1-3, you will have knowledge of around 95% of the *kanji* that are used in newspapers today.

We can also point out that if you have mastered the *kanji* in our Levels 1-3, you will have covered over 90% of the characters that appeared on the old Level 2 (2-*kyū*) Japanese Language Proficiency Test (JLPT), and if you also master Level 4 *kanji*, you will have knowledge of over 97% of the characters tested on the old Level 2 JLPT examination. It is probable that mastery of Levels 3 and 4 of this textbook will prepare you to pass the N2 level of the current JLPT.

Above all else, the objective of *Kanji in Context* is to enable students to master all of the everyday use *kanji*, and the most effective way to reach that objective is to start with Level 1 and then progress steadily to study characters that occur with less frequency. In fact, mastery through Level 3 should enable you to grasp the meaning of most of the writing you will encounter. As you study

Level 4 and higher levels and as you are exposed to a variety of written materials, the speed at which your facility grows will increase.

4. Arrangement of Entries

Not only have the *kanji* in this text been divided into seven levels, but they have also been arranged in order within each level based on consideration of a variety of factors, particularly importance and difficulty, as well as connections in form, meaning, and related vocabulary. In addition, various strategies of arrangement have been applied to the levels as explained below.

Levels 1 & 2: The entries have been arranged mainly around the connections in meaning between each entry's first vocabulary word (the "key word"—see "5. Selection and Arrangement of Vocabulary" below).

Levels 3 & 4: The entries have been arranged comprehensively according the following strategies.

Main strategy: The entries are arranged in order of familiarity and frequency of use of each entry's key word.

Secondary strategies:

· *Kanji* that go together to make up important compounds are placed together.

· *Kanji* that share common components and are similar in form are placed together.

· *Kanji* that do not share common components but are similar enough in form that they might be confused are placed together.

· *Kanji* whose key words make up a distinct group are placed together.

Level 5: The entries are arranged mainly according to similarities in form.

Level 6: The entries are arranged mainly according to similarities in form and vocabulary.

Level 7: *Kanji* that were added in the *Jōyō Kanji* list revision of 2010 are arranged mainly according to similarities in form and vocabulary.

The overall arrangement produced by the above strategies can be seen by perusing the condensed listing of the entries at the end of the text (p. 304).

5. Selection and Arrangement of Vocabulary

The vocabulary words in this text represent the core of *kanji*-based vocabulary, and were carefully selected as the words most essential to meet the needs and interests of adult learners. There are approximately 9,500 words.

Words printed in red are regarded as key vocabulary words, and students must master their readings. As you learn these key vocabulary words, you will gain the ability to master the vast majority of important readings of all the *Jōyō Kanji*. The vocabulary words that follow the key words are arranged according to various factors, including similarities in the meaning of the *kanji* as used in the vocabulary words, similarities in structure, similarities in reading, and degree of difficulty. Among the vocabulary words, there are some compounds that contain *kanji* that have not previously been covered in the text and there are a few *kanji* that are not covered at all in the text, but are considered important enough to warrant their inclusion in the vocabulary listing. Such vocabulary words have been marked with special symbols, such as ＊ or ▲ (see 6, below).

6. Explanation of Entries

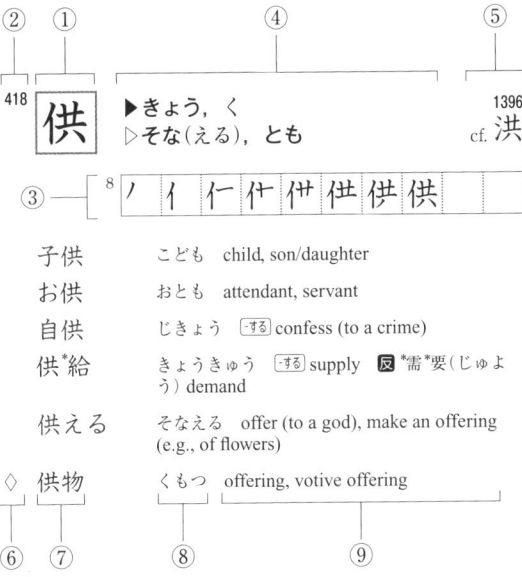

① *Kanji* entry
② **Number of order in text**
③ **Number of strokes and order of strokes**

④ **Readings**

1) All the readings listed in the *Kaitei Jōyō Kanji Hyō* are given. ▶ marks the *on* readings, and ▷ marks the *kun* readings. *Okurigana* are placed in parentheses.

50 学 ▶がく
▷まな（ぶ）

89 長 ▶ちょう
▷なが（い）

2) Readings which according to the *Kaitei Jōyō Kanji Hyō* are limited in usage or to special cases are printed in light font.

44 白 ▶はく，びゃく
▷しろ，しろ（い），しら

58 行 ▶こう，ぎょう，あん
▷い（く），ゆ（く），おこな（う）

⑤ *Kanji* **similar in appearance**

In some cases, *kanji* that are similar in appearance to a particular *kanji* entry are listed on the right side of the heading along with their number in the text, so as to prevent confusion.

605 坂 ▶はん
▷さか

987 1948
cf. 板 阪

⑥ **Notation of difficulty / ⑦ Appearance in text**

Difficult vocabulary words have been marked with special symbols for clear reference.

key vocabulary words (Red)

······Words printed in red are regarded as indispensable key words. If you have mastered these key vocabulary words, you will be able to master most of the readings of all the *Jōyō Kanji*. There are 3,700 of these key vocabulary words.

◇ ⋯⋯ Words that are difficult but are not high on the list of priority of vocabulary words to be learned. (*Kanji* that have not been previously learned are marked with an asterisk (＊))

◇　火＊影　　ほかげ　light of a fire/flame
◇　木立　　こだち　grove, cluster of trees

歴 ⋯⋯ Words that appear in literature or historical writing, or words that are little used today.

歴　大名　　だいみょう　*daimyō*, feudal lord
歴　文　　ふみ　a letter (to someone)

特 ⋯⋯ Extremely rare specialized words, or words that are used only in certain instances.

特　緑青　　ろくしょう　copper/green rust, patina
特　歩　　ふ　pawn (in Japanese chess)

You should begin your study of this textbook by learning the key vocabulary words that are printed in red. Simply by acquiring mastery of these key words, you will be able to read most of the *Jōyō Kanji*. After you have learned the key vocabulary words, you should learn the words that are printed in black and are unmarked by any of the above symbols. By proceeding in this manner, you will be able to expand and strengthen your vocabulary of frequently used, important words. Last of all, you should study the words marked with the symbol ◇, going on to the study of words marked 歴 or 特 as necessary. In this way, beginning from the basic key words and advancing gradually up the various levels of difficulty, and by repetition, you will learn all of the *Jōyō Kanji* and you will be able to fix words in your memory and expand your vocabulary

Vocabulary words which contain a *kanji* that has not yet appeared as an entry or a *kanji* which does not appear as an entry at all are marked with the following symbols:

＊ ⋯⋯ *Kanji* which have not yet appeared as an entry. (Note, however, that *kanji* which soon appear thereafter as an entry are left unmarked, and the *kanji* that appear in Levels 1 and 2 of this textbook [the first 350 *kanji*] are treated as having been previously learned and are left unmarked.)

＊統一　　とういつ　する unify
三つ＊角　　みつかど　three-way junction

▲ ⋯⋯ *Kanji* which are not *Jōyō Kanji*

茶▲碗　　ちゃわん　(rice) bowl, teacup
▲淘汰　　とうた　する select, weed out, screen, sift

⑧ Special readings

The following symbols have been added to vocabulary words which have a special reading:

△ ⋯⋯ Supplementary readings which appear in the appendix to the *Jōyō Kanji*. These represent *ateji* and *jukujikun* which are recognized as *Jōyō Kanji* readings.

一人　　△ひとり　one person
二十＊歳　　△はたち　twenty years old

▲ ⋯⋯ Readings which are not recognized as *Jōyō Kanji* readings.

一寸　　▲ちょっと　(just/for) a moment, slightly
歴　細雪　　▲ささめゆき　light snowfall

⑨ **Meaning**

`[する]` ⋯ This denotes compound verbs (compounds which can be used as verbs by the addition of *suru*).

出発　　しゅっぱつ `[する]` depart, leave

計算　　けいさん `[する]` calculate, compute

vt./vi. ⋯ These are used to indicate whether a verb is transitive or intransitive in cases where it cannot be determined from the English translation alone.

続ける　　つづける　*vt.* continue

続く　　つづく　*vi.* continue

cf. ⋯⋯ This marks notes on usage or related vocabulary.

石けん　　せっけん　soap　cf. 石けん can be written as 石鹸, but 鹸 is not a *Jōyō Kanji*.

作家　　さっか　novelist　cf. 筆者（ひっしゃ）writer, 著者（ちょしゃ）author

abbr. ⋯⋯ This denotes abbreviations of compounds.

日本銀行　　にほんぎんこう　the Bank of Japan　cf. *abbr.* 日銀（にちぎん）

短*期大学　　たんきだいがく　junior college　cf. *abbr.* 短大（たんだい）

反 ⋯⋯ This denotes antonyms.

主*観*的な　　しゅかんてきな　subjective　cf. 反客*観*的な（きゃっかんてきな）objective

本音　　ほんね　real intentions　反*建前（たてまえ）formal principles/policies, a professed position

⑩ **Variant forms of characters**

Variant forms of characters are shown in parentheses (　) next to the current standard forms of those characters. The readings and meanings of these variant forms are exactly the same as those of the current standard forms, but the written forms of the variants are slightly different. Please take note that these variant forms are in common use.

1960　餌（餌）　▶じ
　　　　　　　　▷えさ，え

⑪ **Cross reference with workbook**

To make it easy to see the correspondences between this main book and the workbook, in this main book the number of the relevant workbook lesson is shaded and printed on a separate line.

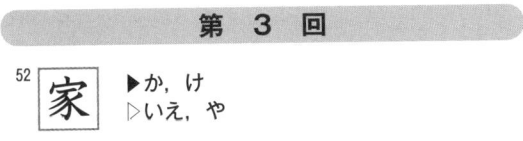

第　3　回

52　家　▶か，け
　　　　▷いえ，や

⑫ **Columns**

In order to help you further expand your knowledge of *kanji* and *kanji*-based vocabulary words, two different types of informative columns have been included in this text.

■ Easily confused *kanji*

　Kanji which can be easily confused due to common components or similarity in appearance are presented together in this column.

■ Related vocabulary

　Vocabulary words which are connected in meaning are presented together in this column.

7. Index

Three types of indexes have been included to allow for speedy reference: *on-kun*, form, and vocabulary. These indexes can be used as described below.

(A) When the reading is known: *On-kun* Index

This index can be used to look up a *kanji* when you know either its *on* or *kun* reading. All the readings for *kanji* entries are contained in the index (arranged in *a-i-u-e-o* order), with the corresponding *kanji* and its number of order in the text. *Okurigana* are included for the *kun* readings.

(B) When the reading is not known: Form Index

The form index can be used to look up a *kanji* when you do not know the reading.

In this index, use the structure of the *kanji* to help you find its location. As most learners know, *kanji* are not random collections of dots and lines; instead, most of them are made up of distinct components. There are a large number of such components, and there is a set pattern to how they are combined to form a *kanji*. The location of the main component can take one of the following nine types of positions.

1	■□	レフト （left）	伝　凝　提
2	□■	ライト （right）	別　敬　断
3	▬	トップ （top）	今　冠　声
4	▬	ボトム （bottom）	先　基　替
5	◰	トップレフト （top & left）	局　広　戻
6	◱	レフトボトム （left & bottom）	道　起　題
7	◳	トップライト （top & right）	句　載
8	∏∐□▭	エンクロージャー （enclosure）	円　凶　区　国
9	■	ソリッド （solid）	弓　止　耳　長

The above types of position are used to look up a *kanji* with the form index as follows:

1) Determine which component is the main component of the *kanji* that you wish to find.
2) Look up the number of the main component by referring to the chart at the end of this text. When the main component of the *kanji* does not take one of the positions shown in types 1-8 above, search for it as type 9 (solid). The main components for each of the nine position types are arranged in order of stroke number. To use this index, you need to carefully check the main component's position and count the number of strokes.
3) Use the component number to find the *kanji* in the index. The *kanji* are arranged under each component heading according to stroke number, and their entry number is given.

There are many cases where two components of a *kanji* are recognized as its main component, and either one can be used in this index to look up the *kanji*. For example, in the case of 休 , both イ on the left and 木 on the right can be used to look up the character. In the same manner, the *kanji* 思 can be referenced with its top component 田 or its bottom component 心 . Further, some characters such as 馬 are in frequent use both as discrete individual characters and as components (as a left component in the case of 馬), but in *Kanji in Context* we have included 馬 among the left components even when it is used as an individual character.

(C) Looking up vocabulary: Vocabulary Index

All the vocabulary contained in the main book are listed in *a-i-u-e-o* order in the vocabulary index with the corresponding entry number of the *kanji* under which they appear. Thus the reference book can serve as a dictionary through the use of the vocabulary index to look up the location of a particular word to find its meaning.

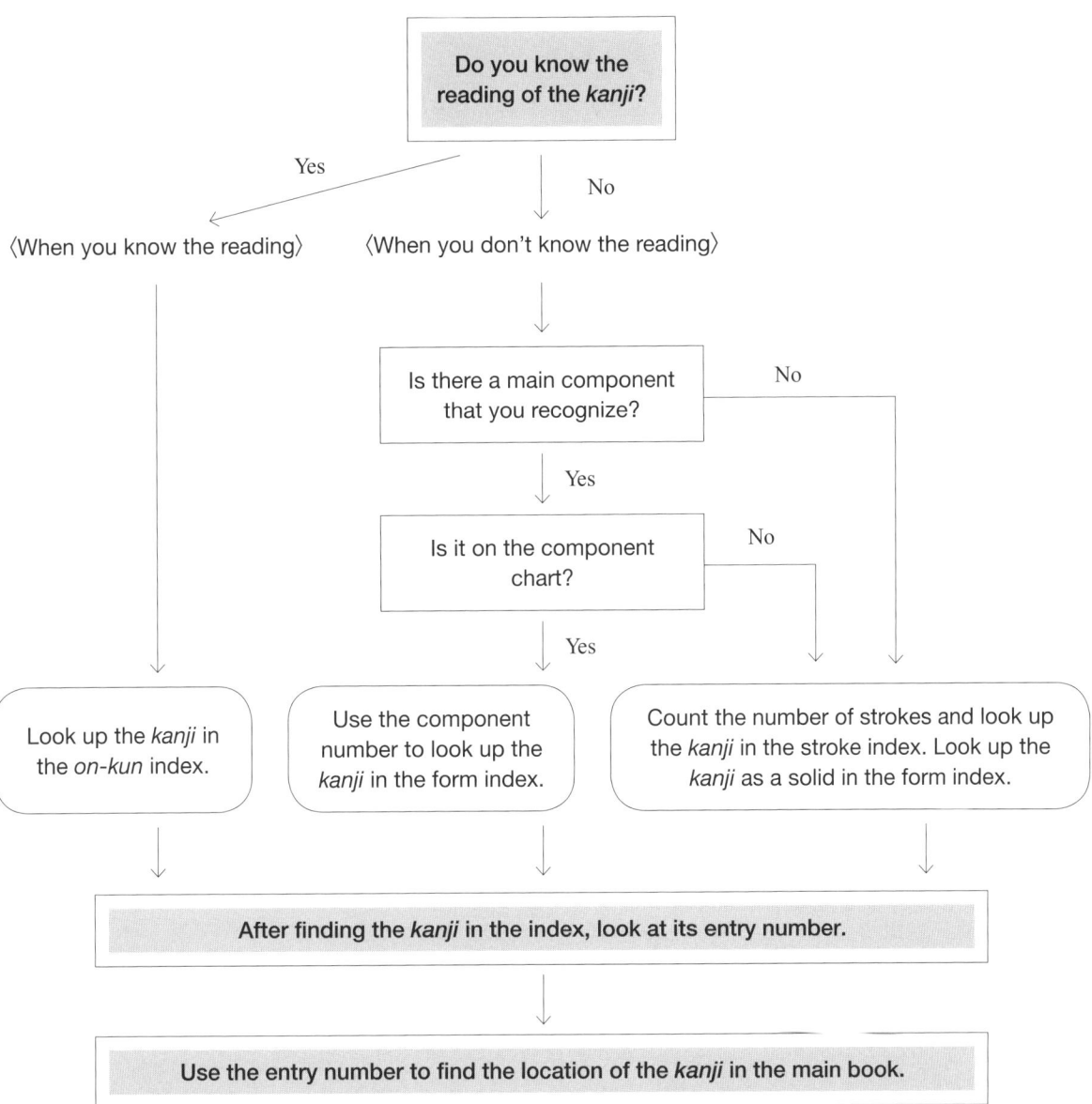

III. Overview of Workbook

1. Main Contents

Each lesson of both volumes of the workbook focuses on approximately 10 to 15 *kanji* (approximately 10 to 30 *kanji* for Levels 1 and 2) from the main book in the order that they appear, and each lesson provides a variety of approaches to help you master the usage of the target vocabulary and expand your overall understanding of *kanji*-based vocabulary. Each lesson is divided into three major sections as listed below:

Section I: Double compounds, idiomatic expressions, and sentence patterns that use the vocabulary.

Section II: Related vocabulary, other related words, contrasting expressions.

Section III: Example sentences using the vocabulary.

Now follow some examples of the material presented in each of the above sections. Underlined words are the vocabulary words from the main book.

Section I: Double compounds, idiomatic expressions, and sentence patterns that use the vocabulary

In this section, the basic usage of the vocabulary words is learned by studying expressions containing them.

1) Double compounds containing the vocabulary:
     e.g. 和平交渉　　団体旅行　　支持率　　技術移転
2) Broad idiomatic expressions using the vocabulary:
     e.g. 平和を守る　　公平な態度　　家具付きの家　　質問に対する答え
3) Sentence patterns using the vocabulary:
     e.g. 男も女も同等の扱いをする　　議論が平行線をたどる
        上体を大きく後ろに反らす　　手紙を封筒に入れて送る

Section II: Related vocabulary, other related words, contrasting expressions

In this section, the connections in meaning between the vocabulary and related words are studied.

1) Related target vocabulary and other related words:
     e.g. 戦争　　平和
        管理職　　平社員
        足し算　　引き算　　掛け算　　割り算
        電車／バス の切符　　映画／コンサート のチケット
2) Contrasting expressions:
     e.g. 収入 ⟷ 支出 (⟷ denotes antonyms)
        意見／提案 に反対する ⟷ 意見／提案 に賛成する
        ビールを冷やす ― ビールが冷える (― denotes intransitive/transitive verbs)

Section III: Example sentences using the vocabulary

In this section, the usage of the vocabulary is learned in the context of example sentences. The example sentences have been chosen so as to be of interest to adult learners, and they are appropriate examples for learning proper usage of the vocabulary. The readings of the underlined vocabulary words are given in the supplemental volume to the the workbook, where these underlined words are all collected together.

2. Vocabulary Covered in Workbook

In the workbook volumes, only vocabulary words that are printed in red (key vocabulary words) in the main book and words that are marked by no symbol or by the symbol ◇ in the main book are treated (see II. 6 "Explanation of Entries.") Key vocabulary words are printed in bold type in the workbook, and we have given item numbers to sentences containing key vocabulary words and printed the numbers in white within black circles. When you are first learning these key vocabulary words, please give priority to these items in the workbook that are encircled in black.

As a general rule, words that contain *kanji* that have not been previously studied (words marked with an asterisk (*)) are treated in the same way as underlined words and are not tested in workbook quizzes. However, although the number of such cases is small, there are some words that we have allowed despite the fact that they include previously unstudied *kanji*; the reason for this is that these words contain a basic reading of a *kanji*. You should regard these words as key vocabulary words, and learn them in the workbook.

With the rare exception of a few words that have become key vocabulary, historical terms marked 歴 and specialized terms marked 特, because they occur infrequently and can be thought of as quite special, are not treated in the workbook.

3. Division of Workbook

The first volume of the workbook covers Levels 1-3 of the main book (*kanji* numbers 1-1200), and the second volume covers Levels 4-7 (*kanji* numbers 1201-2136).

IV. How to use *Kanji in Context*

1. Target Level

The goal of *Kanji in Context* is to foster mastery of all of the *kanji* in everyday use. If you are a student of Japanese who has not yet learned all of the *Jōyō Kanji*, this textbook can be recommended to you.

If one does not know the basic *kanji*, it takes an enormous effort to remember the form of each individual character. To learn over 2,000 characters in a short period of time, it is necessary that you make effective use of characters you have learned previously. If you have acquired command of the basic *kanji*, you will be able to learn new *kanji* effectively by putting together things you know from the basic *kanji* or by noting that characters that are similar in form often have identical pronunciations or similar meanings.

This textbook assumes that the learner has mastered the 300-500 *kanji* normally taught in a typical beginning course. To make effective use of this text, you should already be familiar with most of the key words for the *kanji* entries in Levels 1 and 2 (*kanji* numbers 1-350). If you have mastered these *kanji*, then you should be able to use the main book and the workbook together to systematically learn the *kanji* and vocabulary presented.

If you are still at the beginning level, you can quickly increase your knowledge of compounds and other vocabulary by using the main book to systematically organize the *kanji* that you study in your beginning course textbook. As for the workbook, perhaps you should wait until you have increased your knowledge of *kanji* and vocabulary to a certain extent before you start using it.

2. Where to Start

For the most part, Levels 1 and 2 of the *kanji* entries in the main book represent the beginning level of study, Level 3 represents the intermediate level, Levels 4 and 5 represent the advanced level, and Levels 6 and 7 represent the post-advanced level. While it is possible for you to enter this text at any point in accordance with your current level of proficiency and preferred study method, in order to gain the maximum benefit from the design of *Kanji in Context* (organized so as to bring you to mastery of all of the characters in everyday use), generally it will be best to start at the beginning with Level 1. Although you are most likely already familiar with a large number of the *kanji* in Levels 1 and 2, the material presented in the entries at these levels is not confined to elementary vocabulary words, and we have made a point of presenting vocabulary that is necessary for intermediate and advanced students as well. For that reason, even if you have passed beyond the elementary phase of learning Japanese, study of these levels will almost surely help you expand your knowledge of *kanji*-based vocabulary.

3. Studying *Kanji* and *Kanji*-based Vocabulary with *Kanji in Context*

Below are some pointers that will help you to get the most out of the special features of *Kanji in Context*.

To attain the objective of this text, which is designed to enable students who have already learned some *kanji* to master all of the *Jōyō Kanji*, we recommend that you proceed by dividing your study into three stages and taking four successive steps at each stage.

Stage I: Learn the basics (master the readings of the *Jōyō Kanji*)

Step 1: Acquire a fundamental knowledge of the kanji entries
Fully memorize the forms of the *kanji* that are studied and the meaning and reading of the key words (words printed in red) in the main book and the *kanji* from which they are composed. This study gives you a fundamental knowledge of the *kanji*.

Step 2: Learn the meaning and usage of the kanji entries
Go over the vocabulary listed for each entry in the main book to learn the meaning and usage of the *kanji*. When you are strengthening your vocabulary by at first confining yourself to key words (printed in red), there is no need at this time to memorize the words that are not printed in red.

Step 3: Study the usage of the vocabulary and learn related words
Study the way *kanji* words that you learned are used, and study the way related words are used in the workbook. When you are focusing on key words (printed in red) only, study just the items that are marked by white numbers printed within black circles. Words printed in bold type are key vocabulary words, and you should make certain you memorize their meanings, their readings, and the way in which they are used. If you do not understand something, please go back to the main book and learn it.

Step 4: Check your mastery
Double-check to make certain that you have learned the key vocabulary words. Having your Japanese teacher or a friend make simple quizzes for you or making flashcards are among the effective ways to review. Another way that is useful for confirming your mastery is to try to create your own sentences containing the words in the workbook.

Continuing systematically to follow these four steps, go through the workbook until you have completed all 156 units. When you finish, you will have approximately 3,700 key words in your vocabulary. By mastering all of these, you will be able to read, or at least to infer the meanings and readings of, the vast majority of the *kanji* that appear in everyday Japanese written materials such as newspapers and magazines.

Stage II: Study the words that are unmarked by a symbol (review the readings of the *Jōyō Kanji* and expand your vocabulary)

In Stage II, you will be expanding and strengthening your stock of vocabulary words that incorporate the *kanji* you have learned. Go back to Unit 1 of the main book, and as you review key vocabulary words, follow the four steps described in Stage I, above, to gain mastery of the unmarked words (that is, the words that are not marked with the symbols ◇, 歴, or 特). When you reach Stage II you will have already learned all of the *Jōyō Kanji*, and at this stage you should also study the words in this book that contain characters you have not previously learned, which we have marked with an asterisk (✳). Please note that because not all these unmarked words are treated in the workbook, we have limited the list of such words by selecting words that are important to know but somewhat difficult to use. Although the number of such words is larger than the number of key vocabulary words, you will find that you master them faster than the key vocabulary words because you have already acquired knowledge of the forms and readings of the *Jōyō Kanji*. Continuing to follow this procedure, go through the main book until you have completed all 156 units.

Stage III: Study the words marked with the symbols ◇, 歴, and 特 (learn all the readings of the *Jōyō Kanji* and expand your vocabulary)

In the third and final stage, you will begin again at Unit 1 and learn the words marked with the symbols ◇, 歴, and 特. These words are considered to have relatively low importance than the unmarked words, and generally they are not treated in the workbook (exceptionally, a few words marked ◇ do appear in the workbook). It will be sufficient for you to check the main book and to learn these words as needed to deal with the materials you choose to read. Please be aware, however, that if you wish to attain total mastery of 100% of the readings of *Jōyō Kanji*, you will need to be able to read all of these words.

第 1 水準

（Level 1）

1-250

第 1 回

1
▶いち, いつ
▷ひと, ひと(つ)

一	いち	one
一分	いっぷん	one minute
*統一	とういつ [する] unify	
一*般*的な	いっぱんてきな	general, common
*唯一の	ゆいいつの	only, sole
一人	△ひとり	one person
一人一人	△ひとりひとり	one (person) by one, one (person) at a time
一つ	ひとつ	one (thing)
一目で	ひとめで	at a glance, at first sight
一日	△ついたち	the first day of a month
一日	いちにち	one day

2 二
▶に
▷ふた, ふた(つ)

二	に	two
二分	にふん	two minutes
二人	△ふたり	two persons
二つ	ふたつ	two (things)
二日	△ふつか	the second day of a month, two days
二十日	△はつか	the twentieth day of a month, twenty days
二十*歳	△はたち	twenty years old

3
▶さん
▷み, み(つ), みっ(つ)

三	さん	three
三分	さんぷん	three minutes
三人	さんにん	three persons
三つ	みっつ	three (things)
三日	みっか	the third day of a month, three days
三つ*角	みつかど	three-way junction
三日月	みかづき	crescent moon

4 四
▶し
▷よ, よ(つ), よっ(つ), よん

四	よん, し	four
四分	よんぷん	four minutes
四人	よにん	four persons
四つ	よっつ	four (things)
四日	よっか	the fourth day of a month, four days
四月	しがつ	April
四つ*角	よつかど	crossroads, four-way junction, a (street) corner

5 五
▶ご
▷いつ, いつ(つ)

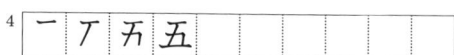

| 五 | ご | five |
| 五分 | ごふん | five minutes |

数え方❶

一分（いっぷん） 二分（にふん） 三分（さんぷん） 四分（よんぷん） 五分（ごふん）

六分（ろっぷん） 七分（ななふん） 八分（はちふん／はっぷん） 九分（きゅうふん）

十分（じっぷん／じゅっぷん）

一人（ひとり） 二人（ふたり） 三人（さんにん） 四人（よにん） 五人（ごにん）

六人（ろくにん） 七人（しちにん／ななにん） 八人（はちにん） 九人（きゅうにん／くにん）

十人（じゅうにん）

第1水準

五人　　ごにん　five persons
五つ　　いつつ　five (things)
五日　　いつか　the fifth day of a month, five days

6 六　▶ろく
▷む, む(つ), むっ(つ), むい

`4` 一 ナ 六 六

六　　　ろく　six
六分　　ろっぷん　six minutes
六人　　ろくにん　six persons
六つ　　むっつ　six (things)
六日　　むいか　the sixth day of a month, six days
六つ切り　むつぎり　cutting into six pieces

7 七　▶しち
▷なな, なな(つ), なの

`2` 一 七

七　　　しち, なな　seven
七分　　ななふん　seven minutes
七人　　しちにん, ななにん　seven persons
七つ　　ななつ　seven (things)
七日　　なのか　the seventh day of a month, seven days
七夕　　△たなばた　the Star <Weaver> Festival

8 八　▶はち
▷や, や(つ), やっ(つ), よう

`2` ノ 八

八　　　はち　eight
八分　　はちふん, はっぷん　eight minutes

八人　　はちにん　eight persons
八つ　　やっつ　eight (things)
八日　　ようか　the eighth day of a month, eight days
八百屋　△やおや　fruit and vegetable shop
八つ*当たり　やつあたり　-する take out one's anger on someone
◇ 八重*桜　やえざくら　double-flowered cherry tree

9 九　▶きゅう, く
▷ここの, ここの(つ)

`2` ノ 九

九　　　きゅう, く　nine
九分　　きゅうふん　nine minutes
九人　　きゅうにん, くにん　nine persons
九つ　　ここのつ　nine (things)
九日　　ここのか　the ninth day of a month, nine days
九月　　くがつ　September

10 十　▶じゅう, じっ
▷とお, と

`2` 一 十

十　　　じゅう　ten
十分　　じっぷん, じゅっぷん　ten minutes
十分な　じゅうぶんな　enough, sufficient
十人　　じゅうにん　ten persons
十*字*架　じゅうじか　cross
十　　　とお　ten (things)
十日　　とおか　the tenth day of a month, ten days
十重　　とえ　tenfold
二十日　△はつか　the twentieth day of a month, twenty days
二十*歳　△はたち　twenty years old

数え方❷

一つ（ひとつ）二つ（ふたつ）三つ（みっつ）四つ（よっつ）五つ（いつつ）
六つ（むっつ）七つ（ななつ）八つ（やっつ）九つ（ここのつ）十（とお）
一日（ついたち）二日（ふつか）三日（みっか）四日（よっか）五日（いつか）
六日（むいか）七日（なのか）八日（ようか）九日（ここのか）十日（とおか）
十九日（じゅうくにち）二十日（はつか）

3

11 百 ▶ひゃく

6 一 ア ア 百 百 百

百	ひゃく	one hundred
百円	ひゃくえん	one hundred yen
〜百	〜ひゃく／びゃく／ぴゃく	〜 hundred
三百六十五日	さんびゃくろくじゅうごにち	365 days
八百屋	△やおや	fruit and vegetable shop

12 千 ▶せん ▷ち

3 ˊ 二 千

千	せん	one thousand
千円	せんえん	one thousand yen
〜千	〜せん／ぜん	〜 thousand
千*島*列*島	ちしまれっとう	the Kuril Islands

13 万 ▶まん, ばん

3 一 ア 万

一万	いちまん	ten thousand
一万円	いちまんえん	ten thousand yen
万年*筆	まんねんひつ	fountain pen
万一	まんいち	by any chance, if anything should happen
万全の	ばんぜんの	thorough, all possible (means/etc.)

14 円 ▶えん ▷まる(い)

4 1 冂 冃 円

一万円	いちまんえん	ten thousand yen
円	えん	circle, yen
円高	えんだか	rise in the exchange rate of the yen
円安	えんやす	fall in the exchange rate of the yen
円い	まるい	circular cf. *丸い（まるい）spherical, globular, round

15 人 ▶じん, にん ▷ひと

2 ノ 人

アメリカ人	アメリカじん	an American
中国人	ちゅうごくじん	a Chinese
日本人	にほんじん	a Japanese
外国人	がいこくじん	foreigner
一人	△ひとり	one person
二人	△ふたり	two persons
三人	さんにん	three persons
〜人	〜にん	〜 persons
人	ひと	person
男の人	おとこのひと	man
女の人	おんなのひと	woman
人々	ひとびと	people
大人	△おとな	adult
*仲人	△なこうど	go-between, matchmaker
*素人	△しろうと	amateur, layman
*玄人	△くろうと	expert, professional, specialist cf. *素人（△しろうと）amateur

16 日 ▶にち, じつ ▷ひ, か

4 1 冂 冃 日

日曜日	にちようび	Sunday

百から一万

百（ひゃく）　二百（にひゃく）　三百（さんびゃく）　四百（よんひゃく）　五百（ごひゃく）
六百（ろっぴゃく）　七百（ななひゃく）　八百（はっぴゃく）　九百（きゅうひゃく）
千（せん）　二千（にせん）　三千（さんぜん）　四千（よんせん）　五千（ごせん）
六千（ろくせん）　七千（ななせん）　八千（はっせん）　九千（きゅうせん）　一万（いちまん）

日	ひ　day, sun
日ざし	ひざし　sunlight
毎日	まいにち　every day
日本	にほん，にっぽん　Japan
休日	きゅうじつ　holiday, day off
*祝日	しゅくじつ　national holiday
一日	△ついたち　the first day of a month
二日	△ふつか　the second day of a month, two days
三日	みっか　the third day of a month, three days
*昨日	さくじつ，△きのう　yesterday
今日	△きょう　today
明日	みょうにち，△あす，▲あした　tomorrow

17 月　▶げつ，がつ　▷つき

4　丿 几 月 月

月曜日	げつようび　Monday
月	つき　month, moon
月見	つきみ　moon-viewing
三日月	みかづき　crescent moon
一月	いちがつ　January
一か月	いっかげつ　one month
歴 五月	△さつき　name for fifth month of lunar calendar
歴 五月雨	△さみだれ　early summer rain

18 火　▶か　▷ひ，ほ

4　丶 丷 少 火

火曜日	かようび　Tuesday
火	ひ　fire, flame
火事	かじ　fire
火*星	かせい　Mars
◇ 火*影	ほかげ　light of a fire/flame

19 水　▶すい　▷みず

4　丿 刀 水 水

水曜日	すいようび　Wednesday
水	みず　water
水道	すいどう　waterworks, water service, tap water
水*星	すいせい　Mercury
*清水寺	きよみずでら　Kiyomizu Temple (in Kyoto)

20 木　▶ぼく，もく　▷き，こ

4　一 十 才 木

木曜日	もくようび　Thursday
木	き　tree
木々	きぎ　trees
大木	たいぼく　big tree
木*星	もくせい　Jupiter
木*綿	△もめん　cotton
◇ 木立	こだち　grove, cluster of trees

21 金　▶きん，こん　▷かね，かな

8　丿 入 入 今 全 仝 金 金

金曜日	きんようび　Friday
金	きん　gold
（お）金	（お）かね　money
お金持ち	おかねもち　rich person, wealthy people
金*星	きんせい　Venus
金物屋	かなものや　hardware store
◇ 金*堂	こんどう　main hall of a temple, golden pavilion
*黄金	おうごん，こがね　gold

「々」の使い方

々, as in 人々, is a sign to repeat the preceding *kanji*.

ex.　木々（きぎ）　時々（ときどき）　方々（かたがた，ほうぼう）

22 土 ▶ど，と ▷つち

3 | 一 | 十 | 土

土曜日	どようび	Saturday
土	つち	soil, earth
土地	とち	land
土*星	どせい	Saturn
(お)土*産	△(お)みやげ	souvenir

23 曜 ▶よう

18 | 1 | 冂 | 日 | 日 | 日¬ | 日⁷ | 日⁷ | 日⁷¬ | 日⁷⁷ |
| 日⁷⁷ | 昭 | 昭 | 昭 | 暗 | 曜 | 曜 | 曜

| 日曜日 | にちようび | Sunday |
| 曜日 | ようび | day of the week |

24 年 ▶ねん ▷とし

6 | ノ | ト | ヒ | 午 | 年 | 年

来年	らいねん	next year
去年	きょねん	last year
今年	△ことし	this year
年	とし	year, age
〜年	〜ねん	〜 year(s)
二千年	にせんねん	the year two thousand, two thousand years
三年生	さんねんせい	third-year student
年月	ねんげつ，としつき	months and years, time
年中	ねんじゅう	the whole year, throughout the year
生年月日	せいねんがっぴ	date of birth
年金	ねんきん	pension

25 時 ▶じ ▷とき

10 | 1 | 冂 | 日 | 日 | 日¬ | 日⁺ | 昨 | 昨 | 時 | 時

一時	いちじ	one o'clock, for a while, once
時間	じかん	time
〜時間	〜じかん	〜 hour(s)

時々	ときどき	sometimes
時	とき	time
時計	△とけい	clock, watch
歴 時雨	△しぐれ	rain shower in late autumn or early winter

26 分 ▶ぶん，ふん，ぶ ▷わ(ける)，わ(かれる)，わ(かる)，わ(かつ)

4 | ノ | 八 | 分 | 分

〜分	〜ふん／ぷん	〜 minute(s)
十分な	じゅうぶんな	enough, sufficient
水分	すいぶん	moisture, water
分かる	わかる	understand, realize, find out
分ける	わける	divide, separate, share
分かれる	わかれる	branch off from 〜 cf. *別れる(わかれる) part from, separate from a person
五分五分	ごぶごぶ	fifty-fifty, even
◇ 分かつ	わかつ	share, separate

第 2 回

27 今 ▶こん，きん ▷いま

4 | ノ | 八 | 今 | 今

今	いま	now
今週	こんしゅう	this week
今月	こんげつ	this month
今日	こんにち	today, nowadays
今日	△きょう	today
今年	△ことし	this year
今朝	△けさ	this morning
歴 今上*陛下	きんじょうへいか	the reigning emperor

28 午 ▶ご

4 | ノ | ト | 二 | 午

午前	ごぜん	morning
午後	ごご	afternoon
午後5時	ごごごじ	five o'clock p.m.

第1水準

第1水準

29 前　▶ぜん　▷まえ

9　丶　丷　丷　斺　斺　斺　前　前　前

前	まえ　in front of, before
名前	なまえ　name
人前で	ひとまえで　in public
一人前	いちにんまえ　grown-up, independent, full-fledged
午前	ごぜん　morning

30 後　▶ご，こう　▷のち，うし(ろ)，あと，おく(れる)

9　ノ　ク　彳　彳　往　往　徫　徫　後

後ろ	うしろ　behind, back
午後	ごご　afternoon
その後	そのご，そのあと　after that
前後	ぜんご　front and behind, before and after, about　するget out of order
明後日	みょうごにち，▲あさって　the day after tomorrow
後で	あとで　later
～(した)後	～(した)あと　after (doing) ～
後ほど	のちほど　later
後れる	おくれる　be behind (in one's work/schedule/ etc.)　cf. 遅れる(おくれる) be late (for)
後続の	こうぞくの　following (vehicle/etc.)

31 上　▶じょう，しょう　▷うえ，かみ，あ(げる)，あ(がる)，のぼ(る)，のぼ(せる)，のぼ(す)，うわ

3　丨　卜　上

上	うえ　top, on, above
上着	うわぎ　coat, jacket
上手な	△じょうずな　skilled, good (tennis player/ drawing/etc.)
地上	ちじょう　on the ground
川上	かわかみ　upper reaches of a river, upstream
*値上げ	ねあげ　price increase　するraise prices
上げる	あげる　raise
上がる	あがる　rise, go up
上り電車	のぼりでんしゃ　inbound train
上る	のぼる　rise, go up (stairs)　cf. *登る(のぼる) go up, climb
上回る	うわまわる　be more than, surpass, exceed
特 上せる	のぼせる　bring up something for discussion
特 上す	のぼす　put on, put something on (top of)
歴 上人	しょうにん　saint

32 下　▶か，げ　▷した，しも，もと，さ(げる)，さ(がる)，くだ(る)，くだ(す)，くだ(さる)，お(ろす)，お(りる)

3　一　丅　下

下	した　bottom, under, beneath
下書き	したがき　rough copy, draft
*靴下	くつした　socks
下見	したみ　preliminary visit, inspection　するget a preview of
川下	かわしも　lower reaches of a river, downstream
～の下で	～のもとで　under the supervision of ～
地下鉄	ちかてつ　subway, underground railway
下水	げすい　sewage, drainage
下車	げしゃ　するget off (a train), get out of (a car)
上下	じょうげ　up and down, top and bottom　するgo up and down
*値下げ	ねさげ　price reduction　するlower prices
下げる	さげる　bring down, lower
下ろす	おろす　put down　cf. 降ろす(おろす) unload, drop off (a passenger)
下りる	おりる　go down　cf. 降りる(おりる) get off (a train, etc.)
下り電車	くだりでんしゃ　outbound train
下る	くだる　go down, descend
下さる	くださる　give [honorific]
見下す	みくだす　despise, look down on (in contempt)
下手な	△へたな　unskillful, poor (tennis player/drawing/ etc.)

33 中　▶ちゅう，じゅう　▷なか

4　丨　冂　口　中

中	なか　the inside, in the middle
中学校	ちゅうがっこう　junior high school
中国	ちゅうごく　China

中東	ちゅうとう	the Middle East
中年の	ちゅうねんの	middle-aged
日中	にっちゅう	in the daytime
日中*関*係	にっちゅうかんけい	Sino-Japan relations
一日中	いちにちじゅう	all day long
世界中	せかいじゅう	throughout the world
心中	しんじゅう	double suicide [-する] commit suicide together
中小*企業	ちゅうしょうきぎょう	small and medium-sized enterprises

34 横 ▶おう ▷よこ

15 一 十 才 木 栌 栌 栌 桜 桜 枻 梏 椲 横 横 横 横

横	よこ	side, beside, the width
横切る	よこぎる	cross, traverse
横*顔	よこがお	side (of one's face), profile
横*断	おうだん	[-する] cross, go across

35 右 ▶う, ゆう ▷みぎ

5 ノ ナ オ 右 右

右	みぎ	right
右手	みぎて	right hand/arm
右足	みぎあし	right foot/leg
右*翼	うよく	the right wing, rightist
左右する	さゆうする	control, affect

36 左 ▶さ ▷ひだり

5 一 ナ 圡 圥 左

左	ひだり	left
左手	ひだりて	left hand/arm
左足	ひだりあし	left foot/leg
左右する	さゆうする	control, affect
左*翼	さよく	the left wing, leftist

37 本 ▶ほん ▷もと

5 一 十 才 木 本

本	ほん	book
～本	～ほん／ぼん／ぽん	counter for long objects
日本	にほん, にっぽん	Japan
本心	ほんしん	one's real intention/mind
本来	ほんらい	originally, essentially, naturally
本*当に	ほんとうに	truly, really
本*当の	ほんとうの	true, real
本	もと	the beginning, the origin

38 机 ▶き ▷つくえ

6 一 十 才 木 机 机

机	つくえ	desk
◇ 机上の*空*論	きじょうのくうろん	armchair theory

39 東 ▶とう ▷ひがし

8 一 厂 厅 戸 戸 申 東 東

東	ひがし	east
東ヨーロッパ	ひがしヨーロッパ	Eastern Europe
東アジア	ひがしアジア	East Asia
中東	ちゅうとう	the Middle East
東京	とうきょう	Tokyo
東*洋	とうよう	the East
*関東	かんとう	the Kanto region

40 西 ▶せい, さい ▷にし

6 一 冂 襾 两 西 西

西	にし	west
西ヨーロッパ	にしヨーロッパ	Western Europe
西アジア	にしアジア	West Asia
東西南北	とうざいなんぼく	north, south, east and west
西*洋	せいよう	the West
*関西	かんさい	the Kansai region

41 南 ▶なん，な
▷みなみ

9 一 十 十 内 内 丙 両 南 南

南	みなみ	south
南アメリカ	みなみアメリカ	South America
東南アジア	とうなんアジア	Southeast Asia
南下	なんか	-する go south

歴 南*無*妙*法*蓮*華*経　なむみょうほうれんげきょう
chant of the Tendai and Nichiren sects of Buddhism, taken from the Lotus Sutra

42 北 ▶ほく
▷きた

5 一 十 屮 北 北

北	きた	north
北アメリカ	きたアメリカ	North America
北風	きたかぜ	north wind
東北	とうほく	the Tohoku region, (the) northeast
北*海*道	ほっかいどう	Hokkaido
南北問題	なんぼくもんだい	North-South problem
北方*領土	ほっぽうりょうど	the Northern Territories

43 方 ▶ほう
▷かた

4 、 一 方 方

方	ほう	direction, way
方*向	ほうこう	direction
方々	ほうぼう	here and there, various places
食べ方	たべかた	way of eating, table manners
あの方	あのかた	the person over there [honorific]
行方	△ゆくえ	(one's) whereabouts

44 白 ▶はく，びゃく
▷しろ，しろ(い)，しら

5 ノ イ 白 白 白

白い	しろい	white
白	しろ	white
真っ白い／な	まっしろい／な	pure white, as white as snow
明白な	めいはくな	clear, obvious
白夜	びゃくや	nights under the midnight sun
白む	しらむ	grow light

45 黒 ▶こく
▷くろ，くろ(い)

11 丶 ロ 戸 甲 甲 里 里 黒 黒 黒
黒

黒い	くろい	black
黒	くろ	black
白黒テレビ	しろくろテレビ	black-and-white television
黒*字	くろじ	surplus, black (as in "be in the black") 反赤*字（あかじ）deficit, red (as in "be in the red")
真っ黒い／な	まっくろい／な	pitch-black
黒*板	こくばん	blackboard

46 赤 ▶せき，しゃく
▷あか，あか(い)，あか(らむ)，あか(らめる)

7 一 十 土 チ 赤 赤 赤

赤い	あかい	red
赤	あか	red
赤らめる	あからめる	blush
真っ赤な	△まっかな	bright/deep red
赤道	せきどう	the equator
赤外*線	せきがいせん	infrared light/ray
赤十*字	せきじゅうじ	the Red Cross
◇ 赤*銅色	しゃくどういろ	bronze(-colored), copper(-colored)

47 青 ▶せい，しょう
▷あお，あお(い)

8 一 十 キ 主 青 青 青 青

青い	あおい	blue
青	あお	blue
青白い	あおじろい	pale
真っ青な	△まっさおな	deep blue, pale
青春時*代	せいしゅんじだい	youth, springtime of life
青少年	せいしょうねん	juveniles, young people
特 *緑青	ろくしょう	copper/green rust, patina

48 先 ▶せん ▷さき

6 ノ ⺊ ⺊ 牛 生 牜 先

先生	せんせい	teacher, master
先週	せんしゅう	last week
先々週	せんせんしゅう	the week before last
先月	せんげつ	last month
先々月	せんせんげつ	the month before last
先日	せんじつ	the other day
先に	さきに	previously, beforehand
先ほど	さきほど	a little while ago, some time ago

49 生 ▶せい, しょう ▷い(きる), い(かす), い(ける), う(まれる), う(む), お(う), は(える), は(やす), き, なま

5 ノ ⺊ 牛 生 生

先生	せんせい	teacher, master
学生	がくせい	student
生*徒	せいと	pupil, student
生*活	せいかつ	[-する] live, make a living
生長	せいちょう	growth (of a plant) [-する] grow
一生	いっしょう	one's (whole) life
*誕生日	たんじょうび	birthday
生まれる	うまれる	be born
生む	うむ	yield, produce cf. *産む(うむ) bear
生きる	いきる	live
生き生きした	いきいきした	lively, fresh
生かす	いかす	make the most of, make the best use of
生け花	いけばな	the art of flower arrangement
生ビール	なまビール	draft beer
生*野*菜	なまやさい	fresh vegetables
生える	はえる	sprout, spring up
*芝生	△しばふ	lawn, plot of grass
生地	きじ	cloth, clothing materials
◇ 生*糸	きいと	raw silk
生い立ち	おいたち	one's background, one's personal history

50 学 ▶がく ▷まな(ぶ)

8 丶 ⺍ ⺍ ⺌ 巛 学 学 学

学校	がっこう	school
学生	がくせい	student
大学	だいがく	university, college
学長	がくちょう	president (of a university)
～学部	～がくぶ	department of ～ , school of ～
入学	にゅうがく	[-する] enter a school
学ぶ	まなぶ	learn

51 校 ▶こう

10 一 十 才 木 木' 栌 栌 栌 栌 校

学校	がっこう	school
小学校	しょうがっこう	elementary school
中学校	ちゅうがっこう	junior high school
高校	こうこう	high school
校長	こうちょう	principal, schoolmaster

第 3 回

52 家 ▶か, け ▷いえ, や

10 丶 ⺆ 宀 宀 宁 宇 宇 家 家 家

家	いえ, ▲うち	house, home
家族	かぞく	family
家*庭	かてい	one's home
家事	かじ	housework, housekeeping
家内	かない	my wife
国家	こっか	state, nation
作家	さっか	novelist cf. *筆者(ひっしゃ) writer, *著者(ちょしゃ) author
～家	～け	the ～ family
大家	おおや	landlord, owner of a rented house/apartment

53 部 ▶ぶ

11 丶 ⺊ 立 立 立 音 音 音 音 音⻏ 部

部

部長　　　　ぶちょう　department head
人事部　　　じんじぶ　personnel department
部下　　　　ぶか　subordinate, one's men
本部　　　　ほんぶ　headquarters, head office
外部の　　　がいぶの　outside, external, exterior
内部の　　　ないぶの　inside, internal, interior
全部　　　　ぜんぶ　all, whole
一部　　　　いちぶ　a portion, a part of
部分　　　　ぶぶん　one portion, one part
大部分　　　だいぶぶん　most of 〜, the majority of 〜
部屋　　　　△へや　room

54 屋 ▶おく
　　　▷や

9　一　コ　尸　尸　尸　层　层　屋　屋

本屋　　　　ほんや　bookstore
花屋　　　　はなや　flower shop, flower stall
八百屋　　　△やおや　fruit and vegetable shop
部屋　　　　△へや　room
小屋　　　　こや　hut, shed, shack
屋*根　　　　やね　roof
屋上　　　　おくじょう　housetop, roof
屋内プール　おくないプール　indoor (swimming) poor
屋外　　　　おくがい　outdoor, open-air
家屋　　　　かおく　houses
歴 母屋　　　△おもや　main building/house　cf. can be
　　　　　　written as 母家

55 店 ▶てん
　　　▷みせ

8　丶　宀　广　广　庁　店　店　店

店　　　　　みせ　store, shop
夜店　　　　よみせ　night stall/stand
店屋　　　　みせや　shops and stores
店長　　　　てんちょう　store manager
本店　　　　ほんてん　the main (office/store)
*支店　　　　してん　branch office/store
*支店長　　　してんちょう　branch manager

56 駅 ▶えき

14　1　厂　厂　F　F　馬　馬　馬　馬
　　馬　馬　馬　駅　駅

駅　　　　　えき　station
駅前　　　　えきまえ　in front of the station
東京駅　　　とうきょうえき　Tokyo Station
駅長　　　　えきちょう　stationmaster

57 銀 ▶ぎん

14　ノ　ハ　ト　乍　午　牟　金　金　鈩
　　釗　鈩　鈩　銀　銀

銀行　　　　ぎんこう　bank
日本銀行　　にほんぎんこう　the Bank of Japan　cf. *abbr.*
　　　　　　日銀（にちぎん）
銀　　　　　ぎん　silver
水銀　　　　すいぎん　mercury, quicksilver
銀色　　　　ぎんいろ　silver, silvery

58 行 ▶こう, ぎょう, あん
　　　▷い(く), ゆ(く), おこな(う)

6　ノ　ク　彳　彳　行　行

銀行　　　　ぎんこう　bank
旅行　　　　りょこう　する make a trip, travel
行動　　　　こうどう　behavior, conduct, action　する act,
　　　　　　behave
行く　　　　いく, ゆく　go
行方　　　　△ゆくえ　(one's) whereabouts
行う　　　　おこなう　do, carry out, hold　cf. 行われる（お
　　　　　　こなわれる) be carried out, be held
行い　　　　おこない　act, action, deed, behavior
行事　　　　ぎょうじ　event
行*政　　　　ぎょうせい　administration
行　　　　　ぎょう　line (in a text)
〜行目　　　〜ぎょうめ　line (one/two/etc.)
歴 行*脚　　　あんぎゃ　する make a pilgrimage, go on a
　　　　　　(walking) tour

11

59 会

▶かい，え
▷あ（う）

6 ノ 入 ム 会 会 会

会社	かいしゃ company
社会	しゃかい society
会話	かいわ conversation -する talk
国会	こっかい the Diet
学会	がっかい academic conference, academic society
大会	たいかい convention, general meeting, tournament, rally
会う	あう meet
会*釈	えしゃく -する bow slightly
会*得	えとく -する understand (the meaning of), learn how to do

60 社

▶しゃ
▷やしろ

7 丶 ラ ネ ネ ネ 社 社

会社	かいしゃ company
社会	しゃかい society
社長	しゃちょう company president
社*員	しゃいん company employee
本社	ほんしゃ headquarters, main office
支社	ししゃ branch (office)
歴 社	やしろ Shinto shrine

61 電

▶でん

13 一 ｢ 戸 币 而 而 兩 雨 雨 雨 雪 雷 電

電車	でんしゃ train
電話	でんわ telephone -する call
電気	でんき electricity, (electric) lights
発電	はつでん (electric) power generation -する generate electricity
電子	でんし electron
電*池	でんち battery

62 車

▶しゃ
▷くるま

7 一 ｢ 戸 戸 亘 亘 車

電車	でんしゃ train
自転車	じてんしゃ bicycle
車	くるま car
歴 山車	△だし float, festival car

63 自

▶じ，し
▷みずか（ら）

6 丶 ｢ 白 白 自 自

自動車	じどうしゃ car
自転車	じてんしゃ bicycle
自分	じぶん self, oneself, I
自分で	じぶんで by oneself, personally
自*由	じゆう freedom, liberty
自*然	しぜん nature, natural
自ら	みずから (for) oneself, in person

64 動

▶どう
▷うご（く），うご（かす）

11 一 二 戸 百 盲 盲 重 重 重 動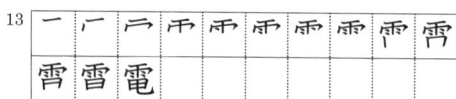

自動車	じどうしゃ car
自動	じどう automatic
動物	どうぶつ animal
行動	こうどう behavior, conduct, action -する act, behave
動く	うごく move, work, run, operate

65 転

▶てん
▷ころ（がる），ころ（げる），ころ（がす），ころ（ぶ）

11 一 ｢ 戸 戸 亘 亘 車 車 転 転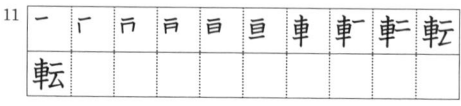

自転車	じてんしゃ bicycle
運転	うんてん -する drive (a car), operate (a machine, train, etc.)
転ぶ	ころぶ tumble, fall down

転がす　　ころがす　roll (a stone/tire/etc.)

転がる　　ころがる　roll (over), tumble

転々とする　てんてんとする　go rolling, wander (from one place/job to another)

66 **道**　▶どう，とう
　　　▷みち

12 ｀　ｿ　ｿ　ｿ　产　肖　肖　首　首　首
道　道

道　　　　みち　road, street, a way, a path

水道　　　すいどう　waterworks, water service, tap water

国道　　　こくどう　national road

道*路　　　どうろ　road, street

北*海道　　ほっかいどう　Hokkaido

茶道　　　さどう，ちゃどう　the art of the tea ceremony

*神道　　　しんとう　Shintoism, Shinto

67 **男**　▶だん，なん
　　　▷おとこ

7 ｜　口　四　甲　田　里　男

男の人　　おとこのひと　man

男　　　　おとこ　man

山男　　　やまおとこ　mountaineer, alpinist, woodsman

男*性　　　だんせい　man, male

長男　　　ちょうなん　the eldest son

68 **女**　▶じょ，にょ，にょう
　　　▷おんな，め

3 く　女　女

女の人　　おんなのひと　woman

女　　　　おんな　woman

女*性　　　じょせい　woman, female

長女　　　ちょうじょ　the eldest daughter

女*房　　　にょうぼう　(my/one's) wife

*老若男女　ろうにゃくなんにょ，ろうじゃくなんにょ
　　　　　　men and women of all ages

特 女人　　にょにん　woman

　女*神　　めがみ　goddess

歴 *乙女　　△おとめ　maiden, (young) girl, virgin

◇ *海女　　△あま　woman diver (for shellfish or seaweed, etc.)　cf. *海*士（あま）is used for male divers.

69 **子**　▶し，す
　　　▷こ

3 ｱ　了　子

子ども　　こども　child, son/daughter　cf. written either 子ども or 子供

男の子　　おとこのこ　boy

女の子　　おんなのこ　girl

*迷子　　　△まいご　lost child

*息子　　　△むすこ　son

帰国子女　きこくしじょ　children who have returned to Japan after living abroad for some time

男子社*員　だんししゃいん　male employee

女子社*員　じょししゃいん　female employee

*扇子　　　せんす　folding fan

70 **主**　▶しゅ，す
　　　▷ぬし，おも

5 ｀　亠　ナ　主　主

主人　　　しゅじん　master, proprietor, my husband

主語　　　しゅご　subject　cf. *述語（じゅつご）predicate

主題　　　しゅだい　subject, theme

主*観*的な　しゅかんてきな　subjective　反客*観*的な（きゃっかんてきな）objective

主な　　　おもな　main, chief, principal, leading

持ち主　　もちぬし　owner, possessor

地主　　　じぬし　landlord, landowner

*坊主　　　ぼうず　Buddhist priest, shaven head, boy

71 **奥**　▶おう
　　　▷おく

12 ｀　ｲ　冂　冂　冂　向　帠　帠　奧　奧
奥　奥

奥さん　　おくさん　(your/his) wife

奥　　　　おく　inside, inner part

山奥　　　やまおく　deep in the mountains

奥行き　　おくゆき　depth

◇ 奥*義　　おうぎ　secrets, key principles

13

72 私 ▶し ▷わたくし, わたし

7 ノ 二 千 千 禾 私 私

私	わたくし, わたし I, me cf. わたくし formally used, わたし used in conversation
私立大学	しりつだいがく private university/college cf. 国立大学(こくりつだいがく) national university/college, 公立高校(こうりつこうこう) public high school

73 父 ▶ふ ▷ちち

4 ノ ハ グ 父

父	ちち father
お父さん	△おとうさん father [polite]
父母	ふぼ father and mother

74 母 ▶ぼ ▷はは

5 ㇄ 口 口 母 母

母	はは mother
お母さん	△おかあさん mother [polite]
母語	ぼご mother tongue
*乳母	△うば wet nurse
歴 母屋	△おもや main building/house cf. can be written as 母家

75 兄 ▶けい, きょう ▷あに

5 ㇉ 口 口 尸 兄

兄	あに elder brother
お兄さん	△おにいさん elder brother [polite]
兄弟	きょうだい brother(s) and sister(s)
◇ 長兄	ちょうけい one's oldest brother

76 弟 ▶てい, だい, で ▷おとうと

7 ㇔ ㇌ ㇒ ㇒ 弓 弟 弟

弟	おとうと younger brother

兄弟	きょうだい brother(s) and sister(s)
子弟	してい children, young people
弟子	でし disciple, pupil

77 姉 ▶し ▷あね

8 ㇉ 女 女 女' 妒 妒 姉 姉

姉	あね elder sister
お姉さん	△おねえさん elder sister [polite]
姉妹	しまい sisters

78 妹 ▶まい ▷いもうと

8 ㇉ 女 女 女' 妹 妹 妹 妹

妹	いもうと younger sister
姉妹	しまい sisters
姉妹*都*市	しまいとし sister city

79 友 ▶ゆう ▷とも

4 一 ナ 方 友

友だち	ともだち friend, can be written as 友達
友人	ゆうじん friend (more formal than 友だち)
友好*関*係	ゆうこうかんけい friendly relations

第 4 回

80 何 ▶か ▷なに, なん

7 ノ イ イ 仁 仃 何 何

何	なに what
何時	なんじ what time cf. 何人(なんにん), 何回(なんかい), 何日(なんにち), etc.
何でも	なんでも whatever
何で	なんで why (used in casual speech)
何とか	なんとか one way or another, somehow
◇ *幾何学	きかがく geometry

81 誰 ▷だれ

15 丶 亠 宀 言 言 言 言 言 訂 訂
訂 訂 訓 誰 誰

誰　　　だれ　who

82 名 ▶めい，みょう
▷な

6 ノ ク タ タ 名 名

名前　　　なまえ　name
人名　　　じんめい　personal name
地名　　　ちめい　place name
名人　　　めいじん　master, expert
*仮名　　△かな　kana, Japanese syllabary
名残　　△なごり　remains, vestiges
歴 大名　　だいみょう　daimyō, feudal lord

83 高 ▶こう
▷たか(い)，たか，たか(まる)，たか(める)

10 丶 亠 广 吂 吂 吂 高 高 高 高

高い　　　たかい　high, expensive
円高　　　えんだか　rise in the exchange rate of the yen
売上高　　うりあげだか　sales, turnover
高まる　　たかまる　rise, be raised
高校　　　こうこう　high school
高気*圧　こうきあつ　high atmospheric pressure

84 安 ▶あん
▷やす(い)

6 丶 丷 宀 灾 安 安

安い　　　やすい　cheap, inexpensive
ドル安　　ドルやす　fall in the exchange rate of the dollar
安心　　　あんしん [-する] feel relieved, stop worrying, feel at ease 反 心*配(しんぱい) [-する] be worried, be anxious
安全　　　あんぜん　safety
*不安　　　ふあん　anxiety

85 新 ▶しん
▷あたら(しい)，あら(た)，にい

13 ' 亠 立 立 立 辛 辛 亲 亲 新
新 新 新

新しい　　あたらしい　new
新聞　　　しんぶん　newspaper
新車　　　しんしゃ　new car　cf. 中古車(ちゅうこしゃ) used car
新入生　　しんにゅうせい　new student
新入社*員　しんにゅうしゃいん　new employee
新たな　　あらたな　new
歴 新*妻　にいづま　newly married woman

86 古 ▶こ
▷ふる(い)，ふる(す)

5 一 十 十 古 古

古い　　　ふるい　old
古本　　　ふるほん　used book
使い古す　つかいふるす　wear out (by use)
中古車　　ちゅうこしゃ　used car
古*典文学　こてんぶんがく　classical literature
古文　　　こぶん　ancient writings, classics
古今東西　ここんとうざい　all ages and countries/places

87 大 ▶だい，たい
▷おお，おお(きい)，おお(いに)

3 一 ナ 大

大きい　　おおきい　big, large
大いに　　おおいに　very, exceedingly
大学　　　だいがく　university, college
大小　　　だいしょう　large and small, various size
大*丈夫　だいじょうぶ　all right, okay, safe
大*豆　　だいず　soybean
大国　　　たいこく　big/powerful nation
大金　　　たいきん　large amount of money
大した　　たいした　great, serious, important, considerable (as in 大した問題(もんだい)ではない)
大して　　たいして　not very ～, not so much ～
大人　　△おとな　adult

歴 大*和*朝*廷 △やまとちょうてい *Yamato Chōtei*, the ancient Japanese Imperial Court

歴 大*和*絵 △やまとえ *Yamato-e* painting

88 小 ▶しょう
▷ちい(さい)，こ，お

3 亅 小 小

小さい　　　ちいさい　small, little
小学校　　　しょうがっこう　elementary school
大小　　　　だいしょう　large and small, various sizes
小人　　　　しょうにん　children (used in bus fares, etc.)
小人　　　　しょうじん　insignificant person, small-minded person
小人　　　　こびと　dwarf, sprite, pygmy
小*指　　　　こゆび　the little finger, the little toe
小*鳥　　　　ことり　little bird
小切手　　　こぎって　check
小川　　　　おがわ　(small) stream
◇ 小*豆　　　△あずき　adzuki beans

89 長 ▶ちょう
▷なが(い)

8 丨 厂 厂 F 厒 長 長 長

長い　　　　ながい　long
長年　　　　ながねん　for a long time
社長　　　　しゃちょう　company president
部長　　　　ぶちょう　department head
長時間　　　ちょうじかん　for a long time
長所　　　　ちょうしょ　strong point, merit 反短所(たんしょ) weak point, shortcoming

90 短 ▶たん
▷みじか(い)

12 丿 亠 ヒ 乍 矢 矢 短 短 短 短
短 短

短い　　　　みじかい　short, brief
短気な　　　たんきな　short-tempered, easily angered
短所　　　　たんしょ　weak point, shortcoming
長短　　　　ちょうたん　strong points and weak points
短*期大学　　たんきだいがく　junior college cf. *abbr.* 短大 (たんだい)
短*期の　　　たんきの　short-term

91 朝 ▶ちょう
▷あさ

12 一 十 十 古 吉 吉 直 卓 卓 朝
朝 朝

朝　　　　　あさ　morning
朝ごはん　　あさごはん　breakfast
毎朝　　　　まいあさ　every morning
朝日　　　　あさひ　morning sun
朝食　　　　ちょうしょく　breakfast
今朝　　　　△けさ　this morning

92 昼 ▶ちゅう
▷ひる

9 ⊃ コ 尸 尺 尺 昇 昇 昼 昼

昼　　　　　ひる　daytime, noon, midday
昼ごはん　　ひるごはん　lunch
昼休み　　　ひるやすみ　lunch break
昼間　　　　ひるま　daytime
昼食　　　　ちゅうしょく　lunch

93 夜 ▶や
▷よ，よる

8 ⼀ 亠 广 广 疒 夜 夜 夜

夜　　　　　よる　night
夜明け　　　よあけ　dawn, daybreak
夜中　　　　よなか　in the night
今夜　　　　こんや　tonight
夜食　　　　やしょく　midnight snack
夜行*列車　　やこうれっしゃ　night train
*昨夜　　　　さくや，▲ゆうべ　last evening, last night

94 晩 ▶ばん

12 丨 冂 日 日 日' 日? 日? 昭 晱 晩
晱 晩

晩　　　　　ばん　evening, night
晩ごはん　　ばんごはん　dinner, supper
今晩　　　　こんばん　tonight

毎晩	まいばん	every night
一晩	ひとばん	one night
一晩中	ひとばんじゅう	all night (long)
晩年	ばんねん	late in life, one's later years

95 夕 ▶せき ▷ゆう

3 ノ ク 夕

夕方	ゆうがた	evening
夕日	ゆうひ	evening/setting sun
夕べ	ゆうべ	evening
七夕	△たなばた	the Star <Weaver> Festival
◇ 一朝一夕	いっちょういっせき	in a day, in a short time

96 春 ▶しゅん ▷はる

9 一 二 三 丰 夫 耒 耒 春 春

春	はる	spring
春休み	はるやすみ	spring vacation
春分の日	しゅんぶんのひ	Vernal Equinox Day
◇ 立春	りっしゅん	the first day of spring (in the lunar calendar)
青春時*代	せいしゅんじだい	youth, springtime of life
売春	ばいしゅん	[-する] prostitute
歴 春画	しゅんが	erotic painting or print (early modern)

97 夏 ▶か, げ ▷なつ

10 一 一 一 一 百 百 百 頁 夏 夏

夏	なつ	summer
夏休み	なつやすみ	summer vacation
春夏秋冬	しゅんかしゅうとう	the four seasons
◇ 夏*至	げし	summer solstice

98 秋 ▶しゅう ▷あき

9 ノ 二 千 禾 禾 利 科 秋 秋

秋	あき	autumn, fall

秋風	あきかぜ	autumn breeze
秋分の日	しゅうぶんのひ	Autumnal Equinox Day

99 冬 ▶とう ▷ふゆ

5 ノ ク タ 冬 冬

冬	ふゆ	winter
冬休み	ふゆやすみ	winter vacation
冬*空	ふゆぞら	winter sky, wintry weather
冬*眠	とうみん	[-する] hibernate

100 山 ▶さん ▷やま

3 | 山 山

山	やま	mountain
入山	にゅうざん	[-する] begin to climb a mountain
下山	げざん	[-する] climb down a mountain
火山	かざん	volcano
歴 山水画	さんすいが	(Chinese-style) landscape paintings
歴 山車	△だし	float, festival car
歴 *築山	△つきやま	artificial hill (in a landscape garden)

101 川 ▶せん ▷かわ

3 ノ 川 川

川	かわ	river
〜川	〜がわ／かわ	〜 River
川上	かわかみ	upper reaches of a river, upstream
川下	かわしも	lower reaches of a river, downstream
小川	おがわ	(small) stream
川原	△かわら	dry riverbed
*河川	かせん	rivers
川*柳	せんりゅう	satirical poem in 17 syllables

102 石 ▶せき, しゃく, こく ▷いし

5 一 ア 不 石 石

石	いし	stone

小石	こいし	small stone, pebbles
石田	いしだ	Ishida (a surname)
石けん	せっけん	soap　cf. 石けん can be written as 石鹸, but 鹸 is not a *Jōyō Kanji*.
*宝石	ほうせき	jewels, precious stones
*磁石	じしゃく	magnet, compass
歴 ～石	～こく／ごく	*koku* (unit of volume, approx. 180 liters)

103 田

▶でん
▷た

5 | 一 | 冂 | 冂 | 用 | 田 | | | | |

山田	やまだ	Yamada (a surname)
田中	たなか	Tanaka (a surname)
田	た	rice paddy, rice field
水田	すいでん	rice paddy, rice field
*油田	ゆでん	oil field
田*舎	△いなか	countryside, rural district, one's hometown

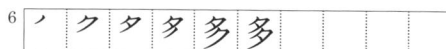

第 5 回

104 多

▶た
▷おお(い)

6 | ノ | ク | タ | タ | 多 | 多 | | | |

多い	おおい	many, plenty
多少	たしょう	to a certain extent, somewhat, quantity, amount
多*数の	たすうの	many, a lot of

105 少

▶しょう
▷すく(ない), すこ(し)

4 | 丿 | 小 | 小 | 少 | | | | | |

少ない	すくない	few
少し	すこし	a little, a few
少年	しょうねん	boy
少女	しょうじょ	girl
少々	しょうしょう	a little, a bit
少*数の	しょうすうの	a little, a few
*減少	げんしょう	する decrease

106 明

▶めい, みょう
▷あ(かり), あか(るい), あか(るむ), あか(らむ), あき(らか), あ(ける), あ(く), あ(くる), あ(かす)

8 | 一 | 冂 | 日 | 日 | 町 | 明 | 明 | 明 | |

明るい	あかるい	bright, light, cheerful
明るむ	あかるむ	become light
明らかな	あきらかな	clear, obvious
明白な	めいはくな	clear, obvious
説明	せつめい	する explain
*証明	しょうめい	する prove, certify
明日	みょうにち, △あす, ▲あした	tomorrow
夜が明ける	よがあける	day breaks
夜明け	よあけ	dawn, daybreak
明け方	あけがた	dawn, daybreak
明くる日	あくるひ	the next day
明かり	あかり	light
明かす	あかす	stay up all night, reveal (one's identity/intentions)

107 暗

▶あん
▷くら(い)

13 | 一 | 冂 | 日 | 日 | 日' | 日立 | 日立 | 日立 | 暗 | 暗 |
| 暗 | 暗 | 暗 | | | | | | | |

暗い	くらい	dark, gloomy
明暗	めいあん	light and shade
暗*示	あんじ	する hint, suggest

108 低

▶てい
▷ひく(い), ひく(める), ひく(まる)

7 | ノ | イ | イ | 仁 | 仳 | 低 | 低 | | |

低い	ひくい	low, short
高低	こうてい	rise and fall, pitch, undulations
低気*圧	ていきあつ	low atmospheric pressure
低める	ひくめる	lower

109 近

▶きん
▷ちか(い)

7 | ノ | イ | ア | 斤 | 沂 | 近 | 近 | | |

18

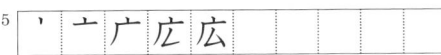

近い	ちかい	near
近道	ちかみち	shortcut
近づく	ちかづく	approach, come near
近々	ちかぢか	shortly, before long
近所	きんじょ	neighborhood
近日中に	きんじつちゅうに	soon, one of these days
近*代*化	きんだいか	modernization

110 遠 ▶えん, おん ▷とお(い)

13　一 十 土 キ 吉 吉 声 克 克 克 袁
袁 遠 遠

遠い	とおい	far, distant, remote
*永遠の	えいえんの	eternal
遠足	えんそく	(a day) excursion, (school) trip
遠心力	えんしんりょく	centrifugal force
遠近*法	えんきんほう	perspective (drawing)
特 *久遠の	くおんの	eternal

111 強 ▶きょう, ごう ▷つよ(い), つよ(まる), つよ(める), し(いる)

11　フ フ 弓 子 弹 弹 弹 弹 強 強
強

強い	つよい	strong, powerful
強まる	つよまる	become strong
強み	つよみ	strong point
勉強	べんきょう	する study
強力な	きょうりょくな	strong, powerful
強*制	きょうせい	する compel, force
強引な	ごういんな	forcible, overbearing, coercive
強いる	しいる	compel, force

112 弱 ▶じゃく ▷よわ(い), よわ(る), よわ(まる), よわ(める)

10　フ フ 弓 弓 弓 弓 弓 弱 弱 弱

弱い	よわい	weak, feeble, faint
弱まる	よわまる	vi. weaken, abate
弱*点	じゃくてん	weak point
弱*肉強食	じゃくにくきょうしょく	(a world where) the weak are victims of the strong

113 広 ▶こう ▷ひろ(い), ひろ(まる), ひろ(める), ひろ(がる), ひろ(げる)

5　' 亠 广 広 広

広い	ひろい	wide, broad, large
広場	ひろば	plaza, (public) square, open space
広まる	ひろまる	vi. spread, be diffused, become popular
広がる	ひろがる	vi. spread, extend, stretch
広める	ひろめる	vt. spread, diffuse, disseminate, make something popular
広げる	ひろげる	vt. widen, unfold, unroll, spread, extend, expand
広々とした	ひろびろとした	wide, spacious
広大な	こうだいな	vast

114 悪 ▶あく, お ▷わる(い)

11　一 ㇏ 冖 旦 甲 甲 亜 亜 悪 悪
悪

悪い	わるい	bad, wrong, evil, harmful
悪口を言う	わるくち／わるぐちをいう	speak ill of
悪人	あくにん	wicked/bad person
悪意	あくい	ill will, malice
悪*化	あっか	する vi. worsen
*憎悪	ぞうお	する hate, abhor
*嫌悪*感	けんおかん	hatred, aversion

115 重 ▶じゅう, ちょう ▷え, おも(い), かさ(ねる), かさ(なる)

9　一 二 亍 亍 亍 盲 重 重 重

重い	おもい	heavy, weighty, serious (illness/injury)
体重	たいじゅう	body weight
重力	じゅうりょく	gravity
重大な	じゅうだいな	serious, important, grave
重*工業	じゅうこうぎょう	heavy industry
重*点	じゅうてん	important point, priority, emphasis
重*役	じゅうやく	company director
重体	じゅうたい	seriously injured/ill, in a critical/serious condition
二重*否定	にじゅうひてい	double negative
*貴重な	きちょうな	valuable, precious

*慎重な　　　しんちょうな　prudent, careful, cautious

重*複　　　ちょうふく　[-する] be repeated/duplicated, overlap

重ねる　　　かさねる　pile up, repeat

◇ 八重*桜　　やえざくら　double-flowered cherry tree

---

116 軽 ▶けい ▷かる(い), かろ(やか)

12	一	厂	戸	百	亘	車	軒	軒	軽
軽	軽								

軽い　　　かるい　light, slight (illness/injury)

手軽な　　　てがるな　easy, simple

気軽に　　　きがるに　lightheartedly, easily, without reserve

◇ 軽やかに　かろやかに　lightly, merrily

軽食　　　けいしょく　light meal

軽自動車　　けいじどうしゃ　compact car

軽*工業　　けいこうぎょう　light industry

軽*率な　　けいそつな　rash, thoughtless, imprudent

---

117 早 ▶そう, さっ ▷はや(い), はや(まる), はや(める)

6	丨	冂	日	日	旦	早

早い　　　はやい　early

早める　　　はやめる　move (the date/time) forward

*素早い　　すばやい　quick, agile, nimble

早朝　　　そうちょう　early in the morning

早春　　　そうしゅん　early spring

早*速　　　さっそく　immediately, right away

早急に　　　さっきゅうに, そうきゅうに　immediately

---

118 遅 ▶ち ▷おく(れる), おく(らす), おそ(い)

12	┐	コ	尸	尸	尸	尸	屖	屖	犀	ˋ犀
遅	遅									

遅い　　　おそい　late, slow

遅れる　　　おくれる　be late, be overdue, be behind the time

遅らす　　　おくらす　delay, put off, postpone

遅*刻　　　ちこく　[-する] be late

---

119 暑 ▶しょ ▷あつ(い)

12	丶	冂	曰	日	昌	早	昱	昇	昇	暑
暑	暑									

暑い　　　あつい　hot

残暑　　　ざんしょ　late summer heat

暑中見*舞い　しょちゅうみまい　midsummer greeting

*避暑地　　ひしょち　summer retreat

---

120 寒 ▶かん ▷さむ(い)

12	丶	宀	宀	宁	宝	审	寒	寒	寒
寒	寒								

寒い　　　さむい　cold

寒気　　　さむけ　chill, (have) the shivers

寒気　　　かんき　the cold, coldness

寒*村　　　かんそん　lonely/impoverished village

◇ 寒*天　　かんてん　agar, vegetable gelatin

*厳寒の　　げんかんの　severe cold, coldest

---

121 深 ▶しん ▷ふか(い), ふか(まる), ふか(める)

11	丶	冫	氵	氵	汐	汐	浮	浮	深	深
深										

深い　　　ふかい　deep, thick, profound

深める　　　ふかめる　deepen, promote (better understanding/etc.)

深まる　　　ふかまる　get deeper, deepen

深夜　　　しんや　midnight

水深　　　すいしん　water depth

---

122 浅 ▶せん ▷あさ(い)

9	丶	冫	氵	氵	汐	汗	浅	浅	浅

浅い　　　あさい　shallow, slight

浅*薄な　　せんぱくな　shallow, superficial

123 **細** ▶さい
▷ほそ(い)，ほそ(る)，こま(か)，こま(かい)

11	く	纟	幺	纟	糸	糸	約	紀	細	細
細										

細い　ほそい　thin, fine, slim, slender
やせ細る　やせほそる　become thin, become emaciated
細かい　こまかい　fine (line), detailed, trifling, small (change)
細部　さいぶ　details
明細書　めいさいしょ　detailed statement
歴 細雪　▲ささめゆき　light snowfall

124 **太** ▶たい，た
▷ふと(い)，ふと(る)

4	一	ナ	大	太				

太い　ふとい　thick, big
太る　ふとる　gain (body) weight, become fat
太*陽　たいよう　the sun
太*郎　たろう　(male given name)
*丸太　まるた　log
歴 太*刀　△たち　sword

125 **若** ▶じゃく，にゃく
▷わか(い)，も(しくは)

8	一	十	サ	ア	芋	若	若	若	

若い　わかい　young
若々しい　わかわかしい　young(-looking)
若者　わかもの　a young person/people
若手(の)　わかて(の)　young (actor/etc.)
特 若人　△わこうど　young person
若年*労働者　じゃくねんろうどうしゃ　young workers
*老若男女　ろうにゃくなんにょ，ろうじゃくなんにょ　men and women of all ages
◇ 若しくは　もしくは　or, otherwise

126 **忙** ▶ぼう
▷いそが(しい)

6	'	'	忄	忄	忙	忙		

忙しい　いそがしい　busy

多忙な　たぼうな　busy
◇ 忙*殺される　ぼうさつされる　be very busy (with work)

第 6 回

127 **寝** ▶しん
▷ね(る)，ね(かす)

13	'	'	宀	宀	宀	疒	疒	疒	疒	疒
疒	寝	寝								

寝る　ねる　fall asleep, go to bed, lie down
昼寝　ひるね　する nap
寝かす　ねかす　put (a child) to bed, lay down
寝室　しんしつ　bedroom
寝*台車　しんだいしゃ　sleeping car

128 **起** ▶き
▷お(きる)，お(こる)，お(こす)

10	一	十	土	キ	キ	走	走	起	起	起

起きる　おきる　get up, happen, occur
早起きする　はやおきする　wake up early
起こす　おこす　wake up (a person), raise, sit up
起こる　おこる　happen, occur
起立　きりつ　する stand up
起*源　きげん　origin, beginning

129 **始** ▶し
▷はじ(める)，はじ(まる)

8	く	夂	女	妙	姁	姁	始	始	

始まる　はじまる　vi. begin, start, commence
始まり　はじまり　beginning
始める　はじめる　vt. begin, start, commence
始め　はじめ　outset, beginning
開始　かいし　する begin, start, commence
始発　しはつ　the first train/bus of the day

130 **終** ▶しゅう
▷お(わる)，お(える)

11	く	纟	幺	纟	糸	糸	紗	紗	終	終
終										

終わる　　おわる　*vi.* end, be completed
終える　　おえる　*vt.* end, finish, complete
終*了　　しゅうりょう　[する] finish, end
終電　　しゅうでん　the last train of the day
終*点　　しゅうてん　the end of the line
終日　　しゅうじつ　all day (long)
始終　　しじゅう　all the time

131 食 ▶しょく，じき
▷く(う)，く(らう)，た(べる)

9　ノ 𠆢 ⺈ 今 今 今 食 食 食

食べる　　たべる　eat, live on (a salary)
食べ物　　たべもの　food
食事　　しょくじ　meal [する] have a meal
朝食　　ちょうしょく　breakfast
昼食　　ちゅうしょく　lunch
夕食　　ゆうしょく　dinner, supper
食料　　しょくりょう　food, provisions
食う　　くう　eat cf. くう can be written as 喰う, but 喰 is not a *Jōyō Kanji.*
◇ *断食　　だんじき　fast, fasting [する] fast

132 飲 ▶いん
▷の(む)

12　ノ 𠆢 ⺈ 今 今 今 食 食 飣 飲
飮 飲

飲む　　のむ　drink, take (medicine), swallow
飲(み)物　　のみもの　drink, beverage
飲み水　　のみみず　drinking water
飲料水　　いんりょうすい　drinking water
飲食店　　いんしょくてん　restaurant
飲酒運転　　いんしゅうんてん　drunken driving

133 来 ▶らい
▷く(る)，きた(る)，きた(す)

7　一 一 ⼗ 平 平 来 来

来る　　くる　come
来月　　らいげつ　next month
来年　　らいねん　next year
来日　　らいにち　[する] come to Japan

本来　　ほんらい　originally, essentially, naturally
来る〜日　　きたる〜にち／か　this coming 〜 (date)
◇ 来す　　きたす　cause, bring about, lead to

134 帰 ▶き
▷かえ(る)，かえ(す)

10　丨 刂 刂 刂 刂 刂 帰 帰 帰 帰

帰る　　かえる　go back, return, leave (from work/etc.)
日帰り旅行　　ひがえりりょこう　day trip
帰国　　きこく　[する] return to one's country

135 乗 ▶じょう
▷の(る)，の(せる)

9　一 二 三 千 丢 乖 乖 乗 乗

乗る　　のる　get on, ride, take (a bus/plane/etc.)
乗り物*酔い　　のりものよい　motion sickness, carsickness, seasickness
乗車*券　　じょうしゃけん　train/bus ticket
[歴] 大乗*仏教　　だいじょうぶっきょう　Mahayanist Buddhism
[歴] 小乗*仏教　　しょうじょうぶっきょう　Hinayana/Theravada Buddhism

136 降 ▶こう
▷お(りる)，お(ろす)，ふ(る)

10　⺀ ⻖ 阝 阝 阝 阶 阦 降 降 降

降りる　　おりる　get off (a train/bus/etc.)
乗り降り　　のりおり　[する] get on and off
降ろす　　おろす　unload, drop off (a passenger)
降車口　　こうしゃぐち　exit on a train/bus
下降　　かこう　[する] descend
降る　　ふる　fall, rain
降雨*量　　こううりょう　(amount of) rainfall

137 作 ▶さく，さ
▷つく(る)

7　ノ 亻 亻 仁 竹 作 作

作る　　つくる　make, produce
手作りの　　てづくりの　handmade
作文　　さくぶん　composition, essay

第
1
水
準

作家	さっか　novelist　cf. *筆者（ひっしゃ）writer, *著者（ちょしゃ）author
作者	さくしゃ　writer, author, artist
名作	めいさく　masterpiece, fine piece (of art)
作*品	さくひん　(artistic, fictional, etc.) works
作物	さくもつ　crops, agricultural products
動作	どうさ　actions, movement, motion　する operate, run
作*法	さほう　manners, form, etiquette

138 休
▶きゅう
▷やす（む），やす（まる），やす（める）
6　ノ イ 仁 什 休 休

休む	やすむ　rest, have a day off, be absent (from school/work)
夏休み	なつやすみ　summer vacation
お休み（なさい）	おやすみ（なさい）　"Good night."
一休み	ひとやすみ　する take a short break
休める	やすめる　rest, give a rest
休日	きゅうじつ　holiday, day off
連休	れんきゅう　consecutive holidays
週休二日*制	△しゅうきゅうふつかせい　the five-day workweek system

139 見
▶けん
▷み（る），み（える），み（せる）
7　丨 冂 冃 月 目 貝 見

見る	みる　look, watch, see
見上げる	みあげる　look up
見下ろす	みおろす　look down (from the roof/etc.)
見下す	みくだす　despise, look down on (in contempt)
見方	みかた　point of view
見本	みほん　sample
見える	みえる　(can) be seen, (can) see, be in sight, appear [honorific]
見せる	みせる　show
意見	いけん　opinion, idea, suggestion
見学	けんがく　する visit (a factory/etc.) to learn something

140 勉
▶べん
10　ノ ク 夕 各 各 免 免 免 勉 勉

勉強	べんきょう　する study
勉学	べんがく　study
*勤勉な	きんべんな　hardworking, diligent, industrious

141 住
▶じゅう
▷す（む），す（まう）
7　ノ イ 仁 仁 住 住 住

住む	すむ　live
住まい	すまい　house, dwelling
住所	じゅうしょ　address
住*民	じゅうみん　inhabitants, residents
住*宅	じゅうたく　house, residence

142 持
▶じ
▷も（つ）
9　一 十 扌 扌 扩 扌 拌 持 持

持つ	もつ　have, take, hold, carry
持ち上げる	もちあげる　lift (up), hold up, flatter, praise
気持ち	きもち　feeling, sensation, mood
*支持	しじ　する support (a political party, etc.), back

143 知
▶ち
▷し（る）
8　ノ 厂 仁 午 矢 知 知 知

知る	しる　know, learn, notice, be acquainted
知人	ちじん　acquaintance, friend
知事	ちじ　(prefectural) governor
知*識	ちしき　knowledge, information

144 酒
▶しゅ
▷さけ，さか
10　丶 冫 氵 沪 沪 沪 洒 洒 酒 酒

酒	さけ　liquor, sake
酒屋	さかや　liquor shop
酒場	さかば　bar, pub
日本酒	にほんしゅ　Japanese sake
飲酒運転	いんしゅうんてん　drunken driving
◇ お*神酒	△おみき　sake offered to the gods

145 茶 ▶ちゃ, さ

9 一 十 サ サ 艾 苾 苳 茶 茶

お茶	おちゃ	tea, Japanese tea
*紅茶	こうちゃ	black tea
茶碗	ちゃわん	(rice) bowl, teacup
茶色	ちゃいろ	brown
茶の間	ちゃのま	living room
茶室	ちゃしつ	tea-ceremony room/house
茶道	さどう, ちゃどう	the art of the tea ceremony

146 地 ▶ち, じ

6 一 十 土 圵 坩 地

地下鉄	ちかてつ	subway, underground railway
地下水	ちかすい	ground water
土地	とち	land
地名	ちめい	place name
地方	ちほう	region, district, province, countryside
*居心地がいい	△いごこちがいい	comfortable/cozy (room), feel at home
地*震	じしん	earthquake
地*面	じめん	surface of the earth, land, ground
意気地のない	△いくじのない	timid, cowardly, spineless

147 鉄 ▶てつ

13 ノ 八 𠂤 𠂤 牟 牟 余 金 鉗 釖 鈝 鈇 鉄

地下鉄	ちかてつ	subway, underground railway
私鉄	してつ	private railway
鉄道	てつどう	railroad
鉄	てつ	iron

148 者 ▶しゃ ▷もの

8 一 十 土 耂 耂 者 者 者

学者	がくしゃ	scholar
医者	いしゃ	doctor
前者	ぜんしゃ	the former
後者	こうしゃ	the latter
*第三者	だいさんしゃ	third person/party
若者	わかもの	young person
うちの者	うちのもの	member of one's family/group cf. よそ者(よそもの) outsider to one's family/group

149 所 ▶しょ ▷ところ

8 一 ㇕ ㇕ 戸 戸 所 所 所

近所	きんじょ	neighborhood
住所	じゅうしょ	address
場所	ばしょ	place
研究所	けんきゅうじょ	(research) laboratory, research institute
所長	しょちょう	head/chief/manager (of an office)
名所	めいしょ	famous place/sight
発電所	はつでんしょ	electric power plant
長所	ちょうしょ	strong point, merit
短所	たんしょ	weak point, shortcoming
所*得	しょとく	income
所	ところ	place, spot, point
*台所	だいどころ	kitchen

150 外 ▶がい, げ ▷そと, ほか, はず(す), はず(れる)

5 ノ ク タ 列 外

外国	がいこく	foreign country
外国人	がいこくじん	foreigner
外国語	がいこくご	foreign language
外来語	がいらいご	loan word
外出	がいしゅつ [する]	go out
*海外旅行	かいがいりょこう	traveling abroad, overseas trip
外	そと	outside
外の	ほかの	another cf. ほかの can be also written 他の
外す	はずす	take off, remove, unfasten
外れる	はずれる	come off/undone, miss (the target)
外*科	げか	surgery

151 国　▶こく　▷くに

8　｜ 冂 冂 冃 冃 国 国 国

外国	がいこく	foreign country
大国	たいこく	big/powerful nation
小国	しょうこく	small nation
中国	ちゅうごく	China
*韓国	かんこく	short form of name of the Republic of Korea
四国	しこく	Shikoku
国家	こっか	state, nation
国	くに	country, nation

152 内　▶ない，だい　▷うち

4　｜ 冂 内 内

国内旅行	こくないりょこう	travel within a country
館内	かんない	in the building
*構内	こうない	in the (train) station, on campus
家内	かない	my wife
内外	ないがい	inside and outside
内*科	ないか	internal medicine
内*側	うちがわ	inside　反 外*側 （そとがわ） outside
*境内	けいだい	precinct (of a temple/shrine)

153 旅　▶りょ　▷たび

10　丶 亠 亍 方 方 方 旅 旅 旅 旅

旅行	りょこう	-する make a trip, travel
旅館	りょかん	Japanese-style inn
旅	たび	journey, trip, travel
旅先	たびさき	destination, place where one is staying while on a journey
旅人	たびびと	traveler

154 語　▶ご　▷かた(る)，かた(らう)

14　丶 亠 亖 言 言 言 訁 訂 語
語 語 語 語

日本語	にほんご	Japanese (language)
英語	えいご	English (language)
中国語	ちゅうごくご	Chinese (language)
外国語	がいこくご	foreign language
語学	ごがく	(foreign) language study
言語	げんご	language, speech
国語	こくご	(the Japanese) language (as a school subject)
物語	ものがたり	tale, story, narrative
物語る	ものがたる	narrate, show (the fact that ～)
語る	かたる	talk, chat, tell (a story)
語り手	かたりて	narrator, storyteller

155 英　▶えい

8　一 十 サ ゲ 苎 苎 英 英

英語	えいご	English (language)
英会話	えいかいわ	English conversation
英国	えいこく	the United Kingdom
大英*帝国	だいえいていこく	the British Empire
英*才教*育	えいさいきょういく	special education for the gifted

第　7　回

156 世　▶せい，せ　▷よ

5　一 十 世 世 世

世界	せかい	world
世話	せわ	-する take care of, care for, tend
世*代	せだい	generation
二世	にせい	second generation (immigrant, etc.)
中世	ちゅうせい	the Middle Ages, the medieval period
この世	このよ	this world, the present life
あの世	あのよ	the next world, the afterlife
世の中	よのなか	the world, life

25

157 界 ▶かい

9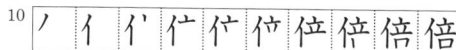

世界	せかい	world
文学界	ぶんがくかい	literary world
*政界	せいかい	political world
*財界	ざいかい	the business world
*限界	げんかい	limit, limitation (ability/capacity/ etc.)

158 倍 ▶ばい

10

| 倍 | ばい | double, twice, two times |
| ～倍 | ～ばい | ～ fold, ～ magnification |

159 半 ▶はん ▷なか(ば)

5 、 ゛ ゛ ⸚ ⸗ 半

十二時半	じゅうにじはん	12:30
半年	はんとし	a half year
半分	はんぶん	half
前半	ぜんはん	the first half
後半	こうはん	the second half
大半	たいはん	the greater part of, the larger portion of, the majority of, for the most part
三十*代半ば	さんじゅうだいなかば	one's middle thirties

160 全 ▶ぜん ▷まった(く), すべ(て)

6 ノ 人 △ 亼 仐 全

全部	ぜんぶ	all, whole
日本全国	にほんぜんこく	all over Japan, all parts of Japan cf. 世界*各国(せかいかっこく) many countries
全体主*義	ぜんたいしゅぎ	totalitarianism
全く	まったく	quite, entirely, thoroughly, completely

| 全うする | まっとうする | carry out (one's duties, mission, etc.), accomplish |
| 全て | すべて | everything, all |

161 間 ▶かん, けん ▷あいだ, ま

12

時間	じかん	time
年間	ねんかん	yearly, a year
夜間	やかん	at night, nighttime
間	あいだ	interval, space, gap, distance
間	ま	time, interval, room
日本間	にほんま	Japanese-style room
*洋間	ようま	Western-style room
茶の間	ちゃのま	living room
人間	にんげん	human beings, mankind
世間	せけん	the world, people

162 回 ▶かい, え ▷まわ(る), まわ(す)

6 丨 冂 冂 冋 回 回

～回	～かい	～ time(s)
前回	ぜんかい	last time
今回	こんかい	this time
*次回	じかい	next time
回答	かいとう	[する] reply, answer
回る	まわる	turn (round), go (round), revolve, rotate
回り道	まわりみち	detour, round-about way
特 回*向	えこう	[する] hold a memorial service

163 週 ▶しゅう

11

先週	せんしゅう	last week
今週	こんしゅう	this week
来週	らいしゅう	next week
～週間	～しゅうかん	～ week(s)

第1水準

週*末　　　　しゅうまつ　weekend

週休二日*制　△しゅうきゅうふつかせい　the five-day workweek system

---

164 毎 ▶まい

6 ノ ー ⸢ 勾 匂 毎

毎日　　　まいにち　every day

毎週　　　まいしゅう　every week

毎月　　　まいつき　every month

毎年　　　まいとし, まいねん　every year

---

165 体 ▶たい, てい
▷からだ

7 ノ イ 仁 什 伜 休 体

体　　　からだ　body

体力　　たいりょく　physical strength

体*格　　たいかく　physique, build

大体　　だいたい　on the whole, by and large, roughly, for the most part, main (points)

一体　　いったい　What on earth (did you do? etc.), a term used to convey excitement, surprise, anger worry, etc.

一体になる　いったいになる　become one with, be united

世間体　　せけんてい　appearance

体*裁　　ていさい　appearance, form, style

---

166 頭 ▶とう, ず, と
▷あたま, かしら

16 一 厂 厂 戸 戸 豆 豆 豆 豆 豆
頭 頭 頭 頭 頭 頭

頭　　　あたま　head

頭痛　　ずつう　headache

先頭　　せんとう　the forefront, the head, the lead, the top

～頭　　～とう　(counter for big animals)

◇ 東京*音頭　とうきょうおんど　*Tokyo Ondo*, Tokyo Dance Song

頭文*字　かしらもじ　the first letter (of a word), initials

---

167 口 ▶こう, く
▷くち

3 丨 冂 口

口　　　くち　mouth

入(り)口　いりぐち　entrance

出口　　でぐち　exit

早口で　はやくちで　(speak) fast

火口　　かこう　(volcanic) crater

口*述試*験　こうじゅつしけん　oral examination

◇ *異口同*音に　いくどうおんに　with one voice, with one accord

---

168 目 ▶もく, ぼく
▷め, ま

5 丨 冂 冃 月 目

目　　　め　eye

お目にかかる　おめにかかる　see [honorific]

目安　　めやす　standard, yardstick, criterion

目上の人　めうえのひと　one's superior, one's senior

目下の人　めしたのひと　one's inferior, one's junior

目前　　もくぜん　before one's eye, immediate, impending

目*的　　もくてき　purpose, aim, goal

目*標　　もくひょう　aim, goal, target

*面目　　めんぼく, めんもく　face, honor, reputation

◇ 目の*当たりに　まのあたりに　before one's eyes

---

169 耳 ▶じ
▷みみ

6 一 丆 丆 E E 耳

耳　　　みみ　ear

早耳　　はやみみ　sharp-eared

---

170 手 ▶しゅ
▷て, た

4 ノ 二 三 手

手　　　て　hand

切手　　きって　(postage) stamp

手前　　てまえ　this side

手間 　　　てま　　time, labor, effort

手伝う 　　△てつだう　help, assist

上手な 　　△じょうずな　skilled, good (tennis player/drawing/etc.)

下手な 　　△へたな　unskillful, poor (tennis player/drawing/etc.)

*選手 　　せんしゅ　athlete, player

◇ 手*綱 　　たづな　reins (for a horse)

---

171 足 ▶そく
▷あし，た(りる)，た(る)，た(す)

足 　　　あし　foot, leg, paw

〜足 　　〜そく／ぞく　〜 pair(s) of (shoes/socks/etc.)

*不足 　　ふそく　insufficiency, shortage 〈する〉 vi. lack, be short of

水*不足 　　みずぶそく　water shortage

足りる 　　たりる　be enough, be sufficient

足す 　　たす　add, supply

◇ 足*袋 　　△たび　Japanese-style socks

---

172 心 ▶しん
▷こころ

4 ＼ 心 心 心

心 　　　こころ　mind, heart, spirit

本心 　　ほんしん　one's real intention/mind

中心 　　ちゅうしん　center, middle, core

*関心 　　かんしん　interest, concern cf. *興味(きょうみ) interest

*感心 　　かんしん　〈する〉admire

*感心な 　　かんしんな　admirable

心中 　　しんじゅう　double suicide 〈する〉commit suicide together

*居心地がいい 　△いごこちがいい　comfortable/cozy (room), feel at home

---

173 力 ▶りょく，りき
▷ちから

2 フ 力

力 　　　ちから　power, force, (physical) strength

力仕事 　　ちからしごと　physical labor, job that requires muscle power

力強い 　　ちからづよい　powerful, mighty, strong

学力 　　がくりょく　academic ability

体力 　　たいりょく　physical strength

全力で 　　ぜんりょくで　with all one's might, to the best of one's ability

*能力 　　のうりょく　ability, capacity

*努力 　　どりょく　〈する〉make efforts

*権力 　　けんりょく　power, authority

*原子力発電所 　　げんしりょくはつでんしょ　nuclear power plant

*馬力 　　ばりき　horsepower, energy (to do work)

力*量 　　りきりょう　ability, capability

第 8 回

174 立 ▶りつ，りゅう
▷た(つ)，た(てる)

5 ＼ 一 十 立 立

立つ 　　たつ　stand up

立ち上がる 　　たちあがる　stand up, stand up and take action, rise (up)

立ち止まる 　　たちどまる　stop, halt, pause

目立つ 　　めだつ　stand out, be conspicuous

立場 　　たちば　standpoint, one's ground, point of view

夕立 　　ゆうだち　sudden shower in the late afternoon

立食パーティー 　　りっしょくパーティー　buffet-style dinner party

国立大学 　　こくりつだいがく　national university

中立国 　　ちゅうりつこく　neutral country

◇ *建立 　　こんりゅう　〈する〉construct a temple or shrine building

---

175 座 ▶ざ
▷すわ(る)

10 ＼ 亠 广 广 庁 庐 应 座 座 座

座る 　　すわる　sit down

座席 　　ざせき　seat

口座 　　こうざ　(bank) account

---

176 歩 ▶ほ，ぶ，ふ
▷ある(く)，あゆ(む)

8 ｜ ト 止 止 牛 歩 歩 歩

歩く	あるく	walk
歩道	ほどう	sidewalk
歩行者	ほこうしゃ	pedestrian
〜歩	〜ほ／ぽ	〜 step(s)
進歩	しんぽ [-する] advance, progress, improve
歩合	ぶあい	percentage, commission
歩み	あゆみ	walking, history (of a company/school/etc.)
特 歩	ふ	pawn (in Japanese chess)

177 走 ▶そう ▷はし（る）

7 一 十 土 キ キ 走 走

走る	はしる	run
走者	そうしゃ	runner
*競走	きょうそう [-する] run in a race
◇ *師走	△しわす	name for twelfth month of lunar calendar

178 話 ▶わ ▷はな（す），はなし

13 丶 亠 ㇜ 言 言 言 言 訅 訐 訐 訐 話 話

話す	はなす	talk, tell, speak
話し手	はなして	speaker
話し中	はなしちゅう	(the line is) busy
話し合う	はなしあう	talk, discuss
話し合い	はなしあい	talk, discussion
立ち話	たちばなし	stand chatting/talking
電話	でんわ	telephone [-する] call
会話	かいわ	conversation [-する] talk

179 聞 ▶ぶん，もん ▷き（く），き（こえる）

14 ｜ ㇕ ㇉ 門 門 門 門 門 門 門 門 聞 聞 聞 聞

聞く	きく	hear, listen
聞き手	ききて	hearer, listener
聞こえる	きこえる	(can) be heard, (can) hear

新聞	しんぶん	newspaper
前*代*未聞の	ぜんだいみもんの	unheard-of, unprecedented

180 読 ▶どく，とく，とう ▷よ（む）

14 丶 亠 ㇜ 言 言 言 言 訁 訅 訐 訪 詩 読 読

読む	よむ	read
読書	どくしょ [-する] read books
読者	どくしゃ	reader
◇ 読*経	△どきょう，どっきょう [-する] chant a sutra
*句読*点	くとうてん	punctuation marks
◇ 読本	とくほん	reader (as in a textbook)

181 書 ▶しょ ▷か（く）

10 ㇕ ㇕ ㇕ ㇕ 聿 聿 書 書 書 書

書く	かく	write
書き手	かきて	writer
書き取り	かきとり	dictation, *kanji* quiz
前書き	まえがき	preface
読書	どくしょ [-する] read books
書名	しょめい	title (of a book)
書店	しょてん	bookstore
書道	しょどう	calligraphy
書物	しょもつ	books

182 借 ▶しゃく ▷か（りる）

10 ノ 亻 亻 仁 仕 借 借 借 借 借

借りる	かりる	borrow, rent
借り	かり	debt, a loan
借金	しゃっきん	debt, loan [-する] borrow money
借家	しゃくや	rented house
◇ 貸借	たいしゃく [-する] lend and borrow, debt and credit

183 貸

▶たい
▷か(す)

12 ノ イ 仁 代 代 代 伐 伐 貸 貸
貸 貸

貸す　　　かす　　lend, loan
貸家　　　かしや　　house for rent
貸間　　　かしま　　room for rent
貸し　　　かし　　debt (as in "I am in his debt.")
貸(し)出し　　かしだし　　lending, loan
◇ 貸借　　たいしゃく　[する] lend and borrow, debt and credit

184 返

▶へん
▷かえ(す), かえ(る)

7 一 厂 反 反 返 返 返

返す　　　かえす　　return, give something back
送り返す　　おくりかえす　　send back, return
返事　　　へんじ　[する] answer, reply
返*却　　へんきゃく　[する] return, repay

185 出

▶しゅつ, すい
▷で(る), だ(す)

5 丨 屮 屮 出 出

出る　　　でる　　go out, attend
出口　　　でぐち　　exit
日の出　　ひので　　sunrise
出かける　　でかける　　go out
出す　　　だす　　put out, take out, send
見出し　　みだし　　headline, dictionary entry
出発　　しゅっぱつ　[する] depart, leave
外出　　がいしゅつ　[する] go out
出国　　しゅっこく　[する] depart from a country
出席　　しゅっせき　[する] attend (a class/meeting/etc.), be present
*提出　　ていしゅつ　[する] present, submit
◇ 出*納*係　　すいとうがかり　　cashier, teller

186 入

▶にゅう
▷い(る), い(れる), はい(る)

2 ノ 入

入る　　　はいる　　enter, be in
入れる　　いれる　　put in/into, let in
気に入る　　きにいる　　get/grow fond of
入(り)口　　いりぐち　　entrance
日の入り　　ひのいり　　sunset
入学　　にゅうがく　[する] enter a school
入社　　にゅうしゃ　[する] enter/join a company
入院　　にゅういん　[する] go into the hospital, be hospitalized
入国　　にゅうこく　[する] enter a country, be admitted into a country
入場　　にゅうじょう　[する] enter, be admitted
*収入　　しゅうにゅう　　income, revenue
参入　　さんにゅう　[する] enter (a market)

187 売

▶ばい
▷う(る), う(れる)

7 一 十 士 声 声 亭 売

売る　　　うる　　sell, deal in
売り場　　うりば　　selling area, sales counter
売り切れる　　うりきれる　　be sold out
売(り)上(げ)　　うりあげ　　sales, proceeds
小売(り)店　　こうりてん　　retail store
前売(り)*券　　まえうりけん　　a ticket sold in advance
売(り)手*市場　　うりてしじょう　　sellers' market
売れる　　うれる　　sell (well) cf. 〜はよく売れる sell well
売れ行き　　うれゆき　　sales
売店　　ばいてん　　stand, kiosk, stall
売春　　ばいしゅん　[する] prostitute
*販売　　はんばい　[する] sell, market, deal in

188 買

▶ばい
▷か(う)

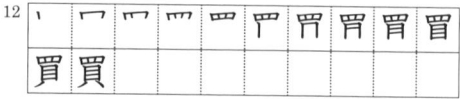

12 丨 冂 冂 罒 罒 罒 胃 胃 買
買 買

買う　　　かう　　buy, purchase
買(い)物　　かいもの　　shopping, a purchase
買(い)手*市場　　かいてしじょう　　buyers' market
売買　　ばいばい　[する] buy and sell, trade/deal in
買*収　　ばいしゅう　[する] buy up, purchase, bribe

189 払 ▶ふつ
▷はら(う)

5 一 十 扌 払 払

払う	はらう pay
*支払う	しはらう pay
*支払(い)	しはらい payment
前払(い)	まえばらい advance payment
払*拭	ふっしょく する sweep away, wipe out
◇ 払*底	ふってい する become scarce, run short

190 着 ▶ちゃく, じゃく
▷き(る), き(せる), つ(く), つ(ける)

12 ` ゛ 丷 䒑 䒑 羊 羊 着 着 着 着

着る	きる put on, wear
着せる	きせる dress someone
着物	きもの kimono
下着	したぎ underwear
水着	みずぎ swimsuit, bathing suit
着く	つく reach, arrive
到着	とうちゃく する arrive
～着	～ちゃく arriving at (time)
～着	～ちゃく counter for clothes
着々と	ちゃくちゃくと steadily, step by step
着手	ちゃくしゅ する start to do, start on
*愛着	あいちゃく, あいじゃく love, attachment, affection
*執着	しゅうちゃく, しゅうじゃく する be attached, stick (to)

191 脱 ▶だつ
▷ぬ(ぐ), ぬ(げる)

11 丿 月 月 月 肛 肌 肌 脐 脐 脐 脱

脱ぐ	ぬぐ take off (clothes, shoes, etc.)
脱水	だっすい する spin-dry (the laundry)
◇ 脱水*症*状	だっすいしょうじょう dehydration
脱出	だっしゅつ する escape, get out of

| 脱*線 | だっせん する be derailed, run off the track, digress (from the subject) |
| 脱*獄 | だつごく する escape from prison |

192 働 ▶どう
▷はたら(く)

13 丿 亻 仁 仟 仟 佇 佇 佇 俥 俥 俥 働 働

働く	はたらく vi. work, labor
働き	はたらき work, workings
働き手	はたらきて worker, laborer
*労働	ろうどう する work, labor
*労働者	ろうどうしゃ worker, laborer
*労働*組合	ろうどうくみあい labor union
*労働人口	ろうどうじんこう working population, work force
*労働力	ろうどうりょく manpower, work force, labor force
*労働力*不足	ろうどうりょくぶそく labor shortage

193 泳 ▶えい
▷およ(ぐ)

8 ` ⺀ 氵 氵 泻 泻 泳 泳

泳ぐ	およぐ swim
水泳	すいえい swimming
遠泳	えんえい long-distance swimming
*平泳ぎ	ひらおよぎ breaststroke

194 写 ▶しゃ
▷うつ(す), うつ(る)

5 丶 冖 写 写 写

写す	うつす copy, take (a picture)
写真	しゃしん photograph, picture
写真家	しゃしんか photographer
写生	しゃせい する sketch

31

195 待
▶たい
▷ま(つ)

9 ノ ノ 彳 彳 什 件 徉 待 待

待つ	まつ	wait
待ち合わせ	まちあわせ	waiting for a person at an appointed place
待ち合わせる	まちあわせる	arrange to meet, meet (at)
待合室	まちあいしつ	waiting room
*期待	きたい	〔する〕 hope for, expect
*招待	しょうたい	〔する〕 invite

196 遊
▶ゆう, ゆ
▷あそ(ぶ)

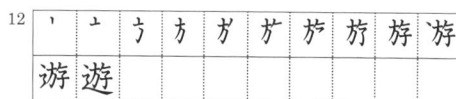

12 ' 丶 う 方 扩 扩 扩 斿 斿 斿 遊 遊

遊ぶ	あそぶ	play
遊園地	ゆうえんち	amusement park, recreational grounds
遊歩道	ゆうほどう	promenade
◇ 物見遊山	ものみゆさん	pleasure trip

197 呼
▶こ
▷よ(ぶ)

8 丶 口 口 口' 口′ 吁 呼 呼

呼ぶ	よぶ	call, call out to
呼び出す	よびだす	ask to come, call somebody up (on the phone), summon, page
呼*吸	こきゅう	respiration, breathing 〔する〕 breathe cf. *息をする(いきをする) breathe

第 9 回

198 洗
▶せん
▷あら(う)

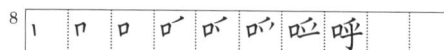

9 丶 冫 冫 冫 汁 泙 浐 浐 洗

洗う	あらう	wash
お手洗い	おてあらい	restroom, lavatory, toilet
洗濯	せんたく	〔する〕 wash, launder
洗濯機	せんたくき	washing machine
水洗トイレ	すいせんトイレ	flushing toilet
洗*脳	せんのう	〔する〕 brainwash

199 使
▶し
▷つか(う)

8 ノ イ 仁 仁 侊 仨 使 使

使う	つかう	use, spend
使い方	つかいかた	how to use, method of use
使用*法	しようほう	how to use, directions for use
大使	たいし	ambassador
歴 使者	ししゃ	messenger

200 歌
▶か
▷うた, うた(う)

14 一 一 一 一 可 可 可 哥 哥 哥 哥 歌 歌 歌

歌	うた	song
歌う	うたう	sing
歌手	かしゅ	singer
国歌	こっか	national anthem
校歌	こうか	school song
短歌	たんか	tanka, Japanese poem of thirty-one syllables
*和歌	わか	waka, Japanese poem of thirty-one syllables

201 習
▶しゅう
▷なら(う)

11 ⁊ ⁊ ⁊ ⁊⁊ ⁊⁊ ⁊⁊ ⁊⁊ 羽 習 習 習

習う	ならう	learn, take lessons
学習	がくしゅう	〔する〕 learn, study
自習	じしゅう	〔する〕 vi. study by oneself
*予習	よしゅう	〔する〕 prepare (one's lessons)
*復習	ふくしゅう	〔する〕 review
習*得	しゅうとく	〔する〕 master
習*字	しゅうじ	calligraphy, penmanship

202 思
▶し
▷おも(う)

9 丶 口 四 田 田 甲 思 思 思

| 思う | おもう | think, guess, believe, feel, consider |

思い出す　おもいだす　remember, recall
思い出　おもいで　memories
思いつく　おもいつく　think of, hit on (an idea)
思いがけない　おもいがけない　unexpected
思い（っ）きり　おもい（っ）きり　to one's heart content, as hard as one can
思わず　おもわず　unconsciously, in spite of oneself
思考力　しこうりょく　ability to think
意思決定　いしけってい　[する] determine (one's) intention

203 言 ▶げん, ごん ▷い（う）, こと

7　丶 二 亠 言 言 言 言

言う　いう　say, talk about, tell
言い*訳　いいわけ　excuse
伝言　でんごん　message　[する] give/send a message
言語　げんご　language, speech
方言　ほうげん　dialect
言*葉　ことば　word, language
一言　ひとこと　a word, single word

204 通 ▶つう, つ ▷とお（る）, とお（す）, かよ（う）

10　フ マ 甬 甬 甬 甬 甬 甬 通 通

通る　とおる　go along, pass through/along
通り　とおり　street
大通り　おおどおり　big street
〜通り　〜どおり　〜 street/avenue
人通り　ひとどおり　pedestrian traffic
（〜した）通り　（〜した）とおり　as (promised, one is told, etc.)
一通り　ひととおり　in a general way, briefly
〜通り　〜とおり　〜 ways (of doing something)
通う　かよう　go to (school/work), go to and from
通学　つうがく　[する] attend/go to school
通*勤　つうきん　[する] commute, go to one's office
通行　つうこう　passing, traffic　[する] pass, go past/through
通知　つうち　[する] notify, announce
文通　ぶんつう　[する] correspond (by letters)
*交通　こうつう　traffic, transportation

通じる　つうじる　be understood, be connected by, be familiar with
通　つう　connoisseur, expert
通夜　つや　wake, vigil

205 渡 ▶と ▷わた（る）, わた（す）

12　丶 氵 氵 氵 汇 汇 浐 浐 浐 浐
渡 渡

渡る　わたる　go across, go over
渡す　わたす　hand in, hand over, build (a bridge) across
渡*米　とべい　[する] go to the United States
◇ 渡*航*費　とこうひ　overseas travel expense
[歴] 渡来人　とらいじん　foreigners who came to ancient Japan, bringing certain expertise

206 送 ▶そう ▷おく（る）

9　丶 丷 丷 兰 羊 关 关 送 送

送る　おくる　send, see somebody (home)
見送る　みおくる　see somebody off
見送り　みおくり　seeing someone off
送り返す　おくりかえす　send back, return
送り*仮名　おくりがな　conjugational/declensional ending added in kana after a kanji
送金　そうきん　[する] remit/send money
運送会社　うんそうがいしゃ　transportation/delivery company
送*別会　そうべつかい　farewell party
*放送局　ほうそうきょく　broadcasting station

207 泊 ▶はく ▷と（まる）, と（める）

8　丶 氵 氵 氵 汀 泊 泊 泊

泊まる　とまる　stay/stop (at a hotel, etc.)
二泊三日　にはくみっか　(trip of) three days and two nights
宿泊*費　しゅくはくひ　charges for accommodations

第 10 回

208 覚 ▶かく
▷おぼ（える），さ（ます），さ（める）

12 丶 ⺍ ⺍ ⺍ ⺍ ⺍ 尚 尚 尚 尚
覚 覚

覚える　　おぼえる　memorize, remember
覚えている　おぼえている　remember, have/keep/bear something in mind
目が覚める　めがさめる　*vi.* wake up
目を覚ます　めをさます　*vi.* wake up
目覚まし時計　めざましどけい　alarm (clock)
知覚　　ちかく　[する] perceive
*感覚　　かんかく　sense, sensation, feeling

209 忘 ▶ぼう
▷わす（れる）

7 丶 亠 亡 亡 忘 忘 忘

忘れる　　わすれる　forget
忘れ物　　わすれもの　thing left behind
忘年会　　ぼうねんかい　year-end (dinner) party

210 調 ▶ちょう
▷しら（べる），ととの（う），ととの（える）

15 丶 亠 讠 訁 言 言 言 訶 訶 訶
調 調 調 調 調

調べる　　しらべる　study, investigate, examine
調子がいい　ちょうしがいい　be in good health, be in good order
強調　　きょうちょう　[する] emphasize, stress　cf. 重
　　　　*視（じゅうし）[する] attach importance to, regard as important
調える　　ととのえる　make preparations, arrange, adjust

211 続 ▶ぞく
▷つづ（く），つづ（ける）

13 く 幺 幺 糸 糸 糸 紒 紒 紒 紒
続 続 続

続ける　　つづける　*vt.* continue
話し続ける　はなしつづける　continue talking/speaking

続く　　つづく　*vi.* continue
降り続く　ふりつづく　continue raining (or snowing)　cf. 続く is used only in 降り続く．〜続ける is used for other verbs
続き　　つづき　continuation, continuance, sequel
手続き　　てつづき　procedures, formalities
連続　　れんぞく　continuation, series　[する] continue, be consecutive
続々と　　ぞくぞくと　one after another, in rapid succession
*相続　　そうぞく　[する] inherit, succeed
*継続　　けいぞく　[する] continue

212 考 ▶こう
▷かんが（える）

6 一 十 土 耂 耂 考

考える　　かんがえる　think, consider
考え方　　かんがえかた　way of thinking, thought, idea
考え　　かんがえ　idea, thought, plan, opinion, intention
思考　　しこう　thinking　[する] *vi.* think
参考書　　さんこうしょ　reference book
考古学　　こうこがく　archeology
考*慮　　こうりょ　[する] consider, give consideration to

213 答 ▶とう
▷こた（える），こた（え）

12 ノ 亠 ⺮ ⺮ ⺮ 竹 竹 灰 灰 灰
答 答

答える　　こたえる　answer, reply, respond
答（え）　　こたえ　answer, reply, response
回答　　かいとう　[する] reply, answer
解答　　かいとう　answer, solution　[する] answer, solve
◇ 答*弁　　とうべん　[する] reply, answer, explain, defend (an answer)

214 教 ▶きょう
▷おし（える），おそ（わる）

11 一 十 土 耂 耂 考 考 孝 孝 教
教

教える　　おしえる　teach, tell

教え方	おしえかた	teaching method
教わる	おそわる	be taught, be told
教室	きょうしつ	classroom
教授	きょうじゅ	professor [する] teach
教*育	きょういく	[する] educate
教会	きょうかい	church
キリスト教	キリストきょう	Christianity
*宗教	しゅうきょう	religion

215 開 ▶かい
▷ひら(く), ひら(ける), あ(く), あ(ける)

12 丨 冂 冂 門 門 門 門 門 閂 開 開

開ける	あける	vt. open
開く	あく	vi. open
開店	かいてん	[する] open a store
開始	かいし	[する] begin, start, commence
開会	かいかい	[する] open a meeting, go into session
開会*式	かいかいしき	opening ceremony
開通	かいつう	[する] vi. be opened to traffic
開発	かいはつ	[する] develop, exploit (natural resources)
*展開	てんかい	[する] develop, unfold
開く	ひらく	open, unfold, establish, hold (a meeting/party), bloom, blossom
*海開き	うみびらき	opening a beach to the public for the summer

216 閉 ▶へい
▷と(じる), と(ざす), し(める), し(まる)

11 丨 冂 冂 門 門 門 門 門 閉 閉

閉める	しめる	shut, close
閉まる	しまる	be shut/closed
閉じる	とじる	close
閉店	へいてん	[する] close a shop
閉会	へいかい	[する] close a meeting
閉会*式	へいかいしき	closing ceremony
開閉	かいへい	[する] open and close, adjourn
閉*鎖	へいさ	[する] shut down, close down
◇ 閉ざす	とざす	shut (one's mouth, a gate, etc.)

217 止 ▶し
▷と(まる), と(める)

4 丨 ト 止 止

止める	とめる	vt. stop, turn off
止まる	とまる	vi. stop, halt, be parked
通行止め	つうこうどめ	(be) closed to traffic
中止	ちゅうし	[する] stop, suspend, discontinue, cancel
*禁止	きんし	[する] forbid, prohibit, ban
歴 *波止場	△はとば	wharf, pier

218 焼 ▶しょう
▷や(く), や(ける)

12 丶 丷 少 火 火 灶 灶 灶 焼 焼 焼 焼

焼く	やく	burn, roast, bake, broil, grill, toast, bake, fire (pottery)
焼ける	やける	be burnt, be baked, be toasted, be roasted, be suntanned
日焼け	ひやけ	[する] be suntanned
夕焼け	ゆうやけ	evening glow
全焼	ぜんしょう	[する] be burnt down, be reduced to ashes
焼*失	しょうしつ	[する] be burnt down, be consumed by fire

219 消 ▶しょう
▷き(える), け(す)

10 丶 丶 氵 氵 氵 汀 汼 消 消 消

消す	けす	extinguish, switch off (a light), turn off (the gas), erase, wipe out, cross out
取り消す	とりけす	cancel, revoke, retract
消しゴム	けしゴム	eraser
消える	きえる	disappear, go out (as in a light/candle), melt (away), die away
消火*器	しょうかき	fire extinguisher
消*化	しょうか	[する] digest
消*費者	しょうひしゃ	consumer(s)

220 直

▶ちょく，じき
▷ただ（ちに），なお（す），なお（る）

8 一 十 十 市 市 直 直 直

直す	なおす repair, fix, correct, revise, improve cf. *治す（なおす）cure, heal
見直す	みなおす look again, reconsider, change for the better
直る	なおる be repaired, be fixed cf. *治る（なおる）get well, be cured
直通電話	ちょくつうでんわ direct (phone) line
直流	ちょくりゅう direct (electrical) current, DC 反*交流（こうりゅう）alternating current, AC
直行便	ちょっこうびん direct flight
直前	ちょくぜん immediately before
直後	ちょくご immediately after
*工場直売	こうじょうちょくばい selling directly from the factory
直*接	ちょくせつ direct, directly
*率直な	そっちょくな frank, candid, straightforward
*正直な	しょうじきな honest, upright
直に	じきに soon, in a short time, before long, immediately
直ちに	ただちに immediately, right away

221 並

▶へい
▷なみ，なら（べる），なら（ぶ），なら（びに）

8 丶 丷 꼭 꼭 꼭 並 並 並

並べる	ならべる line (things) up, put side by side, display, list
並ぶ	ならぶ stand in a line, line up, be parallel, be equal with
並びに	ならびに and, both (A) and (B)
並木	なみき row of trees (along a road/etc.)
並行して	へいこうして (do another thing) at the same time

222 変

▶へん
▷か（わる），か（える）

9 丶 亠 亠 ナ ガ 亦 亦 変 変

変える	かえる vt. change, alter, reform (a system), amend (a regulation)
変わる	かわる vi. change, be altered, vary, be amended, be revised
大変な	たいへんな serious, grave, terrible, dreadful, very

| 変な | へんな odd, strange, queer |
| 変*化 | へんか transition する change, vary, transform, alter |

223 残

▶ざん
▷のこ（る），のこ（す）

10 一 ア 万 歹 歹 歹 残 残 残

残す	のこす leave (behind), save (for later use)
残る	のこる remain, stay
残らず	のこらず all, without exception
残り	のこり remainder, remnant
残りご*飯	のこりごはん leftover rice/food
残業	ざんぎょう overtime work する work overtime
残金	ざんきん remaining money, balance
残*念な	ざんねんな regrettable, unfortunate
名残	△なごり remains, vestiges

224 集

▶しゅう
▷あつ（まる），あつ（める），つど（う）

12 ノ イ イ 尸 竹 竹 隹 隹 隹 隼 集 集

集める	あつめる bring together, gather, collect, call together
集まる	あつまる gather, get together
集会	しゅうかい meeting, gathering, assembly
集金	しゅうきん する collect money/bills
集合	しゅうごう する gather, meet, assemble
集中	しゅうちゅう する concentrate, centralize, center on, focus on
*収集	しゅうしゅう する collect
*特集	とくしゅう feature article する feature (a story)
*特集*号	とくしゅうごう special issue
全集	ぜんしゅう the complete works (of)
◇ 集う	つどう gather, get together, meet

225 倒

▶とう
▷たお（れる），たお（す）

10 ノ イ 亻 仵 仵 仵 侄 侄 倒 倒

| 倒す | たおす knock down, push over, defeat, overthrow, topple |

倒れる	たおれる	fall down, break down, die, be killed, be overthrown
倒*産	とうさん	[する] go bankrupt

第 11 回

226 郵 ▶ゆう

11　｀ ｜ ｀二 ｀亠 `二 `垂 `垂 `垂 `郵
郵

郵便局	ゆうびんきょく	post office
郵送	ゆうそう	[する] mail

227 便 ▶べん，びん
▷たよ(り)

9　丿 亻 亻 仁 仃 信 信 便 便

郵便局	ゆうびんきょく	post office
定*期便	ていきびん	regular service (a flight/etc.)
◇ 便乗*値上げ	びんじょうねあげ	jumping on the bandwagon and increasing prices
便*箋	びんせん	letter paper/pad
便利な	べんりな	convenient, handy
便所	べんじょ	lavatory, toilet
小便	しょうべん	urine
便り	たより	letter, correspondence, news, tidings

228 局 ▶きょく

7　一 コ 尸 弓 局 局 局

郵便局	ゆうびんきょく	post office
*放送局	ほうそうきょく	broadcasting station
北*米局	ほくべいきょく	Bureau for North America
局長	きょくちょう	bureau chief
結局	けっきょく	finally, in the end
*政局	せいきょく	political situation

229 病 ▶びょう，へい
▷や(む)，やまい

10　丶 亠 广 广 疒 疒 疒 病 病 病

病院	びょういん	hospital

病気	びょうき	illness, sickness, disease
病気の	びょうきの	ill, sick
病人	びょうにん	sick person　cf. *患者（かんじゃ）patient
重病	じゅうびょう	serious illness/disease
*不*治の病	ふじのやまい, ふちのやまい	incurable/fatal disease
病む	やむ	fall ill, be taken ill, suffer from
◇ *疾病	しっぺい	disease, illness

230 院 ▶いん

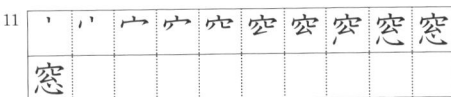
10　｀ ３ ⻖ ⻖' ⻖' ⻖⁺ 阼 陀 陀 院

病院	びょういん	hospital
大学院	だいがくいん	graduate school
入院	にゅういん	[する] go into the hospital, be hospitalized
退院	たいいん	[する] leave the hospital, be discharged from the hospital

231 窓 ▶そう
▷まど

11　｀ ｀ 宀 宀 空 空 空 空 窓 窓
窓

窓	まど	window
窓口	まどぐち	(teller's, etc.) window
同窓会	どうそうかい	alumni association, class reunion

232 雨 ▶う
▷あめ，あま

8　一 ㇀ 冂 丙 雨 雨 雨 雨

雨	あめ	rain
大雨	おおあめ	heavy rain
雨水	あまみず	rainwater
雨*具	あまぐ	rainwear, umbrella
雨*量	うりょう	amount of rainfall, precipitation
*梅雨	△つゆ	rainy season (in June)
*梅雨前*線	ばいうぜんせん	warm front of early summer rain
小雨	こさめ	light rain, drizzle
春雨	はるさめ	spring rain, drizzle

*霧雨　　　　きりさめ　drizzle
歴 五月雨　　　△さみだれ　early summer rain
歴 時雨　　　　△しぐれ　rain shower in late autumn or early winter

233 京 ▶きょう，けい

8 ` 亠 亠 古 古 宁 宁 京

東京　　　とうきょう　Tokyo
京都　　　きょうと　Kyoto
上京　　　じょうきょう　[する]go to Tokyo
帰京　　　ききょう　[する]return to Tokyo
京*阪*神地方　けいはんしんちほう　the Kyoto-Osaka-Kobe area

234 映 ▶えい
▷うつ(る)，うつ(す)，は(える)

9 丨 冂 日 日 旷 旷 旷 映

映画　　　えいが　movie
上映　　　じょうえい　[する]show (a movie)
映る　　　うつる　be reflected
映す　　　うつす　reflect, project
◇ 映える　　はえる　shine, glow, look nice

235 画 ▶が，かく

8 一 厂 冂 冊 冊 両 画 画

映画　　　えいが　movie
画家　　　がか　painter, artist
日本画　　にほんが　Japanese-style painting
*絵画　　　かいが　picture, drawing, painting
*洋画　　　ようが　Western style painting, foreign film
*邦画　　　ほうが　Japanese film
計画　　　けいかく　[する]plan

236 仕 ▶し，じ
▷つか(える)

5 ノ イ 亻 仁 仕

仕事　　　しごと　work, business, job　[する]work

仕上げる　しあげる　finish (off/up), complete
仕上がる　しあがる　be finished, be completed, be ready
仕立てる　したてる　make (clothes), tailor
仕える　　つかえる　serve (a person), work under/for
◇ *給仕　　きゅうじ　waiter, waitress　[する]wait on

237 事 ▶じ，ず
▷こと

8 一 亻 亠 亖 亖 亖 事 事

仕事　　　しごと　work, business, job　[する]work
出来事　　できごと　event, happening, occurrence, incident
見事な　　みごとな　beautiful, splendid, masterful
物事　　　ものごと　things, all things, everything
家事　　　かじ　housework, housekeeping
火事　　　かじ　fire
人事　　　じんじ　personnel affairs
大事な　　だいじな　important, critical
事*件　　　じけん　incident, affair, case
◇ 好事家　　こうずか　a dilettante, a person of unusual tastes

238 質 ▶しつ，しち，ち

15 ` ′ ┌ 斤 斤 斤 斦 斦 斦 斦
斦 斦 斦 質 質

質問　　　しつもん　[する]ask questions
質　　　　しつ　quality　cf. *量(りょう) quantity
本質　　　ほんしつ　real nature, substance, essence
*品質　　　ひんしつ　quality of a product　cf. *性*能(せいのう) capacity/performance (of a machine)
地質　　　ちしつ　nature of the soil, geological features
人質　　　ひとじち　hostage
質屋　　　しちや　pawnshop
特 言質　　げんち　pledge, promise, word (as in "give one's word")

239 問 ▶もん
▷と(う)，と(い)，とん

11 丨 冂 冂 冃 冃 門 門 門 門 問
問

質問	しつもん	[する] ask questions
問題	もんだい	problem, issue, question (in an exam)
学問	がくもん	learning, study, studies
◇ 問答	もんどう	questioning and answering [する] hold a dialogue
問い	とい	question
問い合わせる	といあわせる	make inquiries (at an office)
問い合わせ	といあわせ	inquiry
問屋	とんや，といや	wholesale store

240 料 ▶りょう

10 丶 丷 丷 半 半 米 米 米 米 料

料理	りょうり	cooking, food [する] cook
料金	りょうきん	charge, fee, fare
送料	そうりょう	postage, shipping fee
有料道路	ゆうりょうどうろ	toll road
食料*品	しょくりょうひん	food, groceries

241 理 ▶り

11 一 Ｔ Ｆ 王 玑 玑 玑 玑 理 理
理

料理	りょうり	cooking, food [する] cook
理解	りかい	[する] understand, comprehend cf. 分かる（わかる）understand, realize, find out
心理	しんり	state of mind
心理学	しんりがく	psychology
地理	ちり	geological features
物理学	ぶつりがく	physics
物理*的に	ぶつりてきに	physically
理*論	りろん	theory
*論理	ろんり	logic

242 真 ▶しん ▷ま

10 一 十 广 市 肯 肯 盲 直 真 真

写真	しゃしん	photograph, picture
真理	しんり	truth

真*空	しんくう	vacuum
真っ白い／な	まっしろい／な	pure white, as white as snow
真っ黒い／な	まっくろい／な	pitch-black
真っ赤な	△まっかな	bright/deep red
真っ青な	△まっさおな	deep blue, pale
真っ暗な	まっくらな	pitch-dark
真ん*丸い／な	まんまるい／な	(perfectly) round
真ん中	まんなか	the exact middle
真っ先に	まっさきに	at the very beginning, first of all

243 紙 ▶し ▷かみ

10 乙 幺 幺 糸 糸 糸 糸 糺 紅 紙 紙

手紙	てがみ	letter
紙	かみ	paper
新聞紙	しんぶんし	newspaper
コピー用紙	コピーようし	copying paper
白紙	はくし	blank sheet
*和紙	わし	Japanese paper

244 好 ▶こう ▷この(む)，す(く)

6 く 女 女 好 好 好

好きな	すきな	favorite, be fond of
大好きな	だいすきな	(most) favorite, be very fond of
好き好きだ	すきずきだ	be a matter of taste
好意	こうい	goodwill, kindness, favor, affection
好調な	こうちょうな	satisfactory, in good condition
友好*的な	ゆうこうてきな	friendly
好人物	こうじんぶつ	good-natured person
好む	このむ	like, be fond of cf. 気に入る（きにいる）get/grow fond of
好み	このみ	(personal) preferences/taste

245 元 ▶げん，がん ▷もと

4 一 二 テ 元

元気な	げんきな	healthy, in good spirits
二元*論	にげんろん	dualism

39

足元	あしもと	at one's feet, (one's) step
地元の	じもとの	local/home (team, etc.)
家元	いえもと	head/master of a school (of flower arrangement, tea ceremony, etc.)
元来	がんらい	originally, primarily, by nature
元*旦	がんたん	New Year's Day

246 気 ▶き，け

6　ノ　二　仁　气　気　気

元気な	げんきな	healthy, in good spirits
気持ち	きもち	feeling, sensation, mood
気に入る	きにいる	get/grow fond of
電気	でんき	electricity, (electric) lights
人気	にんき	popularity, popular
大気	たいき	atmosphere, the air
気体	きたい	gas
気*候	きこう	climate
*浮気	△うわき ［-する］ have an affair with
人気のない	ひとけのない	deserted, empty
気*配	けはい	indication, sign
火の気	ひのけ	fire, heat
意気地のない	△いくじのない	timid, cowardly, spineless

247 静 ▶せい，じょう ▷しず，しず(か)，しず(まる)，しず(める)

14　一　十　キ　主　キ　青　青　青　青　青
靑　静　静　静

静かな	しずかな	quiet, silence, calm
静まる	しずまる	become quiet, subside
静けさ	しずけさ	stillness, silence, calm, peace
*冷静な	れいせいな	calm, cool(-headed)
静電気	せいでんき	static electricity
静*脈	じょうみゃく	vein

248 利 ▶り ▷き(く)

7　ノ　二　チ　チ　禾　利　利

| 便利な | べんりな | convenient, handy |

利用	りよう	［-する］use, utilize
勝利	しょうり	［-する］win a victory
利口な	りこうな	wise, clever
利子	りし	interest (on a loan, deposit, etc.)
利*息	りそく	interest (on a loan, deposit, etc.)
利*益	りえき	profit, benefit
*砂利	△じゃり	gravel
右利き	みぎきき	right-handed
左利き	ひだりきき	left-handed

249 親 ▶しん ▷おや，した(しい)，した(しむ)

16　丶　亠　十　立　立　立　辛　辛　辛　亲
亲　亲　亲　亲　親　親

親切な	しんせつな	kind
*両親	りょうしん	one's parents
父親	ちちおや	father
母親	ははおや	mother
親	おや	parent(s)
親子	おやこ	parent(s) and child(ren)
親*指	おやゆび	thumb cf. 人*差し*指(ひとさしゆび)，中*指(なかゆび)，薬*指(くすりゆび)，小*指(こゆび)
親しい	したしい	close, intimate
親友	しんゆう	close friend
◇ 親日家	しんにちか	Japanophile, pro-Japan person

250 切 ▶せつ，さい ▷き(る)，き(れる)

4　一　七　切　切

切る	きる	cut, chop, slice
切手	きって	(postage) stamp
親切な	しんせつな	kind
大切な	たいせつな	important cf. 大事な(だいじな) important
一切	いっさい	(affirmative verb) all, the whole, everything (negative verb) nothing, not at all

第 2 水準
（Level 2）

251-350

第 12 回

251 笑 ▶しょう ▷わら(う)，え(む)

10 ノ ト ケ ゲ ゲ 竹 竹 竺 竿 笑

笑う	わらう	laugh, giggle, smile
笑い	わらい	laughter, a smile
苦笑	くしょう	[する] smile wryly, to give a forced laugh/smile
◇ *微笑	びしょう	faint/subtle smile [する] give a smile
笑*顔	△えがお	smiling face
笑み	えみ	smile

252 泣 ▶きゅう ▷な(く)

8 丶 冫 氵 汀 汁 汁 泣 泣

泣く	なく	cry, weep
泣き*声	なきごえ	cry, tearful voice
◇ *号泣	ごうきゅう	[する] cry bitterly

253 喜 ▶き ▷よろこ(ぶ)

12 一 十 士 吉 吉 吉 吉 青 直 喜
喜 喜

| 喜ぶ | よろこぶ | be glad, be pleased |
| 喜*劇 | きげき | comedy 反悲*劇(ひげき) tragedy, tragic event |

254 困 ▶こん ▷こま(る)

7 丨 冂 冂 円 囝 困 困

| 困る | こまる | have difficulty/trouble, be in/get into trouble, embarrassed |
| 困*難な | こんなんな | difficult, hard |

255 怒 ▶ど ▷いか(る)，おこ(る)

9 乀 夕 女 奴 奴 奴 怒 怒 怒

| 怒る | おこる，いかる | become angry |
| *激怒 | げきど | [する] be enraged, fly into a rage |

256 押 ▶おう ▷お(す)，お(さえる)

8 一 十 扌 扌 扣 押 押 押

押す	おす	push, press
押し入れ	おしいれ	closet
押さえる	おさえる	press/hold down
押*収	おうしゅう	[する] seize, confiscate

257 引 ▶いん ▷ひ(く)，ひ(ける)

4 フ コ 弓 引

引く	ひく	pull, draw (curtain, bowstring, etc.), look up (words in a dictionary)
長引く	ながびく	be prolonged, be protracted, be delayed
引き返す	ひきかえす	turn back, head back, return
引き出す	ひきだす	pull out, take out, withdraw (money)
引き出し	ひきだし	drawer
引っかかる	ひっかかる	be caught in/by ～, be cheated
引っかける	ひっかける	hang/suspend something on ～, hook
引き分け	ひきわけ	a draw, a tie (as in game)
取(り)引(き)	とりひき	[する] trade, deal with
*字引	じびき	dictionary cf. *辞書(じしょ) rather than *字引 is used in modern Japanese
引用	いんよう	[する] quote, cite
引力	いんりょく	gravity, gravitational force
引退	いんたい	[する] retire (from work, an active life, etc.)
強引な	ごういんな	forcible, overbearing, coercive

258 死 ▶し ▷し(ぬ)

6 一 厂 歹 歹 歹 死

死ぬ	しぬ	die, be killed
死者	ししゃ	the deceased, the dead
死人	しにん	dead person, the dead
死体	したい	dead body, corpse
死	し	death
死*亡	しぼう	[する] die, be killed

259 **吹** ▶すい
▷ふ（く）

7 ｜ 口 口 叮 叻 吹 吹

吹く	ふく	blow, exhale
吹*雪	△ふぶき	snowstorm, blizzard
◇ *息吹	△いぶき	a breath (of spring), vigor (of youth)
◇ 吹*奏楽	すいそうがく	wind-instrument music

260 **急** ▶きゅう
▷いそ（ぐ）

9 ノ ク ク 刍 刍 㑊 急 急 急

急ぐ	いそぐ	hurry (up), hasten
急に	きゅうに	suddenly
急行	きゅうこう	express (train) する go in haste
急用	きゅうよう	urgent business
急*速な	きゅうそくな	rapid

261 **咲** ▷さ（く）

9 ｜ 口 口 叱 叱 咩 咲 咲

| 咲く | さく | bloom, blossom |
| 返り咲く | かえりざく | come back (to power), make a comeback |

262 **置** ▶ち
▷お（く）

13 ｜ 冖 罒 罒 罒 罒 甲 甼 胃 胃 胃 置

置く	おく	put, place
置物	おきもの	ornament (for an alcove, entrance way, etc.)
物置	ものおき	storeroom, barn
*位置	いち	position, location する be located cf. 地*位（ちい）(social) position, rank, status

263 **勝** ▶しょう
▷か（つ），まさ（る）

12 丿 刀 月 月 月 月 肝 胖 胖 朕 勝 勝

勝つ	かつ	win
勝利	しょうり	する win a victory
勝者	しょうしゃ	winner, victor
連勝	れんしょう	consecutive victories する keep on winning
*優勝	ゆうしょう	する win (the championship, pennant, etc.)
勝る	まさる	be superior to

264 **選** ▶せん
▷えら（ぶ）

15 ｜ ㇆ 己 弖 弖 弖 吧 吧 罪 罪 巽 `巽 選 選

選ぶ	えらぶ	choose, select, elect
選出	せんしゅつ	する elect
選手	せんしゅ	athlete, player
選*挙	せんきょ	する elect

265 **飛** ▶ひ
▷と（ぶ），と（ばす）

9 ㇂ ㇂ 飞 飞 飞 飛 飛 飛 飛

飛ぶ	とぶ	fly, jump, hop
飛び出す	とびだす	run out, jump out
飛行機	ひこうき	airplane
飛行場	ひこうじょう	airfield cf. *空*港（くうこう）airport

266 **踏** ▶とう
▷ふ（む），ふ（まえる）

15 ｜ 口 口 𝅘 𝅘 𝅗 𝅗 𝅗 𝅗 跡 跡 路 踏 踏

踏む	ふむ	step on, tread on
踏切	ふみきり	railroad crossing
*雑踏	ざっとう	crowd, jam
◇ *舞*踏会	ぶとうかい	a dance/ball
踏まえる	ふまえる	be based on

第 13 回

267 進 ▶しん
▷すす(む), すす(める)

11 ノ イ イ゙ 广 什 件 隹 隹 隹 進
進

進む	すすむ	advance, move forward, make progress
進歩	しんぽ	-する advance, progress, improve
進学	しんがく	-する go on to high school/university
前進	ぜんしん	-する go ahead, advance
先進国	せんしんこく	advanced country, developed nation

268 盗 ▶とう
▷ぬす(む)

11 ヽ ン ソ ソ 次 次 次 盗 盗 盗
盗

盗む	ぬすむ	steal, rob
強盗	ごうとう	burglar, robber
盗作	とうさく	plagiarism, a plagiarism, a crib -する plagiarize

269 受 ▶じゅ
▷う(ける), う(かる)

8 ハ ハ 厂 ᄄ 叩 四 受 受

受ける	うける	receive, be given
引き受ける	ひきうける	undertake, accept (a job, assignment, etc.), take over (a task)
受け取る	うけとる	get, receive, accept, interpret, understand
受け*身	うけみ	passiveness, passivity, passive voice
受*付	うけつけ	reception/information desk, receptionist, receipt
*授受	じゅじゅ	-する give and receive
受理	じゅり	-する accept, receive
受かる	うかる	pass (an exam)

270 取 ▶しゅ
▷と(る)

8  一 Γ F F E 耳 取 取

取る	とる	take, get, hold, remove
取り出す	とりだす	take out, extract
取り入れる	とりいれる	accept, adopt, borrow, harvest, take in
受け取る	うけとる	get, receive, accept, interpret, understand
取*材	しゅざい	-する collect/gather (news materials, data, etc.)

271 合 ▶ごう, がっ, かっ
▷あ(う), あ(わす), あ(わせる)

6 ノ ハ ム 今 合 合

合う	あう	fit, suit, match
話し合う	はなしあう	talk with, discuss
間に合う	まにあう	be in time, be enough
お見合い	おみあい	-する meet a prospective marriage partner
合わせる	あわせる	put together, add, tune (to)
会合	かいごう	meeting, gathering -する meet, gather
集合	しゅうごう	-する gather, meet, assemble
合意	ごうい	agreement -する agree
合*格	ごうかく	-する pass (an entrance/certificate exam)
合*併	がっぺい	-する merge, consolidate
歴 合*戦	かっせん	battle, fight

272 吸 ▶きゅう
▷す(う)

6 Ⅰ ロ ロ ロ゙ 吵 吸

吸う	すう	smoke, inhale, suck (blood), absorb
吸い取る	すいとる	absorb, suck up, soak up, squeeze (money out of someone, etc.)
呼吸	こきゅう	respiration, breathing -する breathe cf. *息をする(いきをする) breathe
吸*収	きゅうしゅう	-する absorb, assimilate

273 拾 ▶しゅう, じゅう
▷ひろ(う)

9 一 十 扌 扩 拎 拎 拾 拾 拾

拾う	ひろう	pick up, gather
拾*得物	しゅうとくぶつ	a find, something found
歴 拾万円	じゅうまんえん	one hundred thousand yen

274 誘

▶ゆう
▷さそ(う)

14 `, ニ 言 言 言 言 言 言 言 計
計 誘 誘 誘

誘う	さそう	invite, tempt
誘発	ゆうはつ	-する induce, cause, trigger
誘*惑	ゆうわく	-する tempt, allure
*勧誘	かんゆう	-する invite, persuade, canvass
誘*拐	ゆうかい	-する kidnap, abduct

275 疲

▶ひ
▷つか(れる)

10 `, 亠 广 广 广 疒 疒 疒 疖 疲

疲れる	つかれる	be tired, grow weary
疲れ	つかれ	tiredness, fatigue, weariness
気疲れ	きづかれ	-する be mentally tired, be a strain on one's nerves
疲*労	ひろう	tiredness, fatigue, weariness -する be tired

276 比

▶ひ
▷くら(べる)

4 一 ヒ 比 比

比べる	くらべる	compare
見比べる	みくらべる	compare (visually)
比*較	ひかく	-する compare
比重	ひじゅう	specific gravity
比*例	ひれい	-する be proportional, be in proportion to

277 決

▶けつ
▷き(める), き(まる)

7 `, ニ ミ シ 汁 汁 決

決める	きめる	decide, fix, settle
決定	けってい	-する decide, settle, determine
決定*的な	けっていてきな	definite, final, decisive
決心	けっしん	-する determine, make up one's mind, resolve
決して	けっして	never, by no means

278 伝

▶でん
▷つた(わる), つた(える), つた(う)

6 ノ イ 仁 仁 伝 伝

伝える	つたえる	tell, report, communicate, notify, transmit
手伝う	△てつだう	help, assist
言い伝え	いいつたえ	legend, tradition
伝う	つたう	go along
伝言	でんごん	message -する give/send a message
伝*統	でんとう	tradition
伝説	でんせつ	legend, folklore

279 流

▶りゅう, る
▷なが(れる), なが(す)

10 `, ニ シ シ 汁 汁 汁 汁 流 流

流れる	ながれる	flow, (time) pass
流す	ながす	pour, let flow, drain, spread (rumors), broadcast
上流	じょうりゅう	upper stream, upper class
上流*階*級	じょうりゅうかいきゅう	upper class
中流	ちゅうりゅう	middle stream, middle class
下流	かりゅう	lower stream, lower class
一流の	いちりゅうの	top-ranking
流行	りゅうこう	fashion, vogue, fad, epidemic -する be in fashion, be popular/prevalent
◇ 流*布	るふ	-する circulate, spread

第 14 回

280 落

▶らく
▷お(ちる), お(とす)

12 一 十 サ サ サ 艾 艾 莎 莈 落
落 落

落ちる	おちる	fall, drop, be omitted
落ち着く	おちつく	settle down, calm down, settle into (a new home)
落とす	おとす	drop, throw down, lose, fail, omit
落とし物	おとしもの	lost article/property
落石	らくせき	falling rock(s)
転落	てんらく	-する fall, roll/tumble down

落*雷　　　らくらい　lightning strike

*墜落　　　ついらく　[する] fall, crash (used for aircraft)

281 晴
▶せい
▷は(れる)，は(らす)

12　１ Ⅱ 日 日 日一 日十 日丰 晴 晴 晴
晴 晴

晴れる　　はれる　clear (up), feel refreshed/better

晴れ　　　はれ　fine weather

秋晴れ　　あきばれ　fine autumn day

晴*天　　　せいてん　fine weather, clear sky

*快晴　　　かいせい　clear sky, fine weather

282 投
▶とう
▷な(げる)

7　一 十 扌 扌 扌 投 投

投げる　　なげる　throw, pitch, give up

投手　　　とうしゅ　pitcher (baseball)

投書　　　とうしょ　contribution, letter from a reader (to an editor) [する] vi. contribute (a letter, poem, etc.) to a publication

投*資　　　とうし　[する] invest

投*票　　　とうひょう　[する] vote

投機　　　とうき　speculation

283 逃
▶とう
▷に(げる)，に(がす)，のが(す)，のが(れる)

9　丿 丿 ㇆ 丬 兆 兆 兆 逃 逃

逃げる　　にげる　run away, get away, escape

逃げ出す　にげだす　run away, flee

逃走　　　とうそう　[する] run away, escape

逃がす　　にがす　release, set free, let escape

取り逃がす　とりにがす　fail to catch

逃す　　　のがす　fail to use (an opportunity)

見逃す　　みのがす　miss, overlook, let go unchallenged/ unpunished

逃れる　　のがれる　escape, get away, avoid, shirk

284 過
▶か
▷す(ぎる)，す(ごす)，あやま(つ)，あやま(ち)

12　１ Ⅱ 冂 冎 冎 咼 咼 咼 咼 '咼
過 過

過ぎる　　すぎる　pass, go past, elapse

通り過ぎる　とおりすぎる　go past, pass (a place/etc.)

飲み過ぎ　のみすぎ　drinking too much, excessive drinking

食べ過ぎ　たべすぎ　eating too much, excessive eating

通過　　　つうか　[する] pass (through/by/etc.)

過半*数　　かはんすう　majority, more than half

過*労死　　かろうし　death caused by overworking

過*程　　　かてい　process

過*失　　　かしつ　error, fault, negligence

過ごす　　すごす　spend (a day, a vacation, etc.)

過ち　　　あやまち　error, fault, mistake

285 捨
▶しゃ
▷す(てる)

11　一 十 扌 扌 扵 捈 捈 捈 捈 捨
捨

捨てる　　すてる　throw away, dispose of, abandon, forsake

見捨てる　みすてる　walk out on, forsake, abandon

捨て犬　　すていぬ　abandoned dog

四捨五入　ししゃごにゅう　[する] round off (to the nearest whole number)

取捨選*択　しゅしゃせんたく　[する] sort out, choose, select

286 発
▶はつ，ほつ

9　フ ㇇ 癶 癶 癶 癶 癶 癶 発

出発　　　しゅっぱつ　[する] depart, leave

発車　　　はっしゃ　[する] depart (as in trains or buses)

〜発　　　〜はつ　departing from/at, shot(s)

発明　　　はつめい　[する] invent

発見　　　はっけん　[する] discover, find

発行　　　はっこう　[する] issue, publish

発足　　　ほっそく　[する] be inaugurated, start

発起人　　ほっきにん　originator, promoter, proposer

第2水準

287 到 ▶とう

8 一 丆 云 至 至 至 到 到

到着	とうちゃく [する] arrive
到*底	とうてい cannot possibly, (not) at all
到来	とうらい [する] come, arrive

288 計 ▶けい
▷はか(る)，はか(らう)

9 ` 二 言 言 言 言 言 計

計画	けいかく [する] plan
時計	△とけい clock, watch
会計	かいけい accounting
家計	かけい household budget
合計	ごうけい a total (amount), the sum [する] add up, total, sum
計る	はかる measure

289 定 ▶てい，じょう
▷さだ(める)，さだ(まる)，さだ(か)

8 ` 宀 宀 宀 宇 宇 定 定

決定	けってい [する] decide, settle, determine
意思決定	いしけってい [する] determine (one's) intention
安定	あんてい [する] be stable/steady
安定した	あんていした stable, steady
*不安定な	ふあんていな unstable, insecure, unsettled
定食	ていしょく a meal of fixed menu
定年	ていねん retirement age
定休日	ていきゅうび regular day off
定める	さだめる decide (on), determine, appoint, establish (a rule/law)
定かではない	さだかではない uncertain
◇ 定石	じょうせき a standard move (in the games of *go* and *shōgi*), standard method

第 15 回

290 注 ▶ちゅう
▷そそ(ぐ)

8 ` 氵 氵 氵 汁 注 注

注意	ちゅうい [する] warn, caution, take notice of
注目	ちゅうもく [する] pay attention, watch, keep one's eyes on
注文	ちゅうもん [する] order
発注	はっちゅう [する] place an order
注ぐ	そそぐ pour

291 意 ▶い

13 ` 亠 亠 立 产 产 咅 咅 音 音
意 意 意

注意	ちゅうい [する] warn, caution, take notice of
意見	いけん opinion, idea, suggestion
好意	こうい goodwill, kindness, favor, affection
用意	ようい [する] prepare (for)
意外な	いがいな unexpected, unforeseen
意地悪な	いじわるな spiteful, nasty
生意気な	なまいきな conceited, impertinent, insolent

292 説 ▶せつ，ぜい
▷と(く)

14 ` 亠 言 言 言 言 言 言' 訝'
訝 訝 訝 説

説明	せつめい [する] explain
解説	かいせつ [する] explain, comment on
小説	しょうせつ novel
社説	しゃせつ editorial
説教	せっきょう [する] preach (a sermon), lecture (a child)
説*得	せっとく [する] persuade
*仮説	かせつ hypothesis
*演説	えんぜつ (political) speech [する] deliver a (political) speech
遊説	ゆうぜい [する] make an election tour, canvass
◇ 説く	とく explain, expound, advocate, persuade

293 解 ▶かい，げ
▷と(く)，と(かす)，と(ける)

13 丿 勹 勹 甬 甬 甬 角 角' 甪' 甪'
甪 甪 解

理解　りかい　-する understand, comprehend　cf. 分かる（わかる） understand, realize, find out

見解　けんかい　opinion, view

解決　かいけつ　-する solve, settle

解く　とく　solve, unfasten

解ける　とける　come untied, melt away, thaw, be solved

解かす　とかす　melt (snow, ice, etc.)

特 解脱　げだつ　emancipation from worldly attachments, salvation from earthly bondage　-する be emancipated

294 参

▶さん
▷まい(る)

8

参加　さんか　-する participate, join

参考書　さんこうしょ　reference book

持参　じさん　-する bring (something) with one

お参り　おまいり　-する visit a shrine/temple

295 加

▶か
▷くわ(える)，くわ(わる)

5

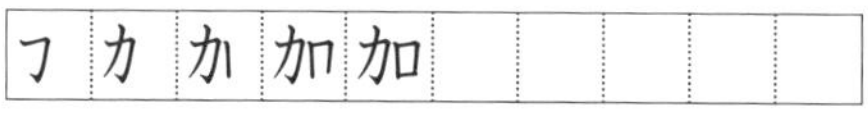

参加　さんか　-する participate, join

加*工　かこう　-する process (food, etc.)

加入　かにゅう　-する join (a club, association, etc.)

加*盟　かめい　-する join (a league, federation, etc.)

加*熱　かねつ　-する heat (up)

加える　くわえる　add, inflict (damage)

加わる　くわわる　join, take part in

296 練

▶れん
▷ね(る)

14

練習　れんしゅう　-する practice, drill, rehearse

洗練された　せんれんされた　sophisticated, refined, polished

*訓練　くんれん　-する train, drill

*熟練*労働者　じゅくれんろうどうしゃ　skilled workers

練る　ねる　knead, elaborate (a scheme)

297 研

▶けん
▷と(ぐ)

9

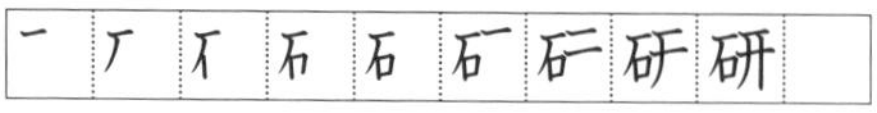

研究　けんきゅう　-する study, research

研究所　けんきゅうじょ　(research) laboratory, research institute

研*修　けんしゅう　-する train, be trained, study

研*修所　けんしゅうじょ　training center

研ぐ　とぐ　-する sharpen (a knife)

298 究

▶きゅう
▷きわ(める)

7

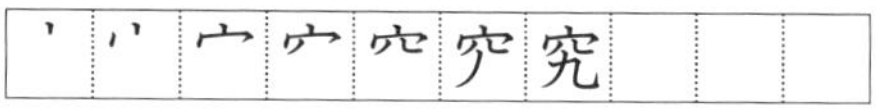

研究　けんきゅう　-する study, research

究明　きゅうめい　-する look deep into, investigate, inquire into

究める　きわめる　master, study thoroughly, get at the truth

299 連

▶れん
▷つら(なる)，つら(ねる)，つ(れる)

10

連絡　れんらく　-する contact, notify

連続　れんぞく　continuation, series　-する continue, be consecutive

国*際連合　こくさいれんごう　the United Nations　cf. *abbr.* 国連（こくれん）

連*想　れんそう　-する call to mind, associated with (in the mind)

*関連　かんれん　relations, connection　-する be connected/associated/correlated　cf. *関*係（かんけい） relations, relationship

*関連した　かんれんした　related, relevant

～に*関連して　～にかんれんして　in connection with, in relation to, with reference to

連れていく　つれていく　take someone along

連なる　つらなる　range, lie/stand in a row

300 絡

▶らく
▷から(む)，から(まる)，から(める)

12

連絡　　　　れんらく　[する] contact, notify
絡む　　　　からむ　coil around, become entwined, involve
絡まる　　　からまる　become entangled
〜絡みの　　〜がらみの　related to
絡める　　　からめる　entwine

301 濯 ▶たく

17	冫	氵	氵	氵	氵	氵	氵	氵	氵
濯	濯	濯	濯	濯	濯	濯			

洗濯　　　　せんたく　[する] wash, launder
洗濯機　　　せんたくき　washing machine
洗濯物　　　せんたくもの　laundry

302 結 ▶けつ
▷むす(ぶ), ゆ(う), ゆ(わえる)

12	く	幺	幺	糸	糸	糸	糸	紆	結
結	結								

結婚　　　　けっこん　[する] marry, get married
結合　　　　けつごう　[する] combine, unite
終結　　　　しゅうけつ　[する] end, conclude
結*論　　　　けつろん　conclusion
結ぶ　　　　むすぶ　tie, fasten (together), bind, enter (a relationship with), make (a contract with)
◇　結*納　　　ゆいのう　betrothal presents
結う　　　　ゆう　dress/do up (one's hair), tie (up), fasten
結わえる　　ゆわえる　bind, fasten, tie

303 婚 ▶こん

11	く	女	女	妒	妒	妮	婚	婚	婚
婚									

結婚　　　　けっこん　[する] marry, get married
新婚旅行　　しんこんりょこう　honeymoon
婚*約　　　　こんやく　[する] get engaged
*離婚　　　　りこん　[する] divorce, get divorced

304 運 ▶うん
▷はこ(ぶ)

12	丶	冖	冖	曰	骨	骨	冒	亘	軍	軍
運	運									

運転　　　　うんてん　[する] drive (a car), operate (a machine, train, etc.)
運転手　　　うんてんしゅ　(bus, taxi, etc.) driver
運動　　　　うんどう　motion, movement, exercise, athletics, (social) movement, campaign [する] exercise
運送会社　　うんそうがいしゃ　transportation/delivery company
運　　　　　うん　fortune
運ぶ　　　　はこぶ　carry, convey, transport, take (something to a place), make progress

305 案 ▶あん

10	丶	宀	宀	安	安	安	宰	案	案

案内　　　　あんない　guidance, information (desk) [する] show around, show the way, give someone a tour of
案　　　　　あん　plan, idea
名案　　　　めいあん　good idea
*提案　　　　ていあん　[する] propose, suggest
案外　　　　あんがい　unexpectedly

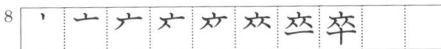

第 16 回

306 卒 ▶そつ

8	丶	宀	宀	交	衣	衣	卒	

卒業　　　　そつぎょう　[する] graduate
卒業生　　　そつぎょうせい　graduate
大卒(者)　　だいそつ(しゃ)　college/university graduate
cf. 高卒(者)(こうそつ(しゃ)) high school graduate
新卒(者)　　しんそつ(しゃ)　recent graduate

307 業 ▶ぎょう, ごう
▷わざ

13	丨	冂	业	业	业	业	业	业	业
茉	業	業							

卒業　　　　そつぎょう　[する] graduate
授業　　　　じゅぎょう　class, lesson

第2水準

事業	じぎょう	business
休業	きゅうぎょう	⌜する⌝ close a business (for a holiday, etc.), suspend business/operations
*職業	しょくぎょう	occupation, profession
*産業	さんぎょう	industry
*実業家	じつぎょうか	businessperson, entrepreneur
自業自*得	じごうじとく	the natural consequences of one's evil deed, getting one's just deserts
早業	はやわざ	quick feat/trick

308 用 ▶よう ▷もち(いる)

5) 冂 月 月 用

利用	りよう	⌜する⌝ use, utilize
使用	しよう	⌜する⌝ use, make use of
通用	つうよう	⌜する⌝ be in use, be accepted
用事	ようじ	errand, something to do, (another) engagement
用	よう	errand (in casual speech)
用意	ようい	⌜する⌝ prepare (for)
用心	ようじん	⌜する⌝ be careful, be on the alert
用語	ようご	(technical) term
用*途	ようと	a use
*費用	ひよう	cost, expense
用いる	もちいる	use, employ, adopt

309 去 ▶きょ, こ ▷さ(る)

5 一 十 土 去 去

去年	きょねん	last year
過去	かこ	past cf. *未来(みらい) future, *現*在(げんざい) present
立ち去る	たちさる	leave (a place)

310 趣 ▶しゅ ▷おもむき

15 一 十 土 キ キ 走 走 走 走 走 起 趄 趣 趣

趣味	しゅみ	interest, hobby, taste
◇ 趣	おもむき	grace, elegance, charm, appearance, taste

311 味 ▶み ▷あじ, あじ(わう)

8) 口 口 口 □ 吽 味 味

趣味	しゅみ	interest, hobby, taste
意味	いみ	meaning, significance ⌜する⌝ mean
*興味	きょうみ	interest cf. *関心(かんしん) interest, concern
地味な	じみな	plain, simple, quiet, subdued 反 *派手な(はでな) showy, bright
*風*邪気味だ	かぜぎみだ	have a slight cold
気味の悪い	きみのわるい	weird, uncanny, creepy
正味	しょうみ	net (weight, quantity, etc.), full (as in "eight full hours")
調味料	ちょうみりょう	(food) seasoning
味覚	みかく	the sense of taste
三味*線	△しゃみせん	shamisen, a three-stringed banjo-like instrument
味	あじ	taste, flavor
味わう	あじわう	taste, experience, go through

312 授 ▶じゅ ▷さず(ける), さず(かる)

11 一 十 扌 扩 扩 护 护 抨 抨 授

授業	じゅぎょう	class, lesson
教授	きょうじゅ	professor ⌜する⌝ teach
授受	じゅじゅ	⌜する⌝ give and receive
授ける	さずける	grant (a license), confer (a title), award (a prize)

313 橋 ▶きょう ▷はし

16 一 十 オ 木 朾 栏 栌 栌 桥 栌 栌 橋 橋 橋 橋

橋	はし	bridge
日本橋	にほんばし	Nihonbashi (a place in Tokyo)
日本橋	にっぽんばし	Nipponbashi (a place in Osaka)
歩道橋	ほどうきょう	pedestrian bridge
鉄橋	てっきょう	railway bridge

314 花 ▶か ▷はな

7 一 十 サ サ ナ 花 花

花	はな	flower
花屋	はなや	flower shop, flower stall
生け花	いけばな	the art of flower arrangement
お花見	おはなみ	cherry blossom viewing
花火	はなび	fireworks
花*壇	かだん	flower bed

315 薬 ▶やく ▷くすり

16 一 十 サ サ ナ 甘 甘 苗 苗 苗
苗 苗 蓮 蓮 薬 薬

薬	くすり	drug, medicine
薬屋	くすりや	pharmacy, drugstore
薬局	やっきょく	pharmacy, drugstore
薬学	やくがく	pharmacology, pharmaceuticals
◇ 薬味	やくみ	spices

316 色 ▶しょく, しき ▷いろ

6 ノ ク 夕 名 名 色

色	いろ	color
茶色	ちゃいろ	brown
～色の	～いろの	～ colored
色紙	いろがみ	colored paper
色づく	いろづく	turn color (as in leaves)
色っぽい	いろっぽい	erotic, seductive, sexy
色気	いろけ	sex appeal
色気がある	いろけがある	sexy, be very interested in, have an inclination for
色紙	しきし	square piece of fancy paper (for writing a poem, etc.)
色*彩	しきさい	hue, tint, coloring, color
*景色	△けしき	view, scenery
*特色	とくしょく	distinguishing characteristics
*原色	げんしょく	primary color
◇ 好色な	こうしょくな	lustful, erotic

317 服 ▶ふく

8 ノ 刀 月 月 肌 服 服 服

服	ふく	clothes
*洋服	ようふく	Western-style clothes
*和服	わふく	Japanese-style clothes, kimono
服*装	ふくそう	(style of) dress, clothes
*征服	せいふく	する conquer
着服	ちゃくふく	する embezzle

318 客 ▶きゃく, かく

9 ヽ ′ 宀 宀 宀 安 safe 客 客

客	きゃく	guest, customer
客間	きゃくま	guest room (in a house)
乗客	じょうきゃく	passenger
旅客機	りょかくき	passenger airplane
お客*様	おきゃくさま	customer, guest [honorific]
客*観*的な	きゃっかんてきな	objective 反 主*観*的な (しゅかんてきな) subjective

319 犬 ▶けん ▷いぬ

4 一 ナ 大 犬

犬	いぬ	dog
小犬／子犬	こいぬ	puppy
*野犬	やけん	stray dog

320 文 ▶ぶん, もん ▷ふみ

4 ヽ 一 ナ 文

文	ぶん	sentence, passage
作文	さくぶん	composition, essay
文学	ぶんがく	literature
文体	ぶんたい	style (of writing)
文語	ぶんご	literary language/expression
文明	ぶんめい	civilization
文*化	ぶんか	culture

人文*科学　じんぶんかがく　humanities
文*字　もじ　letter (of the alphabet, etc.)
歴 文　ふみ　a letter (to someone)

321 物　▶ぶつ, もつ
　　　▷もの

8 ﾉ ｰ ｾ ㇰ 牛 ﾀ 物 物 物

物　もの　thing, object, substance, article
飲(み)物　のみもの　drink, beverage
食べ物　たべもの　food
本物　ほんもの　genuine article, real thing
*偽物　にせもの　imitation, fake
生き物　いきもの　living thing, creature, animal, life
動物　どうぶつ　animal
*植物　しょくぶつ　plants
生物　せいぶつ　living things, organisms, life
生物学　せいぶつがく　biology
物理*的に　ぶつりてきに　physically
物理学　ぶつりがく　physics
物質　ぶっしつ　matter, substance
物*価　ぶっか　prices (of commodities, etc.)
名物　めいぶつ　local specialty, well-known product
食物　しょくもつ　food

第 17 回

322 族　▶ぞく

11 ﾉ ﾗ ﾌ 方 ﾎ 扩 ㇭ 㡀 旅
族

家族　かぞく　family
部族　ぶぞく　tribe
*民族　みんぞく　people, ethnic group
◇ 族*議*員　ぞくぎいん　Diet member who works on policy-making in a particular field

323 公　▶こう
　　　▷おおやけ

4 ﾉ 八 公 公

公園　こうえん　park, square

公立高校　こうりつこうこう　public high school
公*共*施*設　こうきょうしせつ　public/community facilities
公*共事業　こうきょうじぎょう　government enterprise
公*共*交通システム　こうきょうこうつうシステム public transportation system
公言　こうげん　-する declare
公*平な　こうへいな　fair, impartial
公*正な　こうせいな　just, fair, righteous
主人公　しゅじんこう　main character (of a story, etc.)
公の　おおやけの　public, official, formal

324 園　▶えん
　　　▷その

13 一 冂 冃 門 門 鬥 周 周 袁 袁
袁 園 園

公園　こうえん　park, square
動物園　どうぶつえん　zoo
*植物園　しょくぶつえん　botanical garden
遊園地　ゆうえんち　amusement park, recreational grounds
日本*庭園　にほんていえん　Japanese garden
◇ 園*芸　えんげい　gardening
◇ 花園　はなぞの　flower garden

325 医　▶い

7 一 ㇒ 匚 匞 歹 歹 医

医者　いしゃ　doctor
医*師　いし　doctor
医学　いがく　medical science
医学部　いがくぶ　medical department
名医　めいい　great doctor, skilled physician
女医　じょい　female doctor

326 宿　▶しゅく
　　　▷やど, やど(る), やど(す)

11 ﾉ 宀 宀 宀 宇 宇 宿 宿 宿 宿
宿

宿題　しゅくだい　homework

下宿　　　げしゅく　lodging　-する lodge at, room at someone

宿*泊　　　しゅくはく　-する stay at, lodge

宿　　　　やど　inn, lodgings

雨宿り　　あまやどり　-する take cover from the rain (under the eaves of a house)

◇ 宿す　　やどす　be pregnant

---

327 題 ▶だい

18 丨 冂 日 日 旦 早 早 是 是 是 是 題 題 題 題 題 題

宿題　　　しゅくだい　homework

問題　　　もんだい　problem, issue, question (in an exam)

出題　　　しゅつだい　-する make questions (for an exam)

話題　　　わだい　topic, subject (of a conversation)

題名　　　だいめい　title

---

328 寺 ▶じ ▷てら

6 一 十 土 土 寺 寺

寺　　　　てら　temple

山寺　　　やまでら　mountain temple

寺院　　　じいん　temple

---

329 図 ▶ず, と ▷はか(る)

7 丨 冂 冂 冂 図 図 図

図書館　　としょかん　library

意図　　　いと　intention　-する intend

地図　　　ちず　map

図　　　　ず　figure, diagram, illustration

図*表　　　ずひょう　chart, graph, diagram

図*形　　　ずけい　figure, diagram

合図　　　あいず　-する signal, sign, beckon

図る　　　はかる　plan, attempt, aim (at/for)

---

330 館 ▶かん ▷やかた

16 丿 𠂉 𠂉 今 今 今 飠 飠 飠' 飠' 飤 飤 節 館 館 館

図書館　　としょかん　library

旅館　　　りょかん　Japanese-style inn

学生会館　がくせいかいかん　students' hall

水族館　　すいぞくかん　aquarium

館長　　　かんちょう　director (of a museum, aquarium, etc.), chief librarian

本館　　　ほんかん　main building

*別館　　　べっかん　(hotel, etc.) annex

◇ 館　　　やかた　mansion, palace

---

331 室 ▶しつ ▷むろ

9 丶 丷 广 宀 宀 宀 宕 宰 室

教室　　　きょうしつ　classroom

研究室　　けんきゅうしつ　office (of a professor/researcher)

病室　　　びょうしつ　sickroom

客室　　　きゃくしつ　guest room, passenger cabin

待合室　　まちあいしつ　waiting room

室内　　　しつない　indoor-(pool, plumbing, etc.), in a room

*洋室　　　ようしつ　Western-style room

*和室　　　わしつ　Japanese-style room

歴 室町時代　むろまちじだい　Muromachi era (14-16th century)

---

332 席 ▶せき

10 丶 亠 广 户 庁 庐 庐 庐 唐 席

出席　　　しゅっせき　-する attend (a class, a meeting, etc.), be present

*欠席　　　けっせき　-する be absent (from school, etc.)

席　　　　せき　seat

座席　　　ざせき　seat

着席　　　ちゃくせき　-する sit down

*首席　　　しゅせき　top/first in the class

主席　　　しゅせき　head, chief

333 度 ▶ど，と，たく ▷たび

9 ` 亠 广 广 庐 庐 庐 度 度

～度	～ど	～ time(s), ～ degree(s)
今度	こんど	shortly, soon, this time, next time
毎度	まいど	each time, always
年度	ねんど	(school, fiscal, etc.) year
高度な	こうどな	high, advanced, high-grade
高度*経*済*成長	こうどけいざいせいちょう	high economic growth
*温度	おんど	temperature
*速度	そくど	speed, velocity
*制度	せいど	system, institution
*限度	げんど	limit, limitation (quantity)
度々	たびたび	often, frequently
この度	このたび	this time, now
*支度	したく	preparation 〔する〕 get ready
歴 *法度	はっと	regulation, ban

334 機 ▶き ▷はた

16 一 十 才 木 杉 杉 杉 杉 桦 桦
桦 桦 榉 機 機 機

飛行機	ひこうき	airplane
機内	きない	inside an airplane
機内食	きないしょく	inflight meal
機*関	きかん	organization, institution, engine
機*関車	きかんしゃ	locomotive
機*械	きかい	machine
機会	きかい	opportunity, occasion
歴 機	はた	loom

335 場 ▶じょう ▷ば

12 一 十 土 圹 圹 坦 坦 坦 坦 場
場 場

場所	ばしょ	place
場合	ばあい	occasion, case
場	ば	field, place, spot, space

立場	たちば	standpoint, one's ground, point of view
*市場	いちば	local marketplace
*工場	こうば	small factory
*工場	こうじょう	factory, plant
飛行場	ひこうじょう	airfield cf. *空*港（くうこう） airport
出場	しゅつじょう	〔する〕 take part, participate
*市場	しじょう	a market

336 県 ▶けん

9 丨 冂 日 日 目 甼 県 県 県

県	けん	prefecture, prefectural government
～県	～けん	～ Prefecture
県立（の）	けんりつ（の）	prefectural
県道	けんどう	prefectural road
県*庁	けんちょう	prefectural office

337 府 ▶ふ

8 ` 亠 广 广 广 庐 府 府

京都府	きょうとふ	Kyoto Prefecture
大*阪府	おおさかふ	Osaka Prefecture
府立（の）	ふりつ（の）	prefectural (used only for Osaka and Kyoto)
府*庁	ふちょう	prefectural office (used only for Osaka and Kyoto)
歴 *幕府	ばくふ	the shogunate

338 都 ▶と，つ ▷みやこ

11 一 十 土 耂 耂 者 者 者 者 都
都

東京都	とうきょうと	Tokyo metropolis
都立（の）	とりつ（の）	metropolitan
都内	とない	within Tokyo
都道府県	とどうふけん	Tokyo, Hokkaido, Osaka, Kyoto, and the prefectures
都会	とかい	city, town
*首都	しゅと	capital

都*庁　とちょう　Tokyo Metropolitan Government (Office)

都合　つごう　circumstances, convenience 〔-する〕 arrange (for), see to (something)

〔歴〕都　みやこ　capital (historical)　cf. *首都（しゅと）

第 18 回

339 暖
▶だん
▷あたた（か），あたた（かい），あたた（まる），あたた（める）

13 ｜ 冂 日 日 日' 日' 日'' 日'' 昈 昈 | 暖 暖 暖

暖かい　あたたかい　warm
暖める　あたためる　vt. warm, heat (up)
暖まる　あたたまる　get warm, be warmed
暖冬　だんとう　mild winter
暖*房　だんぼう　heating, a heater 〔-する〕 heat (a room)
*温暖な　おんだんな　warm, mild, temperate

340 涼
▶りょう
▷すず（しい），すず（む）

11 ｀ ｀ シ ゛ 汁 汻 泸 泸 涼 涼 | 涼

涼しい　すずしい　cool
夕涼み　ゆうすずみ　enjoying the cool of evening
涼む　すずむ　cool oneself, cool off
涼*風　りょうふう　cool/refreshing breeze
*清涼飲料（水）　せいりょういんりょう（すい）　refreshing beverage, soft drink

341 悲
▶ひ
▷かな（しい），かな（しむ）

12) ナ ヲ ヲ ヺ 非 非 非 非 悲 | 悲 悲

悲しい　かなしい　sad, sorrowful
悲しむ　かなしむ　feel sad, grieve, lament
悲*劇　ひげき　tragedy, tragic event 〔反〕喜*劇（きげき）comedy
悲運　ひうん　misfortune, bad luck

342 苦
▶く
▷くる（しい），くる（しむ），くる（しめる），にが（い），にが（る）

8 一 十 艹 芏 苎 芢 苦 苦

苦しい　くるしい　painful, difficult, hard
重苦しい　おもくるしい　oppressive, gloomy
苦しむ　くるしむ　suffer, be in pain
苦しめる　くるしめる　cause pain, cause distress, torment, annoy
苦心　くしん　〔-する〕 take pains, work hard
苦*労　くろう　〔-する〕 suffer, go through difficult times
苦い　にがい　bitter
苦り切る　にがりきる　be disgusted/displeased

343 楽
▶がく，らく
▷たの（しい），たの（しむ）

13 ' イ 冂 白 白 白 泊 泊 泊 泊 | 楽 楽 楽

楽しい　たのしい　fun, enjoyable
楽しむ　たのしむ　enjoy, have fun
楽しみ　たのしみ　pleasure, joy, fun
音楽　おんがく　music
楽*器　がっき　musical instrument
楽な　らくな　easy, comfortable
気楽に　きらくに　without worry/hesitation
安楽死　あんらくし　euthanasia, mercy killing
楽園　らくえん　paradise
*快楽主*義　かいらくしゅぎ　hedonism, epicureanism
*娯楽　ごらく　amusement, entertainment
〔特〕*神楽　△かぐら　kagura (sacred Shinto music and dancing)

344 辛
▶しん
▷から（い）

7 ` 一 ヤ 立 立 辛 辛

辛い　からい　(spicy) hot, salty
辛口の　からくちの　dry (wine, sake), harsh (criticism)
*塩辛い　しおからい　(too) salty
辛うじて　かろうじて　barely, narrowly, with difficulty
*香辛料　こうしんりょう　spices

第2水準

345 甘 ▶かん
▷あま(い)，あま(える)，あま(やかす)

5 一 十 廿 廿 甘

甘い	あまい	sweet, indulgent
甘える	あまえる	behave like a spoiled child, demand attention
甘やかす	あまやかす	indulge, pamper, spoil (a child)
甘口の	あまくちの	sweet (wine, sake, etc.)
甘味料	かんみりょう	sweetener
◇ 甘*美な	かんびな	sweet

346 痛 ▶つう
▷いた(い)，いた(む)，いた(める)

12 丶 亠 广 广 疒 疒 疒 疒 病 病 痛 痛

痛い	いたい	hurt, be painful
痛み	いたみ	pain, ache
痛む	いたむ	hurt, ache, have a pain
痛ましい	いたましい	pitiful, sad, miserable
痛手	いたで	serious injury, damage
頭痛	ずつう	headache
苦痛	くつう	pain, agony
痛*快な	つうかいな	delightful, jolly, exciting, thrilling

347 有 ▶ゆう，う
▷あ(る)

6 ノ ナ 才 冇 有 有

有名な	ゆうめいな	famous
国有地	こくゆうち	national land
私有地	しゆうち	privately-owned land
所有	しょゆう	[する] own, possess
有る	ある	have, exist
有り金	ありがね	money on hand, all the money one has
有*無	うむ	existence, presence, yes or no
◇ *希有な	けうな	rare, uncommon

348 退 ▶たい
▷しりぞ(く)，しりぞ(ける)

9 コ ヨ ヨ 艮 艮 艮 艮 退 退

退屈な	たいくつな	tedious, boring, monotonous
早退	そうたい	[する] leave school/the office early
退院	たいいん	[する] leave the hospital, be discharged from the hospital
退学	たいがく	[する] withdraw from school
退席	たいせき	[する] leave one's seat/the room
引退	いんたい	[する] retire (from work, an active life, etc.)
退*却	たいきゃく	[する] retreat, withdraw
退く	しりぞく	retreat, step back
立ち退く	△たちのく	move out, evacuate, vacate, withdraw

349 屈 ▶くつ

8 ⁊ ⁊ 尸 尸 尸 屈 屈 屈

退屈な	たいくつな	tedious, boring, monotonous
理屈	りくつ	argument, reason, logic; unreasonable argument
*不屈の	ふくつの	indomitable (spirit), unyielding
屈する	くっする	yield to, give in to
屈*伸	くっしん	[する] bend and stretch
屈*辱	くつじょく	humiliation

350 同 ▶どう
▷おな(じ)

6 丨 冂 冂 冋 同 同

同じ	おなじ	same, identical
同一の	どういつの	same, identical
同一人物	どういつじんぶつ	the same person
同時に	どうじに	at the same time
同意	どうい	[する] agree, consent
同*情	どうじょう	[する] sympathize
同*居	どうきょ	[する] live with, room together with 反 *別*居（べっきょ）[する] live separately
*共同*声明	きょうどうせいめい	joint statement
*協同*組合	きょうどうくみあい	co-op, cooperative (association/union)
*混同	こんどう	[する] confuse, mix up

第 3 水準

（Level 3）

351-1200

第 19 回

351 平
▶へい，びょう
▷たい(ら)，ひら

5 一 丆 丆 立 平

平和	へいわ	peace
和平	わへい	peace (conference, etc.)
平行な	へいこうな	parallel
水*平線	すいへいせん	horizontal line, the horizon
平日	へいじつ	week days
平気な	へいきな	calm, indifferent
公平な	こうへいな	fair, impartial
*不公平な	ふこうへいな	unfair, unjust
*不平	ふへい	complaint, grievance
平*等	びょうどう	equality
平らな	たいらな	flat, even, level
平社員	ひらしゃいん	ordinary employee, non-managerial employee
歴 平家物語	へいけものがたり	*Heike Monogatari, The Tale of the Heike*

352 和
▶わ，お
▷やわ(らぐ)，やわ(らげる)，なご(む)，なご(やか)

8 ノ 二 千 禾 禾 和 和

平和	へいわ	peace
和	わ	peace, harmony
和文	わぶん	Japanese script, writing in Japanese
和*風	わふう	Japanese style
◇ *不和	ふわ	disharmony, discord
和らげる	やわらげる	soften, alleviate
和らぐ	やわらぐ	soften, relax
和やかな	なごやかな	peaceful, mild
和む	なごむ	thaw
歴 和*尚	おしょう	Buddhist priest
歴 大和	△やまと	*Yamato*, ancient Japan

353 等
▶とう
▷ひと(しい)

12 ノ 二 午 午 竹 竹 竺 竺 笙 笙

等 等

平等	びょうどう	equality
同等の	どうとうの	equal, equivalent
上等な／の	じょうとうな／の	one of the best, fine, superior
等分	とうぶん	equal parts ［する］ divide into equal parts
高等教*育	こうとうきょういく	higher education
一等	いっとう	first class, first-rate
等しい	ひとしい	be equal to

354 第
▶だい

11 ノ 二 午 午 竹 竹 竺 笁 笁 第

第

第一に	だいいちに	first, first of all
第〜	だい〜	No. 〜 (prefix for ordinals)
第一人者	だいいちにんしゃ	the leading person (in a field, etc.)
第三者	だいさんしゃ	third person/party
*次第に	しだいに	gradually
〜*次第	〜しだい	as soon as 〜, depending on 〜
落第	らくだい	［する］ flunk, fail

355 筆
▶ひつ
▷ふで

12 ノ 二 午 午 竹 竹 竺 竺 笁 筥

笋 筆

筆	ふで	writing brush
万年筆	まんねんひつ	fountain pen
自筆	じひつ	one's own handwriting
*鉛筆	えんぴつ	pencil
筆*記*試*験	ひっきしけん	written examination

356 算
▶さん

14 ノ 二 午 午 竹 竹 竹 笁 筥 筥

筥 笁 算 算

計算	けいさん	［する］ calculate, compute
足し算	たしざん	addition
引き算	ひきざん	subtraction

暗算	あんざん	mental arithmetic/calculation [する] calculate in one's head
*予算	よさん	budget
算*数	さんすう	arithmetic
公算	こうさん	probability, likelihood

357 符 ▶ふ
570
cf. 荷

11 ノ 亻 𠂉 𠂉 竺 竺 笁 笁 符 符

符

切符	きっぷ	ticket
*音符	おんぷ	musical note(s)
符*号	ふごう	mark, sign, code

358 簡 ▶かん

18 ノ 亻 𠂉 𠂉 竺 竺 笁 笁 節 節

節 節 節 節 節 簡 簡 簡

簡単な	かんたんな	easy, brief
簡*潔な	かんけつな	concise, succinct
簡*素な	かんそな	plain, simple
簡*略な	かんりゃくな	simple, brief
書簡	しょかん	letter

359 単 ▶たん

9 丶 丷 丷 �田 �田 肖 肖 単 単

単語	たんご	word
単なる	たんなる	mere
単に	たんに	only, merely, simply
単*数の	たんすうの	singular [反]*複*数の(ふくすうの) plural
単*位	たんい	unit, denomination
単*独で	たんどくで	by oneself

360 戦 ▶せん
▷いくさ, たたか(う)

13 丶 丷 丷 𤰔 𤰔 肖 肖 単 単

戦 戦 戦

戦争	せんそう	war [する] fight, go to war
内戦	ないせん	civil war
休戦	きゅうせん	cease-fire, truce [する] implement a cease-fire
戦前	せんぜん	prewar, before the war
戦後	せんご	postwar, after the war
第二*次(世界)大戦	だいにじ(せかい)たいせん	World War II
戦う	たたかう	fight with, compete with
[歴] 戦	いくさ	war, battle

361 争 ▶そう
▷あらそ(う)

6 ノ ク 勹 ⺈ 乌 争

戦争	せんそう	war [する] fight, go to war
言い争う	いいあらそう	quarrel, argue
*論争	ろんそう	controversy, dispute [する] argue, dispute, take issue with
争*点	そうてん	point of contention, issue (at stake)
争*議	そうぎ	a dispute, a (work) strike

第 20 回

362 反 ▶はん, ほん, たん
▷そ(る), そ(らす)

4 一 厂 厅 反

反対	はんたい	[する] object, oppose
反日運動	はんにちうんどう	anti-Japanese movement
反発	はんぱつ	[する] repulse, repel, oppose
反*省	はんせい	[する] reflect upon, examine one's conscience
反*面	はんめん	on the other hand
◇ *謀反	むほん	rebellion, treason
反る	そる	be bent/warped/arched
反らす	そらす	bend back
[特] 反物	たんもの	a roll of cloth for kimono

363 対 ▶たい, つい

7 丶 亠 ナ 文 文 対 対

反対	はんたい	[する] object, oppose

第3水準

59

対立　　　たいりつ [-する] *vi.* be opposed to, be confronted with

対話　　　たいわ　dialogue [-する] have a dialogue/talk/conversation

〜に対する　〜にたいする　to 〜, toward 〜, against 〜

一対の　　　いっついの　a pair of

364 村 ▶そん ▷むら

7 一 十 オ 木 木' 村 村

村　　　　　むら　village
村長　　　　そんちょう　village mayor
村*民　　　　そんみん　villager
*市*町村　　しちょうそん　cities, towns and villages

365 付 ▶ふ ▷つ(ける), つ(く)

5 ノ イ 仁 付 付

付く　　　　つく　be attached, stick to
日付　　　　ひづけ　date (of a letter, document, etc.)
付近の　　　ふきんの　adjacent, nearby, neighboring
◇ *交付　　こうふ [-する] issue, deliver, grant

366 団 ▶だん, とん

6 丨 冂 日 旧 団 団

団体　　　　だんたい　group (of tourists, etc.), organization
集団　　　　しゅうだん　group, mob, mass-(suicide, etc.) cf. 集団心理（しゅうだんしんり）group psychology, グループ has a wider usage than 団体 or 集団
団結　　　　だんけつ [-する] be unified, stand together
団地　　　　だんち　housing complex

*布団　　　　ふとん　futon
座*布団　　　ざぶとん　floor cushion

367 寸 ▶すん

3 一 寸 寸

寸　　　　　すん　sun (old Japanese measure of length, 3.03 cm)
寸*法　　　　すんぽう　measurements, size
一寸　　　　▲ちょっと　(just/for) a moment, slightly

368 支 ▶し ▷ささ(える)

4 一 十 ナ 支

支店　　　　してん　branch (office/store)
支社　　　　ししゃ　branch (office)
支部　　　　しぶ　branch, local chapter
支出　　　　ししゅつ　expenditure, disbursement [-する] pay out, expend
支持　　　　しじ [-する] support (a political party, etc.), back
支持者　　　しじしゃ　supporter(s)
支*給　　　　しきゅう [-する] supply (money, food, etc.), pay (for)
支える　　　ささえる　support, sustain
差し支える　△さしつかえる　interfere with

369 技 ▶ぎ ▷わざ

7 一 十 扌 扌 扩 技 技

技術　　　　ぎじゅつ　technique, technology
技*師　　　　ぎし　engineer　cf. エンジニア has a wider usage than 技*師
技*能　　　　ぎのう　(professional, etc.) skills
技　　　　　わざ　art, skill, technique

漢字の形に気をつけましょう❶

368	369	972	1443	2127
支	技	*枝	*岐	*伎
本店と支店	技術の進歩	木の*枝（えだ）	分*岐点（ぶんきてん）	歌舞*伎（かぶき）

370

術 ▶じゅつ

11	ノ	ノ	彳	彳	什	休	休	休	術	術
術										

技術　　　ぎじゅつ　technique, technology
手術　　　しゅじゅつ　(surgical) operation　する have an operation, operate (on a patient)
手術室　　しゅじゅつしつ　operating room
学術用語　がくじゅつようご　technical term

371

街 ▶がい, かい
▷まち

12	ノ	ノ	彳	彳	彳	彳	往	往	往	往
往	街									

街　　　　まち　street, district
地下街　　ちかがい　underground shopping mall
五*番街　　ごばんがい　Fifth Avenue
歴 街道　　かいどう　main road

372

封 ▶ふう, ほう

9	一	十	土	土	圭	圭	圭	封	封

封筒　　　ふうとう　envelope
開封　　　かいふう　する open (a letter)
封*鎖　　　ふうさ　する block (off), blockade, block (up)
封*建*制度　ほうけんせいど　feudalism

373

筒 ▶とう
▷つつ

12	ノ	ト	ケ	ケ	竹	竹	竹	筒	筒	筒
筒	筒									

封筒　　　ふうとう　envelope
水筒　　　すいとう　canteen, flask
筒　　　　つつ　pipe, tube, cylinder

第 21 回

374

竹 ▶ちく
▷たけ

6	ノ	ヒ	ケ	ケ	竹	竹			

竹　　　　たけ　bamboo
竹*林　　　たけばやし, ちくりん　bamboo grove

375

替 ▶たい
▷か(える), か(わる)

12	一	二	夫	夫	夫一	夫二	夫夫	夫夫	替一	替
替	替									

両替　　　りょうがえ　する exchange/change money
替える　　かえる　replace, substitute
着替え　　きがえ　a change of clothes
着替える　きかえる, きがえる　change one's clothes
取り替える　とりかえる　change (parts, etc.), replace, renew
*代替エネルギー　だいたいエネルギー　alternative energy

376

賛 ▶さん

15	一	二	夫	夫	夫一	夫二	夫夫	夫夫	替一	替
替	替	替	賛	賛						

賛成　　　さんせい　する agree, approve
*賞賛　　　しょうさん　する praise, admire
◇ 賛*美歌　さんびか　hymn, psalm

漢字の形に気をつけましょう❷

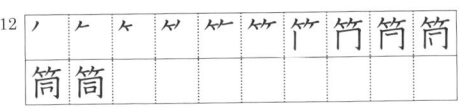

370	371	1388	1449
術	街	*衝	*衡
手術	地下街	*衝*突する	*貿*易*不*均*衡
		しょうとつ	ぼう えき ふ きん こう

377 成

▶せい, じょう
▷な(る), な(す)

6 丿 厂 厂 成 成 成

成功	せいこう	[する] succeed, prosper
成長	せいちょう	[する] grow, mature
成立	せいりつ	[する] be established, be founded
成人	せいじん	adult [する] become an adult
成分	せいぶん	ingredient, component
成り立つ	なりたつ	be composed of
成し*遂げる	なしとげる	accomplish
◇ 成*就	じょうじゅ	[する] accomplish, attain, realize

378 功

▶こう, く

5 一 T エ 功 功

成功	せいこう	[する] succeed, prosper
功*労者	こうろうしゃ	a person who performed distinguished services
◇ 功*徳	くどく	charitable act

379 工

▶こう, く

3 一 T エ

工場	こうじょう	factory
工場	こうば	small factory
工事	こうじ	construction [する] construct
人工の	じんこうの	man-made, artificial
電子工学	でんしこうがく	electrical engineering
大工	だいく	carpenter
細工	さいく	craftsmanship [する] manipulate (a situation)

380 的

▶てき
▷まと

8 ′ ′ 白 白 白 的 的 的

目的	もくてき	purpose, aim, goal
技術的な	ぎじゅつてきな	technological, technical
人工的な	じんこうてきな	man-made, artificial
*民主的な	みんしゅてきな	democratic
理*想的な	りそうてきな	ideal
～的な	～てきな	-tic, -al, etc.
的	まと	target

381 約

▶やく

9 ′ ′ 幺 幺 糸 糸 約 約 約

約束	やくそく	promise, appointment [する] promise
公約	こうやく	public pledge, (campaign) promise [する] promise publicly
先約	せんやく	previous appointment
約～	やく～	about, approximately

382 束

▶そく
▷たば

7 一 厂 厂 吉 束 束 束

約束	やくそく	promise, appointment [する] promise
結束	けっそく	[する] unite, band together
束	たば	bundle, bunch
花束	はなたば	bouquet
束ねる	たばねる	tie in a bundle

383 速

▶そく
▷はや(い), はや(める), はや(まる), すみ(やか)

漢字の形に気をつけましょう❸

380	381	1014	1335
的	約	*均	*釣
社会的な立場	約束する	平*均 へい きん	*釣りをする つ

第3水準

| 10 | 一 | 「 | 戸 | 日 | 車 | 束 | 束 | 涑 | 速 | 速 |

速い	はやい	fast, quick, swift
速まる	はやまる	quicken, speed up
速度	そくど	speed, velocity
速力	そくりょく	speed, velocity
時速	じそく	speed per hour cf. *秒速(びょうそく)，分速(ふんそく)
加速	かそく	-する accelerate
加速度	かそくど	acceleration
高速道*路	こうそくどうろ	expressway, freeway
早速	さっそく	immediately, right away
◇ 速やかに	すみやかに	immediately, promptly

384 達 ▶たつ

| 12 | 一 | 十 | 土 | 圥 | 圥 | 去 | 杢 | 杢 | 幸 | 辛 |
| | 達 | 達 |

速達	そくたつ	express mail, special delivery
上達	じょうたつ	-する vi. improve, become proficient in
発達	はったつ	-する develop, progress
達成	たっせい	-する achieve
友達	△ともだち	friend
達する	たっする	reach, arrive, amount to

第 22 回

385 違 ▶い ▷ちが(う)，ちが(える)

| 13 | ノ | ナ | 圥 | 屯 | 吾 | 吾 | 韋 | 韋 | 韋 | 韋 |
| | 韋 | 違 | 違 |

間違い	まちがい	a mistake, error, accident, mishap
間違って	まちがって	by mistake/accident
間違える	まちがえる	make a mistake
違う	ちがう	be different, be wrong
違い	ちがい	difference
違反	いはん	-する violate (a law, treaty, etc.)
違*法	いほう	illegal
違*憲	いけん	unconstitutional
*相違*点	そういてん	point of difference

386 逆 ▶ぎゃく ▷さか, さか(らう)

| 9 | 、 | ゛ | 丷 | 屰 | 屰 | 逆 | 逆 | 逆 | 逆 |

逆の	ぎゃくの	reverse, opposite
逆説	ぎゃくせつ	paradox
反逆	はんぎゃく	rebellion, insurrection -する rebel, revolt
逆らう	さからう	oppose, disobey
逆さ(ま)	さかさ(ま)	upside-down, inverted

387 整 ▶せい ▷ととの(える)，ととの(う)

| 16 | 一 | 「 | 戸 | 日 | 車 | 束 | 束 | 束 | 敕 |
| 敕 | 敕 | 敕 | 整 | 整 | 整 |

整理	せいり	-する arrange, reorganize
調整	ちょうせい	-する adjust
整*然と	せいぜんと	in a orderly fashion
整*数	せいすう	integer, whole number
整える	ととのえる	arrange

388 務 ▶む ▷つと(める)，つと(まる)

| 11 | マ | マ | ヌ | 予 | 矛 | 矛 | 矛 | 敄 | 務 |
| 務 |

事務	じむ	clerical work
事務室	じむしつ	administrative office
事務*員	じむいん	office worker, clerk
外務省	がいむしょう	Ministry of Foreign Affairs of Japan
国務省	こくむしょう	the State Department (of the U.S. government)
公務*員	こうむいん	public official/servant
務める	つとめる	serve, play the role (of)
務まる	つとまる	befit, be qualified (for)

389 省 ▶せい, しょう ▷かえり(みる)，はぶ(く)

| 9 | ノ | 丿 | 小 | 少 | 少 | 省 | 省 | 省 | 省 |

| 外務省 | がいむしょう | Ministry of Foreign Affairs of Japan |

文部科学省	もんぶかがくしょう Ministry of Education, Culture, Sports, Science and Technology-Japan
省エネ	しょうエネ saving energy
反省	はんせい [する] reflect upon, examine one's conscience
省*略	しょうりゃく [する] omit, abbreviate
省く	はぶく omit, leave out
省みる	かえりみる reflect upon (one's self, what one did, etc.)

390 談 ▶だん

15

相談	そうだん [する] ask a person's advice, consult, talk over
会談	かいだん conference, talks [する] talk together, have a conference
談話	だんわ conversation, informal talking [する] talk, chat
対談	たいだん face-to-face talk [する] have a conversation

391 相 ▶そう，しょう ▷あい

9 一 十 才 木 机 机 机 相 相

相談	そうだん [する] ask a person's advice, consult, talk over
相続	そうぞく [する] inherit, succeed
*首相	しゅしょう prime minister
外相	がいしょう abbr. foreign minister cf. this is an abbreviation of 外務大臣（がいむだいじん）
文科相	もんかしょう abbr. Ministry of Education, Culture, Sports, Science and Technology-Japan cf. this in an abbreviation of 文部科学大臣（もんぶかがくだいじん）
相手	あいて the other party, partner, opponent
相変わらず	あいかわらず as usual, as ever, as before

392 想 ▶そう，そ

1287 cf. 憩

13 一 十 才 木 机 机 相 相 相 想 想 想

理想	りそう ideal
思想	しそう ideas, thought, ideology
連想	れんそう [する] call to mind, associated with (in the mind)
発想	はっそう idea, way of thinking
*空想	くうそう [する] fantasy, daydream
回想	かいそう [する] look back on, recollect, recall
*予想	よそう [する] expect, foresee
*愛想	あいそ amiability, affability, sociability

393 首 ▶しゅ ▷くび

9 、 ソ 艹 六 首 首 首 首 首

首	くび neck, head
手首	てくび wrist
首席	しゅせき top/first in the class
首相	しゅしょう prime minister
国家元首	こっかげんしゅ sovereign of a nation, head of state
部首	ぶしゅ radical of a Chinese character

394 身 ▶しん ▷み

7 ' イ 勺 勺 身 身 身

出身	しゅっしん (be) from (California, Kyoto, etc.), one's place of origin
自身	じしん (one's) self
心身	しんしん mind and body
全身	ぜんしん whole body
単身*赴*任	たんしんふにん [する] work in a distant place away from one's family
身分	みぶん one's social standing
中身	なかみ contents

第 23 回

395 員 ▶いん

10 、 丨 冂 冂 尸 尸 冐 冐 員 員

社員	しゃいん company employee
会社員	かいしゃいん company worker
銀行員	ぎんこういん bank employee

教員	きょういん	teacher
工員	こういん	factory worker
会員	かいいん	member (of a club/society)
全員	ぜんいん	all members, entire staff
定員	ていいん	(seating) capacity, quota
◇ 人員*削*減	じんいんさくげん	personnel cut/reduction, layoff

396

損 ▶そん
▷そこ(なう)，そこ(ねる)

13 一　十　扌　扩　扩　扩　捐　捐　捐
　　捐　捐　損

損	そん	loss, deficit 〔する〕lose
損*失	そんしつ	loss, deficit
損なう	そこなう	hurt, damage

397

別 ▶べつ
▷わか(れる)

7 丨　口　口　号　另　別　別

別の	べつの	different, separate, another
*区別	くべつ	〔する〕distinguish, differentiate
別*居	べっきょ	〔する〕live apart
別人	べつじん	different person
*差別	さべつ	〔する〕discriminate against
別*荘	べっそう	country villa, summer house
別れる	わかれる	part from, be separated

398

特 ▶とく

10 丿　ト　牛　牛　牜　牜　牪　特　特　特

特別な	とくべつな	special
特急	とっきゅう	special/limited express (train)

特色	とくしょく	distinguishing characteristics
特長	とくちょう	merit, strong point, strength, forte
特*徴	とくちょう	special feature, distinguishing characteristic
特売	とくばい	bargain/special sale
特に	とくに	specially, particularly
特有の	とくゆうの	characteristic of, peculiar to, distinctive
*独特な／の	どくとくな／の	peculiar to, characteristic of

399

点 ▶てん

9 丨　卜　ト　占　占　占　点　点　点

点	てん	point, mark, score
百点	ひゃくてん	full marks, perfect score (on a test)
出発点	しゅっぱつてん	starting point
*原点	げんてん	origin (of coordinates/axes), starting point
点*字	てんじ	Braille
点火	てんか	〔する〕ignite
点*検	てんけん	〔する〕inspect, check
点々と	てんてんと	here and there, scattered, sporadically, in drops

400

無 ▶む，ぶ
▷な(い)

12 丿　匸　匚　午　午　無　無　無　無
　　無　無

無理な	むりな	impossible, unreasonable
無名の	むめいの	unknown
無地の	むじの	plain, solid (blue, etc.)
無料の	むりょうの	free (of charge)
無口な	むくちな	taciturn, reticent

第3水準

漢字の形に気をつけましょう❹

328	195	142	398	1878
寺	待	持	特	*侍
お寺	友達を待つ	バッグを持つ	特別なやり方	*侍 さむらい

無心に　　むしんに　be innocently at (play)

無事に　　ぶじに　safely, with no problems

無い　　　ない　not have, not exist

401 然 ▶ぜん，ねん

12 ノ クタタ タ゛ タ゛゛ 外 外 妷 然
然 然

自然　　　しぜん　nature, natural

当然　　　とうぜん　naturally, as a matter of course

全然　　　ぜんぜん　not at all

*必然的な　ひつぜんてきな　inevitable

*天然ガス　てんねんガス　natural gas

402 当 ▶とう
▷あ(たる)，あ(てる)

6 丨 ⺍ ⺍ 当 当 当

本当の　　ほんとうの　true, real

当分　　　とうぶん　for the time being　cf. しばらく for a while

当時　　　とうじ　at that time, then

見当　　　けんとう　estimate, guess

手当　　　てあて　(housing, food, etc.) allowance, medical treatment　-する treat (a cut/wound/etc.)

当たる　　あたる　hit (a target, person), win

日当たりがいい　ひあたりがいい　be sunny, have lots of sunshine

当たり前　あたりまえ　natural, proper

当てはめる　あてはめる　apply (a rule, etc.)

一人当たり　ひとりあたり　per person, per capita

心当たり　こころあたり　(have) an idea

403 予 ▶よ

4 フ マ 予 予

予定　　　よてい　plan, schedule　-する make a plan, prearrange

予約　　　よやく　-する reserve, make an appointment

予想　　　よそう　-する expect, foresee

地*震予知　じしんよち　earthquake prediction

*天気予*報　てんきよほう　weather forecast

404 野 ▶や
▷の

11 丨 冂 日 日 甲 里 里 野 野
野

分野　　　ぶんや　field (of study, etc.)

野生の　　やせいの　wild (animals, etc.)

野*菜　　　やさい　vegetables

平野　　　へいや　flat land, plains

野原　　　のはら　field (of grass, etc.)

第 24 回

405 原 ▶げん
▷はら

10 一 厂 厂 厂 厈 盾 原 原 原 原

原因　　　げんいん　cause, origin

原理　　　げんり　principles

原料　　　げんりょう　(raw) materials

原書　　　げんしょ　the original work/text

原案　　　げんあん　original draft/plan/proposal/bill

原野　　　げんや　(uncultivated) field, (wild) plains

原始時*代　げんしじだい　primitive age

野原　　　のはら　field (of grass, etc.)

*河原／川原　△かわら　dry riverbed

◇ *海原　　△うなばら　ocean, sea

漢字の形に気をつけましょう❺

254	406	1717
困	因	*囚
困る	原因	*囚人
		しゅうじん

406　因　▶いん　▷よ(る)

6　一　冂　冃　円　円　因

原因	げんいん	cause, origin
死因	しいん	cause of death
*要因	よういん	(primary) factor
因*果*関*係	いんがかんけい	causal relationship
◇ 因る	よる	be caused by, be due to

407　正　▶せい, しょう　▷ただ(しい), ただ(す), まさ

5　一　丁　下　正　正

正しい	ただしい	right, correct, just
正解	せいかい	right answer　する answer correctly
校正	こうせい	する proofread
*訂正	ていせい	する correct
正*義	せいぎ	justice
正*確な	せいかくな	exact, precise
正直な	しょうじきな	honest, upright
正午	しょうご	noon
お正月	おしょうがつ	the New Year
正*面	しょうめん	front, facade
正*夢	まさゆめ	prophetic dream, a dream which later comes true
正に	まさに	just/exactly, surely, certainly
正す	ただす	rectify, correct

408　幾　▶き　▷いく

12　一　幺　幺　幺　幺幺　幺幺　幺幺　幺幺　幾

幾　幾

| 幾つ | いくつ | how many |

幾つかの	いくつかの	several, some
幾分	いくぶん	somewhat, to some extent
◇ 幾何学	きかがく	geometry

409　糸　▶し　▷いと

6　く　幺　幺　乡　糸　糸

糸	いと	thread
生糸	きいと	raw silk
◇ *綿糸	めんし	cotton thread

410　級　▶きゅう

9　く　幺　幺　乡　糸　糸　紹　級　級

高級な	こうきゅうな	high-grade
同級生	どうきゅうせい	classmate
初級	しょきゅう	elementary level
中級	ちゅうきゅう	intermediate level
上級	じょうきゅう	advanced level
学級	がっきゅう	school class

411　能　▶のう

10　ム　ム　乍　台　台　肖　肖　能　能　能

能力	のうりょく	ability, capacity
本能	ほんのう	instinct
能	のう	Noh drama
◇ 能*面	のうめん	Noh mask

第3水準

漢字の形に気をつけましょう❻

409	410	243	744
糸	級	紙	*氏
くもの糸	高級車	手紙	*氏名 しめい

412 可 ▶か

5 一 丁 丌 可 可

可能な	かのうな	possible
可決	かけつ [する] approve, adopt
可能*性	かのうせい	possibility, potential, likelihood
*不可能な	ふかのうな	impossible
*不可*欠な	ふかけつな	indispensable
*不可*分な／の	ふかぶんな／の	indivisible

413 代 ▶だい, たい ▷か(わる), か(える), よ, しろ

5 ノ イ 仁 代 代

世代	せだい	generation
時代	じだい	era, period
古代	こだい	ancient times, antiquity
*現代	げんだい	modern times, the present day, modern, contemporary
〜年代	〜ねんだい	-ties (as in "the sixties")
代理	だいり	proxy, deputy [する] represent, act for
代金	だいきん	price, charge
*交代	こうたい	[する] take turns
代わりに	かわりに	in place of, in return/exchange for
お代わり	おかわり	[する] have a second helping (of food), have another cup
千代田*区	ちよだく	Chiyoda Ward (in Tokyo)
◇ 飲み代	のみしろ	money for drinking

414 化 ▶か, け ▷ば(ける), ば(かす)

4 ノ イ 仁 化

文化	ぶんか	culture
化学	かがく	chemistry
強化	きょうか	[する] strengthen
合理化	ごうりか	[する] rationalize, streamline
*民主化	みんしゅか	[する] democratize
自*由化	じゆうか	[する] deregulate
〜化	〜か	-ize, -en, etc.
化*粧	けしょう	[する] makeup, put on make up
化ける	ばける	take the form/shape of, disguise oneself

415 他 ▶た ▷ほか

5 ノ イ 什 仲 他

他の	たの, ほかの	another, other
他人	たにん	other persons
他国	たこく	other countries
その他	そのた, そのほか	"etc.", miscellaneous
他方	たほう	the other party/direction, on the other hand

416 仏 ▶ぶつ ▷ほとけ

4 ノ イ 仏 仏

仏教	ぶっきょう	Buddhism
大仏	だいぶつ	large statue of Buddha
日仏*関*係	▲にちふつかんけい	Japanese-French relations
仏	ほとけ	Buddha

第 25 回

417 位 ▶い ▷くらい

7 ノ イ 亻 仁 什 价 位

地位	ちい	(one's social, an important, etc.) position, rank, status
学位	がくい	academic degree
位置	いち	position, location [する] be located cf. 地位(ちい) (social) position, rank, status
位	くらい	position, rank

418 供 ▶きょう, く ▷そな(える), とも

1396 cf. 洪

8 ノ イ 仁 什 供 供 供 供

子供	こども	child, son/daughter
お供	おとも	attendant, servant
自供	じきょう	[する] confess (to a crime)
供*給	きょうきゅう	[する] supply [反] *需*要(じゅよう) demand
供える	そなえる	offer (to a god), make an offering (e.g., of flowers)
◇ 供物	くもつ	offering, votive offering

419 **共** ▶きょう ▷とも

6 一 十 艹 土 共 共

共通の きょうつうの common, mutual
共通点 きょうつうてん something in common
男女共学 だんじょきょうがく coeducation
公共の こうきょうの public
公共事業 こうきょうじぎょう government enterprise
共和国 きょうわこく republic
共に ともに together, both

420 **以** ▶い

5 丨 レ レ 以 以

～以上 ～いじょう greater than or equal to ～
～以下 ～いか less than or equal to ～
～以内 ～いない within ～
以前 いぜん formerly

421 **性** ▶せい, しょう

8 ・ ・ 忄 忄 忄 性 性 性

女性 じょせい woman, female
男性 だんせい man, male
性 せい sex, gender
性別 せいべつ gender
中性洗*剤 ちゅうせいせんざい neutral detergent
本性 ほんしょう one's true nature

422 **不** ▶ふ, ぶ

4 一 ア 不 不

不足 ふそく insufficiency, shortage [-する] *vi.* lack, be short of
水不足 みずぶそく water shortage
不安な ふあんな uneasy, insecure
不十分な ふじゅうぶんな inadequate
不正な ふせいな unfair, unjust
不利な ふりな disadvantageous
不運 ふうん misfortune, bad luck
不通になる ふつうになる be interrupted (train service, etc.)
行方不明 ^ゆくえふめい missing, lost
不気味な ぶきみな weird, eerie
不可 ふか failure (in an exam, etc.)

423 **必** ▶ひつ ▷かなら(ず)

5 丶 ソ 义 义 必

必要な ひつような necessary
必死に ひっしに desperately
必然的な ひつぜんてきな inevitable
必ず かならず surely, without fail
必ずしも かならずしも not always

424 **要** ▶よう ▷かなめ, い(る)

9 一 ㄒ 丙 覀 覀 覀 要 要 要

必要な ひつような necessary
重要な じゅうような important
主要な しゅような main, leading
要点 ようてん main point
要約 ようやく [-する] summarize
要*素 ようそ element, factor
要*求 ようきゅう [-する] demand, request, claim
要するに ようするに in short
要る いる be required/needed
要 かなめ the main/vital point, pivot

425 **価** ▶か ▷あたい

8 ノ 亻 亻 亻 侕 価 価 価

物価 ぶっか prices (of commodities, etc.)
地価 ちか land prices
単価 たんか unit price
定価 ていか list/labeled price
高価な こうかな expensive, high-priced, valuable
価*格 かかく price
価 あたい price, value [-する] be worth (doing, seeing, etc.)

第3水準

426 値

▶ち
▷ね，あたい

10 ノ イ イ一 イ十 イ止 イ占 佶 值 值

値上げ	ねあげ	price increase [する] raise prices
値下げ	ねさげ	price reduction [する] lower prices
値*段	ねだん	price
価値	かち	value, worth
値	あたい	value (as in the value of the variable "x" in mathematics) [する] be worth (doing, seeing, etc.)

第 26 回

427 普

▶ふ

12 丶 ソ ソ一 ソ丷 ソ丷 丱 丱 並 普 普
普 普

普通の	ふつうの	ordinary, common
普*段の	ふだんの	usual, everyday
普*段着	ふだんぎ	everyday clothes
普*遍的な	ふへんてきな	universal
普*及	ふきゅう	[する] spread, become popular/widely-used

428 昔

▶せき，しゃく
▷むかし

8 一 十 卝 卌 芾 昔 昔 昔

昔	むかし	long ago, before (in contrast to "at present")
昔話	むかしばなし	old tale
大昔	おおむかし	ancient times
◇ 昔日	せきじつ	old days
歴 今昔物語集	こんじゃくものがたりしゅう	Konjaku Monogatari Shū (a collection of folktales edited in the 12th century)

429 増

▶ぞう
▷ま(す)，ふ(える)，ふ(やす)

14 一 十 士 圫 圹 圹 圤 圤 增 増
増 増 増 増

| 増える | ふえる | vi. increase, multiply |

増やす	ふやす	vt. increase, add to
増加	ぞうか	[する] vi. increase, multiply
増大	ぞうだい	[する] vi. increase, enlarge
倍増	ばいぞう	[する] double
増*税	ぞうぜい	tax increase/hike [する] increase/raise taxes
増*産	ぞうさん	[する] increase production
増す	ます	vt. vi. increase

430 減

▶げん
▷へ(る)，へ(らす)

12 丶 ミ 氵 氵 汀 汀 沶 沶 減 減
減 減

減る	へる	vi. decrease
減らす	へらす	vt. decrease, reduce
減少	げんしょう	[する] decrease
半減	はんげん	[する] reduce by half
増減	ぞうげん	[する] increase and decrease, rise and fall
加減	かげん	addition and subtraction, state, condition [する] adjust, regulate
減*税	げんぜい	[する] reduce taxes
減*産	げんさん	[する] reduce production

431 感

▶かん

13 ノ 厂 厂 F 厈 咸 咸 咸 咸
感 感 感

感じる	かんじる	feel, sense
感想	かんそう	impressions, one's thoughts
感心	かんしん	[する] admire
五感	ごかん	the five senses
感受性	かんじゅせい	sensibility, sensitivity
感*情	かんじょう	emotion, feeling

432 留

▶りゅう，る
▷と(める)，と(まる)

10 ノ ト ム 幻 卯 卯 留 留 留 留

留学	りゅうがく	[する] study abroad
書留	かきとめ	registered mail
留*守	るす	absence from home

留*守*番電話　るすばんでんわ　answering machine
留める　とめる　fix, fasten, detain

433 貿　▶ぼう

12　丿　ナ　午　与　与　留　留　留　留
　　貿　貿

貿易　ぼうえき　する　trade
貿易*摩*擦　ぼうえきまさつ　trade friction

434 易　▶えき，い
　　▷やさ（しい）　　　　　　335
　　　　　　　　　　　　　cf. 場

8　丨　口　日　日　甲　号　易　易

貿易　ぼうえき　する　trade
易しい　やさしい　easy, simple
*容易な　よういな　easy, simple
*難易度　なんいど　degree of difficulty
◇ *交易　こうえき　する　trade, exchange, barter
◇ 易者　えきしゃ　fortune-teller

435 量　▶りょう
　　▷はか（る）

12　丨　口　日　日　旦　早　昌　昌　昌　量
　　量　量

量　りょう　quantity, amount　反 質（しつ）quality
大量の　たいりょうの　large amount of
少量の　しょうりょうの　small amount of
分量　ぶんりょう　quantity, dose
雨量　うりょう　amount of rainfall, precipitation
重量　じゅうりょう　weight (of a thing, vehicle, machine, etc.)
大量生*産　たいりょうせいさん　mass production する mass produce
量る　はかる　measure (an amount, weight)

436 裏　▶り
　　▷うら

13　丶　亠　宀　宀　㐬　亩　亩　車　裏　裏
　　裏　裏　裏

裏　うら　reverse side, the back

裏返す　うらがえす　turn the other way
裏口　うらぐち　back door
裏切る　うらぎる　betray
表裏のない人　ひょうりのないひと　honest person
表裏一体の　ひょうりいったいの　one and the same, closely related

437 表　▶ひょう
　　▷おもて，あらわ（す），あらわ（れる）

8　一　十　丰　主　圭　耒　表　表

表　おもて　surface, front
裏表のある人　うらおもてのあるひと　double-dealer
表　ひょう　table, list, chart
表紙　ひょうし　cover (of a book/magazine)
発表　はっぴょう　する　announce, make public, present (findings, etc.)
公表　こうひょう　する　make public, publicly announce
代表的な　だいひょうてきな　representative, typical
表*情　ひょうじょう　facial expression
表す　あらわす　express, show
表れる　あらわれる　be expressed
表れ　あらわれ　manifestation, expression

438 面　▶めん
　　▷おも，おもて，つら

9　一　ア　アア　石　而　而　面　面

面白い　おもしろい　interesting, entertaining, fun
真面目な　△まじめな　serious, earnest, grave
面　めん　mask, surface, aspect　する face, confront
表面　ひょうめん　surface, exterior
水面　すいめん　water's surface
洗面所　せんめんじょ　lavatory, washroom, toilet
場面　ばめん　situation, scene
面倒　めんどう　trouble, nuisance, care
～方面　～ほうめん　～ direction, ～ side
面会人　めんかいにん　visitor to a hospitalized/imprisoned person
面目　めんぼく，めんもく　face, honor, reputation
◇ 面*影　おもかげ　visage, looks, image
◇ 面　おもて　face, surface
◇ 面　つら　face [impolite]

第3水準

第 27 回

439 **最** ▶さい ▷もっと(も)

12 丨 冂 日 日 旦 早 早 昰 㝡 最 最 最

最初	さいしょ	start, beginning
最後	さいご	the last, the end
最近	さいきん	recently, lately
最高の	さいこうの	the best, the maximum
最低の	さいていの	the worst, the minimum
(〜の)最中に	(〜の)さいちゅうに	in the midst/middle of
最も	もっとも	most 〜, -est
最*寄りの	△もよりの	nearest, nearby

440 **初** ▶しょ ▷はじ(め), はじ(めて), はつ, うい, そ(める)

7 丶 ラ ネ ネ ネ 初 初

初め	はじめ	beginning, early period
初めに	はじめに	First of all . . . , first
初めて	はじめて	for the first time
最初	さいしょ	start, beginning
初歩	しょほ	first steps, the ABCs of, basic elements of
初日の出	はつひので	the first sunrise of the year
初*恋	はつこい	one's first love
◇ 書き初め	かきぞめ	first (calligraphy) writing of the New Year
◇ 初々しい	ういういしい	innocent, naive

441 **刀** ▶とう ▷かたな 1774 cf. 刃

2 フ 刀

刀	かたな	sword
日本刀	にほんとう	Japanese sword

442 **号** ▶ごう

5 丨 冂 口 旦 号

〜号	〜ごう	〜 issue (of a magazine/journal/etc.)
今週号	こんしゅうごう	this week's issue
先週号	せんしゅうごう	last week's issue
３号室	さんごうしつ	Room No. 3
号外	ごうがい	an extra (edition of a newspaper)
年号	ねんごう	name of a reign era
*番号	ばんごう	(identification) number
*信号	しんごう	signal, traffic lights

443 **労** ▶ろう

7 丶 丷 ⺍ ⺍ 𫝀 学 労

労働	ろうどう	-する work, labor
労働時間	ろうどうじかん	working hours
労働力	ろうどうりょく	manpower, work force, labor force
労働者	ろうどうしゃ	worker, laborer
労働*組合	ろうどうくみあい	labor union
労力	ろうりょく	trouble, effort
心労	しんろう	worries, concerns

444 **協** ▶きょう

8 一 十 十 忄 协 协 協 協

「最〜」の表現

最新の（さいしんの）	最古の（さいこの）
最大の（さいだいの）	最小の（さいしょうの）
最*良の（さいりょうの）	最悪の（さいあくの）

協力　　　きょうりょく　[-する] cooperate
協力者　　きょうりょくしゃ　collaborator
協同　　　きょうどう　[-する] cooperate, collaborate
協会　　　きょうかい　society, association
生協　　　せいきょう　co-op
*農協　　　のうきょう　agricultural cooperative

445 門　▶もん
　　　▷かど

8 丨 冂 冂 冂 冃 門 門 門

門　　　もん　gate
正門　　　せいもん　front gate
名門　　　めいもん　distinguished/illustrious family
入門　　　にゅうもん　introduction, primer　[-する] become a pupil
部門　　　ぶもん　group, section, class
*専門　　　せんもん　specialty, area of expertise
◇ 門*松　　　かどまつ　pine branch decoration for the New Year

446 関　▶かん
　　　▷せき, かか(わる)

14 丨 冂 冂 冃 冃 門 門 門 門 門
　　門 関 関 関

関係　　　かんけい　relation, relationship　[-する] be related/connected
関連　　　かんれん　relations, connection　[-する] be connected/associated/correlated　cf. 関係（かんけい）
関心　　　かんしん　interest, concern　cf. *興味（きょうみ）interest
関東　　　かんとう　the Kanto region
関西　　　かんさい　the Kansai region
[歴] 関所　　　せきしょ　border gate (in the Edo period), barrier
関わる　　　かかわる　have to do (with), be involved in

447 係　▶けい
　　　▷かか(る), かかり

9 丿 亻 亻 仨 仨 仫 係 係 係

関係　　　かんけい　relation, relationship　[-する] be related/connected

係(り)　　　かかり　person in charge
係長　　　かかりちょう　subsection chief
◇ 係る　　　かかる　be related to

448 孫　▶そん
　　　▷まご

10 了 了 孑 孑 孖 孖 孫 孫 孫 孫

孫　　　まご　grandchild
子孫　　　しそん　descendants, offspring

449 系　▶けい

7 一 亠 亖 玄 糸 系 系

日系人　　　にっけいじん　a person of Japanese descent
体系　　　たいけい　system
系*統　　　けいとう　system, lineage
太*陽系　　　たいようけい　solar system
◇ 系*列子会社　　　けいれつこがいしゃ　subsidiary company

450 懸　▶けん, け
　　　▷か(ける), か(かる)

20 丨 冂 冃 月 月 且 旦 県 県 県
　県 影 県 県 県 県 県 懸 懸 懸

懸案　　　けんあん　pending issue
一生懸*命(に)　　　いっしょうけんめい(に)　with all one's efforts
懸*念　　　けねん　[-する] worry, be anxious
*命懸けの　　　いのちがけの　(at the) risk of one's life

451 態　▶たい
2000
cf. 熊

14 厶 厶 宀 台 台 育 育 能 能 能
　能 態 態 態

態度　　　たいど　attitude, behavior, one's position/stance
事態　　　じたい　the state of affairs
生態系　　　せいたいけい　ecosystem
*実態　　　じったい　actual situation

第3水準

第 28 回

452 池
▶ち
▷いけ

6 `丶 氵 沪 池 池

| 池 | いけ | pond |
| 電池 | でんち | battery |

453 湖
▶こ
▷みずうみ

12 `丶 氵 沪 沪 汁 汁 浩 浩 湖 湖 湖 湖

湖	みずうみ	lake
ミシガン湖	ミシガンこ	Lake Michigan
湖水	こすい	lake water
湖面	こめん	the surface of a lake

454 海
▶かい
▷うみ

9 `丶 氵 沪 汽 汼 海 海 海

海	うみ	sea, ocean
海外	かいがい	overseas
日本海	にほんかい	the Japan Sea
東シナ海	ひがしシナかい	the East China Sea
海*洋	かいよう	ocean cf. 太平*洋(たいへいよう) the Pacific Ocean, 大西*洋(たいせいよう) the Atlantic Ocean

455 島
▶とう
▷しま

10 ` ⺉ 冖 户 户 臼 鸟 鸟 島 島

島	しま	island
島国	しまぐに	island country
島*民	とうみん	islander
無人島	むじんとう	uninhabited island
半島	はんとう	peninsula
*淡*路島	あわじしま	Awaji Island (the largest island in the Seto Inland Sea)

456 岸
▶がん
▷きし

8 `⺍ 山 屵 户 户 岸 岸

西海岸	にしかいがん	west coast
東海岸	ひがしかいがん	east coast
海岸	かいがん	coast, beach
対岸	たいがん	opposite bank
岸	きし	riverbank, shore

457 岩
▶がん
▷いわ

8 `⺍ 山 屵 户 岩 岩 岩

| 岩 | いわ | rock |
| 岩石 | がんせき | stone, rock |

458 谷
▶こく
▷たに

7 ` ハ グ 父 父 谷 谷

谷	たに	valley
谷間	たにま	(inside of) a valley
谷川	たにがわ	mountain stream
谷*底	たにぞこ	the bottom of a ravine/valley
*渓谷	けいこく	(steep-walled) valley, ravine, canyon

漢字の形に気をつけましょう❼

146	415	452
地	他	池
地下鉄	他人	池

四(ツ)谷　▲よつや　Yotsuya (a place in Tokyo)

長谷川　▲はせがわ　(surname)

459 林　▶りん　▷はやし

8　一　十　オ　才　木　村　材　林

林	はやし	small forest
山林	さんりん	mountain forest
林業	りんぎょう	forestry (industry)

460 森　▶しん　▷もり

12　一　十　オ　木　木　杏　森　森　枩　森　森　森

| 森 | もり | woods, a forest |
| 森林 | しんりん | forest |

461 空　▶くう　▷そら，あ(く)，あ(ける)，から

8　'　宀　空　空　空　空　空

空	そら	sky
青空	あおぞら	blue sky, open-air (market, concert, etc.)
大空	おおぞら	sky, firmament
空気	くうき	air, the atmosphere
空間	くうかん	space, room
空中	くうちゅう	in the air
空く	あく	be unoccupied/not in use
空室	くうしつ	unoccupied room
空車	くうしゃ	empty taxi/cab
空の	からの	empty
空っぽの	からっぽの	empty
空手	からて	karate

462 天　▶てん　▷あめ，あま

4　一　二　チ　天

| 天気 | てんき | weather |

天文学　てんもんがく　astronomy

天国　てんごく　heaven, paradise

天性の　てんせいの　natural (attributes), innate

天の川　あまのがわ　the Milky Way

天下り　あまくだり　appointment of a former government official to a high post in a company (through influence from above)

463 星　▶せい，しょう　▷ほし

9　丨　口　日　日　旦　甲　甼　星　星

星	ほし	star
星空	ほしぞら	starry sky
流れ星	ながれぼし	shooting star, meteor
火星	かせい	Mars
金星	きんせい	Venus
歴 明星	みょうじょう	Venus

464 光　▶こう　▷ひか(る)，ひかり

6　丨　丬　丬　半　半　光

光	ひかり	light, a beam/ray
光る	ひかる	shine, glitter, twinkle
日光	にっこう	sunlight, sunshine, Nikko (a tourist spot north of Tokyo)
光*線	こうせん	ray/beam of light

465 風　▶ふう，ふ　▷かぜ，かざ

9　丿　几　凡　凡　凨　風　風　風

風	かぜ	wind
そよ風	そよかぜ	gentle breeze
風土	ふうど	climate
風*向き	かざむき	wind direction
風*呂	ふろ	bath
歴 風土記	ふどき	old records and descriptions of a region's culture and geographic features <record of culture, geography>
風*邪	△かぜ	a cold

466 虫

▶ちゅう
▷むし

6 ｜ 口 口 中 虫 虫

虫	むし	bug, insect
*毛虫	けむし	hairy caterpillar
虫*歯	むしば	decayed tooth
*害虫	がいちゅう	harmful insects
*殺虫*剤	さっちゅうざい	insecticide

第 29 回

467 凡

▶ぼん，はん

3 ｜ 几 凡

平凡な	へいぼんな	commonplace
凡人	ぼんじん	ordinary person
凡*例	はんれい	explanatory note, map legend

468 冗

▶じょう

4 ｜ 冖 冖 冗

| 冗談 | じょうだん | joke |
| 冗長な | じょうちょうな | lengthy, verbose |

469 個

▶こ

10 ｜ 亻 亻 们 们 個 個 個 個 個

個人	こじん	an individual
個人主*義	こじんしゅぎ	individualism
個性	こせい	individuality, one's personality
個別的な	こべつてきな	individual, specific
～個	～こ	(counter for various objects)

470 固

▶こ
▷かた(める)，かた(まる)，かた(い)

8 ｜ 冂 冂 円 円 周 固 固

| 固い | かたい | hard, stiff |
| 固まる | かたまる | *vi.* harden, stiffen |

固体	こたい	solid
固定	こてい	[する] fix, settle
強固な	きょうこな	firm, solid, strong
固有の	こゆうの	peculiar, inherent, characteristic of
固*執	こしつ，こしゅう	[する] hold fast to, persist in, insist on

471 豆

▶とう，ず
▷まめ

7 ｜ 一 冖 冂 曰 豆 豆 豆

豆	まめ	beans, peas
コーヒー豆	コーヒーまめ	coffee beans
*枝豆	えだまめ	green soybeans, cooked green soybeans
*納豆	なっとう	fermented soybeans
豆*腐	とうふ	tofu, soybean curd
大豆	だいず	soybean
◇ 小豆	△あずき	adzuki beans

472 登

▶とう，と
▷のぼ(る)

12 ｜ フ フ ヌ メ メ 癶 癶 脊 脊 登 登

登る	のぼる	climb
登山	とざん	[する] climb a mountain
登場	とうじょう	[する] appear (on stage, in the marketplace, etc.)
登*録	とうろく	[する] register, enroll in
◇ 登用	とうよう	[する] promote, appoint

473 祭

▶さい
▷まつ(る)，まつり

11 ｜ ク タ 夕 夗 夗 忽 祭 祭 祭

（お）祭り／（お）祭	（お）まつり	festival
秋祭(り)	あきまつり	fall festival
文化祭	ぶんかさい	cultural festival
百年祭	ひゃくねんさい	100th Anniversary
祝祭日	しゅくさいじつ	national holiday
祭る	まつる	deify, enshrine

474 **際** ▶さい ▷きわ

14
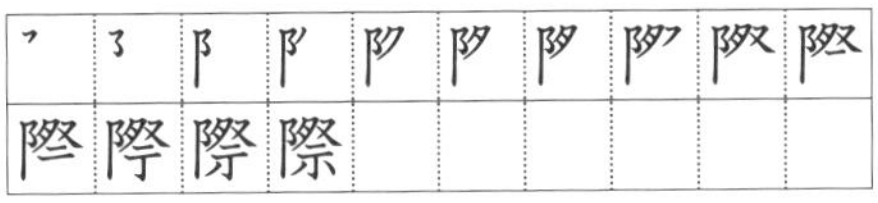

国際的な	こくさいてきな	international
学際的な	がくさいてきな	interdisciplinary
*交際	こうさい	-する keep company with, associate with
*実際	じっさい	actual state (of things), in fact, in truth
水際	みずぎわ	water's edge
際立つ	きわだつ	be conspicuous

475 **察** ▶さつ

14
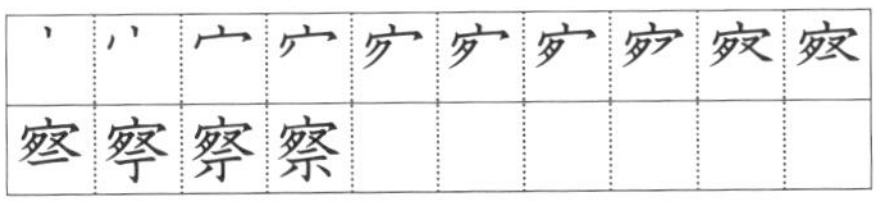

警察	けいさつ	police
*観察	かんさつ	-する observe, watch
考察	こうさつ	-する examine, study (as an academic inquiry)
*視察	しさつ	-する visit to observe/inspect
*検察*庁	けんさつちょう	Public Prosecutors Office

476 **警** ▶けい

19
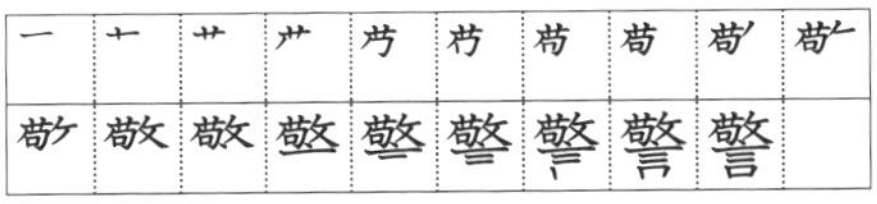

警察	けいさつ	police
警*官	けいかん	police officer
警*告	けいこく	-する warn, caution
警*報	けいほう	warning (signal), alarm (signal)
警*備	けいび	-する guard, defend
警*視*庁	けいしちょう	Metropolitan Police Department

477 **驚** ▶きょう ▷おどろ(く), おどろ(かす)

22
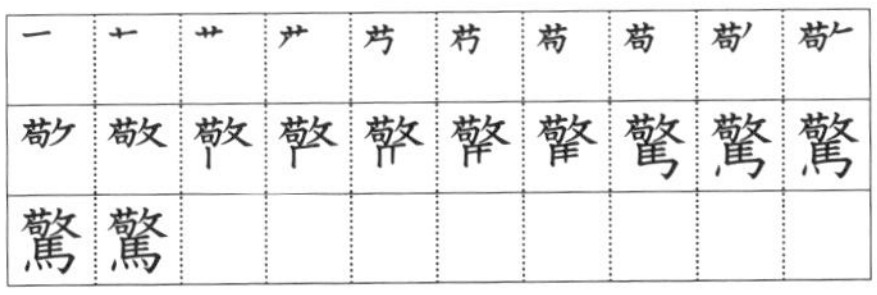

驚く	おどろく	be surprised
驚かす	おどろかす	surprise
驚*異的な	きょういてきな	astonishing
驚*嘆	きょうたん	-する be struck with admiration, marvel at

第 30 回

478 **敬** ▶けい ▷うやま(う)

12
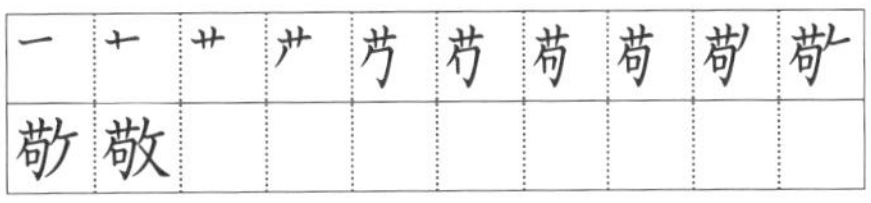

尊敬	そんけい	-する respect
敬意	けいい	respect, reverence
敬語	けいご	honorific expressions
敬*老の日	けいろうのひ	Respect-for-the-Aged Day
敬*具	けいぐ	Sincerely yours, (closing words for letters)
敬遠	けいえん	-する keep at a distance
敬う	うやまう	respect, hold in high esteem

479 **尊** ▶そん ▷たっと(い), とうと(い), たっと(ぶ), とうと(ぶ)

12
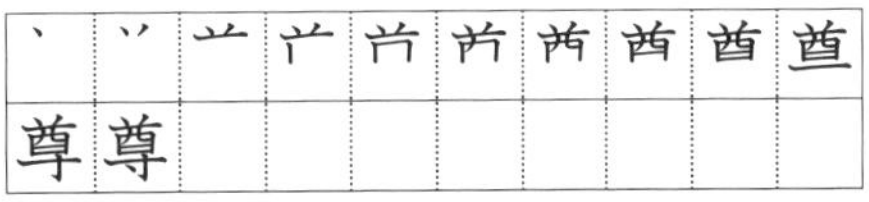

尊敬	そんけい	-する respect
尊重	そんちょう	-する respect, value
自尊心	じそんしん	pride, self-respect
尊大な	そんだいな	arrogant
尊ぶ	たっとぶ, とうとぶ	respect, honor
尊い	たっとい, とうとい	noble, precious

480 **導** ▶どう ▷みちび(く)

15
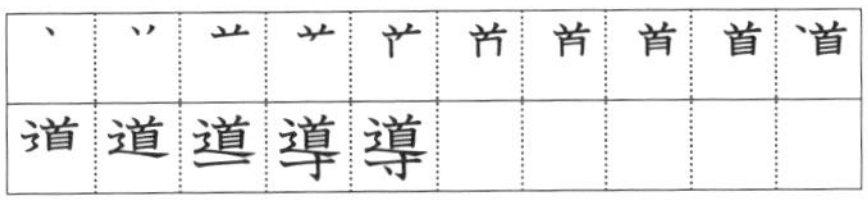

導入	どうにゅう	-する introduce (a new system, technology, etc.)
半導体	はんどうたい	semiconductor
先導	せんどう	-する lead, guide

*指導　　　しどう　[する] lead, guide, instruct
*指導者　　しどうしゃ　leader
主導*権　　しゅどうけん　initiative, leadership
導く　　　みちびく　lead, guide

481 停 ▶てい

cf. 亭 1652

11　ノ イ イ` 广 广 俨 俨 倬 倬 停
停

バス停　　　バスてい　bus stop
停留所　　　ていりゅうじょ　bus stop
停止　　　　ていし　[する] stop, suspend (service, etc.)
停車　　　　ていしゃ　[する] stop (as in buses or trains)
停電　　　　ていでん　power failure/cut [する] have a power failure
*各駅停車　　かくえきていしゃ　local train
調停　　　　ちょうてい　[する] mediate
停*滞　　　　ていたい　[する] be stagnant

482 件 ▶けん

6　ノ イ イ 仁 仨 件

事件　　　じけん　incident, affair, case
用件　　　ようけん　business (as in "let's get down to the business")
件　　　　けん　matter, case
*条件　　　じょうけん　condition

483 牛 ▶ぎゅう ▷うし

4　ノ 乚 二 牛

牛　　　　うし　cow, bull, cattle
子牛　　　こうし　calf
牛小屋　　うしごや　cowshed, barn
水牛　　　すいぎゅう　water buffalo
野牛　　　やぎゅう　buffalo
牛*肉　　　ぎゅうにく　beef

484 馬 ▶ば ▷うま, ま

10　丨 厂 厂 厈 厈 馬 馬 馬 馬 馬

馬　　　　うま　horse
小馬／子馬　こうま　pony
馬小屋　　うまごや　stable
馬車　　　ばしゃ　horse-drawn carriage
馬力　　　ばりき　horsepower, energy (to do work)
馬術　　　ばじゅつ　horseback riding, equestrianism
出馬　　　しゅつば　[する] stand or run as a candidate

485 魚 ▶ぎょ ▷うお, さかな

11　ノ ク ⺈ 凸 备 角 鱼 鱼 魚 魚
魚

魚　　　　さかな　fish
魚屋　　　さかなや　fish shop
金魚　　　きんぎょ　goldfish
魚*市場　　うおいちば　fish market

486 鳥 ▶ちょう ▷とり

11　′ 亻 冂 户 户 户 鳥 鳥 鳥 鳥
鳥

鳥　　　　とり　bird
小鳥　　　ことり　little bird
野鳥　　　やちょう　wild bird
白鳥　　　はくちょう　swan
一石二鳥　いっせきにちょう　killing two birds with one stone
鳥*居　　　とりい　Shinto shrine archway

487 鳴 ▶めい ▷な(く), な(る), な(らす)

14　丶 口 口 口′ 叮 𠮷 𠮷 唣 嗖 鳴
鳴 鳴 鳴 鳴

鳴く　　　なく　(birds) sing, (other animals) meow, neigh, croak, etc.

鳴き*声　なきごえ　singing of a bird, crying of an animal

鳴る　なる　ring, sound, thunder

共鳴　きょうめい　[する] resonate with, sympathize with, agree with

488 羊 ▶よう ▷ひつじ

6 ヽ ソ ´´ 兰 兰 羊

羊　ひつじ　sheep

小羊／子羊　こひつじ　baby sheep

羊毛　ようもう　wool

489 群 ▶ぐん ▷む(れる), む(れ), むら

13 フ ヲ ヨ 尹 尹 君 君 君 君ッ 君ッ
君⺹ 君⺹ 群

群集　ぐんしゅう　large group of people, throng, mob

群集心理　ぐんしゅうしんり　mob psychology

群*衆　ぐんしゅう　crowd of people, multitude

*抜群の　ばつぐんの　outstanding, distinguished (performance)

群れ　むれ　herd, flock, group

群れる　むれる　crowd together, swarm

群がる　むらがる　gather, flock, crowd together

490 毛 ▶もう ▷け

4 一 二 三 毛

毛　け　hair

毛糸　けいと　wool yarn

まゆ毛　まゆげ　eyebrows

羊毛　ようもう　wool

不毛な　ふもうな　unproductive/fruitless, barren, sterile

491 羽 ▶う ▷は, はね

6 フ ヲ ヲ 羽 羽 羽

羽毛　うもう　down, feathers, plumage

羽田空*港　はねだくうこう　Haneda Airport

羽　はね　wing(s)

羽*根　はね　a feather, plumage

～羽　～わ／ば／ぱ (counter for birds) cf. 一羽(いちわ), 二羽(にわ), 三羽(さんば／さんわ), 六羽(ろっぱ／ろくわ)

羽音　はおと　wing beat

第 31 回

492 翌 ▶よく

11 フ ヲ 羽 羽 羽 羽 羽 翌 翌 翌
翌

翌日　よくじつ　the following day

翌週　よくしゅう　the following week

翌月　よくげつ　the following month

翌年　よくねん，よくとし　the following year

翌朝　よくちょう，よくあさ　the following morning

493 義 ▶ぎ

13 ヽ ソ ´´ 羊 羊 羊 差 差 羊
義 義 義

～主義　～しゅぎ　-cy, -ism

社会主義　しゃかいしゅぎ　socialism

漢字の形に気をつけましょう❽

455 島　486 鳥　487 鳴

島まで泳ぐ　鳥が鳴く

第3水準

79

個人主義　こじんしゅぎ　individualism
*民主主義　みんしゅしゅぎ　democracy
共*産主義　きょうさんしゅぎ　communism
義務　　　ぎむ　obligation, duty　cf. *権利（けんり）right
同義語　　どうぎご　synonym
*類義語　　るいぎご　synonym

494　議　▶ぎ

20　丶 亠 亠 言 言 言 言 言 計 訳
訳 誹 譁 譁 譁 詳 詳 議 議 議

会議　　　かいぎ　meeting, conference
議長　　　ぎちょう　chairperson
議会　　　ぎかい　congress, parliament
議員　　　ぎいん　member of an assembly/congress/parliament
協議　　　きょうぎ　-する confer with
不思議な　ふしぎな　strange, mysterious

495　講　▶こう

17　丶 亠 亠 言 言 言 言 計 誹
誹 誹 誹 講 講 講 講

講義　　　こうぎ　lecture　-する give a lecture
休講　　　きゅうこう　-する cancel a lecture
講*師　　　こうし　lecturer
講*演　　　こうえん　lecture　-する give a lecture
講*堂　　　こうどう　lecture hall, auditorium (of a school)
◇ 講和*条約　こうわじょうやく　peace treaty

496　論　▶ろん

15　丶 亠 亠 言 言 言 言 言 訣 訣
訣 訣 論 論 論

理論　　　りろん　theory
論理　　　ろんり　logic
議論　　　ぎろん　-する discuss, argue
世論　　　よろん, せろん　public opinion
世論調*査　よろんちょうさ　public opinion survey/poll
論文　　　ろんぶん　thesis, essay
結論　　　けつろん　conclusion
〜論　　　〜ろん　〜 theory, theory of 〜　e.g., 進化論（しんかろん）theory of evolution, *資本論（しほんろん）the Capital
論じる　　ろんじる　discuss, argue

497　倫　▶りん

10　ノ イ イ 仟 伶 伶 伶 伶 倫 倫

倫理　　　りんり　ethics, morals
倫理学　　りんりがく　ethics
不倫の　　ふりんの　immoral, adulterous

498　輪　▶りん　▷わ

15　一 厂 厅 厅 百 亘 車 車 軒 軒
軒 軒 軒 輪 輪

三輪車　　さんりんしゃ　tricycle　cf. 一輪車（いちりんしゃ）, 二輪車（にりんしゃ）, 三輪車（さんりんしゃ）, 四輪車（よんりんしゃ）
車輪　　　しゃりん　wheel
*競輪　　　けいりん　bicycle race
*指輪　　　ゆびわ　(finger) ring

漢字の形に気をつけましょう❾

496	497	498	499	1579	1458
論	倫	輪	輸	*諭	*愉
議論する	倫理	三輪車	輸出と輸入	子供を*諭す（さと）	*愉*快な*仲間（ゆ・かい・なか・ま）

499 輸 ▶ゆ

16 一 ｢ 戸 百 月 車 車 軩 輪

輪 輪 輪 輸 輸 輸

輸入　　ゆにゅう　[する] import
輸出　　ゆしゅつ　[する] export
輸送　　ゆそう　　[する] transport
空輸　　くうゆ　　[する] send by air

500 較 ▶かく

13 一 ｢ 戸 百 月 車 車 車 軡

軡 軡 較

比較　　ひかく　[する] compare
比較的　ひかくてき　comparatively, relatively

501 効 ▶こう
▷き(く)

8 ' 亠 亠 六 方 交 刻 効

効果　　　こうか　　effect, effectiveness
効果的な　こうかてきな　effective
有効な　　ゆうこうな　effective, valid
無効の　　むこうの　invalid, void
効力　　　こうりょく　effectiveness
時効　　　じこう　prescription (in statute of limitations)
効く　　　きく　be effective, work
効き目　　ききめ　effectiveness (of a medicine)

502 果 ▶か
▷は(たす)，は(てる)，は(て)

8 ' 冂 曰 曰 旦 甲 果 果

結果　　　けっか　result, consequence
成果　　　せいか　result, outcome
効果　　　こうか　effect, effectiveness
果*汁　　　かじゅう　fruit juice
果物　　　△くだもの　fruit
果たす　　はたす　accomplish, fulfill
果たして　はたして　really, actually (as in "Is it really/actually useful?")
果てる　　はてる　(come to an) end, die
地の果て　ちのはて　end of the land

第 32 回

503 郊 ▶こう

9 ' 亠 亠 六 方 交 交7 交3 郊

郊外　　こうがい　suburbs, outskirts
近郊　　きんこう　suburbs, outskirts, environs

504 交 ▶こう
▷まじ(わる)，まじ(える)，ま(じる)，ま(ざる)，ま(ぜる)，か(う)，か(わす)

6 ' 亠 六 六 方 交

交通　　こうつう　traffic, transportation
外交　　がいこう　diplomacy
国交　　こっこう　diplomatic relations
交ざる　まざる　be mingled
交わす　かわす　exchange (opinions, handshakes, letters, etc.)
交わる　まじわる　associate with

第3水準

漢字の形に気をつけましょう❿

504　　51　　501　　503
交　校　効　郊

交通手*段　　学校　　効果的な教え方　　郊外に住む
しゅだん

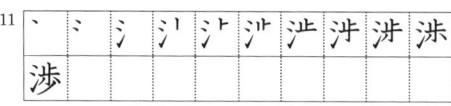

505 渉 ▶しょう

2088
cf. 捗

11 丶 冫 氵 氵 氵 汁 泙 泙 泙 渉
渉

交渉　こうしょう　[する] negotiate

506 干 ▶かん
▷ほ(す), ひ(る)

3 一 二 干

干渉　かんしょう　[する] interfere, meddle
干す　ほす　dry (damp clothing, etc.)
[特] 干る　ひる　get dry, become parched

507 汗 ▶かん
▷あせ

6 丶 冫 氵 汀 汗 汗

汗　あせ　sweat, perspiration
*冷汗　ひやあせ　cold sweat
◇ 発汗　はっかん　[する] perspire

508 軒 ▶けん
▷のき

10 一 厂 厂 百 亘 亘 車 車 軒 軒

〜軒　〜けん／げん　(counter for houses)
軒並(み)　のきなみ　all (stores, prices, etc.), one after another
軒　のき　eaves
◇ 軒先　のきさき　edge of the eaves, the front of the house

509 形 ▶けい, ぎょう
▷かた, かたち

7 一 二 テ 开 开 形 形

人形　にんぎょう　doll
形　かたち　shape, form, figure
三*角形　さんかくけい　triangle
正方形　せいほうけい　square
長方形　ちょうほうけい　rectangle
無形の　むけいの　invisible, intangible
◇ 手形　てがた　promissory note

510 枠 ▷わく

1069
cf. 粋

8 一 十 オ 木 朳 朾 枠 枠

枠　わく　frame, quota
窓枠　まどわく　window frame
輸入枠　ゆにゅうわく　import quota
枠*組　わくぐみ　framework

511 械 ▶かい

11 一 十 オ 木 杧 杧 杭 柹 械 械
械

機械　きかい　machine
機械化　きかいか　[する] mechanize, introduce machinery

512 識 ▶しき

19 丶 亠 亖 言 言 言 訁 訚 訚
訃 誵 誵 諳 諳 諳 識 識 識

漢字の形に気をつけましょう⓫

408	334	511	1334
幾	機	械	*戒

幾つ時計を持っていますか　機械　*戒*律
かい りつ

知識	ちしき	knowledge, information
意識	いしき	[-する] be conscious/aware, feel
識別	しきべつ	[-する] discriminate, distinguish between, discern
*常識	じょうしき	common sense
*認識	にんしき	[-する] recognize, understand, perceive

513 職 ▶しょく

18 一 T F F E 耳 耳' 耶 耶 耶
耶 耴 聄 聄 聈 職 職 職

職業	しょくぎょう	occupation, profession
職場	しょくば	place of work
職員	しょくいん	personnel, staff, staff member
職	しょく	employment, job
職人	しょくにん	artisan, craftsman
*現職の	げんしょくの	current (Diet member/governor/mayor, etc.)
無職の	むしょくの	unemployed

514 就 ▶しゅう, じゅ
▷つ(く), つ(ける)

12 ' 一 亠 古 占 亨 京 京 京 尉
就 就

就職	しゅうしょく	[-する] get a job
就業時間	しゅうぎょうじかん	working hours
就*任	しゅうにん	inauguration [-する] assume (a post)
就く	つく	[-する] gain a position, engage
◇ 成就	じょうじゅ	[-する] accomplish, attain, realize

第 33 回

515 経 ▶けい, きょう
▷へ(る)

11 く ㇑ 幺 幺 幺 糸 糸 紅 絅 経
経

経済	けいざい	economy
経理	けいり	accounting
経*験	けいけん	[-する] experience, go through
経*歴	けいれき	one's personal history, one's career

*神経	しんけい	one's nerves
経*由	けいゆ	[-する] go via/by way of
経度	けいど	longitude [反] *緯度(いど) latitude
(お)経	(お)きょう	sutra
経る	へる	go through, elapse

516 済 ▶さい
▷す(む), す(ます)

11 丶 冫 氵 沪 沪 泸 浐 済 済
済

経済	けいざい	economy
返済	へんさい	[-する] repay, return
決済	けっさい	[-する] settle (a bill)
使用済みの	しようずみの	used/spent (batteries, plastic bags, etc.)
済む	すむ	come to an end

517 活 ▶かつ

9 丶 冫 氵 沪 汗 汗 活 活

生活	せいかつ	[-する] live, make a living
活動	かつどう	activities [-する] be active, take an active part in
活気	かっき	vigor, liveliness
活力	かつりょく	vitality, energy, vigor
活性化	かっせいか	[-する] activate, (re-)vitalize
活発な	かっぱつな	lively, active
活用	かつよう	[-する] make (full) use
活*字	かつじ	printing/movable type

518 法 ▶ほう, はっ, ほっ

8 丶 冫 氵 沪 汁 汢 法 法

方法	ほうほう	method, way
文法	ぶんぽう	grammar
法律	ほうりつ	(national) laws, the law
法案	ほうあん	legislative proposal, a bill
[特] 法*被	はっぴ	workman's jacket (today worn primarily in festivals)
[特] 法主	ほうしゅ, ほっしゅ, ほっす	head of a Buddhist sect

第3水準

83

519 律 ▶りつ, りち

9 ノ ク イ 彳 彳 彳 彳 律 律

法律	ほうりつ	(national) laws, the law
*規律	きりつ	order, discipline
自律*神経	じりつしんけい	autonomic nerve
律*儀な	りちぎな	dutiful, conscientious

520 往 ▶おう

8 ノ ク イ 彳 彳 行 往 往

往復切符	おうふくきっぷ	round-trip ticket
往来	おうらい	traffic, comings and goings [する] come and go
立ち往生	たちおうじょう	[する] be brought to a standstill/halt, be stalled
往々にして	おうおうにして	often

521 復 ▶ふく

12 ノ ク イ 彳 彳 行 行 行 復 復 復

往復切符	おうふくきっぷ	round-trip ticket
往復	おうふく	[する] make a round trip, go to a place and return
回復	かいふく	[する] recover
復習	ふくしゅう	[する] review
反復	はんぷく	[する] repeat
復活	ふっかつ	revival, resurrection [する] revive, come back to life
復*興	ふっこう	[する] revive, reconstruct

522 複 ▶ふく

14 丶 ラ ネ ネ ネ ネ 衤 衤 衤 衤 衤 複 複

複雑な	ふくざつな	complicated, complex, intricate
複写機	ふくしゃき	copying machine cf. コピー機 is normally used
重複	ちょうふく	[する] be repeated/duplicated, overlap
◇ 複合*汚*染	ふくごうおせん	contamination from multiple sources
複*数の	ふくすうの	plural 反 単*数の(たんすうの) singular
複*製	ふくせい	[する] reproduce, replicate

523 雑 ▶ざつ, ぞう

14 ノ 九 九 卆 卆 杂 杂 杂 朵 朵 杂 雑 雑

雑誌	ざっし	magazine, journal
雑*音	ざつおん	noise
雑*草	ざっそう	weeds
雑木林	ぞうきばやし	copse

524 誌 ▶し

14 丶 亠 亖 亖 言 言 言 計 計 誌 誌 誌 誌

雑誌	ざっし	magazine, journal
日誌	にっし	diary, journal

漢字の形に気をつけましょう⓬

521	522	1088
復	複	*腹
往復切符	複雑な仕事	*腹痛 ふくつう

第 34 回

525 勤 ▶きん，ごん
▷つと（める），つと（まる）

12 一 十 艹 艹 芑 苦 昔 莒 革 堇 勤 勤

勤める	つとめる	work for
通勤	つうきん	する commute, go to one's office
出勤	しゅっきん	する go to work
勤務時間	きんむじかん	working hours
転勤	てんきん	する be transferred to another office of the company
歴 勤行	ごんぎょう	(Buddhist) religious service

526 難 ▶なん
▷かた（い），むずか（しい）

18 一 十 艹 艹 芑 苦 莒 莒 莫 黄 菓 葉 糞 葉 難 難 難

難しい	むずかしい	difficult
難解な	なんかいな	difficult (to understand)
難易度	なんいど	degree of difficulty
困難な	こんなんな	difficult, hard
難病	なんびょう	intractable disease
難点	なんてん	defect, drawback
*非難	ひなん	する blame, criticize
難*民	なんみん	refugee
盗難	とうなん	burglary, robbery
*許し難い	ゆるしがたい	unforgivable

527 漢 ▶かん

13 丶 冫 氵 氵 汁 汁 浩 漢 漢 漢 漢 漢 漢

漢字	かんじ	Kanji, Chinese character
漢文	かんぶん	Chinese writing, Chinese classics
漢和*辞*典	かんわじてん	Japanese dictionary of Chinese characters
門外漢	もんがいかん	outsider (to a field)
◇ *熱*血漢	ねっけつかん	hot-blooded man
歴 漢	かん	Han dynasty

528 字 ▶じ
▷あざ

6 丶 丷 宀 宁 字 字

漢字	かんじ	kanji, Chinese character
数字	すうじ	numeral, figure
ローマ字	ローマじ	Roman alphabet
文字	もじ	letter (of the alphabet, etc.)
字	じ	character/symbol used in a writing system
赤十字	せきじゅうじ	the Red Cross
名字	みょうじ	surname, last name
特 字	あざ	section of a town/village

529 数 ▶すう，す
▷かず，かぞ（える）

13 丶 丷 丬 半 半 米 米 娄 娄 娄 数 数

数字	すうじ	numeral, figure
数学	すうがく	mathematics
人数	にんずう	number of people
点数	てんすう	points, score
分数	ぶんすう	fractions (in mathematics)
無数の	むすうの	countless, innumerable
単数の	たんすうの	singular
複数の	ふくすうの	plural 反 単数の（たんすうの）
手数料	てすうりょう	fee, commission

第3水準

漢字の形に気をつけましょう⓭

525	526	527	1436	1582
勤	難	漢	嘆	*謹
勤務時間	難しい漢字	感*嘆する かん たん	*謹*賀新年 きん が	

数　　　かず　number
数える　　かぞえる　count
◇ 数*寄屋橋△すきやばし　Sukiyabashi (a place near Ginza)

530 政 ▶せい，しょう ▷まつりごと

9 一 T F F 正 正 政 政 政

政治　　せいじ　politics
政治家　　せいじか　politician
政府　　せいふ　government
政局　　せいきょく　political situation
行政　　ぎょうせい　administration
政*権　　せいけん　political power, administration (e.g., クリントン政権)
歴 *摂政　　せっしょう　regent, regency
歴 政　　まつりごと　affairs of state

531 治 ▶じ，ち ▷おさ(める)，おさ(まる)，なお(る)，なお(す)　cf. 治 2081

8 ` 丶 氵 汀 沿 治 治 治

政治　　せいじ　politics
明治　　めいじ　Meiji (era)
地方自治体　ちほうじちたい　local government
治る　　なおる　heal, be cured, get well
治める　　おさめる　rule over, govern

532 台 ▶だい，たい

5 厶 厶 台 台 台

台所　　だいどころ　kitchen
台本　　だいほん　script, screenplay
台　　だい　base, stand
〜台　　〜だい　counter for machines, level, mark
天文台　　てんもんだい　astronomical observatory
台風　　たいふう　typhoon

533 路 ▶ろ ▷じ

13 丶 口 口 口 早 卲 趵 趵 跻 路 路 路

道路　　どうろ　road, street
水路　　すいろ　waterway
通路　　つうろ　aisle, passage
十字路　　じゅうじろ　crossroads
路上　　ろじょう　on the road/street
歴 大路　　おおじ　main street　cf. 大通り(おおどおり) rather than 大路 is used in modern Japanese

534 戸 ▶こ ▷と

4 一 ラ ヨ 戸

戸　　と　door
雨戸　　あまど　storm door, shutter
戸外　　こがい　outdoors, open air
◇ 下戸　　げこ　nondrinker

535 居 ▶きょ ▷い(る)

8 フ コ 尸 尸 尸 层 居 居

居間　　いま　living room
居る　　いる　be present, exist (used for humans, animals, etc.)
居座る　　いすわる　linger, stay on (in office)
居直る　　いなおる　take on a threatening/defiant attitude
住居　　じゅうきょ　dwelling place

第 35 回

536 民 ▶みん ▷たみ

5 フ コ 尸 尸 民

民主主義　みんしゅしゅぎ　democracy
国民　　こくみん　people, nation
住民　　じゅうみん　inhabitants, residents
人民　　じんみん　the people, citizens
難民　　なんみん　refugee

民間の	みんかんの	private, non-governmental
民族	みんぞく	people, ethnic group
歴 民	たみ	the people, citizens

537 守 ▶しゅ, す ▷まも(る), もり

6 　'　'　宀　宀　守　守

留守	るす	absence from home
留守*番電話	るすばんでんわ	answering machine
守る	まもる	protect, keep (a promise), obey (a rule)
見守る	みまもる	keep an eye on
子守歌	こもりうた	lullaby
*保守的な	ほしゅてきな	conservative

538 宅 ▶たく

6 　'　'　宀　宀　宅　宅

住宅	じゅうたく	house, residence
住宅地	じゅうたくち	residential area
宅地	たくち	land for housing
自宅	じたく	one's own home
帰宅	きたく	する go home, return home
宅*配便	たくはいびん	home delivery service

539 管 ▶かん ▷くだ

14 　ノ　ト　ト　ヶ　竺　竺　竺　竺　竺　笞
　笞　笞　管　管

水道管	すいどうかん	water pipe
気管	きかん	windpipe, trachea
管理	かんり	する manage, supervise
管理職	かんりしょく	manager, management
管	くだ	pipe, tube

540 官 ▶かん

8 　'　'　宀　宀　宀　官　官　官

| 外交官 | がいこうかん | diplomat |

半官半民	はんかんはんみん	semi-governmental
国務長官	こくむちょうかん	the Secretary of State (of the U.S.)
官*房長官	かんぼうちょうかん	the Chief Cabinet Secretary (of Japan)
*次官	じかん	vice-minister

541 庁 ▶ちょう

5 　'　亠　广　广　庁

県庁	けんちょう	prefectural office
官庁街	かんちょうがい	civic center, the district where lots of government offices are located
文化庁	ぶんかちょう	Agency for the Cultural Affairs
警察庁	けいさつちょう	the National Police Agency
警*視庁	けいしちょう	Metropolitan Police Department
気*象庁	きしょうちょう	the Meteorological Agency

542 庭 ▶てい ▷にわ

10 　'　亠　广　广　庁　庐　庭　庭　庭　庭

庭	にわ	garden, yard, backyard
家庭	かてい	one's home
校庭	こうてい	schoolyard, playground, campus
日本庭園	にほんていえん	Japanese garden
歴 庭*球	ていきゅう	tennis cf. テニス is normally used

543 床 ▶しょう ▷とこ, ゆか

7 　'　亠　广　广　庁　床　床

床	ゆか	floor
床の間	とこのま	alcove in a Japanese-style room
床屋	とこや	barber (shop)
◇ 病床	びょうしょう	sickbed

544 庫 ▶こ, く

10 　'　亠　广　广　庁　启　启　盲　亘　庫

| 車庫 | しゃこ | garage cf. ガレージ is also used. |
| 金庫 | きんこ | a safe, strongbox |

書庫	しょこ	library, stack (room)
文庫本	ぶんこぼん	paperback, pocket edition
*冷*蔵庫	れいぞうこ	refrigerator
*倉庫	そうこ	warehouse, storehouse
*在庫	ざいこ	goods in stock
特 庫裏	くり	priest's living quarters at a Buddhist temple

545 廊 ▶ろう

12 丶 亠 广 广 庐 庐 庐 庐 庐 廊 廊

廊下	ろうか	hallway, corridor
画廊	がろう	art gallery
歴 回廊	かいろう	corridor

546 郎 ▶ろう

9 丶 ㇒ ㇕ ㇕ 自 良 郎 郎 郎

| 太郎 | たろう | (male given name) cf. *次郎／二郎(じろう), 三郎(さぶろう), 四郎(しろう), 五郎(ごろう) |
| 新郎 | しんろう | bridegroom 反新*婦(しんぷ) bride |

第 36 回

547 市 ▶し ▷いち

5 丶 亠 广 方 市

市	し	city
ロサンゼルス市	ロサンゼルスし	(the City of) Los Angeles
ニューヨーク市	ニューヨークし	New York City
市長	しちょう	mayor
市民	しみん	citizens
市立	しりつ	municipal
市場	いちば	local marketplace
市場	しじょう	a market

548 区 ▶く

4 一 フ ヌ 区

区	く	ward, e.g., 千代田区(ちよだく), *港区(みなとく), 新宿区(しんじゅくく), *渋谷区(しぶやく)
区民	くみん	inhabitants of a ward
地区	ちく	district, area, zone
区分	くぶん	する divide, demarcate
区切る	くぎる	punctuate, divide

549 町 ▶ちょう ▷まち

7 丨 冂 冂 田 田 田 町

～町	～ちょう	town, e.g., 人形町(にんぎょうちょう), *永田町(ながたちょう)
町民	ちょうみん	townspeople
歴 町人	ちょうにん	townspeople (in Edo period)
町	まち	town
下町	したまち	traditional working-class neighborhood
歴 室町時代	むろまちじだい	Muromachi era (14-16th century)

550 丁 ▶ちょう, てい

2 一 丁

| ～丁目 | ～ちょうめ | ～ block (in the numbering system for addresses) |
| 丁字路 | ていじろ | T junction cf. T字路(ティーじろ) T junction |

551 番 ▶ばん

12 丿 ㇒ ㇇ 丷 平 平 来 来 番 番 番 番

～番	～ばん	number/# ～
番地	ばんち	a lot/block number
番号	ばんごう	(identification) number
電話番号	でんわばんごう	telephone number
郵便番号	ゆうびんばんごう	zip/postal code

局番	きょくばん	area code
交番	こうばん	police box
当番	とうばん	person on duty, (be on) duty

552 郡 ▶ぐん

10 コ フ ヨ ヲ 尹 尹 君 君ァ 君ァ 郡

| 郡 | ぐん | county (e.g., カリフォルニア州オレンジ郡) |

553 州 ▶しゅう ▷す

6 ' ノ ノ 州 州 州

州	しゅう	state
カリフォルニア州	カリフォルニアしゅう	(the State of) California
本州	ほんしゅう	Honshu, the largest of the four main islands of Japan
九州	きゅうしゅう	Kyushu, the southwesternmost of the four main islands of Japan
◇ 中州	なかす	sandbank in a river

554 欧 ▶おう　1625 cf. 殴

8 一 フ ヌ 区 区 欧 欧 欧

欧州	おうしゅう	Europe
欧州連合	おうしゅうれんごう	European Union
欧*米	おうべい	Europe and the U.S.
西欧*諸国	せいおうしょこく	western European countries cf. 西*洋*諸国（せいようしょこく）western countries

555 満 ▶まん ▷み（ちる），み（たす）

12 ` ㇇ ㇒ 汀 汁 洪 洪 満 満　満 満

満足	まんぞく	する be satisfied
不満	ふまん	dissatisfaction
満員	まんいん	be full (as in trains, theaters, etc.)
満点	まんてん	perfect score (on a test)
円満な	えんまんな	harmonious, peaceful
満たす	みたす	fill, satisfy
満ちる	みちる	become full (of)

556 両 ▶りょう

6 一 丆 丏 丙 両 両

両親	りょうしん	one's parents
両手	りょうて	both hands
両足	りょうあし	both legs, feet
両方	りょうほう	both
両立	りょうりつ	する be compatible with

557 向 ▶こう ▷む（く），む（ける），む（かう），む（こう）

6 ' ㇒ 冂 向 向 向

方向	ほうこう	direction
向上	こうじょう	する improve, become better, make progress
意向	いこう	intention, one's idea
向かう	むかう	face (towards), head for, trend towards
向く	むく	face, turn/tend (toward), suit (one's preferences)
*振り向く	ふりむく	look back, turn around
向き	むき	(wind, etc.) direction cf. 南向き southern exposure (to the sun)
〜向きの	〜むきの	for 〜, suitable for 〜

漢字の形に気をつけましょう⓮

365 付　80 何　557 向　1245 *伺

日付　何を食べたいですか　方向　先生のお宅に*伺う（うかが）

向ける　　むける　turn something (to)
向こう　　むこう　opposite side
子供向けの　こどもむけの　(intended for/marketed at) children

狭い　　せまい　narrow, small (room, etc.)
狭める　せばめる　narrow, reduce
狭まる　せばまる　become narrow
◇ 狭心*症　きょうしんしょう　angina

---

558 周 ▶しゅう
▷まわ(り)

8) 刀 月 冃 冃 用 周 周

一周　　いっしゅう　one lap, one circuit [する] go around once
半周　　はんしゅう　semicircle [する] go halfway around
百周年　ひゃくしゅうねん　100th anniversary
円周　　えんしゅう　circumference
周り　　まわり　surroundings

第 37 回

559 独 ▶どく
▷ひと(り)

9 ノ 犭 犭 犭 狆 犸 狆 独 独

独身　　どくしん　single, unmarried
独立　　どくりつ　[する] be independent
独学　　どくがく　[する] study by oneself
独特な／の　どくとくな／の　peculiar to, characteristic of
日独関係　にちどくかんけい　relations between Japan and Germany
独り　　ひとり　alone, solitary
独り立ち　ひとりだち　[する] stand on one's own feet
独り言　ひとりごと　talking to oneself

560 狭 ▶きょう
▷せま(い), せば(める), せば(まる)

9 ノ 犭 犭 犭 狆 犸 狭 狭

---

561 肉 ▶にく

6) 冂 内 内 内 肉

牛肉　　ぎゅうにく　beef
*豚肉　ぶたにく　pork
肉　　にく　meat, flesh
肉屋　　にくや　butcher (shop)
肉体　　にくたい　the body, the flesh

562 米 ▶べい, まい
▷こめ

6 丶 丷 二 半 米 米

米　　こめ　rice
新米　しんまい　new rice, a novice
白米　はくまい　polished rice
米国　べいこく　the United States
日米関係　にちべいかんけい　relations between Japan and the U.S.
北米　ほくべい　North America
南米　なんべい　South America

563 類 ▶るい
▷たぐ(い)

529 cf. 数

18 丶 丷 二 半 米 米 米 米 类
类 籾 籾 類 類 類 類 類

種類　しゅるい　kind, type, sort
親類　しんるい　relatives, kin

漢字の形に気をつけましょう⑮

14　　350　　308　　558
円　　同　　用　　周

一万円　同じやり方　使用法　地*球を一周する
　　　　　　　　　　　　ち きゅう

人類　　　じんるい　the human race
人類学　　じんるいがく　anthropology
書類　　　しょるい　documents, papers
分類　　　ぶんるい　［する］classify
類い　　　たぐい　a kind, an equal
類いまれな　たぐいまれな　rare, unique

564 種　▶しゅ　▷たね

14 ノ 二 千 禾 禾 禾' 禾' 秆 秆 和
稲 種 種 種

種類　　　しゅるい　kind, type, sort
一種の　　いっしゅの　a kind/sort of
人種　　　じんしゅ　ethnic group, a race
種　　　　たね　seed
不安の種　ふあんのたね　cause of unease

565 科　▶か　240 cf. 料

9 ノ 二 千 禾 禾 禾 禾 秆 科

科学　　　かがく　science
学科　　　がっか　subject of study
理科　　　りか　science (as a school subject)　cf. 社会（しゃかい）social studies (as a school subject)
科目　　　かもく　subject, course (of study)
教科書　　きょうかしょ　textbook
外科　　　げか　surgery
内科　　　ないか　internal medicine

566 芸　▶げい　1665 cf. 芳

7 一 十 艹 艹 芸 芸 芸

芸術　　　げいじゅつ　art
民芸*品　　みんげいひん　folk craft
文芸*批*評　ぶんげいひひょう　literary criticism
工芸　　　こうげい　industrial arts, handicrafts

567 草　▶そう　▷くさ

9 一 十 艹 艹 艻 芍 苩 苷 草

草　　　　くさ　grass, plants
草原　　　そうげん　grassy plain
雑草　　　ざっそう　weeds
草案　　　そうあん　a (rough) draft

568 芝　▷しば　860 cf. 乏

6 一 十 艹 艹 艻 芝

芝生　　　△しばふ　lawn, plot of grass
芝　　　　しば　lawn
人工芝　　じんこうしば　artificial turf
芝居　　　しばい　a (stage) play, play-acting　［する］put on an act

569 葉　▶よう　▷は　1653 cf. 棄

12 一 十 十 芏 芏 苹 苹 苹 莘 莘
葺 葉

言葉　　　ことば　word, language
葉書　　　はがき　postcard
葉　　　　は　leaf, foliage
木の葉　　このは　tree leaves
落ち葉　　おちば　fallen leaves
千葉県　　ちばけん　Chiba prefecture

第3水準

「〜科学」の例

自然科学（しぜんかがく）　natural science
社会科学（しゃかいかがく）　social science
人文科学（じんぶんかがく）　humanities

◇ 青葉　　　あおば　green foliage
*紅葉　　　こうよう　colored leaves [する] turn red
*紅葉　　　△もみじ　maple tree, autumn/colored leaves

570 荷
▶か
▷に

cf. 何 符 苛　80 357 2115

10 一 十 艹 艹 艹 艾 芢 荷 荷 荷

荷物　　　にもつ　luggage, baggage
重荷　　　おもに　burden
出荷　　　しゅっか　[する] vt. ship/forward (goods)
入荷　　　にゅうか　[する] vi. (goods) arrive

第 38 回

571 預
▶よ
▷あず(ける)，あず(かる)

13 マ マ ヌ 予 予 予 預 預 預 預
預 預 預

預ける　　あずける　leave in someone's care, deposit, entrust
預かる　　あずかる　receive for safekeeping, take care of
預金　　　よきん　[する] deposit

572 頼
▶らい
▷たの(む)，たの(もしい)，たよ(る)

16 一 ┌ 冂 冃 申 束 束 束 剌
刺 頼 頼 頼 頼 頼

頼む　　　たのむ　ask (a favor), request
頼る　　　たよる　rely on
*信頼　　　しんらい　[する] trust in, rely on
*依頼　　　いらい　[する] ask, request
頼もしい　たのもしい　dependable

573 顔
▶がん
▷かお

18 ' 十 立 立 立 产 彦 彦 彦
彦 䶮 顔 顔 顔 顔 顔

顔　　　　かお　(a person's) face
顔色　　　かおいろ　complexion, color of one's face

新顔　　　しんがお　a new face, newcomer
笑顔　　　△えがお　smiling face
*素顔　　　すがお　face without makeup
*童顔　　　どうがん　childlike face
顔面　　　がんめん　(a person's) face

574 産
▶さん
▷う(む)，う(まれる)，うぶ

11 ' 亠 亠 立 立 产 产 产 产 産
産

産業　　　さんぎょう　industry
水産業　　　すいさんぎょう　marine products industry
生産　　　せいさん　[する] produce
生産物　　　せいさんぶつ　products
産地　　　さんち　place of production
出産　　　しゅっさん　[する] give birth, be delivered
共産主義　きょうさんしゅぎ　communism
不動産　　ふどうさん　real estate
原産国　　げんさんこく　country of origin (production)
産む　　　うむ　give birth to
（お）土産　△(お)みやげ　souvenir
産声　　　うぶごえ　the first cry of a newborn baby
歴 産湯　　うぶゆ　baby's first bath

575 玉
▶ぎょく
▷たま

5 一 丅 干 王 玉

玉子　　　たまご　egg
十円玉　　じゅうえんだま　10-yen coin
玉　　　　たま　gem, jewel, ball
歴 玉　　　ぎょく　jewel, jade

576 宝
▶ほう
▷たから

8 ' 宀 宀 宀 宀 宇 宝 宝

宝石　　　ほうせき　jewels, precious stones
国宝　　　こくほう　a national treasure
宝物　　　たからもの，ほうもつ　treasure, precious thing
宝　　　　たから　treasure

577 王　▶おう

4　一 丁 干 王

王	おう	king
王国	おうこく	kingdom
王子	おうじ	prince
王女	おうじょ	princess
女王	じょおう	queen
王*様	おうさま	king
法王	ほうおう	a pope
ローマ法王	ローマほうおう	the Pope

578 現　▶げん
▷あらわ（れる），あらわ（す）

11　一 丁 干 王 担 担 珇 珇 珇 現
現

現代	げんだい	modern times, the present day, modern, contemporary
現*在	げんざい	present, current
表現	ひょうげん	する express
現金	げんきん	cash
*実現	じつげん	する realize, come true
現れる	あらわれる	appear, come out, emerge, become visible
現す	あらわす	make an appearance, reveal

579 皇　▶こう，おう

9　′ ′ ′ 白 白 白 皁 皁 皇

天皇	てんのう	(Japanese) emperor
皇居	こうきょ	imperial palace
皇室	こうしつ	imperial family
皇位	こうい	imperial throne
皇*帝	こうてい	emperor　cf. 天皇（てんのう）
歴 法皇	ほうおう	ex-emperor who has become a monk

580 聖　▶せい

13　一 丁 F F 王 耳 耴 耵 耵
聖 聖 聖

聖書	せいしょ	the Bible
聖人	せいじん	saint
*神聖な	しんせいな	sacred, holy
聖母マリア	せいぼマリア	the Virgin Mary

581 望　▶ぼう，もう
▷のぞ（む）

11　′ 亠 亡 也 切 朝 胡 胡 胡 望
望

要望	ようぼう	する demand, request
*失望	しつぼう	する be disappointed
*希望	きぼう	する hope, wish
*志望校	しぼうこう	the school one hopes to enter
望む	のぞむ	hope, wish
望み	のぞみ	hopes, desires, wishes
本望	ほんもう	complete satisfaction

582 亡　▶ぼう，もう
▷な（い）

3　′ 亠 亡

死亡	しぼう	する die, be killed
死亡者	しぼうしゃ	the deceased
*亡命	ぼうめい	する flee (from) one's own country (for a political reason)
◇ 金の亡者	かねのもうじゃ	a person who desires only/mainly money
亡くなる	なくなる	die, pass away

第 39 回

583 未　▶み　
1768
cf. 朱

5　一 二 キ 才 未

未来	みらい	(the) future
未婚の	みこんの	unmarried
未知の	みちの	unknown
未亡人	みぼうじん	widow
未明	みめい	early dawn, before daybreak
前代未聞の	ぜんだいみもんの	unheard-of, unprecedented

584 末

▶まつ，ばつ
▷すえ

5 一 二 キ 才 末

週末	しゅうまつ	weekend
月末	げつまつ	end of the month
年末	ねんまつ	end of the year
末っ子	すえっこ	youngest child
特 末子	ばっし，まっし	youngest child

585 申

▶しん
▷もう(す)

1816
cf. 甲

5 丨 口 日 日 申

申し上げる	もうしあげる	say, tell [humble]
申し入れ	もうしいれ	offer, proposal
答申	とうしん	report (by a committee) する submit a report

586 神

▶しん，じん
▷かみ，かん，こう

1299 2022
cf. 紳 袖

9 ` ラ オ ネ ネ ネ 初 神 神

神	かみ	a god, deity, God
歴 神風	かみかぜ	kamikaze, divine wind
神社	じんじゃ	shrine
神話	しんわ	myth, mythology
神父	しんぷ	Catholic priest, Father
神主	かんぬし	Shinto priest
歴 神楽	△かぐら	kagura (sacred Shinto music and dancing)
特 神々しい	こうごうしい	divine, holy

587 存

▶そん，ぞん

6 一 ナ ナ 存 存 存

存在	そんざい	する exist, be
生存	せいぞん	する exist, survive
生存者	せいぞんしゃ	survivor
共存	きょうぞん	する coexist
ご存じだ	ごぞんじだ	know [honorific]
存じる	ぞんじる	know, think [humble]

588 在

▶ざい
▷あ(る)

6 一 ナ イ 右 在 在

存在	そんざい	する exist, be
現在	げんざい	present, current
在日外国人	ざいにちがいこくじん	foreigners residing in Japan
在学	ざいがく	する be in school, be enrolled (at)
不在だ	ふざいだ	be away, be absent
在る	ある	exist, be

589 禅

▶ぜん

13 ` ラ オ ネ ネ ネ 初 初 初 初 襌 襌 禅

座禅	ざぜん	Zen meditation (in a cross-legged position)
禅寺	ぜんでら	Zen temple
禅*宗	ぜんしゅう	Zen sect
禅*僧	ぜんそう	Zen priest/monk

590 弾

▶だん
▷ひ(く)，はず(む)，たま

12 フ コ 弓 弓 弓 弓 弓 弾 弾 弾 弾 弾

弾	たま	bullet
弾薬	だんやく	ammunition
弾頭	だんとう	warhead
*核弾頭	かくだんとう	nuclear warhead
*爆弾	ばくだん	bomb
弾力	だんりょく	elasticity
弾む	はずむ	bounce, rebound
弾く	ひく	play (string instrument)

591 丸

▶がん
▷まる，まる(い)，まる(める)

3 ノ 九 丸

丸い	まるい	round, circular
丸太	まるた	log

丸　　　まる　circle, whole
丸める　まるめる　make round, make into a ball
弾丸　　だんがん　bullet

592
弓　▶きゅう　▷ゆみ
3　フ　コ　弓

弓　　ゆみ　a bow
弓道　きゅうどう　Japanese archery

593
矢　▶し　▷や
5　ノ　ヒ　ヒ　午　矢

矢　　や　an arrow
弓矢　ゆみや　bow and arrow
◇　一矢を*報いる　いっしをむくいる　retaliate, fight back

594
失　▶しつ　▷うしな（う）
5　ノ　ヒ　ヒ　牛　失

失業　　しつぎょう　[する] lose one's job
失*恋　　しつれん　[する] be unlucky in love, have a broken heart
失望　　しつぼう　[する] be disappointed
失神　　しっしん　[する] faint
失*敗　　しっぱい　[する] fail
失*礼な　しつれいな　impolite, rude
失う　　うしなう　lose
見失う　みうしなう　lose sight of

第 40 回

595
夫　▶ふ, ふう　▷おっと
4　一　二　チ　夫

夫　　　おっと　husband
〜夫人　〜ふじん　Mrs. 〜
夫婦　　ふうふ　husband and wife, married couple
工夫　　くふう　[する] devise, work out (a plan)

596
妻　▶さい　▷つま　cf. 毒 **788**
8　一　ラ　ヨ　ヨ　事　妻　妻　妻

妻　　　つま　wife
妻子　　さいし　wife and child(ren)
〜夫妻　〜ふさい　Mr. and Mrs. 〜
歴 *良妻*賢母　りょうさいけんぼ　good wife and wise mother

597
婦　▶ふ
11　く　女　女　女'　妒　妒　妒　婦　婦　婦　婦

夫婦　　ふうふ　husband and wife, married couple
主婦　　しゅふ　housewife
婦人服　ふじんふく　women's clothes

598
姓　▶せい, しょう
8　く　女　女　女'　妒　姈　姓　姓

姓　　せい　surname, last name

第3水準

漢字の形に気をつけましょう⑯

462　天　593　矢　594　失　595　夫

いい天気　弓と矢　失業者　妻と夫

同姓　　　どうせい　the same surname
夫婦別姓　ふうふべっせい　use of different surnames by a married couple
*旧姓　　きゅうせい　one's maiden name
歴 百姓　ひゃくしょう　farmer

599 嫁
▶か
▷よめ，とつ（ぐ）
1232 cf. 稼

13　く　タ　タ　女'　女'　女ケ　女ケ　女ケ　女ケ　嫁
嫁　嫁　嫁

花嫁　　　はなよめ　bride
嫁　　　　よめ　bride, daughter-in-law
*責*任転嫁　せきにんてんか　する shift the responsibility (for something on somebody)
嫁ぐ　　　とつぐ　get married

600 婿
▶せい
▷むこ

12　く　タ　タ　女'　女ケ　女ケ　女ケ　女ケ　女ケ　婿
婿　婿

花婿　　　はなむこ　bridegroom
婿*養子　むこようし　son-in-law who has taken wife's family name
◇ 女婿　じょせい　son-in-law

601 娘
▷むすめ

10　く　タ　タ　女'　女ケ　女ケ　女ケ　女ケ　女ケ　娘

娘　　　　むすめ　(my) daughter, young woman

602 良
▶りょう
▷よ（い）

7　'　ヮ　ヨ　ヨ　自　自　良

良い　　　よい　good, nice, fine
最良の　　さいりょうの　best
消化不良　しょうかふりょう　indigestion
不良　　　ふりょう　delinquency
不良*品　ふりょうひん　sub-standard product
良心　　　りょうしん　one's conscience
野良犬　　△のらいぬ　ownerless/stray dog

603 飾
▶しょく
▷かざ（る）

13　ノ　ヘ　ケ　今　今　今　倉　食　食　飣
飣　飾　飾

飾る　　　かざる　decorate, adorn
着飾る　　きかざる　get dressed up
*修飾　しゅうしょく　する modify (in grammar)
*装飾*品　そうしょくひん　ornaments, decorations

604 飯
▶はん
▷めし

12　ノ　ヘ　ケ　今　今　今　倉　食　食　飣
飯　飯

ご飯　　　ごはん　cooked rice, a meal
夕飯　　　ゆうはん　dinner
赤飯　　　せきはん　rice cooked with adzuki (red) beans
飯　　　　めし　cooked rice, a meal, food (informal/rough)　cf. ご飯（ごはん）

605 坂
▶はん
▷さか

987 1948
cf. 板 阪

7　一　十　土　圵　圷　坂　坂

坂　　　　さか　slope
◇ 登坂　とうはん，とはん　する go up a slope

606 皆
▶かい
▷みな

9　一　ヒ　ヒ'　比　比　比　皆　皆　皆

皆さん　　みなさん　everybody
皆勤　　　かいきん　する have perfect attendance (at work)
皆無　　　かいむ　none, nothing

第 41 回

607 階
▶かい

12　'　3　阝　阝-　阯　阯'　阰　阰　階
階　階

階段	かいだん　stairs
〜階	〜かい／がい　〜 floor
階級	かいきゅう　social class

608 段 ▶だん　　　　　　622 cf. 暇

9　　丿 亻 ŕ 乍 乍 乍 ₹ 段 段 段

階段	かいだん　stairs
段	だん　steps, rungs
石段	いしだん　flight of stone steps
段階	だんかい　stage (in a project), step (in a plan)
手段	しゅだん　a means, a measure
一段と	いちだんと　further, even more

609 役 ▶やく，えき　　　　1977 cf. 股

7　　丿 ク 彳 彳 犭 役 役

役所	やくしょ　government office
役人	やくにん　government official
役員	やくいん　officer, executive
役者	やくしゃ　actor
役目	やくめ　duty, function
主役	しゅやく　the star/leading role (in a play, etc.)
役	やく　role
役に立つ	やくにたつ　useful, helpful
役*割	やくわり　role, part
*兵役	へいえき　military service

610 殺 ▶さつ，さい，せつ　　2111 ▷ころ(す)　　　　　cf. 刹

10　　丿 メ 彡 乎 杀 杀 杀 新 殺 殺

殺す	ころす　kill, murder
人殺し	ひとごろし　murder, murderer
自殺	じさつ [する] commit suicide
暗殺	あんさつ [する] assassinate
殺人	さつじん　murder, homicide
◇ 相殺	そうさい [する] offset
特 殺生	せっしょう [する] destroy/take life

611 設 ▶せつ ▷もう(ける)

11　　丶 ㇐ 亠 亖 言 言 言 訂 訳 設 設

施設	しせつ　facilities, an institution
設立	せつりつ [する] establish, found
新設校	しんせつこう　newly-established school
設置	せっち [する] install, organize
設ける	もうける　establish, provide

612 施 ▶し，せ ▷ほどこ(す)

9　　丶 ㇐ 亍 方 方 扩 㐅 施 施

施設	しせつ　facilities, an institution
施行	しこう [する] enforce, put in force, carry out
*実施	じっし [する] put into practice
施工	せこう [する] construct, carry out a construction project
施す	ほどこす　give, give alms

613 備 ▶び ▷そな(える)，そな(わる)

12　　丿 亻 亻 仕 仕 伊 伊 伊 借 借 借 備 備

第3水準

漢字の形に気をつけましょう⓱

153　旅　　322　族　　612　施

旅行　　家族　　計画を実施する

準備　　　じゅんび　[する] prepare for
設備　　　せつび　equipment, facilities　[する] equip with, furnish with
予備の　　よびの　reserve, spare
備考　　　びこう　notes, remarks
*軍備　　ぐんび　armaments, military preparedness
整備　　　せいび　[する] service (an airplane), maintain (a car engine), adjust(a machine)
備える　　そなえる　prepare for, be furnished with/ equipped with

公演　　こうえん　public performance　[する] perform in public
出演　　しゅつえん　[する] appear (in a movie, play, etc.)
上演　　じょうえん　[する] put (a play) on the stage, present (a drama)
演技　　えんぎ　performance　[する] perform, act
演習　　えんしゅう　seminar
演*奏　えんそう　musical performance　[する] give a musical performance
演じる　えんじる　perform, act

614 準 ▶じゅん

13 丶 氵 氵 氵' 氵 氵' 汁 汁 淮 淮　淮 淮 準

準備　　　じゅんび　[する] prepare for
水準　　　すいじゅん　a level, a standard
*基準　　きじゅん　standards, basis
*規準　　きじゅん　criterion, standard
準決勝　　じゅんけっしょう　semifinal match

615 率 ▶そつ, りつ　▷ひき(いる)　306 cf. 卒

11 亠 亠 十 玄 玄 玄 泫 泫 泫 率　率

成長率　　せいちょうりつ　(economic) growth rate
出生率　　しゅっしょうりつ　birthrate
率　　　　りつ　rate, proportion
倍率　　　ばいりつ　degree of magnification
効率　　　こうりつ　efficiency
能率　　　のうりつ　efficiency (work)
率直な　　そっちょくな　frank, candid, straightforward
軽率な　　けいそつな　rash, thoughtless, imprudent
率いる　　ひきいる　lead, command

616 演 ▶えん

14 丶 氵 氵 氵 氵 沪 沪 沪 涫　演 演 演 演

講演　　こうえん　lecture　[する] give a lecture

617 絵 ▶かい, え

12 く 幺 幺 糸 糸 糸 糸 紣 紾 紿　絵 絵

絵　　　え　painting, drawing
絵本　　えほん　an illustrated book, a picture book
絵画　　かいが　picture, drawing, painting

618 給 ▶きゅう

12 く 幺 幺 糸 糸 糸 糸 紣 紷 給　給 給

給料　　きゅうりょう　salary, one's pay
月給　　げっきゅう　monthly salary
供給　　きょうきゅう　[する] supply　[反] *需要(じゅよう) demand

第 42 回

619 声 ▶せい, しょう　▷こえ, こわ

7 一 十 士 吉 吉 吉 声

声　　　こえ　voice
音声　　おんせい　voice, sound
声明　　せいめい　statement
共同声明　きょうどうせいめい　joint statement
◇ 声色　こわいろ　voice impersonation, a tone of voice
特 大音声　だいおんじょう　very loud voice

620 音
▶おん, いん
▷おと, ね

9　'　一　ナ　ヤ　立　产　咅　音　音

発音	はつおん　[する] pronounce
足音	あしおと　the sound of footsteps
物音	ものおと　(unidentified) sound
音	おと　sound
母音	ぼいん　vowel
子音	しいん　consonant
本音	ほんね　real intentions　[反] *建前（たてまえ） formal principles/policies, a professed position

621 昨
▶さく
137 cf. 作

9　l　冂　月　日　日'　旷　旷　旷　昨

昨年	さくねん　last year
昨日	さくじつ, △きのう　yesterday
一昨日	いっさくじつ　the day before yesterday
一昨年	いっさくねん　the year before last

622 暇
▶か
▷ひま
608 cf. 段

13　l　冂　月　日　日'　旷　旷　昍　旷

旷　昄　暇

暇な	ひまな　not busy, free, available
暇つぶし	ひまつぶし　killing time
暇	ひま　free time
休暇	きゅうか　vacation, holiday
*余暇	よか　leisure, spare time

623 由
▶ゆ, ゆう, ゆい
▷よし

5　l　冂　巾　由　由

理由	りゆう　reason
自由	じゆう　freedom, liberty
不自由な	ふじゆうな　inconvenient, uncomfortable, handicapped
由来	ゆらい　origin　[する] originate from
由*緒ある	ゆいしょある　be from a noble family, historic
◇　〜の由	〜のよし　I heard that 〜 (used in letters)

624 油
▶ゆ
▷あぶら
1254 cf. 抽

8　、　ミ　シ　氵　汈　油　油　油

石油	せきゆ　oil, petroleum
原油	げんゆ　crude oil
油田	ゆでん　oil field
油	あぶら　oil (from fish, etc.)
油絵	あぶらえ　oil painting

625 曲
▶きょく
▷ま(がる), ま(げる)

6　l　冂　巾　曲　曲　曲

曲	きょく　music, a tune
作曲	さっきょく　[する] compose music
名曲	めいきょく　famous tune/music
曲がる	まがる　make a turn, bend
曲がり*角	まがりかど　(street) corner, turning point
曲*線	きょくせん　curve, curved line

626 農
▶のう
847 cf. 震

13　、　冂　巾　曲　冊　曲　曹　芦　芦

農　農　農

第3水準

漢字の形に気をつけましょう⑱

585　　623　　1816
申　　由　　*甲

申し上げる　　理由を言う　　*甲*乙つけがたい
　　　　　　　　　　　　　　　　こう　おつ

農業　　　　のうぎょう　agriculture, farming
農村　　　　のうそん　a farming village
農家　　　　のうか　farming family, a farm
農民　　　　のうみん　farmer, peasant
農産物　　　のうさんぶつ　agricultural products
農薬　　　　のうやく　agricultural chemicals
農協　　　　のうきょう　agricultural cooperative

627 濃　▶のう
　　　▷こ(い)

16 `丶氵氵氵沪沪沪沪沪沪
濃濃濃濃濃濃

濃い　　　　こい　dark (color), strong (coffee, tea, etc.), dense (fog)
濃度　　　　のうど　density, thickness　cf. 人口*密度(じんこうみつど) population density
濃*霧　　　　のうむ　dense fog

628 豊　▶ほう
　　　▷ゆた(か)

13 丶冂冊冊冊曲曲曲曲豊
豊豊豊

豊かな　　　ゆたかな　abundant, affluent
豊富な　　　ほうふな　abundant, rich
豊作　　　　ほうさく　good harvest
豊*漁　　　　ほうりょう　good catch of fish

629 富　▶ふ, ふう
　　　▷と(む), とみ

12 丶冖宀宀宁宝宮宮富富
富富

豊富な　　　ほうふな　abundant, rich
富*士山　　　ふじさん　Mt. Fuji
富　　　　　とみ　wealth, riches
富む　　　　とむ　be wealthy/rich
富*貴　　　　ふうき　riches and honors

第 43 回

630 典　▶てん

8 丶冂冂冊冊曲典典

古典　　　　こてん　classics
百科事典　　ひゃっかじてん　encyclopedia

631 興　▶こう, きょう
　　　▷おこ(る), おこ(す)

16 丶冂冂冂目目臼臼臼
臼臼臼臼興興興

興味　　　　きょうみ　interest　cf. 関心(かんしん) interest, concern
*即興　　　　そっきょう　improvisation
興*奮　　　　こうふん　する get excited
◇ 興る　　　　おこる　prosper, emerge

632 己　▶こ, き
　　　▷おのれ

3 𠃊コ己

自己中心的な　じこちゅうしんてきな　egocentric, self-centered
自己　　　　じこ　ego, self
利己的な　　りこてきな　selfish, egotistical
◇ 知己　　　　ちき　acquaintance
◇ 己　　　　　おのれ　oneself

633 記　▶き
　　　▷しる(す)

10 丶亠言言言言訂訂記

日記　　　　にっき　diary
記事　　　　きじ　article (in newspaper etc.)
記者　　　　きしゃ　journalist
記号　　　　きごう　sign, mark, symbol
暗記　　　　あんき　する memorize
記*憶　　　　きおく　memory, recollection　する memorize, remember
記す　　　　しるす　write down

634 紀 ▶き

9 〈 纟 幺 糹 糹 糸 紅 糺 紀

20世紀	にじっせいき，にじゅっせいき	twentieth century
紀元前	きげんぜん	B.C.
歴 紀行文	きこうぶん	account of a journey

635 組 ▶そ ▷く(む)，くみ

11 〈 纟 幺 糹 糹 糸 糿 紀 細 組 組

組み立てる	くみたてる	assemble
組み合わせ／組合せ	くみあわせ	a combination, matching/pairing
労働組合	ろうどうくみあい	labor union
組長	くみちょう	a gang leader
組*織	そしき	-する organize, set up

636 素 ▶そ，す

10 一 十 キ 主 キ 主 麦 麦 素 素

水素	すいそ	hydrogen
元素	げんそ	chemical element
質素な	しっそな	simple, plain
素質	そしつ	aptitude for, the makings of
素直な	すなおな	gentle, docile, obedient
素晴らしい	すばらしい	wonderful, splendid
素人	△しろうと	amateur, layman
素*肌	すはだ	bare skin

637 麦 ▶ばく ▷むぎ

7 一 十 キ 主 キ 歩 麦

小麦	こむぎ	wheat
大麦	おおむぎ	barley
麦	むぎ	wheat, barley, rye, oats
麦茶	むぎちゃ	barley tea
麦*畑	むぎばたけ	wheat/barley field
麦*芽	ばくが	malt

638 責 ▶せき ▷せ(める)

11 一 十 キ 主 キ 青 青 青 青 責

責任	せきにん	responsibility
責務	せきむ	duty, job
責める	せめる	blame

639 任 ▶にん ▷まか(せる)，まか(す)

6 ノ イ 仁 仁 任 任

責任	せきにん	responsibility
主任	しゅにん	person in charge, head of a team, chief
就任	しゅうにん	inauguration -する assume (a post)
後任の	こうにんの	succeeding (president, etc.)
任務	にんむ	duty, office, mission
一任	いちにん	-する leave entirely to another person's responsibility
任意に	にんいに	voluntarily, by one's own choice, at will
任*期	にんき	term of office

第3水準

漢字の形に気をつけましょう⑲

437	636	637	788
表	素	麦	*毒
本の表紙	素質がある	米と麦	食中*毒 しょくちゅうどく

任*命　　　にんめい　[-する] appoint, nominate
任せる　　まかせる　entrust

640 信 ▶しん

9 ノ イ イ´ イ⌐ イ⌐ 信 信 信 信

信じる　　しんじる　believe (in), trust
信者　　　しんじゃ　believer (of a religion)
自信　　　じしん　(self-)confidence
通信　　　つうしん　[-する] communicate
信用　　　しんよう　[-する] trust, believe
不信　　　ふしん　distrust
信号　　　しんごう　signal, traffic lights

第 44 回

641 徒 ▶と

10 ノ ク 彳 彳´ 彳丄 彳土 彳キ 彳キ 徒 徒

生徒　　　せいと　pupil, student
キリスト教徒　キリストきょうと　Christian
仏教徒　　ぶっきょうと　Buddhist
イスラム教徒　イスラムきょうと　Muslim

642 従 ▶じゅう，しょう，じゅ
▷したが(う)，したが(える)

10 ノ ク 彳 彳 彳′ 彳″ 彳″ 彳″ 従 従

従来の　　じゅうらいの　usual, past
従業員　　じゅうぎょういん　employee, worker
服従　　　ふくじゅう　[-する] obey
従*順な　　じゅうじゅんな　obedient
従事　　　じゅうじ　[-する] engage in
従う　　　したがう　obey, comply with, follow
従える　　したがえる　be attended by, be accompanied by, conquer
歴 従～位　じゅ～い　rank in the system of office grades first established in ancient Japan
特 従容として　しょうようとして　calmly, with composure/serenity

643 得 ▶とく
▷え(る)，う(る)

11 ノ ク 彳 彳 彳⌐ 彳⌐ 彳⌐ 彳⌐ 得 得
得

得　　　とく　gain, advantage　[-する] gain, make a profit
得意な／の　とくいな／の　good, strong, favorite (subject), proud
損得　　　そんとく　loss and gain
得点　　　とくてん　point, score　[-する] score, count
所得　　　しょとく　income
得る　　　える，うる　gain, acquire
やむを得ない　やむをえない　inevitable
心得る　　こころえる　understand, recognize, have knowledge of

644 徳 ▶とく

14 ノ ク 彳 彳 彳⌐ 彳⌐ 彳⌐ 彳⌐ 彳⌐ 徳
徳 徳 徳 徳

道徳　　　どうとく　morality, morals
人徳　　　じんとく　one's natural virtue
歴 徳川時代　とくがわじだい　Tokugawa era

645 聴 ▶ちょう
▷き(く)

17 一 丅 丆 F E 耳 耳′ 耳⌐ 耳⌐ 耳
耳⌐ 耴 耴 耴 聴 聴 聴

聴講　　　ちょうこう　[-する] audit (a course)
聴講生　　ちょうこうせい　auditing student
聴解　　　ちょうかい　listening comprehension
公聴会　　こうちょうかい　public hearing
聴覚　　　ちょうかく　sense of hearing
*視聴率　　しちょうりつ　audience rating
*視聴者　　しちょうしゃ　TV viewer
聴*衆　　　ちょうしゅう　audience
◇ 事*情聴取　じじょうちょうしゅ　investigative inquiry (by the police)
聴く　　　きく　listen, hear

646 舟
▶しゅう
▷ふね，ふな

6 `丿 力 刀 力 舟

舟　　　　ふね　boat
小舟　　　こぶね　small boat
歴 舟遊び　　ふなあそび　boating
歴 雪舟　　　せっしゅう　(name of a famous Japanese painter in the medieval period)

647 船
▶せん
▷ふね，ふな

11 `丿 力 刀 力 舟 舟' 舟八 船 船
船

船　　　　ふね　ship, vessel
風船　　　ふうせん　(toy) balloon
客船　　　きゃくせん　passenger ship
船員　　　せんいん　sailor, crew
船長　　　せんちょう　captain (of a ship)
船室　　　せんしつ　cabin (of a ship)
船旅　　　ふなたび　voyage
船便　　　ふなびん　surface mail　cf. *航空便(こうくうびん) air mail

648 般
▶はん

10 `丿 力 刀 力 舟 舟' 舟几 船 般

一般的な　いっぱんてきな　general, common
一般の　　いっぱんの　general, ordinary
一般化　　いっぱんか　する generalize
全般的に　ぜんぱんてきに　generally, on the whole
◇ *諸般の事*情により　しょはんのじじょうにより　for various reasons

649 航
▶こう

10 `丿 力 刀 力 舟 舟' 舟亠 航 航

航空便　　こうくうびん　air mail
航空機　　こうくうき　aircraft
航空*券　　こうくうけん　airline ticket

航海　　　こうかい　navigation, voyage　する sail, make a voyage
航路　　　こうろ　route, line, service
◇ *巡航ミサイル　じゅんこうミサイル　cruise missile

650 億
▶おく

15 `亻 亻' 亻宀 亻㐅 亻立 倅 倅 倍 倍
倍 倍 億 億 億

〜億　　　〜おく　hundred million

651 憶
▶おく

16 `丶 亻 亻' 亻宀 忄忄 忄忄 忄音 悟 悟
悟 悟 悟 憶 憶 憶

記憶　　　きおく　memory, recollection　する memorize, remember

652 漫
▶まん

14 `丶 冫 氵 氵冂 氵日 氵日 氵旦 渭 渭
渭 渭 漫 漫

漫画　　　まんが　comics, cartoon
漫然と　　まんぜんと　aimlessly
*散漫な　　さんまんな　scattered (attention), diffuse (style)
漫*才　　　まんざい　Japanese comic dialogue

第 45 回

653 慢
▶まん

14 `丶 忄 忄 忄 忄' 忄宀 忄甲 忄甲 悍
悍 悍 慢 慢

自慢　　　じまん　する boast, be proud of
慢性の　　まんせいの　chronic
*我慢　　　がまん　する endure, bear
*怠慢　　　たいまん　negligence, neglect

第3水準

103

654 情

▶じょう，せい
▷なさ(け)

11 丶 ハ 忄 忄 忙 忰 忰 情 情 情 情

感情	かんじょう	emotion, feeling
感情的な	かんじょうてきな	emotional
同情	どうじょう	する sympathize
友情	ゆうじょう	friendship
苦情	くじょう	complaint
情	じょう	emotion, sympathy
無情の	むじょうの	heartless, cruel
事情	じじょう	circumstances, situation
*実情	じつじょう	actual situation
◇ 風情	ふぜい	manners, elegance, taste
情け	なさけ	sympathy, mercy

655 慣

▶かん
▷な(れる)，な(らす)

14 丶 ハ 忄 忄 忙 忰 慣 慣 慣 慣 慣 慣 慣 慣

慣れる	なれる	get used to
見慣れた	みなれた	familiar
習慣	しゅうかん	custom, practice, habit
慣習	かんしゅう	customs, conventions
慣*例	かんれい	custom, precedent

656 快

▶かい
▷こころよ(い)

7 丶 ハ 忄 忙 忙 快 快

| 快適な | かいてきな | comfortable |
| 快晴 | かいせい | clear sky, fine weather |

全快	ぜんかい	する recover from an illness completely
快速(電車)	かいそく(でんしゃ)	rapid train
*愉快な	ゆかいな	joyful, pleasant, delightful
快い	こころよい	pleasant

657 適

▶てき

14 丶 一 十 冉 产 产 肖 商 商 商 商 商 滴 適

適当な	てきとうな	suitable, appropriate, adequate
適度な	てきどな	a moderate amount of
適切な	てきせつな	appropriate, proper
適用	てきよう	する apply (a rule)
適*材適所	てきざいてきしょ	the right person in the right job/place
適する	てきする	be suitable for

658 敵

▶てき
▷かたき

15 丶 一 十 冉 产 产 肖 商 商 商 商 商 敵 敵 敵

敵	てき	enemy, opponent 反味方(みかた) ally, friend
強敵	きょうてき	formidable enemy
敵意	てきい	hostility
敵対	てきたい	する be hostile to
不敵な	ふてきな	fearless, bold
◇ 敵	かたき	enemy, foe, rival

659 欠

▶けつ
▷か(ける)，か(く)

4 ノ 欠 欠 欠

漢字の形に気をつけましょう⑳

657 適	1256 *摘	1504 *滴	658 敵	684 *商
適当な人	*摘出手術 てきしゅつ	一*滴 二*滴 三*滴 いってき にてき さんてき	敵と味方	*商業 しょうぎょう

欠席　　　けっせき　［する］be absent (from school/etc.)
欠員　　　けついん　vacancy
欠ける　　かける　lack
欠く　　　かく　lack, be missing

660 次 ▶じ，し
▷つ(ぐ)，つぎ

6 ⟍ 丶 冫 冫 汐 次

次の　　　つぎの　next, following
次男　　　じなん　second son
目次　　　もくじ　table of contents
〜次第　　〜しだい　as soon as 〜, depending on 〜
次いで　　ついで　subsequently
〜に次ぐ　〜につぐ　follow 〜 in rank, come after 〜

661 姿 ▶し
▷すがた

9 ⟍ 丶 冫 汐 汐 次 姿 姿 姿

姿　　　　すがた　figure, appearance
後ろ姿　　うしろすがた　one's appearance from behind
姿*勢　　　しせい　posture, stance
*容姿　　　ようし　face and figure, appearance

662 冷 ▶れい
▷つめ(たい)，ひ(える)，ひ(や)，ひ(やす)，ひ(やかす)，さ(める)，さ(ます)

7 ⟍ 冫 冫 汃 汄 冷 冷

冷たい　　つめたい　cold (to the touch or feelings)　cf. 寒い cold (temperature)
冷える　　ひえる　become cold
冷やす　　ひやす　cool, chill
冷戦　　　れいせん　cold war
冷水　　　れいすい　cold water
冷静な　　れいせいな　calm, cool(-headed)
冷*蔵庫　　れいぞうこ　refrigerator
冷やかす　ひやかす　tease, poke fun at
冷める　　さめる　cool off, cool down
冷ます　　さます　cool, let cool

第 46 回

663 句 ▶く

5 ノ 勹 勺 句 句

文句　　　もんく　grumblings, complaints, a phrase/series of words
語句　　　ごく　words and phrases

664 旬 ▶じゅん，しゅん

6 ノ 勹 勺 句 旬 旬

上旬　　　じょうじゅん　the first ten days of a month
中旬　　　ちゅうじゅん　the middle ten days of a month
下旬　　　げじゅん　the last ten days of a month
初旬　　　しょじゅん　(during) the first ten days of a month
◇ 旬　　　しゅん　height of the season

665 保 ▶ほ
▷たも(つ)

9 ノ 亻 亻 仴 仴 仴 伴 保 保

保証　　　ほしょう　［する］guarantee
保証人　　ほしょうにん　guarantor
保存　　　ほぞん　［する］preserve, conserve
保*険　　　ほけん　insurance
保*健　　　ほけん　preservation of health
保*障　　　ほしょう　［する］secure
保*育園　　ほいくえん　nursery school
保つ　　　たもつ　keep, maintain

666 証 ▶しょう

12 ⟍ 亠 言 言 言 言 言 訂 訂 訂 訨 証

証明　　　しょうめい　［する］prove, certify
証人　　　しょうにん　a witness
証言　　　しょうげん　testimony　［する］testify
証*拠　　　しょうこ　evidence, proof

第3水準

667 許 ▶きょ ▷ゆる(す)

11 丶 亠 ﾆ 三 言 言 言 許 許 許 許 許

許可	きょか	[する] allow, permit
特許	とっきょ	patent
許*容	きょよう	[する] allow, permit
*免許	めんきょ	license
許す	ゆるす	forgive, allow, permit

668 認 ▶にん ▷みと(める)

14 丶 亠 ﾆ 三 言 言 言 訒 認 認 認 認 認 認

認める	みとめる	acknowledge, admit
認識	にんしき	[する] recognize, understand, perceive
公認の	こうにんの	officially recognized/authorized/certified
*確認	かくにん	[する] confirm

669 課 ▶か

15 丶 亠 ﾆ 三 言 言 言 訓 課 訓 訓 課 課 課

課長	かちょう	head of a section
課	か	section, department
人事課	じんじか	personnel department
経理課	けいりか	the accounting department
第〜課	だい〜か	section (#), lesson (#)
課題	かだい	assignment, problems
日課	にっか	daily work
課する	かする	impose (a tax, duty, etc.)

670 税 ▶ぜい

12 丶 ﾆ 千 千 禾 禾 秆 秆 秒 税 税 税

税金	ぜいきん	taxes, duties
関税	かんぜい	customs duties
税関	ぜいかん	customs
所得税	しょとくぜい	income tax
無税	むぜい	tax-free, duty-free
課税	かぜい	[する] impose a tax
*免税	めんぜい	tax exemption

671 程 ▶てい ▷ほど   1657 cf. 呈

12 丶 ﾆ 千 千 禾 禾 秆 秆 秆 秆 程 程

程度	ていど	degree, extent
課程	かてい	a course of, a program (of education)
過程	かてい	process
日程	にってい	schedule, agenda
程々に	ほどほどに	moderately

672 実 ▶じつ ▷み, みの(る)

8 丶 丷 宀 宀 宀 宁 実 実

事実	じじつ	fact
真実	しんじつ	truth, reality
口実	こうじつ	excuse
実習	じっしゅう	[する] practice
実感	じっかん	[する] actually feel, realize
実行	じっこう	[する] put into practice, carry out
実力	じつりょく	actual ability
実物	じつぶつ	the real thing
実際に	じっさいに	as a matter of fact, actually
実用的な	じつようてきな	practical
実は	じつは	actually, to tell the truth
実*例	じつれい	example
実に	じつに	surely, really
特 果実酒	かじつしゅ	fruit wine
実	み	fruit
実る	みのる	bear fruit

673 美 ▶び ▷うつく(しい)

9 丶 丷 丷 丷 羊 羊 羊 美 美

美人	びじん	beautiful woman
美術館	びじゅつかん	art museum
美学	びがく	aesthetics
美しい	うつくしい	beautiful, pretty

親善	しんぜん	friendship, goodwill
善悪	ぜんあく	good and evil
*改善	かいぜん	[する] improve, make better
善い	よい	good

第 47 回

674 差 ▶さ ▷さ(す)

10　丶 丷 丷 甾 甾 羊 羊 差 差 差

差	さ	(a) difference
時差	じさ	time difference
時差ぼけ	じさぼけ	jet lag
差別	さべつ	[する] discriminate against
交差点	こうさてん	an intersection
差す	さす	shine into/upon, hold (an umbrella) over one's head
差し上げる	さしあげる	give [humble]
差し引く	さしひく	deduct, take away
物差し	ものさし	ruler, measure
差し支える	△さしつかえる	interfere with

675 養 ▶よう ▷やしな(う)

15　丶 丷 丷 甾 甾 羊 羊 美 美 美
善 善 養 養 養

休養	きゅうよう	[する] rest
教養	きょうよう	culture
養子	ようし	adopted child
養育	よういく	[する] nurture
養分	ようぶん	nourishment
養う	やしなう	foster, support

676 善 ▶ぜん ▷よ(い)

12　丶 丷 丷 丷 兰 羊 羊 羔 盖 善
善 善

善	ぜん	good, goodness, virtue
善意	ぜんい	good intentions
善良な	ぜんりょうな	good(-natured), honest

677 様 ▶よう ▷さま

14　一 十 オ 木 木 栌 栏 栏 栏 様
様 様 様 様

様子	ようす	state of affairs, situation, appearance
多様性	たようせい	diversity
多様化	たようか	diversification (of lifestyle, needs, etc.) [する] be diversified　cf. 多*角化(たかくか) diversification (of business operations)
多様な	たような	diverse, various
同様の	どうようの	same, alike
神様	かみさま	God, gods
～様	～さま	Mr./Mrs. ～ (mainly used in writing)

678 植 ▶しょく ▷う(える)，う(わる)

12　一 十 オ 木 木 柜 柿 枯 柿 植
植 植

植物	しょくぶつ	plants 反動物(どうぶつ) animals
植民地	しょくみんち	colony
植える	うえる	plant
田植え	たうえ	transplanting of rice shoots

679 極 ▶きょく，ごく ▷きわ(める)，きわ(まる)，きわ(み)

12　一 十 オ 木 木 柯 柯 柯 柯 極
極 極

北極	ほっきょく	the North Pole
南極	なんきょく	the South Pole
極東	きょくとう	the Far East
極端な	きょくたんな	extreme
極める	きわめる	master
見極める	みきわめる	see through, discern
極まる	きわまる	reach an extreme

第3水準

107

極み　きわみ　extremity of some kind
極*秘　ごくひ　strict secrecy, top secret

680 端 ▶たん ▷はし，は，はた
14 `丶 亠 士 寺 寺 寺 寺 蛘 蛘 蛘` `蛘 端 端 端`

極端な　きょくたんな　extreme
先端技術　せんたんぎじゅつ　high technology
*異端　いたん　heresy, paganism
端　はし　end, the edge, tip
端数　はすう　a fraction
半端な　はんぱな　odd, incomplete
中*途半端な　ちゅうとはんぱな　half-done, unfinished, unsatisfactory
道端　みちばた　the roadside

681 需 ▶じゅ
14 `一 厂 户 乕 乕 乕 雫 雫 雫` `雫 雫 需 需`

需要　じゅよう　demand 反供給（きょうきゅう）-する supply
需給　じゅきゅう　demand and supply
◇ 特需　とくじゅ　special procurement
必需*品　ひつじゅひん　necessities
◇ *軍需*品　ぐんじゅひん　munitions, war supplies
◇ *軍需産業　ぐんじゅさんぎょう　war industry

682 器 ▶き ▷うつわ
15 `丶 吅 吅 吅 吅 吅 吅 哭 哭` `器 器 器 器 器`

楽器　がっき　musical instrument
食器　しょっき　tableware
受話器　じゅわき　telephone receiver
器用な　きような　skillful, dexterous
不器用な　ぶきような　awkward, clumsy
器*具　きぐ　appliances, utensils
器　うつわ　container, vessel

683 品 ▶ひん ▷しな
9 `丶 口 口 品 品 品 品 品 品`

品質　ひんしつ　quality of a product　cf. *性*能（せいのう）capacity/performance (of a machine)
部品　ぶひん　part(s) (auto-part, etc.)
日用品　にちようひん　daily necessities
薬品　やくひん　medicines, chemicals
洋品店　ようひんてん　Western-style apparel shop
品物　しなもの　merchandise, goods, commodities
品　しな　goods, articles
手品　てじな　magic (show)
上品な　じょうひんな　refined, elegant, graceful
下品な　げひんな　vulgar, indecent
品　ひん　grace, elegance, dignity

684 商 ▶しょう ▷あきな（う）
11 `丶 亠 亠 产 产 产 商 商 商 商` `商`

商業　しょうぎょう　commerce
商品　しょうひん　merchandise, commodity
商人　しょうにん　merchant
商売　しょうばい　business, commerce -する engage in business
商社　しょうしゃ　trading company
商店　しょうてん　shop, store, firm
◇ 商い　あきない　dealing, business

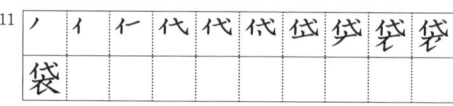

685 袋 ▶たい ▷ふくろ
11 `ノ イ イ 代 代 代 代 伐 袋 袋` `袋`

袋　ふくろ　sack, bag
紙袋　かみぶくろ　paper bag
手袋　てぶくろ　glove
袋小路　ふくろこうじ　blind alley
特 有袋類　ゆうたいるい　marsupial, pouched animal

686 製 ▶せい

14 ノ ← ㇗ ⼆ 与 制 制 制 制 製
製 製 製 製

日本製	にほんせい	made in Japan
製品	せいひん	product
製作	せいさく	[する] make (a product)
製鉄	せいてつ	iron manufacturing
製鉄所	せいてつしょ, せいてつじょ	ironworks

687 制 ▶せい

8 ノ ← ㇗ ⼆ 与 制 制 制

制度	せいど	system, institution
制作	せいさく	[する] produce/make (a work of art)
強制	きょうせい	[する] compel, force
強制労働	きょうせいろうどう	forced labor
税制	ぜいせい	taxation system

688 誕 ▶たん

15 ヽ ㇀ ㇀ ㇀ ㇀ ㇀ 言 言 言 言
証 証 証 誕 誕

| 誕生日 | たんじょうび | birthday |
| 誕生 | たんじょう | birth [する] be born |

689 延 ▶えん　▷の(びる), の(べる), の(ばす)

8 ㇀ ノ 千 征 正 延 延 延

延期	えんき	[する] postpone, put off
延長	えんちょう	[する] extend
延びる	のびる	be postponed, be prolonged
延ばす	のばす	postpone, prolong

| 引き延ばす | ひきのばす | put off (an appointment, payment, etc.) |
| [特] 延べる | のべる | lay out (a futon), make (a bed) |

690 期 ▶き, ご

12 一 十 ㇜ 甘 甘 甘 其 其 期 期
期 期

期間	きかん	period of time, a term
前期	ぜんき	first semester, previous term
後期	こうき	second semester, the latter term
学期	がっき	semester, term
短期大学	たんきだいがく	junior college cf. *abbr.* 短大 (たんだい)
定期的に	ていきてきに	regularly
短期的な	たんきてきな	short-term
中期的な	ちゅうきてきな	medium-term
長期的な	ちょうきてきな	long-term
画期的な	かっきてきな	epoch-making
定期*券	ていきけん	pass (for trains etc., for a period of time)
予期	よき	[する] anticipate, foresee
最期	さいご	one's last moment

691 基 ▶き　▷もと, もとい　1156 cf. 墓

11 一 十 ㇜ 甘 甘 甘 其 其 其 基
基

基本	きほん	basis, foundation, ABCs, fundamentals
基礎	きそ	foundation, basis, groundwork
基金	ききん	foundation, a fund
基地	きち	(military) base
基づく	もとづく	be based on
基	もと, もとい	basis

692 礎 ▶そ　▷いしずえ

18 一 ㇀ 丆 石 石 石 石 石 石
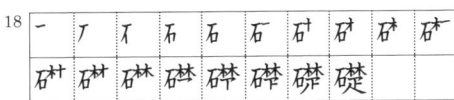

| 基礎 | きそ | foundation, basis, groundwork |
| ◇ 礎 | いしずえ | cornerstone |

693 疑 ▶ぎ
▷うたが(う)

14 `ノ ヒ ヒ ヒ ヒ 毕 毕 毕 毕 疑`
`紆 紆 疑 疑`

疑う	うたがう	doubt, be suspicious of, distrust
疑い	うたがい	doubt, suspicion
疑問	ぎもん	doubt, question
質*応答	しつぎおうとう	questions and answers
疑*念	ぎねん	doubt, suspicion
*容疑者	ようぎしゃ	a suspect
*容疑	ようぎ	suspicion
疑*惑	ぎわく	suspicion, doubt
◇ 疑*獄	ぎごく	(bribery) scandal

694 紹 ▶しょう

11 `く ㄠ ㄠ ㄠ 糸 糸 紆 紹 紹 紹`
`紹`

| 紹介 | しょうかい | -する introduce, present |
| 自己紹介 | じこしょうかい | -する introduce oneself |

695 介 ▶かい

4 `ノ 八 介 介`

紹介	しょうかい	-する introduce, present
介入	かいにゅう	-する intervene
介在	かいざい	-する stand between
魚介類	ぎょかいるい	marine products, seafood

696 招 ▶しょう
▷まね(く)

8 `一 十 扌 扩 扟 扟 招 招`

招待	しょうたい	-する invite
招く	まねく	invite, bring about
手招き	てまねき	-する beckon

第 49 回

697 委 ▶い
▷ゆだ(ねる)

8 `一 二 千 千 禾 秀 委 委`

委員会	いいんかい	committee
委員	いいん	member of a committee
委*託	いたく	-する entrust, consign
委ねる	ゆだねる	entrust

698 季 ▶き

8 `一 二 千 千 禾 禾 季 季`

季節	きせつ	season
季節風	きせつふう	monsoon
四季	しき	four seasons

699 節 ▶せつ, せち
▷ふし

13 `ノ ヶ ヶ ㄠ 竹 竹 竹 竺 筲 筲`
`筲 節 節`

季節	きせつ	season
調節	ちょうせつ	-する adjust
使節	しせつ	a mission, an envoy
節約	せつやく	-する economize, save (money, time, water, electricity, etc.)

漢字の形に気をつけましょう㉑

694	696	867	1691
紹	招	*昭	*召
友だちを家族に紹介する	友だちを家に招待する	*昭和 20 年 しょうわ	*召し上がる め

関節	かんせつ a joint
お節料理	おせちりょうり traditional Japanese New Year's cuisine
節目	ふしめ a swelled part of a stick (joint, bamboo)

700 即 ▶そく

7 フ ヨ ヨ 目 目 即 即

即興	そっきょう improvisation
即座に	そくざに immediately, promptly
即時に	そくじに instantly, immediately

701 企 ▶き
▷くわだ(てる)

6 ノ 人 个 个 企 企

企業	きぎょう enterprise
大企業	だいきぎょう a large company
中小企業	ちゅうしょうきぎょう small and medium-sized enterprises
企画	きかく -する make a plan
企てる	くわだてる plan, scheme, attempt
企て	くわだて plan, project, scheme

702 歯 ▶し
▷は

12 ١ ⊢ ⊦ 止 止 止 止 歩 歩 柴
歯 歯

歯	は tooth
虫歯	むしば decayed tooth
前歯	まえば a front tooth
歯医者	はいしゃ dentist

| 歯車 | はぐるま cogwheel, gear |
| 歯科医 | しかい dentist |

703 歳 ▶さい, せい

13 ١ ⊢ ⊦ 止 广 芦 芦 芦 岦 岢
岁 歳 歳

～歳	～さい ～ years old
歳出	さいしゅつ annual expenditures
歳入	さいにゅう annual revenue
歳末大売出し	さいまつおおうりだし big year-end sale
万歳	ばんざい *banzai*, Long live (the emperor/king, etc.), Hurrah! -する cry *banzai*
二十歳	△はたち twenty years old
お歳*暮	おせいぼ year-end gift

704 歴 ▶れき
1720
cf. 暦

14 一 厂 厂 斤 斤 厤 厤 厤 厤 麻
麻 厤 歴 歴

歴史	れきし history
学歴	がくれき (one's) educational history, academic background
職歴	しょくれき (one's) work experience
経歴	けいれき one's personal history, one's career
前歴	ぜんれき (one's) past record

705 史 ▶し

5 ١ 冂 口 史 史

| 歴史 | れきし history |
| 日本史 | にほんし Japanese history |

漢字の形に気をつけましょう㉒

697 698 1171
委 季 *秀

予算委員会 季節 *優*秀な学生
ゆう しゅう

世界史　　せかいし　world history
文学史　　ぶんがくし　history of literature

常に　　　つねに　always, at all times
◇ 常夏の国　とこなつのくに　a land of everlasting summer

706 央　▶おう

5 丶 冂 凸 央 央

中央　　ちゅうおう　center

第 50 回

707 非　▶ひ

8 丿 ナ ヺ ヺ 非 非 非 非

非常口　　ひじょうぐち　emergency exit
非公開の　ひこうかいの　private, closed to the public, unpublished
非人道的な　ひじんどうてきな　inhumane
非合法的な　ひごうほうてきな　illegal
非合法な　ひごうほうな　illegal
非公式の　ひこうしきの　unofficial

708 常　▶じょう　▷つね, とこ

11 丶 丷 丷 丷 屵 屵 尚 尚 常 常
常

日常会話　にちじょうかいわ　daily conversation
日常生活　にちじょうせいかつ　daily life
正常な　せいじょうな　normal
*異常な　いじょうな　unusual, abnormal 反正常な（せいじょうな）
通常の　つうじょうの　usual, ordinary
非常の　ひじょうの　emergency
非常口　ひじょうぐち　emergency exit
常識　じょうしき　common sense

709 堂　▶どう

11 丶 丷 丷 丷 屵 屵 尚 尚 堂 堂
堂

食堂　　しょくどう　a diner (restaurant), a dining room
本堂　　ほんどう　main hall of a temple
国会議事堂　こっかいぎじどう　the Diet Building

710 党　▶とう

10 丶 丷 丷 丷 屵 屵 尚 尚 尚 党

自民党　じみんとう　the Liberal Democratic Party, LDP cf. this is an abbreviation of 自由民主党（じゆうみんしゅとう）
民主党　みんしゅとう　the Democratic Party, the Democratic Party of Japan
共和党　きょうわとう　the Republican Party
保守党　ほしゅとう　the Conservative Party
労働党　ろうどうとう　the Labor Party
政党　せいとう　political party
*与党　よとう　party in power
野党　やとう　opposition party
党首　とうしゅ　political party head

711 賞　▶しょう

15 丶 丷 丷 丷 屵 屵 尚 尚 尚 尚
営 営 営 賞 賞

ノーベル賞　ノーベルしょう　Nobel Prize　cf. アカデミー賞 Academy Award, グラミー賞 Grammy Award

代表的な日本の政党

自民党（じみんとう）　民主党（みんしゅとう）　公明党（こうめいとう）
日本共産党（にほんきょうさんとう）　社民党（しゃみんとう）

賞　　　　　しょう　prize, award
賞品　　　　しょうひん　prize
賞金　　　　しょうきん　prize money
受賞者　　　じゅしょうしゃ　prize winner

712 **償**　▶しょう
　　　　▷つぐな(う)

17 ノ イ イ イ゙ イ゙ イ゙ 價 價 價
價 價 償 償 償 償 償

代償　　　　だいしょう　compensation, price
*賠償金　　　ばいしょうきん　compensation, reparations,
　　　　　　　damages
損*害*賠償　　そんがいばいしょう　compensation for
　　　　　　　damages
償う　　　　つぐなう　atone for, expiate
償い　　　　つぐない　atonement, compensation

713 **与**　▶よ
　　　　▷あた(える)

3 一 ケ 与

与党　　　　よとう　party in power
与える　　　あたえる　give, provide
給与　　　　きゅうよ　salary, pay
◇ 供与　　　きょうよ　provide
関与　　　　かんよ　する be involved in

714 **券**　▶けん

8 、 ゛ 丷 丷 半 半 券 券

定期券　　　ていきけん　pass (for trains etc., for a period of
　　　　　　　time)
回数券　　　かいすうけん　a book of tickets (for trains,
　　　　　　　buses, etc.)

入場券　　　にゅうじょうけん　admission ticket
証券会社　　しょうけんがいしゃ　securities firm
旅券　　　　りょけん　passport

715 **巻**　▶かん
　　　　▷ま(く)，まき

9 、 ゛ 丷 丷 半 半 券 巻 巻

第～巻　　　だい～かん　volume no. ～
上巻　　　　じょうかん　the first volume (of two or three)
中巻　　　　ちゅうかん　the middle volume
下巻　　　　げかん　the last volume
巻く　　　　まく　wind (up), roll (up), coil
葉巻　　　　はまき　cigar
寝巻き　　　ねまき　Japanese nightclothes
歴 絵巻物　　えまきもの　picture scroll

716 **角**　▶かく
　　　　▷かど，つの

7 ノ ク ア 凢 角 角 角

角　　　　　かど　corner, edge
街角　　　　まちかど　street (corner)
角度　　　　かくど　angle
直角　　　　ちょっかく　right angle
三角形　　　さんかっけい　triangle
三角関係　　さんかくかんけい　love triangle
方角　　　　ほうがく　direction
角　　　　　つの　horns, antlers

第 51 回

717 **負**　▶ふ
　　　　▷ま(ける)，ま(かす)，お(う)

9 ノ ク イ 凢 角 角 負 負 負

いろいろな形の言い方

三角形（さんかくけい）　四角形（しかくけい）　　五角形（ごかくけい）

正方形（せいほうけい）　　長方形（ちょうほうけい）　　ひし形（ひしがた）　　　円（えん）

直方体（ちょくほうたい）　　立方体（りっぽうたい）　　*球（きゅう）

第3水準

113

負ける	まける　lose, be defeated
勝負	しょうぶ　winning or losing 〔する〕 have a match/contest/game
自負	じふ　self-confidence, pride 〔する〕 take pride in, be proud of
負*担	ふたん　burden, responsibility 〔する〕 bear (expenses, responsibility, etc.)
負う	おう　take (responsibility), bear (a burden), suffer (an injury)

718 敗　▶はい　▷やぶ(れる)

11

失敗	しっぱい　〔する〕 fail
敗戦	はいせん　lose a war, be defeated in battle
敗者	はいしゃ　the loser
勝敗	しょうはい　victory or defeat
敗れる	やぶれる　be defeated, lose

719 貝　▷かい

 7

| 貝 | かい　shellfish |
| 貝*殻 | かいがら　seashell |

720 具　▶ぐ

8

家具	かぐ　furniture
道具	どうぐ　tools, instruments
具体的な	ぐたいてきな　concrete, specific
具合	ぐあい　condition, state

721 散　▶さん　▷ち(る), ち(らす), ち(らかす), ち(らかる)

12

| 散歩 | さんぽ　〔する〕 take a walk |

解散	かいさん　〔する〕 break up, dissolve
散文	さんぶん　prose
散漫な	さんまんな　scattered (attention), diffuse (style)
散る	ちる　scatter, fall (as in blossoms/leaves/paper, etc.)
散らかす	ちらかす　scatter about, leave messed up, put in disorder

722 故　▶こ　▷ゆえ

9 | 一 十 十 古 古 击 故 故 故

事故	じこ　an accident
交通事故	こうつうじこ　traffic accident
故国	ここく　one's native land/country
故意に	こいに　intentionally, purposefully, deliberately
故に	ゆえに　therefore, hence

723 放　▶ほう　▷はな(す), はな(つ), はな(れる), ほう(る)

8 | ' 亠 宀 方 ガ ガ 扩 放

放送	ほうそう　〔する〕 to broadcast
解放	かいほう　〔する〕 release, liberate
開放	かいほう　〔する〕 throw (a door) open, open to the public
放火	ほうか　arson 〔する〕 set on fire
放置	ほうち　〔する〕 leave something as it is, neglect, ignore
放す	はなす　let go, release
◇ 放れる	はなれる　get free
放つ	はなつ　shoot, emit, let loose
◇ 放る	ほうる　throw, toss

724 敷　▶ふ　▷し(く)

15

敷石	しきいし　paving stone, flagstone
◇ 屋敷	やしき　mansion, premises
敷地	しきち　a (building) site

敷く　　　　しく　pave, cover, spread/lay out (a futon, mat, etc.)

敷設　　　　ふせつ　-する lay (a pipe, etc.), construct a railroad)

725 **致**　▶ち
　　　　▷いた（す）

10 一 Ｔ 至 至 至 至 致 致 致 致

一致　　　　いっち　-する agree, be consistent
合致　　　　がっち　-する agree, be consistent
致死量　　　ちしりょう　lethal dose
致*命*傷　　ちめいしょう　fatal wound
致す　　　　いたす　do [polite]

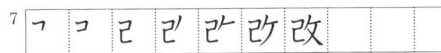

726 **改**　▶かい
　　　　▷あらた（める），あらた（まる）

7 フ コ 己 己 己 改 改

改良　　　　かいりょう　-する improve
改正　　　　かいせい　-する revise, amend
改善　　　　かいぜん　-する improve, make better
改める　　　あらためる　revise, change, renew
改めて　　　あらためて　newly, again, on another time

727 **配**　▶はい
　　　　▷くば（る）

10 一 Ｔ 斤 斤 両 西 酉 酉 配 配

心配　　　　しんぱい　-する worry
支配　　　　しはい　-する control, rule over
配達　　　　はいたつ　-する deliver
配る　　　　くばる　distribute, deliver

728 **酔**　▶すい
　　　　▷よ（う）

11 一 Ｔ 斤 斤 两 西 酉 酉 酉 酔 酔

酔う　　　　よう　get drunk
酔っ払い　　よっぱらい　drunk
*麻酔　　　　ますい　anesthesia

729 **針**　▶しん
　　　　▷はり

10 ノ 人 ム 合 牟 牟 余 金 金 針

方針　　　　ほうしん　policy, guidelines
針路　　　　しんろ　course, direction (of a ship/airplane/etc.)　cf. 進路（しんろ）course, direction (in general)
針　　　　　はり　needle
針金　　　　はりがね　a wire

730 **録**　▶ろく

16 ノ 人 ム 合 牟 牟 余 金 針 針
　　 針 針 針 録 録 録

録音　　　　ろくおん　-する record (speech, sound, etc.)
録画　　　　ろくが　-する record (video)
記録　　　　きろく　-する record
付録　　　　ふろく　supplement, appendix

731 **緑**　▶りょく, ろく
　　　　▷みどり

14 く ㇙ 幺 糸 糸 糸 紀 紀 紀
　　 紀 紀 緑 緑

緑　　　　　みどり　green
緑色　　　　みどりいろ　green
新緑　　　　しんりょく　fresh verdure
緑地　　　　りょくち　green tract of land
葉緑素　　　ようりょくそ　chlorophyll
特 緑青　　　ろくしょう　copper/green rust, patina

732 **縁**　▶えん
　　　　▷ふち

15 く ㇙ 幺 糸 糸 糸 紀 紀 紀
　　 紀 紀 緑 縁 縁

縁　　　　　えん　fate, karma, a relation
因縁　　　　いんねん　fate, connection
縁*側　　　えんがわ　veranda
縁　　　　　ふち　edge

733 納

▶のう，なっ，な，なん，とう
▷おさ（める），おさ（まる）

10 〈 幺 幺 幺 糸 糸 糸 糸 糸 納 納

納得	なっとく [する]	understand, give one's consent to
納税	のうぜい [する]	pay a tax
納める	おさめる	pay, supply, store
納屋	なや	barn, shed cf. *倉庫（そうこ）warehouse, storehouse
出納	すいとう	revenues and expenditures
出納係	すいとうがかり	cashier, teller
納戸	なんど	storage room, closet

734 絶

▶ぜつ
▷た（える），た（やす），た（つ）

12 〈 幺 幺 幺 糸 糸 糸 紵 紵 紵 絢
絢 絶

絶対に	ぜったいに	definitely
絶望	ぜつぼう [する]	despair
絶望的な	ぜつぼうてきな	hopeless
絶大な	ぜつだいな	enormous, tremendous
*根絶	こんぜつ [する]	exterminate, eradicate
絶*滅	ぜつめつ [する]	vi. vt. become extinct, exterminate
絶えず	たえず	continuously, incessantly, all the time
絶える	たえる	become extinct
絶やす	たやす	run out of, exhaust
絶つ	たつ	stop/abstain from (drinking, smoking, etc.)

735 総

▶そう

1000
cf. 統

14 〈 幺 幺 幺 糸 糸 糸 糸 紵 紵
紵 総 総 総

総合的な	そうごうてきな	comprehensive
総計	そうけい	grand total [する] total
総会	そうかい	general meeting
国内総生産	こくないそうせいさん	gross domestic product, GDP
総理大*臣	そうりだいじん	prime minister

736 為

▶い

9 丶 ソ ⺈ ⺹ 为 為 為 為 為

行為	こうい	act, deed, behavior, conduct
人為的な	じんいてきな	artificial
無作為	むさくい	random (sampling)
◇ 為政者	いせいしゃ	statesman, ruler
為替相場	△かわせそうば	exchange rate
為替レート	△かわせレート	exchange rate
為替	△かわせ	currency

737 老

▶ろう
▷お（いる），ふ（ける）

6 一 十 土 耂 耂 老

老人	ろうじん	an old person
長老	ちょうろう	(a village, etc.) elder
歴 老子	ろうし	Laozi
老ける	ふける	grow old (in terms of appearance)
老いる	おいる	grow old

738 孝

▶こう

7 一 十 土 耂 耂 考 孝

親孝行	おやこうこう	filial piety [する] be filial to one's parents
親不孝	おやふこう	lack of filial piety

第 53 回

739 才

▶さい

3 一 十 才

～才	～さい	～ years old cf. 歳（さい），rather than 才, is normally used
天才	てんさい	genius
才能	さいのう	talent, gift, ability
多才な	たさいな	versatile (person)

740 材

▶ざい

7 　一　十　オ　木　木　村　材

材料	ざいりょう	materials
教材	きょうざい	study materials
取材	しゅざい	[する] collect/gather (news materials, data, etc.)
題材	だいざい	theme, subject matter
材木	ざいもく	lumber, timber
木材	もくざい	wood
新素材	しんそざい	new materials

741 財 ▶ざい，さい

10 　｜　冂　円　月　日　目　貝　貝　貝ー　貯　財

財産	ざいさん	assets, property
財政	ざいせい	finances, financial affairs
財界	ざいかい	the business world
財務省	ざいむしょう	Ministry of Finance Japan
財団	ざいだん	foundation
文化財	ぶんかざい	cultural asset
財*布	さいふ	wallet, pocketbook

742 貯 ▶ちょ

12 　｜　冂　円　月　日　目　貝　貝　貝'　貝'　貯　貯貯

貯金	ちょきん	savings, a deposit [する] vi. save money
貯水池	ちょすいち	reservoir
貯*蔵	ちょぞう	[する] store

743 蓄 ▶ちく ▷たくわ（える） 1274 cf. 畜

13 　一　十　艹　艹　芊　芊　荃　荃　莕蓄蓄

貯蓄	ちょちく	savings [する] vi. save (money)
備蓄	びちく	[する] store/save (something for an emergency)
蓄*積	ちくせき	[する] accumulate
蓄える	たくわえる	store, save, reserve

744 氏 ▶し ▷うじ

4 　ノ　亡　ビ　氏

氏名	しめい	(person's) full name
～氏	～し	～ Mr./Ms. ～
[歴] 氏神	うじがみ	local guardian deity

745 底 ▶てい ▷そこ

8 　ヽ　亠　广　广　庐　庐　底底

海底	かいてい	bottom of the sea
*根底	こんてい	basis, foundation, bottom [abstract]
底	そこ	bottom
◇ 底値	そこね	(rock-)bottom price

746 抵 ▶てい

8 　一　十　扌　扌'　扒　抂　抵抵

抵抗	ていこう	[する] resist
大抵	たいてい	generally, usually
抵当	ていとう	a mortgage
抵*触	ていしょく	[する] conflict (with), be against (the law, etc.)

747 抗 ▶こう 1925 cf. 坑

7 　一　十　扌　扌'　扩　扩　抗

抵抗	ていこう	[する] resist
反抗	はんこう	[する] oppose, disobey
反抗的な	はんこうてきな	rebellious
抗議	こうぎ	[する] protest, object
◇ 抗争	こうそう	struggle, rivalry
抗ガン*剤	こうガンざい	anticancer drug

748 接 ▶せつ ▷つ（ぐ）

11 　一　十　扌　扌'　扩　扩　护　护接接接

第3水準

117

直接	ちょくせつ	direct, directly
間接的に	かんせつてきに	indirectly
面接	めんせつ	[する] interview
接近	せっきん	[する] approach
接続	せつぞく	[する] connect
接待	せったい	[する] entertain (usually for business clients)
◇ 接ぐ	つぐ	join together

749 換 ▶かん
▷か（える），か（わる）

12 一 十 扌 扌 扩 扩 护 护 捣 換 換 換

乗り換える	のりかえる	transfer (to another train, bus, etc.)
交換	こうかん	[する] exchange, replace
変換	へんかん	[する] change, convert
転換期	てんかんき	a turning point, a transition
換気	かんき	[する] ventilate
換算	かんさん，かんざん	[する] convert (from one currency to another)

第 54 回

750 条 ▶じょう

7 ノ ク 夂 冬 冬 条 条

条約	じょうやく	treaty
条文	じょうぶん	text/provisions (of legal documents, treaties, etc.)
第～条	だい～じょう	Article # ～
*憲法第九条	けんぽうだいきゅうじょう	Article 9 of the (Japanese) Constitution
条件	じょうけん	condition
信条	しんじょう	belief, principle

751 契 ▶けい
▷ちぎ（る）

9 一 十 キ キ 契 契 契 契 契

契約	けいやく	[する] sign a contract
契機	けいき	opportunity, (serve as an) impetus
[歴] 契る	ちぎる	pledge (one's love, etc.)

752 喫 ▶きつ

12 丨 口 口 口 叩 呫 咭 唖 啺 喫
喫 喫

喫茶店	きっさてん	coffee shop
喫*煙	きつえん	[する] smoke
満喫	まんきつ	[する] enjoy fully

753 潔 ▶けつ
▷いさぎよ（い）

15 丶 冫 氵 氵 汁 汼 渎 潔 潔 潔
潔 潔 潔 潔 潔

清潔な	せいけつな	clean, neat
不潔な	ふけつな	unclean, dirty, filthy
潔白	けっぱく	innocence
潔い	いさぎよい	graceful, sportsmanlike

754 清 ▶せい，しょう
▷きよ（い），きよ（まる），きよ（める）

11 丶 冫 氵 汀 汁 汢 浐 清 清 清
清

清潔な	せいけつな	clean, neat
清書	せいしょ	[する] make a clean copy
清算	せいさん	[する] liquidate, settle, clear (a debt), atone for
清涼飲料（水）	せいりょういんりょう（すい）	refreshing beverage, soft drink
清水	△しみず	spring water
清水寺	きよみずでら	Kiyomizu Temple (in Kyoto)
清い	きよい	pure, clean
清める	きよめる	purify, cleanse
[特] 六*根清*浄	ろっこんしょうじょう	be completely purified

755 士 ▶し

3 一 十 士

会計士	かいけいし	licensed accountant
税理士	ぜいりし	licensed tax accountant
代議士	だいぎし	Diet member

学士	がくし	bachelor's degree holder
学士号	がくしごう	bachelor's degree
弁*護士	べんごし	lawyer
歴*武士	ぶし	warrior (in medieval Japan), samurai

---

756 志 ▶し
▷こころざ(す)，こころざし

7 一 十 士 士 志 志 志

意志	いし	will, volition
有志	ゆうし	a volunteer, a supporter, someone who is interested
同志	どうし	like-minded people
志向	しこう	orientation, inclination 〔する〕intend, aim at
志す	こころざす	aspire (to do or become)
志	こころざし	one's will, ambition

---

757 恩 ▶おん

10 丨 冂 冃 円 因 因 凩 恩 恩 恩

恩	おん	favor, debt of gratitude
恩人	おんじん	benefactor
恩返し	おんがえし	〔する〕repay a person's kindness
恩知らず	おんしらず	ingrate
恩給	おんきゅう	pension
恩*師	おんし	respected former teacher

---

758 忠 ▶ちゅう

1367
cf. 患

8 丨 冂 口 中 忠 忠 忠 忠

忠実な	ちゅうじつな	loyal, faithful
忠*告	ちゅうこく	〔する〕advise
忠*誠	ちゅうせい	loyalty

---

759 恐 ▶きょう
▷おそ(れる)，おそ(ろしい)

10 一 丁 エ 刃 巩 巩 巩 恐 恐 恐

| 恐ろしい | おそろしい | terrible, scary |
| 恐れる | おそれる | fear |

恐*縮	きょうしゅく	feel obliged, be very grateful, be sorry
恐*怖	きょうふ	fear, terror, horror
恐*慌	きょうこう	panic (in the stock market, etc.)

第 55 回

760 翻 ▶ほん
▷ひるがえ(る)，ひるがえ(す)

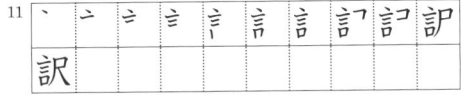

翻訳	ほんやく	〔する〕translate
翻案	ほんあん	〔する〕adapt (from novel/etc.)
◇ 翻意	ほんい	〔する〕change one's mind
翻す	ひるがえす	turn (one's body) around quickly, change (one's mind)
翻る	ひるがえる	flutter, wave, fly (as in flag movements)

---

761 訳 ▶やく
▷わけ

11 丶 亠 亍 言 言 言 訂 訂 訳
訳

通訳	つうやく	interpretation, an interpreter 〔する〕interpret (speech, etc.)
訳	やく	a translation
英訳	えいやく	English translation 〔する〕translate into English
和訳	わやく	Japanese translation 〔する〕translate into Japanese
訳者	やくしゃ	translator
訳す	やくす	translate
訳	わけ	reason, cause
言い訳	いいわけ	〔する〕excuse
申し訳	もうしわけ	apology
申し訳ない	もうしわけない	be very sorry, apologize for

---

762 尺 ▶しゃく

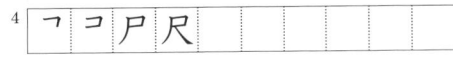

| 尺度 | しゃくど | measure, criterion |
| 尺 | しゃく | *shaku* (unit of length, approx. 30.3 cm) |

第3水準

763 釈 ▶しゃく

11 一 ⺥ ⺫ ⽶ ⺤ 采 釈 釈 釈 釈

解釈	かいしゃく	interpretation [する] interpret (a text/etc.)
注釈	ちゅうしゃく	[する] annotate
釈明	しゃくめい	[する] explain, offer clarification
釈放	しゃくほう	[する] release (a suspect/etc.)
保釈	ほしゃく	bail [する] release on bail

764 択 ▶たく

7 一 十 扌 扩 护 护 択

選択	せんたく	[する] select, choose
選択科目	せんたくかもく	elective (subject), optional (subject)
二者択一	にしゃたくいつ	either-or, alternative
*採択	さいたく	[する] adopt (a proposal/a bill/act, etc.)

765 描 ▶びょう ▷えが(く), か(く)

11 一 十 扌 扌 扩 扩 扩 措 描 描 描

描写	びょうしゃ	[する] describe, depict
心理描写	しんりびょうしゃ	a psychological description
描く	えがく	describe, draw, paint, sketch, depict
描く	かく	draw, paint

766 拝 ▶はい ▷おが(む)

8 一 十 扌 扌 扩 拝 拝 拝

拝見	はいけん	[する] see, have a look at [humble]
参拝	さんぱい	[する] go and worship (at a shrine/temple)
参拝者	さんぱいしゃ	visitor (to a shrine/temple)
*礼拝	れいはい	church service [する] worship
拝*啓	はいけい	Dear Sir, Dear Madam (opening word for letters)
拝む	おがむ	pray, worship

767 提 ▶てい ▷さ(げる) 1852 1670 cf. 堤 是

12 一 十 扌 扌 扩 护 押 押 押 捍 捍 提

提案	ていあん	[する] propose, suggest
提出	ていしゅつ	[する] present, submit
前提	ぜんてい	premise
提供	ていきょう	an offer, sponsorship [する] offer, furnish, supply, provide, sponsor (a television program, etc.)
提げる	さげる	carry in one's hand

768 拡 ▶かく

8 一 十 扌 扩 扩 扩 拡 拡

拡大	かくだい	[する] expand, enlarge
拡散	かくさん	[する] diffuse
拡声器	かくせいき	loudspeaker
拡*張	かくちょう	[する] extend, expand
拡*充	かくじゅう	[する] expand, enlarge, amplify

769 抜 ▶ばつ ▷ぬ(く), ぬ(ける), ぬ(かす), ぬ(かる)

7 一 十 扌 扩 扩 抜 抜

抜群の	ばつぐんの	outstanding, distinguished (performance)
選抜	せんばつ	[する] select, pick out
抜く	ぬく	pull out, pass/surpass

第 56 回

770 振 ▶しん ▷ふ(る), ふ(るう), ふ(れる)

10 一 十 扌 扩 扩 护 拆 拆 振 振

振動	しんどう	[する] vibrate, swing, oscillate
三振	さんしん	[する] be struck out
振興	しんこう	[する] promote
振る	ふる	wave, shake (one's head)
振れる	ふれる	vi. shake, swing
振り返る	ふりかえる	look back

振る*舞う　ふるまう　behave, act

振り*仮名△ふりがな　*kana* that are used to show the reading of *kanji*

771 打
▶だ
▷う(つ)

5　一　十　扌　扩　打

打つ　うつ　hit, strike, slap

打ち合わせ　うちあわせ　(prior) arrangement, a meeting

打ち消す　うちけす　deny

打算的な　ださんてきな　calculating, selfish

打開　だかい　-する achieve a breakthrough, resolve (a situation)

打*撃　だげき　blow, shock, batting

772 折
▶せつ
▷お(る)，おり，お(れる)

7　一　十　扌　扌　扩　扩　折

折る　おる　fold, bend, break

折り紙　おりがみ　origami, paper for origami

折　おり　occasion, opportunity

右折　うせつ　-する turn right

左折　させつ　-する turn left

折半　せっぱん　-する (literally) divide into halves, split (the cost 50-50)

773 採
▶さい
▷と(る)

11　一　十　扌　扌　扩　扩　扩　押　採
採

採用　さいよう　-する adopt, employ

採決　さいけつ　-する vote, take a vote

採集　さいしゅう　-する collect (butterflies, etc.)

採算　さいさん　profit, pay (as in hard work pays, but crime doesn't pay)

採点　さいてん　-する grade (exams, etc.)

採る　とる　employ, collect, adopt

774 菜
▶さい
▷な

11　一　十　艹　艹　艼　艼　莯　荽　菜
菜

野菜　やさい　vegetables

菜食主義　さいしょくしゅぎ　vegetarianism

菜園　さいえん　vegetable garden

山菜　さんさい　edible wild plants

菜の花　なのはな　rape blossoms

青菜　あおな　green vegetables

775 指
▶し
▷ゆび，さ(す)

9　一　十　扌　扌　扩　扞　指　指　指

指　ゆび　fingers, toes

親指　おやゆび　thumb　cf. 人差し指(ひとさしゆび)，中指(なかゆび)，薬指(くすりゆび)，小指(こゆび)

指輪　ゆびわ　(finger) ring

指導　しどう　-する lead, guide, instruct

指導員　しどういん　instructor

指名　しめい　-する nominate, designate

指定席　していせき　reserved seat (in a train)　cf. 予約席(よやくせき) reserved seat (in a restaurant)

指*示　しじ　-する direct, instruct

指す　さす　point to, indicate

目指す　めざす　aim at, head for

776 揮
▶き

12　一　十　扌　扌　扩　护　护　拐　揎
揎　揮

指揮　しき　-する conduct, command

指揮者　しきしゃ　conductor (of an orchestra)

発揮　はっき　-する display (one's power, potential, etc.), show

777 輝
▶き
▷かがや(く)

15　丨　刂　屮　屮　屮　光　光　炉　炉　炉
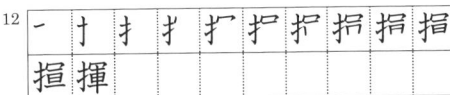
炉　炉　焙　焙　輝

輝く	かがやく	shine, glitter
輝かしい	かがやかしい	splendid, brilliant
輝き	かがやき	brilliance, radiance, a shine, glitter
特 光輝	こうき	brilliance, luster

778 軍 ▶ぐん

9 丨 冖 冖 冖 冒 冒 軍 軍

軍隊	ぐんたい	military, armed forces
*陸軍	りくぐん	army
空軍	くうぐん	air force
海軍	かいぐん	navy
軍人	ぐんじん	service (wo)man
軍	ぐん	military, troops
十字軍	じゅうじぐん	the Crusades
軍国主義	ぐんこくしゅぎ	militarism

779 隊 ▶たい

12 ヌ 3 阝 阝 阝' 阡 阡 阽 阽 隊 隊

軍隊	ぐんたい	military, armed forces
部隊	ぶたい	a squad
隊	たい	a group of soldiers (squad, flotilla, etc.)
隊長	たいちょう	commander, captain, leader, chief

第 57 回

780 衛 ▶えい

16 ノ ク イ イ 彳 彳 彳 併 併 彳 彳 衛 衛 衛 衛

自衛隊	じえいたい	the Self-Defense Forces (of Japan)
衛星	えいせい	satellite
衛生	えいせい	hygiene, sanitation

781 防 ▶ぼう ▷ふせ(ぐ)

7 ヌ 3 阝 阝' 阽 防 防

防衛

防衛	ほうえい	する defend
防衛省	ほうえいしょう	Ministry of Defense (of Japan)
国防省	こくぼうしょう	the Department of Defense
国防総省	こくぼうそうしょう	the Department of Defense (of the U.S.)
防止	ぼうし	する prevent, hold in check
予防	よぼう	する prevent, protect against, take precautions
消防車	しょうぼうしゃ	fire engine
防火*訓練	ぼうかくんれん	fire drill
防ぐ	ふせぐ	prevent, defend

782 坊 ▶ぼう, ぼっ

7 一 十 土 圵 圷 坊 坊

お坊さん	おぼうさん	Buddhist priest
坊主	ぼうず	Buddhist priest, shaven head, boy
赤ん坊	あかんぼう	baby
坊ちゃん	ぼっちゃん	(your/his/her) son, boy [honorific]
坊や	ぼうや	son, boy [polite]
朝寝坊	あさねぼう	する oversleep in the morning, sleep late

783 訪 ▶ほう ▷おとず(れる), たず(ねる)

11 ` ㇒ ㇒ ㇒ 言 言 言 言 訁 訪 訪

訪問	ほうもん	する visit
訪米	ほうべい	する visit the U.S.
訪ねる	たずねる	visit
訪れる	おとずれる	visit (a place)

784 妨 ▶ぼう ▷さまた(げる)

7 ㇚ 女 女 女' 圹 妨 妨

妨害	ぼうがい	する obstruct, hinder
妨げる	さまたげる	obstruct, hinder

785 害 ▶がい

10 ′ 宀 宀 宀 宀 宀 宀 害 害 害

損害	そんがい	damage, loss
公害	こうがい	environmental pollution, a public hazard
水害	すいがい	a flood, flood damage
利害	りがい	interests (as in a clash of interests)
*被害	ひがい	damage, harm, injury

786 割 ▶かつ
▷わ(る), わり, わ(れる), さ(く)

12 ′ 宀 宀 宀 宀 宀 宀 害 害
割 割

割る	わる	divide, split, break
割合	わりあい	ratio, proportion
割引	わりびき	[する] discount
二割引(き)	にわりびき	20% discount
時間割	じかんわり	class schedule
役割	やくわり	role, part
割り算	わりざん	division (in mathematics)
分割	ぶんかつ	[する] divide
割く	さく	spare (some time, money, etc.) (for someone/something), tear, split

787 憲 ▶けん

16 ′ 宀 宀 宀 宀 宀 宀 害 害
宀 宀 宀 憲 憲 憲

憲法	けんぽう	constitution
憲法改正	けんぽうかいせい	revision/amendment of the constitution, abbreviated as 改憲
改憲	かいけん	[する] revise the constitution
違憲	いけん	unconstitutional
立憲政治	りっけんせいじ	constitutional government
立憲*君主制	りっけんくんしゅせい	constitutional monarchy

788 毒 ▶どく

596
cf. 妻

8 一 十 主 主 未 青 青 毒

毒	どく	poison, venom
中毒	ちゅうどく	poisoning, addiction
食中毒	しょくちゅうどく	food-poisoning
消毒	しょうどく	[する] disinfect
有毒な	ゆうどくな	poisonous
気の毒な	きのどくな	pitiable, unfortunate

789 危 ▶き
▷あぶ(ない), あや(うい), あや(ぶむ)

6 ′ ク 厃 产 危 危

危ない	あぶない	dangerous, risky
危険な	きけんな	dangerous, risky
危機	きき	crisis
石油危機	せきゆきき	oil crisis, oil shock
危害	きがい	harm, injury
◇ 危急の	ききゅうの	critical, imminent
危*惧	きぐ	[する] feel misgivings about, be apprehensive about
危うい	あやうい	dangerous
危ぶむ	あやぶむ	have misgivings about

790 険 ▶けん
▷けわ(しい)

11 ′ ⻖ ⻖ ⻖ ⻖ 険 険 険 険
険

危険な	きけんな	dangerous, risky
保険	ほけん	insurance
険悪な	けんあくな	hostile, threatening
*陰険な	いんけんな	sly, sneaky
険しい	けわしい	steep, stern

第 58 回

791 剣 ▶けん
▷つるぎ

10 ′ ⺉ ⺈ 合 合 合 争 食 剣 剣

第3水準

真剣な　　　しんけんな　serious, earnest
剣道　　　　けんどう　*kendō*, (Japanese) fencing
剣　　　　　けん，つるぎ　sword

792 検 ▶けん

12

一	十	才	木	术	杧	朴	杦	栓	栓
栓	検								

点検　　　　てんけん　［する］inspect, check
検*討　　　　けんとう　［する］examine, consider
検定　　　　けんてい　official approval (of school textbooks, etc.)
検証　　　　けんしょう　［する］verify, inspect
検察庁　　　けんさつちょう　Public Prosecutors Office
検事　　　　けんじ　a public prosecutor

793 験 ▶けん，げん

18

1	厂	厂	尸	馬	馬	馬	馬	馬	馬
馭	駼	駼	験	験	験	験	験	馬	

経験　　　　けいけん　［する］experience, go through
体験　　　　たいけん　［する］experience
*試験　　　　しけん　［する］test, experiment
実験　　　　じっけん　［する］experiment
受験　　　　じゅけん　［する］take an exam
特 験　　　　げん　omens

794 騒 ▶そう ▷さわ(ぐ)

18

1	厂	厂	尸	馬	馬	馬	馬	馬	馬
馭	駼	駼	騒	騒	騒	騒	騒		

騒ぐ　　　　さわぐ　be noisy, make a fuss
騒がしい　　さわがしい　noisy, boisterous
大騒ぎ　　　おおさわぎ　uproar, big fuss
騒音　　　　そうおん　noise
騒々しい　　そうぞうしい　noisy, boisterous
物騒な　　　ぶっそうな　dangerous, frightening

795 試 ▶し ▷こころ(みる)，ため(す)

13

、	ー	二	言	言	言	言	言	言	訂
訂	試	試							

試験　　　　しけん　［する］test, experiment
試合　　　　しあい　［する］have a match/game
試食　　　　ししょく　［する］try/taste (food)
試運転　　　しうんてん　［する］make a trial run, test out
試す　　　　ためす　try, test, experiment
試みる　　　こころみる　try, attempt, test

796 式 ▶しき

6

一	二	テ	王	式	式

結婚式　　　けっこんしき　wedding
入学式　　　にゅうがくしき　(school) entrance ceremony
卒業式　　　そつぎょうしき　commencement/graduation ceremony
正式な　　　せいしきな　formal, official
公式の　　　こうしきの　official
方式　　　　ほうしき　system, method
形式　　　　けいしき　a formality, a form
方程式　　　ほうていしき　equation

797 専 ▶せん ▷もっぱ(ら)

9

一	厂	戸	戸	自	由	車	専	専

専門　　　　せんもん　specialty, area of expertise
専門家　　　せんもんか　expert, specialist
専任の　　　せんにんの　full-time (lecturer, instructor, etc.)
専制政治　　せんせいせいじ　autocracy
バス専用レーン　バスせんようレーン　"buses-only" lane
専ら　　　　もっぱら　mainly, chiefly

798 博 ▶はく，ばく

12

一	十	ナ	尸	忖	恒	恒	博	博	博
博	博								

博士	はくし，△はかせ　Ph.D., Doctor
博士号	はくしごう，△はかせごう　doctorate
博士課程	はくしかてい，△はかせかてい　a Ph.D. program
博物館	はくぶつかん　museum
万博	ばんぱく　world exposition　cf. this is an abbreviation of 万国博*覧会(ばんこくはくらんかい)
*賭博	とばく　gambling, gaming

799 薄 ▶はく
▷うす(い)，うす(める)，うす(まる)，うす(らぐ)，うす(れる)
cf. 簿 1684

16　一 十 艹 艹 艹 艹 艹 芦 芦 芦 薄 薄 薄 薄 薄 薄

薄い	うすい　light (color), weak (tea, etc.), thin (book, etc.)
薄暗い	うすぐらい　dim, gloomy
薄める	うすめる　make thin, dilute
薄利多売	はくりたばい　(gaining profit by) selling many items with a small profit margin on each item
薄情な	はくじょうな　heartless, cold-hearted, unfeeling

800 夢 ▶む
▷ゆめ

13　一 十 艹 艹 芍 芍 芍 茜 茜 萝 夢 夢

夢	ゆめ　dream
悪夢	あくむ　nightmare, bad dream
夢中になる	むちゅうになる　be fascinated with, be crazy about

801 葬 ▶そう
▷ほうむ(る)

12　一 十 艹 艹 芦 芍 芗 芗 莚 莚 葬

葬式	そうしき　funeral
葬*儀	そうぎ　funeral
火葬	かそう　する cremate
土葬	どそう　する bury (a dead body)
◇ *副葬品	ふくそうひん　items buried with the dead
葬る	ほうむる　bury (a dead person)

802 蒸 ▶じょう
▷む(す)，む(れる)，む(らす)

13　一 十 艹 艹 芽 芽 芽 茏 莁 莁 蒸 蒸 蒸

蒸気	じょうき　steam
蒸気船	じょうきせん　steamboat
水蒸気	すいじょうき　steam, water vapor
蒸し暑い	むしあつい　muggy
蒸す	むす　steam, be muggy
蒸れる	むれる　become stuffy
蒸らす	むらす　steam (rice, etc.)

第 59 回

803 確 ▶かく
▷たし(か)，たし(かめる)

15　一 丆 丆 石 石 石 矿 矿 矿 矿 矿 硝 碲 確 確

正確な	せいかくな　exact, precise
確実な	かくじつな　certain, sure
確率	かくりつ　probability
確信	かくしん　する believe firmly, be sure of, be convinced that
確かな	たしかな　certain, definite
確かめる	たしかめる　make sure

804 権 ▶けん，ごん

15　一 十 才 木 木 柠 柠 柠 柠 栌 栌 栌 権 権

権利	けんり　right, claim
人権	じんけん　human rights
特権	とっけん　a privilege
権力	けんりょく　power, authority
主権	しゅけん　sovereignty
三権分立	さんけんぶんりつ　the separation of powers
有権者	ゆうけんしゃ　voter(s)
◇ 権化	ごんげ　incarnation

805 観 ▶かん

18 ノ ⺊ ⺕ ⺉ ⺊ 午 午 年 年 隹
隹 奞 奞 観 観 観 観 観

観光	かんこう	[する] go sightseeing
観客	かんきゃく	spectator, audience
観点	かんてん	point of view
外観	がいかん	appearance
主観的な	しゅかんてきな	subjective
客観的な	きゃっかんてきな	objective
楽観的な	らっかんてきな	optimistic
悲観的な	ひかんてきな	pessimistic
人生観	じんせいかん	one's view of life
世界観	せかいかん	one's view of the world

806 視 ▶し

11 ヽ ⺈ ネ ネ ネ ネ 初 初 初 視
視

無視	むし	[する] ignore, disregard
重視	じゅうし	[する] attach importance to
視野	しや	field of vision
視界	しかい	range of vision
視力	しりょく	eyesight, vision, sight
近視	きんし	near-sightedness
視察	しさつ	[する] visit to observe/inspect
*監視	かんし	[する] watch, keep watch over, surveillance

807 規 ▶き

11 一 二 ナ 夫 知 扣 扣 抑 相 抑
規

規則	きそく	rule, regulation
規則的な	きそくてきな	regular
不規則な	ふきそくな	irregular
規定	きてい	rules, regulations [する] prescribe, stipulate
定規	じょうぎ	ruler, measure
規準	きじゅん	criterion, standard

808 則 ▶そく

9 丨 冂 冂 冃 目 目 貝 則 則

規則	きそく	rule, regulation
法則	ほうそく	laws (of nature, etc.)
原則	げんそく	principle
変則的な	へんそくてきな	irregular
校則	こうそく	school regulations
会則	かいそく	rules of a society

809 側 ▶そく ▷がわ

11 ノ イ 亻 仍 仍 但 但 但 倶 側
側

右側	みぎがわ	right-hand side
左側	ひだりがわ	left-hand side
反対側	はんたいがわ	the opposite side
両側	りょうがわ	both sides
側面	そくめん	side, aspect
側近	そっきん	close aide/associate

漢字の形に気をつけましょう㉓

719	718	808	809	810
貝	敗	則	側	測
海岸で貝を拾う	失敗と成功	規則を守る	右側を歩く	水質を測定する

810 測

▶そく
▷はか（る）

12　丶　氵　氵　氵　沪　沪　沪　沪　沪　淠
測　測

予測	よそく	[する] predict, forecast
観測	かんそく	[する] observe
測定	そくてい	[する] measure
測る	はかる	measure

811 例

▶れい
▷たと（える）

8　ノ　イ　イ　仃　仍　伤　例　例

例	れい	example, instance
前例	ぜんれい	precedent
例外	れいがい	exception
特例	とくれい	special case, exception
例年	れいねん	every year, (in an) average year, (in a) normal year
例えば	たとえば	for example
例える	たとえる	liken to, compare

812 列

▶れつ

6　一　ア　歹　夕　列　列

列	れつ	a line/row (of people, cars, etc.)
列車	れっしゃ	a train
夜行列車	やこうれっしゃ	night train
日本列島	にほんれっとう	the Japanese Archipelago
行列	ぎょうれつ	column [する] line up

813 殊

▶しゅ
▷こと

10　一　ア　歹　夕　歺　歼　殀　殊　殊

| 特殊な | とくしゅな | special, peculiar |
| 殊に | ことに | especially, particularly |

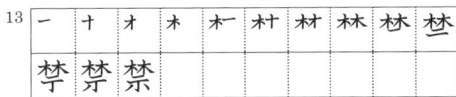

第 60 回

814 示

▶じ, し
▷しめ（す）

5　一　二　亍　示　示

指示	しじ	[する] direct, instruct
明示	めいじ	[する] state/specify clearly
暗示	あんじ	[する] hint, suggest
公示	こうじ	[する] announce publicly
*掲示	けいじ	a notice [する] put up a notice
*掲示*板	けいじばん	bulletin board
示*唆	しさ	[する] suggest, hint at
示す	しめす	show, display

815 禁

▶きん

13　一　十　オ　木　木　村　材　林　林　埜
埜　禁　禁

禁止	きんし	[する] forbid, prohibit, ban
立入禁止	たちいりきんし	No Trespassing, Do Not Enter
発禁	はっきん	ban on publication
禁じる	きんじる	forbid, prohibit
禁*煙	きんえん	No Smoking [する] give up smoking

816 宗

▶しゅう, そう

8　丶　丷　宀　宀　宀　宗　宗　宗

宗教	しゅうきょう	religion
改宗	かいしゅう	[する] be converted (in a religious sense)
[特] 宗家	そうけ	the head family, the originator (of a sect)

817 完

▶かん

7　丶　丷　宀　宀　宀　宇　完

完成	かんせい	[する] complete
未完成の	みかんせいの	incomplete
完全な	かんぜんな	perfect
完敗	かんぱい	[する] be totally defeated

第3水準

127

818 了 ▶りょう

2 一 了

終了	しゅうりょう -する finish, end
完了	かんりょう -する complete
任期満了	にんきまんりょう the expiration of a term in office
了解	りょうかい -する understand, consent, agree

819 承 ▶しょう ▷うけたまわ（る）

8 一 了 了 手 手 承 承 承

承認	しょうにん -する approve
承知	しょうち -する consent to, agree to accept
了承	りょうしょう -する acknowledge
伝承	でんしょう oral tradition -する transmit by word of mouth
承る	うけたまわる hear, be told [humble]

820 浮 ▶ふ ▷う（く），う（かれる），う（かぶ），う（かべる）

10 丶 冫 氵 氵 泛 泛 浮 浮 浮 浮

浮く	うく float
浮世絵	うきよえ *ukiyoe*
浮力	ふりょく buoyancy
浮気	△うわき -する have an affair with
浮かぶ	うかぶ float, rise to the surface, cross one's mind
浮かべる	うかべる set afloat, put ~ on one's face

821 乳 ▶にゅう ▷ちち，ち

8 一 乊 乊 乊 母 虿 乳 乳

牛乳	ぎゅうにゅう milk
母乳	ぼにゅう mother's milk
乳首	ちくび nipple
◇ 乳母車	△うばぐるま baby carriage
乳	ちち milk, breasts

822 礼 ▶れい，らい

984
cf. 札

5 丶 ラ ネ ネ 礼

お礼	おれい gratitude, thanks
失礼な	しつれいな impolite, rude
無礼な	ぶれいな rude
礼拝	れいはい，らいはい church service, worship -する worship
礼*儀	れいぎ etiquette, good manners

823 祈 ▶き ▷いの（る）

8 丶 ラ ネ ネ ネ 祈 祈 祈

祈る	いのる pray
（お）祈り	（お）いのり prayer
祈*願	きがん -する pray

824 祖 ▶そ

9 丶 ラ ネ ネ 礼 礽 衵 衵 祖

祖父	そふ grandfather cf. お祖父さん（▲おじいさん）[polite]
祖母	そぼ grandmother cf. お祖母さん（▲おばあさん）[polite]
祖先	そせん ancestor(s), forebears
先祖	せんぞ ancestor, ancestry

第 61 回

825 査 ▶さ

9 一 十 才 木 木 杏 杏 杳 査

調査	ちょうさ -する investigate
検査	けんさ -する examine, inspect

826 助 ▶じょ ▷たす（ける），たす（かる），すけ

7 丨 冂 月 月 且 助 助

助ける	たすける help, assist, rescue

助かる　　　たすかる　　be helped, assisted, rescued
助け合う　　たすけあう　　help each other
助手　　　　じょしゅ　　assistant, helper
助言　　　　じょげん　　-する advise
助力　　　　じょりょく　　assistance, aid
*援助　　　　えんじょ　　-する help, assist, aid
特 助六　　　すけろく　　name of a famous character in Kabuki drama

827 努　▶ど
▷つと(める)　　　　　　　　255　1871
cf. 怒　奴

7　く　タ　タ　夕刀　奴　努　努

努力　　　　どりょく　　-する make efforts
努力家　　　どりょくか　　hard worker
努める　　　つとめる　　exert oneself

828 収　▶しゅう
▷おさ(める)，おさ(まる)

4　丨　乢　収　収

収入　　　　しゅうにゅう　　income, revenue
買収　　　　ばいしゅう　　-する buy up, purchase, bribe
貿易収支　　ぼうえきしゅうし　　trade balance
収*益　　　　しゅうえき　　profit, gains
収*容　　　　しゅうよう　　-する accommodate
収支決算　　しゅうしけっさん　　settlement of accounts
収める　　　おさめる　　obtain (profit, etc.), gain (a good result, etc.)
収まる　　　おさまる　　be put (back) in place, settle down, calm down

829 状　▶じょう

7　丨　丬　丬　丬　丬　状　状

状態　　　　じょうたい　　state, condition
現状　　　　げんじょう　　present circumstances, present conditions
招待状　　　しょうたいじょう　　invitation
(お)礼状　　(お)れいじょう　　thank-you letter

830 将　▶しょう

10　丨　丬　丬　扩　折　肸　护　护　将　将

将来　　　　しょうらい　　(in the) future
将軍　　　　しょうぐん　　shogun, general
将校　　　　しょうこう　　military officer
将*棋　　　　しょうぎ　　*shōgi*, Japanese chess

831 奨　▶しょう

13　丨　丬　丬　扩　折　折　肸　护　护　将
将　奨　奨

奨学金　　　しょうがくきん　　scholarship
奨学生　　　しょうがくせい　　student on scholarship
奨励　　　　しょうれい　　-する encourage, promote

832 励　▶れい
▷はげ(む)，はげ(ます)

7　一　厂　厈　厉　厉　励　励

奨励　　　　しょうれい　　-する encourage, promote
◇ 励行　　　　れいこう　　-する observe strictly
励む　　　　はげむ　　do diligently
励み　　　　はげみ　　encouragement
励ます　　　はげます　　encourage, cheer up

833 陸　▶りく

11　フ　3　阝　阝一　阝十　阡　阡　阦　陆　陸
陸

大陸　　　　たいりく　　a continent
陸　　　　　りく　　land, the shore
陸地　　　　りくち　　land
上陸　　　　じょうりく　　-する land, go ashore
陸軍　　　　りくぐん　　army

834 陽 ▶よう

12 ｀ 3 3 β 3¬ 3Π 3ϰ 3ϭ 3ϭ 陽
陽 陽

太陽　　　　たいよう　the sun
陽気な　　　ようきな　cheerful, merry
◇ 陽光　　　　ようこう　sunlight
陽子　　　　ようし　proton

835 傷 ▶しょう
▷きず, いた(む), いた(める)

13 ノ イ イ´ 仁 仁 仵 侮 侮 傴 傴
傷 傷 傷

傷　　　　　きず　injury (e.g., a cut)
無傷の　　　むきずの　uninjured
負傷　　　　ふしょう　[する] be injured, be wounded
重傷　　　　じゅうしょう　serious injury
軽傷　　　　けいしょう　slight injury
死傷者　　　ししょうしゃ　casualties
傷害事件　　しょうがいじけん　incident involving bodily injury
中傷　　　　ちゅうしょう　[する] slander
傷む　　　　いたむ　be damaged, be worn out, rot, go bad

第 62 回

836 湯 ▶とう
▷ゆ

12 ｀ ｀ ｀ ｀ ｀ ｀ ｀ 湯 湯 湯
湯 湯

湯　　　　　ゆ　hot water
湯ぶね　　　ゆぶね　bathtub

湯元　　　　ゆもと　the source of a hot spring
茶の湯　　　ちゃのゆ　tea ceremony
湯気　　　　ゆげ　steam, vapor
湯飲み　　　ゆのみ　cup (for drinking tea)
*熱湯　　　　ねっとう　boiling water
◇ 湯治　　　　とうじ　hot-spring cure [する] bathe in a hot spring as a remedy

837 混 ▶こん
▷ま(じる), ま(ざる), ま(ぜる), こ(む)　　cf. 昆 1859

11 ｀ ｀ ｀ ｀ ｀ ｀ ｀ ｀ ｀ 混
混

混雑　　　　こんざつ　[する] be crowded, be congested
混*乱　　　　こんらん　[する] be confused, be thrown into confusion
混合　　　　こんごう　[する] mix, blend
混同　　　　こんどう　[する] confuse, mix up
混ぜる　　　まぜる　mix, blend
かき混ぜる　かきまぜる　mix together, stir up
混む　　　　こむ　be crowded

838 湿 ▶しつ
▷しめ(る), しめ(す)

12 ｀ ｀ ｀ ｀ ｀ ｀ ｀ ｀ ｀ 湿
湿 湿

湿度　　　　しつど　humidity
湿気　　　　しっけ　moisture, humidity
◇ 湿*布　　　　しっぷ　(cold/hot) compress [する] apply a compress
湿る　　　　しめる　become damp

漢字の形に気をつけましょう㉔

335	834	836	1481	835
場	陽	湯	*揚	傷
入場券	太陽と月	茶の湯	気持ちが高*揚する こう よう	重傷を負う

839 温

▶おん
▷あたた(か)，あたた(かい)，あたた(まる)，あたた(める)

12　丶 氵 氵 氵 沪 沪 沪 浬 温 温
温 温

温度	おんど	temperature
気温	きおん	air temperature
水温	すいおん	water temperature
体温	たいおん	body temperature
温室	おんしつ	greenhouse
温和な	おんわな	gentle, mild
温かい	あたたかい	warm　cf. 温かい is used for things warm to the touch, whereas 暖かい is used for air temperature
温める	あたためる	warm (up) something

840 泉

▶せん
▷いずみ

9　丶 丆 宀 白 白 自 身 身 泉

| 温泉 | おんせん | hot spring, spa |
| 泉 | いずみ | a spring, fountain |

841 線

▶せん

15　く 纟 纟 糸 糸 糸 糸 糽 紟 紳
紳 紳 綧 線 線

線	せん	a line
直線	ちょくせん	straight line
曲線	きょくせん	curve, curved line
下線	かせん	underline
地平線	ちへいせん	the horizon
水平線	すいへいせん	horizontal line, the horizon
線路	せんろ	railway track/line
電線	でんせん	electric wire
無線	むせん	wireless, radio
内線	ないせん	telephone extension
赤外線	せきがいせん	infrared light/ray

842 雪

▶せつ
▷ゆき

11　一 厂 宀 示 示 示 示 雪 雪 雪
雪

雪	ゆき	snow
初雪	はつゆき	the first snowfall of the season
雪祭り	ゆきまつり	snow festival
大雪	おおゆき	heavy snow
新雪	しんせつ	fresh snow
*積雪	せきせつ	accumulated snow
*除雪	じょせつ	[-する] remove snow
吹雪	△ふぶき	snowstorm, blizzard

843 雷

▶らい
▷かみなり

13　一 厂 宀 示 示 示 示 示 雫 雫
雫 雫 雷

雷	かみなり	thunder
雷雨	らいう	thunderstorm
雷鳴	らいめい	thunderclap
落雷	らくらい	lightning strike　[-する] be struck by lightning
地雷	じらい	(land) mine
魚雷	ぎょらい	torpedo

844 雲

▶うん
▷くも

12　一 厂 宀 示 示 示 示 示 示 雫
雲 雲

雲	くも	cloud
雨雲	あまぐも	rain cloud
暗雲	あんうん	dark clouds

[歴] 出雲大社　△いずもたいしゃ　Izumo Shrine

845 霧

▶む
▷きり

19　一 厂 宀 示 示 示 示 示 示 雫
雫 雫 霚 霚 霚 霧 霧 霧

霧	きり	fog, mist
霧雨	きりさめ	drizzle
濃霧	のうむ	dense fog

846 露 ▶ろ, ろう
▷つゆ

21 一 ア 戸 币 币 币 雫 雫 雫 雫 雫 雫 雫 雫 雫 霄 霄 霞 露 露
露

露店　　　ろてん　　street stall
露天*風呂　ろてんぶろ　open-air bath
露天　　　ろてん　　open air
露出　　　ろしゅつ　-する expose
*暴露　　　ばくろ　　-する bring to light, expose, disclose
*披露*宴　　ひろうえん　(wedding) reception, banquet
露　　　　つゆ　　dew
夜露　　　よつゆ　　evening dew

847 震 ▶しん
▷ふる(う), ふる(える)
cf. 農 626

15 一 ア 戸 币 币 币 雫 雫 雫 雫 雫 雫 雫 雫 震

地震　　　じしん　　earthquake
震度　　　しんど　　seismic intensity (e.g., 震度4の地震 earthquake of the 4th degree on the Japanese seismic scale)
震動　　　しんどう　-する vibrate, shake
震*源地　　しんげんち　epicenter
震える　　ふるえる　tremble
特 震う　　　ふるう　　shake

第 63 回

848 厚 ▶こう
▷あつ(い)

9 一 厂 厂 厈 戶 戶 厚 厚 厚

厚い　　　あつい　　thick, warmhearted
厚かましい　あつかましい　shameless, impudent
厚生労働省　こうせいろうどうしょう　Ministry of Health, Labour and Welfare

849 宴 ▶えん

10 ' 宀 宀 宀 宀 宀 宴 宴 宴

宴会　　　えんかい　dinner party, banquet
特 酒宴　　　しゅえん　feast

850 宣 ▶せん
cf. 宜 1658

9 ' 宀 宀 宀 宀 宀 宣 宣

宣言　　　せんげん　-する declare
独立宣言　どくりつせんげん　declaration of independence
宣伝　　　せんでん　publicity, advertisement, propaganda -する propagate, publicize
宣教*師　　せんきょうし　missionary

851 各 ▶かく
▷おのおの

6 ノ ク 夂 夂 各 各

各地　　　かくち　　many/various places
世界各国　せかいかっこく　many countries (around the world)
各種の　　かくしゅの　a large variety of
各自　　　かくじ　　each person, individually
各々　　　おのおの　each (one)

852 格 ▶かく, こう

10 一 十 才 才 才 杉 杉 柊 格 格

価格　　　かかく　　price
性格　　　せいかく　personality, character
合格　　　ごうかく　-する pass (an entrance/certificate exam)
人格　　　じんかく　personality, character
格好　　　かっこう　shape, appearance
同格の　　どうかくの　equal (in rank)
本格的な　ほんかくてきな　full-scale
格別な／の　かくべつな／の　particular, special, exceptional
格子　　　こうし　　lattice, grille

853 資　▶し

13　丶　冫　冫　沪　沪　次　次　咨　咨
資　資　資

資源	しげん	(natural) resources
資本	しほん	capital
資金	しきん	funds
資格	しかく	qualification
物資	ぶっし	goods, commodities

854 源　▶げん　▷みなもと

13　丶　冫　氵　氵　沪　沪　沪　沪　沥　沥
沪　源　源

資源	しげん	(natural) resources
起源	きげん	origin, beginning
財源	ざいげん	financial resources
歴 源氏物語	げんじものがたり	*The Tale of Genji*
源	みなもと	source, origin

855 貴　▶き　▷たっと(い)，とうと(い)，たっと(ぶ)，とうと(ぶ)

12　丶　一　口　中　串　串　貴　貴　青　青
貴　貴

貴重な	きちょうな	valuable, precious
貴重品	きちょうひん	valuables
貴族	きぞく	nobleman, the nobility
貴い	とうとい，たっとい	noble
◇ 貴ぶ	とうとぶ，たっとぶ	esteem

856 賃　▶ちん

13　ノ　亻　仁　仁　任　任　任　侊　侊
賃　賃　賃

| 家賃 | やちん | rent (real estate) |
| 運賃 | うんちん | fare (bus, etc.) |

| 賃金 | ちんぎん | wages, pay |
| 賃上げ | ちんあげ | a wage increase |

857 貨　▶か

11　ノ　亻　亻　化　化　竹　貨　貨　貨　貨
貨

通貨	つうか	(monetary) currency
外貨	がいか	foreign currency
金貨	きんか	gold coin
貨物	かもつ	freight, cargo

858 費　▶ひ　▷つい(やす)，つい(える)

12　一　ニ　弓　弗　弗　弗　弗　青　青　青
費　費

費用	ひよう	cost, expense
経費	けいひ	cost, expense
人件費	じんけんひ	labor costs
旅費	りょひ	traveling expenses
生活費	せいかつひ	cost of living
食費	しょくひ	food expenses
光*熱費	こうねつひ	heating and lighting expenses
費やす	ついやす	spend, waste, use up
◇ 費える	ついえる	be used up/wasted

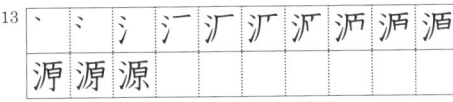

第　64　回

859 貧　▶ひん，びん　▷まず(しい)　2067　cf. 貪

11　ノ　八　今　分　分　谷　谷　谷　貧　貧
貧

貧乏な	びんぼうな	poor, needy
貧富の差	ひんぷのさ	gap between the rich and the poor
貧困	ひんこん	poverty
貧弱な	ひんじゃくな	poor, scanty
貧しい	まずしい	poor, needy

第3水準

860 乏

▶ぼう
▷とぼ(しい)

cf. 芝 568

4 一 ノ 三 乏

貧乏な	びんぼうな	poor, needy
欠乏	けつぼう [する] run short of
乏しい	とぼしい	scarce, scant

861 額

▶がく
▷ひたい

18 ` 宀 宀 宀 宀 安 宓 客 客 客
客 額 額 額 額 額 額 額

額	がく	picture frame, framed picture, amount of money
金額	きんがく	amount of money
総額	そうがく	total amount
半額	はんがく	half price
差額	さがく	balance (as in "Please pay the balance.")
額	ひたい	forehead

862 願

▶がん
▷ねが(う)

19 一 厂 厂 厂 斤 斤 盾 原 原 原
原 原 原 願 願 願 願 願 願

お願い	おねがい	[する] request
願う	ねがう	hope, wish, ask
願書	がんしょ	application (form)
志願者	しがんしゃ	applicant

863 塾

▶じゅく

14 ` 亠 亠 六 古 亨 享 享 刳 孰
孰 孰 塾 塾

| (学習)塾 | (がくしゅう)じゅく | private prep school attended after regular school hours <cram school> |

◇ *慶^應義塾大学 | けいおうぎじゅくだいがく | Keio University

864 熟

▶じゅく
▷う(れる)

---

15 ` 亠 六 六 古 亨 享 享 刳 孰
孰 孰 孰 熟 熟

未熟な	みじゅくな	immature, inexperienced, unskilled
成熟	せいじゅく	[する] mature, ripen
熟す	じゅくす	ripen, mature
熟語	じゅくご	idiom, *kanji* compound
熟れる	うれる	ripen, be ripe

865 勢

▶せい
▷いきお(い)

13 一 十 土 尹 尹 走 幸 坴 坴丿 埶
埶 勢 勢

大勢	おおぜい	a lot of (people)
大勢	たいせい	general tendency
勢力	せいりょく	influence, power
情勢	じょうせい	state of affairs
国勢調査	こくせいちょうさ	national census
勢い	いきおい	vigor, force, towards

866 熱

▶ねつ
▷あつ(い)

15 一 十 土 尹 尹 走 坴 坴 刔 埶
埶 埶 熱 熱 熱

熱い	あつい	hot cf. 熱い is used for things hot to the touch, whereas 暑い is used for air temperature
熱	ねつ	a fever, heat
高熱	こうねつ	high fever
熱湯	ねっとう	boiling water
情熱	じょうねつ	enthusiasm, passion
熱中	ねっちゅう	[する] be crazy about
熱心な	ねっしんな	earnest, eager

867 昭

▶しょう

9 丨 冂 月 日 旷 旷 昭 昭 昭

| 昭和 | しょうわ | *Shōwa* (imperial era, 1926 -1989) |

868 **照** ▶しょう
▷て(る)，て(らす)，て(れる)

13 | 丨 | 冂 | 日 | 日 | 日⁷ | 即 | 昭 | 昭 | 昭 |
照 | 照 | 照 |

参照　　　さんしょう　[する] refer to
対照的に　たいしょうてきに　in contrast
照明　　　しょうめい　lighting
◇ 東照宮　とうしょうぐう　Toshogu Shrine (the shrine in Nikko where the first shogun is enshrined)
照る　　　てる　shine
照れる　　てれる　feel embarrassed

869 **黙** ▶もく
▷だま(る)

15 | 丨 | 冂 | 甲 | 日 | 甲 | 甲 | 里 | 里ˉ | 野 | 默 |
默 | 默 | 默 | 默 | 默 |

黙る　　　だまる　become silent
*沈黙　　ちんもく　[する] become silent
黙認　　　もくにん　[する] permit tacitly
黙*秘権　もくひけん　the right of silence
黙殺　　　もくさつ　[する] ignore deliberately

870 **燃** ▶ねん
▷も(える)，も(やす)，も(す)

16 | 丿 | 丶 | 丷 | 火 | 火 | 炒 | 炒 | 炒 | 炒 | 燃 |
燃 | 燃 | 燃 | 燃 | 燃 | 燃 |

燃える　　もえる　vi. burn, blaze
燃やす　　もやす　vt. burn
燃料　　　ねんりょう　fuel
可燃性の　かねんせいの　flammable
不燃性の　ふねんせいの　nonflammable

871 **灯** ▶とう
▷ひ

6 | 丶 | 丶 | 丷 | 火 | 灯 | 灯 |

灯台　　　とうだい　lighthouse
点灯　　　てんとう　[する] turn a light on
◇ 灯　　　ひ　light

872 **畑** ▷はた，はたけ

9 | 丶 | 丶 | 丷 | 火 | 炒 | 炒 | 畑 | 畑 | 畑 |

畑　　　　はたけ　field, vegetable field
みかん畑　みかんばたけ　mikan orchard
田畑　　　たはた　the fields, rice paddies and vegetable fields

873 **災** ▶さい
▷わざわ(い)

1803
cf. 炎

7 | く | 巛 | 巛 | 巛 | 巛 | 巛 | 災 |

災害　　　さいがい　disaster, calamity
災難　　　さいなん　misfortune, mishap
火災　　　かさい　a fire (in the building, etc.)
天災　　　てんさい　natural disaster
人災　　　じんさい　man-made disaster
[歴] 関東大震災　かんとうだいしんさい　the great earthquake that struck the Kanto area in 1923
災い　　　わざわい　misfortune, mishap　[する] cause misfortune

874 **灰** ▶かい
▷はい

6 | 一 | 厂 | 厂 | 厂 | 灰 | 灰 |

灰　　　　はい　ash
灰*皿　　はいざら　ashtray
火山灰　　かざんばい　volcanic ash
灰色　　　はいいろ　gray
石灰　　　せっかい　lime (chemical)
石灰岩　　せっかいがん　limestone

875 **炭** ▶たん
▷すみ

9 | 丨 | 屮 | 山 | 屮 | 产 | 炭 | 炭 | 炭 | 炭 |

石炭　　　せきたん　coal
炭素　　　たんそ　carbon
二*酸化炭素　にさんかたんそ　carbon dioxide
炭*酸飲料　たんさんいんりょう　carbonated drinks
炭　　　　すみ　charcoal

第 65 回

876 鉱 ▶こう

13 ノ ハ ト ト 午 午 午 金 釒 釘
釟 鉱 鉱

鉱山 こうざん mine
炭鉱 たんこう coal mine
鉱業 こうぎょう mining
鉱物 こうぶつ a mineral

877 精 ▶せい，しょう

14 ` ` ` ` ` ` ` ` ` `
精 精 精 精

精神 せいしん spirit, mind
精力 せいりょく energy, vigor
精子 せいし spermatozoon cf. *卵子（らんし） ovum
筆不精 ふでぶしょう someone who doesn't write letters often
精進 しょうじん する devote oneself
◇ 精進料理 しょうじんりょうり vegetarian food (served at a temple)

878 請 ▶せい，しん ▷こ(う)，う(ける)

15 ` ` ` ` ` ` ` ` ` `
請 請 請 請 請

申請書 しんせいしょ application form (for a grant, permission, etc.)
要請 ようせい する request, demand
下請け したうけ する subcontract
請う こう ask for (help)
特 普請 ふしん する build, construct, make repairs

879 育 ▶いく ▷そだ(つ)，そだ(てる)，はぐく(む)

8 ` 一 ナ 云 六 育 育 育

教育 きょういく する educate
体育 たいいく physical education
発育 はついく growth (of an animal) する grow
生育 せいいく growth (of a plant) する grow
育つ そだつ grow up
育てる そだてる bring up, raise
育む はぐくむ bring up, cultivate, foster

880 絹 ▶けん ▷きぬ

13 く ㄠ ㄠ 幺 糸 糸 糹 糹 紆 絹
絹 絹 絹

絹 きぬ silk
特 人絹 じんけん artificial silk

881 綿 ▶めん ▷わた

14 く ㄠ ㄠ 幺 糸 糸 糸 紀 紀 紀
綿 綿 綿 綿

綿 めん cotton
木綿 △もめん cotton
◇ 綿糸 めんし cotton thread
◇ 海綿 かいめん sponge
綿*密な めんみつな detailed (plan, etc.)
綿 わた cotton wadding

882 織 ▶しょく，しき ▷お(る)

512
cf. 識

漢字の形に気をつけましょう㉕

47	281	754	877	878
青	晴	清	精	請
青春時代	今日は快晴だ	清潔なキッチン	精神的なダメージ	申請書

| 18 | く | 幺 | 幺 | 糸 | 糸 | 糸 | 糸′ | 約 | 紵 | 紵 |
| | 紵 | 紵 | 紵 | 縋 | 縋 | 織 | 織 | 織 | | |

組織	そしき	[する] organize, set up
織物	おりもの	textiles
織る	おる	weave (a fabric, etc.)
特 織機	しょっき	a (clothing) loom

883 編 ▶へん
▷あ(む)

| 15 | く | 幺 | 幺 | 糸 | 糸 | 糸 | 約′ | 約 | 約′ | 紵 |
| | 紵 | 絹 | 絹 | 編 | 編 | | | | | |

編集	へんしゅう	[する] edit, compile
編集長	へんしゅうちょう	chief editor
短編小説	たんぺんしょうせつ	short story
編む	あむ	knit
手編みの	てあみの	hand-knit
編み物	あみもの	knitting

第 66 回

884 縮 ▶しゅく
▷ちぢ(む)，ちぢ(まる)，ちぢ(める)，ちぢ(れる)，ちぢ(らす)

| 17 | く | 幺 | 幺 | 糸 | 糸 | 糸 | 糸′ | 糸′ | 紵 |
| | 紵 | 紵 | 紵 | 縮 | 縮 | 縮 | 縮 | | |

縮む	ちぢむ	shrink, become short
縮める	ちぢめる	shorten, shrink
縮れる	ちぢれる	be frizzled or curly
縮れ毛	ちぢれげ	curly hair
縮小	しゅくしょう	[する] curtail, cut (down)
短縮	たんしゅく	[する] reduce (time), curtail, shorten, abridge, abbreviate

縮図	しゅくず	a reduced drawing
軍縮	ぐんしゅく	disarmament, arms reduction
*伸縮自在の	しんしゅくじざいの	elastic

885 績 ▶せき

| 17 | く | 幺 | 幺 | 糸 | 糸 | 糸 | 糸′ | 紵′ | 絆 | 絜 |
| | 絜 | 績 | 績 | 績 | 績 | 績 | 績 | | | |

成績	せいせき	results, grades, performance
成績表	せいせきひょう	school transcript, report card
業績	ぎょうせき	achievements, business results
実績	じっせき	actual results
功績	こうせき	achievement, merit
*紡績	ぼうせき	spinning (of yarn/thread)

886 積 ▶せき
▷つ(む)，つ(もる)

| 16 | ノ | 二 | 千 | 禾 | 禾 | 禾 | 秆 | 秆 | 秸 | 積 |
| | 積 | 積 | 積 | 積 | 積 | 積 | | | | |

積む	つむ	load, pile up
積もる	つもる	accumulate (as in snow, dust, etc.)
積極的な	せっきょくてきな	positive (attitude, etc.), active 反 消極的な (しょうきょくてきな) negative (attitude, etc.), passive
面積	めんせき	area, square measure
体積	たいせき	cubic volume
*容積	ようせき	volume, capacity
見積(も)り	みつもり	estimate

887 布 ▶ふ
▷ぬの

| 5 | ノ | ナ | ナ | 右 | 布 | | | | | |

第3水準

漢字の形に気をつけましょう㉖

638	885	886	1249	1506
責	績	積	*債	*漬
責任を果たす	テストの成績	積極的に仕事をする	*債権 さいけん	*漬物 つけもの

毛布　　　　もうふ　blanket
分布　　　　ぶんぷ　[する] vi. be distributed
配布　　　　はいふ　[する] vt. distribute
公布　　　　こうふ　[する] promulgate
布　　　　　ぬの　cloth

888 **希** ▶き

7 ノ メ ヌ チ チ 希 希

希望　　　　きぼう　[する] hope, wish
希少価値　　きしょうかち　scarcity value

889 **衣** ▶い
▷ころも

6 ' 亠 ナ ★ 衣 衣

衣食住　　　いしょくじゅう　food, clothing and shelter
衣類　　　　いるい　clothing
[特] 法衣　　ほうえ，ほうい　vestment, a clerical robe
衣　　　　　ころも　clothes, robe, gown

890 **依** ▶い，え

8 ノ イ 亻 忄 忬 佊 佐 依

依頼　　　　いらい　[する] ask, request
依存　　　　いそん，いぞん　[する] depend on
依然として　いぜんとして　still, as ever
[特] 帰依　　きえ　[する] become a believer (in a religion)

891 **報** ▶ほう　　　　　1823
▷むく(いる)　　cf. 執

12 一 十 土 キ 圭 幸 幸 幸 郣 郣
報 報

報告　　　　ほうこく　[する] report
天気予報　　てんきよほう　weather forecast
情報　　　　じょうほう　information
電報　　　　でんぽう　telegram
報道機関　　ほうどうきかん　the news media, the press
報道　　　　ほうどう　news [する] inform, report

報復　　　　ほうふく　[する] retaliate
報*酬　　　　ほうしゅう　a reward, remuneration, a fee
報い　　　　むくい　a reward, retribution
報いる　　　むくいる　reward, repay (a kindness)

892 **告** ▶こく
▷つ(げる)

7 ノ 𠂉 牛 生 牛 告 告

報告　　　　ほうこく　[する] report
告白　　　　こくはく　[する] confess
告*訴　　　　こくそ　[する] accuse, sue, lodge a complaint, charge
告発　　　　こくはつ　[する] indict, prosecute, accuse
申告　　　　しんこく　[する] declare, report
告げる　　　つげる　tell, announce

893 **吉** ▶きち，きつ

6 一 十 士 古 吉 吉

吉日　　　　きちじつ，きつじつ　lucky day
吉報　　　　きっぽう　good news
不吉な　　　ふきつな　ill-omened, ominous
吉田　　　　▲よしだ　(surname)

第 67 回

894 **幸** ▶こう
▷さいわ(い)，さち，しあわ(せ)

8 一 十 土 キ 𡴐 幸 幸 幸

幸福　　　　こうふく　happiness
不幸　　　　ふこう　unhappiness
幸運　　　　こううん　good fortune
幸せ　　　　しあわせ　happiness
◇ 幸　　　　さち　happiness, fortune
◇ 海の幸　　うみのさち　food/delicacies from the sea
幸い　　　　さいわい　happiness, fortunately [する] cause good fortune

895 **福** ▶ふく

13	丶	ラ	ネ	ネ	ネ	ネ	ネ	ネ	福
	福	福	福						

幸福　こうふく　happiness
福祉　ふくし　welfare, well-being
*祝福　しゅくふく　[する] bless, wish somebody well
福音書　ふくいんしょ　the Gospel

896 社 ▶し

8	丶	ラ	ネ	ネ	ネ	ネ	ネ	社

福祉　ふくし　welfare, well-being
社会福祉　しゃかいふくし　social/public welfare
福祉国家　ふくしこっか　a welfare state

897 幅 ▶ふく ▷はば

12	丨	口	巾	巾	巾	巾	巾	巾	幅	幅
	幅	幅								

幅　はば　width, breadth
大幅な　おおはばな　big (increase, decrease, improvement, etc.)
振幅　しんぷく　amplitude (of a swing)

898 副 ▶ふく

11	一	冖	戸	戸	戸	冨	畐	畐	畐	副
	副									

副社長　ふくしゃちょう　vice president (of a company)
副業　ふくぎょう　side business, side job
副産物　ふくさんぶつ　by-product
副作用　ふくさよう　side effect
副題　ふくだい　a subtitle　cf. 字*幕(じまく) (movie) subtitles

899 判 ▶はん, ばん

7	丶	ソ	ソ	半	半	判

判断　はんだん　[する] judge

*裁判　さいばん　trial　[する] judge, try
判事　はんじ　a judge
判決　はんけつ　a judgment, a judicial decision, a sentence
公判　こうはん　a (public) trial
判明　はんめい　[する] become clear, be identified, prove (to be true)
判(子)　はん(こ)　seal (equivalent to a signature)

900 断 ▶だん ▷た(つ), ことわ(る)

11	丶	ソ	ソ	半	半	迷	迷	迷	断
	断								

判断　はんだん　[する] judge
決断　けつだん　[する] decide, determine
油断　ゆだん　[する] be careless or inattentive or off guard
断定　だんてい　[する] conclude
横断歩道　おうだんほどう　pedestrian crossing
横断　おうだん　[する] cross, go across
断水　だんすい　suspension of the water supply [する] vi. the water supply is cut off
断*念　だんねん　[する] give up, abandon
断る　ことわる　decline, refuse, reject, ask to be excused
断つ　たつ　cut off, sever

901 継 ▶けい ▷つ(ぐ)

13	乚	幺	幺	幺	糸	糸	糸	糸	絆
	絆	絆	継						

継続　けいぞく　[する] continue
後継者　こうけいしゃ　successor
衛星中継　えいせいちゅうけい　transmission via satellite
継ぐ　つぐ　inherit, succeed to
受け継ぐ　うけつぐ　succeed to, inherit

902 繰 ▷く(る)

19	乚	幺	幺	幺	糸	糸	糸	絎	絎
	絎	絎	繰	繰	繰	繰	繰	繰	

第3水準

139

繰り返す　　くりかえす　repeat

引っ繰り返す　ひっくりかえす　turn upside down, overturn, upset, tip over

引っ繰り返る　ひっくりかえる　topple over, fall on one's back, be upset

---

903 **燥** ▶そう

1485
cf. 操

17 ⎸ ⎹ ⺌ 火 火 炉 炉 炉 炉 炉
焯 焯 焯 焯 焊 燥 燥

乾燥　　　かんそう　[する] dry up, dry out
乾燥機　　かんそうき　clothes dryer
乾燥地*帯　かんそうちたい　arid region

---

904 **乾** ▶かん
▷かわ（く），かわ（かす）

11 一 十 古 古 古 甴 直 卓 卓 乾
乾

乾燥　　かんそう　[する] dry up, dry out
乾電池　　かんでんち　dry cell battery
乾*杯　　かんぱい　[する] drink a toast, "Cheers!"
乾く　　かわく　become dry, dry out

第 68 回

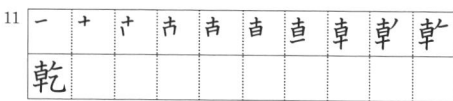

905 **江** ▶こう
▷え

6 丶 冫 氵 氵 汀 江

江戸　　えど　Edo (the old name for Tokyo)
入り江　いりえ　inlet, cove
江ノ島　えのしま　Enoshima (an island near Kamakura)
特 *揚子江　ようすこう　the Yangtze River

---

906 **液** ▶えき

11 丶 冫 氵 氵 泸 泸 泸 泸 液 液
液

液体　　えきたい　liquid　cf. 固体（こたい）solid, 気体（きたい）gas

液化　　えきか　[する] vi. vt. liquefy
*唾液　　だえき　saliva, sputum

---

907 **汚** ▶お
▷けが（す），けが（れる），けが（らわしい），よご（す），よご（れる），きたな（い）

6 丶 冫 氵 氵 汚 汚

汚染　　おせん　[する] pollute, contaminate
大気汚染　たいきおせん　air pollution
汚職　　おしょく　corruption
汚名　　おめい　stigma, disgrace
汚点　　おてん　stain, blot, blemish
汚い　　きたない　dirty
汚す　　よごす　make dirty, taint
汚れる　よごれる　get dirty, become stained, become foul
汚す　　けがす　dishonor, disgrace
汚れた　けがれた　impure, unclean

---

908 **染** ▶せん
▷そ（める），そ（まる），し（みる），し（み）

9 丶 冫 氵 氵 氿 染 染 染 染

汚染　　おせん　[する] pollute, contaminate
大気汚染　たいきおせん　air pollution
伝染病　でんせんびょう　contagious disease
感染　　かんせん　[する] vi. vt. infect
染色　　せんしょく　[する] dye
染める　そめる　dye (something a color)
染み　　しみ　stain, blotch
染みる　しみる　permeate, soak into

---

909 **港** ▶こう
▷みなと

12 丶 冫 氵 氵 沣 汼 洪 汼 洪 洪
港 港

空港　　くうこう　airport
横*浜港　よこはまこう　the port of Yokohama
港　　　みなと　harbor, port
港町　　みなとまち　port town

910 湾　▶わん

12　丶　氵　氵　氵　氿　汽　沪　沙　湾　湾　湾　湾

東京湾　　とうきょうわん　Tokyo Bay
湾　　　　わん　bay, gulf
台湾　　　たいわん　Taiwan

911 浜　▶ひん
　　　▷はま

10　丶　氵　氵　氵　汇　汇　沪　泸　浜　浜

横浜　　　よこはま　Yokohama (port city near Tokyo)
浜*辺　　　はまべ　beach, seashore
海浜公園　かいひんこうえん　seashore park

912 沖　▶ちゅう
　　　▷おき

7　丶　氵　氵　氵　汀　沪　沖

沖　　　　おき　offshore
特 沖積*層　ちゅうせきそう　alluvial layer

913 波　▶は
　　　▷なみ

8　丶　氵　氵　氵　汇　沪　波　波

波　　　　なみ　wave, ripple
電波　　　でんぱ　radio wave, a (mobile phone) signal
短波　　　たんぱ　shortwave (radio)
波長　　　はちょう　wavelength

914 漁　▶ぎょ, りょう

14　丶　氵　氵　氵　氵　沪　沪　漁　漁　漁　漁　漁　漁　漁

漁業　　　ぎょぎょう　fishing industry
漁船　　　ぎょせん　fishing boat
漁村　　　ぎょそん　fishing village
漁場　　　ぎょじょう　fishing ground

漁民　　　ぎょみん　fishermen
漁　　　　りょう　fishing
漁*師　　　りょうし　fisherman

915 鯨　▶げい
　　　▷くじら

19　ノ　ク　ク　名　角　角　角　角　魚　魚
　　魚　魚'　鮁　鮁　鯨　鮫　鯨　鯨　鯨

鯨　　　　くじら　whale
*捕鯨　　　ほげい　whaling
鯨油　　　げいゆ　whale oil
鯨肉　　　げいにく　whale meat
白鯨　　　はくげい　white whale, Moby Dick

916 鮮　▶せん
　　　▷あざ(やか)

17　ノ　ク　ク　名　角　角　角　角　魚　魚
　　魚　魚　魚'　鮮　鮮　鮮　鮮

新鮮な　　しんせんな　fresh
鮮魚　　　せんぎょ　fresh fish
鮮度　　　せんど　freshness (level)
鮮明な　　せんめいな　clear, vivid
朝鮮半島　ちょうせんはんとう　the Korean Peninsula
鮮やかな　あざやかな　vivid, bright, brilliant

917 洋　▶よう

9　丶　氵　氵　氵　汁　沣　泮　洋　洋

太平洋　　たいへいよう　the Pacific Ocean
大西洋　　たいせいよう　the Atlantic Ocean
海洋　　　かいよう　ocean　cf. 太平洋(たいへいよう),
　　　　　大西洋(たいせいよう)
西洋　　　せいよう　the West
東洋　　　とうよう　the East
洋書　　　ようしょ　foreign/Western book

第 69 回

918 卸 ▷おろ(す)，おろし

9 ｜ ノ ┌ ┌ 午 午 缶 缶 釦 卸

卸値　　　　おろしね　wholesale price
卸売(り)　　おろしうり　wholesale
卸売物価　　おろしうりぶっか　wholesale prices
卸す　　　　おろす　sell wholesale

919 御 ▶ぎょ，ご
▷おん

12 ｜ ノ ク イ イ 彳 犳 犳 件 徃 徃
御 御

御飯　　　　ごはん　cooked rice, a meal
京都御所　　きょうとごしょ　the Kyoto Imperial Palace
御礼　　　　おれい，おんれい　gratitude, thanks
制御　　　　せいぎょ　[する] control

920 缶 ▶かん

6 ｜ ノ ┌ ┌ 午 缶 缶

空き缶　　　あきかん　empty can
缶ビール　　かんビール　canned beer

921 益 ▶えき，やく

10 ｜ 、 丷 丷 产 兴 关 兴 益 益 益

利益　　　　りえき　profit, benefit
収益　　　　しゅうえき　profit, gains
有益な　　　ゆうえきな　useful, beneficial
無益な　　　むえきな　useless, futile
公益　　　　こうえき　the public interest/good
公益法人　　こうえきほうじん　public corporation
ご利益　　　ごりやく　divine assistance

922 盛 ▶せい，じょう
▷も(る)，さか(る)，さか(ん)

11 ｜ ノ ┌ 厂 成 成 成 成 咸 盛 盛
盛

盛大な　　　せいだいな　grand(party, etc.)
*繁盛　　　　はんじょう　[する] prosper (used for business)
盛り*込む　　もりこむ　incorporate (one's idea into a plan),
　　　　　　　include
盛る　　　　もる　heap up, fill up (a bowl with rice), pile up
盛んな　　　さかんな　active, prosperous
花盛り　　　はなざかり　in full bloom

923 盟 ▶めい

13 ｜ 丨 冂 日 日 旫 明 明 明 明 明
明 盟 盟

同盟国　　　どうめいこく　allied nations
国際連盟　　こくさいれんめい　the League of Nations
連盟　　　　れんめい　league
加盟　　　　かめい　[する] join (a league/federation/etc.)
盟主　　　　めいしゅ　leading power, leader
◇ 盟約　　　めいやく　pledge, pact　[する] form an alliance
　　　　　　　(with)

924 塩 ▶えん
▷しお

13 ｜ 一 十 土 𡈼 扩 圹 圹 坊 坊 塩
塩 塩 塩

塩　　　　　しお　salt
塩分　　　　えんぶん　salt content
食塩　　　　しょくえん　(table) salt
塩水　　　　しおみず，えんすい　salt water, brine

925 監 ▶かん

15 ｜ 丨 厂 广 𠂆 𡰪 臣 臥 臥 臥
臥 𣪘 臥 監 監

監督　　　　かんとく　(film) director, manager (of a sport)
　　　　　　　[する] supervise

監視	かんし　[する] watch, keep watch over, surveillance
監禁	かんきん　[する] confine, imprison
監査	かんさ　[する] inspect, audit

926　督　▶とく

13　｜　ﾄ　上　ヤ　赤　赤　叔　叔　叔　叔

督　督　督

監督	かんとく　(film) director, manager (of a sport) [する] supervise
督*促	とくそく　[する] demand/urge (payment of a debt)
◇ 家督	かとく　headship of a family, a family's estate

927　皿　▷さら

5　｜　口　皿　皿　皿

皿	さら　plate, dish, saucer
皿洗い	さらあらい　dishwashing
灰皿	はいざら　ashtray

928　血　▶けつ　▷ち

6　ノ　イ　白　血　血　血

血	ち　blood
血液	けつえき　blood
血管	けっかん　blood vessel
出血	しゅっけつ　[する] bleed
輸血	ゆけつ　[する] give a blood transfusion
血*圧	けつあつ　blood pressure
高血*圧	こうけつあつ　high blood pressure
*献血	けんけつ　[する] donate blood
流血	りゅうけつ　bloodshed

第 70 回

929　宮　▶きゅう，ぐう，く　▷みや

10　ノ　ソ　宀　宀　宀　宮　宮　宮　宮　宮

明治神宮　めいじじんぐう　Meiji Shrine

宮*殿	きゅうでん　palace　cf. バッキンガム宮殿，ベルサイユ宮殿
子宮	しきゅう　uterus, womb
お宮参り	おみやまいり　the custom of taking one's baby to a shrine (to pray the blessing)
宮内庁	くないちょう　the Imperial Household Agency

930　営　▶えい　▷いとな(む)

12　丶　丷　丷　丷　丷　営　営　営　営

営　営

経営	けいえい　[する] manage, run (a company)
経営者	けいえいしゃ　manager
運営	うんえい　[する] manage, operate
営業	えいぎょう　[する] do business
非営利団体	ひえいりだんたい　non-profit organization
公営住宅	こうえいじゅうたく　government-built apartment complex
営む	いとなむ　run (a business)

931　辞　▶じ　▷や(める)

13　ノ　二　千　千　舌　舌　舌'　舌　舌　舌

辞　辞　辞

辞書	じしょ　dictionary
辞職	じしょく　[する] resign (a job)
辞表	じひょう　letter of resignation
お世辞	おせじ　flattery
辞める	やめる　resign, quit

932　乱　▶らん　▷みだ(れる)，みだ(す)

7　ノ　二　千　千　舌　舌　乱

混乱	こんらん　[する] be confused, be thrown into confusion
反乱	はんらん　rebellion, revolt
内乱	ないらん　civil war
[歴] 乱	らん　rebellion, disturbance
乱筆	らんぴつ　hasty handwriting
乱れる	みだれる　fall into disorder

第3水準

933 求

▶きゅう
▷もと(める)

7 一 十 寸 寸 求 求 求

要求	ようきゅう	する demand, request, claim
請求	せいきゅう	する claim, bill
求人	きゅうじん	help wanted (ad), job offer する offer a job
求職	きゅうしょく	する look for a job
探求	たんきゅう	する search for, pursue
求める	もとめる	demand, request, seek

934 救

▶きゅう
▷すく(う)

11 一 十 寸 寸 求 求 求 求 救 救

救急車	きゅうきゅうしゃ	ambulance
救助	きゅうじょ	する rescue
救*命具	きゅうめいぐ	life preserver
救う	すくう	save, rescue, help

935 球

▶きゅう
▷たま

11 一 丁 干 王 王 坷 坷 坷 球 球

地球	ちきゅう	the earth
野球	やきゅう	baseball
(野)球場	(や)きゅうじょう	baseball stadium
電球	でんきゅう	electric bulb
気球	ききゅう	balloon
球	たま	ball

936 儀

▶ぎ

15 丿 亻 亻 亻 伫 伫 伫 伴 伴 伴 伴 儀 儀 儀

礼儀	れいぎ	etiquette, good manners
礼儀正しい	れいぎただしい	courteous, polite
行儀	ぎょうぎ	manners

| 儀式 | ぎしき | ceremony, ritual |
| 地球儀 | ちきゅうぎ | terrestrial globe |

937 犠

▶ぎ

17 丿 亠 牛 牛 牜 牜 牜 牜 牜 牜 牜 牜 牜 牜 犠 犠 犠

| 犠牲 | ぎせい | sacrifice, victim |
| 犠牲者 | ぎせいしゃ | victim |

938 牲

▶せい

9 丿 亠 牛 牛 牛 牜 牜 牲 牲

| 犠牲 | ぎせい | sacrifice, victim |

第 71 回

939 象

▶しょう, ぞう

12 丿 勹 勹 凸 凸 乸 象 象 象 象 象

対象	たいしょう	subject (of investigation), object (of study), target (of criticism)
現象	げんしょう	phenomenon
気象庁	きしょうちょう	the Meteorological Agency
気象学	きしょうがく	meteorology
象	ぞう	elephant

940 像

▶ぞう

14 丿 亻 亻 亻 伫 伫 俛 俛 俛 像 像 像 像

想像	そうぞう	する imagine
現像	げんぞう	する develop (a film)
映像	えいぞう	picture, image
仏像	ぶつぞう	statue/image of Buddha
自画像	じがぞう	self-portrait

941 免

▶めん
▷まぬか(れる)

8 ノ ク 夕 召 召 召 免

免税	めんぜい	tax exemption
免税店	めんぜいてん	duty-free shop
免許	めんきょ	permission, license
免れる	まぬかれる	be exempted

942 城

▶じょう
▷しろ

9 一 十 扌 圵 圹 圻 城 城 城

城	しろ	castle
江戸城	えどじょう	Edo Castle
城下町	じょうかまち	castle town
歴 城主	じょうしゅ	castle lord

943 誠

▶せい
▷まこと

13 丶 ㇑ 二 言 言 言 言 訂 訪 誠 誠 誠

誠実な	せいじつな	sincere, faithful
誠意	せいい	sincerity, faith
誠に	まことに	truly

944 詳

▶しょう
▷くわ(しい)

13 丶 ㇑ 二 言 言 言 訂 訂 詳 詳 詳

詳しい	くわしい	detailed, well-informed
詳細な	しょうさいな	detailed
◇ 詳報	しょうほう	detailed report [する] make a full report

945 詩

▶し

13 丶 ㇑ 二 言 言 言 訂 計 詰 詩 詩

詩	し	poetry, poem
詩人	しじん	poet
詩集	ししゅう	collection of poems
漢詩	かんし	Chinese poem/poetry
詩歌	しいか, しか	poetry

946 討

▶とう
▷う(つ)

10 丶 ㇑ 二 言 言 言 言 訂 討 討

討論	とうろん	[する] vi. debate, discuss
検討	けんとう	[する] examine, consider
討議	とうぎ	[する] vi. discuss, deliberate
歴 討つ	うつ	attack, defeat

947 謝

▶しゃ
▷あやま(る)

17 丶 ㇑ 二 言 言 言 言 訂 訪 訓 詢 謝 謝 謝 謝 謝

謝る	あやまる	apologize
感謝	かんしゃ	[する] thank
謝*罪	しゃざい	[する] apologize
謝礼	しゃれい	remuneration, honorarium, fee, reward
◇ 新*陳代謝	しんちんたいしゃ	metabolism [する] metabolize

948 評

▶ひょう

12 丶 ㇑ 二 言 言 言 訂 訂 評 評 評

評価	ひょうか	[する] evaluate, assess
評判	ひょうばん	reputation
*批評	ひひょう	[する] criticize, critique
論評	ろんぴょう	[する] comment, criticize
書評	しょひょう	book review

第3水準

第 72 回

949 誤
▶ご
▷あやま（る）
1329 1926
cf. 娯 呉

14　丶 亠 亠 亖 言 言 言 訁 訚 誤 誤 誤 誤 誤

誤解	ごかい	する misunderstand
誤報	ごほう	erroneous report/information
誤算	ごさん	miscalculation する miscalculate, miscount
誤植	ごしょく	misprint, typo
誤り	あやまり	mistake, error
見誤る	みあやまる	fail to recognize, mistake (for someone/something else), misread

950 誇
▶こ
▷ほこ（る）

13　丶 亠 亠 亖 言 言 言 訡 訝 誇 誇 誇

誇大広告	こだいこうこく	exaggerated advertisement
誇*張	こちょう	する exaggerate
誇り	ほこり	pride

951 訓
▶くん

10　丶 亠 亠 亖 言 言 言 訓 訓 訓

訓練	くんれん	する train, drill
教訓	きょうくん	teachings, precept, lesson, moral
訓読み	くんよみ	Japanese reading of a *kanji*

952 順
▶じゅん

12　丿 丿 川 川 川 順 順 順 順 順 順 順

順番	じゅんばん	order, turn
順位	じゅんい	ranking, standing
順序	じゅんじょ	order, procedure
順	じゅん	order, sequence
道順	みちじゅん	route, course
順調な	じゅんちょうな	smooth, favorable, satisfactory
順(々)に	じゅん(じゅん)に	in order, by turns, in turns, one after another

953 序
▶じょ

7　丶 亠 广 庁 序 序 序

秩序	ちつじょ	(public, world, etc.) order
順序	じゅんじょ	order, procedure
序列	じょれつ	ranking, grade
年功序列	ねんこうじょれつ	seniority system
序文	じょぶん	preface, foreword
序論	じょろん	introduction, first chapter (of a book, article, etc.)
序曲	じょきょく	overture, prelude

954 秩
▶ちつ

10　丿 二 千 千 禾 禾 秒 秋 秩 秩

| 秩序 | ちつじょ | (public, world, etc.) order |

955 矛
▶む
▷ほこ

5　フ マ 孖 予 矛

漢字の形に気をつけましょう㉗

403	953	955	388	1310
予	序	矛	務	*柔
予約する	順序	矛盾	事務室	*柔道 じゅうどう

矛盾　　　　むじゅん　[する] contradict, conflict
矛先　　　　ほこさき　spearhead, brunt of an attack
[歴] 矛　　　ほこ　halberd

956 **盾**　▶じゅん
　　　　　▷たて
　　　　　　　　　　　　　　　　　　　　　1969
　　　　　　　　　　　　　　　　　　　cf. 眉

9　一 厂 厅 厈 盾 盾 盾 盾

矛盾　　　　むじゅん　[する] contradict, conflict
矛盾した　　むじゅんした　contradictory
後ろ盾　　　うしろだて　supporter, support
盾　　　　　たて　shield

957 **掃**　▶そう
　　　　　▷は(く)

11　一 十 扌 扌 扩 扫 扫 扫 掃 掃

掃除　　　　そうじ　[する] clean
一掃　　　　いっそう　[する] sweep away, eradicate
掃く　　　　はく　sweep

958 **除**　▶じょ, じ
　　　　　▷のぞ(く)

10　⁊ 孑 阝 阝 阩 险 险 除 除

掃除　　　　そうじ　[する] clean
取り除く　　とりのぞく　remove
免除　　　　めんじょ　[する] vt. exempt
除外　　　　じょがい　[する] exclude
除名　　　　じょめい　expulsion　[する] expel (from a club), remove a name from a list
解除　　　　かいじょ　[する] lift (a ban, siege, etc.), release

959 **余**　▶よ
　　　　　▷あま(る), あま(す)

7　ノ 人 𠆢 今 今 余 余

余る　　　　あまる　be left over
余り　　　　あまり　remainder, surplus
余す　　　　あます　leave (over)
余分な　　　よぶんな　surplus, excess
余計な　　　よけいな　unnecessary, more than enough
余地　　　　よち　room (for doubt, discussion, etc.), space (for)
余波　　　　よは　aftereffect, aftermath
余*裕　　　　よゆう　leeway, spare (time, money, etc.)
余*命　　　　よめい　one's remaining days

第 73 回

960 **途**　▶と

10　ノ 人 𠆢 今 今 余 余 涂 途

途中　　　　とちゅう　on the way, midway
中途半端な　ちゅうとはんぱな　half-done, unfinished, unsatisfactory
開発途上国　かいはつとじょうこく　developing countries
前途　　　　ぜんと　one's future
途絶える　　とだえる　stop, cease
〜した途端に　〜したとたんに　just as 〜, the moment that 〜

961 **込**　▷こ(む), こ(める)

5　ノ 入 込 込 込

込む　　　　こむ　be crowded　cf. 混む is also used
飛び込む　　とびこむ　dive, plunge into
引っ込む　　ひっこむ　draw back, withdraw

漢字の形に気をつけましょう㉘

134　　　597　　　957
帰　　　**婦**　　　**掃**

家に帰る　　夫婦　　　掃除をする

147

払い込む　はらいこむ　pay (into an account)

申し込む　もうしこむ　apply (for/to)

申(し)込み　もうしこみ　an application

人込み　ひとごみ　crowd, throng, crowded place

見込み　みこみ　prospects, hope, likelihood, expectation

込める　こめる　load (a gun), include

962　辺　▷へん　▷あた(り)，べ

5　フ　刀　刃　辺　辺

この辺り　このあたり　around here

この辺　このへん　this neighborhood

近辺　きんぺん　vicinity

周辺　しゅうへん　periphery, environs

底辺　ていへん　base, bottom

海辺　うみべ　seashore, beach

水辺　みずべ　waterside, shore

◇　辺*境地　へんきょうち　frontier, remote region

963　述　▷じゅつ　▷の(べる)

8　一　十　オ　ホ　ボ　゙ホ　述　述

述べる　のべる　state, mention

記述　きじゅつ　する describe

口述試験　こうじゅつしけん　oral examination

述語　じゅつご　predicate

上述の　じょうじゅつの　above-mentioned

964　迫　▷はく　▷せま(る)

8　′　亻　白　白　白　゙白　泊　迫

迫る　せまる　press someone to do something, be imminent

迫力　はくりょく　force, power

迫害　はくがい　する persecute

切迫した　せっぱくした　pressing, imminent

965　造　▷ぞう　▷つく(る)

10　′　゚　牛　生　生　告　告　゙告　造　造

製造　せいぞう　する manufacture

製造業　せいぞうぎょう　manufacturing (industry)

造船　ぞうせん　shipbuilding

改造　かいぞう　する remodel, rebuild

木造の　もくぞうの　wooden

人造湖　じんぞうこ　man-made lake

造る　つくる　make, build

966　追　▷つい　▷お(う)

9　′　亻　广　卢　自　自　゙自　追　追

追いかける　おいかける　chase, pursue

追いつく　おいつく　catch up with

追い*越す　おいこす　pass, get ahead of

追う　おう　chase, pursue, drive away

追い風　おいかぜ　favorable wind

追加　ついか　する add, supplement

追求　ついきゅう　する pursue, seek

追放　ついほう　する drive away, banish, purge

967　師　▷し

10　′　亻　广　卢　自　自　゙自　帥　帥　師

教師　きょうし　teacher

家庭教師　かていきょうし　home tutor

医師　いし　doctor

師*匠　ししょう　master (in contrast to disciples)

◇　師走　△しわす　December

968　桜　▷おう　▷さくら　　1887　cf. 楼

10　一　十　オ　木　术　゙术　゙゙术　桜　桜　桜

桜　さくら　cherry (tree, blossoms)

八重桜　やえざくら　double-flowered cherry tree

桜*桃　おうとう　cherry fruit

969　梅　▷ばい　▷うめ

10　一　十　オ　木　术　゙术　杧　柙　梅　梅

梅	うめ	*ume*, Japanese apricot
梅酒	うめしゅ	*ume* wine
梅干(し)	うめぼし	pickled *ume*/Japanese apricot
白梅	はくばい	*ume* tree with white blossoms
*紅梅	こうばい	*ume* tree with red blossoms
梅園	ばいえん	*ume* tree orchard
梅雨	△つゆ	rainy season (in June)
梅雨前線	ばいうぜんせん	warm front of early summer rain

970 松 ▶しょう ▷まつ

8 一 十 オ 木 札 松 松 松

松	まつ	pine tree
松林	まつばやし	pine woods
松島	まつしま	Matsushima (scenic coastal area near Sendai)
松竹梅	しょうちくばい	pine, bamboo and plum (decorations at a celebration)

971 桃 ▶とう ▷もも

10 一 十 オ 木 杁 杁 杁 机 桃 桃

桃	もも	peach (fruit, tree)
桃色	ももいろ	pink
桜桃	おうとう	cherry fruit
特 桃源*郷	とうげんきょう	earthly paradise

第 74 回

972 枝 ▶し ▷えだ

8 一 十 オ 木 村 村 杉 枝

枝	えだ	(tree) branch, bough
小枝	こえだ	twig, sprig
枝葉	えだは	branches and leaves, minor details
枝葉末節	しようまっせつ	trivial details

973 株 ▷かぶ

10 一 十 オ 木 村 村 柈 株 株 株

株	かぶ	stock, share, tree stump
株式	かぶしき	stock, shares
株式会社	かぶしきがいしゃ	joint-stock corporation
株主	かぶぬし	stockholder
株主総会	かぶぬしそうかい	stockholders' meeting
切り株	きりかぶ	tree stump, (grain) stubble

974 根 ▶こん ▷ね

10 一 十 オ 木 木 杓 柯 椏 根 根

屋根	やね	roof
根	ね	root, origin
根強い	ねづよい	deep-rooted
大根	だいこん	Japanese radish
根本的な	こんぽんてきな	fundamental, basic
根気	こんき	perseverance, endurance

975 限 ▶げん ▷かぎ(る)

9 ⁊ ⻖ ⻖ ⻖ ⻖ ⻖ 阳 阴 限

制限	せいげん	する restrict, limit
限度	げんど	limit, limitation (quantity)
限界	げんかい	limit, limitation (ability/capacity/ etc.)
期限	きげん	deadline, time limit
権限	けんげん	authority, power, competence
無限の	むげんの	unlimited, endless, infinite, boundless
有限の	ゆうげんの	limited, finite
限る	かぎる	restrict, limit

976 眼 ▶がん，げん ▷まなこ

11 丨 冂 冂 月 目 目 眀 眀 眼 眼 眼

主眼	しゅがん	chief aim, main purpose
眼球	がんきゅう	eyeball
開眼	かいがん，かいげん	する be spiritually enlightened, be initiated into the mysteries of an art
◇ 眼	まなこ	eye
血眼になって	ちまなこになって	frantically

977 睡 ▶すい

13 丨 冂 冃 目 目 旷 旷 旺 眡 睡 睡 睡

睡眠　　　すいみん　sleep
睡眠不足　すいみんぶそく　lack of sleep
熟睡　　　じゅくすい　-する have a sound/deep sleep

978 眠 ▶みん
▷ねむ(る)，ねむ(い)

10 丨 冂 冃 目 目 旷 旷 肝 眠 眠

睡眠　　すいみん　sleep
安眠　　あんみん　-する sleep soundly
冬眠　　とうみん　-する hibernate
不眠*症　ふみんしょう　insomnia
眠る　　ねむる　sleep
居眠り　いねむり　-する doze, take a nap
眠い　　ねむい　sleepy

979 瞬 ▶しゅん
▷またた(く)

18 丨 冂 冃 目 目 旷 旷 旷 旷 旷
　 眹 眹 眹 眹 眹 瞬 瞬 瞬

瞬間　　しゅんかん　moment
瞬時に　しゅんじに　instantaneously
一瞬　　いっしゅん　moment
瞬き　　またたき　twinkling　cf. 輝き(かがやき)
　　　　glittering

980 隣 ▶りん
▷とな(る)，となり

16 ㇇ 阝 阝 阝 阝 阡 阡 阡 阡 阡
　 阡 阡 阡 阡 隣 隣

隣の　　　　となりの　neighboring
隣人　　　　りんじん　neighbor
隣国　　　　りんごく　neighboring country
近隣*諸国　きんりんしょこく　neighboring countries
隣り合う　　となりあう　be next door to each other,
　　　　　　adjacent, adjoining

981 舞 ▶ぶ
▷ま(う)，まい

15 ノ 一 二 キ 午 無 無 無 無 舞
　 舞 舞 舞 舞 舞

舞台　　　ぶたい　stage
お見舞い　おみまい　inquiry after a person's health
見舞う　　みまう　inquire after a person's health
舞う　　　まう　dance, whirl
特 舞　　　まい　dancing, a dance

第 75 回

982 枚 ▶まい
　　　　　　　　　　　1273
　　　　　　　　　cf. 牧

8 一 十 才 木 朾 朾 朾 枚

～枚　　～まい　(counter for thin, flat objects)
枚数　　まいすう　number of sheets (of paper, etc.)

983 杯 ▶はい
▷さかずき

8 一 十 才 木 朾 朾 朾 杯

～杯　　～はい／ばい／ぱい　～ glass/cup of cf. 一杯
　　　　(いっぱい)，二杯(にはい)，三杯(さんばい)
乾杯　　かんぱい　"Cheers!"　-する drink a toast
*祝杯　　しゅくはい　toast
杯　　　さかずき　sake cup

984 札 ▶さつ
▷ふだ
　　　　　　　　　　　822
　　　　　　　　　cf. 礼

5 一 十 才 木 札

千円札　　　せんえんさつ　1,000-yen bill
(お)札　　　(お)さつ　paper money, bill, note
札束　　　　さつたば　roll of bills
改札口　　　かいさつぐち　ticket gate
表札　　　　ひょうさつ　nameplate (on a house or door)
*競争入札　きょうそうにゅうさつ　public tender,
　　　　　　competitive bidding
名札　　　　なふだ　name card

985 析 ▶せき

8 一 十 才 才 术 杧 析 析

分析　ぶんせき　[する] analyze
解析　かいせき　[する] analyze (used in mathematics)
◇ 析出　せきしゅつ　[する] educe, extract

986 核 ▶かく

10 一 十 才 才 术 杧 杧 栌 栌 核

核エネルギー　かくエネルギー　nuclear energy
核戦争　かくせんそう　nuclear war
核燃料　かくねんりょう　nuclear fuel
核*兵器　かくへいき　nuclear weapon
核*廃*棄物　かくはいきぶつ　nuclear waste
原子核　げんしかく　nucleus (of an atom)
核　かく　nucleus, core
核家族　かくかぞく　nuclear family
核心　かくしん　core, heart, point
結核　けっかく　tuberculosis

987 板 ▶はん，ばん
▷いた　　　　　cf. 坂 605

8 一 十 才 才 术 杧 板 板

黒板　こくばん　blackboard
板　いた　board
合板　ごうはん，ごうばん　plywood
*甲板　かんぱん　deck (of a ship)

988 棒 ▶ぼう

12 一 十 才 才 术 杧 栌 栟 榛 棒
棒 棒

棒　ぼう　stick, rod, club
鉄棒　てつぼう　iron bar/rod, horizontal bar
棒グラフ　ぼうグラフ　bar graph

989 柄 ▶へい
▷がら，え

9 一 十 才 才 术 杧 枛 柄 柄

柄　がら　pattern, design
人柄　ひとがら　character, personality
家柄　いえがら　social standing of a family, lineage, birth
横柄な　おうへいな　haughty
柄　え　handle (of an umbrella, etc.)

990 柱 ▶ちゅう
▷はしら

9 一 十 才 才 术 杧 杧 柱 柱

電柱　でんちゅう　telephone/utility pole
柱　はしら　pillar, column
大黒柱　だいこくばしら　the main pillar (of a house), breadwinner

991 構 ▶こう
▷かま（える），かま（う）

14 一 十 才 才 术 杧 栉 栝 構
構 構 構 構

構造　こうぞう　structure
構成　こうせい　[する] form, compose
構想　こうそう　a conception, idea　[する] plan, plot, design

第3水準

漢字の形に気をつけましょう㉙

821	822	984	1881
乳	礼	札	*孔

牛乳　お礼を言う　千円札　鼻*孔（び こう）

機構	きこう	organization, system
心構え	こころがまえ	one's mental attitude, mental readiness
構える	かまえる	set up (an office, store, etc.), stand ready for
構う	かまう	mind, care about

第 76 回

992 再 ▶さい，さ ▷ふたた（び）

6 一 𠄌 冂 币 再 再

再会	さいかい	する meet again
再婚	さいこん	する remarry
再開	さいかい	する reopen, resume
再編成	さいへんせい	する reorganize, restructure, reshuffle
再三	さいさん	again and again
再来週	さらいしゅう	the week after next
再び	ふたたび	again

993 黄 ▶こう，おう ▷き，こ

11 一 十 卄 芒 芏 芇 带 昔 苗 黄
黄

黄色	きいろ	yellow
黄身	きみ	egg yolk
黄*河	こうが	Hwang Ho, the Yellow River
黄熱病	おうねつびょう	yellow fever
*硫黄	△いおう	sulfur
黄金	おうごん，こがね	gold

994 兵 ▶へい，ひょう

7 ノ イ 斤 斤 丘 兵 兵

兵器	へいき	weapons, arms
核兵器	かくへいき	nuclear weapon
兵士	へいし	soldier
兵役	へいえき	military service
歴 兵*糧	ひょうろう	military provisions

995 靴 ▶か ▷くつ

13 一 十 卄 廿 廿 苩 苩 苗 革 革
靬 靬' 靴

靴	くつ	shoes
靴屋	くつや	shoe store
革靴	かわぐつ	leather shoes
靴下	くつした	socks
特 軍靴	ぐんか	army boots

996 革 ▶かく ▷かわ

9 一 十 卄 廿 廿 苩 苩 苩 革

革命	かくめい	revolution
改革	かいかく	する reform, reorganize
変革	へんかく	する reform, change
革新	かくしん	する innovate, reform
技術革新	ぎじゅつかくしん	technological innovation
*皮革製品	ひかくせいひん	leather goods
革	かわ	leather

997 命 ▶めい，みょう ▷いのち

8 ノ 人 𠆢 合 合 合 命 命

革命	かくめい	revolution
命令	めいれい	する order, command
生命	せいめい	life
生命保険	せいめいほけん	life insurance
人命	じんめい	(human) life
運命	うんめい	fate
使命	しめい	a mission
任命	にんめい	する appoint, nominate
*寿命	じゅみょう	life span
命	いのち	life

998 令 ▶れい

5 ノ 人 𠆢 令 令

命令	めいれい [-する] order, command	
法令	ほうれい law, ordinance	
政令	せいれい government ordinance, cabinet order	

999 領 ▶りょう

14 ノ 人 々 今 令 令 令 领 領 領
領 領 領 領

大統領	だいとうりょう president (of a country)	
領事	りょうじ consul	
総領事	そうりょうじ consul general	
領土	りょうど territory (of a nation)	
領地	りょうち feudal estate	
領主	りょうしゅ feudal lord	
領収書	りょうしゅうしょ receipt	
要領	ようりょう point, gist, knack	
横領	おうりょう [する] misappropriate, embezzle	

1000 統 ▶とう ▷す(べる) 735 cf. 総

12 く 幺 幺 幺 糸 糸 糸' 紅 統 統
紵 統

大統領	だいとうりょう president (of a country)	
統治	とうち [する] reign, rule, govern	
統制経済	とうせいけいざい controlled economy	
統一	とういつ [する] unify	
統合	とうごう [する] unite, combine	
伝統	でんとう tradition	
統計	とうけい statistics	
特 統べる	すべる govern	

1001 補 ▶ほ ▷おぎな(う) 1049 cf. 捕

12 、 ラ ネ ネ ネ 衤 初 初 袖 補
補 補

補助	ほじょ [する] assist, help	
補助金	ほじょきん subsidy	
補給	ほきゅう [する] supply, replenish	
補習	ほしゅう supplementary lessons	

補正	ほせい [する] revise, correct, supplement (a budget, etc.)	
補*充	ほじゅう [する] fill a vacancy, replenish, supplement	
補う	おぎなう make up for, supplement, complement	

1002 佐 ▶さ

7 ノ イ 仁 什 佐 佐 佐

補佐	ほさ assistance, an assistant [する] assist, aid	
補佐官	ほさかん (presidential) aide	
大佐	たいさ colonel (army), captain (navy)	
歴 佐*幕	さばく supporting the Shogunate government	

1003 臣 ▶しん, じん

7 一 厂 厂 厍 臣 臣 臣

大臣	だいじん (government) minister	
総理大臣	そうりだいじん prime minister	
歴 臣民	しんみん subjects (in contrast to royalty)	

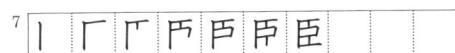

第 77 回

1004 巨 ▶きょ

5 一 厂 厂 戸 巨

巨大な	きょだいな gigantic	
巨人	きょじん giant, Yomiuri Giants (a professional baseball team)	

1005 拒 ▶きょ ▷こば(む)

8 一 十 扌 扪 拒 拒 拒 拒

拒否	きょひ [する] reject, refuse, veto	
拒絶	きょぜつ [する] refuse, reject	
拒む	こばむ refuse, decline	

1006 否 ▶ひ ▷いな

7 一 ア オ 不 不 否 否

否定	ひてい	-する deny, negate
否認	ひにん	-する deny, repudiate
否決	ひけつ	-する vote down, reject
賛否	さんぴ	approval or disapproval, yes or no
否めない	いなめない	undeniable

1007 距 ▶きょ

12 ' ロ ロ ロ ロ ロ ロ ロ 距 距
距 距

距離	きょり	distance

1008 離 ▶り ▷はな(れる), はな(す)　2130 cf. 璃

18 ' ㅗ ㅗ ㅗ 卤 卤 卤 离 离
离 离 离 离 離 離 離

距離	きょり	distance
離婚	りこん	-する divorce, get divorced
離陸	りりく	-する take off
離反	りはん	-する secede, break away from
離れる	はなれる	be separated/apart
切り離す	きりはなす	cut off, sever

1009 推 ▶すい ▷お(す)

11 一 十 オ 扌 扌 扩 扩 抌 拌 推
推

推理小説 すいりしょうせつ detective story, mystery story

推理	すいり	-する infer, reason, deduce
推論	すいろん	-する reason, infer, deduce
推測	すいそく	-する guess, suppose, surmise
推定	すいてい	-する estimate, presume, infer
類推	るいすい	-する analogize
推進	すいしん	-する promote, propel, push forward
推し量る	おしはかる	guess, conjecture

1010 哲 ▶てつ

10 一 十 オ 扌 扩 抃 折 折 折 哲

哲学	てつがく	philosophy
哲学者	てつがくしゃ	philosopher

1011 揭 ▶けい ▷かか(げる)

11 一 十 オ 扌 扩 扫 担 担 揭 揭
揭

揭示	けいじ	a notice -する put up a notice
揭示板	けいじばん	bulletin board
揭*載	けいさい	-する publish, carry an article
揭げる	かかげる	hoist (a flag), hang out (a sign, notice, etc.)

1012 抱 ▶ほう ▷だ(く), いだ(く), かか(える)

8 一 十 オ 扌 扩 扚 抭 抱

抱く	だく	hug, hold in one's arms
抱く	いだく	embrace, harbor (hope/ambition/etc.)
抱える	かかえる	carry in one's arms, employ, have (a problem)

漢字の形に気をつけましょう㉚

1013	1012	1629	1630	1631	1632
包	抱	*泡	*胞	*砲	*飽
包丁	介抱する	気*泡 (き ほう)	細*胞 (さい ぼう)	大*砲 (たい ほう)	*飽和状態 (ほう わ じょうたい)

介抱	かいほう	[する] nurse, care for
抱負	ほうふ	ambition, aspiration
抱*擁	ほうよう	[する] embrace, hug

1013 包 ▶ほう
▷つつ(む)

5 ノ ク 勺 匀 包

包む	つつむ	wrap
包み紙	つつみがみ	wrapping paper
小包	こづつみ	(postal) package
包丁	ほうちょう	kitchen knife
包*容力	ほうようりょく	broad-mindedness, tolerance
包*装紙	ほうそうし	wrapping paper

1014 均 ▶きん

7 一 十 土 圤 均 均 均

平均	へいきん	average, mean [する] average
均等に	きんとうに	equally, evenly
均一価格	きんいつかかく	uniform price

第 78 回

1015 射 ▶しゃ
▷い(る)
947
cf. 謝

10 ノ イ 勺 白 白 身 身 身 射 射

注射	ちゅうしゃ	injection, inoculation [する] inject, give a shot
発射	はっしゃ	[する] launch, fire
反射	はんしゃ	[する] reflect (light, heat, etc.)
射殺	しゃさつ	[する] kill with a gun
放射能	ほうしゃのう	radioactivity
射る	いる	shoot (an arrow, a bird, etc.)

1016 占 ▶せん
▷し(める), うらな(う)

5 ト ト 占 占

| 独占 | どくせん | [する] monopolize, keep a thing to oneself |

占領	せんりょう	[する] occupy (another country/territory)
*寡占市場	かせんしじょう	oligopolistic market
買い占める	かいしめる	buy up (all the goods), corner a market
占める	しめる	occupy, hold
占う	うらなう	tell a fortune, predict the future

1017 況 ▶きょう

8 丶 冫 氵 沪 沪 沪 況

不況	ふきょう	recession, depression
好況	こうきょう	brisk market, prosperity 反不況 (ふきょう)
状況／情況	じょうきょう	condition, situation cf. 状態 (じょうたい) state
実況放送	じっきょうほうそう	[する] broadcast on the spot

1018 祝 ▶しゅく, しゅう
▷いわ(う)
2099
cf. 呪

9 丶 ネ ネ ネ 初 祁 祁 祝

お祝い	おいわい	celebration
結婚祝い	けっこんいわい	wedding gift
祝う	いわう	celebrate, congratulate
祝日	しゅくじつ	national holiday
祝電	しゅくでん	telegram of congratulations
祝辞	しゅくじ	congratulatory address, speech
祝儀	しゅうぎ	celebration, tip

1019 賀 ▶が

12 フ カ カ 加 加 加 賀 賀 賀 賀 賀 賀

年賀状	ねんがじょう	New Year's card
祝賀会	しゅくがかい	celebration, congratulatory banquet
志賀高原	しがこうげん	Shigakogen (famous resort area in Nagano Prefecture)

第3水準

155

1020 競

▶きょう, けい
▷きそ(う), せ(る)

20 ` 亠 丿 立 立 立 产 音 音 竞 竞
竞' 竞 竞` 竞 竞 竞 竞 竞 竞 競

競走	きょうそう	する run in a race
競争	きょうそう	する compete, vie
競売	きょうばい	する sell by auction
競馬	けいば	horse racing
競う	きそう	compete
◇ 競る	せる	compete, bid

1021 景

▶けい

12) 冂 日 日 曰 旦 早 昙 昙 昙 景
景 景

景色	△けしき	view, scenery
景気	けいき	business conditions
不景気	ふけいき	business depression/recession
不景気な	ふけいきな	gloomy, cheerless
風景	ふうけい	landscape, scenery
光景	こうけい	sight, spectacle

1022 影

▶えい
▷かげ

15) 冂 日 日 旦 旦 昙 昙 昙 景
景 景 影' 影 影

影響	えいきょう	する vi. influence, affect
影	かげ	shadow, silhouette, figure
◇ 面影	おもかげ	visage, looks, image

1023 響

▶きょう
▷ひび(く)

20 く 纟 纟 幺 幺ヨ 纟ヨ 纟ヨ 紅 紎 紎
鄉` 鄉` 鄉 鄉 鄉 響 響 響 響 響

影響	えいきょう	する vi. influence, affect
反響	はんきょう	する echo, resound
音響効果	おんきょうこうか	sound effect

| 交響曲 | こうきょうきょく | symphony |
| 響く | ひびく | echo, resound, affect |

1024 郷

▶きょう, ごう

11 く 纟 纟 幺 幺ヨ 纟ヨ 纟日 紅 紅` 紅ヨ
郷

故郷	こきょう	hometown
郷土	きょうど	native province
歴 近郷	きんごう	neighboring villages

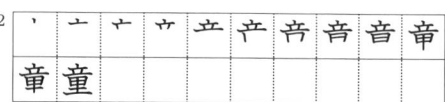
第 79 回

1025 里

▶り
▷さと

7) 冂 日 日 甲 甲 里

里	さと	village, one's parents' home
～里	～り	～ ri (unit of distance, approx. 3.9 km)
海里	かいり	nautical mile

1026 童

▶どう
▷わらべ

12 ` 亠 立 立 产 产 音 音 音 童
童 童

童話	どうわ	children's story
童心	どうしん	child's mind
*児童	じどう	pupil (in a primary school), child, juvenile
歴 童	わらべ	child
◇ 童歌	わらべうた	children's song

1027 章

▶しょう

11 ` 亠 立 立 产 产 音 音 音 章
章

章	しょう	chapter
第～章	だい～しょう	chapter no. ～
文章	ぶんしょう	composition, writing, sentence

1028 障

▶しょう
▷さわ（る）

14 ｜ ｀ 3 β β' β⁻ β⁻ β⁻ 陷 陷 陷
陷 陷 障 障

故障	こしょう	[する] break down, fail, (be) out of order
障害	しょうがい	obstacle, impediment, handicap
保障	ほしょう	[する] secure
支障	ししょう	hindrance, obstacle, problem
障子	しょうじ	*shōji*, sliding paper door
障る	さわる	harm, hurt, hinder

1029 壁

▶へき
▷かべ

2075
cf. 璧

16 ｜ コ ア ア 尼 臣 臣' 臣⁻ 臣⁻ 臣⁻
臣⁻ 臣⁻ 辟 辟 壁 壁

壁	かべ	wall
壁紙	かべがみ	wallpaper
壁画	へきが	wall painting, mural
障壁	しょうへき	barrier, obstacle

1030 卓

▶たく

8 ｜ ｜ ト ⼘ 占 占 卣 卓 卓

食卓	しょくたく	dining table
卓球	たっきゅう	ping-pong
電卓	でんたく	calculator
卓*越した	たくえつした	excellent, eminent, prominent

1031 著

▶ちょ
▷あらわ（す），いちじる（しい）

1316 1963
cf. 署 箸

11 一 十 艹 艹 芏 苎 芚 芚 著 著
著

著者	ちょしゃ	author, writer
著書	ちょしょ	(literary) work, book, one's writings
名著	めいちょ	famous/great book
著名な	ちょめいな	well-known, distinguished, celebrated

著作権	ちょさくけん	copyright
*顕著な	けんちょな	remarkable
著しい	いちじるしい	remarkable
著す	あらわす	write, publish

1032 諸

▶しょ

15 ｀ 二 ㇉ 三 言 言 言 計 計 計
誁 誁 諸 諸 諸

| アジア諸国 | アジアしょこく | Asian countries |
| マリアナ諸島 | マリアナしょとう | the Mariana Islands |

1033 緒

▶しょ，ちょ
▷お

14 ｜ ㇉ 幺 乡 糸 糸 糸 糸 紵 紵
紵 緒 緒 緒

一緒に	いっしょに	together, with
情緒	じょうちょ	emotion, feeling, atmosphere
[特] *鼻緒	はなお	thongs on *geta*

1034 鏡

▶きょう
▷かがみ

19 ノ 八 𠆢 ㇈ 乍 乍 乍 金 金 金
鈩 鈩 鈩 鈩 鈩 鏡 鏡 鏡 鏡

鏡	かがみ	mirror
望遠鏡	ぼうえんきょう	telescope
眼鏡	△めがね	eyeglasses

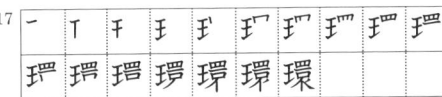
第 80 回

1035 環

▶かん

17 一 丁 千 王 王 玌 玌 玌 玌
玌 玌 玌 玌 環 環 環

| 環境 | かんきょう | environment |
| 環状線 | かんじょうせん | loop (belt) line |

1036 境

▶きょう，けい
▷さかい

14 一 十 土 圵 圹 圻 圻 培 埣 埣

培 培 埴 境

環境	かんきょう	environment
国境	こっきょう	national border
境界	きょうかい	boundary, border
境	さかい	boundary
境目	さかいめ	borderline
境内	けいだい	precinct (of a temple/shrine)

1037 破

▶は
▷やぶ(る)，やぶ(れる)

10 一 厂 丆 石 石 矴 矿 砂 砂 破

環境破壊	かんきょうはかい	destruction of the environment
破産	はさん	-する go bankrupt
破る	やぶる	break (a promise, rule, etc.), tear (paper, clothing, etc.), defeat
見破る	みやぶる	see through (a plot), see (into someone's heart)
破く	やぶく	tear (paper)
破れる	やぶれる	be torn, be defeated

1038 壊

▶かい
▷こわ(す)，こわ(れる)

16 一 十 圵 圹 圹 圹 圹 圹 圹 壊

壊 壊 壊 壊 壊 壊

環境破壊	かんきょうはかい	destruction of the environment
破壊	はかい	-する destroy
壊す	こわす	break, destroy
壊れる	こわれる	be broken
*崩壊	ほうかい	-する collapse, disintegrate

1039 激

▶げき
▷はげ(しい)

16 丶 丷 氵 沪 沪 沪 沪 沪 渆 渇

漫 潪 潪 濁 激 激

激しい	はげしい	fierce, intense
急激な	きゅうげきな	sudden, abrupt
過激な	かげきな	radical
過激*派	かげきは	radicals, extremists
激増	げきぞう	-する increase sharply
感激	かんげき	-する be moved (emotionally)
激動	げきどう	-する shake violently, be tumultuous
激流	げきりゅう	swift current, rapid stream, torrent

1040 攻

▶こう
▷せ(める)

378
cf. 功

7 一 丁 工 工 攻 攻 攻

攻撃	こうげき	-する attack
専攻	せんこう	(one's) academic specialty -する major (in a subject)
攻める	せめる	attack

1041 撃

▶げき
▷う(つ)

15 一 厂 冃 冃 冃 車 軎 軎 軎

軎 軎 撃 撃 撃

攻撃	こうげき	-する attack
反撃	はんげき	-する counterattack
打撃	だげき	blow, shock, batting
目撃者	もくげきしゃ	eyewitness
撃つ	うつ	fire, shoot

漢字の形に気をつけましょう㉛

291	1020	1034	1036
意	競	鏡	境
意見	競争	望遠鏡	国境

1042 襲
▶しゅう
▷おそ（う）

22 ｀ 亠 亠 亠 立 产 音 音 音 音

龍 龍 龍 龍 龍 龍 龍 龍 襲 襲

襲 襲

世襲の	せしゅうの	hereditary
襲撃	しゅうげき	する raid, attack
襲う	おそう	raid, attack

1043 暴
▶ぼう, ばく
▷あば（く）, あば（れる）

15 丶 口 曰 曰 旦 早 昇 昂 昂 昇

暴 暴 暴 暴 暴

暴力	ぼうりょく	violence
暴力団	ぼうりょくだん	organized group of gangsters
乱暴な	らんぼうな	violent, rough
暴風雨	ぼうふうう	violent storm
暴走族	ぼうそうぞく	motorcycle gang, hot rodders
暴徒	ぼうと	rioters, mob, insurgents
暴れる	あばれる	act violently
暴露	ばくろ	する bring to light, expose, disclose
暴く	あばく	bring to light, expose, disclose

1044 爆
▶ばく

19 丶 丿 ⺌ 火 炉 炉 炉 炉 炉 炉

炉 煁 煁 煠 爆 爆 爆 爆 爆

爆発	ばくはつ	する explode
爆撃	ばくげき	する bomb
爆破	ばくは	blast する blow up
爆弾	ばくだん	bomb
原爆	げんばく	atomic bomb
*被爆者	ひばくしゃ	victims of the atomic bomb

1045 煙
▶えん
▷けむ（る）, けむり, けむ（い）

13 丶 丿 ⺌ 火 炉 炉 炉 煙 煙 煙

煙 煙 煙

煙	けむり	smoke
煙い	けむい	smoky
喫煙	きつえん	する smoke
禁煙	きんえん	No Smoking する give up smoking
黒煙	こくえん	black smoke
煙*突	えんとつ	chimney, smokestack

第 81 回

1046 犯
▶はん
▷おか（す）

5 丿 犭 犭 犭 犯

犯罪	はんざい	crime
犯罪者	はんざいしゃ	criminal, offender
犯人	はんにん	culprit, criminal
犯行	はんこう	crime, offense
共犯者	きょうはんしゃ	accomplice
防犯カメラ	ぼうはんカメラ	surveillance camera
犯す	おかす	commit (a crime), violate (the law), rape

1047 罪
▶ざい
▷つみ
1317
cf. 罰

13 丶 口 冂 罒 罒 罒 罪 罪 罪 罪

罪 罪 罪

犯罪	はんざい	crime
有罪	ゆうざい	guilty
無罪	むざい	not guilty
罪	つみ	crime, sin, guilt

1048 逮
▶たい
1054
cf. 康

11 ⼁ ⼂ ⼅ 肀 肀 肀 肀 隶 逮 逮

逮

| 逮捕 | たいほ | する arrest |
| 逮捕状 | たいほじょう | arrest warrant |

1049 捕

▶ほ
▷と(らえる)，と(らわれる)，
　と(る)，つか(まえる)，つか(まる)

cf. 補 1001

10　一　十　扌　扌　扩　折　折　捅　捕　捕

逮捕	たいほ	[する] arrest
捕鯨	ほげい	whaling
[特] 拿捕	だほ	[する] capture (a ship)
捕る	とる	catch
捕まえる	つかまえる	catch, arrest
捕まる	つかまる	be caught
捕らえる	とらえる	catch, seize

1050 担

▶たん
▷かつ(ぐ)，にな(う)

cf. 胆 1344

8　一　十　扌　扌　扣　扣　担　担

担当	たんとう	[する] take charge of
担任の先生	たんにんのせんせい	homeroom teacher, teacher in charge of a class
負担	ふたん	burden, responsibility [する] bear (expenses, responsibility, etc.)
担保	たんぽ	security, mortgage, guarantee [する] guarantee
担ぐ	かつぐ	carry on one's shoulder
担う	になう	bear/shoulder (responsibility)

1051 批

▶ひ

7　一　十　扌　扌　批　批　批

批判	ひはん	[する] criticize
批判的な	ひはんてきな	critical
文芸批評	ぶんげいひひょう	literary criticism

1052 刑

▶けい

cf. 形 509

6　一　二　开　开　刑　刑

刑法	けいほう	criminal law
死刑	しけい	capital punishment
刑事	けいじ	(police) detective, criminal (case, liability, etc.)
刑*罰	けいばつ	punishment, penalty

| 刑 | けい | punishment, penalty, sentence |
| 刑務所 | けいむしょ | prison |

1053 健

▶けん
▷すこ(やか)

11　ノ　イ　イフ　イヨ　イヨ　イヨ　イ彐　律　律　健
　　健

健康	けんこう	health
保健	ほけん	preservation of health
健在	けんざい	in good health
健勝	けんしょう	(excellent) health
*穏健な	おんけんな	moderate
健やかな	すこやかな	healthy

1054 康

▶こう

cf. 逮 1048

11　、　亠　广　广　庐　序　序　序　序　康
　　康

健康	けんこう	health
健康な	けんこうな	healthy
不健康な	ふけんこうな	unhealthy
◇ 小康	しょうこう	(temporary) lull, breathing space

1055 建

▶けん，こん
▷た(てる)，た(つ)

9　フ　ヨ　ヨ　彐　彐　聿　律　建　建

建てる	たてる	build, construct
建物	たてもの	a building
～階建て	～かいだて／がいだて	～ story (building)
建前	たてまえ	formal principle/policy, professed position [反] 本音(ほんね) real intentions
建設	けんせつ	[する] construct, build
◇ 建立	こんりゅう	[する] construct a temple or shrine building

1056 築

▶ちく
▷きず(く)

16　ノ　ト　ケ　チ　ケ　竹　竹　竺　竺
　　筑　筑　筑　筑　築　築

新築の　しんちくの　newly-constructed

改築　かいちく　[-する] rebuild

建築　けんちく　architecture, construction　[-する] build, construct

建築家　けんちくか　architect

築く　きずく　build, construct

[歴] 築山　△つきやま　artificial hill (in a landscape garden)

1057 策　▶さく

12　ノ　ト　ト　ゲ　竺　竺　竺　竿　竿　竿
策　策

政策　せいさく　policy

対策　たいさく　measure, countermeasure

第 82 回

1058 籍　▶せき

20　ノ　ト　ケ　ゲ　竺　竺　竺　竿　竿　竿
笋　笋　笋　笄　籍　籍　籍　籍　籍　籍

国籍　こくせき　nationality

本籍　ほんせき　place where one's family records are registered

籍　せき　family register, membership (in a club)

在籍　ざいせき　[-する] be enrolled/registered (at a school)

除籍　じょせき　[-する] remove from a register, expel

書籍　しょせき　books

1059 筋　▶きん　▷すじ

12　ノ　ト　ケ　ゲ　竺　竺　竺　竺　筋　筋
筋　筋

筋肉　きんにく　muscle

筋道　すじみち　logic/reasoning behind an argument

筋　すじ　story line, plot

筋書　すじがき　synopsis, outline, plan

1060 箱　▷はこ

15　ノ　ト　ケ　ゲ　竺　竺　竺　竿　竿　竿
筋　筋　箱　箱　箱

箱　はこ　box, case

本箱　ほんばこ　bookcase

箱根　はこね　Hakone (scenic mountain spot near Mt. Fuji)

1061 範　▶はん

範囲　はんい　scope, range, sphere

広範な　こうはんな　extensive, broad

規範　きはん　norm, criterion

1062 囲　▶い　▷かこ(む)，かこ(う)

7　│　冂　冃　冃　冄　囲　囲

範囲　はんい　scope, range, sphere

周囲の　しゅういの　the surrounding ～

包囲　ほうい　[-する] besiege, surround, encircle

囲む　かこむ　surround, enclose

1063 雰　▶ふん

雰囲気　ふんいき　atmosphere (of a party, restaurant, etc.)

1064 井　▶せい，しょう　▷い　　　1964　cf. 丼

井戸　いど　(water) well

天井　てんじょう　ceiling

軽井*沢　かるいざわ　Karuizawa (summer resort area northwest of Tokyo)

[特] 市井の人　しせいのひと　ordinary citizens, the common people

1065 帯

▶たい
▷お（びる）, おび

10 一 十 卅 卅 丗 丗 丗 芾 带 帯

温帯	おんたい	temperate zone
寒帯	かんたい	frigid zone
熱帯	ねったい	tropical zone, the tropics
熱帯雨林	ねったいうりん	tropical rain forest
安全地帯	あんぜんちたい	safety zone
包帯	ほうたい	a bandage
世帯	せたい	household
帯	おび	belt, sash (for kimono)
帯びる	おびる	wear, have

1066 帝

▶てい

9 ` 亠 亠 产 产 产 产 帝 帝

帝国主義	ていこくしゅぎ	imperialism
皇帝	こうてい	emperor cf. 天皇（てんのう） (Japanese) emperor
ローマ帝国	ローマていこく	the Roman Empire
帝政	ていせい	imperial rule
特 カール大帝	カールたいてい	Emperor Charlemagne

1067 締

▶てい
▷し（まる）, し（める）
2102
cf. 諦

15 ｸ 幺 幺 糸 糸 糸 糸' 紵 紵 紵
紵 紵 締 締 締

締（め）切り	しめきり	deadline, closing date
締結	ていけつ する conclude (a treaty with)
取締役	とりしまりやく	(executive) director (of a company)

締める	しめる	tighten, tie up, fasten
金融引（き）締め	きんゆうひきしめ	financial tightening

1068 純

▶じゅん
1916
cf. 屯

10 ｸ 幺 幺 糸 糸 糸 紅 紅 紀 純

単純な	たんじゅんな	simple
純金	じゅんきん	pure gold
純毛	じゅんもう	pure wool
純文学	じゅんぶんがく	pure literature
純日本風の	じゅんにほんふうの	classical Japanese style
純情な	じゅんじょうな	pure in heart
純益	じゅんえき	net profit

1069 粋

▶すい
▷いき
510
cf. 枠

10 ` ` ` 半 半 米 籵 籵 粋 粋

純粋な	じゅんすいな	pure, genuine
特 粋人	すいじん	person of refined taste
粋な	いきな	smart, refined

1070 迷

▶めい
▷まよ（う）

9 ` ` ` 半 半 米 米 迷 迷

迷う	まよう	get lost, be unable to decide
迷子	△まいご	lost child
迷路	めいろ	maze
迷信	めいしん	superstition
低迷	ていめい する be stagnant/sluggish

漢字の形に気をつけましょう㉜

510 枠
1069 粋
1550 *砕

窓枠　純粋な人　岩を*砕く
くだ

第3水準

1071 惑
▶わく
▷まど(う)

12 一 丆 丆 戸 戸 或 或 或 或 惑 惑 惑

迷惑	めいわく	trouble, inconvenience [する] be troubled/annoyed
迷惑な	めいわくな	annoying
当惑	とうわく	[する] be perplexed
困惑	こんわく	[する] be dismayed
思惑	おもわく	intention, expectation, speculation
惑星	わくせい	planet
戸惑う	とまどう	be bewildered, be flustered
惑う	まどう	go astray, be misguided/tempted

1072 域
▶いき

11 一 十 土 士 圹 圹 圻 垣 垣 域 域

地域	ちいき	region, area, zone
領域	りょういき	territory, domain
区域	くいき	zone, district
流域	りゅういき	(river) basin, valley
聖域	せいいき	sanctuary, holy ground

1073 越
▶えつ
▷こ(す), こ(える)

12 一 十 土 キ キ 走 走 走 赴 越 越 越

| 引っ越し | ひっこし | moving (to a new house) |
| 引っ越す | ひっこす | move (to a new house) |

乗り越す	のりこす	ride past (one's stop)
越える	こえる	go over, go beyond
超越	ちょうえつ	[する] transcend
越権行為	えっけんこうい	overstepping one's authority

1074 超
▶ちょう
▷こ(える), こ(す)

12 一 十 土 キ キ 走 走 起 起 超 超 超

超大国	ちょうたいこく	superpower (nation)
超満員	ちょうまんいん	overcrowded, overflowing (with people)
超音速	ちょうおんそく	supersonic speed
超過	ちょうか	[する] exceed
超える	こえる	exceed, go over

1075 赴
▶ふ
▷おもむ(く)

9 一 十 土 キ キ 走 走 赴 赴

赴任	ふにん	[する] leave for/arrive in one's new post
単身赴任	たんしんふにん	[する] work in a distant place away from one's family
赴く	おもむく	proceed, go

第 84 回

1076 更
▶こう
▷さら, ふ(ける), ふ(かす)

7 一 丆 百 百 百 更 更

| 変更 | へんこう | [する] change, alter |
| 更衣室 | こういしつ | dressing room, changing room, locker room |

漢字の形に気をつけましょう㉝

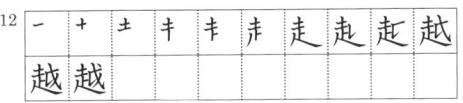

| 431 | 1071 | 1072 | 942 | 430 | 1333 | 1500 |
| 感 | 惑 | 域 | 城 | 減 | *威 | *滅 |

不安を感じる 　迷惑をかける 　地域社会 　名古屋城 　減少する 　日本史の権*威(けん い)

ローマ帝国の*滅亡(めつぼう)

163

更新	こうしん [する] renew, establish a new record, update
更に	さらに furthermore, again
夜更かし	よふかし [する] stay up late at night
更ける	ふける grow late

1077 恵 ▶けい, え ▷めぐ(む)

10 一 厂 冖 百 百 宙 声 恵 恵 恵

恩恵	おんけい a favor, a benefit
知恵	ちえ wisdom, intelligence
恵まれる	めぐまれる be blessed with
恵む	めぐむ bestow a favor, bless
恵み	めぐみ a blessing

1078 恋 ▶れん ▷こ(う), こい, こい(しい) 222 cf. 変

10 、 宀 ナ オ 方 亦 亦 恋 恋 恋

恋	こい (romantic) love [する] be in love
恋人	こいびと boyfriend, girlfriend, lover
恋心	こいごころ love
恋しい	こいしい dearest, beloved
恋愛	れんあい (passionate) love [する] be in love

1079 愛 ▶あい

13 一 一 一 一 一 一 一 愛 愛 愛
愛 愛 愛

恋愛	れんあい (passionate) love [する] be in love
愛	あい [する] love
愛情	あいじょう love, affection

| 愛国心 | あいこくしん patriotic sentiment, patriotism |
| 愛読書 | あいどくしょ favorite book |

1080 互 ▶ご ▷たが(い)

4 一 工 互 互

お互いに	おたがいに mutually
相互理解	そうごりかい mutual understanding
交互に	こうごに alternately

1081 涙 ▶るい ▷なみだ 1201 cf. 戻

10 、 丶 氵 氵 汽 沪 沪 沪 沪 涙

涙	なみだ teardrop, tears [する] drop tears, weep
涙声	なみだごえ tearful voice
◇ 感涙	かんるい tears (of strong emotion)

1082 房 ▶ぼう ▷ふさ

8 一 一 一 戸 戸 戸 房 房

冷房	れいぼう [する] air condition
暖房	だんぼう heating, a heater [する] heat (a room)
文房具	ぶんぼうぐ stationery
官房長官	かんぼうちょうかん the Chief Cabinet Secretary (of Japan)
女房	にょうぼう (my/one's) wife
乳房	ちぶさ, にゅうぼう breasts cf. in medical usage, pronounced にゅうぼう
房	ふさ bunch, cluster, tassel, tuft

漢字の形に気をつけましょう㉞

1076 更 227 便 199 使 1883 *吏

予定を変更する 便利な辞書 パソコンを使う 官*吏 かん り

1083

雇

▶こ
▷やと(う)

12 　一　一　ヨ　戸　戸　戸　戸　戸　戸　雇

雇　雇

雇用制度	こようせいど　employment system
雇用	こよう　[する] employ, hire
解雇	かいこ　[する] fire (an employee)　cf. 首にする（くびにする）fire, 首になる（くびになる）be fired
雇用主	こようぬし　employer
雇用者	こようしゃ　employee, in official documents and statistics, "employer"
雇う	やとう　employ, hire

1084

肩

▶けん
▷かた

8 　一　一　ヨ　戸　戸　肩　肩　肩

肩	かた　shoulder
肩書き	かたがき　(one's) title
肩代わり	かたがわり　[する] pay in someone's stead, take on someone's obligation
肩身が狭い	かたみがせまい　feel ashamed, feel small
特　肩章	けんしょう　epaulet

1085

背

▶はい
▷せ，せい，そむ(く)，そむ(ける)

9 　一　ナ　ユ　キ　北　北　背　背　背

背中	せなか　back
背	せ　back (of a person's body/a chair/a book)
背	せい，せ　stature, height
背広	せびろ　(men's) business suit
背景	はいけい　background, setting
背後	はいご　back, rear

◇ 背信行為	はいしんこうい　betrayal, breach of trust
背く	そむく　disobey, betray, revolt
背ける	そむける　avert (one's eyes from), turn (one's face) away

1086

胸

▶きょう
▷むね，むな

10 　丿　刀　月　月　月'　肕　肕　胸　胸　胸

胸	むね　chest, breast, bosom
胸毛	むなげ　chest hair
胸囲	きょうい　girth of the chest
胸中	きょうちゅう　inner feelings
度胸	どきょう　courage, nerve, guts

1087

腰

▶よう
▷こし

13 　丿　刀　月　月　肝　肝　腭　腭　腭　腰

腰　腰　腰

腰	こし　lower back, waist, hips
物腰	ものごし　demeanor, manner
本腰を入れる	ほんごしをいれる　set about (a task) in earnest
腰痛	ようつう　backache, pain in the lower back

1088

腹

▶ふく
▷はら

13 　丿　刀　月　月　肝　肝　胪　胪　胪

胪　胪　腹

空腹な	くうふくな　hungry
立腹	りっぷく　[する] get angry
腹が立つ	はらがたつ　get angry

漢字の形に気をつけましょう㉟

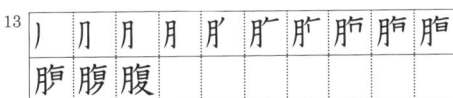

797	798	1077	1856
専	博	恵	*穂
専門は文学だ	大学院の博士課程	恩恵を受ける	麦の*穂

| 腹 | はら | stomach, belly, abdomen |
| お腹 | ▲おなか | stomach |

1089 豚 ▶とん / ▷ぶた   cf. 家 52

11 ノ 几 月 月 肝 肝 肝 肝 豚 豚
豚

豚	ぶた	pig, hog
豚肉	ぶたにく	pork
豚カツ	とんカツ	pork cutlet
養豚	ようとん	hog/pig raising

第 85 回

1090 届 ▷とど(ける), とど(く)

8 ┐ コ コ 尸 尸 吊 届 届

欠席届	けっせきとどけ	report of absence (from school)
欠勤届	けっきんとどけ	report of absence (from work)
届ける	とどける	report, send, deliver
届け先	とどけさき	where to report, receiver's address
届く	とどく	be delivered, reach, arrive at

1091 属 ▶ぞく

12 ┐ コ コ 尸 尸 戸 戸 戸 属 属
属 属

属す（る）	ぞくす（る）	belong to (an organization, etc.), fall under/within (a given category)
所属	しょぞく	[する] belong to (an organization, etc.)
金属	きんぞく	metal
属性	ぞくせい	attributes, properties

1092 展 ▶てん

10 ┐ コ コ 尸 尸 尸 屏 屏 屏 展

| 発展 | はってん | [する] develop |
| 発展途上国 | はってんとじょうこく | developing countries |

展示	てんじ	[する] exhibit, display
展望	てんぼう	prospects, view [する] have a view of, look over
展開	てんかい	[する] develop, unfold

1093 殿 ▶でん, てん / ▷との, どの

13 ┐ コ 尸 尸 尸 戸 屈 屏 展 屏
屏 殿 殿

宮殿	きゅうでん	palace cf. バッキンガム宮殿, ベルサイユ宮殿
御殿	ごてん	palace
殿下	でんか	His/Her Highness
皇太子殿下	こうたいしでんか	His Imperial Highness the Crown Prince
歴 殿様	とのさま	feudal lord
〜殿	〜どの	Mr./Ms. 〜 (used in official documents, etc.)

1094 凍 ▶とう / ▷こお(る), こご(える)

10 丶 冫 广 汗 汗 汗 凍 凍 凍 凍

凍る	こおる	freeze, be frozen (up, over)
冷凍食品	れいとうしょくひん	frozen food
凍結	とうけつ	[する] be frozen, freeze (assets, etc.)
凍傷	とうしょう	frostbite
凍死	とうし	[する] freeze to death
凍える	こごえる	be frozen, be numb with cold

1095 氷 ▶ひょう / ▷こおり, ひ

5 ﹄ 丁 引 氺 氷

氷	こおり	ice
氷山	ひょうざん	iceberg
氷*河	ひょうが	glacier
流氷	りゅうひょう	drift ice, floes
氷点下	ひょうてんか	below the freezing point
特 氷室	ひむろ	icehouse

1096 永 ▶えい / ▷なが(い)

| 5 | ﹨ | ｺ | ｺ | 永 | 永 | | | | |

永住　　　　えいじゅう　[する] reside permanently
永遠に　　　えいえんに　eternally
永眠　　　　えいみん　[する] pass away, die
永続　　　　えいぞく　[する] last for a long time
永い　　　　ながい　long (time)
永田町　　　ながたちょう　Nagatacho (the area in Tokyo where the Diet Building is located)

1097

久　▶きゅう, く
　▷ひさ(しい)

| 3 | ノ | ク | 久 | | | |

久しぶりに　　ひさしぶりに　after a long time
永久に　　　　えいきゅうに　permanently, perpetually
持久力　　　　じきゅうりょく　tenacity, stamina, staying power
[特] 久遠の　　くおんの　eternal

1098

及　▶きゅう
　▷およ(ぶ), およ(び), およ(ぼす)

| 3 | ノ | 乃 | 及 | | | |

普及　　　ふきゅう　[する] spread, become popular/widely-used
言及　　　げんきゅう　[する] refer to, mention
及ぶ　　　およぶ　reach, extend to, amount to
及び　　　および　and/as well as (formal)
及ぼす　　およぼす　exert (influence on)

1099

幼　▶よう
　▷おさな(い)

1814
cf. 幻

| 5 | く | 幺 | 幺 | 幻 | 幼 | | | |

幼稚園　　ようちえん　kindergarten
幼稚な　　ようちな　childish, infantile, unrefined
幼い　　　おさない　very young, childish, infantile

1100

稚　▶ち

1297
cf. 維

| 13 | ノ | ニ | 千 | 千 | 禾 | 禾 | 利 | 利 | 利 | 利 |
| | 秆 | 稚 | 稚 | | | | | | |

幼稚園　　ようちえん　kindergarten
幼稚な　　ようちな　childish, infantile, unrefined

第 86 回

1101

移　▶い
　▷うつ(る), うつ(す)

| 11 | ノ | ニ | 千 | 千 | 禾 | 禾 | 利 | 利 | 移 | 移 |
| | 移 | | | | | | | | | |

移民　　　いみん　immigrant, immigration, emigrant, emigration　[する] immigrate, emigrate
移住　　　いじゅう　[する] migrate, immigrate, emigrate, move to
移動　　　いどう　[する] move, transfer
移転　　　いてん　[する] vi. move/change (offices, schools, etc.)
移植　　　いしょく　[する] transplant, graft
移る　　　うつる　vi. move to, change, pass
移す　　　うつす　vt. move, infect (someone else)

1102

秘　▶ひ
　▷ひ(める)

| 10 | ノ | ニ | 千 | 千 | 禾 | 禾 | 利 | 秘 | 秘 | 秘 |

秘密　　　　ひみつ　a secret, secrecy
秘書　　　　ひしょ　secretary, work assistant
神秘的な　　しんぴてきな　mysterious, mystical
極秘　　　　ごくひ　strict secrecy, top secret
秘められた　ひめられた　hidden, secret

1103

密　▶みつ

1957
cf. 蜜

| 11 | ﹅ | ﹅ | 宀 | 宀 | 宓 | 宓 | 宓 | 宓 | 宓 | 密 |
| | 密 | | | | | | | | | |

秘密　　　　ひみつ　a secret, secrecy
密輸　　　　みつゆ　[する] smuggle
人口密度　　じんこうみつど　population density
精密な　　　せいみつな　precise, detailed, minute
密接な　　　みっせつな　close
親密な　　　しんみつな　close, intimate

1104 骨 ▶こつ
▷ほね

10 丨 冖 冂 冂 冎 冎 冎 骨 骨 骨

骨　　　ほね　bone
骨折　　こっせつ　-する break a bone
鉄骨　　てっこつ　steel frame
骨子　　こっし　main point, gist

1105 胃 ▶い

9 丨 冂 冂 田 田 胃 胃 胃 胃

胃　　　い　stomach
胃がん　いがん　stomach cancer

1106 腸 ▶ちょう

13 丿 刀 月 月 月 肝 肥 胆 胆 胆
腸 腸 腸

腸　　　ちょう　intestines, bowels
胃腸　　いちょう　stomach and intestines
小腸　　しょうちょう　small intestines
大腸　　だいちょう　large intestines

1107 肝 ▶かん
▷きも

7 丿 刀 月 月 肝 肝 肝

肝臓　　かんぞう　liver
肝心な　かんじんな　main, essential
◇ 肝　　きも　liver, guts

1108 臓 ▶ぞう

19 丿 刀 月 月 肝 肝 肝 肝 肝 肝
肝 肝 肝 肝 臓 臓 臓 臓 臓

肝臓　　かんぞう　liver
心臓　　しんぞう　heart

内臓　　ないぞう　internal organs
臓器　　ぞうき　internal organs

1109 脳 ▶のう

11 丿 刀 月 月 月 肝 肝 肝 脳 脳
脳

脳　　　のう　brain
洗脳　　せんのう　-する brainwash
◇ 脳卒中　のうそっちゅう　a stroke, cerebral hemorrhage
首脳会談　しゅのうかいだん　summit meeting
頭脳　　ずのう　brains, head

1110 悩 ▶のう
▷なや(む), なや(ます)

10 丨 丷 忄 忄 忄 忄 悩 悩 悩 悩

悩む　　なやむ　be troubled, be worried, be distressed
悩み　　なやみ　trouble, worry, agony
伸び悩む　のびなやむ　make little progress, show little growth
悩ます　なやます　annoy, pester, harass
苦悩　　くのう　-する suffer, be distressed, be in agony
◇ 悩殺　のうさつ　-する charm, bewitch

第 87 回

1111 蔵 ▶ぞう
▷くら

15 一 十 艹 艹 芹 芹 芹 芹 芹 芹
芹 芹 蔵 蔵 蔵

冷蔵庫　れいぞうこ　refrigerator
貯蔵　　ちょぞう　-する store
蔵書　　ぞうしょ　collection of books
蔵　　　くら　storehouse, warehouse

1112 倉 ▶そう
▷くら

10 丿 人 入 今 今 合 合 倉 倉 倉

| 倉庫 | そうこ | warehouse, storehouse |
| 倉 | くら | storehouse, warehouse |

1113 創 ▶そう ▷つく(る)

創る	つくる	create
創造性	そうぞうせい	creativity, originality
創造	そうぞう	[する] create
創作	そうさく	original work [する] create
創立	そうりつ	[する] establish, found
独創的な	どくそうてきな	original, creative

1114 看 ▶かん

| 9 | 一 二 三 丢 丢 丢 看 看 看 |

看護師	かんごし	nurse
看病	かんびょう	[する] nurse, look after
看板	かんばん	signboard
看守	かんしゅ	prison guard
◇ 看破	かんぱ	[する] see through, detect

1115 護 ▶ご

| 20 | ヽ 二 三 三 訁 訁 訁 訁 言 訒 |
| | 訰 訳 訝 訝 謹 謹 謹 護 護 護 |

看護師	かんごし	nurse
弁護士	べんごし	lawyer
弁護	べんご	[する] defend, plead for, speak for
保護	ほご	[する] protect, preserve
護衛	ごえい	bodyguard, guard, escort [する] guard, escort

1116 弁 ▶べん

| 5 | ㇗ ㇛ ㇛ 弁 弁 |

| 弁護士 | べんごし | lawyer |

弁解	べんかい	[する] explain, justify, make an excuse
◇ 答弁	とうべん	[する] reply, answer, explain (in a formal setting, e.g., parliament)
関西弁	かんさいべん	Kansai dialect/accent
弁当	べんとう	box lunch
駅弁	えきべん	box lunch sold at a train station

1117 念 ▶ねん

信念	しんねん	belief, faith
理念	りねん	idea, concept
念頭に	ねんとうに	(keep, bear, etc.) in mind
念入りに	ねんいりに	carefully, elaborately
記念	きねん	[する] commemorate
記念日	きねんび	memorial day, anniversary

1118 息 ▶そく ▷いき

1285 cf. 臭

| 10 | ㇒ ㇗ 冖 白 白 自 自 息 息 息 |

休息	きゅうそく	[する] rest, take a rest
利息	りそく	interest (on a loan, deposit, etc.)
消息	しょうそく	news, information
息子	△むすこ	son
息	いき	a breath, breathing
◇ 息吹	△いぶき	a breath (of spring), vigor (of youth)

1119 応 ▶おう ▷こた(える)

| 7 | ㇒ 一 广 广 応 応 応 |

反応	はんのう	[する] react, respond to
応答	おうとう	[する] answer, response
質疑応答	しつぎおうとう	questions and answers
応用	おうよう	[する] apply, put to practical use
応接室	おうせつしつ	reception room
応える	こたえる	respond, answer

第3水準

1120 寄

▶き
▷よ（る），よ（せる）

1292
cf. 奇

11　｀　宀　宀　宀　宀　宇　宯　宯　害　寄
寄

寄る	よる	approach, draw near, drop in
近寄る	ちかよる	draw near, approach
立ち寄る	たちよる	stop by, pay a visit,
最寄りの	△もよりの	nearest, nearby
寄付	きふ [する] contribute, donate
寄付金	きふきん	a contribution, a donation, gift of money
◇ 寄生	きせい	[する] be parasitic (on a tree, animal, etc.), live upon
寄せる	よせる	bring near, gather together, move (a thing) to

1121 突

▶とつ
▷つ（く）

8　｀　宀　宀　宀　空　空　空　突

突然	とつぜん	suddenly
突入	とつにゅう	[する] storm (a building), rush (into), dash (into)
突破	とっぱ	[する] break through, exceed (100,000, etc.)
突く	つく	poke, thrust
突き当たり	つきあたり	the end of a street/hall/passage, etc.
突き当たる	つきあたる	come to the end of a street, run/ bump against
突っ込む	つっこむ	thrust into, rush into

1122 穴

▶けつ
▷あな

5　｀　宀　宀　穴　穴

穴	あな	hole, opening
落とし穴	おとしあな	pitfall
◇ *洞穴	どうけつ	cave, cavern

第 88 回

1123 容

▶よう

1501
cf. 溶

10　｀　宀　宀　宀　宍　宍　突　突　容　容

内容	ないよう	content(s)
容器	ようき	container, vessel
容量	ようりょう	volume, capacity
美容	びよう	beauty (treatment)
美容院	びよういん	beauty parlor
受容	じゅよう	[する] accept
形容詞	けいようし	adjective

1124 欲

▶よく
▷ほっ（する），ほ（しい）

11　ノ　ハ　グ　父　穴　谷　谷　谷　谷　欲
欲

欲	よく	greed, desire, volition
食欲	しょくよく	appetite
性欲	せいよく	sexual desire
欲望	よくぼう	desire, greed
無欲な	むよくな	indifferent to (monetary/personal) gain, unselfish
欲しい	ほしい	want
欲する	ほっする	want, desire

1125 裕

▶ゆう

12　｀　ラ　ネ　ネ　ネ　衤　衤　衤　衤
裕　裕

| 余裕 | よゆう | leeway, spare (time/money/etc.) |
| 裕福な | ゆうふくな | wealthy, rich |

1126 浴

▶よく
▷あ（びる），あ（びせる）

10　｀　シ　シ　シ　沙　沙　浴　浴　浴

入浴	にゅうよく	[する] take a bath
浴室	よくしつ	bathroom
海水浴	かいすいよく	sea bathing
日光浴	にっこうよく	sun bathing
浴衣	△ゆかた	yukata (cotton kimono worn in summer)
浴びる	あびる	be bathed in, take (a shower)
浴びせる	あびせる	pour over, douse, bombard (with criticism, questions, etc.)

1127 河 ▶か ▷かわ

8 丶 亠 氵 汀 沪 沪 河 河 河

河	かわ	river
運河	うんが	canal
銀河	ぎんが	the Milky Way
黄河	こうが	Hwang Ho, the Yellow River
河川	かせん	rivers
河原	△かわら	dry riverbed

1128 沿 ▶えん ▷そ(う)

8 丶 亠 氵 氵 沙 汾 沿 沿

～に沿って	～にそって	along (the coast/river, etc.)
川沿いの	かわぞいの	along the river
沿岸	えんがん	(on/along) the coast/shore
沿線	えんせん	along the train line

1129 沈 ▶ちん ▷しず(む), しず(める) cf. 枕 2029

7 丶 氵 氵 氵 汗 沙 沈

沈没	ちんぼつ	[する] sink, founder
沈着冷静な	ちんちゃくれいせいな	composed, calm
沈む	しずむ	sink

1130 没 ▶ぼつ

7 丶 氵 氵 氵 沉 汐 没

沈没	ちんぼつ	[する] sink, founder
没落	ぼつらく	[する] be ruined/bankrupt
没収	ぼっしゅう	[する] confiscate
◇ 出没	しゅつぼつ	[する] appear frequently, haunt, infest

1131 添 ▶てん ▷そ(える), そ(う)

11 丶 氵 氵 氵 汗 汗 沃 添 添 添 添

付き添う	つきそう	attend on, accompany, escort
添える	そえる	add, attach, garnish
添加物	てんかぶつ	additive
添*削	てんさく	[する] correct

1132 歓 ▶かん cf. 勧 1615

15 ノ 亻 二 チ 牟 牟 牟 斉 雈 雈 雚 勧 歓 歓

歓迎	かんげい	[する] welcome
歓待	かんたい	[する] give a warm reception
歓声	かんせい	shout of joy, cheer
歓楽街	かんらくがい	entertainment district

1133 迎 ▶げい ▷むか(える)

7 ノ 亻 幻 卬 卬 迎 迎

歓迎	かんげい	[する] welcome
送迎バス	そうげいバス	shuttle bus
出迎える	でむかえる	go to greet (someone at the front door, train station, etc.)
迎えに行く	むかえにいく	go to meet (someone at the airport, etc.), pick up
迎合	げいごう	[する] cater to somebody's wishes, accommodate oneself

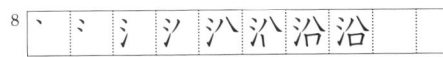

第 89 回

1134 仰 ▶ぎょう, こう ▷あお(ぐ), おお(せ)

6 ノ 亻 亻 化 仰 仰

信仰	しんこう	religious faith
仰向け	あおむけ	facing upward [反]うつ*伏せ(うつぶせ) facing downward
仰ぐ	あおぐ	look up at, ask for (advice/support), etc.
◇ 仰天	ぎょうてん	[する] be astonished
[特] 仰せ	おおせ	your wish [honorific]

第3水準

171

1135 卵
▶らん
▷たまご

7 ノ L ビ 5 5 5 卵

卵	たまご	egg, spawn
卵子	らんし	egg/ovum　cf. 精子（せいし）sperm/spermatozoon
卵*巣	らんそう	ovary

1136 印
▶いん
▷しるし

6 ノ イ F E 臼 印

印刷	いんさつ	-する print
印象	いんしょう	impression
調印	ちょういん	-する sign (a treaty, etc.), affix one's seal/signature
印税	いんぜい	(publishing) royalties
印	しるし	mark, sign
矢印	やじるし	(directional) arrow
目印	めじるし	mark, landmark, signpost

1137 刷
▶さつ
▷す(る)

8 フ コ P P 局 吊 刷 刷

印刷	いんさつ	-する print
印刷物	いんさつぶつ	printed matter
刷新	さっしん	-する to reform, renovate
刷る	する	print

1138 刊
▶かん

5 一 二 干 刊 刊

週刊誌	しゅうかんし	weekly magazine
朝刊	ちょうかん	morning edition (of a newspaper)
夕刊	ゆうかん	evening edition (of a newspaper)
新刊書	しんかんしょ	a new publication (as in new books or magazines)

1139 刻
▶こく
▷きざ(む)

8 ` 宀 ナ ガ 亥 亥 刻 刻

深刻な	しんこくな	grave, serious
時刻	じこく	time, the hour
*彫刻	ちょうこく	sculpture, a sculpture　-する carve, engrave
刻む	きざむ	cut, chop up, engrave

1140 劇
▶げき

15 ` 宀 广 广 庐 庐 庐 虍 虍
虏 虏 虏 劇 劇

劇	げき	drama, play, theatrical performance
演劇	えんげき	drama, play, theatrical performance
歌劇	かげき	opera
劇場	げきじょう	theater
喜劇	きげき	comedy　反悲劇（ひげき）
悲劇	ひげき	tragedy, tragic event
劇的な	げきてきな	dramatic
劇薬	げきやく	powerful drug, poison

1141 仮
▶か, け
▷かり

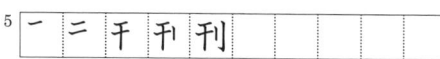
6 ノ イ 仁 仮 仮 仮

漢字の形に気をつけましょう㊱

1133	1134	1264	1135	1136	918
迎	仰	*抑	卵	印	卸
ホテルの送迎バス	信仰を捨てる	核の*抑止力 よくしりょく	カエルの卵	印刷する	卸値

仮定　かてい　する suppose, assume
仮説　かせつ　hypothesis
仮面　かめん　mask
平仮名　△ひらがな　*hiragana*
仮の　かりの　provisional, tentative, temporary
仮病　けびょう　faked illness

1142 版 ▶はん

8 ノ 丿 广 片 片 斤 斨 版 版

出版　しゅっぱん　する publish
出版社　しゅっぱんしゃ　publisher, publishing company
版権　はんけん　copyright
初版　しょはん　first edition
改訂版　かいていばん　revised edition
版画　はんが　woodblock print

1143 片 ▶へん ▷かた

4 ノ 丿 片 片

破片　はへん　fragment, splinter
断片的な　だんぺんてきな　fragmentary
断片　だんぺん　fragment, scrap
片道　かたみち　one-way (ticket) cf. 一方通行（いっぽうつうこう）one-way traffic
片手　かたて　one hand
片仮名　△かたかな　*katakana*
片付く　かたづく　be put in order, be settled, be finished
片付ける　かたづける　put in order, tidy (up), put away, settle, finish
片寄る　かたよる　lean to, incline toward

第 90 回

1144 皮 ▶ひ ▷かわ

5 ノ 厂 广 皮 皮

皮　かわ　skin, hide leather, bark, rind, peel
毛皮　けがわ　fur
皮革製品　ひかくせいひん　leather goods
皮肉　ひにく　irony, sarcasm
皮相的な　ひそうてきな　superficial, shallow

1145 被 ▶ひ ▷こうむ（る）

10 丶 ラ 才 衤 衤 初 初 袯 袯 被

被害　ひがい　damage, harm, injury
被害者　ひがいしゃ　victim, sufferer
被告　ひこく　defendant
被選挙権　ひせんきょけん　eligibility (for)
被る　こうむる　suffer

1146 彼 ▶ひ ▷かれ, かの

8 ノ ク イ 彳 犳 犷 彿 彼

彼　かれ　he, boyfriend
彼女　かのじょ　she, girlfriend
彼岸　ひがん　equinoctial week

1147 徹 ▶てつ

15 ノ ク イ 彳 彳 疒 疒 祜 祜 徟 徟 徟 徹 徹

第3水準

漢字の形に気をつけましょう㊲

1144 皮	913 波	1037 破	1145 被	1146 彼	1468 *披
皮革製品	電波	環境破壊	被害を受ける	お彼岸	*披露宴 ひろうえん

173

徹夜 てつや 〔-する〕 stay up all night

徹底的に てっていてきに thoroughly

冷徹な れいてつな cool-headed

◇ *貫徹 かんてつ 〔-する〕 accomplish, carry out

1148 徴 ▶ちょう

14 ノ ク イ 彳 彳 彷 彷 徃 徨 徨 徨 徴 徴

象徴 しょうちょう 〔-する〕 symbolize

特徴 とくちょう special feature, distinguishing characteristic

徴*候 ちょうこう sign, indication, symptom

徴兵 ちょうへい 〔-する〕 conscript, draft

徴税 ちょうぜい 〔-する〕 collect taxes

1149 微 ▶び

13 ノ ク イ 彳 彳 彷 彷 佛 微 微 微 微

微妙な びみょうな subtle, delicate, fine

◇ 微笑 びしょう faint/subtle smile 〔-する〕 give a smile

微熱 びねつ slight fever

微生物 びせいぶつ microbes, microorganisms

1150 妙 ▶みょう

7 く タ 女 刘 如 如 妙

微妙な びみょうな subtle, delicate, fine

*奇妙な きみょうな strange, curious, odd

妙な みょうな strange, curious, odd

妙案 みょうあん excellent idea, bright idea

絶妙な ぜつみょうな exquisite, superb

神妙な しんみょうな meek, docile

*巧妙な こうみょうな skillful, ingenious, clever

1151 秒 ▶びょう

9 ノ 二 千 手 禾 利 利 秒 秒

～秒 ～びょう ～ second(s)

1152 砂 ▶さ, しゃ ▷すな

9 一 フ 丆 石 石 刷 刷 砂 砂

砂 すな sand

砂浜 すなはま sandy beach

砂時計 すなどけい sandglass

砂利 △じゃり gravel

土砂 どしゃ earth and sand

土砂降り どしゃぶり downpour

土砂*崩れ どしゃくずれ landslide

砂金 さきん gold dust

砂*糖 さとう sugar

砂*漠 さばく desert

砂*丘 さきゅう sand hill, dune

1153 劣 ▶れつ ▷おと(る)

6 丨 ⺌ 小 少 岁 劣

劣等感 れっとうかん inferiority complex

劣等生 れっとうせい poor student

*優劣 ゆうれつ superior or inferior, relative merit

劣勢 れっせい inferiority in strength/numbers

劣る おとる be inferior (to)

第 91 回

1154 勇 ▶ゆう ▷いさ(む)

9 フ マ 丏 丙 丙 甬 甬 勇 勇

勇気 ゆうき courage

勇退 ゆうたい 〔-する〕 retire voluntarily to open the way for younger people

勇ましい いさましい brave, courageous, valiant

1155 **募** ▶ぼ
▷つの(る)
1660 cf. 寡

12	一	十	艹	艹	莊	莊	苔	草	草	莫
	募	募								

募集　ぼしゅう　recruitment, solicitation　する recruit, invite (person to join)
応募　おうぼ　する apply for
応募者　おうぼしゃ　applicant
募金運動　ぼきんうんどう　fund-raising campaign
公募　こうぼ　advertise for a post, invite public participation
募る　つのる　recruit, invite (donations), raise (funds), grow intense

1156 **墓** ▶ぼ
▷はか
691 cf. 基

13	一	十	艹	艹	莊	莊	苔	草	草	莫
	莫	墓	墓							

墓　はか　grave, tomb
墓参り　はかまいり　する visit a grave
墓石　はかいし，ぼせき　tombstone, gravestone
墓地　ぼち　cemetery, graveyard
墓穴を掘る　ぼけつをほる　dig one's own grave, bring about one's own ruin

1157 **幕** ▶まく，ばく

13	一	十	艹	艹	莊	莊	苔	草	草	莫
	莫	幕	幕							

幕　まく　(stage) curtain, act (of a play)
開幕　かいまく　する (an event) begin
閉幕　へいまく　する (an event) end

字幕　じまく　subtitles
内幕　うちまく　behind-the-scenes story
歴 幕府　ばくふ　the shogunate

1158 **暮** ▶ぼ
▷く(れる)，く(らす)

14	一	十	艹	艹	莊	莊	苔	草	草	莫
	莫	幕	幕	暮						

暮らす　くらす　live, make a living
一人暮らし　ひとりぐらし　living alone
夕暮れ　ゆうぐれ　dusk, twilight, evening
暮れる　くれる　grow dark
お歳暮　おせいぼ　year-end gift

1159 **漠** ▶ばく

13	丶	丶	氵	氵	氵	汁	沣	沣	渖
	渖	漠	漠						

砂漠　さばく　desert
漠然とした　ばくぜんとした　vague, obscure

1160 **模** ▶も，ぼ

14	一	十	才	木	栌	栌	栌	栌	栖	栖
	栖	榟	模	模						

規模　きぼ　scale
大規模な　だいきぼな　large-scale
模*型　もけい　a model, a miniature
模範　もはん　model, exemplar
模造品　もぞうひん　imitation (goods)
模様　もよう　pattern, figure, design, appearance, look

漢字の形に気をつけましょう38

1159 **漠**　1160 **模**　1546 ***膜**

砂漠　大規模な調査　油の*膜
　　　　　　　　　　　　まく

第3水準

1161 概 ▶がい

14　一 十 オ 木 杆 杆 杆 栂 栂 栂
　　栂 椚 椚 概

概念	がいねん	concept, notion
概要	がいよう	outline
概*略	がいりゃく	outline, summary
概算	がいさん	-する make a rough estimate
概論	がいろん	introduction (to philosophy, astronomy, etc.), outline (of modern literature), survey course
大概	たいがい	generally, mostly, probably

1162 既 ▶き ▷すで(に)

10　コ ヨ ヨ 臼 臼 臤 臤 臤 郎 既

既に	すでに	already, before
既成事実	きせいじじつ	established fact, fait accompli
既成概念	きせいがいねん	preconceived notion, stereotype, accepted idea
既製の	きせいの	ready-made
既婚の	きこんの	married
既存の	きそんの	existing

1163 裁 ▶さい ▷た(つ), さば(く)

12　一 十 土 キ 丰 丰 走 走 表 裁
　　裁 裁

裁判	さいばん	trial -する judge, try
裁判官	さいばんかん	a judge, the court, the bench
裁判所	さいばんしょ	court of law
独裁者	どくさいしゃ	dictator

総裁	そうさい	president, governor, general director
裁く	さばく	judge, decide (a case)
洋裁	ようさい	(western-style) dressmaking
裁つ	たつ	cut (cloth, leather, etc.)

1164 我 ▶が ▷われ, わ

7　ノ 二 千 手 扎 我 我

我々	われわれ	we
我が国	わがくに	our country
自我	じが	self, ego
無我夢中で	むがむちゅうで	desperately, like mad, crazily

1165 武 ▶ぶ, む

8　一 二 亍 亍 疒 正 武 武

武器	ぶき	weapon, arms
武力	ぶりょく	military force/power
武道	ぶどう	martial arts
歴 武士	ぶし	warrior (in medieval Japan), samurai
歴 武者	むしゃ	warrior

第 92 回

1166 輩 ▶はい

15　ノ 丿 ヨ ヨ ヨ| ヨ| ヨ| ヨ| ヨ| ヨ|
　　背 背 背 軰 輩

先輩	せんぱい	one's senior (at school, work, etc.)
後輩	こうはい	one's junior (at school, work, etc.)
年輩の	ねんぱいの	elderly

漢字の形に気をつけましょう❸⓿

796	1165	377	1164	1163	1821	1307
式	武	成	我	裁	*栽	*載
結婚式	武士	成功する	我々	裁判	草花を*栽培する さいばい	論文が掲*載される けいさい

1167 俳 ▶はい

10　ノ イ イ′ イ″ イ‡ イ∔ 俳 俳 俳 俳

俳優	はいゆう	actor
俳句	はいく	haiku, Japanese short poem consisting of 17 syllables
俳人	はいじん	haiku poet

1168 優 ▶ゆう
▷やさ(しい), すぐ(れる)　　cf. 憂 1829

17　ノ イ イ′ イ″ イ″ 俨 俨 俨 俨 俥
俥 傻 傻 傻 傻 優 優

俳優	はいゆう	actor
女優	じょゆう	actress
優勝	ゆうしょう	[する] win (the championship, pennant, etc.)
優先	ゆうせん	[する] have priority (over), take precedence (over)
優*秀な	ゆうしゅうな	excellent, superior
優れた	すぐれた	excellent, superior
優しい	やさしい	gentle, tender, sweet, kindhearted

1169 仲 ▶ちゅう
▷なか　　cf. 伸 1246

6　ノ イ イ′ 仁 仁 仲

仲がいい	なかがいい	be on good terms (with someone)
仲	なか	relations, relationship
仲人	△なこうど	go-between, matchmaker
仲介	ちゅうかい	[する] mediate
仲裁	ちゅうさい	[する] arbitrate, mediate

1170 促 ▶そく
▷うなが(す)　　cf. 捉 2080

9　ノ イ イ′ 仁 仴 仴 仴 伊 促

促進	そくしん	[する] promote, quicken, hasten
*催促	さいそく	[する] press (a person for), urge (a person to do)
◇ 促成*栽*培	そくせいさいばい	artificially accelerated growth
促す	うながす	urge (a person to do something), press, prompt

1171 秀 ▶しゅう
▷ひい(でる)

7　一 二 千 千 禾 禾 秀

優秀な	ゆうしゅうな	excellent, superior
秀才	しゅうさい	brilliant person, talented student
秀でる	ひいでる	excel (at), surpass

1172 似 ▶じ
▷に(る)

7　ノ イ イ′ 化 化 似 似

似ている	にている	resemble
似顔絵	にがおえ	likeness, portrait
似合う	にあう	be suitable for, go well (with)
類似品	るいじひん	similar product, imitation (goods)
◇ 疑似体験	ぎじたいけん	simulated experience

1173 傾 ▶けい
▷かたむ(く), かたむ(ける)

13　ノ イ イ′ 化 化 佗 伫 伫 佰 傾
傾 傾 傾

傾向	けいこう	tendency, trend
傾*斜	けいしゃ	[する] slant, slope, incline
傾倒	けいとう	[する] respect (the master of an art), devote oneself (to)
傾く	かたむく	lean, incline, slant

第3水準

「仲～」の表現

・仲がいい←→仲が悪い　　・仲が良くなる←→仲が悪くなる
・けんかする←→仲直りする　　・AとBは仲良しだ　　・仲間

1174
候
▶こう
▷そうろう

1876
cf. 侯

10 ノ 亻 亻 仾 仾 伊 伊 俟 候 候

気候　きこう　climate
天候　てんこう　weather
候補者　こうほしゃ　candidate
立候補　りっこうほ [する] run in an election　cf. 出馬 (しゅつば)[する] stand as a candidate (for election)
特 居候　いそうろう　freeloader [する] live off others, freeload
歴 候文　そうろうぶん　*sōrō*-style writing (epistolary style Japanese, formal writing style in the Edo period)

1175
修
▶しゅう, しゅ
▷おさ(める), おさ(まる)

10 ノ 亻 亻 亻 俏 俏 攸 修 修 修

修理　しゅうり [する] repair, mend
修正　しゅうせい [する] amend, revise, modify, correct, retouch
修了　しゅうりょう [する] complete (a course of study, etc.)
修了証　しゅうりょうしょう　certificate for the completion of a course
研修　けんしゅう [する] train, be trained, study
修める　おさめる　master (a field of study), complete (a course of studies)
修行　しゅぎょう　(religious, artistic, etc.) training, apprenticeship [する] train oneself

1176
偏
▶へん
▷かたよ(る)

11 ノ 亻 仢 仢 伊 伊 伊 偏 偏 偏
偏

偏見　へんけん　prejudice
偏食　へんしょく [する] have an unbalanced diet
偏差値　へんさち　deviation value/score
偏る　かたよる　lean, incline, be prejudiced

第 93 回

1177
遍
▶へん

12 一 ㇕ ㇌ 戸 戸 肩 肩 扁 扁 ㇂扁
遍 遍

普遍的な　ふへんてきな　universal
遍歴　へんれき [する] wander, travel about

1178
遇
▶ぐう

12 丿 口 日 日 甲 禺 禺 禺 禺 ㇂禺
遇 遇

待遇　たいぐう　treatment, pay
優遇　ゆうぐう [する] treat someone well, give favorable treatment to
冷遇　れいぐう [する] treat someone coldly, give a cold reception to

1179
遺
▶い, ゆい

1214
cf. 遣

15 丿 口 日 中 虫 虫 串 貴 貴 貴
貴 貴 遺 遺 遺

遺伝　いでん　heredity [する] be inherited
遺産　いさん　inheritance, estate (left by a departed person), heritage
遺族　いぞく　family of the deceased, surviving family members
遺体　いたい　corpse, a person's remains
遺言　ゆいごん, いごん　will, last wishes [する] leave a will

1180
貢
▶こう, く
▷みつ(ぐ)

10 一 丅 ㇒ 㢩 㣺 吉 吉 音 貢 貢

貢献　こうけん [する] contribute, serve
特 貢ぐ　みつぐ　pay tribute, supply (a person) with money
特 貢ぎ物　みつぎもの　tribute
歴 年貢　ねんぐ　annual tribute, land tax paid in kind

1181 献 ▶けん，こん

13　一 十 广 古 古 古 南 南 南 南
献 献 献

貢献　こうけん　[-する] contribute, serve
献金　けんきん　gift of money, contribution, donation [-する] contribute, donate
献血　けんけつ　[-する] donate blood
文献　ぶんけん　literature, bibliography
献立　こんだて　menu

1182 僚 ▶りょう

14　ノ イ 仁 广 伩 伩 伩 侒 侒
侒 伩 僚 僚

同僚　どうりょう　colleague, coworker
官僚　かんりょう　bureaucrat
官僚制度　かんりょうせいど　bureaucracy
*閣僚　かくりょう　cabinet member

1183 寮 ▶りょう

15　丶 丷 宀 宀 宀 灾 灾 灾 灾 寀
寀 容 寮 寮 寮

寮　りょう　dormitory
学生寮　がくせいりょう　student dormitory
社員寮　しゃいんりょう　company dormitory
独身寮　どくしんりょう　dormitory for single men or women
寮長　りょうちょう　dormitory director
寮生　りょうせい　students living in a dormitory

1184 帳 ▶ちょう

11　丨 冂 巾 巾 𢂁 帕 帬 帳 帳 帳
帳

電話帳　でんわちょう　telephone directory
手帳　てちょう　pocket notebook
通帳　つうちょう　bankbook, passbook
帳消し　ちょうけし　cancellation of a debt

1185 張 ▶ちょう　▷は(る)

11　丁 弓 弓 引 弘 弤 弤 張 張 張
張

緊張　きんちょう　[-する] feel tension/strain
主張　しゅちょう　[-する] assert, claim that, insist (on/that)
出張　しゅっちょう　[-する] take a business trip
出張所　しゅっちょうじょ　branch office, agency
拡張　かくちょう　[-する] extend, expand
引っ張る　ひっぱる　pull, drag, stretch over
見張る　みはる　keep watch, be on the lookout
張る　はる　spread (a net, wall paper, etc.), stretch (a rope), paste (a paper, poster, etc.)
張り切る　はりきる　be in high spirits, be full of pep
欲張り　よくばり　greedy person, greed, a miser
欲張りな　よくばりな　greedy

1186 緊 ▶きん　　1711 cf. 紫

15　丨 丆 冖 丆 丆 丆 臣 臤 臤 𦥑
𦥑 臤 臤 緊 緊

緊張　きんちょう　[-する] feel tension/strain

第3水準

漢字の形に気をつけましょう㊵

1182	1183	1362	2109
僚	寮	*療	*瞭
会社の同僚	大学の寮	病気を治*療する	明*瞭な音声
		ち　りょう	めい　りょう

緊急の　　きんきゅうの　urgent, pressing
緊密な　　きんみつな　close, intimate
緊迫　　　きんぱく　[する] become tense, grow strained

1187

繁　▶はん

16	ノ	一	ヒ	与	句	毎	毎	毎ヒ	毎ヶ	敏
敏	繁	繁	繁	繁	繁					

繁栄　　　はんえい　[する] prosper (used for nations, civilizations, etc.)
繁盛　　　はんじょう　[する] prosper (used for business)
繁*華街　　はんかがい　busy shopping area

1188

栄　▶えい
▷さか(える)，は(え)，は(える)

9	丶	丷	⺍	⺍	兴	学	学	栄	栄

繁栄　　　はんえい　[する] prosper (used for nations, civilizations, etc.)
栄養　　　えいよう　nutrition
栄光　　　えいこう　glory
栄える　　さかえる　thrive, prosper
◇ 栄えある　はえある　honorable, glorious
◇ 栄える　　はえる　shine, be bright, glow

1189

挙　▶きょ
▷あ(げる)，あ(がる)
1973 cf. 拳

10	ノ	丶	⺍	⺍	兴	兴	兴	举	挙	挙

選挙　　　せんきょ　[する] elect
挙手　　　きょしゅ　[する] raise one's hand
検挙　　　けんきょ　[する] arrest
[歴] 挙兵　きょへい　[する] raise an army
一挙に　　いっきょに　at a stroke, at once
挙げる　　あげる　raise (one's hand), provide (examples), enumerate (reasons), arrest

1190

厳　▶げん，ごん
▷おごそ(か)，きび(しい)

17	丶	丷	⺍	⺍	产	产	产	产	产	产
肖	肖	肖	肖	厳	厳	厳			

厳しい　　きびしい　strict, severe, harsh
厳重な　　げんじゅうな　strict, severe
厳格な　　げんかくな　strict, stern
厳禁　　　げんきん　[する] prohibit strictly, forbid
尊厳　　　そんげん　dignity
*威厳　　　いげん　dignity, stateliness
厳かな　　おごそかな　solemn, grave
*荘厳な　　そうごんな　solemn, sublime

第 94 回

1191

派　▶は
1353 cf. 脈

9	丶	丷	氵	氵	沪	沪	派	派	派

派閥　　　はばつ　faction
右派　　　うは　right-wing faction
左派　　　さは　left-wing faction
〜派　　　〜は　〜 faction
宗派　　　しゅうは　religious sect
特派員　　とくはいん　(special) correspondent (as in a journalist)
派手な　　はでな　showy, flashy, gaudy　[反] 地味な(じみな) plain, quiet
立派な　　りっぱな　fine, splendid, admirable, respectable, magnificent
派*遣　　　はけん　[する] dispatch, send

1192

閥　▶ばつ

14	l	⺆	⺆	尸	尸'	門	門	門	門	門
閂	閥	閥	閥						

派閥　　　はばつ　faction
財閥　　　ざいばつ　*zaibatsu*, financial combine/group/clique
軍閥　　　ぐんばつ　militarists, military clique

1193

閣　▶かく

14	l	⺆	⺆	尸	尸'	門	門	門	門	閂
閉	閣	閣	閣						

内閣　　　ないかく　cabinet (of the Prime Minister)

閣議　　　　かくぎ　cabinet meeting

閣僚　　　　かくりょう　cabinet member

組閣　　　　そかく　[する] form a cabinet

金閣寺　　　きんかくじ　Kinkakuji Temple, Temple of the Golden Pavilion

1194 衆 ▶しゅう, しゅ

52 cf. 家

12 ノ ィ ゥ ㇆ 血 血 虫 哟 衆 衆 衆

大衆文化　　たいしゅうぶんか　popular culture

公衆電話　　こうしゅうでんわ　public telephone

アメリカ合衆国　アメリカがっしゅうこく　the United States of America

民衆　　　　みんしゅう　the people, the masses

[歴] 衆生　　しゅじょう　humankind, the world (in Buddhism)

1195 略 ▶りゃく

11 丨 冂 𤴓 甲 田 田' 畋 畋 略 略

省略　　　　しょうりゃく　[する] omit, abbreviate

略す　　　　りゃくす　abbreviate, shorten, omit

略語　　　　りゃくご　abbreviation

略歴　　　　りゃくれき　brief personal history

略式の　　　りゃくしきの　informal　[反] 正式の(せいしきの) formal　cf. 公式の(こうしきの) official, 非公式の(ひこうしきの) unofficial, private

戦略　　　　せんりゃく　strategy

1196 異 ▶い ▷こと

11 丨 口 田 田 田 𱁬 甲 畀 畀 異 異

異常な　　　いじょうな　unusual, abnormal　[反] 正常な(せいじょうな) normal, usual

異質な／の　いしつな／の　heterogeneous　[反] 同質な／の(どうしつな／の) homogeneous

異国　　　　いこく　foreign country

異民族　　　いみんぞく　other tribe, other ethnic group

異教徒　　　いきょうと　heathen, heretic

異議　　　　いぎ　objection

突然変異　　とつぜんへんい　[する] mutate

異なる　　　ことなる　be different, vary

1197 圧 ▶あつ

5 一 厂 厂 圧 圧

圧力　　　　あつりょく　pressure

気圧　　　　きあつ　atmospheric pressure

高気圧　　　こうきあつ　high atmospheric pressure

低気圧　　　ていきあつ　low atmospheric pressure

圧縮　　　　あっしゅく　[する] compress, condense

圧迫　　　　あっぱく　[する] oppress, press

*抑圧　　　よくあつ　[する] oppress, suppress

圧倒的に　　あっとうてきに　overwhelmingly

1198 至 ▶し ▷いた(る)

6 一 云 云 云 至 至

至急　　　　しきゅう　urgently, immediately

◇ 夏至　　　げし　summer solstice

◇ 冬至　　　とうじ　winter solstice

必至の　　　ひっしの　inevitable

至る　　　　いたる　lead to, extend to, come to

1199 票 ▶ひょう

11 一 厂 厅 币 西 西 西 票 票 票 票 票

投票　　　　とうひょう　[する] vote

開票　　　　かいひょう　[する] count votes, open ballot boxes

得票率　　　とくひょうりつ　percentage of votes obtained

票　　　　　ひょう　vote, ballot, slip of paper

1200 標 ▶ひょう

15 一 十 才 木 杧 柙 枦 桓 標 標 標 標 標 標

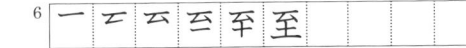

目標	もくひょう	aim, goal, target
標準的な	ひょうじゅんてきな	standard, average
標準語	ひょうじゅんご	standard language
標語	ひょうご	motto, slogan
標本	ひょうほん	specimen, sample
道路標識	どうろひょうしき	traffic signs, road signs

第 4 水準

(Level 4)

1201-1420

第 95 回

1201 戻
▶れい
▷もど(す)，もど(る)

cf. 涙 1081

7 一 一 ヲ 戸 戸 尸 戻

戻る	もどる	return, go back
後戻り	あともどり	[する] go/turn back
戻す	もどす	give/pay back, vomit
差し戻す	さしもどす	send back, remand (a case)
◇ 返戻	へんれい	[する] give back, return

1202 丘
▶きゅう
▷おか

5 ノ イ 仁 斤 丘

丘	おか	hill
自由が丘	じゆうがおか	Jiyugaoka (an area in Tokyo)
砂丘	さきゅう	sand hill, dune

1203 匹
▶ひつ
▷ひき

4 一 フ 兀 匹

| ～匹 | ～ひき／びき／ぴき | (counter for animals) cf. 一匹(いっぴき), 二匹(にひき), 三匹(さんびき) |
| 匹敵 | ひってき | [する] be a match for |

1204 司
▶し

5 フ 刁 司 司 司

司会	しかい	emcee, chairperson [する] chair (a conference, etc.)
上司	じょうし	one's boss/superior
司法	しほう	judiciary

1205 詞
▶し

12 丶 亠 亖 言 言 言 言 訂 訂 詞 詞 詞

| 歌詞 | かし | lyrics, words to a song |
| 品詞 | ひんし | part of speech |

1206 訂
▶てい

9 丶 亠 亖 言 言 言 訂 訂

| 訂正 | ていせい | [する] correct |
| 改訂 | かいてい | [する] revise |

1207 訴
▶そ
▷うった(える)

12 丶 亠 亖 言 言 言 訂 訂 訴 訴

訴える	うったえる	sue, appeal
訴訟	そしょう	lawsuit
起訴	きそ	[する] prosecute, charge
告訴	こくそ	[する] accuse, sue, lodge a complaint, charge
勝訴	しょうそ	[する] win a lawsuit/case
敗訴	はいそ	[する] lose a lawsuit/case

1208 訟
▶しょう

11 丶 亠 亖 言 言 言 言 訟 訟 訟

| 訴訟 | そしょう | lawsuit |

いろいろな品詞

名詞（めいし） noun　　動詞（どうし） verb　　形容詞（けいようし） adjective

副詞（ふくし） adverb　　代名詞（だいめいし） pronoun

1209 譲 ▶じょう
▷ゆず（る）

20 `、 ㇒ ㇇ 言 言 言 言 言 言 言 言
言 言 言 言 言 諄 諄 諄 譲 譲

譲る　　　ゆずる　transfer, yield, sell
親譲りの　おやゆずりの　inherent from a parent
譲歩　　　じょうほ 〔する〕compromise, concede
譲渡　　　じょうと 〔する〕transfer, assign, convey, cede
歴 割譲　　かつじょう 〔する〕cede (territory)

1210 購 ▶こう

17 丨 冂 冂 月 目 貝 貝 貝 貝 貝
貝 貝 貝 購 購 購 購

購読　　　こうどく 〔する〕subscribe (to a newspaper, etc.)
購読料　　こうどくりょう　cost of a subscription
購買力　　こうばいりょく　purchasing power
購入　　　こうにゅう 〔する〕purchase

第 96 回

1211 廷 ▶てい

7 ノ 二 千 壬 任 廷 廷

法廷　　　ほうてい　court of law, tribunal
開廷　　　かいてい 〔する〕open court proceedings
出廷　　　しゅってい 〔する〕appear in court
宮廷　　　きゅうてい　imperial palace

1212 処 ▶しょ

5 ノ ク タ 処 処

処理　　　しょり 〔する〕deal with, manage, treat, dispose of
対処　　　たいしょ 〔する〕cope with (a difficult situation, etc.), deal with, treat
処分　　　しょぶん 〔する〕dispose of, deal with, punish
処置　　　しょち 〔する〕deal with, take measures, give medical treatment
処女　　　しょじょ　virgin (female)

1213 拠 ▶きょ, こ

8 一 十 扌 扐 扐 拠 拠 拠

証拠　　　しょうこ　evidence, proof
根拠　　　こんきょ　basis, grounds
拠点　　　きょてん　foothold, base
準拠　　　じゅんきょ 〔する〕conform to (guidelines, etc.), be based on

1214 遣 ▶けん
▷つか（う）, つか（わす）

13 丶 丨 口 中 虫 串 串 串 串 貴
貴 遣 遣

派遣　　　はけん 〔する〕dispatch, send
小遣い　　こづかい　pocket money
仮名遣い　△かなづかい　kana usage
言葉遣い　ことばづかい　wording, phraseology
特 遣わす　つかわす　send, dispatch, give

1215 還 ▶かん

16 丶 丨 冂 罒 罒 罒 罒 罒 罟 罟
罘 罘 景 睘 環 還

返還　　　へんかん 〔する〕return, restore

第4水準

漢字の形に気をつけましょう㊶

1209	495	991	1210	1499
譲	講	構	購	*溝
譲歩する	講義をする	流通機構	家を購入する	*溝を*掘る
				みぞ　ほ

生還　　　せいかん　[する] come back alive

還元　　　かんげん　[する] return (the company's profits to the consumers)

1216 逐 ▶ちく

10 一 ブ 丁 丏 豕 豕 豕 豕 `豕 逐 逐

逐語訳　　ちくごやく　[する] translate word for word

逐一　　　ちくいち　one by one, in detail

逐次　　　ちくじ　one after another, one by one, in succession

[特] *駆逐　　くちく　[する] expel, drive away

1217 遂 ▶すい
▷と(げる)

12 丶 丷 丷 丷 芐 芣 芣 芟 芟 `芟
遂 遂

遂行　　　すいこう　[する] accomplish, execute, perform

自殺未遂　じさつみすい　attempted suicide

やり遂げる　やりとげる　carry out, accomplish, complete

1218 墜 ▶つい
1693
cf. 堕

15 ⁊ ⻖ 阝 阝 阝 阝 阝 阾 陊 隊
隊 隊 墜 墜 墜

墜落　　　ついらく　[する] fall, crash (used for aircraft)

撃墜　　　げきつい　[する] shoot down (an airplane)

失墜　　　しっつい　[する] lose (prestige, credit, etc.), fall (from power, etc.)

1219 悔 ▶かい
▷く(いる)，く(やむ)，くや(しい)

9 丶 丷 忄 忄 忙 忙 恈 悔 悔

後悔　　　こうかい　[する] regret, repent

悔しい　　くやしい　mortifying, vexing, regrettable

悔やむ　　くやむ　regret, repent, lament

悔いる　　くいる　repent, regret, be sorry for

1220 慎 ▶しん
▷つつし(む)

13 丶 丷 忄 忄 忄 忄 恈 恈 慎 慎
慎 慎 慎

慎重な　　しんちょうな　prudent, careful, cautious

慎む　　　つつしむ　be prudent, be careful, refrain from

第 97 回

1221 頻 ▶ひん

17 卜 上 上 止 屯 牛 米 步 步 歩
炉 炉 頻 頻 頻 頻 頻

頻繁に　　ひんぱんに　frequently

頻発　　　ひんぱつ　[する] occur frequently

頻出　　　ひんしゅつ　[する] appear frequently

頻度　　　ひんど　frequency

1222 項 ▶こう

12 一 丅 丁 工 工 功 項 項 項 項
項 項

漢字の形に気をつけましょう 42

1212	1213	1211	542	689	688
処	拠	廷	庭	延	誕

適切な処置　　証拠を提出する　　　法廷に出る　　日本庭園　　　　延長戦　　誕生日

事項	じこう	matter, item
項目	こうもく	item, heading
条項	じょうこう	article, clause, provision
要項	ようこう	guidelines, handbook (on applying to a school, etc.), the essential points

1223　販　▶はん

11　｜ 冂 冂 月 目 月 貝 貯 舨 販 販

販売	はんばい	-する sell, market, deal in
自動販売機	じどうはんばいき	vending machine
市販	しはん	-する put on the market
販路	はんろ	a market (for goods), outlet

1224　贈　▶ぞう，そう　▷おく(る)

18　｜ 冂 冂 月 目 月 貝 貝 貯 貯 貯 贈 贈 贈 贈 贈 贈 贈

贈(り)物	おくりもの	gift, present
贈る	おくる	give a present
贈与税	ぞうよぜい	gift tax
贈答品	ぞうとうひん	gift
寄贈	きぞう，きそう	-する give a present, donate

1225　賄　▶わい　▷まかな(う)

13　｜ 冂 冂 月 目 月 貝 貝 貯 賄 賄 賄 賄

賄賂	わいろ	bribe, corruption
贈賄	ぞうわい	-する give a bribe

収賄	しゅうわい	-する accept a bribe
贈収賄事件	ぞうしゅうわいじけん	bribery case
賄う	まかなう	cover the cost of, provide (meals, etc.)

1226　賂　▶ろ

13　｜ 冂 冂 月 目 月 貝 貯 貯 賂 賂 賂

賄賂	わいろ	bribe, corruption

1227　賢　▶けん　▷かしこ(い)　1987　cf. 腎

16　｜ 冖 冖 亚 臣 臣 臣 臣 臣 臥 賢 賢 賢 賢 賢 賢 賢

賢明な	けんめいな	wise, prudent
歴 良妻賢母	りょうさいけんぼ	good wife and wise mother
賢い	かしこい	wise, clever, smart

1228　堅　▶けん　▷かた(い)

12　｜ 冖 冖 亚 臣 臣 臣 臣 臥 堅 堅 堅

堅い	かたい	hard, solid, reliable
堅固な	けんごな	strong, solid, firm
堅実な	けんじつな	steady, reliable, sound, solid
中堅企業	ちゅうけんきぎょう	medium-sized companies
堅持	けんじ	-する hold fast to, adhere to

第4水準

漢字の形に気をつけましょう❹

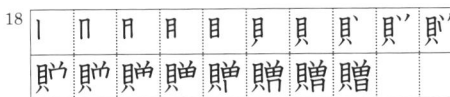

1179	1214	1215	1035
遺	遣	還	環

遺伝の法則　　使節を派遣する　　領土を返還する　　環境破壊

1229 臨 ▶りん ▷のぞ(む)

18

| 丨 | 厂 | 厂 | 臣 | 臣 | 臣 | 臣 | 臣 | 臨 | 臨 |
| 臨 | 臨 | 臨 | 臨 | 臨 | 臨 | 臨 | 臨 | | |

臨時の　りんじの　temporary, extraordinary, special

臨時国会　りんじこっかい　extraordinary session of the Diet

臨床心理学　りんしょうしんりがく　clinical psychology

臨終　りんじゅう　one's last moments, one's death

臨む　のぞむ　face (the ocean, a tough situation, etc.)

1230 幹 ▶かん ▷みき

13

| 一 | 十 | 十 | 古 | 古 | 古 | 直 | 卓 | 卓 | 幹 |
| 幹 | 幹 | 幹 | | | | | | | |

幹部　かんぶ　managing staff, executive members, key officers

新幹線　しんかんせん　the *Shinkansen*, Japan's bullet train

幹事長　かんじちょう　secretary-general/executive secretary (of a party)

根幹　こんかん　basis, root, nucleus

語幹　ごかん　stem of a word

幹　みき　tree trunk, important part

第 98 回

1231 稿 ▶こう　　83　313　cf. 高 橋

15

| ノ | 二 | 千 | 千 | 禾 | 禾 | 秆 | 秆 | 秆 | 秆 |
| 秆 | 稿 | 稿 | 稿 | 稿 | | | | | |

原稿　げんこう　manuscript, draft

草稿　そうこう　rough draft

投稿　とうこう　contribution (of one's writing) [する] contribute (to a magazine, newspaper, etc.)

1232 稼 ▶か ▷かせ(ぐ)　　52　599　cf. 家 嫁

15

| ノ | 二 | 千 | 千 | 禾 | 禾' | 禾' | 秅 | 秅 | 秅 |
| 秷 | 秷 | 稼 | 稼 | 稼 | | | | | |

稼ぐ　かせぐ　earn money

稼ぎ　かせぎ　earnings, income

稼働　かどう　[する] work, operate

1233 稲 ▶とう ▷いね, いな

14

| ノ | 二 | 千 | 千 | 禾 | 禾 | 秆 | 秆 | 秆 | 秆 |
| 稻 | 稲 | 稲 | 稲 | | | | | | |

稲　いね　rice plant

稲作　いなさく　rice growing

[特] 水稲　すいとう　paddy rice

◇ 早稲田大学　わせだだいがく　Waseda University

1234 穏 ▶おん ▷おだ(やか)

16

| ノ | 二 | 千 | 禾 | 禾 | 秆 | 秅 | 秅 | 秅 | 稆 |
| 稆 | 稆 | 稆 | 穏 | 穏 | 穏 | | | | |

穏やかな　おだやかな　gentle, calm, peaceful, tranquil

平穏な　へいおんな　peaceful, uneventful

穏和な　おんわな　gentle, moderate, mild

◇ 安穏な　あんのんな　easy and peaceful

1235 隠 ▶いん ▷かく(す), かく(れる)

14

| ⻖ | ⻖ | ⻖ | ⻖ | ⻖ | ⻖ | ⻖ | 陷 | 陷 | 陷 |
| 隱 | 隠 | 隠 | 隠 | | | | | | |

漢字の形に気をつけましょう ㊹

1216	1217	1218	1693
逐	遂	墜	*堕
逐語訳	任務を遂行する	旅客機が墜落する	*堕落した生活 だらく

隠す	かくす hide, conceal, put (something) out of sight
隠れる	かくれる hide, disappear
歴 隠居	いんきょ retirement, a person retired from active life する retire from active life

1236 隔 ▶かく ▷へだ(てる)，へだ(たる)

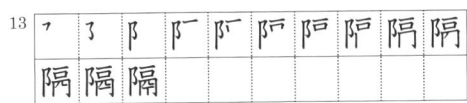

間隔	かんかく space, interval
隔離	かくり する isolate, quarantine
隔てる	へだてる part, separate, partition, screen
隔たる	へだたる be distant from, be remote, be estranged

1237 融 ▶ゆう

金融	きんゆう finance, financing
金融機関	きんゆうきかん financial institutions
融資	ゆうし する vi. finance, loan, furnish funds
融通	ゆうずう する lend (money)
融通がきく	ゆうずうがきく flexible, adaptable
融合	ゆうごう する fuse, merge
核融合	かくゆうごう nuclear fusion

1238 邸 ▶てい

| 邸宅 | ていたく a residence, mansion |

私邸	してい private residence (in contrast to official residence)
公邸	こうてい official residence
首相官邸	しゅしょうかんてい official residence of the prime minister

1239 隅 ▶ぐう ▷すみ

隅	すみ corner, nook
隅田川	すみだがわ Sumida River
特 一隅	いちぐう corner, nook

1240 偶 ▶ぐう

偶然	ぐうぜん by chance, by coincidence
偶発的な	ぐうはつてきな accidental
偶数	ぐうすう even number 反 *奇数(きすう) odd number
配偶者	はいぐうしゃ spouse
偶像	ぐうぞう idol, icon

第 99 回

1241 僕 ▶ぼく

| 僕 | ぼく I (in masculine speech) |

第4水準

漢字の形に気をつけましょう㊺

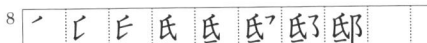

74	164	454	969	1219	1801
母	毎	海	梅	悔	*悔
父と母	毎日	青い海	梅の花	悔しい思いをする	人を*侮*辱する

特 下僕　　　げぼく　a male servant
特 従僕　　　じゅうぼく　servant, valet

1242 偉 ▶い
▷えら(い)

12 ノ イ イ′ イ″ 仵 偉 偉 偉 偉 偉 偉

偉大な　　いだいな　great, grand
偉人　　　いじん　great person
偉い　　　えらい　great, eminent

1243 俗 ▶ぞく
1126 cf. 浴

9 ノ イ イ′ 伀 伀 俗 俗 俗 俗

風俗　　　ふうぞく　manners, customs, public morals
cf. 風俗営業(ふうぞくえいぎょう)
entertainment and amusement business
俗語　　　ぞくご　slang
民俗学　　みんぞくがく　folklore

1244 侵 ▶しん
▷おか(す)
1496 cf. 浸

9 ノ イ イ′ 仴 仴 伊 侵 侵 侵

侵略　　　しんりゃく　する invade, aggress
侵入　　　しんにゅう　する invade, trespass
侵害　　　しんがい　する infringe on
侵攻　　　しんこう　する invade
侵す　　　おかす　invade, violate, infringe on (someone's rights)

1245 伺 ▶し
▷うかが(う)

7 ノ イ 门 伺 伺 伺 伺

伺う　　　うかがう　visit, ask/inquire, hear/be told [humble]
歴 伺候　　しこう　する attend (one's lord), make a courtesy call

1246 伸 ▶しん
▷の(びる)，の(ばす)，の(べる) cf. 申 仲
585 1169

7 ノ イ 仃 仃 伬 伸 伸

伸びる　　のびる　vi. stretch, lengthen, grow, extend
伸ばす　　のばす　vt. stretch, lengthen, increase
差し伸べる　さしのべる　reach out (one's hand)
追伸　　　ついしん　postscript, P.S.
屈伸　　　くっしん　する bend and stretch

1247 倣 ▶ほう
▷なら(う)

10 ノ イ イ′ 仁 仿 仿 伨 倣 倣 倣

模倣　　　もほう　imitation, an imitation　する imitate
例に倣って　れいにならって　in the same manner as the example

1248 催 ▶さい
▷もよお(す)

13 ノ イ イ′ 仴 伬 伬 伬 催 催 催 催 催

開催　　　かいさい　する hold (an event)
主催　　　しゅさい　する sponsor, promote
主催者　　しゅさいしゃ　sponsor, promoter
催す　　　もよおす　hold (an event), feel (sleepy, cold, etc.)
催し物　　もよおしもの　entertainment, special event

漢字の形に気をつけましょう㊻

238　　433　　853　　1227
質　貿　資　賢

質問をする　　外国との貿易　　教員の資格　　賢明なやり方

催眠術　　　さいみんじゅつ　hypnotism
◇ 催涙ガス　さいるいガス　tear gas

南極圏　　　なんきょくけん　the Antarctic Circle
大気圏　　　たいきけん　the atmosphere

1249 債 ▶さい

cf. 積 責　886 638

13　ノ イ イ― イ＋ イ＋ 伴 倩 倩 債 債 債 債

負債　　　　ふさい　debt, liabilities
国債　　　　こくさい　government bond
社債　　　　しゃさい　(corporate) bond/debenture
債券　　　　さいけん　bonds, debentures
債権(者)　　さいけん(しゃ)　credit(or)
債務(者)　　さいむ(しゃ)　debt(or)

1250 併 ▶へい
▷あわ(せる)

8　ノ イ イ イ′ 伫 伫 併 併

合併　　　　がっぺい　する merge, consolidate
併用　　　　へいよう　する use together, use two things at the same time
併発　　　　へいはつ　する have a complication (from surgery, a disease, etc.)
併せる　　　あわせる　put together, combine

第 100 回

1251 圏 ▶けん

12　｜ 冂 冂 冂 罒 罒 罒 圀 圏 圏 圏 圏

首都圏　　　しゅとけん　metropolitan area
共産圏　　　きょうさんけん　the Communist bloc
北極圏　　　ほっきょくけん　the Arctic Circle

1252 宇 ▶う

6　｀ ヽ 宀 宀 宁 宇

宇宙　　　　うちゅう　the universe, the cosmos, space

1253 宙 ▶ちゅう

8　｀ ヽ 宀 宀 宁 审 宙 宙

宇宙　　　　うちゅう　the universe, the cosmos, space
宙返り　　　ちゅうがえり　する somersault

1254 抽 ▶ちゅう

cf. 油　624

8　一 十 扌 扣 扣 抽 抽 抽

抽象的な　　ちゅうしょうてきな　abstract
抽出　　　　ちゅうしゅつ　する extract, sample
抽選　　　　ちゅうせん　lottery, a drawing (of lots)　する draw lots

1255 拍 ▶はく, ひょう

8　一 十 扌 扌′ 扩 拍 拍 拍

拍手　　　　はくしゅ　する clap one's hands, applaud
拍車　　　　はくしゃ　spur
*脈拍　　　　みゃくはく　pulse
拍子　　　　ひょうし　tempo, time, chance, the moment

第4水準

漢字の形に気をつけましょう㊼

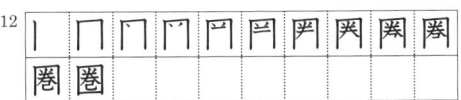

1178　1239　1240
遇　隅　偶

社員の待遇　　部屋の隅　　街で偶然友達に会った

1256 摘 ▶てき
▷つ(む)

14 一 十 扌 扌 扩 扩 扩 扩 摍 摘
摘 摘 摘 摘

指摘	してき	[する] point out
摘出	てきしゅつ	[する] extract, take out, remove
摘発	てきはつ	[する] disclose, expose
摘む	つむ	pick (flowers/berries, etc.)
茶摘み	ちゃつみ	tea picking

1257 握 ▶あく
▷にぎ(る)

12 一 十 扌 扩 护 护 护 捏 捏 握
握 握

握手	あくしゅ	[する] shake hands
握力	あくりょく	grasping power, (the strength of one's) grip
*掌握	しょうあく	[する] control, command
握る	にぎる	grip, grasp, take hold of

1258 探 ▶たん
▷さぐ(る)，さが(す)

11 一 十 扌 扌 扩 护 护 挥 挥 探
探

探す	さがす	look for, look up (a word)
探る	さぐる	grope for, probe, search
探求	たんきゅう	[する] search for, pursue
探知機	たんちき	detector, device used for detection

1259 掘 ▶くつ
▷ほ(る)
349
cf. 屈

11 一 十 扌 扩 护 折 拆 掘 掘 掘
掘

掘る	ほる	dig, excavate
発掘	はっくつ	[する] excavate
採掘	さいくつ	[する] mine

1260 堀 ▷ほり
349
cf. 屈

11 一 十 土 扩 圷 圹 圻 坭 坭 堀
堀

堀	ほり	moat
内堀	うちぼり	inner moat
外堀	そとぼり	outer moat
◇ *釣堀	つりぼり	fishing pond

1261 埋 ▶まい
▷う(める)，う(まる)，う(もれる)

10 一 十 土 圤 圽 坭 坦 坢 埋 埋

埋める	うめる	bury, inter, fill up (a hole)
埋立地	うめたてち	reclaimed land
埋もれる	うもれる	be buried, sink into obscurity
埋葬	まいそう	[する] inter
埋没	まいぼつ	[する] be buried
[特] 埋蔵金	まいぞうきん	money buried in the ground

第 101 回

1262 排 ▶はい

11 一 十 扌 扪 扫 抈 捈 挑 排 排
排

漢字の形に気をつけましょう㊽

307　　1241　　1489
業　　僕　　*撲

大企業と中小企業　　*君と僕　　打*撲傷
　　　　　　　　　　きみ　ぼく　　だ ぼくしょう

排気ガス	はいきガス	exhaust (fumes)
排水	はいすい	drainage ［する］ vi. drain
排他的な	はいたてきな	exclusive
排日運動	はいにちうんどう	anti-Japanese movement

1263 拓 ▶たく

8 　一 十 扌 扩 拓 拓 拓 拓

開拓	かいたく	［する］ open up, bring (land) under cultivation
開拓者	かいたくしゃ	pioneer, settler
干拓	かんたく	［する］ reclaim land by drainage
特 拓本	たくほん	rubbing (of an inscription)

1264 抑 ▶よく ▷おさ(える) 　1854 cf. 柳

7 　一 十 扌 扩 扣 扣 抑

抑制	よくせい	［する］ control, restrain, suppress
抑圧	よくあつ	［する］ oppress, suppress
抑止力	よくしりょく	deterrent
抑える	おさえる	hold down, suppress (a rebellion), repress

1265 拐 ▶かい

8 　一 十 扌 扌 护 护 拐 拐

誘拐	ゆうかい	［する］ kidnap, abduct

1266 扱 ▷あつか(う)

6 　一 十 扌 扱 扱 扱

扱う	あつかう	handle, deal with, conduct, manage, treat

取り扱う	とりあつかう	deal in, handle
取扱注意	とりあつかいちゅうい	Handle With Care

1267 撮 ▶さつ ▷と(る) 　439 cf. 最

15 　一 十 扌 扌 扩 护 押 押 押 押 押 揖 撮 撮

撮影	さつえい	［する］ make a film, take a picture
撮影所	さつえいじょ	film studio
撮る	とる	take (a picture), make (a film)

1268 挑 ▶ちょう ▷いど(む)

9 　一 十 扌 扪 払 扴 扒 挑 挑

挑戦	ちょうせん	［する］ challenge
挑戦者	ちょうせんしゃ	challenger
挑発	ちょうはつ	［する］ provoke, arouse
挑発的な	ちょうはつてきな	provocative, suggestive
挑む	いどむ	challenge, defy

1269 兆 ▶ちょう ▷きざ(す), きざ(し)

6 　丿 丿 丬 北 兆 兆

一兆円	いっちょうえん	one trillion yen cf. 一億円 (いちおくえん) one hundred million yen
前兆	ぜんちょう	omen, sign
兆し	きざし	signs, symptoms, indications

1270 援 ▶えん 　1950 cf. 媛

12 　一 十 扌 扩 扩 护 护 押 押 揺 援

第4水準

漢字の形に気をつけましょう❹❾

385　違　1242　偉　110　遠　1865　*猿

規則に違反する　偉大な人物　遠心力　類人*猿
るいじん えん

援助　　　えんじょ　［する］help, assist, aid

応援　　　おうえん　［する］cheer, root for, aid, support

声援　　　せいえん　shout of encouragement/support
　　　　　［する］cheer, encourage

援軍　　　えんぐん　reinforcements

後援会　　こうえんかい　group supporting a politician, fan club

1271 緩 ▶かん
▷ゆる（い），ゆる（やか），ゆる（む），ゆる（める）

15 く　幺　幺　糸　糸　糸　紀　紓　緩
緩　緩　緩　緩　緩

緩和　　　かんわ　［する］relieve, ease, relax

規制緩和　きせいかんわ　deregulation, relaxation of restrictions

緩やかな　ゆるやかな　loose, slack, slow

緩い　　　ゆるい　loose, slack, lax

緩める　　ゆるめる　loosen, relieve, relax, slacken

第 102 回

1272 丈 ▶じょう
▷たけ

3 一　ナ　丈

大丈夫　　だいじょうぶ　all right, okay, safe

丈夫な　　じょうぶな　healthy, strong, durable

背丈　　　せたけ　one's height, stature

1273 牧 ▶ぼく
▷まき
982 cf. 枚

8 ノ　ヒ　ヒ　牛　牛　牛　牧　牧

牧場　　　ぼくじょう　ranch, pasture

牧草　　　ぼくそう　grass, pasture

放牧　　　ほうぼく　［する］pasture, graze

遊牧　　　ゆうぼく　nomadism

牧師　　　ぼくし　clergyman, minister, pastor

◇ 牧場　　まきば　pasture

1274 畜 ▶ちく
743 cf. 蓄

10 ' 一 亠 玄 玄 产 斉 斉 斋 畜

家畜　　　かちく　livestock, domestic animals

牧畜業　　ぼくちくぎょう　stock farming

1275 充 ▶じゅう
▷あ（てる）

6 ' 一 ナ 玄 充 充

充電　　　じゅうでん　［する］charge/recharge (electricity)

充実した　じゅうじつした　full, complete, satisfying

充満　　　じゅうまん　［する］be full of (poisonous gas, smoke, etc.)

充足　　　じゅうそく　［する］suffice, satisfy

充血　　　じゅうけつ　［する］be bloodshot, be congested

拡充　　　かくじゅう　［する］expand, enlarge, amplify

充てる　　あてる　assign, allot

1276 玄 ▶げん

5 ' 一 亠 玄 玄

玄関　　　げんかん　front door/entrance, porch

玄米　　　げんまい　brown rice

玄人　　　△くろうと　expert, professional, specialist　cf. 素人（△しろうと）amateur

---

漢字の形に気をつけましょう 50

312　授　　339　暖　　1270　援　　1271　緩

面白い授業　　暖房　　海外経済援助　　規制緩和

1277 **豪**　▶ごう　　52 cf. 家

14
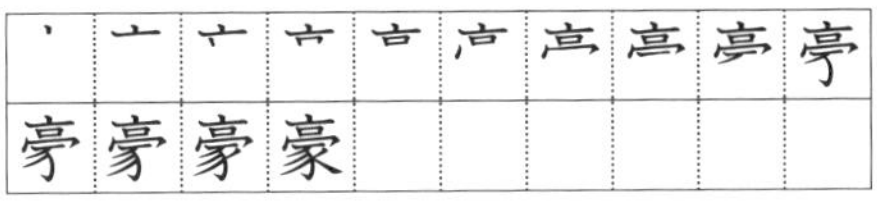

豪雨　ごうう　heavy rainfall, torrential downpour
豪遊　ごうゆう　-する spend extravagantly, live it up
豪*華な　ごうかな　gorgeous, deluxe, magnificent
豪勢な　ごうせいな　luxurious, grand
豪州　ごうしゅう　Australia

1278 **盲**　▶もう

8

盲人　もうじん　blind person, the blind
盲目の　もうもくの　blind
盲点　もうてん　blind spot, (legal) loophole

1279 **帽**　▶ぼう　　1669 cf. 冒

12
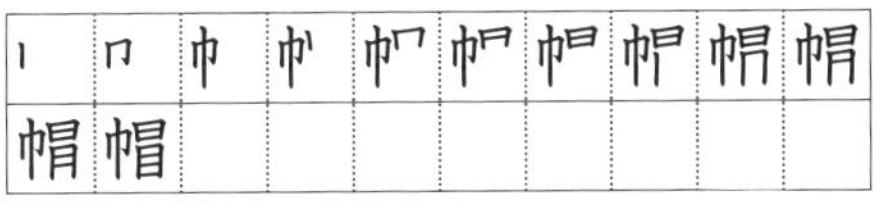

帽子　ぼうし　hat, cap

1280 **昇**　▶しょう　▷のぼ(る)　　1915 cf. 升

8

上昇　じょうしょう　-する rise, ascend
昇進　しょうしん　-する be promoted (in rank, at work, etc.)
昇格　しょうかく　-する be promoted (to a higher rank)
昇給　しょうきゅう　salary increase　-する get a pay raise
昇る　のぼる　rise, ascend

第　103　回

1281 **曇**　▶どん　▷くも(る)

16

曇り　くもり　cloudy
曇る　くもる　get cloudy
曇天　どんてん　cloudy weather

1282 **糧**　▶りょう，ろう　▷かて

18
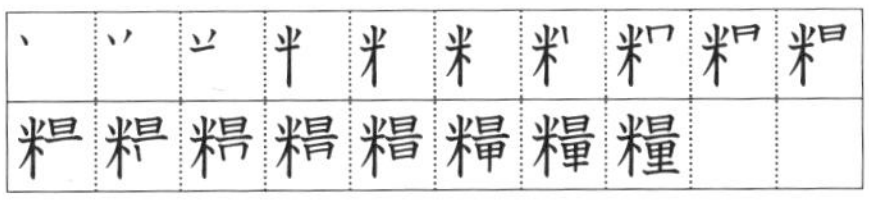

食糧　しょくりょう　provisions, food
歴 兵糧　ひょうろう　military provisions
◊ 日々の糧　ひびのかて　one's daily bread

1283 **糖**　▶とう

16

砂糖　さとう　sugar
糖分　とうぶん　sugar content

漢字の形に気をつけましょう(51)

87	320	1272
大	文	丈
大きい家	文学と歴史	丈夫な体

1284 粧 ▶しょう

12 丶 丷 丬 半 米 米 米' 籵 籵 粧 粧

化粧	けしょう [する] makeup, put on make up
化粧品	けしょうひん cosmetics, makeup
化粧室	けしょうしつ dressing room, rest room, powder room

1285 臭 ▶しゅう ▷くさ(い)，にお(う) cf. 息 1118

9 ノ 丨 冂 甶 甶 自 皁 臭 臭

臭い	くさい smelly, suspicious, fishy
臭う	におう smell
悪臭	あくしゅう bad smell, offensive odor

1286 鼻 ▶び ▷はな

14 ノ 丨 冂 甶 甶 自 自 皁 鳥 鳥 畠 畠 鼻 鼻

鼻	はな nose
鼻血	はなぢ nosebleed
耳鼻科	じびか ear and nose (medical specialty)
特 鼻*孔	びこう nostril

1287 憩 ▶けい ▷いこ(い)，いこ(う) cf. 想 392

16 一 二 千 千 舌 舌 舌' 舌 舌 舌 舌 舌 憩 憩 憩

休憩	きゅうけい [する] rest, take a break
休憩時間	きゅうけいじかん recess, intermission, break time
憩い	いこい relaxation, rest
憩う	いこう rest

1288 舌 ▶ぜつ ▷した

6 一 二 千 千 舌 舌

| 舌 | した tongue |

二枚舌	にまいじた forked tongue, two-faced, duplicity
舌打ち	したうち [する] cluck one's tongue
舌戦	ぜっせん verbal warfare, heated discussion
弁舌	べんぜつ eloquence
毒舌	どくぜつ malicious tongue

1289 君 ▶くん ▷きみ

7 フ ⼂ ヨ 尹 尹 君 君

君	きみ you, lord (sovereign)
君主	くんしゅ monarch, sovereign
立憲君主制	りっけんくんしゅせい constitutional monarchy
◇ 君臨	くんりん [する] reign over (a country), rule over

1290 含 ▶がん ▷ふく(む)，ふく(める)

7 ノ 人 ⼈ 今 今 含 含

含む	ふくむ contain, include, hold (inside)
含める	ふくめる include
含有量	がんゆうりょう amount contained, (alcohol, etc.) content
含蓄	がんちく implication, significance, overtone

第 104 回

1291 叫 ▶きょう ▷さけ(ぶ) cf. 収 828

6 丨 冂 口 叫 叫 叫

叫ぶ	さけぶ shout, cry out, scream
叫び声	さけびごえ shout, cry, scream
絶叫	ぜっきょう [する] cry out loudly

1292 奇 ▶き cf. 寄 1120

8 一 ナ 大 ⼤ 杏 杏 杏 奇

奇妙な	きみょうな strange, curious, odd
好奇心	こうきしん curiosity
奇数	きすう odd number 反 偶数（ぐうすう）even number

1293 **崎**　▷さき　1945 cf. 埼

11
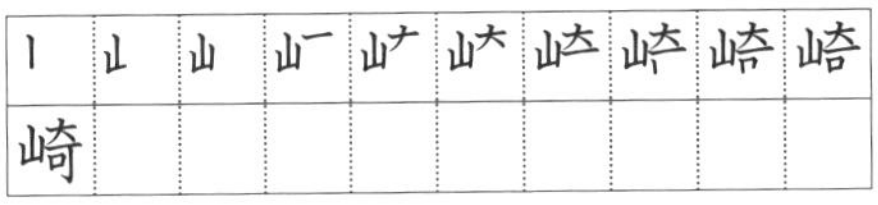

長崎　ながさき　Nagasaki (a city on the western coast of Kyushu)

宮崎　みやざき　Miyazaki (a city on the eastern coast of Kyushu)

1294 **峡**　▶きょう　560 cf. 狭

9
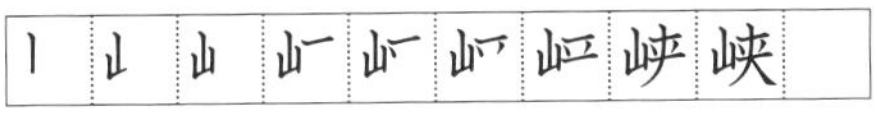

海峡　かいきょう　strait, channel

ドーバー海峡　ドーバーかいきょう　the Strait of Dover

1295 **紅**　▶こう，く　▷べに，くれない

9
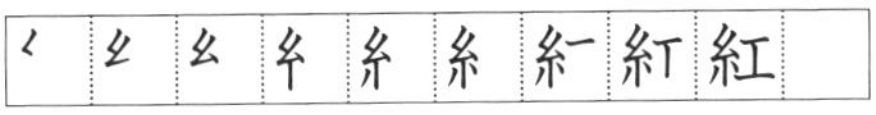

紅茶　こうちゃ　black tea

紅葉　こうよう　colored leaves　-する turn red

紅葉　△もみじ　maple tree, autumn/colored leaves

真紅の　しんくの　deep crimson

口紅　くちべに　lipstick

◇ 紅　くれない　crimson

1296 **繊**　▶せん　882 cf. 織

17

繊維　せんい　fiber, textiles

繊維工業　せんいこうぎょう　textile industry

合成繊維　ごうせいせんい　synthetic fiber

化学繊維　かがくせんい（かせん）　synthetic fiber　cf. *abbr.* 化繊

繊細な　せんさいな　delicate, fine

1297 **維**　▶い　81 1100 cf. 誰 稚

14

維持　いじ　-する maintain, sustain

維持費　いじひ　maintenance costs

歴 明治維新　めいじいしん　the Meiji Restoration

1298 **紛**　▶ふん　▷まぎ(れる)，まぎ(らす)，まぎ(らわす)，まぎ(らわしい)　1557 cf. 粉

10

国境紛争　こっきょうふんそう　border dispute

内紛　ないふん　internal trouble/strife

紛失　ふんしつ　-する lose (an object), be lost, be missing

紛れる　まぎれる　be mistaken (for), be mixed with, be diverted

紛らす　まぎらす　divert (attention, one's mind)

紛らわしい　まぎらわしい　confusing, easily confused, hard to distinguish

1299 **紳**　▶しん　586 cf. 神

11

紳士　しんし　gentleman

紳士服　しんしふく　men's clothing

特 紳士協定　しんしきょうてい　gentleman's agreement

第4水準

漢字の形に気をつけましょう(52)

532	892	893	1006	1288	1289	1290
台	告	吉	否	舌	君	含

台所　報告をする　大安吉日　犯行を否認する　毒舌家　君と僕　税を含んだ料金

1300 縦 ▶じゅう ▷たて

16

縦の	たての	vertical, longitudinal
縦線	たてせん	vertical line
縦断	じゅうだん	する travel down/up through
*操縦	そうじゅう	する steer, operate, pilot, maneuver

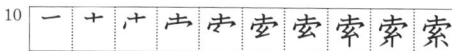
第 105 回

1301 索 ▶さく

10 一 十 卞 壶 壶 壶 宏 突 索 索

索引	さくいん	index
思索	しさく	する contemplate
*捜索	そうさく	する search/look for
探索	たんさく	する search for, explore

1302 累 ▶るい

11 ' 口 田 田 甲 罗 罗 罗 累 累

累計	るいけい	(grand) total する total
累積赤字	るいせきあかじ	cumulative deficit
累積債務	るいせきさいむ	cumulative debts
特 累進課税	るいしんかぜい	progressive/graduated taxation

1303 畳 ▶じょう ▷たた(む)，たたみ   1922 cf. 且

12 ' 口 田 田 甲 甲 畀 畀 畳 畳 畳

畳	たたみ	tatami, Japanese straw mat
～畳	～じょう	~ tatami-mat (room)
折り畳み式	おりたたみしき	collapsible
畳む	たたむ	fold up

1304 翼 ▶よく ▷つばさ

17

右翼	うよく	the right wing, rightist
左翼	さよく	the left wing, leftist
翼	つばさ	wing

1305 裸 ▶ら ▷はだか

13 ` ラ ネ ネ ネ ネ ネ 衤 衤 衤 裡 裸 裸

裸	はだか	nude, naked
裸足	▲はだし	barefoot
裸婦	らふ	nude woman
裸体画	らたいが	nude pictures

1306 軌 ▶き

9 一 厂 厅 冇 目 亘 車 軋 軌

| 軌道 | きどう | orbit, (railroad) tracks |

1307 載 ▶さい ▷の(せる)，の(る)

13 一 十 圭 圭 声 青 青 青 壹 車 載 載 載

掲載	けいさい	する publish, carry an article
◇ 積載	せきさい	する load, carry
載せる	のせる	place (on), load, publish

1308 軟 ▶なん ▷やわ(らか)，やわ(らかい)

11 一 厂 厅 冇 目 亘 車 軒 軒 軟 軟

| 軟らかい | やわらかい | soft |
| *柔軟な | じゅうなんな | flexible, limber, supple |

軟弱な	なんじゃくな	weak, feeble
軟骨	なんこつ	cartilage
軟化	なんか	-する soften, weaken

1309
硬　▶こう
　　▷かた（い）

| 12 | 一 | ア | エ | 石 | 石 | 石 | 石 | 砠 | 硴 |
| | 硬 | 硬 | | | | | | | |

硬い	かたい	hard, solid, stiff
硬貨	こうか	coins, hard currency
硬度	こうど	(degree of) hardness
強硬な	きょうこうな	firm (attitude), stubborn, uncompromising
硬化	こうか	-する stiffen, harden

1310
柔　▶じゅう，にゅう　　1855
　　▷やわ（らか），やわ（らかい）　cf. 桑

| 9 | フ | マ | ユ | 予 | 矛 | 予 | 柔 | 柔 | 柔 |

柔らかい	やわらかい	soft, tender, gentle
柔軟な	じゅうなんな	flexible, limber, supple
柔道	じゅうどう	Judo
◇ 柔和な	にゅうわな	gentle, mild, tender, soft

第 106 回

1311
炊　▶すい
　　▷た（く）

| 8 | ' | ' | ソ | 火 | 火 | 炊 | 炊 | 炊 | |

炊事	すいじ	cooking, kitchen work -する vi. do the cooking
自炊	じすい	-する do one's own cooking
炊飯器	すいはんき	rice cooker
炊く	たく	cook (rice)

1312
冊　▶さつ，さく

| 5 | 丨 | 冂 | 册 | 冊 | 冊 | | | | |

| ～冊 | ～さつ | (counter for books) |
| 別冊 | べっさつ | separate volume supplement |

| 分冊 | ぶんさつ | separate volume |
| ◇ 短冊 | たんざく | strip of fancy paper (for writing haiku, etc.) |

1313
盤　▶ばん　　648
　　　cf. 般

| 15 | ' | 丿 | 力 | 角 | 舟 | 舟 | 舡 | 船 | 般 |
| | 般 | 般 | 盤 | 盤 | 盤 | | | | |

基盤	きばん	foundation, basis, base
地盤	じばん	foundation (of a home/building), the ground, constituency
円盤	えんばん	disk
終盤戦	しゅうばんせん	final stage (of a game, election campaign, etc.)

1314
盆　▶ぼん

| 9 | 丿 | 八 | 分 | 分 | 分 | 盆 | 盆 | 盆 | 盆 |

（お）盆	（お）ぼん	the *Bon* Festival, tray
盆地	ぼんち	basin
盆*栽	ぼんさい	bonsai, potted dwarf tree

1315
煮　▶しゃ
　　▷に（る），に（える），に（やす）

| 12 | 一 | 十 | 土 | 耂 | 耂 | 者 | 者 | 者 | 者 |
| | 煮 | 煮 | | | | | | | |

煮る	にる	boil, simmer, cook
煮える	にえる	boil, cook, be boiled, be cooked
業を煮やす	ごうをにやす	become irritated, lose patience
◇ 煮*沸	しゃふつ	-する vt. boil, scald

1316
署　▶しょ　　1031
　　　cf. 著

| 13 | 丶 | 冂 | 冂 | 罒 | 罒 | 罒 | 罕 | 罜 | 署 |
| | 署 | 署 | 署 | | | | | | |

署名	しょめい	signature -する sign
警察署	けいさつしょ	police station
消防署	しょうぼうしょ	fire station
税務署	ぜいむしょ	tax office

第4水準

1317 罰 ▶ばつ, ばち

1047
cf. 罪

14 丶 冖 冖 罒 罒 罒 罰 罰 罰 罰
罰 罰 罰 罰

罰	ばつ	punishment, penalty
罰する	ばっする	punish, penalize
罰金	ばっきん	a fine, monetary penalty
体罰	たいばつ	corporal/physical punishment
罰が当たる	ばちがあたる	receive divine punishment, pay for it

1318 型 ▶けい ▷かた

9 一 二 干 开 开 刑 刑 型 型

型	かた	model, pattern, mold, type
大型	おおがた	large (truck, machine, etc.)
中型	ちゅうがた	medium (truck, machine, etc.)
小型	こがた	small (truck, machine, etc.)
典型的な	てんけいてきな	typical
原型	げんけい	prototype, model
類型的な	るいけいてきな	stereotypical

1319 刺 ▶し ▷さ(す), さ(さる)

8 一 厂 冖 市 束 束 刺 刺

刺す	さす	stab, pierce; sting
刺さる	ささる	stick, get stuck
刺し身	さしみ	sliced raw fish
名刺	めいし	business card
風刺	ふうし	-する satirize
刺激	しげき	-する stimulate, irritate

1320 削 ▶さく ▷けず(る)

9 丷 丷 ハ ゲ 肖 肖 肖 削 削

| 削減 | さくげん | -する reduce, cut down |
| 削除 | さくじょ | -する delete |

| 削る | けずる | sharpen (a pencil), curtail, cut down, delete |
| *鉛筆削り | えんぴつけずり | pencil sharpener |

第 107 回

1321 剰 ▶じょう

11 一 二 三 千 丰 垂 乗 乗 乗 剰
剰

過剰な	かじょうな	excessive
余剰人員	よじょうじんいん	superfluous personnel
剰余金	じょうよきん	surplus (funds)

1322 垂 ▶すい ▷た(れる), た(らす)

8 一 二 三 千 丰 垂 垂 垂

垂直の	すいちょくの	vertical, perpendicular
垂線	すいせん	perpendicular line
雨垂れ	あまだれ	raindrops (from a tree, roof, etc.)
垂らす	たらす	drip (with sweat, saliva, blood)

1323 華 ▶か, け ▷はな

10 一 二 艹 艹 芏 芒 苎 莒 莒 華

中華料理	ちゅうかりょうり	Chinese food
中華思想	ちゅうかしそう	Sinocentrism
中華人民共和国	ちゅうかじんみんきょうわこく	People's Republic of China
中華民国	ちゅうかみんこく	Republic of China
華道	かどう	the Japanese art of flower arrangement
華やかな	はなやかな	flowery, brilliant
歴 *香華	こうげ	incense and flowers

1324 兼 ▶けん ▷か(ねる)

10 丶 丷 丷 兰 岂 兰 羊 兼 兼 兼

兼任	けんにん	-する hold two posts simultaneously
～兼～	～けん～	and, in addition
兼ねる	かねる	double as

1325 嫌

▶けん, げん
▷きら(う), いや

1649 cf. 嬢

13
| く | 女 | 女 | 女' | 妒 | 妒 | 娏 | 娏 | 娏 | 娏 |
| 嫌 | 嫌 | 嫌 | | | | | | | |

嫌いな	きらいな	disliked, disgusting, disagreeable
好き嫌い	すききらい	likes and dislikes
嫌う	きらう	dislike, hate
嫌悪感	けんおかん	hatred, aversion
機嫌	きげん	mood
嫌な	いやな	disagreeable, unpleasant, disgusting

1326 尋

▶じん
▷たず(ねる)

12
| コ | ヨ | ヨ | ヨ | ヨ | ヨ | ヨ | 尋 | 尋 | 尋 |
| 尋 | 尋 | | | | | | | | |

尋ねる	たずねる	ask, inquire
尋問	じんもん	-する question, examine
◇ 尋常な	じんじょうな	ordinary, common

1327 寿

▶じゅ
▷ことぶき

7
| 一 | 二 | 三 | 寿 | 寿 | 寿 | 寿 | | | |

寿命	じゅみょう	life span
長寿	ちょうじゅ	a long life, longevity
特 寿	ことぶき	congratulations, longevity
寿司	▲すし	sushi

1328 闘

▶とう
▷たたか(う)

18
| | | | | | | | | | |
| | | | | | | | | | |

戦闘	せんとう	battle, combat
戦闘機	せんとうき	fighter planes
階級闘争	かいきゅうとうそう	class struggle
春闘	しゅんとう	spring labor offensive (union initiative to negotiate higher wages, etc.)
◇ 闘う	たたかう	fight, struggle

1329 娯

▶ご

949　1926
cf. 誤 呉

10
| く | 女 | 女 | 女' | 妒 | 妒 | 娯 | 娯 | 娯 | 娯 |

| 娯楽 | ごらく | amusement, entertainment |

1330 妊

▶にん

7
| く | 女 | 女 | 妊' | 妊 | 妊 | 妊 | | | |

妊娠	にんしん	-する get pregnant, conceive a child
妊婦	にんぷ	pregnant woman
*避妊	ひにん	-する prevent conception

1331 娠

▶しん

10
| く | 女 | 女 | 娠' | 娠 | 娠 | 娠 | 娠 | 娠 | 娠 |

| 妊娠 | にんしん | -する get pregnant, conceive a child |
| 人工妊娠中絶 | じんこうにんしんちゅうぜつ | abortion cf. 人工妊娠中絶 is very often abbreviated as 人工中絶 or even simply 中絶 |

漢字の形に気をつけましょう53

1322	226	977
垂	郵	睡
垂線	郵便局	睡眠時間

第4水準

第 108 回

1332 **妥** ▶だ

cf. 受(269) 安(84)

7	一	𠂊	爫	爫	妥	妥	妥		

妥協 だきょう -する compromise
妥当な だとうな proper, appropriate, adequate
妥結 だけつ -する come to terms, reach an agreement

1333 **威** ▶い

9	ノ	厂	厂	反	反	反	威	威	威	

権威 けんい authority, an authority
威厳 いげん dignity, stateliness
威信 いしん prestige
威力 いりょく (overwhelming) power
威張る いばる be haughty, be arrogant, boast, brag
◇ 示威行動 じいこうどう threatening action
*脅威 きょうい threat, menace

1334 **戒** ▶かい ▷いまし(める)

cf. 械(511)

7	一	二	〒	开	戒	戒	戒		

警戒 けいかい -する be on guard, watch out for, take precautions against
厳戒態勢 げんかいたいせい high alert
十戒 じっかい，じゅっかい the Ten Commandments
戒律 かいりつ (religious) precepts
戒め いましめ admonition, lesson

1335 **釣** ▶ちょう ▷つ(る)

11	ノ	𠆢	亼	仐	令	牟	余	金	釒	釣
	釣									

釣り つり fishing
釣る つる fish
釣(り)合い つりあい balance, proportion
釣り合う つりあう be balanced, match well, be in proportion
お釣り おつり change (i.e., money that you get back after making a purchase)
特 釣果 ちょうか catch (in fishing)

1336 **鈴** ▶れい，りん ▷すず

13	ノ	𠆢	亼	仐	令	牟	余	金	釒	鈴
	鈴	鈴	鈴							

鈴 すず bell (that tinkles/jingles) cf. *鐘(かね) bell (like those used at a temple/church)
鈴虫 すずむし a kind of cricket
鈴木 すずき (surname)
風鈴 ふうりん wind-bell
呼び鈴 よびりん doorbell
特 電鈴 でんれい electric bell

1337 **鋼** ▶こう ▷はがね

16	ノ	𠆢	亼	仐	令	牟	余	金	釒	釦
	釦	鈤	鈤	鋼	鋼	鋼				

鉄鋼 てっこう (iron and) steel
鉄鋼業 てっこうぎょう steel industry
◇ 鋼 はがね steel

漢字の形に気をつけましょう(54)

84	269	1332	661
安	受	妥	姿
安心する	受付	妥協する	姿を見せる

1338 鎖
▶さ
▷くさり

18 ノ ノ ム ム 牟 牟 牟 金 金' 釒'
釒" 釒" 釗 鎖 鎖 鎖 鎖 鎖

鎖	くさり	chain
鎖国	さこく	[する] close the country
閉鎖	へいさ	[する] shut down, close down
封鎖	ふうさ	[する] block (off), blockade, block (up)
連鎖反応	れんさはんのう	chain reaction

1339 鉛
▶えん
▷なまり

13 ノ ノ ム ム 牟 牟 牟 金 金 釤ハ
鉛 鉛 鉛

| 鉛筆 | えんぴつ | pencil |
| 鉛 | なまり | lead |

1340 銅
▶どう

14 ノ ノ ム ム 牟 牟 牟 金 釘 釘
釘 釘 銅 銅

銅	どう	copper
銅像	どうぞう	bronze statue
銅メダル	どうメダル	bronze medal

第 109 回

1341 胴
▶どう

10 ノ 刀 月 月 月 肌 肌 胴 胴 胴

胴	どう	trunk, torso, waist
胴体	どうたい	body, trunk, torso
胴上げ	どうあげ	[する] hoist shoulder-high
胴回り	どうまわり	girth

1342 腕
▶わん
▷うで

979 2039
cf. 瞬 宛

12 ノ 刀 月 月 月' 月' 肸 肸 肸 胪
胪 腕

腕	うで	arm, skill, ability
腕時計	うでどけい	wristwatch
腕力	わんりょく	physical strength, (brute) force
手腕	しゅわん	ability, capability

1343 肺
▶はい

9 ノ 刀 月 月 月' 肸 肸 肺 肺

肺	はい	lung
肺病	はいびょう	lung disease
肺結核	はいけっかく	pulmonary tuberculosis
肺*炎	はいえん	pneumonia

1344 胆
▶たん

1050
cf. 担

9 ノ 刀 月 月 肌 肌 胆 胆 胆

大胆な	だいたんな	bold, daring
落胆	らくたん	[する] be disappointed, be discouraged
胆石	たんせき	gallstone

第4水準

漢字の形に気をつけましょう㉟

1086	1342	1630	1526
胸	腕	*胞	*陶
胸囲	腕力	細*胞 さい ぼう	*陶器 とう き

1345 肌 ▷はだ

6 ﾉ 刀 月 月 肌 肌

肌	はだ	(human) skin, disposition, character, temperament
肌寒い	はだざむい	chilly
地肌	じはだ	bare skin (without makeup), (the surface of) the ground
肌着	はだぎ	underwear
肌*触り	はだわり	(pleasant to the) touch, (a nice/unpleasant) feel

1346 飢 ▶き ▷う（える）

10 ﾉ 入 ㇒ 今 今 令 飠 食 創 飢

| 飢餓 | きが | hunger, starvation |
| 飢える | うえる | starve |

1347 餓 ▶が

15 ﾉ 入 ㇒ 今 今 令 飠 食 食 飠
飠 飠 餓 餓 餓

| 飢餓 | きが | hunger, starvation |
| 餓死 | がし | する starve to death |

1348 飼 ▶し ▷か（う）

13 ﾉ 入 ㇒ 今 今 令 飠 食 飣 飼
飼 飼 飼

飼う	かう	keep as pets/have/raise (animals)
飼い主	かいぬし	(pet) owner
羊飼い	ひつじかい	shepherd
飼育	しいく	する raise/breed (animals)
飼料	しりょう	feed, fodder

1349 旨 ▶し ▷むね

6 一 ヒ ヒ 占 旨 旨

趣旨	しゅし	purport, aim, meaning
要旨	ようし	gist, point, substance
論旨	ろんし	point of an argument
旨	むね	to the effect that, principle

1350 脂 ▶し ▷あぶら

10 ﾉ 刀 月 月 肪 肥 脂 脂 脂 脂

脂肪	しぼう	fat, grease, lard
脂	あぶら	fat, grease, lard
脂っこい	あぶらっこい	oily, fatty, greasy

1351 肪 ▶ぼう

8 ﾉ 刀 月 月 肛 肪 肪 肪

| 脂肪 | しぼう | fat, grease, lard |

第 110 回

1352 肥 ▶ひ ▷こ（える），こえ，こ（やす），こ（やし）

8 ﾉ 刀 月 月 肥 肥 肥 肥

肥料	ひりょう	fertilizer, manure
肥満	ひまん	obesity する grow fat
肥大化	ひだいか	する enlarge, grow
肥える	こえる	grow fat, become fertile/rich
肥やす	こやす	fertilize, fatten
肥やし	こやし	manure, fertilizer
◇ 肥	こえ	manure, night soil

1353 脈 ▶みゃく

cf. 派 1191

10 ﾉ 刀 月 月 肝 肝 肵 脈 脈 脈

脈	みゃく	pulse, pulsation, vein
文脈	ぶんみゃく	context
人脈	じんみゃく	personal network
動脈	どうみゃく	artery
静脈	じょうみゃく	vein

不整脈　ふせいみゃく　irregular pulse
山脈　さんみゃく　mountain range

1354 **膨** ▶ぼう
▷ふく（らむ），ふく（れる）

16 丿 几 月 月 肜 肜 肝 胖 胖 胖 胖 胖 脂 膨 膨 膨

膨大な　ぼうだいな　enormous (amount of)
膨張　ぼうちょう　［する］expand, swell
膨らむ　ふくらむ　swell, expand, bulge
膨らます　ふくらます　blow up (a balloon with air), inflate

1355 **肢** ▶し

8 丿 几 月 月 肝 肝 肢 肢

選択肢　せんたくし　choices, options
四肢　しし　the limbs, arms and legs

1356 **枯** ▶こ
▷か（れる），か（らす）

9 一 十 オ 木 札 柿 枯 枯 枯

枯れる　かれる　wither
枯れ葉　かれは　dead/withered leaf
枯れ木　かれき　dead/withered tree
◇ 栄枯盛*衰　えいこせいすい　prosperity and decline, vicissitudes

1357 **杉** ▷すぎ

7 一 十 オ 木 朾 杉 杉

杉　すぎ　Japanese cedar
杉並木　すぎなみき　row of cedar trees
杉並区　すぎなみく　Suginami Ward (in Tokyo)

1358 **彫** ▶ちょう
▷ほ（る）

11 丿 刀 月 月 月 用 周 周 周 彫 彫

彫刻　ちょうこく　sculpture, a sculpture　［する］carve, engrave
彫金　ちょうきん　metal engraving
彫る　ほる　carve, engrave, chisel
木彫り　きぼり　wood carving
浮き彫り　うきぼり　a carving in relief, relief

1359 **髪** ▶はつ
▷かみ

14 丿 厂 厂 厈 耂 長 長 髟 髟 髟 髟 髪 髪 髪

髪の毛　かみのけ　hair (on the head)
白髪の　はくはつの，△しらがの　gray-haired, white-haired

1360 **珍** ▶ちん
▷めずら（しい）

9 一 丁 王 王 珎 珎 珍 珍 珍

珍しい　めずらしい　rare, unusual, precious
珍品　ちんぴん　rare article, rarity
珍味　ちんみ　delicacies
珍客　ちんきゃく　unexpected visitor, welcome guest

第 111 回

1361 **診** ▶しん
▷み（る）

12 丶 亠 亍 言 言 言 言 診 診 診 診

診察　しんさつ　medical examination　［する］examine (a patient)
診断　しんだん　［する］diagnose
検診　けんしん　［する］examine (a person's body)
打診　だしん　［する］sound out (a person on a matter)
往診　おうしん　(doctor's) house call　［する］make a house call
診る　みる　examine (a patient)

第4水準

1362 療 ▶りょう

17 ｀ 一 广 广 广 疒 疒 疒 疒
疒 疠 痦 痦 瘄 療 療

治療　ちりょう　medical treatment, therapy ［-する］ treat, cure, remedy
医療費　いりょうひ　medical expenses
診療所　しんりょうじょ　clinic
療養　りょうよう ［する］ get medical treatment, recuperate

1363 症 ▶しょう

10 ｀ 一 广 广 广 广 疒 疔 疔 症

症状　しょうじょう　a symptom, the condition of a patient
病症　びょうしょう　condition of a disease/patient, nature of a disease
不眠症　ふみんしょう　insomnia
自閉症　じへいしょう　autism
症候群　しょうこうぐん　syndrome

1364 癖 ▶へき ▷くせ

18 ｀ 一 广 广 广 疒 疒 疒 疒 疒
疒 疒 疒 疒 癖 癖 癖 癖

癖　くせ　(personal) habit
◇ 盗癖　とうへき　propensity to steal, kleptomania
潔癖な　けっぺきな　cleanly, scrupulous

1365 避 ▶ひ ▷さ(ける)

16 ｀ ７ ７ ７ 尸 启 启 启 启 啓
辟 辟 辟 避 避 避

避難　ひなん ［する］ take refuge, take shelter
避妊　ひにん ［する］ prevent conception
回避　かいひ ［する］ avoid, evade, shirk
不可避の　ふかひの　unavoidable, inevitable
避ける　さける　avoid, evade, shirk

1366 恥 ▶ち ▷は(じる), はじ, は(じらう), は(ずかしい)

10 一 丅 丆 丆 王 耳 耳 恥 恥 恥

恥ずかしい　はずかしい　be embarrassed, be ashamed
恥　はじ　shame, disgrace, dishonor
恥じる　はじる　feel shame
恥じらう　はじらう　be shy, be bashful
＊羞恥心　しゅうちしん　sense of shame

1367 患 ▶かん ▷わずら(う) 758 cf. 忠

11 ｀ 口 口 尸 吕 吕 串 串 患 患
患

患者　かんじゃ　a patient
患部　かんぶ　affected/diseased part
患う　わずらう　suffer (illness), worry
長患い　ながわずらい ［する］ suffer from a long illness

1368 菌 ▶きん

11 一 十 艹 艹 芍 芍 芮 萄 菌 菌
菌

菌　きん　germs, bacteria, fungus
細菌　さいきん　germs, bacteria
殺菌　さっきん ［する］ sterilize, pasteurize
無菌の　むきんの　germ-free, sterilized

1369 荘 ▶そう

9 一 十 艹 艹 艹 艾 荘 荘 荘

別荘　べっそう　country villa, summer house
山荘　さんそう　mountain villa/retreat
◇ 荘重な　そうちょうな　solemn, grave
荘厳な　そうごんな　solemn, sublime

1370 装 ▶そう, しょう ▷よそお(う)

12 | ` | ` | ` | ` | ` | ` | ` | ` | ` |
装 装

服装　　ふくそう　(style of) dress, clothes
変装　　へんそう　[する] disguise oneself
武装　　ぶそう　armament　[する] arm
装飾　　そうしょく　ornament, decoration　[する] decorate
装置　　そうち　device, apparatus
衣装　　いしょう　costume, (wedding) dress
装う　　よそおう　wear, feign, pretend

1371 裂　▶れつ
　　　▷さ(く)，さ(ける)

12 | ` | ` | ` | ` | ` | ` | ` | ` | ` |
裂 裂

分裂　　ぶんれつ　[する] break up, disunite
破裂　　はれつ　[する] burst, explode, rupture
決裂　　けつれつ　[する] break down (in negotiations)
裂く　　さく　*vt.* tear, split, rip
裂ける　さける　*vi.* tear, split, rip
裂け目　さけめ　slit, crack, tear, rip

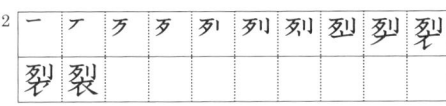

第 112 回

1372 鈍　▶どん
　　　▷にぶ(い)，にぶ(る)

12 | ` | ` | ` | ` | ` | ` | ` | ` | ` |
鈍 鈍

鈍感な　どんかんな　dull, insensitive
鈍い　　にぶい　dull, slow-witted, slow-moving, blunt
鈍る　　にぶる　become dull

1373 鋭　▶えい
　　　▷するど(い)

15 | ` | ` | ` | ` | ` | ` | ` | ` | ` |
鋭 鋭 鋭 鋭 鋭

鋭い　　するどい　sharp, acute (pain, etc.)
鋭利な　えいりな　sharp, sharp-edged (knife, etc.)

最新鋭の　さいしんえいの　newest and most powerful, most advanced
鋭気　　えいき　spirit, energy

1374 克　▶こく

7 | 一 | 十 | 十 | 古 | 古 | 声 | 克 | | |

克服　　こくふく　[する] conquer, overcome (a handicap/obstacle)
克明に　こくめいに　in detail, scrupulously

1375 児　▶じ，に

7 | ' | '' | '冂 | '旧 | '旧 | '臼 | 児 | | |

育児　　いくじ　child care, nursing
産児制限　さんじせいげん　birth control
児童　　じどう　pupil (in a primary school), child, juvenile
小児科　しょうにか　pediatrics

1376 旧　▶きゅう

5 | ` | `` | `冂 | 旧 | 旧 | | | | |

旧約聖書　きゅうやくせいしょ　the Old Testament　cf. 新約聖書（しんやくせいしょ）the New Testament
旧式の　きゅうしきの　old-fashioned, outdated
新旧　　しんきゅう　(both) old and new
復旧工事　ふっきゅうこうじ　work done to repair broken buildings, etc.

1377 慮　▶りょ

1884
cf. 虜

15 | ` | ' | 广 | 广 | 广 | 卢 | 虎 | 虎 | 庸 |
庸 庸 慮 慮 慮

遠慮　　えんりょ　[する] refrain, hesitate, show reserve
考慮　　こうりょ　[する] consider, give consideration to
配慮　　はいりょ　consideration, care, concern　[する] give attention to, take into consideration
*憂慮　　ゆうりょ　[する] be anxious/apprehensive/concerned, worry

1378 寧 ▶ねい

14	'	'	宀	宀	忉	忉	宓	宓	宓	寍
	寍	寍	寗	寧						

丁寧な　ていねいな　polite, careful

1379 寛 ▶かん

13	'	'	宀	宀	宀	审	审	宵	宵	宵
	宵	寛	寛							

寛容な　かんような　tolerant
寛大な　かんだいな　broad-minded

1380 寂 ▶じゃく，せき
▷さび，さび(しい)，さび(れる)

11	'	'	宀	宀	宀	宁	宇	宋	宋	寂
	寂									

寂しい　さびしい　lonely, lonesome
寂れる　さびれる　decline (in prosperity)
寂　さび　elegant simplicity
静寂　せいじゃく　silence, stillness
◇ 寂然とした　せきぜんとした，じゃくねんとした
　　　　　　　 lonesome, desolate

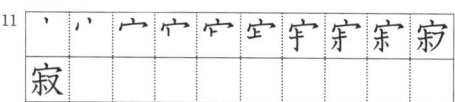
第 113 回

1381 孤 ▶こ
1447
cf. 弧

9	了	了	孑	孑	孔	孤	孤	孤	孤

孤独な　こどくな　lonely, solitary
孤立　こりつ　[する] be isolated, be friendless
孤島　ことう　isolated island
孤児　こじ　orphan
孤児院　こじいん　orphanage

1382 触 ▶しょく
293
▷ふ(れる)，さわ(る)
cf. 解

13	ノ	ク	ケ	角	角	角	角	角	鮋	鮋
	触	触	触							

触る　さわる　touch
触れる　ふれる　touch, mention
接触　せっしょく　[する] touch, make contact with
感触　かんしょく　(the sense of) touch, feel
抵触　ていしょく　[する] conflict (with), be against (the law, etc.)

1383 踊 ▶よう
▷おど(る)，おど(り)

14	'	口	口	呈	足	足	足	跙	跙	趵
	踊	踊	踊	踊						

踊る　おどる　dance
特 踊り子　おどりこ　dancer, dancing girl
日本舞踊　にほんぶよう　Japanese dancing

1384 躍 ▶やく
▷おど(る)

21	'	口	口	呈	足	足	足	跙	跙	趵
	踔	踔	踵	踽	躍	躍	躍	躍	躍	躍
	躍									

活躍　かつやく　[する] be active, play an active (important) role
暗躍　あんやく　[する] be active behind the scenes
躍進　やくしん　[する] make remarkable progress
飛躍　ひやく　[する] leap, jump, progress rapidly
躍動　やくどう　[する] be full of life, throb with energy
躍り出る　おどりでる　jump (to first place)

1385 焦 ▶しょう
▷こ(げる)，こ(がす)，こ(がれる)，あせ(る)

12	ノ	イ	イ'	仁	什	什	隹	隹	隹	焦
	焦	焦								

焦点　しょうてん　focal point, focus
焦げる　こげる　become burnt/scorched
焦がす　こがす　burn, scorch
焦る　あせる　be in a hurry, be impatient
焦がれる　こがれる　yearn for, pine for

1386 駐 ▶ちゅう

15 一 Γ Γ Γ Γ 馬 馬 馬 馬 馬 馬 馬 駐 駐 駐

駐車場　ちゅうしゃじょう　parking lot
駐日大使　ちゅうにちたいし　Ambassador to Japan

1387 循 ▶じゅん

12 ノ ク イ イ 彳 彳 彳 彳 循 循 循 循

悪循環　あくじゅんかん　vicious circle
血液循環　けつえきじゅんかん　blood circulation
循環器　じゅんかんき　circulatory organs

1388 衝 ▶しょう

15 ノ ク イ イ 彳 彳 行 行 徟 徟 徟 衝 衝 衝 衝

衝突　しょうとつ　[する] collide, conflict with
衝撃　しょうげき　shock, impact
衝動的な　しょうどうてきな　impulsive
折衝　せっしょう　[する] negotiate
◇ 緩衝地帯　かんしょうちたい　buffer zone

1389 征 ▶せい

8 ノ ク イ 彳 行 行 征 征

征服　せいふく　[する] conquer
征服者　せいふくしゃ　conqueror
◇ 出征　しゅっせい　[する] go to the war front

1390 徐 ▶じょ

10 ノ ク イ 彳 彳 彳 彳 徐 徐 徐

徐々に　じょじょに　gradually, slowly
徐行　じょこう　[する] drive slowly

1391 斜 ▶しゃ　▷なな(め)　1918 cf. 斗

11 ノ ハ ム ム 午 会 余 余 余 斜 斜

斜面　しゃめん　slope, slant
斜線　しゃせん　slanting line, slash
◇ 斜陽産業　しゃようさんぎょう　declining industry
斜めの　ななめの　slanting, diagonal

第 114 回

1392 滑 ▶かつ, こつ　▷すべ(る), なめ(らか)

13 丶 冫 氵 氵 氵 汩 汩 汩 汩 滑 滑 滑 滑

滑る　すべる　slide, slip, skate
滑らかな　なめらかな　smooth
滑走　かっそう　[する] slide, roll, glide
滑走路　かっそうろ　runway
円滑な　えんかつな　smooth
◇ 滑*稽な　こっけいな　funny, comical, ludicrous

第4水準

漢字の形に気をつけましょう㊱

190 着　1114 看　956 盾　1387 循

服を着る　看護師　矛盾した考え　悪循環

1393 潜

▶せん
▷ひそ(む), もぐ(る)

15 丶 氵 氵 氵 氵 汢 洪 洪 洪 洪
洪 洪 潜 潜 潜

潜在的な	せんざいてきな	latent, potential, hidden
潜入	せんにゅう	[する] infiltrate, enter secretly
潜水	せんすい	[する] dive, submerge
潜水夫	せんすいふ	diver
潜水*艦	せんすいかん	submarine
潜る	もぐる	dive into (the ocean)
潜む	ひそむ	lurk, be in hiding

1394 渇

▶かつ
▷かわ(く)

11 丶 氵 氵 氵 汜 沪 浔 渇 渇
渇

渇く	かわく	be thirsty, get dry
枯渇	こかつ	[する] run dry, be exhausted
渇水	かっすい	drought, water shortage
渇望	かつぼう	[する] crave, long for

1395 沢

▶たく
▷さわ
761 cf. 訳

7 丶 氵 氵 沪 沪 沢 沢

金沢	かなざわ	Kanazawa (the capital city of Ishikawa Prefecture)
沢田	さわだ	(surname)
沢	さわ	mountain stream, swamp
光沢	こうたく	luster, gloss
毛沢東	もうたくとう	Mao Tse-Tung
*潤沢な	じゅんたくな	abundant (money, profits, etc.), ample
▲贅沢な	ぜいたくな	extravagant, luxurious

1396 洪

▶こう
418 cf. 供

9 丶 氵 氵 沪 汁 沖 泄 洪 洪

| 洪水 | こうずい | flood |

1397 津

▶しん
▷つ

9 丶 氵 氵 沪 沪 沪 津 津 津

津波	つなみ	tsunami, tidal wave
津軽半島	つがるはんとう	Tsugaru Peninsula (the peninsula at the northern tip of Honshu)
◇ 興味津々	きょうみしんしん	very interested

1398 浪

▶ろう

10 丶 氵 氵 沪 汸 沪 泊 泊 浪 浪

| 浪費 | ろうひ | [する] waste, squander |
| 浪人 | ろうにん | masterless samurai, a student who has failed the university entrance examinations and will retake them the following year [する] be forced to retake university examinations |

1399 汁

▶じゅう
▷しる

5 丶 氵 氵 汁 汁

みそ汁	みそしる	miso soup
汁	しる	juice, sap, broth, soup
果汁	かじゅう	fruit juice

1400 渋

▶じゅう
▷しぶ, しぶ(い), しぶ(る)

漢字の形に気をつけましょう㊺

959	958	1390	1391
余	除	徐	斜
余分なお金	除外する	徐々に増えてきた	山の斜面

11	、	ミ	シ	シ	シ-	沪	渋	渋	渋
渋									

渋い	しぶい	astringent, bitter, quiet and cool
渋谷	しぶや	Shibuya (an area in downtown Tokyo)
渋	しぶ	astringent/bitter juice
渋る	しぶる	be reluctant (to do)
渋*滞	じゅうたい	traffic jam ［する］ be congested, be delayed
苦渋	くじゅう	anguish
◇ 渋面	じゅうめん	grimace, sour face

1401

 淡
▶たん
▷あわ(い)

11	、	ミ	シ	シ	シ`	沙	淡	淡	淡
淡									

淡い	あわい	light, pale
淡路島	あわじしま	Awaji Island (the largest island in the Seto Inland Sea)
冷淡な	れいたんな	cold-hearted, cold
淡泊な	たんぱくな	plain (food), aloof/indifferent (person)
濃淡	のうたん	light and shade, shading
淡水	たんすい	fresh water
淡水魚	たんすいぎょ	freshwater fish

1402

滞
▶たい
▷とどこお(る)

13	、	ミ	シ	氵	泄	滞	滞	滞	滞
滞	滞	滞							

| 滞在 | たいざい | ［する］ stay |
| 滞納 | たいのう | ［する］ default in payment, fail to keep up payment |

渋滞	じゅうたい	traffic jam ［する］ be congested, be delayed
沈滞	ちんたい	［する］ stagnate, become dull
滞る	とどこおる	be left undone, be in arrears

第 115 回

1403

肯
▶こう
cf. 背
1085

8	ィ	ト	ト	止	屵	肯	肯	肯

| 肯定 | こうてい | ［する］ affirm, acknowledge |
| 特 首肯 | しゅこう | ［する］ agree, consent |

1404

齢
▶れい

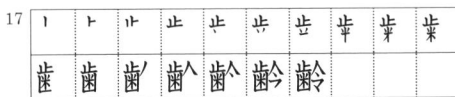

17	ィ	ト	止	止	止	止	歩	歩	崇
歯	歯	歯	歯	歯	齢	齢			

年齢	ねんれい	age
高齢者	こうれいしゃ	senior citizen, old person
高齢化社会	こうれいかしゃかい	aging society

1405

履
▶り
▷は(く)

15	一	コ	尸	尸	尸	尼	尼	屟	屟
屟	屟	屟	履	履					

履歴書	りれきしょ	résumé, curriculum vitae
履行	りこう	［する］ fulfill, implement, perform (duties in a contract)
草履	△ぞうり	(Japanese) sandals
履く	はく	wear/put on (shoes, pants, a skirt, etc.)

第4水準

漢字の形に気をつけましょう㊽

335	834	836	1394	1011	1434	1556
場	陽	湯	渇	掲	*喝	*褐

入場券　太陽と月　茶の湯

渇水の被害　論文が掲載される　 恐*喝 *褐色
きょう かつ　かっしょく

1406 奮

▶ふん
▷ふる(う)

16　一 ナ 大 太 本 杏 杏 杏 杏 奞
奮 奮 奮 奮 奮 奮

興奮	こうふん	[する] get excited
奮起	ふんき	[する] rouse oneself (to action), be inspired, be stirred up
奮発	ふんぱつ	[する] exert oneself, splurge
奮い立つ	ふるいたつ	rouse oneself (to action)

1407 奪

▶だつ
▷うば(う)

14　一 ナ 大 太 本 杏 杏 杏 杏 奞
奞 奞 奪 奪

奪う	うばう	snatch away, take (a thing) by force
強奪	ごうだつ	[する] seize, rob
略奪	りゃくだつ	[する] plunder, pillage
奪回	だっかい	[する] recapture, win back
争奪戦	そうだつせん	competition, contest for (power, a trophy, etc.)

1408 獲

▶かく
▷え(る)

16　ノ 丿 犭 犭 犷 犷 犷 犷 犷 犷
犷 犷 犷 獲 獲 獲

獲得	かくとく	[する] acquire, gain
捕獲	ほかく	[する] catch (an animal, a big fish, etc.)
乱獲	らんかく	[する] overfish, overhunt
漁獲高	ぎょかくだか	catch of fish
獲物	えもの	game, catch, take
◇ 獲る	える	get (wild game, etc.)

1409 穫

▶かく

18　ノ 二 千 禾 禾 禾 秆 秆 秆 秆
秆 秆 秆 秆 稚 稚 穫 穫

収穫	しゅうかく	[する] harvest, reap
収穫高	しゅうかくだか	crop, harvest
収穫期	しゅうかくき	harvest time

1410 猫

▶びょう
▷ねこ

11　ノ 丿 犭 犭 犷 犷 犵 猫 猫 猫
猫

猫	ねこ	cat
山猫	やまねこ	wildcat, lynx
◇ 愛猫家	あいびょうか	cat lovers

第 116 回

1411 薦

▶せん
▷すす(める)

16　一 十 艹 艹 芦 芦 芦 芦 芦 薦
薦 薦 薦 薦 薦 薦

推薦状	すいせんじょう	letter of recommendation
推薦	すいせん	[する] recommend
推薦者	すいせんしゃ	recommender
薦める	すすめる	recommend

1412 廃

▶はい
▷すた(れる), すた(る)

12　丶 亠 广 广 庐 庐 庐 庐 庐 庐
庬 廃

廃止	はいし	[する] abolish, repeal
廃する	はいする	abolish, repeal
廃人	はいじん	disabled person
退廃的な	たいはいてきな	decadent
廃れる	すたれる	go out of fashion, fall into disuse

1413 庶

▶しょ

332　333
cf. 席 度

11　丶 亠 广 广 庐 庐 庐 庐 庐 庶
庶

庶民	しょみん	common people
庶民的な	しょみんてきな	popular, common
庶務	しょむ	general affairs
庶務課	しょむか	general affairs section

1414 麻 ▶ま ▷あさ

11 丶 亠 广 广 庁 床 床 床 床 麻
麻

麻薬	まやく	(narcotic) drugs
大麻	たいま	marijuana
麻	あさ	hemp, flax, linen

1415 摩 ▶ま cf. 歴 704

15 丶 亠 广 广 庁 庀 床 床 麻
麻 麻 麼 麼 摩

| 摩擦 | まさつ | rubbing, friction, trouble -する rub against |

1416 擦 ▶さつ ▷す(る), す(れる)

17 一 十 扌 扌 扩 扩 扩 扩 扩
扩 擦 擦 擦 擦 擦 擦

摩擦	まさつ	rubbing, friction, trouble -する rub against
擦れる	すれる	rub, chafe
擦(り)傷	すりきず	abrasion, scrape

1417 邪 ▶じゃ cf. 雅 1638

8 一 厂 工 牙 牙 牙' 邪 邪

風邪	△かぜ	a cold
邪魔な	じゃまな	obstructive, hindering
邪魔	じゃま	-する interfere, disturb
邪道	じゃどう	evil ways, the wrong path
邪教	じゃきょう	heretical religion

1418 魔 ▶ま cf. 摩 1415

21 丶 亠 广 广 庁 庀 床 床 麻
麻 麻 麼 麿 麿 麿 魔 魔 魔
魔

邪魔な	じゃまな	obstructive, hindering
悪魔	あくま	devil, demon, Satan
魔術	まじゅつ	magic
魔法	まほう	magic, witchcraft, sorcery

1419 魅 ▶み

15 丶 亻 宀 宀 由 甶 鬼 鬼 鬼
鬼 鬽 魅 魅 魅

魅力	みりょく	charm, appeal, attraction, fascination
魅力的な	みりょくてきな	charming, attractive
魅惑の	みわくの	fascinating, charming, seductive, captivating

1420 酸 ▶さん ▷す(い)

14 一 厂 厂 丙 西 酉 酉 酊 酊
酘 酘 酸 酸

酸性雨	さんせいう	acid rain
酸性の	さんせいの	acid
酸素	さんそ	oxygen
酸化	さんか	oxidation -する vi. vt. oxidize
塩酸	えんさん	hydrochloric acid
酸っぱい	すっぱい	sour

第4水準

漢字の形に気をつけましょう59

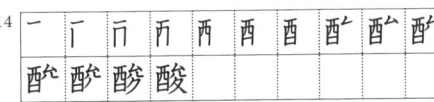

704	1720	1414	1415	1418	1731
歴	*暦	麻	摩	魔	*磨
日本の歴史	太陽*暦 たいよう れき	麻薬	経済摩擦	仕事の邪魔をする	研*磨する けん ま

第 5 水準

（Level 5）

1421-1832

第 117 回

1421 伏
▶ふく
▷ふ(せる)，ふ(す)
829 cf. 状

6 ノ イ 亻 仁 伏 伏

伏せる	ふせる	lie on the ground, hide
伏す	ふす	lie down (on the ground), prostrate oneself
うつ伏せになる	うつぶせになる	lie on one's stomach
起伏	きふく	ups and downs, undulations [する] rise and fall
潜伏	せんぷく	[する] hide oneself, lie dormant
潜伏期間	せんぷくきかん	incubation period, latent period
伏線	ふくせん	foreshadowing (in a story, movie, etc.)

1422 伐
▶ばつ
413 cf. 代

6 ノ イ 亻 代 伐 伐

伐採	ばっさい	[する] cut/hew down, fell
殺伐とした	さつばつとした	inhuman, brutal
[歴] 征伐	せいばつ	[する] subjugate, conquer

1423 伴
▶はん，ばん
▷ともな(う)

7 ノ イ 亻 伴 伴 伴 伴

伴う	ともなう	accompany, go with
伴*奏	ばんそう	accompaniment (of a piano, guitar, etc.) [する] play an accompaniment
同伴	どうはん	[する] accompany, go with, bring (one's spouse to a party, etc.)
伴*侶	はんりょ	partner, companion
◇ 言語随伴行動	げんごずいはんこうどう	language-accompanying behavior

1424 俊
▶しゅん
2033 cf. 挨

9 ノ イ 亻 仁 伩 伀 俊 俊 俊

俊才	しゅんさい	brilliant person
俊*敏な	しゅんびんな	swift, agile

1425 倹
▶けん
790 cf. 険

10 ノ イ 亻 仁 伶 伶 俭 俭 倹 倹

倹約	けんやく	[する] be thrifty, economize

1426 俵
▶ひょう
▷たわら

10 ノ イ 亻 仁 件 伊 俵 俵 俵 俵

土俵	どひょう	sumo ring
～俵	～ひょう／びょう／ぴょう	(counter for straw bags of rice)
俵	たわら	straw bag, bale (of straw)
米俵	こめだわら	straw rice bag

1427 俸
▶ほう

10 ノ イ 亻 仁 佳 伊 俸 俸 俸 俸

年俸	ねんぽう	annual salary
俸給	ほうきゅう	salary, one's pay
本俸	ほんぽう	basic salary

1428 偽
▶ぎ
▷いつわ(る)，にせ
736 cf. 為

11 ノ イ 亻 伆 伊 偽 偽 偽 偽 偽

偽物	にせもの	imitation, fake
偽札	にせさつ	counterfeit bills (money)
偽の	にせの	false, forged, counterfeit
偽る	いつわる	tell a lie, deceive, feign
偽りの	いつわりの	false, counterfeit
偽名	ぎめい	false name, alias
真偽	しんぎ	truth or falsehood
*虚偽の	きょぎの	false (statement, answer, etc.)

1429 傍
- ▶ぼう
- ▷かたわ（ら）

748 cf. 接

12　ノ イ イ´ 仢 仢 仢 伫 倅 傍 傍 傍

傍聴	ぼうちょう	[-する] attend/listen to (a court trial, etc.)
傍観	ぼうかん	[-する] look on, watch (from the side)
傍線	ぼうせん	a sideline (next to a word in vertical writing)
[特] 路傍	ろぼう	the roadside
傍ら	かたわら	the side

1430 僧
- ▶そう

13　ノ イ イ´ 仴 仴 伫 僧 僧 僧 僧 僧 僧

僧	そう	Buddhist priest/monk
僧院	そういん	monastery
高僧	こうそう	high-ranking monk
僧*侶	そうりょ	(Buddhist) priest, bonze, monk
*尼僧	にそう	nun, sister

1431 傑
- ▶けつ

980 cf. 隣

13　ノ イ イ´ 仸 仸 伫 傑 傑 傑 傑 傑 傑

傑作	けっさく	masterpiece
◇ 豪傑	ごうけつ	hero, daring person
傑物	けつぶつ	outstanding person

1432 吐
- ▶と
- ▷は（く）

6　丨 口 口 口` 吁 吐

吐く	はく	vomit, spew, spit
吐き気	はきけ	nausea, sickness
吐血	とけつ	[-する] vomit blood
◇ *嘔吐	おうと	[-する] vomit
吐露	とろ	[-する] speak (one's mind)

1433 唆
- ▶さ
- ▷そそのか（す）

1424 cf. 俊

10　丨 口 口 口" 口" 吣 唆 唆 唆 唆

示唆	しさ	[-する] suggest, hint at
教唆	きょうさ	[-する] instigate, incite
唆す	そそのかす	instigate, coax into, entice

1434 喝
- ▶かつ

11　丨 口 口 口¹ 吖 吗 吗 喝 喝

| 恐喝 | きょうかつ | [-する] blackmail, intimidate |
| 一喝 | いっかつ | [-する] scold, yell at (someone) |

1435 喚
- ▶かん

12　丨 口 口 口² 口² 吙 吙 吣 唤 喚 喚

証人喚問	しょうにんかんもん	summons of a witness
喚声	かんせい	excited (or surprised) cry
*召喚	しょうかん	[-する] summon, call

1436 嘆
- ▶たん
- ▷なげ（く）, なげ（かわしい）

527 cf. 漢

13　丨 口 口 口¯ 口¹ 吐 哕 哕 哕 哻 嘆 嘆

感嘆	かんたん	[-する] admire, marvel at
驚嘆	きょうたん	[-する] be struck with admiration, marvel at
嘆願	たんがん	[-する] entreat, petition
嘆息	たんそく	[-する] sigh, grieve
嘆く	なげく	grieve, lament, deplore
嘆き	なげき	sorrow, grief
嘆かわしい	なげかわしい	regrettable, lamentable

第5水準

1437 嘱 ▶しょく

15　｜ 冂 口 口ˊ 口ˉ 呎 呎 呎 呢 嘱
呢 嘱 嘱 嘱 嘱

委嘱　　　いしょく　［する］entrust (someone with a matter)
嘱*託　　　しょくたく　contract-based employee, temporary employee

1438 塔 ▶とう

12　一 十 土 圹 圹 圹 坮 垯 垯 塔
塔 塔

五重の塔　ごじゅうのとう　five-storied pagoda
石塔　　　せきとう　stone pagoda

1439 塀 ▶へい
　　　　　　　　　　　　1250 1260
　　　　　　　　　　　cf. 併 堀

12　一 十 土 圹 圹 圹 圬 圬 垉 塀
塀 塀

塀　　　　へい　wall, fence
板塀　　　いたべい　wooden wall/fence

1440 壇 ▶だん，たん
　　　　　　　　　　　　1888
　　　　　　　　　　　cf. 墳

16　一 十 土 圹ˊ 圹 圹 圹 垆 垆 垆
垆 垆 垆 壇 壇 壇

花壇　　　かだん　flower bed
演壇　　　えんだん　platform (for speaking), dais
壇上　　　だんじょう　(on) the platform/stage (used during a speech/presentation, etc.)
文壇　　　ぶんだん　the literary world
土壇場　　どたんば　(at) the last moment

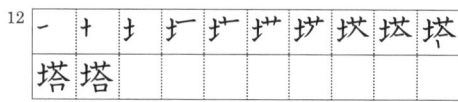

第 118 回

1441 如 ▶じょ，にょ

6　く タ 女 如 如 如

欠如　　　けつじょ　［する］vi. lack

突如　　　とつじょ　suddenly, all at once
如実に　　にょじつに　realistically, vividly
歴 如来　　にょらい　Buddha

1442 姻 ▶いん

9　く タ 女 如 如 姻 姻 姻 姻

婚姻届　　こんいんとどけ　marriage registration
姻*戚関係　いんせきかんけい　a relation by marriage

1443 岐 ▶き

7　｜ 山 山 山ˊ 山ˉ 岐 岐

岐路に立つ　きろにたつ　stand at a turning point/crossroads
分岐点　　　ぶんきてん　a turning point, point of divergence
多岐にわたる　たきにわたる　range widely, cover a variety (e.g. of topics)

1444 帆 ▶はん ▷ほ
　　　　　　　　　　　　467
　　　　　　　　　　　cf. 凡

6　｜ 冂 巾 巾ˊ 帆 帆

帆　　　　ほ　sail
帆船　　　はんせん　sailing ship
出帆　　　しゅっぱん　［する］sail, set sail
帆走　　　はんそう　［する］sail

1445 壮 ▶そう
　　　　　　　　　　　　829
　　　　　　　　　　　cf. 状

6　丨 丬 丬 丬ˊ 壮ˉ 壮

壮大な　　そうだいな　magnificent, grand
壮健な　　そうけんな　very healthy

1446 弦 ▶げん ▷つる

8　一 フ 弓 弓ˊ 弦ˊ 弦ˉ 弦 弦

弦　　　　げん　string (on an instrument), bowstring
特 弦　　　つる　bowstring, string (on an instrument)
特 上弦の月　じょうげんのつき　waxing crescent moon

1447 弧　▶こ　1381 cf. 弧

9　フ コ 弓 弓' 弧' 弧 弧 弧 弧

弧	こ	arc
弧状の	こじょうの	arc-shaped
*括弧	かっこ	parentheses

1448 径　▶けい

8　ノ ク イ 彳 彳 径 径 径

| 直径 | ちょっけい | diameter |
| 半径 | はんけい | radius |

1449 衡　▶こう

16　ノ ク イ 彳 彳 衎 衡 衡 衡

衡 衡 衡 衡 衡 衡

均衡	きんこう	balance, equilibrium
貿易不均衡	ぼうえきふきんこう	trade imbalance
平衡感覚	へいこうかんかく	sense of balance

1450 怪　▶かい　▷あや(しい), あや(しむ)

8　ノ ハ 忄 忄 怪 怪 怪 怪

怪しい	あやしい	suspicious, doubtful
怪しげな	あやしげな	suspicious, dubious
怪しむ	あやしむ	vt. suspect, doubt
怪物	かいぶつ	monster
怪談	かいだん	ghost story
奇怪な	きかいな	weird, mysterious, strange

1451 怖　▶ふ　▷こわ(い)

8　丶 ハ 忄 忄 忙 怖 怖 怖

怖い	こわい	scary, be afraid of
怖がる	こわがる	be afraid of, be scared of
恐怖	きょうふ	fear, terror, horror
◇ *畏怖の念	いふのねん	awe, fear

1452 恨　▶こん　▷うら(む), うら(めしい)　974 cf. 根

9　丶 ハ 忄 忄 忖 忖 恨 恨 恨

恨む	うらむ	hold a grudge, feel resentment, think ill of
恨み	うらみ	a grudge, resentment
恨めしい	うらめしい	reproachful, rueful
悔恨	かいこん	remorse, regret
◇ 遺恨	いこん	grudge, spite, enmity
痛恨の	つうこんの	deeply regrettable

1453 悦　▶えつ

10　丶 ハ 忄 忄 忄 忄 悦 悦 悦 悦

| 悦楽 | えつらく | joy, pleasure |
| 喜悦 | きえつ | joy, ecstasy |

1454 悟　▶ご　▷さと(る)

10　丶 ハ 忄 忄 忄 悟 悟 悟 悟 悟

| 悟り | さとり | spiritual enlightenment |
| 悟る | さとる | be enlightened spiritually, realize |

第5水準

漢字の形に気をつけましょう⑳

116	515	1448	1450
軽	経	径	怪
軽工業	経済発展	直径	奇怪な事件

覚悟 かくご readiness of mind [する] be prepared/determined (to do)

悟性 ごせい understanding, intelligence

1455 惜
▶せき
▷お(しい)，お(しむ)

11 画

惜しむ おしむ be reluctant to part with, spare/hold back (efforts), regret

惜しい おしい regrettable, precious

負け惜しみ まけおしみ refusal to acknowledge defeat, a case of sour grapes

惜敗 せきはい [する] lose a close game

愛惜 あいせき [する] be reluctant to (part)

愛惜の情 あいせきのじょう the sorrow of parting

1456 悼
▶とう
▷いた(む)
1030
cf. 卓

11 画

追悼式 ついとうしき memorial service

悼辞 とうじ words of condolence

*哀悼の念 あいとうのねん sorrow over someone's death

悼む いたむ mourn

1457 惨
▶さん，ざん
▷みじ(め)

11 画

悲惨な ひさんな miserable, wretched

惨劇 さんげき tragedy, tragic event

惨殺 ざんさつ [する] kill without mercy

惨めな みじめな miserable, wretched

1458 愉
▶ゆ

12 画

愉快な ゆかいな joyful, pleasant, delightful

1459 慌
▶こう
▷あわ(てる)，あわ(ただしい)

12 画

慌てる あわてる be flustered, lose one's presence of mind, be in a hurry

大慌て おおあわて (in a) great hurry

慌ただしい あわただしい hurried, busy

恐慌 きょうこう panic (in the stock market, etc.)

1460 惰
▶だ

12 画

惰性 だせい (by force of) habit

*怠惰な たいだな lazy, idle

第 119 回

1461 慨
▶がい
1161 1162
cf. 概 既

13 画

感慨 かんがい deep emotion

慨嘆 がいたん [する] deplore, regret

*憤慨 ふんがい [する] be indignant, resent

1462 憎
▶ぞう
▷にく(む)，にく(い)，にく(らしい)，にく(しみ)

14 画

憎しみ にくしみ hatred

憎らしい にくらしい hateful, detestable

憎い にくい hateful, detestable, provoking

憎む にくむ hate, detest, feel hatred towards

憎悪 ぞうお [する] hate, abhor

愛憎 あいぞう love and hatred

1463 懐
▶かい
▷ふところ，なつ（かしい），
　なつ（かしむ），なつ（く），なつ（ける）

1038
cf. 壊

16　丶 丶 忄 忄 忄 忄 忷 忷 忷
　　悙 悙 悙 懐 懐 懐

懐中電灯	かいちゅうでんとう	flashlight
◇ 懐古趣味	かいこしゅみ	nostalgia for the good old days
述懐	じゅっかい [する]	reminisce, speak about recollections
懐かしい	なつかしい	dear old, fondly-remembered, yearn
懐かしむ	なつかしむ	remember fondly, miss, long for
懐く	なつく	be tamed, get attached to
手懐ける	てなずける	tame
◇ 懐	ふところ	bosom, breast pocket

1464 憾
▶かん

16　丶 丶 忄 忄 忄 忄 忄 恼 恼 憾
　　憾 憾 憾 憾 憾 憾

遺憾に思う	いかんにおもう	feel sorry, regret (formal)

1465 抄
▶しょう

1151
cf. 秒

7　一 十 扌 扌 扚 抄 抄

抄訳	しょうやく	abridged translation, a translation of selected passages [する] make an abridged translation
抄本	しょうほん	an abstract (i.e., a partial copy), an extract
抄録	しょうろく [する]	extract, summarize

1466 扶
▶ふ

7　一 十 扌 扌 扞 扶 扶

扶養家族	ふようかぞく	one's dependents
◇ 扶助	ふじょ [する]	help, aid, support

1467 把
▶は

7　一 十 扌 扌 扪 扣 把

把握	はあく [する]	grasp (the meaning)
特 把持	はじ [する]	hold firm
～把	～わ／ぱ	(counter for bundles/bunches) cf. 一把（いちわ），十把（じっぱ）

1468 披
▶ひ

1144
cf. 皮

8　一 十 扌 扌 扩 护 披 披

披露宴	ひろうえん	(wedding) reception, banquet
披露	ひろう [する]	announce, introduce

1469 拘
▶こう

8　一 十 扌 扌 扚 拘 拘 拘

拘束	こうそく [する]	restrain (a person), confine, bind
拘留	こうりゅう [する]	detain, take someone into custody
拘置所	こうちしょ	detention center, jail

1470 拙
▶せつ
▷つたな（い）

8　一 十 扌 扌 扪 拙 拙 拙

稚拙な	ちせつな	childish, unskillful

漢字の形に気をつけましょう㉛

429 増　1224 贈　1430 僧　1462 憎

赤字が増大する　　蔵書を学校に寄贈する　　僧　　憎悪

拙速な　　せっそくな　rough-and-ready

◇　拙劣な　　せつれつな　badly-done, ill-managed, unskillful, blundering

◇　*巧拙　　　こうせつ　skill, dexterity

拙い　　　　つたない　unskillful, clumsy

1471 抹 ▶まつ

8　一 十 才 扌 扩 抃 抹 抹

抹消　　　まっしょう　[する] erase, strike (from a list)

抹殺　　　まっさつ　[する] wipe out, kill

◇　一抹の不安　いちまつのふあん　slight anxiety

1472 括 ▶かつ

9　一 十 才 扌 扩 托 拝 括 括

包括的な　　ほうかつてきな　comprehensive, inclusive

括弧　　　かっこ　parentheses

一括　　　いっかつ　[する] lump together

1473 挟 ▶きょう　▷はさ(む), はさ(まる)

9　一 十 才 扌 扩 护 挟 挟

挟む　　　はさむ　put in/between, pinch

挟まる　　はさまる　be caught in/between

挟撃　　　きょうげき　[する] attack on/from both sides

1474 拷 ▶ごう

9　一 十 才 扩 扩 挧 拷 拷

拷問　　　ごうもん　[する] torture

1475 捜 ▶そう　▷さが(す)　　1982 cf. 痩

10　一 十 才 扌 扣 护 押 捜 捜

捜査　　　そうさ　[する] search for a criminal

捜索　　　そうさく　[する] search/look for

捜す　　　さがす　seek, look for, search

1476 措 ▶そ

11　一 十 才 扌 扩 扩 挩 挫 措 措

措置　　　そち　measures, steps

◇　挙措　　　きょそ　movement, behavior

1477 掛 ▷か(ける), か(かる), かかり　　371 cf. 街

11　一 十 才 扌 扩 扗 拌 挂 掛

掛ける　　かける　hang, suspend from, cover

見掛ける　みかける　(happen to) see, find

掛け算　　かけざん　multiplication (mathematics)

掛かる　　かかる　hang from, be suspended

◇　掛　　　　かかり　section　cf. 係 is normally used

1478 挿 ▶そう　▷さ(す)　　256 cf. 押

10　一 十 才 扌 扩 扩 拈 掐 挿

挿入　　　そうにゅう　[する] insert, put into

挿話　　　そうわ　episode, incident

漢字の形に気をつけましょう㊲

1288　178　517　1472
舌　話　活　括

毒舌家　話題　日常生活　包括的なプラン

| 挿絵 | さしえ | illustrations (in a book, etc.) |
| 挿す | さす | insert, put in |

1479 控 ▶こう ▷ひか（える）

11 一 十 扌 扌 扌 护 护 抣 控 控 控

控除	こうじょ	［する］ deduct, subtract
控訴	こうそ	［する］ appeal (to a higher court of law)
控室	ひかえしつ	waiting room, anteroom
控える	ひかえる	refrain, restrain oneself, wait (in another room)
控え	ひかえ	a note, memorandum, duplicate, copy

1480 据 ▷す（える）, す（わる）

11 一 十 扌 护 护 护 护 拐 据 据

据える	すえる	put into position, set, place, lay, install
据え置く	すえおく	leave (something) as it is, leave (something) untouched
◇ 目が据わる	めがすわる	have glazed eyes (when drunk, angry, etc.)

第 120 回

1481 揚 ▶よう ▷あ（げる）, あ（がる）

12 一 十 扌 扌 护 护 押 押 押 揚 揚 揚

| 意気揚々と | いきようようと | triumphantly, elatedly, in high spirits |
| 抑揚 | よくよう | intonation, modulation |

揚げる	あげる	(deep-)fry, hoist (sails, a flag)
荷揚げ	にあげ	［する］ unload (freight)
揚がる	あがる	be (deep-)fried, go up, rise (into the air)

1482 摂 ▶せつ

13 一 十 扌 护 护 护 护 拒 拝 拝 摂 摂 摂

摂取	せっしゅ	［する］ ingest, take in/adopt (foreign customs, etc.)
包摂	ほうせつ	［する］ subsume
摂氏	せっし	centigrade, Celsius cf. 華氏（かし） Fahrenheit
歴 摂政	せっしょう	regent, regency

1483 搭 ▶とう

12 一 十 扌 扌 扩 扩 护 扶 抶 搭 搭

| 搭乗券 | とうじょうけん | boarding pass |
| 搭載 | とうさい | ［する］ be armed with (missiles, etc.), carry, take in/on |

1484 搾 ▶さく ▷しぼ（る）

13 一 十 扌 扌 扌 护 护 护 搾 搾 搾

搾取	さくしゅ	［する］ exploit, squeeze (money out of a person)
特 圧搾機	あっさくき	(hydraulic, etc.) press, compressor
搾る	しぼる	squeeze (a lemon), milk (a cow)

第5水準

漢字の形に気をつけましょう㊸

428	182	1455	1476
昔	借	惜	措
今と昔	借金	惜敗する	措置

1485 操

▶そう　902 903
▶みさお，あやつ（る）　cf. 繰 燥

16　一 十 扌 扩 护 护 护 押 押 押
操 操 捛 捛 操 操

操作	そうさ [する] operate (a machine, vehicle, etc.), manipulate, handle
操縦	そうじゅう [する] steer, operate, pilot, maneuver
体操	たいそう gymnastics
節操	せっそう constancy, fidelity
操り人形	あやつりにんぎょう puppet
操る	あやつる work (puppets), handle
歴 操	みさお chastity, virginity

1486 携

▶けい
▶たずさ（える），たずさ（わる）

13　一 十 扌 扩 扩 扩 护 拌 拌 拌
携 携 携

携帯電話	けいたいでんわ mobile phone, cellular phone
技術提携	ぎじゅつていけい technological cooperation (among businesses)
業務提携	ぎょうむていけい business cooperation
携える	たずさえる bring/take/carry (something) with (someone)
携わる	たずさわる participate in, have a hand in, be involved in

1487 搬

▶はん　648
cf. 般

13　一 十 扌 扩 扩 扚 扚 拍 拍 拍
拍 搬 搬

運搬	うんぱん [する] transport
搬入	はんにゅう [する] carry in, bring (something) in
搬出	はんしゅつ [する] carry out, take (something) out

1488 撤

▶てつ　1147
cf. 徹

15　一 十 扌 扩 扩 护 护 护 捛 捛
捛 捛 捛 撤 撤

撤回	てっかい [する] vt. withdraw, take back, retract (a statement)
撤去	てっきょ [する] vt. remove, take away
◇ 撤退	てったい [する] vi. withdraw, evacuate, pull out
撤兵	てっぺい [する] withdraw soldiers

1489 撲

▶ぼく

15　一 十 扌 扩 扩 扩 护 护 护 护
扠 拌 拌 撲 撲

相撲	△すもう sumo (Japanese wrestling)
打撲傷	だぼくしょう bruise, contusion
◇ 撲殺	ぼくさつ [する] beat (a person) to death
撲*滅	ぼくめつ [する] eradicate

1490 擁

▶よう

16　一 十 扌 扩 扩 扩 扩 护 护 护
护 拥 拥 擁 擁 擁

擁護	ようご [する] protect, defend
擁立	ようりつ [する] have one's leader stand as a candidate <give support to>
抱擁	ほうよう [する] embrace, hug
擁する	ようする hold in one's arms, have

1491 汽

▶き

7　丶 冫 氵 氵 汽 汽 汽

汽船	きせん steamship
汽車	きしゃ (railroad) train, steam locomotive
汽*笛	きてき (steam) whistle

1492 泌

▶ひつ，ひ　1102
cf. 秘

8　丶 冫 氵 氵 汃 汃 泌 泌

分泌	ぶんぴつ，ぶんぴ [する] secrete
内分泌	ないぶんぴつ，ないぶんぴ internal secretion
◇ 泌*尿器科	ひにょうきか urology department

1493 泥 ▶でい ▷どろ

8 丶 氵 氵 氵 沪 沪 沪 泥

泥棒	どろぼう	thief, robber
泥	どろ	mud
泥*沼	どろぬま	bog, quagmire, morass (of difficulties)
雲泥の差	うんでいのさ	a great/marked difference (in quality)
◇ 泥土	でいど	mud, muddy soil
◇ 拘泥	こうでい	する adhere/stick to

1494 沸 ▶ふつ ▷わ(く), わ(かす)

8 丶 氵 氵 氵 沪 沸 沸 沸

沸く	わく	vi. boil, be ready (as in bath water)
沸かす	わかす	vt. heat up, boil
湯沸(かし)器	ゆわかしき	water heater
沸点	ふってん	boiling point
◇ 煮沸	しゃふつ	する vt. boil, scald
沸*騰	ふっとう	する vi. come to a boil

1495 浄 ▶じょう

9 丶 氵 氵 氵 沪 沪 浄 浄 浄

浄化	じょうか	する purify, clean up
浄化*槽	じょうかそう	water purification tank
清浄な	せいじょうな	clean and pure
不浄な	ふじょうな	unclean, impure

1496 浸 ▶しん ▷ひた(す), ひた(る) cf. 侵 1244

10 丶 氵 氵 沪 沪 沪 浸 浸 浸 浸

浸す	ひたす	immerse, dunk
浸る	ひたる	be soaked, be immersed
水浸しになる	みずびたしになる	be inundated with water
浸水	しんすい	する be flooded/inundated
浸*透	しんとう	する penetrate, infiltrate, permeate

1497 涯 ▶がい

11 丶 氵 氵 沪 沪 沪 沪 涯 涯 涯 涯

| 生涯 | しょうがい | one's life/lifetime |

1498 渦 ▶か ▷うず cf. 過 284

12 丶 氵 氵 氵 沪 沪 沪 沪 渦 渦 渦 渦

渦	うず	eddy, whirlpool, vortex
渦巻(き)	うずまき	eddy, whirlpool, vortex
渦巻く	うずまく	eddy, swirl
渦中の人	かちゅうのひと	the person involved in (a scandal, etc.)

1499 溝 ▶こう ▷みぞ cf. 講 495 構 991

13 丶 氵 氵 氵 沪 沪 沪 溝 溝 溝 溝 溝 溝

溝	みぞ	drain, ditch, gutter
排水溝	はいすいこう	drainage ditch
下水溝	げすいこう	sewer

1500 滅 ▶めつ ▷ほろ(びる), ほろ(ぼす)

13 丶 氵 氵 氵 沪 沪 沪 沪 沪 滅 滅 滅 滅

絶滅	ぜつめつ	する become extinct, exterminate
消滅	しょうめつ	する be extinguished, disappear
滅亡	めつぼう	する fall into ruin
滅多に	めったに	seldom, rarely
*幻滅	げんめつ	する be disillusioned (with)
滅びる	ほろびる	fall into ruin
滅ぼす	ほろぼす	ruin, destroy, overthrow

第5水準

225

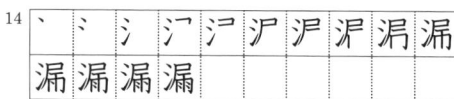

第　121　回

1501

溶　▶よう　1126

▷と(ける)，と(かす)，と(く)　cf. 浴

13　丶　氵　シ　ジ　沪　沪　沪　沪　容

溶　溶　溶

水溶液	すいようえき	(a water-based) solution
溶液	ようえき	solution
溶解	ようかい	[-する] vi. vt. melt, dissolve
溶岩	ようがん	lava
溶ける	とける	vi. melt, dissolve (as in salt in water)
溶け込む	とけこむ	adapt oneself to, blend into, melt into
溶かす	とかす	vt. melt, dissolve
溶く	とく	vt. dissolve (paint, flour)

1502

漏　▶ろう

▷も(る)，も(れる)，も(らす)

14　丶　氵　シ　沪　沪　沪　沪　沪　涓　漏

漏　漏　漏　漏

雨漏り	あまもり	leaking of rain (through the roof) [-する] (the roof) leak
漏る	もる	leak
漏れる	もれる	leak out, escape, come through, be heard outside (a window, etc.)
漏らす	もらす	reveal, divulge, express (one's feelings)
漏電	ろうでん	[-する] short circuit
[特] *疎漏な	そろうな	careless, heedless

1503

漸　▶ぜん　2061

cf. 斬

14　丶　氵　シ　ジ　沪　沪　沪　洹　淖　淖

渐　渐　漸　漸

| 漸次 | ぜんじ | gradually, step by step |
| 漸進的に | ぜんしんてきに | step by step, gradually |

1504

滴　▶てき

▷しずく，したた(る)

14　丶　氵　シ　ジ　沪　沪　沪　沪　渧　渧

滴　滴　滴　滴

～滴	～てき	(counter for drops)
水滴	すいてき	waterdrop
点滴	てんてき	intravenous drip
滴	しずく	a drop (of rain, etc.)
滴る	したたる	drip, drop, trickle
滴り	したたり	dripping, drop, trickle

1505

漆　▶しつ

▷うるし

14　丶　氵　シ　汁　汁　沐　沐　沐　沐　漆

漆　漆　漆　漆

漆器	しっき	lacquer ware
◇ 漆黒	しっこく	pitch-black, jet-black
漆	うるし	lacquer

1506

漬　▷つ(ける)，つ(かる)　886　638

cf. 積 責

14　丶　氵　シ　汁　汁　汗　渍　清　清

清　清　清　漬

漬物	つけもの	pickled vegetables
漬ける	つける	pickle, salt, soak, preserve
漬かる	つかる	be soaked in, be seasoned (with seasonings), be pickled

1507

漂　▶ひょう　1199

▷ただよ(う)　cf. 票

14　丶　氵　シ　沪　沪　沪　沪　潭　潭　潭

潭　潭　潭　漂

漂白	ひょうはく	[-する] bleach
漂流	ひょうりゅう	[-する] drift, be adrift
漂着	ひょうちゃく	[-する] be washed ashore
漂う	ただよう	drift, float

1508

潮　▶ちょう

▷しお

15　丶　氵　シ　シ　汁　汁　沽　沽　沽　渲

淖　潮　潮　潮　潮

| 風潮 | ふうちょう | public trend, the current of the times |

満潮	まんちょう	high tide
干潮	かんちょう	low tide
潮流	ちょうりゅう	tidal current, current of the times
潮	しお	tide, sea water
潮風	しおかぜ	sea breeze

1509 潤 ▶じゅん ▷うるお(う)，うるお(す)，うる(む)

15 ` 冫 氵 汀 汀 汀 浐 潤 潤 潤 潤 潤 潤 潤

潤滑油	じゅんかつゆ	lubricant
潤滑に	じゅんかつに	smoothly
潤沢な	じゅんたくな	abundant (money, profits, etc.), ample
湿潤な	しつじゅんな	wet, damp, moist
◇ 潤色	じゅんしょく [する]	embellish, add color to (a story)
潤う	うるおう	be moistened, profit from, benefit from
潤い	うるおい	moisture
潤す	うるおす	moisten, wet, benefit (someone)
潤む	うるむ	be moist, be emotional/teary-eyed

1510 澄 ▶ちょう ▷す(む)，す(ます)

15 ` 冫 氵 汐 汐 浐 浐 浐 澄 澄 澄 澄 澄 澄

澄む	すむ	become clear
上澄み	うわずみ	the top/clear layer (of soup, etc.)
澄ます	すます	look serious/prim, look unconcerned/indifferent, listen for
澄まし顔	すましがお	indifferent/unconcerned look
特 清澄な	せいちょうな	clear

1511 濁 ▶だく ▷にご(る)，にご(す)

16 ` 冫 氵 汐 汐 汐 汐 汐 汐 濁 濁 濁 濁 濁 濁

| 濁る | にごる | be muddy, become impure, have a voiced/flat sound |

濁り	にごり	muddiness, impurity
言葉を濁す	ことばをにごす	speak ambiguously, give a vague answer
濁流	だくりゅう	muddy stream
濁音	だくおん	sonant, voiced sound

1512 濫 ▶らん

925 cf. 監

18 ` 冫 氵 彐 汀 汀 汿 沪 沪 浬 潤 潤 濫 濫 濫 濫 濫 濫

濫伐	らんばつ [する]	cut down trees indiscriminately
職権濫用	しょっけんらんよう [する]	abuse authority
特 濫費	らんぴ [する]	waste, squander, dissipate
*氾濫	はんらん [する]	inundate, overflow, flood

1513 狂 ▶きょう ▷くる(う)，くる(おしい)

7 ノ 犭 犭 犭 狂 狂 狂

熱狂的な	ねっきょうてきな	enthusiastic, ardent
狂気	きょうき	madness, insanity
狂人	きょうじん	madman, lunatic
狂言	きょうげん	a Noh comic play or a farce presented between Noh plays, a made-up affair, sham/mock (suicide, etc.)
狂喜	きょうき [する]	go wild with joy
狂う	くるう	go mad, get out of order
◇ 狂おしい	くるおしい	mad/crazy (with love, grief, etc.)

1514 狩 ▶しゅ ▷か(る)，か(り)

9 ノ 犭 犭 犭 犭 狩 狩 狩 狩

狩り	かり	hunting
ぶどう狩り	ぶどうがり	picking grapes
狩る	かる	hunt
狩猟	しゅりょう [する]	vi. hunt

第5水準

1515 猟 ▶りょう

11　ノ　丬　犭　犭　犷　犷゛犷゛猟　猟　猟
猟

猟師	りょうし	hunter
猟犬	りょうけん	hound, hunting dog
狩猟	しゅりょう	-する vi. hunt
猟*銃	りょうじゅう	hunting gun, shotgun

1516 猛 ▶もう

11　ノ　丬　犭　犭゛犷　狞　猛　猛　猛
猛

勇猛な	ゆうもうな	valiant, brave
猛*獣	もうじゅう	fierce animal
猛*烈な	もうれつな	fierce, intense, violent

1517 猶 ▶ゆう

12　ノ　丬　犭　犭゛犷゛狞　狳　猗　猶
猶　猶

| 猶予 | ゆうよ | -する postpone, delay, grant a reprieve |
| *執行猶予 | しっこうゆうよ | stay of execution, suspended sentence |

1518 獄 ▶ごく

14　ノ　丬　犭　犭　犭゛犷　狞　狞　猗
猗　狱　獄　獄

地獄	じごく	hell, the inferno 反 天国(てんごく) heaven, paradise
◇ 疑獄	ぎごく	(bribery) scandal
監獄	かんごく	jail, prison
◇ 獄*舎	ごくしゃ	jail, cage

1519 阻 ▶そ
▷はば(む)

8　フ　丬　阝　阝|　阠　阻　阻　阻

阻止	そし	-する obstruct, hinder, prevent
阻害	そがい	-する obstruct, hamper, hinder, impede
阻む	はばむ	obstruct, hinder, prevent

1520 附 ▶ふ

8　フ　丬　阝　阝|　阝|　阣　阠　附

| 附属 | ふぞく | -する be attached to (as in a hospital attached to a university) cf. 付属 is more often used in modern Japanese |

第 122 回

1521 陛 ▶へい

10　フ　丬　阝　阝-　阯　阰　陞　陞　陛　陛

| 陛下 | へいか | His/Her Majesty |

1522 陥 ▶かん
▷おちい(る)，おとしい(れる)　cf. 稲 1233

10　フ　丬　阝　阝'　阝ク　阶　阶　陥　陥　陥

欠陥	けっかん	defect, flaw, fault
陥落	かんらく	-する surrender, fall
陥没	かんぼつ	-する subside, sink, cave in
陥る	おちいる	fall into (a trap, difficulties, etc.)
陥れる	おとしいれる	entrap (a person), ensnare

1523 陣 ▶じん

10　フ　丬　阝　阝-　阣　阣　陌　陌　陣　陣

報道陣	ほうどうじん	group of reporters, press
陣頭	じんとう	the front, vanguard, lead
東側陣営	ひがしがわじんえい	Eastern bloc/communist camp
陣	じん	camp, (battle) formation
陣痛	じんつう	labor pains

1524 陳 ▶ちん

11　了 了 阝 阝⌐ 阝￢ 阿 阿 阿 陣 陳
陳

陳列	ちんれつ	する exhibit, display
陳謝	ちんしゃ	する apologize
陳*腐な	ちんぷな	commonplace, trite, stale
陳情	ちんじょう	する petition, lobby

1525 陰 ▶いん ▷かげ，かげ(る)

11　了 了 阝 阝⌐ 阝＾ 阝⌐ 险 险 陰 陰
陰

陰気な	いんきな gloomy, melancholic　反 陽気な(ようきな) cheerful
陰性	いんせい negative (in a medical test)　反 陽性 (ようせい) positive (in a medical test)
山陰地方	さんいんちほう　the San'in region (the Japan Sea-side of the western part of Honshu)
陰	かげ shade　cf. 陰で behind the scenes
日陰	ひかげ the shade, shady spot
陰る	かげる be shaded (by a cloud)
陰り	かげり cloud (on one's happiness/business prospects, etc.)

1526 陶 ▶とう

11　了 了 阝 阝 阝⌐ 阝⌐ 陶 陶 陶
陶

陶器	とうき pottery, earthenware, ceramics
陶酔	とうすい する be charmed/fascinated/ intoxicated (by)
特 *薫陶	くんとう guidance, education

1527 旋 ▶せん

11　丶 亠 う 方 ㅏ 方⌐ 扩 斿 斿 旋
旋

旋律	せんりつ melody
旋回	せんかい する circle, revolve, rotate
特 周旋	しゅうせん する mediate, act as an agent

1528 旗 ▶き ▷はた

14　丶 亠 う 方 ㅏ 方⌐ 扩 斿 斿
斿 旗 旗 旗

国旗	こっき national flag
校旗	こうき school flag
旗*艦	きかん flagship
旗	はた flag, banner, pennant
手旗	てばた semaphore flag
旗色	はたいろ tide of war, odds, outlook

1529 朴 ▶ぼく

6　一 十 才 木 札 朴

| 素朴な | そぼくな simple, artless |
| 純朴な | じゅんぼくな simple and honest |

1530 枢 ▶すう

8　一 十 才 木 朾 朾 枢 枢

| 中枢 | ちゅうすう center, mainstay |
| 中枢神経系 | ちゅうすうしんけいけい the central nervous system |

第5水準

漢字の形に気をつけましょう㊿

|153|612|1527|1528|
|旅|施|施|旗|

海外旅行　　新しい税制が実施される　　ピアノの旋律　　国旗

歴 枢密院　　すうみついん　the Privy Council
歴 枢*軸国　すうじくこく　the Axis Powers (during World War II)

1531 栓　▶せん

10　一 十 才 木 杧 杧 栓 栓 栓 栓

栓抜き　　せんぬき　bottle opener, corkscrew
栓　　　　せん　cork, plug, stopper
消火栓　　しょうかせん　fire hydrant

1532 桟　▶さん
cf. 残　223

10　一 十 才 木 杧 杧 杧 栈 桟 桟

桟橋　　さんばし　pier, jetty, wharf

1533 棟　▶とう
▷むね，むな

12　一 十 才 木 杧 杧 杧 栢 栢 棟 棟 棟

病棟　　びょうとう　hospital ward
別棟　　べつむね　another building
棟　　　むね　ridge of a roof
〜棟　　〜むね　(counter for houses)
特 棟木　むなぎ　ridgepole, rooftree

1534 棺　▶かん

12　一 十 才 木 杧 杧 柠 柠 柠 柠 棺 棺

出棺　　しゅっかん　する carry out a coffin from a house
棺桶　　かんおけ　coffin

1535 棋　▶き
cf. 期　690

12　一 十 才 木 杧 杧 枅 枅 棋 棋 棋 棋

将棋　　しょうぎ　*shōgi*, Japanese chess

1536 棚　▷たな

12　一 十 才 木 杧 初 初 枛 棚 棚 棚 棚

棚　　　たな　shelf, rack
戸棚　　とだな　cupboard, cabinet, locker
棚上げにする　たなあげにする　shelve, pigeonhole

1537 槽　▶そう
cf. 曹　1930

15　一 十 才 木 杧 杧 柿 柿 槽 槽 槽 槽 槽 槽 槽

浴槽　　よくそう　bathtub
水槽　　すいそう　aquarium, water tank

1538 欄　▶らん
cf. 潤　1509

20　一 十 才 木 杧 杧 杧 杧 杧 杧 椚 椚 椚 椚 椚 椚 欄 欄 欄 欄

投書欄　　とうしょらん　letter-to-the-editor column

漢字の形に気をつけましょう⑤

296	1094	1524	1533	1602
練	凍	陳	棟	*錬
発音の練習	冷凍食品	商品を陳列する	小児病棟	アルミ精*錬所 せい れんじょ

欄外	らんがい	margin (on the pages of a book, etc.)
空欄	くうらん	blank (to be filled in)
欄干	らんかん	banister, railing

1539 殉 ▶じゅん

664 cf. 旬

10 一 ア ラ ヌ グ 歹 列 殉 殉 殉

殉職	じゅんしょく	〔する〕die on duty
殉教	じゅんきょう	〔する〕die a martyr
殉教者	じゅんきょうしゃ	martyr
殉死	じゅんし	〔する〕kill oneself after the death of one's lord/master

1540 殖 ▶しょく ▷ふ(える), ふ(やす)

220 678 cf. 直 植

12 一 ア ラ ヌ 歹 歹 歼 殖 殖 殖 殖 殖

養殖	ようしょく	〔する〕cultivate (fish, marine life)
生殖器	せいしょくき	sexual/reproductive organs
◇ 利殖	りしょく	moneymaking
特 殖産	しょくさん	promotion of industry
殖やす	ふやす	vt. increase
殖える	ふえる	vi. increase

第 123 回

1541 班 ▶はん

1994 cf. 斑

10 一 T F 王 王 刊 珂 珏 班 班

班	はん	group
班長	はんちょう	group leader

1542 祥 ▶しょう

917 488 cf. 洋 羊

10 丶 ラ ネ ネ ネ ネ 衤 衤 祥 祥

不祥事	ふしょうじ	disgraceful affair
発祥(の)地	はっしょう(の)ち	place of origin, cradle
清祥	せいしょう	healthy and doing well

1543 禍 ▶か

284 cf. 過

13 丶 ラ ネ ネ ネ 初 袒 禍 禍 禍 禍 禍

禍根	かこん	root of evil, source of trouble
特 禍福	かふく	fortune and misfortune

1544 胎 ▶たい

9 丿 刀 月 月 肝 肝 胎 胎 胎

胎児	たいじ	embryo, fetus
受胎	じゅたい	〔する〕conceive (a child)
*堕胎	だたい	〔する〕have an abortion cf. 人工中絶(じんこうちゅうぜつ), rather than *堕胎, is normally used.

1545 脚 ▶きゃく, きゃ ▷あし

11 丿 刀 月 月 肝 肚 胠 胠 胠 脚 脚

脚本	きゃくほん	scenario, playbook
三脚	さんきゃく	tripod
脚色	きゃくしょく	〔する〕dramatize
脚光	きゃっこう	spotlight, limelight
脚立	きゃたつ	stepladder
脚	あし	leg
歴 行脚	あんぎゃ	〔する〕make a pilgrimage, go on a (walking) tour

1546 膜 ▶まく

1159 cf. 漠

14 丿 刀 月 月 肝 胪 肺 胪 胪 胪 腊 瞙 膜 膜

膜	まく	membrane, film
細*胞膜	さいぼうまく	cell membrane
*粘膜	ねんまく	mucous membrane
*鼓膜	こまく	eardrum

第5水準

1547 騰 ▶とう

263 1934
cf. 勝 騰

20 ノ 刀 月 月 月 月′ 胙 胙 朕 朕
朕 朕 朕 朕 騰 騰 騰 騰 騰 騰

高騰	こうとう	steep rise (in prices) する spike upward
暴騰	ぼうとう	sudden/sharp/abnormal rise (in prices) する soar, rise suddenly
沸騰	ふっとう	する vi. come to a boil
◇ 騰貴	とうき	a rise (in prices) する rise, go up, appreciate (in value)

1548 眺 ▶ちょう ▷なが(める)

1269
cf. 兆

11 丨 冂 冂 月 目 肌 肌 肌 眺 眺
眺

眺望	ちょうぼう	view, prospect
眺め	ながめ	view
眺める	ながめる	gaze at/upon, watch

1549 矯 ▶きょう ▷た(める)

313
cf. 橋

17 ノ ⺊ 仁 午 矢 矢′ 矢′ 矢″ 矫 矫
矫 矫 矫 矯 矯 矯 矯

矯正	きょうせい	する correct (poor eyesight, crooked teeth, etc.), cure (bad habit)
特 奇矯な	ききょうな	eccentric, odd
特 矯める	ためる	correct, cure (a bad habit)

1550 砕 ▶さい ▷くだ(く), くだ(ける)

510 1069
cf. 枠 粋

9 一 丆 イ 石 石 石′ 矽 砕 砕

砕く	くだく	break (into pieces), smash, crush
砕ける	くだける	go to pieces, be shattered
*粉砕	ふんさい	する vt. shatter, smash (into pieces)
砕石	さいせき	crushed/broken stone

1551 硫 ▶りゅう

12 一 丆 イ 石 石 石′ 矿 硫 硫 硫
硫 硫

| 硫酸 | りゅうさん | sulfuric acid |
| 硫黄 | △いおう | sulfur |

1552 硝 ▶しょう

12 一 丆 イ 石 石 石′ 矿 矿 矿 硝
硝 硝

硝酸	しょうさん	nitric acid
硝煙	しょうえん	smoke (from gunpowder)
特 硝石	しょうせき	saltpeter

1553 礁 ▶しょう

17 一 丆 イ 石 石 矿 矿 矿 矿 砫
砫 碓 碓 礁 礁 礁 礁

暗礁	あんしょう	submerged rock, reef
岩礁	がんしょう	shore reef
△珊△瑚礁	さんごしょう	coral reef

1554 称 ▶しょう

10 一 二 千 千 禾 利 秒 秒 称 称

名称	めいしょう	name
愛称	あいしょう	nickname, term of endearment
称する	しょうする	call oneself 〜, pretend, feign
自称	じしょう	self-professed, would-be する call oneself to be
称賛	しょうさん	する praise, admire cf. しょうさん can also be written as 賞賛

1555 襟 ▶きん ▷えり

815
cf. 禁

18 丶 ⼀ ⼎ ⻂ ⻂ 衤 衤′ 衤卄 衤朮 衤朮
衤朮 衤林 衤林 襟 襟 襟 襟

襟　えり　collar, neckband, lapel
襟首　えりくび　nape, scruff
◇ 開襟シャツ　かいきんシャツ　open-necked shirt
胸襟を開く　きょうきんをひらく　bare one's heart, confide in (someone)

1556 **褐**
▶かつ

13
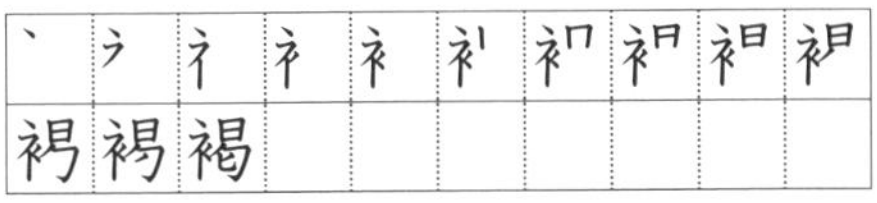

褐色の　かっしょくの　brown

1557 **粉**
▶ふん
▷こ，こな
cf. 紛 1298

10

小麦粉　こむぎこ　(wheat) flour
パン粉　パンこ　bread crumbs
粉雪　こなゆき　powder snow
粉　こな　powder
粉末　ふんまつ　powder
粉砕　ふんさい　[-する] *vt.* shatter, smash (into pieces)
粉飾　ふんしょく　[-する] embellish

1558 **粒**
▶りゅう
▷つぶ

11
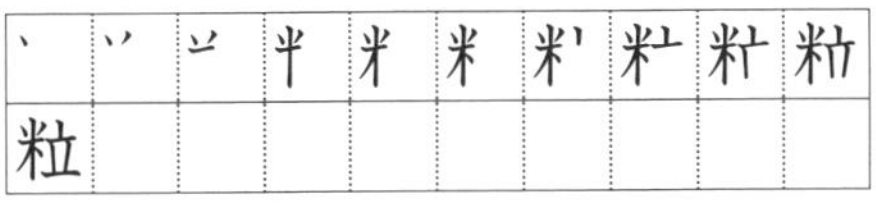

粒　つぶ　grain (of rice), granule (of sugar)
粒子　りゅうし　(atomic) particle, grain (of sand)
▲顆粒　かりゅう　granule (of sugar, medicine, etc.)

1559 **粘**
▶ねん
▷ねば(る)

11
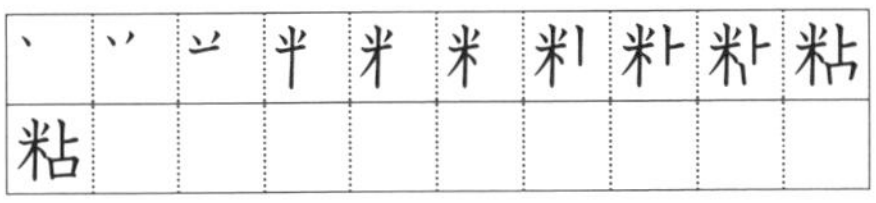

粘土　ねんど　clay
粘着テープ　ねんちゃくテープ　adhesive tape
粘液　ねんえき　mucus
粘る　ねばる　be sticky, be adhesive, persevere
粘り　ねばり　stickiness, tenacity
粘り強い　ねばりづよい　tenacious

1560 **粗**
▶そ
▷あら(い)

11
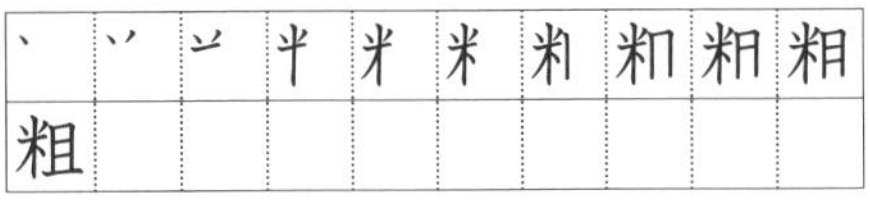

粗大ゴミ　そだいゴミ　large/bulky garbage
粗末な　そまつな　shabby, simple, humble
粗野な　そやな　rustic, boorish, unrefined
粗い　あらい　coarse, rough
粗筋　あらすじ　outline, synopsis

第 124 回

1561 **糾**
▶きゅう

9

紛糾　ふんきゅう　[-する] become entangled
糾弾　きゅうだん　[-する] impeach, denounce

1562 **紺**
▶こん

11

紺　こん　dark blue, navy blue
濃紺　のうこん　dark blue, navy blue

1563 **紡**
▶ぼう
▷つむ(ぐ)

10

紡績業　ぼうせきぎょう　the spinning industry
[特] 混紡　こんぼう　mixed yarn, mixed spinning
紡ぐ　つむぐ　spin, make yarn

1564 紋 ▶もん

10 〈 ⟨ ⟨ ⟨ 幺 幺 糸 糸 糸 糸゛ 糸' 紋 紋 紋

波紋	はもん	ripple, stir
指紋	しもん	fingerprint
紋章	もんしょう	coat of arms, crest
紋切り型の	もんきりがたの	conventional, stereotyped, formal

1565 絞 ▶こう ▷しぼ(る), し(める), し(まる)

12 〈 ⟨ ⟨ 幺 幺 糸 糸 糸゛ 紋 紋 絞 紋 絞

絞る	しぼる	wring, reduce scope
絞める	しめる	strangle
絞まる	しまる	feel choked
絞殺	こうさつ	[する] strangle to death
絞首刑	こうしゅけい	death by hanging

1566 綱 ▶こう ▷つな

14 〈 ⟨ ⟨ 幺 幺 糸 糸 糸 綱 綱 綱 綱 綱 綱 綱 綱

綱	つな	rope, line
横綱	よこづな	*yokozuna*, the grand-champion of sumo wrestling
大綱	たいこう	outline, general principles
綱領	こうりょう	party's platform, general principles (of a group/organization)
◇ 綱紀*粛正	こうきしゅくせい	enforcement of official discipline

1567 網 ▶もう ▷あみ

14 〈 ⟨ ⟨ 幺 幺 糸 糸 綱 綱 綱 綱 網 網 網 網

網	あみ	net
網戸	あみど	screen door
特 投網	△とあみ	casting net
通信網	つうしんもう	communications network
網膜	もうまく	retina
漁網	ぎょもう	fishing net

1568 縄 ▶じょう ▷なわ

15 〈 ⟨ ⟨ 幺 幺 糸 糸 綱 綱 綱 綱 縄 縄 縄 縄 縄

縄	なわ	rope, cord
沖縄	おきなわ	Okinawa
縄張り	なわばり	one's territory, one's sphere of influence
歴 縄文式土器	じょうもんしきどき	straw-rope pattern pottery
◇ 自縄自縛になる	じじょうじばくになる	lose one's freedom of action as a result of one's own actions

1569 縛 ▶ばく ▷しば(る)

16 〈 ⟨ ⟨ 幺 幺 糸 紋 紋 紋 綱 縛 縛 縛 縛 縛 縛

束縛	そくばく	[する] restrict, restrain, fetter, bind
特 捕縛	ほばく	[する] arrest, capture
縛る	しばる	bind (a person's hands/feet, etc.), tie, restrict, restrain

---

漢字の形に気をつけましょう66

1337	1566	1567
鋼	綱	網
鉄鋼業	党の綱領	通信網

1570 緯 ▶い

16　〈　乡　幺　夅　糸　糸　糸′　紅　紵　絆

紵　紵　緯　緯　緯　緯

経緯　　けいい　circumstances, sequence of events, details

緯度　　いど　latitude　反 経度(けいど) longitude

北緯　　ほくい　north latitude

南緯　　なんい　south latitude

1571 縫 ▶ほう　▷ぬ(う)

16　〈　乡　幺　夅　糸　糸　糸′　紵　終　終

終　終　縫　縫　縫　縫

裁縫　　さいほう　sewing, needlework

縫製　　ほうせい　[する] sew

縫合　　ほうごう　a suture　[する] suture, seam

縫う　　ぬう　sew, stitch

縫い目　ぬいめ　a seam (on clothing), a suture, a stitch

1572 繕 ▶ぜん　▷つくろ(う)

18　〈　乡　幺　夅　糸　糸　糸′　紅′　紺

紺　絆　絆　縒　縒　繕　繕　繕

修繕　　しゅうぜん　[する] mend, repair

繕う　　つくろう　mend, patch, keep up (appearances)

繕い　　つくろい　repairs, mending

1573 舶 ▶はく

11　′　′　力　力　舟　舟　舟′　舟′　舶　舶

舶

船舶　　せんぱく　vessel, ship

◇ 舶来の　はくらいの　foreign-made, imported

1574 託 ▶たく

10　丶　亠　二　言　言　言　言　訂　託

託す　　たくす　entrust (someone with something), commit to the care of

委託　　いたく　[する] entrust, consign

嘱託　　しょくたく　contract-based employee, temporary employee

信託銀行　しんたくぎんこう　trust bank

託児所　たくじしょ　day-care center

特 託宣　たくせん　an oracle

1575 詐 ▶さ

12　丶　亠　二　言　言　言　言　訂　訐

詐　詐

詐称　　さしょう　[する] make a false statement regarding one's educational background, age, name, etc.

詐*欺　　さぎ　fraud, swindling

1576 詰 ▶きつ　▷つ(める), つ(まる), つ(む)　cf. 結 302　吉 893

13　丶　亠　二　言　言　言　言′　計　詰

詰　詰　詰

詰める　　つめる　stuff, cram, pack, plug up

見詰める　みつめる　stare/gaze at, fix one's eyes on

詰め込む　つめこむ　cram, load, squeeze into

缶詰　　かんづめ　canned food

詰め物　つめもの　stuffing, filling, packing

詰まる　つまる　be stuffed, be full, be packed, be blocked

行き詰まる　いきづまる　vi. come to a deadlock

詰む　　つむ　be checkmated (in *shōgi*)

詰問　　きつもん　[する] cross-examine

特 難詰　なんきつ　[する] blame, censure

1577 該 ▶がい　cf. 核 986

13　丶　亠　二　言　言　言　言′　訪　訪

訪　該　該

該当　　がいとう　[する] fall under (an applicable rule/ provision), be applicable, correspond to

当該の　とうがいの　(the persons) concerned

第5水準

235

1578 諾 ▶だく

15 丶 亠 讠 訁 訁 訁 訁 計 計
訳 訝 許 諾 諾

承諾	しょうだく	する consent, agree
受諾	じゅだく	する accept, agree (to do)
快諾	かいだく	する agree willingly
諾否	だくひ	acceptance or refusal

1579 諭 ▶ゆ ▷さと(す)

16 丶 亠 讠 訁 訁 訁 計 訟 諭
諭 諭 諭 諭 諭 諭

教諭	きょうゆ	school teacher
説諭	せつゆ	する admonish
◇ 諭旨免職	ゆしめんしょく	resignation done at the suggestion of one's superior
諭す	さとす	admonish, counsel, reason with

1580 諮 ▶し ▷はか(る)

16 丶 亠 讠 訁 訁 言 計 訃 訃
訟 訟 諮 諮 諮 諮

| 諮問機関 | しもんきかん | advisory body |
| 諮る | はかる | consult, refer (a matter to a committee) |

第 125 回

1581 謙 ▶けん
cf. 1325 嫌 1324 兼 1952 鎌

17 丶 亠 讠 訁 訁 訁 訁 謙' 謙
訲 誠 誠 謙 謙 謙 謙

謙譲の美徳	けんじょうのびとく	virtue of modesty/humility
謙*虚な	けんきょな	modest, humble
謙*遜	けんそん	する be modest, be humble

1582 謹 ▶きん ▷つつし(む)
cf. 525 勤

17 丶 亠 讠 訁 訁 訁 訁 訝 謹
謹 謹 謹 謹 謹 謹 謹

謹賀新年	きんがしんねん	Best wishes in the new year.
謹慎	きんしん	する be confined to one's home (as a form of punishment)
謹む	つつしむ	be modest cf. 謹んで humbly

1583 譜 ▶ふ

19 丶 亠 讠 訁 訁 訁 訁 訁 譜
訝 訝 譜 譜 譜 譜 譜 譜

楽譜	がくふ	(musical) score, music
譜面	ふめん	sheet music
系譜	けいふ	genealogy, pedigree
年譜	ねんぷ	chronological history

1584 賊 ▶ぞく

13 丨 冂 冃 貝 貝 貝 貝 財 財
賊 賊 賊

海賊	かいぞく	pirate
海賊版	かいぞくばん	pirated edition
盗賊	とうぞく	burglar, robber, bandit
賊	ぞく	burglar, robber
特 賊軍	ぞくぐん	rebel army, rebels

1585 賦 ▶ふ

15 丨 冂 冃 貝 貝 貝 貝 財 財
財 財 財 賦 賦

天賦の才	てんぷのさい	natural gifts
特 賦役	ふえき	imposed labor
月賦	げっぷ	monthly installment

1586 跳 ▶ちょう ▷は(ねる), と(ぶ)
cf. 1269 兆

13 丨 冂 口 口 口 趵 趵 跳 跳
跳 跳 跳

跳ぶ	とぶ　jump, leap
縄跳び	なわとび　[する] skip rope
跳ねる	はねる　leap, jump, bounce, splash (onto)
跳躍	ちょうやく　[する] jump, leap

1587 跡 ▶せき ▷あと

足跡	あしあと　footprint
足跡	そくせき　footprint, track, mark
跡	あと　a trace, a mark, ruins, remains
遺跡	いせき　ruins, remains
名所旧跡	めいしょきゅうせき　places of scenic beauty and historic interest
追跡	ついせき　[する] chase, run after, trace

1588 践 ▶せん　223 cf. 残

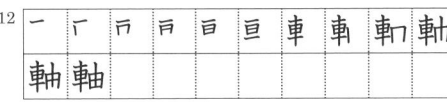

| 実践 | じっせん　[する] put into practice |

1589 軸 ▶じく

軸	じく　pivot, spindle, axle, scroll
地軸	ちじく　earth's axis
車軸	しゃじく　(wheel) axle
[歴] 枢軸国	すうじくこく　the Axis Powers (during World War II)

1590 轄 ▶かつ

| 管轄 | かんかつ　control, jurisdiction　[する] have jurisdiction/have control over |

| 所轄官庁 | しょかつかんちょう　the authorities concerned |
| 直轄領 | ちょっかつりょう　territory under the direct jurisdiction (of some authority) |

1591 酌 ▶しゃく ▷く(む)

晩酌	ばんしゃく　[する] have a drink at supper
情状酌量	じょうじょうしゃくりょう　making allowances in consideration of the circumstances
*媒酌人	ばいしゃくにん　matchmaker, go-between
事情を酌む	じじょうをくむ　take someone's circumstances into consideration <make allowances for>

1592 酢 ▶さく ▷す

酢	す　vinegar
酢の物	すのもの　vinegared food
酢酸	さくさん　acetic acid

1593 酪 ▶らく

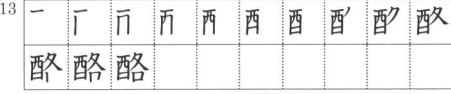

| 酪農 | らくのう　dairy farming |

1594 酬 ▶しゅう

| 報酬 | ほうしゅう　a reward, remuneration, a fee |
| 応酬 | おうしゅう　[する] exchange (heated words), reply |

1595 **酵** ▶こう

14
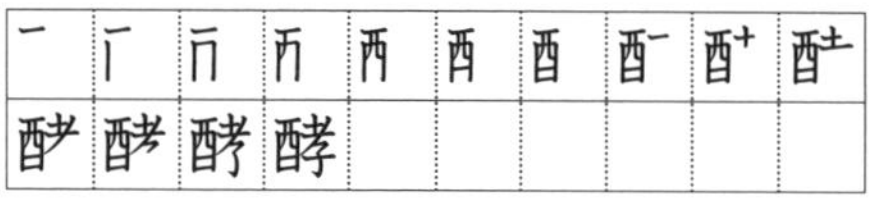

酵素	こうそ	enzyme
発酵	はっこう	-する *vi.* ferment
酵母(菌)	こうぼ(きん)	yeast (fungus)

1596 **酷** ▶こく

14
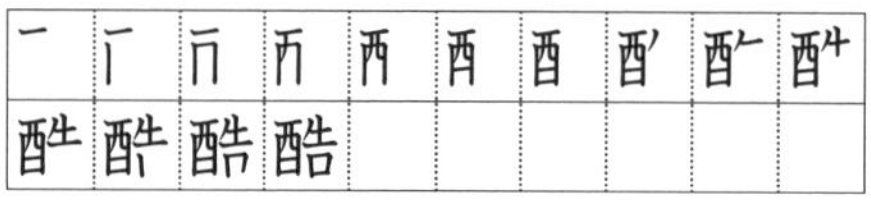

残酷な	ざんこくな	cruel, merciless
冷酷な	れいこくな	heartless, cruel
酷似	こくじ	-する be very much alike, be similar
酷使	こくし	overuse -する work someone very/too hard, overwork

1597 **鉢** ▶はち，はつ

13

植木鉢	うえきばち	(flower/plant) pot
鉢	はち	bowl, pot, flower pot
特 ▲托鉢	たくはつ	religious mendicancy -する go about asking for alms

1598 **銭** ▶せん ▷ぜに cf. 残 223

14

銭湯	せんとう	bathhouse, public bath
金銭の授受	きんせんのじゅじゅ	giving and receiving of money
小銭	こぜに	small change

1599 **銃** ▶じゅう cf. 統 1000 充 1275

14

銃	じゅう	gun, rifle
小銃	しょうじゅう	rifle, small arms
銃弾	じゅうだん	bullet, shot (for a rifle)
銃声	じゅうせい	the sound of gunshot
銃刀法	じゅうとうほう	guns and swords restriction law
*拳銃	けんじゅう	pistol, handgun, revolver

1600 **銘** ▶めい

14

感銘を受ける	かんめいをうける	be deeply impressed
銘柄	めいがら	brand, name, issue
銘記	めいき	-する bear in mind
銘々	めいめい	each, each respectively

第 126 回

1601 **鋳** ▶ちゅう ▷い(る)

15

漢字の形に気をつけましょう(67)

122	223	1532	1588	1598
浅	残	桟	践	銭
浅い川	残念な結果	桟橋	理論と実践	銭湯

鋳造	ちゅうぞう [する] cast (iron), found (metal), mint (coins)
鋳る	いる　cast, mold, coin
鋳物	いもの　casting (of metal)
鋳型	いがた　a mold, a cast

1602 錬 ▶れん

16 ノ 八 厶 亼 牟 余 余 金 金 釘
釘 釘 釘 鍊 鍊 錬

精錬所	せいれんじょ　refinery
錬金術	れんきんじゅつ　alchemy
心身の*鍛錬	しんしんのたんれん　training of mind and body
特 錬*磨	れんま [する] train, drill, practice

1603 錯 ▶さく

16 ノ 八 厶 亼 牟 余 余 金 金 釘
鉗 錯 錯 錯 錯 錯

錯覚	さっかく [する] have the illusion that, be under the mistaken impression
交錯	こうさく [する] intertwine, mix
試行錯誤	しこうさくご　trial and error

1604 錠 ▶じょう

16 ノ 八 厶 亼 牟 余 余 金 金' 金'
鋌 鋌 鋌 鋌 錠 錠

手錠	てじょう　handcuffs
錠前	じょうまえ　a lock (on a door, etc.)
錠*剤	じょうざい　tablet, pill

1605 鍛 ▶たん ▷きた(える)

17 ノ 八 厶 亼 牟 余 余 金 金' 釘
釘 鍁 釮 釮 鍜 鍛 鍛

| 鍛える | きたえる　train, drill, discipline |
| 心身の鍛錬 | しんしんのたんれん　training of mind and body |

1606 鎮 ▶ちん ▷しず(める)，しず(まる)

18 ノ 八 厶 亼 牟 余 余 金 金 釘
鉗 鉗 鎮 鎮 鎮 鎮 鎮 鎮

鎮圧	ちんあつ [する] suppress, repress, quell
鎮火	ちんか [する] vi. vt. be put out, be extinguished, put out, extinguish
特 鎮座	ちんざ [する] be enshrined
鎮静	ちんせい [する] vi. vt. become calm, subside, settle down, quell (a riot, etc.)
鎮静*剤	ちんせいざい　sedative, tranquilizer
重鎮	じゅうちん　leading figure (in business circles, in society, etc.)
鎮める	しずめる　relieve, subdue, suppress, repress
鎮まる	しずまる　subside, be suppressed

1607 鐘 ▶しょう ▷かね

20 ノ 八 厶 亼 牟 余 余 金 金' 釘
釘 鉗 鉗 鍔 鍍 鐘 鐘 鐘 鐘 鐘

教会の鐘	きょうかいのかね　church bell
警鐘	けいしょう　alarm bell, warning
歴 半鐘	はんしょう　fire alarm, alarm bell

1608 鑑 ▶かん ▷かんが(みる)　925 cf. 監

23 ノ 八 厶 亼 牟 余 余 金 釘 釘
釘 鉗 鉗 鉗 鑑 鑑 鑑 鑑 鑑
鑑 鑑 鑑

鑑賞	かんしょう [する] appreciate, enjoy (listening to music, etc.)
鑑定	かんてい [する] appraise, judge (the true nature of an antique's origin, etc.), identify (handwriting, etc.), give an expert opinion (in court)
年鑑	ねんかん　yearbook, almanac
図鑑	ずかん　illustrated reference book
鑑みる	かんがみる　take into account

第5水準

1609 剖 ▶ぼう

10 ｀ 亠 亠 𠆢 立 立 咅 咅 咅 剖

| 解剖 | かいぼう | -する | perform an autopsy, dissect |

1610 駄 ▶だ

14 １ 厂 𠂆 𠂢 𨈐 馬 馬 馬 馬 馬
馬 駄 駄 駄

無駄な	むだな	wasteful, useless, futile
駄目な	だめな	useless, vain, no good
駄作	ださく	poor work, (literary/artistic) trash
駄*菓子	だがし	cheap sweets/candy

1611 駆 ▶く ▷か(ける), か(る)

14 １ 厂 𠂆 𠂢 𨈐 馬 馬 馬 馬 馬
馬 駆 駆 駆

先駆者	せんくしゃ	precursor, pioneer
四輪駆動	よんりんくどう	four-wheel drive
駆使	くし	-する have a good command of, make full use of, use freely
特 駆逐	くちく	-する expel, drive away
駆逐*艦	くちくかん	destroyer (naval vessel)
駆除	くじょ	-する exterminate, destroy, get rid of
駆ける	かける	run, canter, gallop
駆り立てる	かりたてる	drive, urge on, spur

1612 刈 ▷か(る)

4 ノ メ メ 刈

稲刈り	いねかり	-する harvest rice
芝刈り	しばかり	mowing (the grass/lawn)
芝刈り機	しばかりき	mower
刈る	かる	mow, cut, clip
刈り入れ	かりいれ	reaping, harvesting

1613 剛 ▶ごう

10 １ 冂 冂 冂 罓 罓 岡 岡 岡 剛

| 剛健な | ごうけんな | sturdy, robust |
| 特 金剛力 | こんごうりき | Herculean strength |

1614 劾 ▶がい

8 ｀ 亠 𠂇 歺 歺 亥 刻 劾

| 弾劾 | だんがい | -する impeach |

1615 勧 ▶かん ▷すす(める)   1132 cf. 歓

13 ノ 𠂊 𠂉 ケ 午 乍 午 乍 隹 隹
隹 勧 勧

勧誘	かんゆう	-する invite, persuade, canvass
勧告	かんこく	-する give advice to, counsel, recommend
勧奨	かんしょう	-する encourage
勧める	すすめる	advise, encourage, urge
勧め	すすめ	advice, suggestion

1616 却 ▶きゃく

7 一 十 土 𠮷 去 𠮷 却

却下	きゃっか	-する reject, dismiss, overrule (an objection)
売却	ばいきゃく	-する sell, sell off
退却	たいきゃく	-する retreat, withdraw

1617 叙 ▶じょ

9 ノ 𠆢 𠆢 𠂤 𠂤 余 余 叙 叙

叙述	じょじゅつ	-する describe, narrate
叙景	じょけい	descriptions of scenery
叙事詩	じょじし	epic poem/poetry
叙情詩	じょじょうし	lyric poem/poetry
叙*勲	じょくん	-する confer a decorations/medals

1618 耐 ▶たい
▷た（える）

9 一 丆 丆 丆 丆 而 而 耐 耐

耐久性	たいきゅうせい	endurance, durability
耐火構造	たいかこうぞう	fire-resistant structure
耐震構造	たいしんこうぞう	earthquake-resistant structure
耐熱ガラス	たいねつガラス	heat-resistant glass
*忍耐	にんたい	-する be patient, persevere, endure
耐える	たえる	endure, bear, withstand

1619 彩 ▶さい
▷いろど（る）

11 一 ⺊ ⺊ ⻂ ⻂ 平 采 采 采 彩
彩

多彩な	たさいな	various, diversified
色彩	しきさい	color, hue
彩色	さいしき，さいしょく	coloring, painting
彩る	いろどる	color, decorate
彩り	いろどり	coloring, color scheme

1620 彰 ▶しょう

14 ⺀ ⺊ ⺀ ⺾ 立 产 咅 音 音 章
章 章 彰 彰

表彰	ひょうしょう	-する publicly commend
表彰式	ひょうしょうしき	commendation/award ceremony
表彰状	ひょうしょうじょう	certificate of commendation, testimonial

第　127　回

1621 邦 ▶ほう

7 一 ⼆ ⺕ 丰 邦' 邦⁷ 邦

邦画	ほうが	Japanese film 反 洋画（ようが）foreign (Western) film, Western painting
邦楽	ほうがく	(traditional) Japanese music
連邦政府	れんぽうせいふ	federal government
旧ソビエト連邦	きゅうソビエトれんぽう	the former Soviet Union/U.S.S.R.　cf. *abbr.* 旧ソ連（きゅうソれん）
本邦初公開	ほんぽうはつこうかい	first appearance in this country

1622 敢 ▶かん

12 一 ⺊ ⼯ 干 干 乕 肀 耳 耵 耵
敢 敢

勇敢に	ゆうかんに	bravely, courageously
果敢に	かかんに	boldly, daringly
敢然と	かんぜんと	boldly, resolutely, bravely, fearlessly

1623 欺 ▶ぎ
▷あざむ（く）

12 一 ⺊ 廿 廿 甘 甘 其 其 其 其
欺 欺

| 詐欺 | さぎ | fraud, swindling |
| 欺く | あざむく | deceive |

第5水準

漢字の形に気をつけましょう⑱

| 773 | 1357 | 1619 | 1620 |
| 採 | 杉 | 彩 | 彰 |

新しい社員を採用する　　杉の木　　鮮やかな色彩　　表彰状を授与する

1624 款 ▶かん

12 一 十 土 士 吉 吉 吉 吉 款 款
款 款

定款 ていかん articles of an association, certificate of incorporation

円借款 えんしゃっかん yen(-denominated) loan

1625 殴 ▶おう ▷なぐ(る) cf. 欧 区 554 548

8 一 フ ヌ 区 区 区´ 欧 殴

殴る なぐる beat, punch, strike

殴打 おうだ する hit, beat, strike

1626 殻 ▶かく ▷から

11 一 十 土 士 声 声 壳 壳 壳 殻
殻

殻 から shell, husk

貝殻 かいがら seashell

地殻変動 ちかくへんどう alteration of the earth's crust

特 甲殻類 こうかくるい crustaceans

1627 穀 ▶こく

14 一 十 土 士 声 声 声 亭 亭 亭
亭 榖 榖 穀

穀物 こくもつ grain, cereal, corn (British)

特 雑穀 ざっこく cereals

1628 朗 ▶ろう ▷ほが(らか) cf. 郎 546

10 ' ⺆ ⺕ ⺕ 自 良 郎 朗 朗 朗

朗読 ろうどく する recite, read aloud

朗報 ろうほう good news, glad tidings

◇ 朗々と ろうろうと sonorously, clearly

明朗な めいろうな cheerful, clear, fair

朗らかな ほがらかな cheerful, bright

1629 泡 ▶ほう ▷あわ

8 ' ⺀ ⺒ ⺡ 汋 沟 沟 泡

泡 あわ foam, bubble, froth, suds

泡立つ あわだつ vi. foam, lather, froth

水泡 すいほう foam, bubble

気泡 きほう air bubble

発泡スチロール はっぽうスチロール polystyrene, styrene plastic

1630 胞 ▶ほう

9) 刀 月 月 ⺼ 肌 肑 肑 胞

細胞 さいぼう cell

胞子 ほうし spore

同胞 どうほう compatriot, fellow countryman, brothers

1631 砲 ▶ほう

10 一 ⺃ 石 石 石 矿 矿 砲 砲 砲

砲撃 ほうげき する bombard, fire at

大砲 たいほう artillery gun, cannon

鉄砲 てっぽう gun, rifle

1632 飽 ▶ほう ▷あ(きる), あ(かす)

13 ノ 人 ⼇ 今 今 今 食 食 飠
飣 飣 飽

飽きる あきる get tired of, be weary of, lose interest in

飽きっぽい あきっぽい quick to become tired of (something), fickle

暇に飽かして ひまにあかして taking advantage of all the time that one has at one's disposal

飽和状態 ほうわじょうたい saturation, completely full

◇ 飽食の時代 ほうしょくのじだい age of satiation

1633 噴 ▶ふん
▷ふ(く)

15 画筆順: 丨 口 口 ロ⁻ ロ⁺ 吣 叻 哧 哹 唪
噴 噴 噴 噴 噴

噴水　　ふんすい　fountain, jet of water
噴火　　ふんか　(volcanic) eruption ［-する］ erupt
噴出　　ふんしゅつ ［-する］ spew, gush, spurt out, erupt
噴射　　ふんしゃ ［-する］ jet, spray
噴き出す　ふきだす　spurt out, gush out, burst into laughter

1634 憤 ▶ふん
▷いきどお(る)

15 画筆順: 丶 丷 忄 忄⁻ 忄⁺ 忄 忄 忄 惼
憤 憤 憤 憤 憤

憤慨　　ふんがい ［-する］ be indignant, resent
発憤　　はっぷん ［-する］ be roused, be stimulated, be inspired
義憤　　ぎふん　righteous indignation
憤る　　いきどおる　get angry, resent (an insult), be indignant
憤り　　いきどおり　resentment, indignation, anger

1635 准 ▶じゅん

10 画筆順: 丶 冫 冫 冫 冫 冫 冫 淮 准 准

批准　　ひじゅん ［-する］ ratify
准教授　じゅんきょうじゅ　associate professor
准将　　じゅんしょう　brigadier general

1636 唯 ▶ゆい, い

11 画筆順: 丨 口 口 叮 叮 唯 唯 唯 唯
唯

唯一の　　ゆいいつの　only, sole
唯物論　　ゆいぶつろん　materialism (in philosophical terms) 反 唯心論（ゆいしんろん）idealism, spiritualism cf. 物質主義（ぶっしつしゅぎ）materialism (in terms of a way of life), 精神主義（せいしんしゅぎ）spiritualism

唯物史観　ゆいぶつしかん　historical materialism
◇ 唯々諾々として　いいだくだくとして　obediently, tamely, submissively

1637 雄 ▶ゆう
▷お, おす

12 画筆順: 一 ナ 圡 圡 圡 圡 圡 雄 雄
雄 雄

英雄　　えいゆう　hero
雄大な　ゆうだいな　magnificent, majestic, grand
雄　　　おす　male (for animals) 反 *雌（めす）female
雄犬　　おすいぬ　male dog
雄花　　おばな　male flower
雄牛　　おうし　ox, bull
雄しべ　おしべ　stamen (i.e., the male part of a flower)
雄々しい　おおしい　brave, manly
特 雄飛　ゆうひ ［-する］ launch into, embark on (career)

1638 雅 ▶が
1417 cf. 邪

13 画筆順: 一 匚 工 牙 牙 牙 邪 邪 邪 邪
邪 雅 雅

優雅な　ゆうがな　elegant, graceful
特 風雅　ふうが　elegance, refined taste
雅楽　　ががく　gagaku, Japanese ceremonial court music

1639 雌 ▶し
▷め, めす

14 画筆順: 丨 卜 止 止 此 此 此 此 雌
此 此 雌 雌

雌　　　めす　female (for animals) 反 雄（おす）male
雌犬　　めすいぬ　female dog
雌花　　めばな　female flower
雌牛　　めうし　cow
雌しべ　めしべ　pistil (i.e., the female part of a flower)
雌雄　　しゆう　male or female, the two sexes, superior or inferior
特 雌伏　しふく ［-する］ bide one's time, lie low 反 雄飛（ゆうひ）［-する］ launch into

1640 培

▶ばい
▷つちか(う)

11 一 十 土 土 土 土 坪 垃 培 培
培

培養	ばいよう	[する] culture
培養基	ばいようき	culture medium
培養液	ばいようえき	culture solution
*栽培	さいばい	[する] grow (flowers, plants, etc.), cultivate
培う	つちかう	cultivate, nurture, foster, develop

第 128 回

1641 陪

▶ばい

11 ⌐ 阝 阝 阝 阝 阝 阝 阹 陪 陪
陪

陪席	ばいせき	[する] sit with one's superior
陪*審員	ばいしんいん	juror, member of the jury
陪*審制度	ばいしんせいど	jury system

1642 賠

▶ばい

15 丨 冂 冃 冃 目 貝 貝 貝 貯 貯
貯 貯 貯 賠 賠

| 賠償金 | ばいしょうきん | compensation, reparations, damages |
| 損害賠償 | そんがいばいしょう | compensation for damages |

1643 頂

▶ちょう
▷いただ(く), いただき

11 一 丁 丆 丆 πr 顶 顶 顶 頂 頂
頂

頂上	ちょうじょう	top, summit, peak
頂点	ちょうてん	apex, climax, zenith, summit, top
絶頂	ぜっちょう	summit, peak, zenith, climax
頂く	いただく	be given, receive, eat, drink [humble]
頂	いただき	top, summit, peak

1644 頑

▶がん

13 一 二 テ 元 元 元 秖 頑 頑 頑
頑 頑 頑

頑張る	がんばる	try hard, do one's best, hold out
頑固な	がんこな	stubborn, obstinate
頑強な	がんきょうな	strong, tough, stubborn
頑健な	がんけんな	robust, hardy, sturdy
頑丈な	がんじょうな	strong, solid, robust, sturdy

1645 頒

▶はん

13 丿 八 分 分 分 分 分 頒 頒 頒
頒 頒 頒

| 頒布 | はんぷ | [する] distribute |
| 頒価 | はんか | distribution price |

1646 煩

▶はん, ぼん
▷わずら(う), わずら(わす)

13 丶 丷 ソ 火 灯 灯 灯 炉 煩 煩
煩 煩 煩

| 煩雑な | はんざつな | complicated, troublesome |

漢字の形に気をつけましょう❻❾

53	1609	158	1640	1641	1642
部	剖	倍	培	陪	賠
部屋	死体を解剖する	4倍ズーム	草花を栽培する	陪*審制度 ばいしん	賠償金

煩悩	ぼんのう	carnal desire, worldly passions, lust
煩わしい	わずらわしい	troublesome, complicated
煩わす	わずらわす	vt. trouble, bother, annoy
煩う	わずらう	be troubled, be worried
思い煩う	おもいわずらう	worry oneself, feel anxious about

1647 顕 ▶けん

18 〳 冂 冃 日 旦 旱 昦 昦 昦
昦 顕 顕 顕 顕 顕 顕 顕

| 顕微鏡 | けんびきょう | microscope |
| 顕著な | けんちょな | remarkable |

1648 顧 ▶こ ▷かえり(みる)

21 一 ニ ヨ 尸 戸 戸 戸 戸 扉 雇
雇 雇 雇 雇 顧 顧 顧 顧 顧 顧
顧

顧問	こもん	consultant, advisor, counselor, teacher in charge of a school club
回顧	かいこ [する]	look back upon, recollect, reminisce
顧慮	こりょ [する]	take into consideration
顧みる	かえりみる	look back on, reflect upon, think of

1649 嬢 ▶じょう

16 く 夂 女 女' 㚣 㚣 妶 妶 妶 妶
嬢 嬢 嬢 嬢 嬢 嬢

| お嬢さん | おじょうさん | young lady, (your/his/her) daughter [honorific] |
| 令嬢 | れいじょう | a daughter from a good family, a young lady |

1650 壊 ▶じょう

16 一 十 圡 圡 圹 圹 圹 圹 圹 圹
圹 壊 壊 壊 壊 壊

| 土壌 | どじょう | soil |

1651 醸 ▶じょう ▷かも(す)

20 一 厂 亓 丙 西 酉 酉 酉' 酉̄ 酊
酊 酊 酊 酊 酶 醸 醸 醸 醸 醸

醸造酒	じょうぞうしゅ	alcoholic beverage made by fermentation, a brew
醸成	じょうせい [する]	brew, bring about, breed (atmosphere, feelings, etc.)
醸し出す	かもしだす	produce (a pleasant/cheerful atmosphere, etc.)

1652 亭 ▶てい
481 cf. 停

9 ' 一 亠 亠 亠 声 亭 亭 亭

| 料亭 | りょうてい | traditional Japanese-style restaurant |
| 亭主 | ていしゅ | one's husband [vulgar], host (of a tea ceremony) |

1653 棄 ▶き
569 cf. 葉

13 ' 亠 亡 亡 亡 亥 杏 杏 杏
亝 亝 棄

| 放棄 | ほうき [する] | give up, abandon, renounce |
| 廃棄 | はいき [する] | do away with, abolish, abandon, scrap |

漢字の形に気をつけましょう⑦

1325	1581	1209	1649	1650	1651
嫌	謙	譲	嬢	壊	醸
嫌悪感を持つ	謙譲の美徳	譲歩する	お嬢さん	土壌を改良する	醸造酒

第5水準

産業廃棄物　さんぎょうはいきぶつ　industrial waste

核廃棄物　かくはいきぶつ　nuclear waste

死体遺棄　したいいき　abandonment of a dead body

棄権　きけん　－する　abstain (from voting), withdraw (from a race/contest)

棄却　ききゃく　－する　dismiss, remand (to a lower court), reject

1654 舎 ▶しゃ

8　ノ　人　ム　宀　全　全　舎　舎

校舎　こうしゃ　schoolhouse, school building

官舎　かんしゃ　official residence

宿舎　しゅくしゃ　lodgings, quarters

寄宿舎　きしゅくしゃ　dormitory, residence hall

特　舎監　しゃかん　dormitory superintendent

田舎　△いなか　countryside, rural district, one's hometown

1655 傘 ▶さん ▷かさ

12　ノ　人　人　人　今　今　今　今　今　傘　傘

傘　かさ　umbrella, parasol

雨傘　あまがさ　(a rain) umbrella

日傘　ひがさ　parasol, sunshade

傘下　さんか　under the umbrella/banner (of)

◇　落下傘　らっかさん　parachute

1656 冠 ▶かん ▷かんむり

9　冖　冖　冖　完　完　冠　冠

冠詞　かんし　(definite/indefinite) article

王冠　おうかん　crown

栄冠　えいかん　crown, laurels

冠　かんむり　crown, coronet

1657 呈 ▶てい cf. 671 程

7　口　口　旦　早　早　呈

贈呈　ぞうてい　－する　make a gift of

進呈　しんてい　－する　present, offer

露呈　ろてい　－する　vi. vt. reveal, expose, disclose

1658 宜 ▶ぎ cf. 850 宣

8　宀　宀　宀　宀　官　官　宜

便宜　べんぎ　convenience

適宜　てきぎ　properly, suitably, at one's (own) discretion

1659 宰 ▶さい cf. 344 辛

10　宀　宀　宀　宀　宀　宰　宰　宰

宰相　さいしょう　prime minister

主宰　しゅさい　－する　preside over, superintend, run

特　宰領　さいりょう　－する　organize, supervise, oversee

1660 寡 ▶か cf. 1155 募

14　宀　宀　宀　宀　宀　宀　宜　宜　宜　寅　寅　寡　寡

寡占市場　かせんしじょう　oligopolistic market

寡黙な　かもくな　taciturn

寡婦　かふ　widow

特　多寡　たか　quantity, amount

第 129 回

1661 審 ▶しん

15　宀　宀　宀　宀　宀　宰　宰　宷　宷　寀　審　審

審判　しんぱん　umpire, referee, judge

主審　しゅしん　chief umpire, head referee/judge

副審　ふくしん　assistant umpire/judge/referee

審議　しんぎ　－する　discuss (at a government assembly), deliberate

不審な　ふしんな　suspicious, dubious

1662　賓　▶ひん

15　｀　丷　宀　宀　宀　宀　宀　宀　宀
宀　宀　宀　宀　賓

貴賓室　　きひんしつ　VIP room
主賓　　　しゅひん　guest of honor
来賓　　　らいひん　guest/visitor (at an official
　　　　　　　ceremony)

1663　崩　▶ほう
　　　▷くず(れる)，くず(す)

11　｀　屮　屮　屵　屵　屵　屵　屵　崩　崩
崩

崩壊　　　ほうかい　[する] collapse, disintegrate
崩御　　　ほうぎょ　[する] (the emperor) pass away
崩れる　　くずれる　collapse, crumble, break, get out of
　　　　　shape/physical condition
山崩れ　　やまくずれ　landslide
崩す　　　くずす　destroy, level (a hill), change/break (a
　　　　　large bill), write characters in a fluid/cursive
　　　　　style
雪崩　　　△なだれ　snowslide, avalanche

1664　崇　▶すう
　　　　　　　　　　　　　　816
　　　　　　　　　　　　　cf. 宗

11　｀　屮　屮　屮　崇　屵　屵　屵　崇
崇

崇拝　　　すうはい　[する] worship, venerate, adore,
　　　　　admire, idolize
偶像崇拝　ぐうぞうすうはい　idolatry, idol worship
崇高な　　すうこうな　sublime, lofty, noble

1665　芳　▶ほう
　　　▷かんば(しい)
　　　　　　　　　　　　　　566
　　　　　　　　　　　　　cf. 芸

7　一　十　艹　艹　艹　芳　芳

芳香　　　ほうこう　fragrance, sweet smell
芳しくない　かんばしくない　not good, unsavory, poor
　　　　　(performance, reputation, etc.)

1666　荒　▶こう
　　　▷あら(い)，あ(れる)，あ(らす)

9　一　十　艹　艹　艹　芒　芦　芹　荒

荒れる　　あれる　be stormy, be rough, run wild, be
　　　　　dilapidated, get chapped
荒れ地　　あれち　wasteland, barren land
大荒れ　　おおあれ　heavy storm, disorder
荒らす　　あらす　devastate, lay waste, damage
荒い　　　あらい　rude, wild, rough
荒波　　　あらなみ　raging waves, heavy seas
荒々しい　あらあらしい　rough, harsh, rude
荒廃　　　こうはい　[する] fall into ruin, be devastated
◇　荒天　　こうてん　stormy weather
荒涼とした　こうりょうとした　desolate, dreary,
　　　　　deserted, inhospitable

1667　菓　▶か
　　　　　　　　　　　502　1862
　　　　　　　　　　　cf. 果 巣

11　一　十　艹　艹　芇　苸　昔　苩　草　菓
菓

(お)菓子　　(お)かし　confectionery, candy, cake

1668　慕　▶ぼ
　　　▷した(う)
　　　　　　　　　　　　　　1157
　　　　　　　　　　　　　cf. 幕

14　一　十　艹　艹　芇　苩　昔　苩　莫　莫
莫　莫　慕　慕

慕う　　　したう　yearn for, love dearly, adore
◇　慕わしい　したわしい　dear, beloved
敬慕　　　けいぼ　[する] love and respect
特 慕情　　ぼじょう　longing, affection, love
特 思慕　　しぼ　[する] long for, love dearly

1669　冒　▶ぼう
　　　▷おか(す)
　　　　　　　　　　　　　　1279
　　　　　　　　　　　　　cf. 帽

9　｀　冂　冃　冃　冃　冐　冐　冒　冒

冒険　　　ぼうけん　[する] have an adventure, run a risk,
　　　　　take a chance
冒頭　　　ぼうとう　the beginning, the opening
◇　感冒　　かんぼう　a cold
冒す　　　おかす　take a risk, brave, defy
冒される　おかされる　be afflicted (by a disease)

第5水準

1670 是 ▶ぜ

767
cf. 提

9 ｜ 冂 曰 日 旦 早 早 是 是

是正	ぜせい [する]	correct, rectify
是認	ぜにん [する]	approve of
国是	こくぜ	national policy
是非	ぜひ	right or wrong, by all means, without fail

1671 罷 ▶ひ

15 ｜ 冂 冂 冂 罒 罒 罒 罒 罪 罪 罪 罷 罷 罷

罷免	ひめん [する]	dismiss (someone from their job)

1672 羅 ▶ら

19 ｜ 冂 冂 冂 罒 罒 罒 罒 罒 罪 罪 罪 罪 罪 罪 羅 羅 羅

羅列	られつ [する]	enumerate, list
網羅	もうら [する]	contain (everything), cover all (the facts)
羅針盤	らしんばん	(mariner's) compass
*甲羅	こうら	shell, carapace

1673 窃 ▶せつ

9 ｀ ｀ 宀 宀 穴 空 空 窃 窃

窃盗	せっとう	theft, stealing

1674 窒 ▶ちつ

11 ｀ ｀ 宀 宀 穴 空 空 空 窒 窒 窒

窒息	ちっそく [する]	be suffocated, be asphyxiated
窒素	ちっそ	nitrogen

1675 窮 ▶きゅう
▷きわ(める)，きわ(まる)

15 ｀ ｀ 宀 宀 穴 空 空 空 空 空 窮 窮 窮 窮 窮

窮屈な	きゅうくつな	narrow, tight
窮乏生活	きゅうぼうせいかつ	impoverished life, life of destitution
窮状	きゅうじょう	wretched condition, distress, sad plight
困窮	こんきゅう [する]	be in difficulty, be in need
窮極の	きゅうきょくの	ultimate, final cf. きゅうきょくの is normally written as 究極の
窮める	きわめる	carry to extremes, bring to an end
窮まる	きわまる	reach an extreme, come to an end

1676 蛍 ▶けい
▷ほたる

11 ｀ ｀ ｀ ｀ 兴 兴 兴 兴 尚 蛍 蛍

蛍光灯	けいこうとう	fluorescent lamp
蛍光*塗料	けいこうとりょう	fluorescent paint
蛍	ほたる	firefly

1677 掌 ▶しょう

12 ｀ ｀ ｀ ｀ 兴 兴 兴 兴 尚 堂 堂 掌

車掌	しゃしょう	(train) conductor
掌中	しょうちゅう	in one's hands
掌握	しょうあく [する]	control, command
職掌	しょくしょう	(official) duties
分掌	ぶんしょう [する]	share work/tasks, divide up the duties

1678 奉 ▶ほう，ぶ
▷たてまつ(る)

8 一 二 三 声 夫 夫 参 奉

社会奉仕	しゃかいほうし	voluntary service to society
信奉	しんぽう [する]	espouse, follow (a spiritual leader, etc.), believe in

奉納　ほうのう　[する] dedicate/offer (to the gods, Buddha)

 奉公人　ほうこうにん　servant, apprentice, employee

歴 奉行　ぶぎょう　magistrate (in the Edo period)

歴 奉る　たてまつる　offer, present, revere [humble]

1679　奏　▶そう　▷かな（でる）

9　一 二 三 声 夫 表 表 奏 奏

演奏　えんそう　musical performance　[する] give a musical performance

合奏　がっそう　[する] play in concert

伴奏　ばんそう　accompaniment (of a piano, guitar, etc.)　[する] play an accompaniment

奏でる　かなでる　play (musical instrument, especially strings)

1680　泰　▶たい

10　一 二 三 声 夫 未 表 泰 泰 泰

安泰だ　あんたいだ　be stable and secure

特 泰然と　たいぜんと　composedly, calmly

第 130 回

1681　笛　▶てき　▷ふえ　cf. 苗 1837

11　ノ ト ヒ ヒ ヒ ヒ ヒ 竹 竹 竹 笛　笛

笛　ふえ　flute, whistle

口笛　くちぶえ　whistle, whistling sound

警笛　けいてき　warning horn, alarm whistle

汽笛　きてき　(steam) whistle

1682　箇　▶か

14　ノ ト ヒ ヒ ヒ ヒ 竹 竹 竹 笛　笛 笛 箇 箇

箇条書き　かじょうがき　itemized (statement, list, etc.)

箇所　かしょ　place, part, point, spot

1683　篤　▶とく

16　ノ ト ヒ ヒ ヒ 竹 竹 竹 竹 竿　竿 篤 篤 篤 篤 篤

危篤の　きとくの　in critical condition　cf. 重態の／重体の（じゅうたいの）in serious condition

篤実な　とくじつな　sincere, faithful

篤志家　とくしか　charitable person, philanthropist

1684　簿　▶ぼ　cf. 薄 799

19　ノ ト ヒ ヒ ヒ 竹 竹 竹 竹 竿　竿 竿 竿 箔 薄 篷 篷 簿 簿

名簿　めいぼ　name roster, list of members

帳簿　ちょうぼ　account book

簿記　ぼき　bookkeeping

1685　覇　▶は

19　一 一 戸 両 両 西 严 严 严　严 严 严 霏 霏 覇 覇 覇 覇

覇権　はけん　hegemony

覇者　はしゃ　conqueror, champion

制覇　せいは　[する] conquer, dominate, gain supremacy, win the championship

連覇　れんぱ　[する] win the championship consecutively

1686　覆　▶ふく　▷おお（う），くつがえ（す），くつがえ（る）

18　一 一 戸 両 両 西 严 严 严　严 覃 覂 覆 覆 覆 覆 覆

覆う　おおう　cover, conceal, hide

覆い　おおい　a cover/covering (for a chair, machine, etc.)

覆す　くつがえす　overturn, overthrow

覆る　くつがえる　be overturned, be overthrown

覆面　ふくめん　(cloth) mask

転覆　てんぷく　[する] vi. vt. overturn, capsize, overthrow

第5水準

249

1687 零 ▶れい

13 一 ハ 戸 雨 雨 雨 雨 雨 乗 乗
乗 零 零

零細企業	れいさいきぎょう	small business
零下	れいか	below zero (degrees Celsius)
零点	れいてん	zero points (on a test)
特 零落	れいらく	する be reduced to poverty, be ruined

1688 霊 ▶れい, りょう ▷たま

15 一 ハ 戸 雨 雨 雨 雨 雨 雪 雪
雲 雰 雰 雰 霊

霊	れい	spirit, soul
霊*魂	れいこん	soul, spirit
霊園	れいえん	cemetery
霊感	れいかん	inspiration, extra-sensory perception (i.e., ESP) of the supernatural
霊長類	れいちょうるい	primates
霊*枢車	れいきゅうしゃ	hearse
*幽霊	ゆうれい	ghost
悪霊	あくりょう	evil spirit
死霊	しりょう	spirit of a dead person, evil spirit
御霊	みたま	spirit of the dead, departed spirit [honorific]

1689 霜 ▶そう ▷しも

17 一 ハ 戸 雨 雨 雨 雨 雨 雪 雪
霜 霜 霜 霜 霜 霜 霜

霜	しも	frost
初霜	はつしも	the first frost of the season
霜柱	しもばしら	frost columns
霜害	そうがい	frost damage

1690 啓 ▶けい

11 一 ヲ ヲ 戸 戸 戸 戸 所 所 啓 啓
啓

拝啓	はいけい	Dear Sir, Dear Madam (opening word for letters)
自己啓発	じこけいはつ	self-enlightenment
神の啓示	かみのけいじ	revelation by God
啓*蒙	けいもう	する enlighten

1691 召 ▶しょう ▷め(す)

5 ヲ コ コ 召 召

召集	しょうしゅう	する summon, conscript, draft
召集令状	しょうしゅうれいじょう	draft papers
召喚	しょうかん	する summon, call
召し上がる	めしあがる	eat, drink [honorific]
お召しになる	おめしになる	wear, have (a coat) [honorific]

1692 塁 ▶るい

12 ヽ ロ 四 用 田 甲 甲 男 男 畏 畏
畾 塁

一塁	いちるい	first base (in baseball)
塁審	るいしん	base umpire (in baseball)
特 土塁	どるい	earthwork
塁	るい	fort, base (in baseball)

1693 堕 ▶だ

1218
cf. 墜

12 ヲ ヲ 阝 阝 阝 阶 防 阤 隋 隋
堕 堕

| 堕落 | だらく | する become corrupted, degenerate into |
| 堕胎 | だたい | する have an abortion cf. 人工中絶（じんこうちゅうぜつ）, rather than 堕胎, is normally used. |

1694 塗 ▶と ▷ぬ(る)

13 ヽ シ シ 氵 氵 氵 氵 氵 涂 涂
塗 塗 塗

| 塗る | ぬる | apply a coat (of paint, varnish, lacquer, etc.) |

ペンキ塗り立て　ペンキぬりたて　freshly painted, "WET PAINT"

塗料　とりょう　paints

塗装　とそう　-する coat with paint

塗布　とふ　-する apply/spread (paint, ointment, etc.)

1695 墨 ▶ぼく ▷すみ

14　丶 口 戸 戸 甲 甲 里 里 黒 黒 黒 黒 墨 墨

墨　すみ　Indian/Chinese ink, ink stick, the black ink (stick) used in traditional Japanese calligraphy, etc.

墨絵　すみえ　ink drawing using a traditional black ink

お墨付き　おすみつき　approval from a superior/influential person

墨汁　ぼくじゅう　Indian/Chinese ink, the black ink used in traditional Japanese calligraphy, etc.

特 墨守　ぼくしゅ　-する adhere (to tradition, customs, etc.)

1696 妄 ▶もう, ぼう

6　丶 亠 亡 亡 妄 妄

妄想　もうそう　wild fantasy, delusion -する be deluded

妄信　もうしん　-する accept blindly

特 妄言　もうげん, ぼうげん　thoughtless words, falsehood

1697 忌 ▶き ▷い(む), い(まわしい)

7　コ コ 己 已 忌 忌 忌

忌避　きひ　-する evade, shirk (responsibility)

禁忌　きんき　taboo

忌中　きちゅう　in mourning

忌む　いむ　abhor, have a taboo against, avoid

忌まわしい　いまわしい　abominable, disgusting, offensive

1698 怠 ▶たい ▷おこた(る), なま(ける)

9　ㄥ ㄥ 台 台 台 台 怠 怠 怠

怠慢　たいまん　negligence, neglect

怠惰な　たいだな　lazy, idle

怠ける　なまける　be idle/lazy, neglect (one's work, studies, etc.)

怠け者　なまけもの　lazy fellow, idler

怠る　おこたる　be lazy, neglect (one's duties, responsibilities, etc.)

1699 悠 ▶ゆう

11　ノ イ 亻 仃 竹 攸 攸 悠 悠 悠

悠々と　ゆうゆうと　calmly, leisurely, easily, composedly

悠然と　ゆうぜんと　calmly, composedly

悠長に　ゆうちょうに　leisurely, at an easygoing pace

悠久の　ゆうきゅうの　eternal, everlasting

1700 愁 ▶しゅう ▷うれ(える), うれ(い)

13　丿 二 千 禾 禾 禾 利 秒 秋 秋 愁 愁 愁

愁い　うれい　grief, sorrow, sadness

愁える　うれえる　grieve, lament

愁傷　しゅうしょう　grief, lamentation

*哀愁　あいしゅう　sadness, sorrow, grief

*憂愁　ゆうしゅう　melancholy, gloom

1701 愚 ▶ぐ ▷おろ(か)

13　丨 口 冃 日 曰 吕 禺 禺 禺 禺 愚 愚 愚

愚かな　おろかな　foolish, stupid, silly

愚問　ぐもん　stupid question

愚鈍な　ぐどんな　stupid, silly, foolish

愚*痴　ぐち　grumbles, complaints

1702 慰

▶い
▷なぐさ（める），なぐさ（む）

15 一 コ ア ア 尸 尿 尿 尉 尉 尉
尉 尉 尉 慰 慰

慰める	なぐさめる	console, comfort, solace
慰め	なぐさめ	consolation, comfort
慰む	なぐさむ	amuse oneself, make a plaything of
慰み	なぐさみ	diversion, amusement
慰謝料	いしゃりょう	consolation money, compensation money, damages
慰労	いろう	［する］acknowledge a person's services
慰留	いりゅう	［する］persuade someone to stay in office, persuade someone not to resign
慰問	いもん	［する］go to console
慰安旅行	いあんりょこう	a recreation trip taken with one's co-workers, a company trip/outing
自慰行為	じいこうい	masturbation

1703 懲

▶ちょう
▷こ（りる），こ（らす），こ（らしめる） cf. 徴 1148

18 ノ ク イ イ イ゛ 彴 彴 彵 徍 徎
徎 徴 徴 徴 徴 懲 懲 懲

懲役	ちょうえき	penal servitude, imprisonment
懲罰	ちょうばつ	［する］punish, discipline
懲戒免職	ちょうかいめんしょく	disciplinary dismissal
懲らしめる	こらしめる	punish, chastise, discipline
懲らす	こらす	punish, chastise, discipline
懲りる	こりる	learn by experience, have a bitter experience
性懲りもなく	しょうこりもなく	incorrigibly, in spite of one's bitter experience

1704 架

▶か
▷か（ける），か（かる）

9 フ カ カ 加 加 カロ 架 架 架

十字架	じゅうじか	cross
書架	しょか	bookshelf, bookcase, the stacks (in a library)
架橋	かきょう	bridge construction, bridge
架線工事	かせんこうじ	(work done to install) wiring
架空の	かくうの	fictitious, imaginary

架ける	かける	construct/build (a bridge)
架かる	かかる	be constructed/built
架け橋	かけはし	bridge, go-between

1705 香

▶こう，きょう
▷か，かお（り），かお（る）

9 一 ニ 千 千 禾 禾 香 香 香

香水	こうすい	perfume
線香	せんこう	a stick of incense
香気	こうき	fragrance, perfume, aroma, sweet scent
香り	かおり	scent, fragrance, perfume
香る	かおる	be fragrant, smell sweet
色香	いろか	the charms (of a woman), color and scent
移り香	うつりが	lingering scent
［特］香車	きょうしゃ	lance (in Japanese chess)

1706 暫

▶ざん

15 一 厂 厂 甘 目 旦 車 車 車 斬
斬 斬 斬 暫 暫

暫定的な	ざんていてきな	provisional, temporary, tentative
暫定政権	ざんていせいけん	provisional government
暫時	ざんじ	for a (short) time, (for) a little time

1707 脅

▶きょう
▷おびや（かす），おど（す），おど（かす）

10 フ カ ヲ 力 カ 夯 夯 脅 脅 脅

脅迫	きょうはく	［する］intimidate, threaten, blackmail
脅威	きょうい	threat, menace
脅す	おどす	threaten, browbeat, menace, intimidate, frighten
脅し	おどし	a threat, a menace
脅かす	おどかす	threaten, intimidate, frighten, scare
脅かす	おびやかす	threaten (e.g., the existence of something), menace, intimidate

1708 烈

▶れつ
cf. 列 812

10　一 ア 歹 歹 列 列 列 烈 烈 烈

猛烈な　　　もうれつな　fierce, intense, violent

特　壮烈な　　　そうれつな　heroic, brave

特　烈風　　　　れっぷう　violent winds, gale

特　烈火　　　　れっか　raging fire

1709　勲　▶くん

15　一 ｒ ｆ 彳 彳 血 重 重 重 動
動 動 動 動 勲

勲章　　　　くんしょう　decoration (e.g., military), medal

叙勲式　　　じょくんしき　award(-conferring) ceremony

勲功　　　　くんこう　distinguished services, deeds of valor

最高殊勲選手　さいこうしゅくんせんしゅ　most valuable player, MVP

1710　薫　▶くん
　　　▷かお（る）

16　一 ＋ 艹 艹 芦 芦 苦 苦 苜 苜
苜 萐 蕈 薫 薫 薫

薫製　　　　くんせい　smoked product (such as smoked salmon, herring, etc.) cf. くんせい can be written as 燻製 , but 燻 is not a Jōyō Kanji

薫り　　　　かおり　scent, fragrance, aroma

薫る　　　　かおる　be fragrant, smell sweet

1711　紫　▶し　　　　　　　　1186
　　　▷むらさき　　　　　cf. 緊

12　１ ｔ ｔ 止 此 此 此 些 些 紫
紫 紫

紫外線　　　しがいせん　ultraviolet rays

紫　　　　　むらさき　purple, violet

1712　誓　▶せい
　　　▷ちか（う）

14　一 ｔ ｔ 扌 折 折 折 折 哲 哲
誓 誓 誓 誓

誓う　　　　ちかう　swear (an oath), promise, vow

誓い　　　　ちかい　oath, vow

誓約書　　　せいやくしょ　written oath/pledge

宣誓　　　　せんせい　する take an oath, pledge

1713　誉　▶よ　　　　　　　1189
　　　▷ほま（れ）　　　　cf. 挙

13　、 ゛ ゛ ゛ 产 兴 兴 誉 誉
誉 誉 誉

名誉　　　　めいよ　honor, reputation

栄誉　　　　えいよ　honor, credit, distinction, glory

誉れ　　　　ほまれ　honor, reputation, glory

1714　貫　▶かん
　　　▷つらぬ（く）

11　ｌ ｐ 田 毌 毌 甲 貫 貫 貫 貫
貫

一貫性　　　いっかんせい　consistency

一貫性がある　いっかんせいがある　consistent

貫通　　　　かんつう　する pierce, penetrate, pass through

縦貫　　　　じゅうかん　する run right across, traverse the whole length

貫く　　　　つらぬく　pierce, penetrate, carry out

1715　匠　▶しょう

6　一 ｒ ｒ 厂 斤 匠

意匠権　　　いしょうけん　design rights

巨匠　　　　きょしょう　great master

師匠　　　　ししょう　master (in contrast to disciples)

1716　匿　▶とく

10　一 ｒ 干 开 歼 歼 苪 若 匿 匿

匿名で　　　とくめいで　anonymously

隠匿　　　　いんとく　する conceal, hide (stolen property, etc.)

1717 囚 ▶しゅう

254 406
cf. 困 因

5 丨 冂 囚 囚 囚

| 囚人 | しゅうじん | prisoner, a convict |
| 死刑囚 | しけいしゅう | condemned criminal |

1718 閑 ▶かん

12 丨 冂 冂 冃 冃 門 門 門 門 閑
閑 閑

| 閑静な | かんせいな | quiet (neighborhood), tranquil |

1719 閲 ▶えつ

15 丨 冂 冂 冃 冃 門 門 門 門 門
門 閂 閉 閲 閲

検閲	けんえつ	〔-する〕 censor, inspect
校閲	こうえつ	〔-する〕 proofread, look over and correct (a manuscript)
閲兵	えっぺい	〔-する〕 inspect/review the troops
閲*覧	えつらん	〔-する〕 peruse, inspect, read
閲*覧室	えつらんしつ	reading room

1720 暦 ▶れき ▷こよみ

704
cf. 歴

14 一 厂 厂 斤 斤 斤 厍 厤 厤 厤
厤 暦 暦 暦

西暦	せいれき	the Christian Era, Anno Domini, A.D.
太陽暦	たいようれき	the solar calendar
太陰暦	たいいんれき	the lunar calendar
新暦	しんれき	the new calendar, the solar calendar
旧暦	きゅうれき	the old calendar, the lunar calendar
還暦	かんれき	60th birthday
暦	こよみ	calendar cf. カレンダー, rather than 暦, is used in modern Japanese

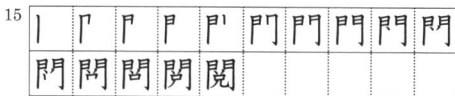

1721 厄 ▶やく

4 一 厂 厃 厄

厄介な	やっかいな	troublesome, burdensome, annoying, difficult
特 厄	やく	misfortune, disaster
災厄	さいやく	misfortune, disaster
厄年	やくどし	unlucky/bad year

1722 尼 ▶に ▷あま

2097
cf. 叱

5 ⁊ ⁹ 尸 尸 尼

尼	あま	nun
尼寺	あまでら	nunnery
尼僧	にそう	nun, sister
修道尼	しゅうどうに	nun

1723 尾 ▶び ▷お

7 ⁊ ⁹ 尸 尸 尸 尾 尾

尾	お	tail (on a dog or other animal)
尾根	おね	mountain ridge
尾行	びこう	〔-する〕 follow/shadow/tail (someone)
首尾一貫した	しゅびいっかんした	consistent
語尾	ごび	ending of a word
末尾	まつび	the end, the close

1724 尿 ▶にょう

7 ⁊ ⁹ 尸 尺 尿 尿 尿

糖尿病	とうにょうびょう	diabetes
尿	にょう	urine
放尿	ほうにょう	〔-する〕 urinate
尿意を催す	にょういをもよおす	have a desire to urinate
尿素	にょうそ	urea
夜尿症	やにょうしょう	enuresis

1725 層 ▶そう　　429 cf. 増

14 ｜ 一 二 尸 尸 尸 尸 尸 尸 屈 屈
屈 層 層 層

高層ビル	こうそうビル	skyscraper
断層	だんそう	fault
低所得層	ていしょとくそう	social stratum with a low level of income
一層	いっそう	even more, all the more
大層	たいそう	very (much), greatly

1726 尽 ▶じん　▷つ(くす), つ(きる), つ(かす)

6 ｜ 一 コ 尸 尺 尽 尽

力を尽くす	ちからをつくす	make an effort, exert oneself
尽くす	つくす	render (service), exert (one's power), use (one's ability)
心尽くし	こころづくし	thoughtfulness, kindness
尽きる	つきる	run out, be exhausted
愛想が尽きる	あいそがつきる	run out of patience (with a person)
無尽蔵の	むじんぞうの	inexhaustible, unlimited
尽力	じんりょく	-する make an effort, endeavor, render service

1727 唐 ▶とう　▷から

10 ｜ 一 亠 广 广 广 肀 肀 唐 唐 唐

唐突な	とうとつな	abrupt, unexpected
唐	とう	the Tang dynasty
唐草模様	からくさもよう	arabesque pattern

1728 庸 ▶よう　　1824 cf. 粛

11 ｜ 一 亠 广 广 广 庐 庐 庐 肩 庸

| 中庸 | ちゅうよう | moderation |
| 凡庸な | ぼんような | mediocre, ordinary, common |

1729 廉 ▶れん　　1324 cf. 兼

13 ｜ 丶 亠 广 广 广 产 肀 庚 彦 庚
庚 庚 廉

清廉潔白な	せいれんけっぱくな	honest, upright, full of integrity
破廉恥な	はれんちな	shameless, infamous
廉価	れんか	low price
廉売	れんばい	a (bargain) sale

1730 腐 ▶ふ　▷くさ(る), くさ(れる), くさ(らす)

14 ｜ 丶 亠 广 广 广 庐 庐 府 府 府
腐 腐 腐 腐

豆腐	とうふ	tofu, soybean curd
腐敗	ふはい	-する decay, rot, become corrupt
腐心	ふしん	-する take pains (to do)
腐食	ふしょく	-する corrode, erode, rot
陳腐な	ちんぷな	commonplace, trite, stale
腐る	くさる	rot, decay, spoil
腐れ縁	くされえん	unfortunate but inescapable relationship, fatal bond
ふて腐れる	ふてくされる	sulk, get sulky
腐らす	くさらす	let rot/spoil

1731 磨 ▶ま　▷みが(く)　　704 cf. 歴

16 ｜ 丶 亠 广 广 广 广 庑 庑 麻 麻
麻 歴 磨 磨 磨 磨

磨く	みがく	brush (teeth), shine (shoes), polish (silver)
歯磨き	はみがき	brushing one's teeth
磨き粉	みがきこ	polishing powder
研磨	けんま	-する grind, polish

1732 慶 ▶けい

15 ｜ 丶 亠 广 广 广 庐 慶 慶 慶 慶
慶 慶 慶 慶 慶

第5水準

255

慶事　けいじ　happy event

◇ 慶*應義塾大学　けいおうぎじゅくだいがく　Keio University

1733 **扇**

▶せん
▷おうぎ

10

扇風機　せんぷうき　electric fan
扇子　せんす　folding fan
扇状地　せんじょうち　(alluvial) fan
扇動　せんどう　[-する] fan, agitate, incite
扇　おうぎ　folding fan, traditional Japanese fan

1734 **扉**

▶ひ
▷とびら

12
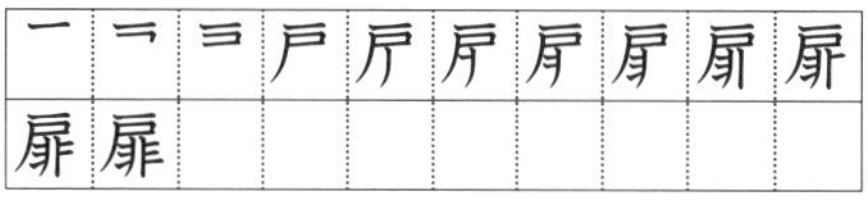

扉　とびら　door (with hinges), title page
門扉　もんぴ　door (of a gate)
[特] 開扉　かいひ　[-する] open the door

1735 **疫**

▶えき，やく

9
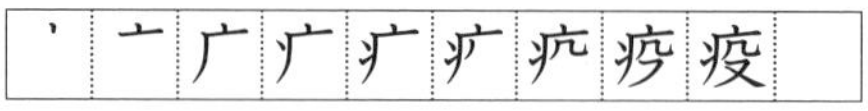

疫病　えきびょう　epidemic, plague
[特] 防疫　ぼうえき　prevention of epidemics
疫病神　やくびょうがみ　plague, jinx

1736 **疾**

▶しつ

10
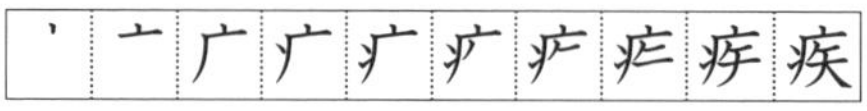

疾走　しっそう　[-する] run at full speed, dash
疾患　しっかん　disease, ailment
◇ 疾病　しっぺい　disease, illness

1737 **痢**

▶り

12
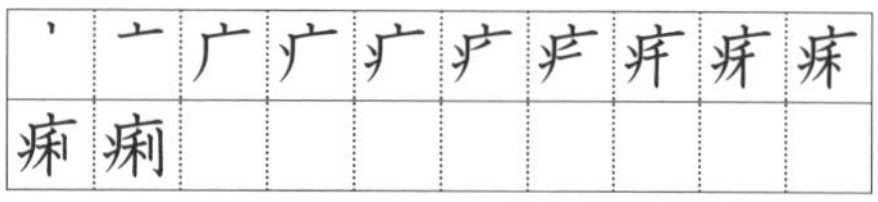

下痢　げり　diarrhea
赤痢　せきり　dysentery

1738 **痴**

▶ち

13

愚痴　ぐち　grumbles, complaints
痴漢　ちかん　molester of woman (on the train, etc.)
[特] 痴情　ちじょう　blind love, insane passion, jealousy

1739 **癒**

▶ゆ
▷い(える)，い(やす)

18

治癒　ちゆ　[-する] *vi.* be cured, recover
癒着　ゆちゃく　adhesion　[-する] adhere
癒える　いえる　get well, be cured, heal
癒やす　いやす　heal, cure

1740 **虐**

▶ぎゃく
▷しいた(げる)

9
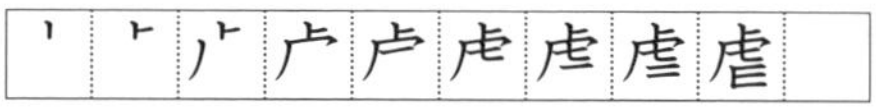

虐殺　ぎゃくさつ　[-する] slaughter, massacre, butcher
虐待　ぎゃくたい　[-する] treat cruelly, abuse
残虐な　ざんぎゃくな　cruel, brutal, heartless
虐げる　しいたげる　oppress, persecute, tyrannize, treat cruelly

第 133 回

1741 **虚**

▶きょ，こ

11

謙虚な　けんきょな　modest, humble

虚偽の　　きょぎの　false (statement, answer, etc.)
空虚な　　くうきょな　empty, vacant, hollow
虚無主義　きょむしゅぎ　nihilism
虚空　　　こくう　empty air, the void

1742 膚　▶ふ

15　`丶 丨 广 广 户 卢 卢 虏 虏 膚 膚 膚 膚 膚 膚`

皮膚　　　ひふ　skin
◇ 完膚なきまで　かんぷなきまで　(defeat the enemy) thoroughly

1743 巡　▶じゅん
　　　　　▷めぐ(る)

6　`く 巛 巛 巡 巡 巡`

巡礼　　　じゅんれい　pilgrimage, pilgrim ［する］make/go on a pilgrimage
巡査　　　じゅんさ　police officer
巡回　　　じゅんかい　［する］go around, patrol, make rounds
巡視　　　じゅんし　［する］patrol, make an inspection
巡業　　　じゅんぎょう　a tour (by a singer/band, theatrical group, etc.) ［する］go on tour
一巡　　　いちじゅん　a round, a tour ［する］make rounds, cover (the grounds) on foot
巡る　　　めぐる　travel around
巡り歩く　めぐりあるく　walk around, travel around
巡り合わせ　めぐりあわせ　(a stroke of) fortune, good/bad luck
お巡りさん　△おまわりさん　police officer

1744 迅　▶じん

6　`乀 コ 刊 刊 迅 迅`

迅速に　　じんそくに　promptly, swiftly
◇ ▲獅子奮迅の努力　ししふんじんのどりょく　desperate effort

1745 迭　▶てつ　　　　206 cf. 送

8　`丿 一 二 牛 失 失 迭 迭`

更迭　　　こうてつ　［する］make a switch (in the Cabinet, etc.)

1746 透　▶とう　　　　1171 cf. 秀
　　　　　▷す(く), す(かす), す(ける)

10　`一 二 千 千 禾 秀 秀 透 透 透`

透明な／の　とうめいな／の　transparent, clear
透視　　　とうし　［する］see through, examine by x-ray
透過性　　とうかせい　permeability
浸透　　　しんとう　［する］penetrate, infiltrate, permeate
透かす　　すかす　look through, hold (a thing) up to the light
透かし　　すかし　watermark, openwork
透ける　　すける　be transparent
透き間　　すきま　small opening/gap, chink
透き通る　すきとおる　be transparent, be seen through

1747 逝　▶せい　　　　772 cf. 折
　　　　　▷ゆ(く), い(く)

10　`一 十 扌 扩 折 折 折 浙 浙 逝`

逝去　　　せいきょ　［する］pass away, die
急逝　　　きゅうせい　［する］die a sudden death
逝く　　　ゆく, いく　pass away, die

1748 逸　▶いつ　　　　941 cf. 免

11　`丿 勹 勹 宀 宀 宀 免 免 逸 逸`

逸

逸話　　　いつわ　anecdote
逸品　　　いっぴん　excellent/fine article
逸材　　　いつざい　person of talent
逸脱　　　いつだつ　［する］deviate, depart from
逸する　　いっする　miss, lose, deviate/stray from

第5水準

1749 遮

▶しゃ
▶さえぎ(る)

14 ｀ 一 广 广 庐 庐 庶 庶 庶 庶
庶 `庶 遮 遮

遮断	しゃだん	[-する] cut off, stop, interrupt (traffic, etc.), block
遮断機	しゃだんき	railroad crossing gate
遮る	さえぎる	interrupt, obstruct, block, intercept, screen

1750 遭

▶そう
▶あ(う)

14 一 厂 厂 戸 币 曲 曲 曹 曹 曹
曹 曹 遭 遭

遭難	そうなん	[-する] meet with disaster, have an accident
遭遇	そうぐう	[-する] encounter, come across
遭う	あう	meet (with disaster), be exposed (to danger)

1751 遵

▶じゅん

479
cf. 尊

15 ｀ ｀ 艹 产 片 片 酋 酋 酋 酋
尊 尊 尊 遵 遵

| 遵守 | じゅんしゅ | [-する] obey (the law) |
| 遵法精神 | じゅんぽうせいしん | spirit of compliance with the law |

1752 鬼

▶き
▶おに

10 ｀ ｀ 宀 宀 宀 由 尹 鬼 鬼 鬼

鬼	おに	devil, demon, fiend, ogre
鬼ごっこ	おにごっこ	tag (children's game)
鬼才	きさい	unusual ability, genius (at)
[特] 餓鬼	がき	hungry ghost, devil, brat

1753 塊

▶かい
▶かたまり

13 一 十 土 圹 圹 圹 坰 坰 塀
塊 塊 塊

団塊の世代	だんかいのせだい	baby boom generation
山塊	さんかい	group of mountains, massif
塊	かたまり	lump, mass, clod, chunk

1754 魂

▶こん
▶たましい

14 一 二 云 云 云' 动' 动 动 魂
魂 魂 魂 魂

霊魂	れいこん	soul, spirit
商魂	しょうこん	commercial enthusiasm, salesmanship
魂胆	こんたん	ulterior motive
魂	たましい	soul, spirit

1755 醜

▶しゅう
▶みにく(い)

17 一 厂 币 币 西 酉 酉 酉' 酉' 酉'
酊 酊 酌 酌 醜 醜 醜

醜聞	しゅうぶん	scandal, bad reputation
醜態	しゅうたい	disgraceful behavior
美醜	びしゅう	beauty or ugliness, looks
醜悪な	しゅうあくな	ugly, mean
醜い	みにくい	ugly, bad-looking

1756 甚

▶じん
▶はなは(だ), はなは(だしい)

9 一 十 廿 廿 甘 甚 其 其 甚

甚大な	じんだいな	serious/heavy (damage, etc.), great, enormous
甚だ	はなはだ	very much, exceedingly
甚だしい	はなはだしい	extreme (suffering), enormous (losses)

1757 勘

▶かん

11 一 十 廿 廿 甘 甚 其 其 甚 甚
勘

| 勘 | かん | intuition, sixth sense |
| 勘定 | かんじょう | counting, calculation, payment (of a bill) [-する] count, calculate |

勘弁　　　かんべん　[する] pardon, forgive, tolerate
勘当　　　かんどう　[する] disinherit, disown, renounce
勘違い　　かんちがい　[する] misunderstand, misinterpret

1758	堪	▶かん ▷た（える）

12　一 十 土 坩 坩 坩 坩 堪 堪 堪
　　堪 堪

堪える　　たえる　endure, bear/stand, be competent to
　　　　　　　　　(the task)
◇ 堪*忍　　かんにん　[する] forgive, be patient with

1759	某	▶ぼう

9　一 十 卄 廿 甘 甚 草 某 某

某国　　　ぼうこく　a certain country
某所　　　ぼうしょ　a certain place
某氏　　　ぼうし　a certain person
某ホテル　ぼうホテル　a certain hotel

1760	媒	▶ばい

12　く 夕 夕 女 女 女 女 女 女
　　媒 媒

媒体　　　ばいたい　media, medium
媒介　　　ばいかい　[する] mediate, act as an agent,
　　　　　　　　　transmit
触媒　　　しょくばい　catalyst
媒酌人　　ばいしゃくにん　matchmaker, go-between

第 134 回

1761	謀	▶ぼう，む ▷はか（る）

16　丶 亠 亠 亖 言 言 言 計 計
　　訨 計 詳 謀 謀 謀

陰謀　　　いんぼう　conspiracy, intrigue, plot
謀略　　　ぼうりゃく　a plot, a scheme
首謀者　　しゅぼうしゃ　ringleader

無謀な　　むぼうな　reckless, thoughtless
◇ 謀反　　むほん　rebellion, treason
謀る　　　はかる　plot, scheme

1762	又	▷また

2　フ 又

又　　　　また　moreover, again, as well
又は　　　または　or

1763	双	▶そう ▷ふた

4　フ 又 刄 双

双方　　　そうほう　both parties, both sides
双方向の　そうほうこうの　two-way, interactive
双子　　　ふたご　twin(s)
双葉　　　ふたば　seed leaf

1764	貞	▶てい

9　丶 ト 上 占 卢 貞 貞 貞 貞

貞操　　　ていそう　chastity, virtue, honor
貞節　　　ていせつ　chastity, faithfulness
◇ 貞*淑な　ていしゅくな　chaste, faithful

1765	偵	▶てい

11　ノ 亻 亻 亻 亻 佔 佔 偵 偵
　　偵

偵察　　　ていさつ　[する] reconnoiter, scout
探偵　　　たんてい　a detective, detective work
内偵　　　ないてい　[する] make secret inquiries

1766	叔	▶しゅく

8　丨 ト 上 才 才 未 叔 叔

叔父　　　△おじ　uncle

叔母 △おば aunt
*伯叔 はくしゅく uncles

1767 淑 ▶しゅく

11 丶 冫 氵 沪 沪 沪 沪 沐 淑
淑

淑女 しゅくじょ lady, gentlewoman
◇ 貞淑な ていしゅくな chaste, faithful
私淑 ししゅく する look up to/model oneself after a person (though not directly studying under that person)

1768 朱 ▶しゅ 583 cf. 未

6 ノ ゝ 二 牛 牛 朱

朱色 しゅいろ vermilion, cinnabar red
朱肉 しゅにく cinnabar/vermilion inkpad (used to ink signature seal)
朱塗りの しゅぬりの vermilion-lacquered

1769 珠 ▶しゅ

10 一 二 千 王 王 玝 珎 珒 珠 珠

真珠 しんじゅ pearl
珠玉 しゅぎょく pearls and gems, excellent/precious works
珠算 しゅざん calculation using an abacus
数珠 △じゅず (Buddhist) rosary

1770 卑 ▶ひ ▷いや(しい), いや(しむ), いや(しめる)

9 丶 丿 甶 甶 由 甶 申 卑 卑

卑屈な ひくつな obsequious, servile
卑近な例 ひきんなれい familiar example
卑下 ひげ する belittle oneself
卑劣な ひれつな mean, sneaky
卑怯な ひきょうな unfair, cowardly
卑猥な ひわいな obscene, indecent
卑しい いやしい vulgar, greedy, low (status)

卑しむべき いやしむべき contemptible
卑しめる いやしめる despise, look down on

1771 碑 ▶ひ

14 一 丆 仄 石 石 石' 矿 矿 砷 砷
砷 砷 砷 碑

石碑 せきひ stone monument, tombstone
記念碑 きねんひ monument
碑文 ひぶん inscription (on a stone monument), epitaph
碑銘 ひめい epitaph

1772 享 ▶きょう

8 丶 亠 宀 宁 古 宣 亨 享

享受 きょうじゅ する enjoy, be given (freedom, etc.)
享有 きょうゆう する be given (talent, etc.) by nature
享楽 きょうらく enjoyment
享楽主義 きょうらくしゅぎ epicurism, hedonism

1773 郭 ▶かく

11 丶 亠 宀 宁 古 宣 亨 享' 郭'
郭

輪郭 りんかく a contour, an outline (of one's face, etc.)
外郭団体 がいかくだんたい government-related institution
城郭 じょうかく castle, fortress

1774 刃 ▶じん ▷は 441 cf. 刀

3 フ 刀 刃

かみそりの刃 かみそりのは razor blade
刃物 はもの cutlery, knives
両刃 りょうば double-edged (blade)
自刃 じじん する commit suicide with a sword

◇ *凶刃　きょうじん　assassin's dagger
特 白刃　はくじん　drawn sword

1775 忍
▶にん
▷しの（ぶ），しの（ばせる）

7　フ 刀 刃 刃 忍 忍 忍

忍耐　にんたい　－する be patient, persevere, endure
残忍な　ざんにんな　brutal, merciless
歴 忍者　にんじゃ　*ninja*, spy warrior in feudal times
忍ぶ　しのぶ　bear, endure, hide
忍び足　しのびあし　stealthy steps
声を忍ばせる　こえをしのばせる　lower one's voice

1776 滋
▶じ

12　、 ⋮ シ ジ ジ 汁 汁 滋 滋 滋
滋 滋

滋養強壮　じようきょうそう　nutrition and health
滋味　じみ　nutritious and tasty (food)
滋賀県　▲しがけん　name of a prefecture

1777 磁
▶じ

14　一 ア エ 石 石 石' 石" 矿 矿 磁
磁 磁 磁 磁

磁石　じしゃく　magnet, compass
磁気　じき　magnetism
磁器　じき　porcelain
陶磁器　とうじき　ceramic ware

1778 慈
▶じ
▷いつく（しむ）

13　、 ⋮ 兰 关 茲 茲 茲 茲 茲 茲
慈 慈 慈

慈悲　じひ　mercy, charity
慈愛　じあい　affection, love
慈善事業　じぜんじぎょう　relief/charitable work

慈しむ　いつくしむ　be tender, love
慈しみ　いつくしみ　love, affection

1779 斉
▶せい

8　、 一 ナ 文 斉 斉 斉 斉

一斉に　いっせいに　all together, simultaneously, all at once
斉*唱　せいしょう　－する sing in chorus

1780 剤
▶ざい

10　、 一 ナ 文 斉 斉 斉 斉 剤 剤

洗剤　せんざい　a detergent, cleanser
錠剤　じょうざい　tablet, pill
消化剤　しょうかざい　digestive
薬剤師　やくざいし　pharmacist

第 135 回

1781 斎
▶さい

11　、 一 ナ 文 斉 斉 斉 斎 斎
斎

書斎　しょさい　a study, a library
斎場　さいじょう　funeral hall

1782 耕
▶こう
▷たがや（す）

10　一 ニ 三 丰 丰 耒 耒 耒 耕 耕

農耕　のうこう　farming
耕地　こうち　arable/cultivated land
耕作　こうさく　－する farm, till, plow
耕す　たがやす　till, plow, cultivate

1783 耗
▶もう，こう

10　一 ニ 三 丰 丰 耒 耗 耗 耗 耗

第5水準

消耗　　　　　しょうもう　[する] consume/exhaust (energy)

摩耗　　　　　まもう　　　[する] be worn away, wear out

心神耗弱　　　しんしんこうじゃく　feeble-mindedness, diminished capacity

1784

垣　▷かき

9　一 十 士 圷 圷 垣 垣 垣 垣

石垣　　　　　いしがき　　stone wall

垣根　　　　　かきね　　　hedge, fence, boundary

1785

恒　▶こう

9　丨 丶 忄 忉 忉 恒 恒 恒 恒

恒常的な　　　こうじょうてきな　constant

恒久の　　　　こうきゅうの　permanent, everlasting

恒例　　　　　こうれい　usual practice, established custom

1786

巧　▶こう
　　▷たく(み)

5　一 丁 工 丂 巧

巧妙な　　　　こうみょうな　skillful, ingenious, clever

◇　巧拙　　　こうせつ　skill, dexterity

技巧　　　　　ぎこう　technique, art

巧みに　　　　たくみに　skillfully, cleverly, ingeniously

1787

朽　▶きゅう
　　▷く(ちる)

6　一 十 オ 木 朽 朽

不朽の名作　　ふきゅうのめいさく　an immortal work

老朽化　　　　ろうきゅうか　[する] become decrepit

◇　朽ちる　　　くちる　rot, decay, crumble

特　朽木　　　くちき　decayed tree, rotted wood

1788

謡　▶よう
　　▷うたい, うた(う)

16　丶 亠 亖 亖 訁 訁 訁 訁 訁
　　訡 訡 謡 謡 謡 謡

童謡　　　　　どうよう　children's song

民謡　　　　　みんよう　folk ballad, folk song

歌謡曲　　　　かようきょく　a popular song

謡曲　　　　　ようきょく　Noh song/chant

謡　　　　　　うたい　Noh chanting

謡う　　　　　うたう　sing without accompaniment, chant

1789

揺　▶よう
　　▷ゆ(れる), ゆ(る), ゆ(らぐ), ゆ(るぐ),
　　ゆ(する), ゆ(さぶる), ゆ(すぶる)

12　一 十 扌 扩 扩 护 护 护 押
　　揺 揺

揺りかご　　　ゆりかご　(baby) cradle

揺れる　　　　ゆれる　vi. shake, sway, quake

揺れ　　　　　ゆれ　shaking, jolting, tremor

揺する　　　　ゆする　vt. shake, swing, sway

揺さぶる　　　ゆさぶる　vt. shake, rock

揺すぶる　　　ゆすぶる　vt. shake, rock

揺らぐ　　　　ゆらぐ　vi. shake, sway, waver

揺るぐ　　　　ゆるぐ　vi. waver

揺るぎない　　ゆるぎない　firm, steady

動揺　　　　　どうよう　[する] waver, be disturbed

漢字の形に気をつけましょう㉑

516	1779	1780	1781
済	斉	剤	斎

自由経済　　　一斉に走り出す　　　洗剤　　　書斎

1790 凝 ▶ぎょう
▷こ(る), こ(らす)
693 cf. 疑

16 画: 丶 冫 冫 冸 冸 冸 冸 冸 冸 冸
冸 冸 冸 冸 凝 凝

凝視	ぎょうし [する] gaze, stare	
凝固	ぎょうこ [する] *vi.* coagulate, congeal, solidify	
凝結	ぎょうけつ [する] *vi.* condense, congeal, coagulate, freeze	
凝る	こる grow stiff (shoulders, etc.), be particularly interested in	
凝り性	こりしょう fastidious, single-minded	
目を凝らす	めをこらす look hard (at), focus intensely on	

1791 擬 ▶ぎ
693 cf. 疑

17 画: 一 十 才 扌 扩 扩 扩 扩 擬
擬 擬 擬 擬 擬 擬 擬

擬人法	ぎじんほう personification
擬声語	ぎせいご onomatopoeia
擬態語	ぎたいご mimetic word
擬態	ぎたい mimesis
擬装	ぎそう [する] camouflage, disguise
模擬テスト	もぎテスト practice exam, mock/simulated test

1792 随 ▶ずい

12 画: 乛 阝 阝 阝 阝 阝 防 防 隋 随
随 随

随筆	ずいひつ an essay, miscellaneous writings
随想録	ずいそうろく memoirs, (occasional) essays
随行	ずいこう [する] accompany (someone of high status)
随員	ずいいん attendant, (members of an) entourage
随時	ずいじ (at) any time, (at) all times
随分	ずいぶん quite, very (much), fairly
追随	ついずい [する] follow (the leader), be trying to catch up

◇ 言語随伴行動 げんごずいはんこうどう language-accompanying behavior
特 随意筋 ずいいきん voluntary muscle

1793 髄 ▶ずい

19 画: 丨 冂 冂 冎 冎 咼 骨 骨 骨
骨 骨 骨 骨 骨 骨 骨 骨 髄 髄

骨髄	こつずい (bone) marrow
脳髄	のうずい the brain, encephalon
延髄	えんずい medulla oblongata
真髄	しんずい essence, quintessence

1794 唇 ▶しん
▷くちびる

10 画: 一 厂 厂 厂 厄 辰 辰 辰 唇 唇

唇	くちびる lips (of the mouth)
口唇	こうしん lips (of the mouth)

1795 辱 ▶じょく
▷はずかし(める)

10 画: 一 厂 厂 厂 厄 辰 辰 辰 辱 辱

屈辱	くつじょく humiliation
恥辱	ちじょく disgrace, dishonor, shame
雪辱を果たす	せつじょくをはたす avenge an insult, get even (with)
*侮辱	ぶじょく [する] insult
辱める	はずかしめる *vt.* humiliate, disgrace, rape
辱め	はずかしめ humiliation, disgrace, shame, rape

1796 幣 ▶へい

15 画: 丨 丬 丬 丬 屵 屵 屵 屵 敝
敝 敝 敝 幣 幣

紙幣	しへい paper money, bills, note
貨幣	かへい currency, money, coin(s)
造幣局	ぞうへいきょく mint, the Mint Bureau

第5水準

1797 弊 ▶へい

15	⺌	⺌	⺌	⺌	⺌	尚	尚	尚	尚	尚
	敝	敝	敝	弊	弊					

弊害　へいがい　harmful effect, evil
疲弊　ひへい　[する] become impoverished, be (physically) exhausted
旧弊　きゅうへい　conventional bad practices, out-dated customs
弊社　へいしゃ　our company [humble]

1798 墾 ▶こん

16	⺈	⺈	⺈	爫	豸	豸	豸	豸	豸	豸
	豸	豸	豸	狠	墾	墾				

開墾　かいこん　[する] cultivate, reclaim (land)

1799 懇 ▶こん ▷ねんご(ろ)

17	⺈	⺈	⺈	爫	豸	豸	豸	豸	豸	豸
	豸	豸	狠	狠	懇	懇	懇			

懇親会　こんしんかい　social gathering
懇談会　こんだんかい　informal talk (with the prime minister, etc.)
懇切丁寧に　こんせつていねいに　kindly (and painstakingly), cordially
懇ろに　ねんごろに　intimately, courteously

1800 敏 ▶びん

10	ノ	⺧	⺧	与	毎	毎	毎	敏	敏	敏

敏感な　びんかんな　sensitive (to), susceptible (to)
敏速に　びんそくに　promptly, quickly
機敏な　きびんな　swift, quick, prompt
鋭敏な　えいびんな　sharp, keen, sensitive

第 136 回

1801 侮 ▶ぶ ▷あなど(る)　164 cf. 毎

侮 (1801 continued)

8	ノ	イ	イ	仁	佐	佑	侮	侮		

侮辱　ぶじょく　[する] insult
[特] 軽侮　けいぶ　[する] scorn, make light of
侮る　あなどる　look down on, make light of
侮り　あなどり　contempt, scorn

1802 炉 ▶ろ

8	⺀	⺀	⺌	火	炉	炉	炉	炉		

原子炉　げんしろ　nuclear reactor
暖炉　だんろ　fireplace, stove
溶鉱炉　ようこうろ　(blast) furnace
[特] 炉辺　ろへん　fireside

1803 炎 ▶えん ▷ほのお　873 cf. 災

8	⺀	⺀	⺌	火	火	炎	炎	炎		

炎天下　えんてんか　under the burning sun
炎上　えんじょう　[する] go up in flames, be burned down
火炎　かえん　flame, blaze
炎　ほのお　flame, fire

1804 哀 ▶あい ▷あわ(れ), あわ(れむ)

9	⺀	⺀	宀	亠	古	声	声	声	哀	

哀れな　あわれな　piteous, pitiable, pathetic
哀れむ　あわれむ　pity, feel sympathy/compassion (for)
哀れみ　あわれみ　pity, compassion, mercy
悲哀　ひあい　grief, sadness, sorrow
哀愁　あいしゅう　sadness, sorrow, grief
哀願　あいがん　[する] entreat, implore, appeal to

1805 衰 ▶すい ▷おとろ(える)

10	⺀	⺀	宀	亠	亩	声	亨	亨	亨	衰

衰弱　すいじゃく　[する] weaken, become feeble, be worn out

衰退	すいたい [する] decline, decay
老衰	ろうすい [する] become senile
盛衰	せいすい rise and fall, ups and down
衰える	おとろえる become weak, lose vigor, waste away, wither, fade
衰え	おとろえ weakening, decline

1806 衰 ▶ちゅう

9 一 ㇐ 宀 亠 声 亠 亠 亠 衰

折衷案	せっちゅうあん a compromise (plan)
折衷主義	せっちゅうしゅぎ eclecticism
折衷	せっちゅう [する] blend, cross, compromise

1807 喪 ▶そう ▷も

12 一 十 忄 什 忄 忄 忄 忄 恭 喪 喪 喪

喪失	そうしつ [する] lose, forfeit
記憶喪失	きおくそうしつ amnesia
喪服	もふく mourning clothing
喪主	もしゅ chief mourner
喪中	もちゅう period of mourning
喪	も mourning

1808 晶 ▶しょう

12 丨 口 日 日 日 旦 旦 晶 晶 晶 晶 晶

| 結晶 | けっしょう a crystal, crystallization, fruit (of one's labors, etc.) [する] vi. crystallize |
| 水晶 | すいしょう (rock) crystal |

1809 唱 ▶しょう ▷とな(える) cf. 唄 2128

11 丨 口 口 叮 叨 明 唱 唱 唱 唱

| 合唱 | がっしょう [する] sing in chorus |
| 唱歌 | しょうか singing, songs |

| 提唱 | ていしょう [する] advocate, propose |
| 唱える | となえる advocate, chant |

1810 尚 ▶しょう cf. 向 557

8

| 高尚な | こうしょうな high, noble, lofty |
| 時期尚早 | じきしょうそう premature, too early |

1811 肖 ▶しょう

7 丶 ⺍ ⺍ 丬 肖 肖 肖

| 肖像画 | しょうぞうが portrait |

1812 凶 ▶きょう

4

凶悪な	きょうあくな atrocious, heinous
凶暴な	きょうぼうな brutal, ferocious
凶器	きょうき deadly weapon
凶作	きょうさく poor harvest
吉凶	きっきょう fortunate or unfortunate, good or bad luck

1813 丹 ▶たん

4 丿 几 凡 丹

| 丹念に | たんねんに carefully, elaborately |
| 丹精込めて | たんせいこめて laboriously, painstakingly, with devotion |

1814 幻 ▶げん ▷まぼろし cf. 幼 1099

4 ㇇ 幺 幺 幻

幻想	げんそう illusion, vision, fantasy
幻覚	げんかく a hallucination
幻滅	げんめつ [する] be disillusioned (with)
幻	まぼろし phantom, illusion, vision

第5水準

1815 弔

▶ちょう
▷とむら(う)

cf. 弟 76

4 一 ユ 弖 弔

弔問	ちょうもん [する] make a call of condolence
弔辞	ちょうじ memorial address, condolence message
弔電	ちょうでん condolatory telegram
慶弔	けいちょう congratulations and condolences
弔う	とむらう mourn, condole, perform a memorial service
弔い	とむらい condolence, funeral, burial

1816 甲

▶こう，かん

cf. 申 585

5 丨 冂 冂 日 甲

甲板	かんぱん deck (of a ship)
甲高い声	かんだかいこえ high-pitched/shrill voice
手の甲	てのこう back of the hand
特 装甲車	そうこうしゃ armored car
特 甲殻類	こうかくるい crustaceans
甲*乙つけがたい	こうおつつけがたい be difficult to distinguish which is better
甲種	こうしゅ A-rank/highest rank cf. *乙種(おつしゅ) B-rank/secondary rank, *丙種(へいしゅ) C-rank/tertiary rank

1817 斥

▶せき

5 ⼃ 厂 斥 斥 斥

| 排斥 | はいせき [する] boycott, exclude |
| 斥候 | せっこう scout, reconnaissance |

1818 亜

▶あ

cf. 悪 114

7 一 亅 冂 曱 甲 西 亜

亜熱帯	あねったい subtropical zone
亜流	ありゅう second-rate imitator
亜鉛	あえん zinc

1819 奔

▶ほん

8 一 ナ 六 杢 本 杢 杢 奔

奔走	ほんそう [する] make every effort
自由奔放な	じゆうほんぽうな free and unrestrained, uninhibited
特 出奔	しゅっぽん [する] run away, flee, elope

1820 幽

▶ゆう

9 丨 ⺊ 外 纟 纵 幺幺 幽 幽

幽霊	ゆうれい ghost
幽玄	ゆうげん subtle profundity, elegant simplicity
幽閉	ゆうへい [する] confine

第 137 回

1821 栽

▶さい

10 一 十 土 圭 圭 丰 未 哉 栽 栽

| 栽培 | さいばい [する] grow (flowers, plants, etc.), cultivate |
| 盆栽 | ぼんさい bonsai, potted dwarf tree |

1822 瓶

▶びん

11 ⼂ ⼆ 亠 亝 羊 并 并 拼 瓶 瓶 瓶

花瓶	かびん (flower) vase
ビール瓶	ビールびん bottle of beer
瓶詰	びんづめ bottled (goods)

1823 執

▶しつ，しゅう
▷と(る)

cf. 報 幸 891 894

11 一 十 土 圭 圭 幸 幸 幸 剌 執 執

| 執筆 | しっぴつ [する] write |
| 執務室 | しつむしつ the (physical) office (of a president, emperor, etc.) |

執行	しっこう [する] execute (a sentence), carry out (an order)
執行猶予	しっこうゆうよ　stay of execution, suspended sentence
確執	かくしつ　discord, feud
執°拗な	しつような　obstinate, persistent
執念	しゅうねん　persistence, tenacity, devotion
執心	しゅうしん [する] be infatuated (with a boy/girl)
執着	しゅうちゃく，しゅうじゃく [する] be attached, stick (to)
執る	とる　do, carry out, handle

1824 粛 ▶しゅく

1728 cf. 庸

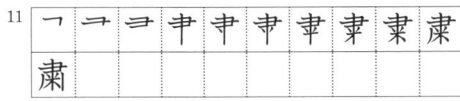

11 ｜ ｢ ｺ ⺺ 肀 肀 肀 肀 肃 肃 粛

自粛	じしゅく [する] voluntarily refrain, practice self-control
◇ 綱紀粛正	こうきしゅくせい　enforcement of official discipline
粛清	しゅくせい [する] clean up, purge
静粛にする	せいしゅくにする　keep quiet, remain silent
◇ 粛然と	しゅくぜんと　silently, quietly, solemnly

1825 蛮 ▶ばん

12 ' 一 亠 亣 亦 亦 亦 亦 变 蛮 蛮

野蛮な	やばんな　barbarous, uncivilized, savage
野蛮人	やばんじん　barbarians, savages
歴 南蛮人	なんばんじん　Europeans (in the usage of 16th-19th c. Japan)
蛮行	ばんこう　barbarous act

1826 疎 ▶そ
▷うと(い)，うと(む)

12 ⺅ 了 ⻊ 平 正 疋 疋 虸 趴 趺 趺 疎

疎外	そがい [する] alienate, shun, estrange
親疎	しんそ　(degree of) closeness (in personal relations)
疎遠になる	そえんになる　drift apart, become estranged

意思の疎通	いしのそつう　communication, mutual understanding
疎い	うとい　knowing little about, (be) unfamiliar with, (be) estranged from
◇ 疎む	うとむ　shun, neglect, estrange
疎ましい	うとましい　disagreeable, offensive

1827 鼓 ▶こ
▷つづみ

13 一 十 土 士 吉 吉 吉 吉 壴 壴
尌 鼓 鼓

太鼓	たいこ　drum
鼓動	こどう [する] beat, throb, pulsate
鼓舞	こぶ [する] inspire (someone to greater efforts), encourage, stimulate
鼓	つづみ　hand drum
舌鼓を打つ	したつづみをうつ　smack one's lips

1828 碁 ▶ご

691 cf. 基

13 一 十 廾 甘 甘 甚 其 其 其 其
萁 碁 碁

碁	ご　go (an East Asian board game)
囲碁	いご　go (an East Asian board game)
碁石	ごいし　a stone/piece used in a game of go
碁盤	ごばん　the game board for go

1829 憂 ▶ゆう
▷うれ(える)，うれ(い)，う(い)

1168 cf. 優

15 一 ｢ 亣 亣 丙 百 百 亘 亘 亙
惪 惪 惪 憂 憂

憂慮	ゆうりょ [する] be anxious/apprehensive/concerned, worry
一喜一憂	いっきいちゆう [する] be alternately glad and sad, be unable to put one's mind at ease
憂°鬱な	ゆううつな　depressed, dejected, gloomy
憂える	うれえる　be distressed, be anxious, grieve
憂い	うれい　anxiety, distress, grief
憂き目をみる	うきめをみる　have a bitter experience
物憂い	ものうい　listless, weary, languid

第5水準

1830 舗 ▶ほ

15 ノ 　ハ 　ム 　牟 　全 　全 　舎 　舎 　舎 　舎

舗 舗 舗 舗 舗

舗装	ほそう	［する］ pave (a road, highway, etc.)
◇ 舗装道路	ほそうどうろ	paved road, pavement
店舗	てんぽ	shop, store
老舗	△しにせ	a store that has been in business for a long time

1831 覧 ▶らん

17 | 　厂 　厂 　厂 　戸 　戸 　臣 　臣 　臣 　臣

臣 臣 臣 臣 臣 覧 覧

ご覧になる	ごらんになる	see, look at [honorific]
閲覧	えつらん	［する］ peruse, inspect, read
一覧表	いちらんひょう	list, table
展覧会	てんらんかい	exhibition, show

1832 麗 ▶れい
▷うるわ(しい)

19 一 　厂 　厉 　厉 　厉 　厉 　厉 　厉 　厉

严 严 严 麗 麗 麗 麗 麗 麗

華麗な	かれいな	splendid, magnificent, gorgeous
◇ 端麗な	たんれいな	graceful, good-looking
美辞麗句	びじれいく	flowery words
特 麗人	れいじん	beautiful woman
麗しい	うるわしい	beautiful, graceful, elegant

第 6 水準
（Level 6）

1833-1942

第 138 回

1833 菊 ▶きく

11 一 一 ++ ++ 芍 芍 芍 苟 菊 菊
菊

| 菊 | きく | chrysanthemum (flower) |
| 白菊 | しらぎく | white chrysanthemum |

1834 芋 ▷いも

6 一 十 ++ 艹 芏 芋

芋	いも	potato, sweet potato
焼き芋	やきいも	roasted sweet potato
里芋	さといも	taro

1835 芽 ▶が ▷め

8 一 十 ++ 芒 芦 芦 芽 芽

芽が出る	めがでる	bud, sprout
芽	め	bud, sprout, shoot
新芽	しんめ	bud, sprout, shoot
発芽	はつが	[する] germinate, bud, sprout
麦芽	ばくが	malt

1836 茎 ▶けい ▷くき

8 一 十 ++ サ 艾 茎 茎 茎

茎	くき	stalk, stem
歯茎	はぐき, しけい	gums
地下茎	ちかけい	underground/subterranean stem

1837 苗 ▶びょう ▷なえ, なわ cf. 笛 1681

8 一 十 ++ 艹 芦 苗 苗 苗

| 苗 | なえ | seedling, sapling, shoot |
| 苗木 | なえぎ | sapling, young tree |

| 特 苗代 | なわしろ | rice nursery |
| 特 種苗 | しゅびょう | seeds and seedlings |

1838 薪 ▶しん ▷たきぎ

16 一 十 ++ ++ 芏 芏 芏 芏 芏 芏
莘 莘 薪 薪 薪 薪

薪	たきぎ	firewood
薪能	たきぎのう	Noh performance beside a fire
特 薪炭	しんたん	firewood and charcoal, winter fuel
特 薪水	しんすい	firewood and water

1839 藻 ▶そう ▷も cf. 燥 903

19 一 十 ++ 艹 艹 芦 芦 茫 茫 茫
茫 茫 茫 薻 薻 薻 薄 藻 藻

藻	も	algae, seaweed
海藻	かいそう	seaweed
藻類	そうるい	algae

1840 茂 ▶も ▷しげ(る)

8 一 十 ++ 芦 芦 芀 茂 茂

茂み	しげみ	bush, thicket
茂る	しげる	grow thickly/luxuriantly
繁茂	はんも	[する] grow thickly/luxuriantly

1841 滝 ▷たき

13 丶 氵 氵 汁 汴 泮 泮 淕 淕
淕 淕 滝

| 滝 | たき | waterfall |
| 滝壷 | たきつぼ | basin of a waterfall |

1842 沼 ▶しょう ▷ぬま

8 丶 氵 氵 沼 沼 沼 沼 沼

沼	ぬま	swamp, marsh, bog
沼地	ぬまち	marshland
湖沼	こしょう	lakes and marshes
特 沼沢地	しょうたくち	marshland, swampy areas

1843 渓 ▶けい

11 `、` `丶` `氵` `氵` `汀` `涇` `涇` `涇` `溪` `渓`
渓

渓谷	けいこく	(steep-walled) valley, ravine, canyon
渓流	けいりゅう	mountain torrent/stream
雪渓	せっけい	snowy valley/ravine

1844 洞 ▶どう　▷ほら

9 `、` `丶` `氵` `汩` `汩` `洞` `洞` `洞` `洞`

空洞	くうどう	hollow, cave
洞穴	どうけつ，ほらあな	cave, cavern
洞察力	どうさつりょく	insight, discernment
洞*窟	どうくつ	cave, cavern

1845 瀬 ▷せ

19 `、` `丶` `氵` `氵` `氵` `沪` `沪` `泸` `沛` `涑`
涑 涑 涑 瀬 瀬 瀬 瀬 瀬 瀬

浅瀬	あさせ	shallows, shoal
瀬	せ	river rapids, shallows
立つ瀬がない	たつせがない	be put in an awkward position
瀬戸物	せともの	earthenware, pottery

1846 浦 ▷うら

10 `、` `丶` `氵` `氵` `汀` `沪` `泀` `涓` `浦` `浦`

三浦半島	みうらはんとう	Miura Peninsula
浦	うら	inlet, bay, shore
津々浦々	つつうらうら	throughout the country, far and wide

1847 潟 ▷かた　836　cf. 湯

15 `、` `丶` `氵` `氵` `沪` `沪` `沪` `泻` `泻`
潟 潟 潟 潟 潟

| 新潟県 | にいがたけん | name of a prefecture |
| 干潟 | ひがた | tideland, tidal flats |

1848 峰 ▶ほう　▷みね

10 `丨` `山` `山` `山'` `山个` `峃` `峃` `峄` `峰` `峰`

峰	みね	peak, summit, top
浅間連峰	あさまれんぽう	the Asama Mountains
特 霊峰	れいほう	sacred mountain

1849 峠 ▷とうげ

9 `丨` `山` `山` `山'` `山+` `峠` `峠` `峠` `峠`

| 峠 | とうげ | mountain pass, the critical point |
| 峠を越す | とうげをこす | cross a ridge, pass the critical point, be over the hump |

1850 岬 ▷みさき

8 `丨` `山` `山` `山'` `山冂` `岬` `岬` `岬`

| 岬 | みさき | cape, promontory |

第 139 回

1851 岳 ▶がく　▷たけ

8 `ノ` `イ` `仁` `丘` `丘` `乒` `岳` `岳`

山岳地帯	さんがくちたい	mountainous region
特 岳父	がくふ	the father of one's wife
北岳	きただけ	Kitadake (a peak in the Southern Alps)

1852 堤

▶てい
▷つつみ

767 1670
cf. 提 是

12 一 十 土 土 圹 坦 坦 坦 埠 埠 堤 堤

堤防	ていぼう	bank, embankment, dike, levee
防波堤	ぼうはてい	breakwater, seawall
歴 堤	つつみ	bank, embankment, dike

1853 樹

▶じゅ

16 一 十 オ 木 木 栉 栉 栉 桔 桔 桔 桔 桔 桔 樹 樹

街路樹	がいろじゅ	roadside trees
果樹園	かじゅえん	orchard
樹木	じゅもく	trees
樹林帯	じゅりんたい	forest
樹立	じゅりつ	する establish (a new government, etc.), found

1854 柳

▶りゅう
▷やなぎ

1264
cf. 抑

9 一 十 オ 木 木 机 机 柳 柳

柳	やなぎ	willow (tree)
川柳	せんりゅう	satirical poem in 17 syllables
特 花柳界	かりゅうかい	the world of *geisha*

1855 桑

▶そう
▷くわ

1310
cf. 柔

10 フ ヌ ヌ ヌ 矛 矛 桒 桑 桑 桑

桑	くわ	mulberry (tree)
桑畑	くわばたけ	mulberry field
特 桑園	そうえん	mulberry plantation

1856 穂

▶すい
▷ほ

1077
cf. 恵

15 一 二 千 千 禾 禾 利 利 和 和 稗 稗 穂 穂 穂

| 穂 | ほ | ear (of corn/rice), head (of wheat) |

| 稲穂 | いなほ | ear of a rice plant |
| 特 穂状の | すいじょうの | ear-shaped |

1857 畔

▶はん

10 丨 冂 冂 田 田 田 田' 畔 畔 畔

| 湖畔 | こはん | shores of a lake |

1858 暁

▶ぎょう
▷あかつき

218
cf. 焼

12 丨 冂 日 日 日一 日十 旷 旷 晓 晓 晓 暁

| 暁 | あかつき | daybreak, dawn |
| 特 早暁 | そうぎょう | early dawn |

1859 昆

▶こん

837
cf. 混

8 丨 冂 冂 日 旦 尾 尾 昆

| 昆虫 | こんちゅう | insects, bugs |
| 昆布 | こんぶ | kelp |

1860 蚊

▷か

10 丨 冂 口 中 虫 虫 虫' 虫' 蚊 蚊

| 蚊 | か | mosquito |

1861 蛇

▶じゃ, だ
▷へび

11 丨 冂 口 中 虫 虫 虫' 虫' 虫' 蚍 蛇

蛇	へび	snake
大蛇	だいじゃ	huge serpent/snake
蛇腹	じゃばら	cornice, bellows
蛇口	じゃぐち	faucet, tap
蛇行	だこう	する wind its way (through), meander
長蛇の列	ちょうだのれつ	long line/queue
蛇足	だそく	superfluity, redundancy

1862 **巣**
▶そう
▷す
1667 502
cf. 菓 果

11 丶 ﾉﾉ ﾉﾉﾉ ﾊ ﾊ 屵 屵 当 単 単
巣

鳥の巣	とりのす	bird's nest
巣箱	すばこ	birdhouse, beehive
巣立つ	すだつ	leave the nest, make one's own start in life
卵巣	らんそう	ovary
病巣	びょうそう	the focus of disease

1863 **鶏**
▶けい
▷にわとり

19 ﾉ ﾉ ﾉ 爫 丞 丞 函 函 函 函
函 函 函 鶏 鶏 鶏 鶏 鶏 鶏

鶏	にわとり	chicken, hen, rooster
鶏卵	けいらん	(hen's) egg
養鶏場	ようけいじょう	poultry/chicken farm
特 闘鶏	とうけい	cockfighting

1864 **獣**
▶じゅう
▷けもの

16 丶 ﾉﾉ ﾉﾉﾉ ﾊ 屵 屵 単 単 単 単
單 嘼 嘼 獣 獣 獣

猛獣	もうじゅう	fierce animal
野獣	やじゅう	wild beast, wild animal
鳥獣	ちょうじゅう	birds and wild animals
珍獣	ちんじゅう	rare animal
獣	けもの	animal, beast

1865 **猿**
▶えん
▷さる
110
cf. 遠

13 ﾉ ﾗ ﾗ 犭 犭 狆 犷 猝 猝 猿
猿 猿 猿

| 猿 | さる | monkey, ape |
| 野猿 | やえん | wild monkey |

| 類人猿 | るいじんえん | anthropoids |
| 犬猿の仲 | けんえんのなか | be like cats and dogs, be on bad terms |

1866 **蚕**
▶さん
▷かいこ

10 一 二 ﾁ 天 天 呑 呑 呑 蚕 蚕

蚕	かいこ	silkworm
養蚕業	ようさんぎょう	sericultural industry
特 蚕糸	さんし	silk thread
特 蚕食	さんしょく	[-する] encroach (upon), make inroads (into)

1867 **竜**
▶りゅう
▷たつ

10 丶 ﾗ ﾗ 立 立 产 音 音 音 竜

竜	りゅう, たつ	dragon
特 竜頭蛇尾	りゅうとうだび	bright beginning and dull ending
竜巻	たつまき	tornado, whirlwind

第 140 回

1868 **姫**
▷ひめ

10 く ﾉ 女 刈 妒 妒 妒 妒 妒 姫

| 姫 | ひめ | princess |

1869 **妃**
▶ひ

6 く ﾉ 女 妒 妒 妃

王妃	おうひ	queen
妃殿下	ひでんか	Her Imperial Highness
▲ 楊貴妃	ようきひ	Yang Kuei-fei (a famous Chinese beauty of the Tang dynasty)

1870 **嫡**
▶ちゃく

14 く ﾉ 女 女' 妒 妒 妒 妒 妒 妒
嫡 嫡 嫡 嫡

| 嫡子 | ちゃくし | one's heir |

273

1871 奴　▶ど　827 cf. 努

5　く　女　女　奴　奴

奴隷	どれい	slave
歴 農奴	のうど	serf
売国奴	ばいこくど	traitor to one's country

1872 隷　▶れい　1048 cf. 逮

16　一　十　土　士　圭　寺　寺　隶　隶　隶
隶　隶　隶　隶　隷　隷

奴隷	どれい	slave
隷属	れいぞく	する be subordinate to, follow orders
隷従	れいじゅう	する be enslaved, be subordinate to

1873 后　▶こう

6　一　厂　戸　斤　后　后

| 皇后 | こうごう | empress, queen |
| 皇太后 | こうたいごう | empress dowager |

1874 騎　▶き

18　｜　厂　厂　厇　厈　馬　馬　馬　馬
馬　馬　駐　駐　騎　騎　騎　騎

騎士	きし	knight
騎手	きしゅ	jockey, rider
騎馬民族	きばみんぞく	equestrian people

1875 爵　▶しゃく

17　爫　爫　爫　爫　爫　爫　爫　爫　爵
爵　爵　爵　爵　爵　爵　爵

| 侯爵 | こうしゃく | marquis |
| 爵位 | しゃくい | title of nobility, peerage |

1876 侯　▶こう　1174 cf. 候

9　ノ　イ　仁　作　作　侯　侯　侯　侯

侯爵	こうしゃく	marquis
王侯貴族	おうこうきぞく	king and feudal lords
諸侯	しょこう	feudal lords

1877 伯　▶はく　1255 cf. 拍

7　ノ　イ　イ′　イ′　伯　伯　伯

伯父	△おじ	uncle
伯母	△おば	aunt
画伯	がはく	painter [honorific]
伯仲	はくちゅう	する be evenly matched

1878 侍　▶じ　▷さむらい　195 cf. 待

8　ノ　イ　イ′　仆　件　侍　侍　侍

侍医	じい	court physician
侍従	じじゅう	chamberlain, lord-in-waiting
歴 侍女	じじょ	lady's maid, lady-in-waiting
特 侍する	じする	attend on (a lord), wait on
侍	さむらい	*samurai*, warrior (in medieval times)

1879 仁　▶じん, に

4　ノ　イ　イ‐　仁

仁義	じんぎ	humanity and justice, duty, a moral code
仁王	におう	the guardian gods of a temple gate, the two Deva kings
特 仁術	じんじゅつ	benevolent act
特 仁	じん	benevolence, compassion

1880 仙　▶せん

5　ノ　イ　仈　仙　仙

| 仙人 | せんにん | hermit, unworldly person |

1881 孔 ▶こう
822
cf. 礼

4 ｜ フ 了 子 孔

孔子　　　　こうし　Confucius
鼻孔　　　　びこう　nostril

1882 尉 ▶い

11 ｜ フ コ 尸 尸 尽 尉 尉 尉 尉 尉
尉

大尉　　　　たいい　captain, lieutenant
尉官　　　　いかん　officers in the army below the rank of major, officers in the navy below the rank of lieutenant commander

1883 吏 ▶り
199
cf. 使

6 ｜ 一 ㄇ 后 吏 吏

官吏　　　　かんり　government official
能吏　　　　のうり　capable (government) official, capable administrator

1884 虜 ▶りょ
1377
cf. 慮

13 ｜ ㇑ ㇏ ㇏ 广 户 卢 虏 虏 虏 虏 虏 虜 虜

捕虜　　　　ほりょ　prisoner (of war), captive

1885 嗣 ▶し

13 ｜ ㇑ ㅁ 尸 尸 咠 咠 咠 嗣 嗣 嗣 嗣 嗣

嗣子　　　　しし　heir, heiress, successor

1886 陵 ▶りょう
▷みささぎ

11 ｜ フ 阝 阝 阝 阡 陟 陟 陟 陵
陵

陵墓　　　　りょうぼ　mausoleum
丘陵　　　　きゅうりょう　hills
陵　　　　　みささぎ　(Imperial) mausoleum

1887 楼 ▶ろう
968
cf. 桜

13 ｜ 一 十 才 木 杧 杧 杣 杣 柣 柣
桜 楼 楼

鐘楼　　　　しょうろう　bell tower, belfry
楼閣　　　　ろうかく　many-storied building
[特]望楼　　ぼうろう　watchtower
[歴]▲妓楼　ぎろう　brothel

1888 墳 ▶ふん
1633 1634
cf. 噴 憤

15 ｜ 一 十 土 扩 扩 坿 坿 坿 坿 垟
垟 垟 墳 墳 墳

古墳　　　　こふん　tumulus, ancient tomb (mound)
墳墓　　　　ふんぼ　grave, tomb

1889 塚 ▷つか
52
cf. 家

12 ｜ 一 十 土 圹 圹 圹 坿 坿 垙 塚
塚 塚

貝塚　　　　かいづか　shell mound
▲蟻塚　　　ありづか　anthill
塚　　　　　つか　mound, hillock, tumulus

1890 藩 ▶はん

18 ｜ 一 十 艹 艹 艹 艹 艹 艹 荖 荖
萍 萍 潂 潂 潂 藩 藩 藩

[歴]藩　　　はん　feudal domain/fief in the Tokugawa era
[歴]藩主　　はんしゅ　feudal lord in the Tokugawa era

第6水準

第 141 回

1891 儒 ▶じゅ 681 cf. 需

16 ノ イ 仁 仁 伊 俨 俨 傊 傊 傊 傊 傊 儒 儒 儒 儒

儒教	じゅきょう	Confucianism (thought; school of thought)
儒学	じゅがく	Confucianism (scholarship; body of knowledge)
儒学者	じゅがくしゃ	Confucian (scholar)

1892 艦 ▶かん 925 cf. 監

21 ノ 刀 刀 月 月 舟 舟 舟 舮 舮 舮 舮 舮 舮 舮 舮 艦 艦 艦 艦

軍艦	ぐんかん	warship
戦艦	せんかん	battleship
艦隊	かんたい	fleet, armada
艦*艇	かんてい	naval vessels

1893 租 ▶そ 635 cf. 組

10 ー 二 千 千 禾 利 和 和 和 租

| 租税 | そぜい | taxes, taxation |

1894 帥 ▶すい 967 cf. 師

9 ノ イ ㇒ 㠯 㠯 自 自 帥 帥

総帥	そうすい	commander
元帥	げんすい	army/air force general, fleet admiral
歴 統帥権	とうすいけん	supreme command authority

1895 勅 ▶ちょく

9 ー 厂 厅 吏 束 束 束 敕 勅

歴 勅語	ちょくご	imperial rescript
歴 勅使	ちょくし	imperial envoy
歴 勅令	ちょくれい	imperial decree
*詔勅	しょうちょく	imperial edict/order/proclamation

1896 遷 ▶せん 1215 cf. 還

15 ー 厂 厅 西 西 西 覀 覀 票 票 覂 塞 墨 遷 遷

| 変遷 | へんせん | change, transition [する] vi. change, undergo change |
| 特 遷都 | せんと | [する] transfer the capital |

1897 赦 ▶しゃ 46 cf. 赤

11 ー 十 土 扌 才 赤 赤 赤 赤 赦 赦

恩赦	おんしゃ	pardon, amnesty
大赦	たいしゃ	a general pardon, amnesty
赦免	しゃめん	[する] pardon, remit a punishment, let someone off

1898 賜 ▶し ▷たまわ（る） 434 335 cf. 易 場

15 丨 冂 𠕁 日 日 日 貝 貝 貝 貶 貶 貶 賜 賜 賜

賜る	たまわる	be given, be honored with
下賜	かし	[する] give [honorific]
恩賜	おんし	gift from the emperor

1899 謁 ▶えつ 1011 cf. 掲

15 ` 亠 言 言 言 言 言 言 訶 訶 訶 謁 謁

拝謁	はいえつ	[する] have an audience (with a noble person)
謁見	えっけん	[する] have an audience (with a noble person, etc.)
特 謁する	えっする	have an audience (with a noble person, etc.)

1900 窯
▶よう
▷かま
1674
cf. 窒

15 `ヽ`｀`宀`宀`宛`宛`宛`窄`窄
窄 窄 窯 窯 窯

窯業　　　ようぎょう　ceramics industry
窯　　　　かま　kiln

1901 戯
▶ぎ
▷たわむ(れる)
1741
cf. 虚

15 `ー`｜`广`广`户`卢`虍`虍`虚`虚
虚 虚 戯 戯 戯

戯曲　　　ぎきょく　a drama, a play
戯れる　　たわむれる　play/frolic, joke/jest, flirt
戯れ　　　たわむれ　(having a bit of) fun, a joke, flirtation
戯作　　　▲げさく　popular/lowbrow literature (latter half of 18th c. - 19th c.)

1902 姿
▶ば
913 661
cf. 波 姿

11 `ヽ`丶`氵`汀`沪`波`波`婆
婆

老婆　　　ろうば　old woman
歴 産婆　　さんば　midwife
お婆さん　▲おばあさん　old woman　cf. お祖母さん(▲おばあさん) grandmother

1903 韻
▶いん

19 `ヽ`亠`六`立`亠`音`音`音`韵
韵 韵 韵 韻 韻 韻 韻 韻 韻

韻　　　　いん　rhyme
韻律　　　いんりつ　meter, rhythm
韻文　　　いんぶん　verse, poetry
音韻　　　おんいん　phoneme

1904 吟
▶ぎん

7 `丨`口`口`口'`吟`吟`吟

吟味　　　ぎんみ　[する] examine closely, select something with care
詩吟　　　しぎん　recitation/chanting of a Chinese poem
吟詠　　　ぎんえい　[する] recite/chant a poem

1905 詠
▶えい
▷よ(む)

12 `丶`二`言`言`言`言`言`言`訂`訠
詠 詠

詠嘆の声　えいたんのこえ　voice filled with admiration
朗詠　　　ろうえい　[する] recite/chant a poem
詠む　　　よむ　compose/chant (a poem)

1906 琴
▶きん
▷こと

12 `一`丆`王`王`珏`玎`珏`珏`珏`珏
琴 琴

琴　　　　こと　koto, Japanese zither-like instrument
木琴　　　もっきん　xylophone
心の琴線　こころのきんせん　one's heartstrings

1907 宵
▶しょう
▷よい
1811
cf. 肖

10 `丶`丷`宀`宀`宀`宀`宵`宵`宵`宵

宵　　　　よい　early evening
特 徹宵　　てっしょう　overnight, without sleep

第 142 回

1908 乙
▶おつ

1 乙

乙　　　　おつ　B, the second (class)
乙種　　　おつしゅ　B-rank/secondary rank　cf. 甲種(こうしゅ) A rank
甲乙つけがたい　こうおつつけがたい　be difficult to distinguish which is better
歴 乙女　　△おとめ　maiden, (young) girl, virgin

第6水準

277

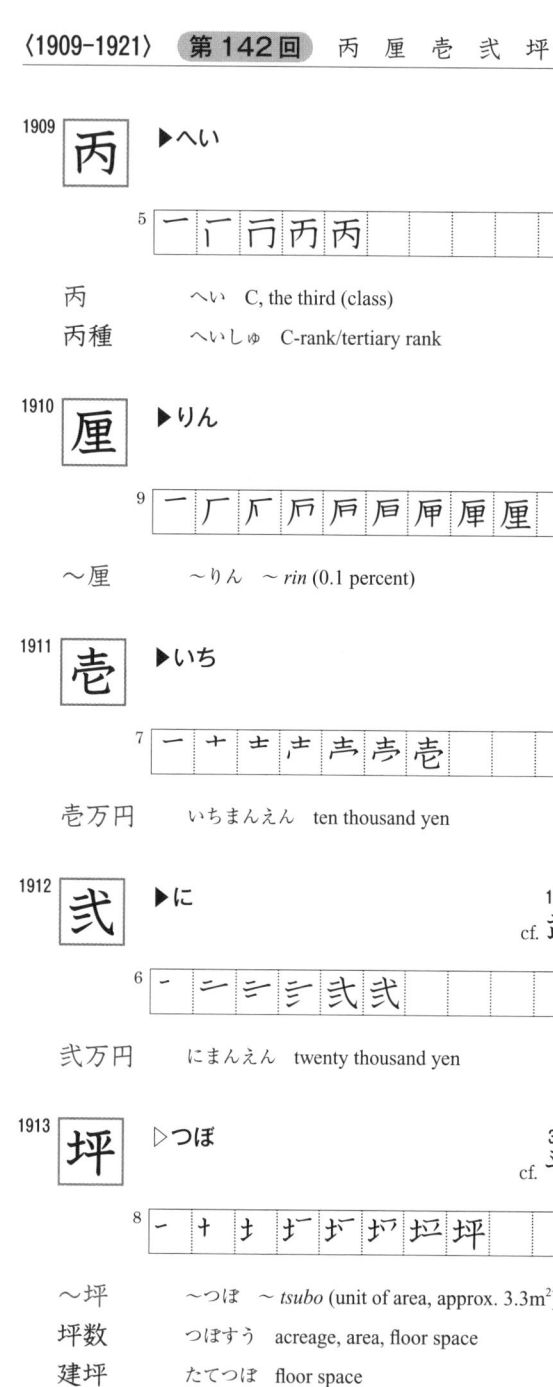

1909 丙 ▶へい

5 一 丆 丙 丙 丙

丙　　　へい　C, the third (class)
丙種　　へいしゅ　C-rank/tertiary rank

1910 厘 ▶りん

9 一 厂 厃 厊 厍 厔 厘 厘 厘

〜厘　　〜りん　〜 rin (0.1 percent)

1911 壱 ▶いち

7 一 十 士 声 声 壱 壱

壱万円　いちまんえん　ten thousand yen

1912 弐 ▶に　1165 cf. 武

6 一 二 二 二 弐 弐

弐万円　にまんえん　twenty thousand yen

1913 坪 ▷つぼ　351 cf. 平

8 一 十 土 圵 圹 圷 坪 坪

〜坪　　〜つぼ　〜 tsubo (unit of area, approx. 3.3m²)
坪数　　つぼすう　acreage, area, floor space
建坪　　たてつぼ　floor space

1914 斤 ▶きん　772 cf. 折

4 ノ 丆 斤 斤

〜斤　　〜きん　〜 kin (unit of weight, approx. 600g)

1915 升 ▶しょう ▷ます　1280 cf. 昇

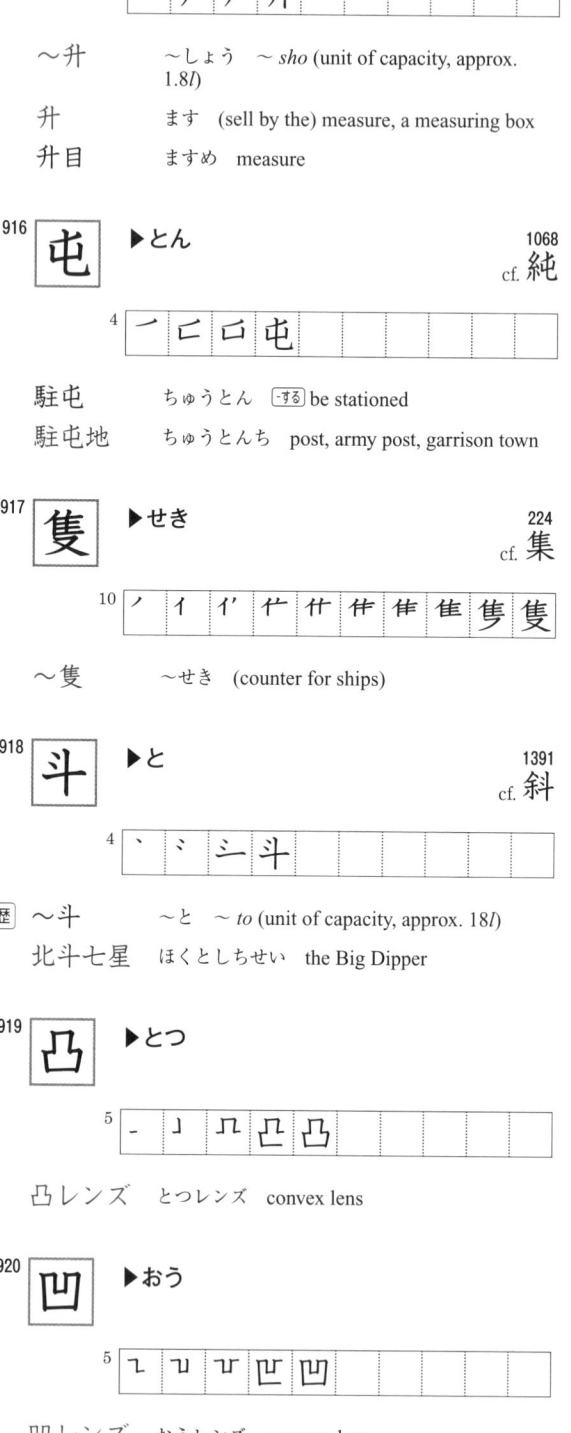

4 ノ 丿 千 升

〜升　　〜しょう　〜 sho (unit of capacity, approx. 1.8l)
升　　　ます　(sell by the) measure, a measuring box
升目　　ますめ　measure

1916 屯 ▶とん　1068 cf. 純

4 一 亡 屯 屯

駐屯　　ちゅうとん　‐する be stationed
駐屯地　ちゅうとんち　post, army post, garrison town

1917 隻 ▶せき　224 cf. 集

10 ノ イ イ' 忄 什 作 隹 隹 隻 隻

〜隻　　〜せき　(counter for ships)

1918 斗 ▶と　1391 cf. 斜

4 、 ゙ 二 斗

歴 〜斗　　〜と　〜 to (unit of capacity, approx. 18l)
北斗七星　ほくとしちせい　the Big Dipper

1919 凸 ▶とつ

5 一 丨 几 凸 凸

凸レンズ　とつレンズ　convex lens

1920 凹 ▶おう

5 乚 冂 冚 凹 凹

凹レンズ　おうレンズ　concave lens
凹凸　　　おうとつ　unevenness, ruggedness, irregularity
凸凹　　　△でこぼこ　unevenness, ruggedness, irregularity

1921 但 ▷ただ(し)　1050 cf. 担

7 ノ イ 仆 们 伯 但 但

但し　　ただし　but, however
但し書き　ただしがき　proviso

1922 且 ▷か(つ)　635 cf. 組

5 丨 冂 日 月 且

且つ　かつ　moreover, besides, and

1923 嚇 ▶かく　46 cf. 赤

17 嚇...

威嚇　いかく　[する] threaten, menace

1924 隆 ▶りゅう

11 隆

隆盛　りゅうせい　prosperity
隆起　りゅうき　[する] rise, be elevated, bulge, protrude
興隆　こうりゅう　[する] rise, prosper, flourish

1925 坑 ▶こう　747 cf. 抗

7 坑

炭坑　たんこう　coal mine
坑道　こうどう　tunnel/shaft (in a mine)
廃坑　はいこう　abandoned mine

1926 呉 ▶ご　949 1329 cf. 誤 娯

7 呉

呉服　ごふく　kimono (fabric)
呉服店　ごふくてん　kimono (fabric) shop

呉越同舟　ごえつどうしゅう　bitter enemies (placed by fate) in the same boat　cf. 呉 and 越 are two rival countries in ancient China

1927 艇 ▶てい　1211 cf. 廷

13 艇 艇 艇

競艇　きょうてい　motorboat race
艦艇　かんてい　naval vessels

第 143 回

1928 佳 ▶か

8 ノ イ 仁 什 件 佳 佳 佳

佳作　かさく　commendable work; honorable mention
佳人　かじん　beautiful woman

1929 痘 ▶とう

12 痘 痘

天然痘　てんねんとう　smallpox
種痘　しゅとう　vaccination for smallpox

1930 曹 ▶そう　1537 cf. 槽

11 曹 曹

法曹界　はうそうかい　judicial circles, legal circles
軍曹　ぐんそう　sergeant

1931 恭 ▶きょう　419 ▷うやうや(しい)　cf. 共

10 一 十 艹 共 共 共 恭 恭 恭

恭順　きょうじゅん　submission, obedience
恭しく　うやうやしく　respectfully, reverently

第6水準

279

1932 詔
▶しょう
▷みことのり
694
cf. 紹

12 丶 亠 ﾆ 言 言 言 言 訒 訒 詔

詔 詔

詔勅　しょうちょく　imperial edict/order/proclamation
詔書　しょうしょ　imperial edict
詔　みことのり　imperial edict

1933 褒
▶ほう
▷ほ(める)
665
cf. 保

15 丶 亠 广 产 产 夲 夲 裆 裆 裆

裆 夲 褒 褒 褒

褒める　ほめる　praise, speak well of
褒美　ほうび　prize, reward

1934 謄
▶とう
263 1547
cf. 勝 騰

17 丿 刀 月 月 月' 脒' 胪 胪 胖 朕

朕 騰 騰 謄 謄 謄 謄

戸籍謄本　こせきとうほん　certified copy of one's family register

1935 朕
▶ちん

10 丿 刀 月 月 月' 月' 肝 胪 胖 朕

歴 朕　ちん　I (traditionally used by the emperor)

1936 畝
▷うね

10 丶 亠 亠 古 亩 亩 亩 畝 畝

畝　うね　ridge, furrow

1937 翁
▶おう

10 ノ 八 公 公 今 爷 爷 翁 翁 翁

老翁　ろうおう　old man

1938 逓
▶てい

10 ノ 厂 厈 后 后 后 乕 乕 浦 逓

逓減　ていげん　する decrease gradually, diminish successively
歴 逓信省　ていしんしょう　Communication Ministry (of the pre-war Japanese government)

1939 塑
▶そ

13 丶 丷 丷 丷 屰 屰 朔 朔 朔 朔

朔 塑 塑

塑像　そぞう　plastic image, clay figure/statue
彫塑　ちょうそ　carvings and sculptures
可塑性　かそせい　plasticity

1940 虞
▷おそれ
1926
cf. 呉

13 丶 ﾄ ﾄ 广 户 卢 虍 虎 虞 虞

虞 虞 虞

虞　おそれ　fear, anxiety

1941 繭
▶けん
▷まゆ

18 一 十 艹 艹 芇 芇 芇 芇 芇 莭

莭 繭 繭 繭 繭 繭 繭 繭

繭　まゆ　cocoon
歴 繭糸　けんし　silk thread

1942 璽
▶じ

19 一 一 尒 尒 夻 夳 尒 尒 尒 尒

尒 尒 尒 尒 尒 璽 璽 璽 璽

国璽　こくじ　seal of state
御璽　ぎょじ　imperial seal

第 7 水準
（Level 7）

1943-2136

第 144 回

1943 茨（茨）　▷いばら

9 一 十 艹 艿 艿 艿 茓 茏 茨

茨　　　　　いばら　　thorn, bramble
茨城県　　▲いばらきけん　name of a prefecture

1944 栃（栃）　▷とち

9 一 十 才 木 杧 杤 杯 栃 栃

栃木県　　とちぎけん　name of a prefecture

1945 埼　▷さい　　　　　　　　1293
　　　　　　　　　　　　　cf. 崎

11 一 十 土 圵 圹 圹 埣 埣 埼
埼

埼玉県　　さいたまけん　name of a prefecture

1946 阜　▶ふ

8 ′ 亻 亡 户 自 自 皀 阜

岐阜県　　▲ぎふけん　name of a prefecture

1947 奈　▶な　　　　　　　131
　　　　　　　　　　　cf. 食

8 一 ナ 大 太 杰 杢 奈 奈

奈良県　　▲ならけん　name of a prefecture
神奈川県　▲かながわけん　name of a prefecture
奈落　　　ならく　hell, abyss, pit

1948 阪　▶はん　　　　　　　605
　　　　　　　　　　cf. 坂

7 ′ 3 阝 阝 阞 阪 阪

大阪府　　▲おおさかふ　Osaka Prefecture
阪神高速道路　はんしんこうそくどうろ　Hanshin
　　　　　　　　　　　　　　　Expressway

1949 岡　▷おか

8 丨 冂 冂 冂 冏 冏 岡 岡

岡山県　　おかやまけん　name of a prefecture
静岡県　　しずおかけん　name of a prefecture
福岡県　　ふくおかけん　name of a prefecture

1950 媛　▶えん　　　　　　　1270
　　　　　　　　　　cf. 援

12 く 夂 女 女 妒 妒 妒 妏 娅 娅
娿 媛

愛媛県　　▲えひめけん　name of a prefecture
才媛　　　さいえん　intelligent/talented woman

1951 畿　▶き　　　　　　　408
　　　　　　　　　　cf. 幾

15 く 幺 幺 幺 幺 幺 丝 丝 丝 絲
絲 絲 畿 畿 畿

近畿　　　きんき　region encompassing Kyoto, Osaka,
　　　　　　　　and five other prefectures
畿内　　　きない　region around old capital, incl. five
　　　　　　　　ancient provinces

1952 鎌　▷かま　　　　　　　1581
　　　　　　　　　　cf. 謙

18 ′ 人 스 亼 全 年 年 金 金 金
鈝 鈝 鈝 鈝 鍏 鎌 鎌 鎌

鎌倉　　　かまくら　name of a city, shogunal capital,
　　　　　　　　1185-1333

1953 弥　▷や

8 フ コ 弓 引 弘 弥 弥 弥

歴 弥生　　△やよい　name for third month of lunar calendar,
　　　　　　　　name of place in Tokyo
歴 弥生時代　△やよいじだい　name of period in prehistory of
　　　　　　　　Japan

1954 韓 ▶かん

18 一 十 さ 古 古 古 直 卓 卓' 卓"
韓 韓 韓 韓 韓 韓 韓 韓

韓国　　　　かんこく　short form of name of the Republic of Korea

大韓民国　　だいかんみんこく　Republic of Korea

第 145 回

1955 柿 ▷かき

9 一 十 才 木 木' 朾 柿 柿 柿

柿　　　　かき　Japanese persimmon

1956 梨 ▷なし

11 一 二 千 禾 禾 利 利 利 梨 梨
梨

梨　　　　なし　pear, pear tree

1957 蜜 ▶みつ
1103
cf. 密

14 ' ' 宀 宀 少 空 空 空 容
容 審 蜜 蜜

蜜　　　　みつ　honey, nectar
*蜂蜜　　　はちみつ　honey
蜜月　　　みつげつ　honeymoon

1958 麺 ▶めん

16 一 十 丰 圭 丰 丰 麦 麦 変 変
麺 麺 麺 麺 麺 麺

麺（類）　　めん（るい）　noodles, *udon* and *soba*

1959 餅（餠）▶へい
▷もち

15 ノ 人 ㇒ 㝵 㿝 食 食 食 食 食
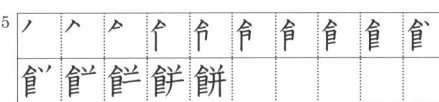
飣 飣 飣 餅 餅

餅　　　　もち　rice cake
*煎餅　　　せんべい　rice cracker
焼き餅　　やきもち　toasted rice cake, jealousy　cf. 焼き餅を焼く　be jealous
*尻餅をつく　しりもちをつく　falling on one's behind/buttocks

1960 餌（餌）▶じ
▷えさ, え

15 ノ 人 ㇒ 㝵 㿝 食 食 食 食 食
飣 飣 飣 飵 餌

餌　　　　えさ　bait, food
餌食　　　えじき　prey, victim
好餌　　　こうじ　easy victim, easy prey
餌付け　　えづけ　-する get (an animal) to feed

1961 酎 ▶ちゅう

10 一 厂 厅 丙 西 酉 酉 酉 酎 酎

焼酎　　　しょうちゅう　*shōchū*, a clear liquor distilled from sweet potatoes, rice, buckwheat, etc.
酎ハイ　　ちゅうハイ　*shōchū* mixed with soda water

1962 串 ▷くし

7 丶 冂 叮 尸 吕 吕 串

串　　　　くし　spit, skewer
串刺し　　くしざし　skewering, transfixing something with a spear

1963 箸（箸）▷はし
1031
cf. 著

15 ノ ノ ㇒ 竹 竹 竹 竹 竹 竺 竺
笁 笁 箸 箸 箸

箸　　　　はし　chopsticks

第7水準

1964 丼 ▷どんぶり, どん

1064
cf. 井

5 一 二 井 井 丼

丼	どんぶり	a porcelain bowl
～丼	～どん	rice in a large bowl with a topping (thin slices of beef, etc.) cf. 牛丼（ぎゅうどん）, 天丼（てんどん）, etc.
丼勘定	どんぶりかんじょう	sloppy/slapdash accounting/book keeping

1965 釜 ▷かま

21
cf. 金

10 ノ ハ ハ 父 父 笒 笒 娑 釜 釜

| 釜 | かま | rice-cooker, teakettle |
| 後釜 | あとがま | successor |

1966 鍋 ▷なべ

17 ノ ハ 亼 亼 乇 乇 乍 金 金 釕
釕 釕 釕 鍋 鍋 鍋 鍋

| 鍋 | なべ | pan, pot |
| 鍋物 | なべもの | hot-pot (cooked at the table) |

1967 煎（煎） ▷せん ▷い(る)

13 ` ` ´ ∵ 广 亡 前 前 前 前
前 煎 煎

煎茶	せんちゃ	green tea (of middle grade)
煎じる	せんじる	make a decoction of, decoct, make an infusion of
煎る	いる	parch, roast
～の肝煎りで	～のきもいりで	through the kind offices, under the auspices of

1968 膳 ▷ぜん

16 ノ 刀 月 月 月゛ 月゛ 月゛ 月゛ 月゛ 脟
脟 脟 腊 膳 膳 膳

| 膳 | ぜん | meal set on a table, small dining table |

～膳	～ぜん	(counter for chopsticks)
配膳	はいぜん	する lay the table for dinner
お膳立て	おぜんだて	preparation, arrangements

第 146 回

1969 眉 ▷び, み ▷まゆ

956
cf. 盾

9 ⺈ ア 尸 尸 尸 尸 眉 眉 眉

眉	まゆ	eyebrow
眉間	みけん	the middle of the forehead, brow
特 眉目秀麗な	びもくしゅうれいな	handsome

1970 瞳 ▷どう ▷ひとみ

17 丨 冂 月 月 目 日゛ 旷 旷 旷 旷
旷 睦 睦 暗 瞳 瞳 瞳

| 瞳 | ひとみ | pupil (of the eye) |
| 瞳孔 | どうこう | pupil (of the eye) |

1971 頬（頰） ▷ほお

16 一 厂 厃 厃 夾 夾 夾 夾 夾 夾
頬 頬 頬 頬 頬 頬

頬	ほお	cheek
頬張る	ほおばる	fill one's mouth with food
頬▲杖をつく	ほおづえをつく	rest one's cheeks in one's hands

1972 顎 ▷がく ▷あご

18 丨 亇 亇 亇 亇 亇 四 罗 罗
罗 罗 罗 罗 顎 顎 顎 顎

| 顎 | あご | chin, jaw |
| 顎関節 | がくかんせつ | jaw joint |

1973 拳 ▷けん ▷こぶし

1189
cf. 拳

10　丶 丷 亠 丷 芈 芈 类 巻 参 拳

拳銃　　　　けんじゅう　pistol, handgun, revolver
拳　　　　　こぶし　fist
拳法　　　　けんぽう　Chinese martial art

1974　爪　▷つめ，つま

4　丿 丨 爪 爪

爪　　　　　つめ　nail, claw, talon
爪先　　　　つまさき　tip of a toe, toe
爪*痕　　　つめあと　nail/claw mark, scar, damage

1975　臼　▶きゅう　▷うす　cf.白 44

6　丿 丨 臼 臼 臼 臼

脱臼　　　　だっきゅう　する be dislocated, be put out of joint
臼歯　　　　きゅうし　molar tooth, grinder
臼　　　　　うす　mortar

1976　肘　▷ひじ

7　丿 刀 月 月 肝 肘 肘

肘　　　　　ひじ　elbow

1977　股　▶こ　▷また　cf.役 609

8　丿 刀 月 月 肝 肥 股 股

股　　　　　また　thigh
股関節　　　こかんせつ　hip joint
内股　　　　うちまた　inside of the thigh, pigeon-toed walk
大股　　　　おおまた　long steps/strides
世界を股にかける　せかいをまたにかける　be active in a great number of places
二股　　　　ふたまた　a fork, (adj.) forked

1978　膝　▷ひざ

15　丿 刀 月 月 肝 肚 肤 胗 胗 胗 胯 胯 膝 膝 膝

膝　　　　　ひざ　knee, lap
膝詰め談判　ひざづめだんぱん　direct negotiations
膝掛け　　　ひざかけ　lap robe
膝元　　　　ひざもと　near one's knees, close by one, under one's care/influence

1979　尻　▷しり

5　丆 コ 尸 尸 尻

尻　　　　　しり　hips, the behind, the backside
尻込みする　しりごみする　recoil, flinch, shrink
目尻　　　　めじり　the corner of one's eye
言葉尻　　　ことばじり　end of one's sentence, slip of the tongue
尻尾　　　　△しっぽ　tail

1980　捻　▶ねん

11　一 十 扌 扩 扚 扲 捡 捡 捻 捻

捻挫　　　　ねんざ　する sprain
捻出　　　　ねんしゅつ　する manage to raise (funds), work out (a time)

1981　挫　▶ざ

10　一 十 扌 扌 扩 挫 挫 挫 挫 挫

捻挫　　　　ねんざ　する sprain
挫折　　　　ざせつ　する suffer a setback, be frustrated

1982　痩　▶そう　▷や(せる)　cf.捜 1475

12　丶 亠 广 广 疒 疒 疒 疒 疒 痩 痩 痩

痩せる　　　やせる　get lean/thin, lose weight
痩身　　　　そうしん　thin body
痩せ我慢　　やせがまん　strained endurance

第7水準

1983 箋 ▶せん

14　ノ ⺊ ⺀ ⺀ ⺮ ⺮ 竺 笺 笺 笺
笺 笺 箋 箋

便箋　　びんせん　letter paper/pad
附箋　　ふせん　tag, label　cf. 付箋 is more often used in modern Japanese.
処方箋　しょほうせん　(medical) prescription

第 147 回

1984 唾 ▶だ ▷つば

11　丨 冂 口 口⁻ 口² 口³ 吽 吽 唾
唾

唾　　つば　spit, spittle, saliva
唾液　　だえき　saliva, sputum
眉唾物　まゆつばもの　a fake, unlikely story
固唾をのむ　△かたずをのむ　hold one's breath

1985 咽 ▶いん

9　丨 冂 口 叮 呪 呮 呬 咽 咽

耳鼻咽喉科　じびいんこうか　otorhinolaryngology; ear, nose, and throat (medical specialty)

1986 喉 ▶こう ▷のど
1174 1876 cf. 候 侯

12　丨 冂 口 叮 叫 吖 呸 呿 呼
喉 喉

喉　　のど　throat
耳鼻咽喉科　じびいんこうか　otorhinolaryngology; ear, nose, and throat (medical specialty)
喉自慢　のどじまん　amateur singing contest, person who is proud of his (singing) voice
喉越し　のどごし　feeling as food or drink passes through the throat
喉元　　のどもと　throat, around the base of the neck
喉仏　　のどぼとけ　Adam's apple

1987 腎 ▶じん
1227 cf. 賢

13　丨 厂 厂 厔 臤 臤 臣 臣⁻ 臤 臤
腎 腎 腎

腎臓　　じんぞう　kidney
肝腎な　かんじんな　essential

1988 脊 ▶せき
1085 cf. 背

10　ノ 人 入 ⺷ 夫 夫 夯 夯 脊 脊

脊髄　　せきずい　the spinal cord
脊*椎動物　せいついどうぶつ　vertebrate animal

1989 腺 ▶せん
841 cf. 線

13　ノ 刀 月 月 月' 月' 肝 脬 脬 脬
腺 腺 腺

涙腺　　るいせん　lachrymal gland, tear duct
汗腺　　かんせん　sweat gland

1990 腫 ▶しゅ ▷は(れる), は(らす)

13　ノ 刀 月 月 肝 肝 肝 肺 脂 脂
腫 腫 腫

腫*瘍　　しゅよう　tumor
腫れる　はれる　swell, get swollen
腫らす　はらす　make something swell
腫れ　　はれ　swelling

1991 骸 ▶がい

16　丨 冂 冋 冎 冎 丹 凸 骨 骨 骨
骨' 骨² 骸 骸 骸 骸

死骸　　しがい　corpse, dead body, carcass
形骸化　けいがいか　する become a mere name
残骸　　ざんがい　wreck, wreckage
骸骨　　がいこつ　skeleton

1992 瘍 ▶よう
835 cf. 傷

14 `丶 亠 广 广 广 广 疒 疒 疒 疸 疸 瘍 瘍 瘍`

| 腫瘍 | しゅよう | tumor |
| *潰瘍 | かいよう | ulcer |

1993 痕 ▶こん ▷あと
974 cf. 根

11 `丶 亠 广 广 广 广 疒 疒 疒 疸 痕`

痕跡	こんせき	trace, marks, vestiges
血痕	けっこん	bloodstain
爪痕	つめあと	nail/claw mark, scar, damage
傷痕	きずあと, しょうこん	scar cf. 痕 was not officially recognized as *Jōyō Kanji*, and 傷跡（きずあと）is often used as a substitute for it in the word 傷痕 . In literary-style Japanese, the word 傷痕 is pronounced しょうこん .

1994 斑 ▶はん
1541 cf. 班

12 `一 丅 王 王 王 王 王 玟 玟 斑 斑 斑`

| 斑点 | はんてん | spot, speckle, speck |

1995 潰 ▶かい ▷つぶ(す), つぶ(れる)

15 `丶 丶 氵 氵 氵 氵 沖 沣 沣 潰 潰 潰 潰 潰`

潰瘍	かいよう	ulcer
潰す	つぶす	crush, smash, baffle, ruin, kill (time)
潰れる	つぶれる	be crushed, be smashed, collapse, go bankrupt

1996 椎 ▶つい

12 `一 十 才 木 木 村 杧 杧 桦 桦 椎 椎`

| 脊椎動物 | せきついどうぶつ | vertebrate animal |

1997 梗 ▶こう
227 cf. 便

11 `一 十 才 木 杧 杧 杧 桓 桓 梗`

| 脳梗*塞 | のうこうそく | cerebral infarction |
| 心筋梗*塞 | しんきんこうそく | myocardial infarction |

第 148 回

1998 鹿 ▷しか, か

11 `丶 亠 广 户 庐 庐 鹿 鹿 鹿 鹿`

| 鹿 | しか | deer |
| 鹿児島県 | かごしまけん | name of a prefecture |

1999 虎 ▶こ ▷とら

8 `丶 丶 广 广 庐 虍 虍 虎`

虎	とら	tiger
虎視*眈々	こしたんたん	with a vigilant eye, vigilantly
虎穴	こけつ	tiger's den cf. 虎穴（こけつ）に入（い）らずんば、虎児（こじ）を得（え）ず "Nothing ventured, nothing gained" (proverb)

2000 熊 ▷くま
451 cf. 態

14 `丶 厶 宀 台 台 台 育 能 能 能 能 能 熊`

| 熊 | くま | bear |
| 熊本県 | くまもとけん | name of a prefecture |

第7水準

287

2001
哺 ▶ほ

10 ｜ 冂 口 叮 叮 叮 叮 叮 哺 哺

哺乳類　ほにゅうるい　mammal
哺乳瓶　ほにゅうびん　feeding/nursing bottle

2002
牙（牙） ▶が, げ
▷きば

4 一 二 亍 牙

牙　きば　tusk, fang
牙城　がじょう　stronghold, bastion, citadel
象牙　ぞうげ　elephant tusk, ivory
（〜の）毒牙にかかる　（〜の）どくがにかかる　have fallen prey to

2003
亀 ▶き
▷かめ

11 ノ ⺈ 甶 甶 甶 备 备 备 备 备 亀

亀　かめ　tortoise, turtle
亀裂　きれつ　crack, crevice, split

2004
鶴 ▷つる

21 ｜ 冖 ⺈ 伊 伊 伊 伊 隹 隹 隹
隺 鹳 鹳 鹳 鹳 鹳 鶴 鶴 鶴 鶴
鶴

鶴　つる　crane

2005
蜂 ▶ほう
▷はち

13 ｜ 口 口 中 虫 虫 虬 虬 蛑 蛑
蛑 蛑 蜂

蜂　はち　bee, wasp, hornet
蜂起　ほうき  する rise in rebellion, revolt
蜂蜜　はちみつ　honey
蜂の巣　はちのす　beehive, honeycomb

2006
虹 ▷にじ

9 ｜ 口 口 中 虫 虫 虹 虹 虹

虹　にじ　rainbow

2007
嵐 ▷あらし

12 ｜ 屮 山 广 屵 屵 屵 嵐 嵐 嵐
嵐 嵐

嵐　あらし　storm

2008
崖 ▶がい
▷がけ
456 cf. 岸

11 ｜ 屮 山 屵 户 户 岸 崖 崖 崖
崖

崖　がけ　precipice, cliff
崖っぷち　がけっぷち　brink
断崖　だんがい　precipice, cliff
断崖絶壁　だんがいぜっぺき　precipitous cliff, sheer precipice

2009
麓 ▶ろく
▷ふもと

19 一 十 ⺊ 木 木 林 林 林 林 林
芦 芦 麓 麓 麓 麓 麓 麓 麓

麓　ふもと　the foot, the base
山麓　さんろく　the foot of a mountain

2010
窟 ▶くつ

13 ｜ 宀 宀 宀 空 空 空 穸 穸 窋
窋 窟 窟

洞窟　どうくつ　cave, cavern
巣窟　そうくつ　den, haunt, nest
石窟　せっくつ　stone cave

2011 **葛（葛）** ▶かつ ▷くず

12 一 十 艹 艹 芎 芦 芎 芦 葛 葛
葛 葛

葛藤	かっとう	[する] conflict, discord
葛	くず	kudzu (vine), arrowroot
葛飾区	▲かつしかく	name of a ward in Tokyo

2012 **藤** ▶とう ▷ふじ

18 一 十 艹 艹 芐 芐 芐 芐 芐
芐 芐 莢 萨 萨 萨 藤 藤

| 葛藤 | かっとう | [する] conflict, discord |
| 藤 | ふじ | (Japanese) wisteria |

2013 **藍** ▶らん ▷あい

18 一 十 艹 艹 芦 芦 莅 莅 莅
莅 莅 莅 莅 莅 莅 莅 藍

| 藍色 | あいいろ | indigo-blue, deep blue |
| [特] 出藍の誉れ | しゅつらんのほまれ | surpassing one's teacher/master |

2014 **堆** ▶たい

1009
cf. 推

11 一 十 土 圵 圵 圵 圵 堆 堆
堆

| 堆積 | たいせき | [する] be piled up, accumulate |

2015 **湧** ▶ゆう ▷わ（く）

12 丶 丶 氵 氵 氵 沪 沪 沪 涌 涌
涌 湧

湧く	わく	gush/spring/flow/out, breed
湧き水	わきみず	spring water
湧水	ゆうすい	spring water

2016 **沃** ▶よく

7 丶 丶 氵 氵 氵 沃 沃

| 肥沃な | ひよくな | fertile, rich |

2017 **闇** ▷やみ

17 丨 冂 冂 冂 門 門 門 門 門
門 門 問 閨 閽 閽 闇 闇

闇	やみ	darkness, the dark
暗闇	くらやみ	darkness, the dark
闇市	やみいち	black market

第 149 回

2018 **玩** ▶がん

8 一 丁 王 王 玗 玗 玩 玩

| 玩具 | がんぐ | toy |
| 愛玩 | あいがん | [する] pet, fondle |

2019 **駒** ▷こま

15 丨 冂 冂 厈 厈 馬 馬 馬 馬
馬 駒 駒 駒 駒

駒	こま	horse, (chess) man, bridge of string instrument
持ち駒	もちごま	captured piece, person available
[特] 若駒	わかごま	young horse

2020 **呂** ▶ろ

7 丨 口 口 吗 呂 呂 呂

風呂	ふろ	bath
語呂	ごろ	combination of sounds, sound harmony
風呂敷	ふろしき	square of cloth for wrapping, cloth wrapper

第7水準

2021 巾 ▶きん

3 丨 冂 巾

雑巾 　ぞうきん　floor cloth, mop
布巾 　ふきん　dish towel, dishcloth
頭巾 　ずきん　hood

2022 袖 ▶しゅう
▷そで　　　　　　586
cf. 神

10 丶 礻 礻 礻 礻 礻 衤 衤 袖 袖

袖 　そで　sleeve, wing
特 領袖 　りょうしゅう　leader, head

2023 裾 ▷すそ

13 丶 礻 礻 礻 礻 礻 礻 裙 裙 裙
裙 裾 裾

裾 　すそ　hem of a skirt, bottom edge, bottom
裾野 　すその　skirts of a mountain, range (of volunteer activities, etc.)

2024 籠 ▶ろう
▷かご, こ(もる)

22 ⺮ ⺮ ⺮ ⺮ ⺮ ⺮ ⺮ ⺮ ⺮ ⺮
筥 筥 箮 箮 箮 箮 箮 籠 籠
籠 籠

籠城 　ろうじょう　する hold a castle, be besieged, be confined to one's home
籠 　かご　cage, coop, basket
籠もる 　こもる　shut oneself up, be full of, blur

2025 蓋 ▶がい
▷ふた　　　　　566
cf. 芸

13 一 艹 艹 艹 茇 茇 莕 莕 蓋
蓋 蓋 蓋

蓋 　ふた　cover, lid, cap
火蓋を切る 　ひぶたをきる　start firing, open fire, start

頭蓋骨 　ずがいこつ　skull
蓋然性 　がいぜんせい　probability

2026 芯 ▶しん

7 一 十 艹 艹 芯 芯 芯

芯 　しん　wick, padding, core lead, core

2027 瓦 ▶が
▷かわら

5 一 丆 瓦 瓦 瓦

瓦 　かわら　tile
瓦解 　がかい　する be ruined, fall down, collapse

2028 鍵 ▶けん
▷かぎ

17 ノ 人 𠆢 𠂉 牟 牟 金 金 鈩 鈩
鈩 鈩 鍵 鍵 鍵 鍵 鍵

鍵 　かぎ　key
鍵盤 　けんばん　clavier

2029 枕 ▷まくら　　　1129
cf. 沈

8 一 十 木 木 朳 枕 枕 枕

枕 　まくら　pillow
枕詞 　まくらことば　conventional epithet (used in Japanese poetry)
枕元 　まくらもと　one's bedside

2030 柵 ▶さく

9 一 十 木 木 朳 朳 柵 柵 柵

柵 　さく　fence, railing

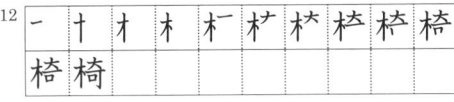
2031 椅 ▶い

12 一 十 オ オ ポ ポ 柊 柊 柊 椅
椅 椅

椅子　　いす　chair

2032 舷 ▶げん

11 ′ ′ 刀 月 月 舟 舟' 舟' 舟' 舷
舷

右舷　　うげん　starboard　cf. 左舷(さげん) port

第 150 回

2033 挨 ▶あい
1424
cf. 俊

10 一 十 扌 扩 扩 护 护 拌 挨 挨

挨拶　　あいさつ　-する greet

2034 拶 ▶さつ

9 一 十 扌 扌 扩 扩 拶 拶 拶

挨拶　　あいさつ　-する greet

2035 沙 ▶さ
1465
cf. 抄

7 、 氵 氵 氵 氿 沙 沙

ご無沙汰　ごぶさた　-する neglect to call or write
音沙汰がない　おとさたがない　haven't heard from
表沙汰になる　おもてざたになる　come into the open, become public knowledge
裁判沙汰になる　さいばんざたになる　take a case to court

2036 汰 ▶た

7 、 氵 氵 氵 氿 汰 汰

ご無沙汰　ごぶさた　-する neglect to call or write
▴淘汰　とうた　-する select, weed out, screen, sift

2037 頃 ▷ころ

11 ′ ヒ ヒ ヒ 圹 圹 圹 圹 頃 頃
頃

〜(の)頃　〜(の)ころ　(the) time, about
日頃　　ひごろ　usually
この頃　このごろ　these days, recently　cf. このころ at this time
食べ頃　たべごろ　be ready/ripe enough to eat

2038 旦 ▶たん，だん

5 丨 冂 日 日 旦

元旦　　がんたん　New Year's Day
旦那　　だんな　one's master, one's husband, patron, sir

2039 宛 ▷あ(てる)
1342
cf. 腕

8 ′ ′ 宀 宀 夗 夗 夗 宛

宛先　　あてさき　addressee, address
宛名　　あてな　addressee
〜宛(の)　あて(の)　addressed to, consigned to
宛てる　あてる　address

2040 隙 ▶げき
▷すき

13 ′ 阝 阝 阝' 阝' 阝'' 阝'' 陥 陥
隙 隙 隙

隙間　　すきま　opening, space between two things, chink
間隙　　かんげき　gap in space or time
お手隙　おてすき　free from things to do

2041 脇 ▷わき

10 丿 刀 月 月 肝 胗 胗 脇 脇 脇

脇　　　　　わき　side, aside, another place
脇道　　　　わきみち　side road, byway, digression
脇見運転　　わきみうんてん　inattentive driving
脇目も振らず　わきめもふらず　wholeheartedly

2042 桁　▷けた

10　一 十 オ ォ ォ ォ 杵 杵 杵 桁

桁　　　　けた　crossbeam, girder, figure, digit, place (as in decimal places)
橋桁　　　はしげた　bridge girder
桁外れ　　けたはずれ　extraordinary, incredible

2043 毀　▶き

13　丶 丷 广 臼 臼 白 臼 皀 皀
毇 皃 毀

毀損　　きそん　[する] damage, injure

2044 錮　▶こ

16　ノ 𠆢 𠆢 亼 牟 牟 金 釒 釘
釘 釦 鉬 錮 錮 錮

禁錮　　きんこ　imprisonment　cf. 錮 was not officially recognized as *Jōyō Kanji*, and 禁固 was used as a substitute for 禁錮

2045 勾　▶こう

4　ノ 勹 勾 勾

勾留　　こうりゅう　[する] detain　cf. 拘留（こうりゅう）custody
勾配　　こうばい　slope, incline, steep

第 151 回

2046 賭（賭）　▶と　▷か（ける）

16　丨 冂 月 月 目 貝 貝 貯 貯 貯
貯 貯 賭 賭 賭 賭

2047 醒　▶せい

16　一 厂 冂 万 西 西 酉 酉 酉
酊 酊 酲 醒 醒 醒 醒

覚醒　　かくせい　[する] awake, come to one's sense
覚醒剤　　かくせいざい　stimulant, pep pill

2048 溺（溺）　▶でき　▷おぼ（れる）

13　丶 冫 氵 氵 汈 汈 泖 弱 溺
溺 溺 溺

溺れる　　おぼれる　drown, be drowned, indulge in, be addicted to
溺死　　できし　[する] die by drowning, drown
溺愛　　できあい　[する] dote on

2049 綻　▶たん　▷ほころ（びる）

14　㇐ 乡 幺 糸 糸 糸 糹 糹 綻 綻
綻 綻 綻 綻

破綻　　はたん　[する] fail, break down, go bankrupt
綻びる　　ほころびる　come apart at the seams, (buds) begin to open, smile
綻び　　ほころび　an open seam, a tear

2050 踪　▶そう

15　丨 口 口 𧾷 𧾷 𧾷 𧾷 跕 跕 跕
踪 踪 踪 踪 踪

失踪　　しっそう　[する] disappear, abscond, run away

2051 謎（謎） ▷なぞ

17 画

謎　　　　　なぞ　　riddle, puzzle, mystery, hint
謎解き　　　なぞとき　　solving a riddle
謎めく　　　なぞめく　　enigmatic

2052 蔽（蔽） ▶へい

15 画

隠蔽　　　　いんぺい　　[する] hide, conceal, cover up
遮蔽　　　　しゃへい　　[する] cover, shelter, screen

2053 詮（詮） ▶せん

13 画

詮索　　　　せんさく　　[する] search, inquire into
所詮　　　　しょせん　　after all, anyway

2054 匂 ▷にお（う）

4 画

匂う　　　　におう　　be fragrant, smell
匂わせる　　におわせる　　suggest, smell

2055 嗅（嗅） ▶きゅう
▷か（ぐ）

13 画

嗅覚　　　　きゅうかく　　sense of smell
嗅ぐ　　　　かぐ　　smell, sniff

2056 狙 ▶そ
▷ねら（う）

8 画

狙う　　　　ねらう　　aim at, sight, aspire
狙撃　　　　そげき　　[する] shoot at, snipe at
狙い　　　　ねらい　　an aim, an objective

2057 拉 ▶ら

8 画

拉致　　　　らち　　[する] take someone away, abduct

2058 乞 ▷こ（う）

3 画

乞う　　　　こう　　beg, ask, solicit, entreat (help/assistance/
　　　　　　　　　　etc.) cf. 請う（こう）ask, request
命乞い　　　いのちごい　　pleading for one's life

2059 蹴 ▶しゅう
▷け（る）

19 画

蹴る　　　　ける　　kick, reject, refuse
一蹴　　　　いっしゅう　　[する] refuse flatly, reject
踏んだり蹴ったり　　ふんだりけったり　　one misfortune
　　　　　　　　　　　　on top of another
足蹴にする　　あしげにする　　kick, treat cruelly

2060 剥（剥） ▶はく
▷は（がす），は（ぐ），は（がれる），
は（げる）

10 画

剥奪　　　　はくだつ　　[する] deprive, divest
剥がす　　　はがす　　peel, tear off
剥がれる　　はがれる　　come/peel off
剥ぐ　　　　はぐ　　tear/peel off, skin, strip, deprive
剥げる　　　はげる　　come/peel off, be worn off, fade,
　　　　　　　　　　discolor
剥製　　　　はくせい　　stuffed animal/bird

2061 斬 ▶ざん ▷き(る) 1503 cf. 漸

11 一 ┌ ┌ ┌ ┌ 亘 車 軒 斬 斬 斬

斬る　きる　cut (kill) with a sword
斬新な　ざんしんな　novel, original

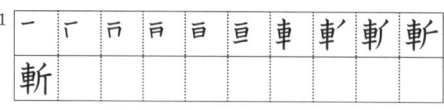

2062 俺 ▷おれ

10 ノ イ イ′ 仁 伫 杁 佅 佅 倍 俺

俺　おれ　I (used between close friends or to younger person in masculine speech)

2063 傲 ▶ごう

13 ノ イ イ′ 仁′ 仹 仹 倠 倣 傲 傲 傲 傲

傲慢な　ごうまんな　haughtiness, arrogance (haughty, arrogant)

2064 遜（遜） ▶そん

14 ┐ 了 子 孑 孖 孖 孫 孫 孫 孫 孫 孫 遜

謙遜　けんそん　する　be modest, be humble
不遜な　ふそんな　insolent, haughty
遜色（が）ない　そんしょく（が）ない　bear comparison with, be equal to

2065 辣 ▶らつ

14 ᐟ 亠 亠 立 立 辛 辛 辛 辛 辣 辣 辣 辣

辛辣な　しんらつな　incisive, trenchant, bitter, harsh
辣腕　らつわん　shrewdness, sharpness, astuteness

2066 凄 ▶せい

10 丶 冫 冫 冱 冱 冱 凄 凄 凄 凄

凄惨な　せいさんな　ghastly, gruesome
凄い　▲すごい　horrible, terrible, superb, fantastic, tremendous, awful

2067 貪 ▶どん ▷むさぼ(る) 859 cf. 貧

11 ノ 人 𠆢 今 今 含 含 貪 貪 貪 貪

貪欲な　どんよくな　greedy, avaricious
貪る　むさぼる　covet, crave, be greedy for, devour

2068 旺 ▶おう

8 丨 冂 日 日 旺 町 旺 旺

旺盛な　おうせいな　be full of energy/strength

2069 淫（淫） ▶いん ▷みだ(ら)

11 丶 氵 氵 𣲾 𣴎 𣴎 𣴎 淫 淫 淫 淫

淫らな　みだらな　obscene, loose, unchaste
淫乱な　いんらんな　lecherous, lascivious
淫行　いんこう　sexual misconduct

2070 艶 ▶えん ▷つや

19 丨 冂 内 曲 曲 曲 曲 豊 豊 豊 豊 豊 豊 豊 艶 艶 艶 艶 艶

妖艶な　ようえんな　fascinating, bewitching, voluptuous
艶　つや　gloss, luster, polish, charm

2071 妖 ▶よう ▷あや(しい)

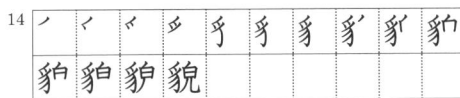

妖精　　ようせい　fairy, sprite, elf

妖艶な　ようえんな　fascinating, bewitching, voluptuous

妖怪　　ようかい　monstrous being, monster, ghost　cf. 幽霊(ゆうれい) ghost

妖しい　あやしい　strange (as of an apparition or a spirit), bewitching, luring　cf. 怪しい(あやしい) strange, questionable, uncertain

2072 貌　▶ぼう

14

容貌　　ようぼう　looks, features

変貌　　へんぼう　[する] change in appearance, transfigure

全貌　　ぜんぼう　full picture, full view

2073 摯　▶し

15

真摯な　しんしな　sincere

2074 爽　▶そう　▷さわ(やか)

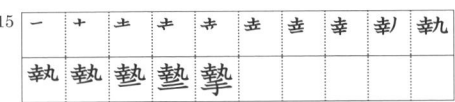

爽やかな　さわやかな　fresh, bracing

爽快な　そうかいな　refreshing, invigorating

2075 璧　▶へき　1029 cf. 壁

16

完璧な　かんぺきな　perfect, flawless

双璧をなす　そうへきをなす　being the two greatest authorities, being the best two

2076 憧　▶しょう　▷あこが(れる)

15

憧れる　あこがれる　long for, yearn for, admire

憧憬　しょうけい　[する] yearn (also pronounced どうけい)

憧れ　あこがれ　longing, yearning

2077 憬　▶けい

15

憧憬　しょうけい　[する] yearn (also pronounced どうけい)

第 153 回

2078 拭　▶しょく　▷ふ(く), ぬぐ(う)

9

拭く　ふく　wipe, mop, rub

払拭　ふっしょく　[する] sweep away, wipe out

拭う　ぬぐう　wipe

尻拭い　しりぬぐい　[する] clear up someone's mess, bear the consequences of someone's mistake

2079 貼　▶ちょう　▷は(る)

12

貼る　はる　paste, stick (a stamp, a poster, etc.)　cf. 張る spread (net, wall paper, etc.), stretch (a rope), paste (a paper, poster, etc.)

貼付　ちょうふ　[する] stick on, paste on, affix on

2080 捉　▶そく　▷とら(える)　1170 cf. 促

10

捉える　とらえる　grasp, catch
捕捉　ほそく　[-する] capture, apprehend

2081 冶　▶や　531　cf. 治

7　丶　冫　冫ㅗ　冫㇒　冶　冶

[特] 陶冶　とうや　[-する] cultivate/build up one's character/ability
[特] 冶金　やきん　metallurgy
鍛冶　△かじ　forging, smithery, a blacksmith

2082 詣　▶けい　▷もう(でる)

13　丶　二　三　言　言　言　言　詣　詣　詣　詣　詣

初詣　はつもうで　first visit of the year to a shrine/temple (made during the New Year)
造詣が深い　ぞうけいがふかい　be conversant with, have great knowledge
詣でる　もうでる　visit a temple

2083 遡（遡）　▶そ　▷さかのぼ(る)

14　丶　ソ　�　朔　朔　遡　遡

遡る　さかのぼる　go upstream, go back in time
遡及　そきゅう　[-する] retroact

2084 塡（填）　▶てん

13　一　十　土　塡　塡　塡　塡

補塡　ほてん　[-する] fill (a deficit), supplement

2085 頓　▶とん

13　𠃌　亡　口　頓　頓　頓　頓

整頓　せいとん　[-する] put something in order, tidy up
無頓着な　むとんちゃくな　indifferent, nonchalant, careless
頓挫　とんざ　[-する] be frustrated, be held up, be checked

2086 氾　▶はん　1046　cf. 犯

5　丶　冫　氵　氾　氾

氾濫　はんらん　[-する] inundate, overflow, flood

2087 勃　▶ぼつ

9　一　十　ナ　圡　㞢　孛　孛　勃　勃

勃発　ぼっぱつ　[-する] break out, occur suddenly
勃興　ぼっこう　[-する] rise suddenly, increase in the power suddenly

2088 捗（捗）　▶ちょく　505　cf. 渉

10　一　十　扌　捗　捗

進捗　しんちょく　[-する] make progress, advance

2089 采　▶さい　774　cf. 菜

8　一　采　采　采

采配　さいはい　[-する] command, direct
喝采　かっさい　[-する] applause, cheers
風采　ふうさい　personal appearance, presence

第 154 回

2090 羨　▶せん　▷うらや(む)，うらや(ましい)

13　丶　ソ　羨　羨　羨

羨ましい　うらやましい　enviable
羨望　せんぼう　[-する] be envious of
羨む　うらやむ　envy, be envious of

2091 嫉 ▶しつ

13 く　タ　女　女`　女ㇾ　女ㇾ　女ㇾ　女ㇾ　女ㇾ　女ㇾ
妒　妒　嫉

嫉妬　　　しっと　[-する] be jealous, envy

2092 妬 ▶と
▷ねた（む）

8 く　タ　女　女ˊ　女ㇾ　女ㇾ　妬　妬

嫉妬　　　しっと　[-する] be jealous, envy
妬む　　　ねたむ　be jealous
嫉妬深い　しっとぶかい　jealous, envious

2093 惧 ▶ぐ

11 ′　′′　忄　忄′　忄′′　忄′′　忄′′　惧　惧
惧

危惧　　　きぐ　[-する] feel misgivings about, be
　　　　　apprehensive about

2094 弄 ▶ろう　　　　　1116
▷もてあそ（ぶ）　cf. 弁

7 一　丁　干　王　王　王　弄

弄ぶ　　　もてあそぶ　play with, make sport of
翻弄　　　ほんろう　[-する] make fun of, play with, trifle
弄する　　ろうする　use sophistry, play a mean trick on
　　　　　someone
愚弄　　　ぐろう　[-する] ridicule, mock

2095 嘲（嘲） ▶ちょう
▷あざけ（る）

15 丨　口　口　口′　叶′　呿′　咾　咾　咾
啈　啈　嘲　嘲　嘲

嘲る　　　あざける　ridicule, sneer, scoff
嘲笑　　　ちょうしょう　[-する] laugh at, scoff, ridicule
自嘲　　　じちょう　[-する] ridicule oneself
嘲笑う　▲あざわらう　laugh at, sneer at, ridicule

2096 蔑（蔑） ▶べつ
▷さげす（む）

14 一　十　艹　艹′　芦　苎　苎　苗　苩　苩
苩　苎　蔑　蔑

軽蔑　　　けいべつ　[-する] contempt, scorn
蔑視　　　べっし　[-する] look down on with contempt
蔑む　　　さげすむ　contempt, scorn

2097 叱 ▶しつ　　　　　1722
▷しか（る）　cf. 尼

5 丨　口　口　口ㇾ　叱

叱る　　　しかる　scold, chide, reprove
叱責　　　しっせき　[-する] scold, reproach, reprove
叱咤激励　しったげきれい　[-する] scold and encourage/spur
　　　　　(on)

2098 罵 ▶ば
▷ののし（る）

15 丨　冂　冂′　罒　罒′　罒′　罒′　罒′　罜
罜　罵　罵　罵　罵

罵る　　　ののしる　abuse, revile, inveigh against, rebuke
罵声　　　ばせい　boos, jeers
罵倒　　　ばとう　[-する] abuse, revile, hurl abuse

2099 呪 ▶じゅ　　　　　1018
▷のろ（う）　cf. 祝

8 丨　口　口　口′　叩′　叩′　呪　呪

呪う　　　のろう　curse
呪文　　　じゅもん　(magic) spell, charm, magic words
呪縛　　　じゅばく　[-する] put a spell on
呪術　　　じゅじゅつ　magic, an occult art

2100 怨 ▶えん，おん

9 ノ　ク　夕　夘′　夗　夗　怨　怨　怨

怨恨　　　えんこん　grudge
怨念　　　おんねん　a deep-seated grudge

第7水準

怨霊 おんりょう　a vengeful ghost

怨み ▲うらみ　grudge　cf. 怨み has a stronger nuance than 恨み(うらみ)

2101 臆 ▶おく

17 ⟨ノ 几 月 月 月' 肜 肜 肜 肜 肜 肜 脂 臆 臆 臆 臆 臆⟩

臆病な　おくびょうな　cowardly, timid

臆測　おくそく　[-する] guess without certain basis　cf. 臆 was not officially recognized as *Jōyō Kanji*, and 憶 was used as a substitute for it.

臆す(る)　おくす(る)　be afraid, be timid, flinch

臆面もなく　おくめんもなく　impudently, shamelessly

2102 諦 ▶てい ▷あきら(める) 1067 cf. 締

16 ⟨丶 亠 二 ミ 言 言 言 言 言 訁 訏 訏 諪 諪 諦 諦⟩

諦める　あきらめる　give up on, abandon, resign oneself to

[特] 諦観　ていかん　[-する] resign oneself

2103 羞 ▶しゅう 674 cf. 差

11 ⟨丶 ソ ソ ソ 兰 羊 羊 差 差 羞 羞⟩

羞恥心　しゅうちしん　sense of shame

2104 鬱 ▶うつ

29 ⟨…⟩

鬱　うつ　depression, low spirits

憂鬱な　ゆううつな　depressed, dejected, gloomy

第 155 回

2105 須 ▶す

12 ⟨ノ ク タ 彡 彡' 泸 沜 須 須 須 須 須⟩

必須の　ひっすの　indispensable, essential, necessary

必須条件　ひっすじょうけん　indispensable condition

2106 汎 ▶はん 467 cf. 凡

6 ⟨丶 氵 氵 汃 汎 汎⟩

汎用(性)　はんよう(せい)　widely used, widely applicable

汎神論　はんしんろん　pantheism

2107 曖 ▶あい

17 ⟨丨 冂 日 日 日 日 日 日 昭 昭 昭 昭 曖 曖 曖⟩

曖昧な　あいまいな　vague, obscure, ambiguous

2108 昧 ▶まい 311 cf. 味

9 ⟨丨 冂 日 日 旷 旷 昒 昧 昧⟩

曖昧な　あいまいな　vague, obscure, ambiguous

〜三昧　〜ざんまい　be absorbed in, give all one's time to

2109 瞭 ▶りょう

17 ⟨丨 冂 日 日 日 旷 旷 旷 旷 眤 睔 睔 睟 睟 瞭 瞭⟩

明瞭な　めいりょうな　clear, plain, lucid

一目瞭然な／の　いちもくりょうぜんな／の　quite obvious

2110 緻 ▶ち

16 ⟨ ⟨ ⟨ ⟨ ⟨ 糸 紅 紀 紵 絆 絆 絆 絆 絆 緻 緻

緻密な　ちみつな　careful
精緻な　せいちな　minute, detailed, fine

2111 刹 ▶さつ, せつ　　cf. 殺 610

8 ノ メ メ ≠ ≠ 希 利 刹

刹那　せつな　moment
刹那的な　せつなてきな　momentary/transient (pleasures)
特 古刹　こさつ　historic old temple

2112 那 ▶な

7 フ ヲ ヲ 月 月' 那' 那

刹那　せつな　moment
那覇　なは　name of a city in Okinawa

2113 恣 ▶し

10 一 ニ 丆 丆 次 次 次 恣 恣

恣意的な　しいてきな　arbitrary, with concern only for oneself

2114 僅（僅） ▶きん
▷わず（か）

13 ノ イ 仁 仁 仁 仔 仔 俗 俗 俗 僅 僅 僅

僅かな／の　わずかな／の　a few, a little, slight
僅差　きんさ　narrow/slim margin

2115 苛 ▶か　　cf. 荷 570

8 一 十 艹 艹 苎 苛 苛 苛

苛酷な　かこくな　harsh, rigorous, cruel, merciless, severe
苛立ち　▲いらだち　irritation

2116 慄 ▶りつ

13 ノ ハ 忄 忄 忄 忄 怖 怖 怖 慄 慄 慄 慄

戦慄　せんりつ　する shiver, shudder
慄然とする　りつぜんとする　be filled with horror, be horrified

2117 畏 ▶い
▷おそ（れる）

9 丨 冂 冂 田 田 甲 甲 畏 畏

畏怖　いふ　する stand/be in awe of
畏敬の念　いけいのねん　awe, reverence
畏れる　おそれる　fear with reverence, be awestruck by (god/lord/nature, etc)　cf. 恐れる（おそれる）be afraid of (an enemy/death, etc.)

2118 萎 ▶い
▷な（える）

11 一 十 艹 艹 艹 芏 芋 苿 萎 萎 萎

萎縮　いしゅく　する wither, shrink, become atrophied
萎える　なえる　lose strength, go numb, wither

2119 塞 ▶さい, そく　　cf. 寒 120
▷ふさ（ぐ）, ふさ（がる）

13 ' ' 宀 宀 宀 宀 审 审 塞 寒 寒 塞

閉塞感　へいそくかん　feeling of being blocked, feeling of being bottled-up
要塞　ようさい　fortress, stronghold
塞ぐ　ふさぐ　close, shut, stop up, stuff up, fill up, clog
塞がる　ふさがる　be closed, be obstructed, be choked, be occupied
塞ぎ込む　ふさぎこむ　deeply depressed

第7水準

第 156 回

2120 曽 ▶そう, ぞ

11 　丶　丷　丷　丷　⺍　凹　冊　兽　曽　曽
曽

曽祖母	そうそぼ	great-grandmother
曾祖父	そうそふ	great-grandfather
未曽有の	みぞうの	unprecedented, unexampled
曽孫	そうそん, ▲ひまご	great-grandchild

2121 戚 ▶せき

11 　ノ　厂　厂　厍　戚　戌　戌　戚　戚　戚
戚

| 親戚 | しんせき | relatives |
| 姻戚 | いんせき | in-laws, relatives by marriage |

2122 冥 ▶めい, みょう

10 　丶　冖　冖　冝　冝　冒　冒　冥　冥　冥

| 冥福 | めいふく | happiness after death |
| ～冥利に尽きる | ～みょうりにつきる | feel happy by obtaining more (of something, e.g., praise) than expected (or deserved) |

2123 侶 ▶りょ

9 　ノ　イ　イ　伫　伫　侣　侣　侶　侶

| 僧侶 | そうりょ | (Buddhist) priest, bonze, monk |
| 伴侶 | はんりょ | partner, companion |

2124 訃 ▶ふ

9 　丶　二　二　言　言　言　言　訃　訃

| 訃報 | ふほう | report of someone's death |

2125 諧 ▶かい

16 　丶　二　二　言　言　言　言　訲　訲
訧　訕　訧　詣　諧　諧

| 俳諧 | はいかい | a poetic genre that includes *haiku*, *renku*, and *senryū* |

2126 楷 ▶かい　2125 cf. 諧

13 　一　十　才　木　杧　桁　桁　桁　桁　桁
楷　楷　楷

| 楷書 | かいしょ | square/printed style (of Chinese characters) |

2127 伎 ▶き

6 　ノ　イ　仁　什　仿　伎

| 歌舞伎 | かぶき | a type of Japanese traditional performing art which was born in Edo era |

2128 唄 ▷うた　1809 cf. 唱

10 　丨　口　口　叮　叮　唄　唄　唄　唄　唄

小唄	こうた	*kouta*, a Japanese ballad accompanied on the *shamisen* cf. 唄 is widely used to denote traditional Japanese folk songs or ballads, e.g., *kouta*, *nagauta*, *funauta* (boatman's chantey)
長唄	ながうた	epic song originally composed for kabuki, accompanied by *shamisen*
島唄	しまうた	folk song of the Amami Islands, Kagoshima Prefecture; loosely, Okinawan folk song

2129 瑠 ▶る

14 　一　丁　王　王　王　玗　玗　珋　珋
瑠　瑠　瑠　瑠

| 浄瑠璃 | じょうるり | *jōruri*, dramatic narrative chanted to a *shamisen* accompaniment |

2130　璃　▶り　1008　cf. 離

15　一　T　F　王　王丶　扩　玙　玙　琂　璃
琂　璃　璃　璃　璃

浄瑠璃　じょうるり　jōruri, dramatic narrative chanted to a *shamisen* accompaniment

2131　稽　▶けい　15

ノ　ニ　千　千　禾　禾　秕　秕　秸　稯
稯　稯　稭　稭　稽

稽古　けいこ　［する］ practice, training, lesson
滑稽な　こっけいな　funny, comical, ludicrous
荒唐無稽な　こうとうむけいな　nonsensical, absurd, preposterous

2132　喩　▶ゆ　499　cf. 輸

12　ｌ　ロ　ロ　ロ丿　ロ入　叭　吟　哈　唸
喩　喩

比喩　ひゆ　metaphor, simile

2133　彙　▶い　13

ㄥ　ㄩ　彐　彐　彐　彐　彐　彐　彙
彙　彙　彙

語彙　ごい　vocabulary, lexicon

2134　錦　▶きん　▷にしき　841　cf. 線

16　ノ　ハ　ム　ム　牟　牟　余　金　金丶　釒
釒　釒　鈤　鈤　錦　錦

錦　にしき　Japanese brocade
錦を飾る　にしきをかざる　return home loaded with honors
錦の御旗　にしきのみはた　Imperial standard or banner (made of gold brocade), a sacred/worthy cause
［特］錦糸　きんし　thread of brocade

2135　睦　▶ぼく　833　cf. 陸

13　ｌ　冂　月　月　目　目　町　町　眸　睦
睦　睦　睦

親睦　しんぼく　mutual friendship, amity

2136　戴　▶たい　1307　cf. 載

17　一　十　士　+　吉　吉　吉　声　壴　壴
壴　壴　壴　戴　戴　戴

頂戴する　ちょうだいする　be given, be presented, enjoy, have
［特］戴冠式　たいかんしき　coronation ceremony

第7水準

301

付 録
（Appendices）

学習漢字一覧表

(List of *Kanji*)

第 1 水 準						250字

1 一	30 後	59 会	88 小	117 早	146 地	175 座
2 二	31 上	60 社	89 長	118 遅	147 鉄	176 歩
3 三	32 下	61 電	90 短	119 暑	148 者	177 走
4 四	33 中	62 車	91 朝	120 寒	149 所	178 話
5 五	34 横	63 自	92 昼	121 深	150 外	179 聞
6 六	35 右	64 動	93 夜	122 浅	151 国	180 読
7 七	36 左	65 転	94 晩	123 細	152 内	181 書
8 八	37 本	66 道	95 夕	124 太	153 旅	182 借
9 九	38 机	67 男	96 春	125 若	154 語	183 貸
10 十	39 東	68 女	97 夏	126 忙	155 英	184 返
11 百	40 西	69 子	98 秋	127 寝	156 世	185 出
12 千	41 南	70 主	99 冬	128 起	157 界	186 入
13 万	42 北	71 奥	100 山	129 始	158 倍	187 売
14 円	43 方	72 私	101 川	130 終	159 半	188 買
15 人	44 白	73 父	102 石	131 食	160 全	189 払
16 日	45 黒	74 母	103 田	132 飲	161 間	190 着
17 月	46 赤	75 兄	104 多	133 来	162 回	191 脱
18 火	47 青	76 弟	105 少	134 帰	163 週	192 働
19 水	48 先	77 姉	106 明	135 乗	164 毎	193 泳
20 木	49 生	78 妹	107 暗	136 降	165 体	194 写
21 金	50 学	79 友	108 低	137 作	166 頭	195 待
22 土	51 校	80 何	109 近	138 休	167 口	196 遊
23 曜	52 家	81 誰	110 遠	139 見	168 目	197 呼
24 年	53 部	82 名	111 強	140 勉	169 耳	198 洗
25 時	54 屋	83 高	112 弱	141 住	170 手	199 使
26 分	55 店	84 安	113 広	142 持	171 足	200 歌
27 今	56 駅	85 新	114 悪	143 知	172 心	201 習
28 午	57 銀	86 古	115 重	144 酒	173 力	202 思
29 前	58 行	87 大	116 軽	145 茶	174 立	203 言

204 通	211 続	218 焼	225 倒	232 雨	239 問	246 気
205 渡	212 考	219 消	226 郵	233 京	240 料	247 静
206 送	213 答	220 直	227 便	234 映	241 理	248 利
207 泊	214 教	221 並	228 局	235 画	242 真	249 親
208 覚	215 開	222 変	229 病	236 仕	243 紙	250 切
209 忘	216 閉	223 残	230 院	237 事	244 好	
210 調	217 止	224 集	231 窓	238 質	245 元	

第 2 水 準　　　　100字／計350字

251 笑	266 踏	281 晴	296 練	311 味	326 宿	341 悲
252 泣	267 進	282 投	297 研	312 授	327 題	342 苦
253 喜	268 盗	283 逃	298 究	313 橋	328 寺	343 楽
254 困	269 受	284 過	299 連	314 花	329 図	344 辛
255 怒	270 取	285 捨	300 絡	315 薬	330 館	345 甘
256 押	271 合	286 発	301 濯	316 色	331 室	346 痛
257 引	272 吸	287 到	302 結	317 服	332 席	347 有
258 死	273 拾	288 計	303 婚	318 客	333 度	348 退
259 吹	274 誘	289 定	304 運	319 犬	334 機	349 屈
260 急	275 疲	290 注	305 案	320 文	335 場	350 同
261 咲	276 比	291 意	306 卒	321 物	336 県	
262 置	277 決	292 説	307 業	322 族	337 府	
263 勝	278 伝	293 解	308 用	323 公	338 都	
264 選	279 流	294 参	309 去	324 園	339 暖	
265 飛	280 落	295 加	310 趣	325 医	340 涼	

第 3 水 準　　　　850字／計1200字

351 平	359 単	367 寸	375 替	383 速	391 相	399 点
352 和	360 戦	368 支	376 賛	384 達	392 想	400 無
353 等	361 争	369 技	377 成	385 違	393 首	401 然
354 第	362 反	370 術	378 功	386 逆	394 身	402 当
355 筆	363 対	371 街	379 工	387 整	395 員	403 予
356 算	364 村	372 封	380 的	388 務	396 損	404 野
357 符	365 付	373 筒	381 約	389 省	397 別	405 原
358 簡	366 団	374 竹	382 束	390 談	398 特	406 因

407	正	443	労	479	尊	515	経	551	番	587	存	623	由
408	幾	444	協	480	導	516	済	552	郡	588	在	624	油
409	糸	445	門	481	停	517	活	553	州	589	禅	625	曲
410	級	446	関	482	件	518	法	554	欧	590	弾	626	農
411	能	447	係	483	牛	519	律	555	満	591	丸	627	濃
412	可	448	孫	484	馬	520	往	556	両	592	弓	628	豊
413	代	449	系	485	魚	521	復	557	向	593	矢	629	富
414	化	450	懸	486	鳥	522	複	558	周	594	失	630	典
415	他	451	態	487	鳴	523	雑	559	独	595	夫	631	興
416	仏	452	池	488	羊	524	誌	560	狭	596	妻	632	己
417	位	453	湖	489	群	525	勤	561	肉	597	婦	633	記
418	供	454	海	490	毛	526	難	562	米	598	姓	634	紀
419	共	455	島	491	羽	527	漢	563	類	599	嫁	635	組
420	以	456	岸	492	翌	528	字	564	種	600	婿	636	素
421	性	457	岩	493	義	529	数	565	科	601	娘	637	麦
422	不	458	谷	494	議	530	政	566	芸	602	良	638	責
423	必	459	林	495	講	531	治	567	草	603	飾	639	任
424	要	460	森	496	論	532	台	568	芝	604	飯	640	信
425	価	461	空	497	倫	533	路	569	葉	605	坂	641	徒
426	値	462	天	498	輪	534	戸	570	荷	606	皆	642	従
427	普	463	星	499	輸	535	居	571	預	607	階	643	得
428	昔	464	光	500	較	536	民	572	頼	608	段	644	徳
429	増	465	風	501	効	537	守	573	顔	609	役	645	聴
430	減	466	虫	502	果	538	宅	574	産	610	殺	646	舟
431	感	467	凡	503	郊	539	管	575	玉	611	設	647	船
432	留	468	冗	504	交	540	官	576	宝	612	施	648	般
433	貿	469	個	505	渉	541	庁	577	王	613	備	649	航
434	易	470	固	506	干	542	庭	578	現	614	準	650	億
435	量	471	豆	507	汗	543	床	579	皇	615	率	651	憶
436	裏	472	登	508	軒	544	庫	580	聖	616	演	652	漫
437	表	473	祭	509	形	545	廊	581	望	617	絵	653	慢
438	面	474	際	510	枠	546	郎	582	亡	618	給	654	情
439	最	475	察	511	械	547	市	583	未	619	声	655	慣
440	初	476	警	512	識	548	区	584	末	620	音	656	快
441	刀	477	驚	513	職	549	町	585	申	621	昨	657	適
442	号	478	敬	514	就	550	丁	586	神	622	暇	658	敵

659 欠	695 介	731 緑	767 提	803 確	839 温	875 炭
660 次	696 招	732 縁	768 拡	804 権	840 泉	876 鉱
661 姿	697 委	733 納	769 抜	805 観	841 線	877 精
662 冷	698 季	734 絶	770 振	806 視	842 雪	878 請
663 句	699 節	735 総	771 打	807 規	843 雷	879 育
664 旬	700 即	736 為	772 折	808 則	844 雲	880 絹
665 保	701 企	737 老	773 採	809 側	845 霧	881 綿
666 証	702 歯	738 孝	774 菜	810 測	846 露	882 織
667 許	703 歳	739 才	775 指	811 例	847 震	883 編
668 認	704 歴	740 材	776 揮	812 列	848 厚	884 縮
669 課	705 史	741 財	777 輝	813 殊	849 宴	885 績
670 税	706 央	742 貯	778 軍	814 示	850 宣	886 積
671 程	707 非	743 蓄	779 隊	815 禁	851 各	887 布
672 実	708 常	744 氏	780 衛	816 宗	852 格	888 希
673 美	709 堂	745 底	781 防	817 完	853 資	889 衣
674 差	710 党	746 抵	782 坊	818 了	854 源	890 依
675 養	711 賞	747 抗	783 訪	819 承	855 貴	891 報
676 善	712 償	748 接	784 妨	820 浮	856 賃	892 告
677 様	713 与	749 換	785 害	821 乳	857 貨	893 吉
678 植	714 券	750 条	786 割	822 礼	858 費	894 幸
679 極	715 巻	751 契	787 憲	823 祈	859 貧	895 福
680 端	716 角	752 喫	788 毒	824 祖	860 乏	896 祉
681 需	717 負	753 潔	789 危	825 査	861 額	897 幅
682 器	718 敗	754 清	790 険	826 助	862 願	898 副
683 品	719 貝	755 士	791 剣	827 努	863 塾	899 判
684 商	720 具	756 志	792 検	828 収	864 熟	900 断
685 袋	721 散	757 恩	793 験	829 状	865 勢	901 継
686 製	722 故	758 忠	794 騒	830 将	866 熱	902 繰
687 制	723 放	759 恐	795 試	831 奨	867 昭	903 燥
688 誕	724 敷	760 翻	796 式	832 励	868 照	904 乾
689 延	725 致	761 訳	797 専	833 陸	869 黙	905 江
690 期	726 改	762 尺	798 博	834 陽	870 燃	906 波
691 基	727 配	763 釈	799 薄	835 傷	871 灯	907 汚
692 礎	728 酔	764 択	800 夢	836 湯	872 畑	908 染
693 疑	729 針	765 描	801 葬	837 混	873 災	909 港
694 紹	730 録	766 拝	802 蒸	838 湿	874 灰	910 湾

307

911	浜	947	謝	983	杯	1019	賀	1055	建	1091	属	1127	河
912	沖	948	評	984	札	1020	競	1056	築	1092	展	1128	沿
913	波	949	誤	985	析	1021	景	1057	策	1093	殿	1129	沈
914	漁	950	誇	986	核	1022	影	1058	籍	1094	凍	1130	没
915	鯨	951	訓	987	板	1023	響	1059	筋	1095	氷	1131	添
916	鮮	952	順	988	棒	1024	郷	1060	箱	1096	永	1132	歓
917	洋	953	序	989	柄	1025	里	1061	範	1097	久	1133	迎
918	卸	954	秩	990	柱	1026	童	1062	囲	1098	及	1134	仰
919	御	955	矛	991	構	1027	章	1063	雰	1099	幼	1135	卵
920	缶	956	盾	992	再	1028	障	1064	井	1100	稚	1136	印
921	益	957	掃	993	黄	1029	壁	1065	帯	1101	移	1137	刷
922	盛	958	除	994	兵	1030	卓	1066	帝	1102	秘	1138	刊
923	盟	959	余	995	靴	1031	著	1067	締	1103	密	1139	刻
924	塩	960	途	996	革	1032	諸	1068	純	1104	骨	1140	劇
925	監	961	込	997	命	1033	緒	1069	粋	1105	胃	1141	仮
926	督	962	辺	998	令	1034	鏡	1070	迷	1106	腸	1142	版
927	皿	963	述	999	領	1035	環	1071	惑	1107	肝	1143	片
928	血	964	迫	1000	統	1036	境	1072	域	1108	臓	1144	皮
929	宮	965	造	1001	補	1037	破	1073	越	1109	脳	1145	被
930	営	966	追	1002	佐	1038	壊	1074	超	1110	悩	1146	彼
931	辞	967	師	1003	臣	1039	激	1075	赴	1111	蔵	1147	徹
932	乱	968	桜	1004	巨	1040	攻	1076	更	1112	倉	1148	徴
933	求	969	梅	1005	拒	1041	撃	1077	恵	1113	創	1149	微
934	救	970	松	1006	否	1042	襲	1078	恋	1114	看	1150	妙
935	球	971	桃	1007	距	1043	暴	1079	愛	1115	護	1151	秒
936	儀	972	枝	1008	離	1044	爆	1080	互	1116	弁	1152	砂
937	犠	973	株	1009	推	1045	煙	1081	涙	1117	念	1153	劣
938	牲	974	根	1010	哲	1046	犯	1082	房	1118	息	1154	勇
939	象	975	限	1011	揭	1047	罪	1083	雇	1119	応	1155	募
940	像	976	眼	1012	抱	1048	逮	1084	肩	1120	寄	1156	墓
941	免	977	睡	1013	包	1049	捕	1085	背	1121	突	1157	幕
942	城	978	眠	1014	均	1050	担	1086	胸	1122	穴	1158	暮
943	誠	979	瞬	1015	射	1051	批	1087	腰	1123	容	1159	漠
944	詳	980	隣	1016	占	1052	刑	1088	腹	1124	欲	1160	模
945	詩	981	舞	1017	況	1053	健	1089	豚	1125	裕	1161	概
946	討	982	枚	1018	祝	1054	康	1090	届	1126	浴	1162	既

1163 裁	1169 仲	1175 修	1181 献	1187 繁	1193 閣	1199 票
1164 我	1170 促	1176 偏	1182 僚	1188 栄	1194 衆	1200 標
1165 武	1171 秀	1177 遍	1183 寮	1189 挙	1195 略	
1166 輩	1172 似	1178 遇	1184 帳	1190 厳	1196 異	
1167 俳	1173 傾	1179 遺	1185 張	1191 派	1197 圧	
1168 優	1174 候	1180 貢	1186 緊	1192 閥	1198 至	

第 4 水 準　　220字／計1420字

1201 戻	1228 堅	1255 拍	1282 糧	1309 硬	1336 鈴	1363 症
1202 丘	1229 臨	1256 摘	1283 糖	1310 柔	1337 鋼	1364 癖
1203 匹	1230 幹	1257 握	1284 粧	1311 炊	1338 鎖	1365 避
1204 司	1231 稿	1258 探	1285 臭	1312 冊	1339 鉛	1366 恥
1205 詞	1232 稼	1259 掘	1286 鼻	1313 盤	1340 銅	1367 患
1206 訂	1233 稲	1260 堀	1287 憩	1314 盆	1341 胴	1368 菌
1207 訴	1234 穏	1261 埋	1288 舌	1315 煮	1342 腕	1369 荘
1208 訟	1235 隠	1262 排	1289 君	1316 署	1343 肺	1370 装
1209 譲	1236 隔	1263 拓	1290 含	1317 罰	1344 胆	1371 裂
1210 購	1237 融	1264 抑	1291 叫	1318 型	1345 肌	1372 鈍
1211 廷	1238 邸	1265 拐	1292 奇	1319 刺	1346 飢	1373 鋭
1212 処	1239 隅	1266 扱	1293 崎	1320 削	1347 餓	1374 克
1213 拠	1240 偶	1267 撮	1294 峡	1321 剰	1348 飼	1375 児
1214 遣	1241 僕	1268 挑	1295 紅	1322 垂	1349 旨	1376 旧
1215 還	1242 偉	1269 兆	1296 繊	1323 華	1350 脂	1377 慮
1216 逐	1243 俗	1270 援	1297 維	1324 兼	1351 肪	1378 寧
1217 遂	1244 侵	1271 緩	1298 紛	1325 嫌	1352 肥	1379 寛
1218 墜	1245 伺	1272 丈	1299 紳	1326 尋	1353 脈	1380 寂
1219 悔	1246 伸	1273 牧	1300 縦	1327 寿	1354 膨	1381 孤
1220 慎	1247 倣	1274 畜	1301 索	1328 闘	1355 肢	1382 触
1221 頻	1248 催	1275 充	1302 累	1329 娯	1356 枯	1383 踊
1222 項	1249 債	1276 玄	1303 畳	1330 妊	1357 杉	1384 躍
1223 販	1250 併	1277 豪	1304 翼	1331 娠	1358 彫	1385 焦
1224 贈	1251 圏	1278 盲	1305 裸	1332 妥	1359 髪	1386 駐
1225 賄	1252 宇	1279 帽	1306 軌	1333 威	1360 珍	1387 循
1226 賂	1253 宙	1280 昇	1307 載	1334 戒	1361 診	1388 衝
1227 賢	1254 抽	1281 曇	1308 軟	1335 釣	1362 療	1389 征

1390 徐	1395 沢	1400 渋	1405 履	1410 猫	1415 摩	1420 酸
1391 斜	1396 洪	1401 淡	1406 奮	1411 薦	1416 擦	
1392 滑	1397 津	1402 滞	1407 奪	1412 廃	1417 邪	
1393 潜	1398 浪	1403 肯	1408 獲	1413 庶	1418 魔	
1394 渇	1399 汁	1404 齢	1409 穫	1414 麻	1419 魅	

第 5 水準　　412字／計1832字

1421 伏	1449 衡	1477 掛	1505 漆	1533 棟	1561 糾	1589 軸
1422 伐	1450 怪	1478 挿	1506 漬	1534 棺	1562 紺	1590 轄
1423 伴	1451 怖	1479 控	1507 漂	1535 棋	1563 紡	1591 酌
1424 俊	1452 恨	1480 据	1508 潮	1536 棚	1564 紋	1592 酢
1425 倹	1453 悦	1481 揚	1509 潤	1537 槽	1565 絞	1593 酪
1426 俵	1454 悟	1482 摂	1510 澄	1538 欄	1566 綱	1594 酬
1427 俸	1455 惜	1483 搭	1511 濁	1539 殉	1567 網	1595 酵
1428 偽	1456 悼	1484 搾	1512 濫	1540 殖	1568 縄	1596 酷
1429 傍	1457 惨	1485 操	1513 狂	1541 班	1569 縛	1597 鉢
1430 僧	1458 愉	1486 携	1514 狩	1542 祥	1570 緯	1598 銭
1431 傑	1459 慌	1487 搬	1515 猟	1543 禍	1571 縫	1599 銃
1432 吐	1460 惰	1488 撤	1516 猛	1544 胎	1572 繕	1600 銘
1433 唆	1461 慨	1489 撲	1517 猶	1545 脚	1573 舶	1601 鋳
1434 喝	1462 憎	1490 擁	1518 獄	1546 膜	1574 託	1602 錬
1435 喚	1463 懐	1491 汽	1519 阻	1547 騰	1575 詐	1603 錯
1436 嘆	1464 憾	1492 泌	1520 附	1548 眺	1576 詰	1604 錠
1437 嘱	1465 抄	1493 泥	1521 陛	1549 矯	1577 該	1605 鍛
1438 塔	1466 扶	1494 沸	1522 陥	1550 砕	1578 諾	1606 鎮
1439 塀	1467 把	1495 浄	1523 陣	1551 硫	1579 諭	1607 鐘
1440 壇	1468 披	1496 浸	1524 陳	1552 硝	1580 諮	1608 鑑
1441 如	1469 拘	1497 涯	1525 陰	1553 礁	1581 謙	1609 剖
1442 姻	1470 拙	1498 渦	1526 陶	1554 称	1582 謹	1610 駄
1443 岐	1471 抹	1499 溝	1527 旋	1555 襟	1583 譜	1611 駆
1444 帆	1472 括	1500 滅	1528 旗	1556 褐	1584 賊	1612 刈
1445 壮	1473 挟	1501 溶	1529 朴	1557 粉	1585 賦	1613 剛
1446 弦	1474 拷	1502 漏	1530 枢	1558 粒	1586 跳	1614 劾
1447 弧	1475 捜	1503 漸	1531 栓	1559 粘	1587 跡	1615 勧
1448 径	1476 措	1504 滴	1532 桟	1560 粗	1588 践	1616 却

1617	叙	1648	顧	1679	奏	1710	薫	1741	虚	1772	享	1803	炎
1618	耐	1649	嬢	1680	泰	1711	紫	1742	膚	1773	郭	1804	哀
1619	彩	1650	壌	1681	笛	1712	誓	1743	巡	1774	刃	1805	衰
1620	彰	1651	醸	1682	箇	1713	誉	1744	迅	1775	忍	1806	衷
1621	邦	1652	亭	1683	篤	1714	貫	1745	迭	1776	滋	1807	喪
1622	敢	1653	棄	1684	簿	1715	匠	1746	透	1777	磁	1808	晶
1623	欺	1654	舎	1685	覇	1716	匿	1747	逝	1778	慈	1809	唱
1624	款	1655	傘	1686	覆	1717	囚	1748	逸	1779	斉	1810	尚
1625	殴	1656	冠	1687	零	1718	閑	1749	遮	1780	剤	1811	肖
1626	殻	1657	呈	1688	霊	1719	閲	1750	遭	1781	斎	1812	凶
1627	穀	1658	宜	1689	霜	1720	暦	1751	遵	1782	耕	1813	丹
1628	朗	1659	宰	1690	啓	1721	厄	1752	鬼	1783	耗	1814	幻
1629	泡	1660	寡	1691	召	1722	尼	1753	塊	1784	垣	1815	弔
1630	胞	1661	審	1692	墾	1723	尾	1754	魂	1785	恒	1816	甲
1631	砲	1662	賓	1693	堕	1724	尿	1755	醜	1786	巧	1817	斥
1632	飽	1663	崩	1694	塗	1725	層	1756	甚	1787	朽	1818	亜
1633	噴	1664	崇	1695	墨	1726	尽	1757	勘	1788	謡	1819	奔
1634	憤	1665	芳	1696	妄	1727	唐	1758	堪	1789	揺	1820	幽
1635	准	1666	荒	1697	忌	1728	庸	1759	某	1790	凝	1821	栽
1636	唯	1667	菓	1698	怠	1729	廉	1760	媒	1791	擬	1822	瓶
1637	雄	1668	慕	1699	悠	1730	腐	1761	謀	1792	随	1823	執
1638	雅	1669	冒	1700	愁	1731	磨	1762	又	1793	髄	1824	粛
1639	雌	1670	是	1701	愚	1732	慶	1763	双	1794	唇	1825	蛮
1640	培	1671	罷	1702	慰	1733	扇	1764	貞	1795	辱	1826	疎
1641	陪	1672	羅	1703	懲	1734	扉	1765	偵	1796	幣	1827	鼓
1642	賠	1673	窃	1704	架	1735	疫	1766	叔	1797	弊	1828	碁
1643	頂	1674	室	1705	香	1736	疾	1767	淑	1798	墾	1829	憂
1644	頑	1675	窮	1706	暫	1737	痢	1768	朱	1799	懇	1830	舗
1645	頒	1676	蛍	1707	脅	1738	痴	1769	珠	1800	敏	1831	覧
1646	煩	1677	掌	1708	烈	1739	癒	1770	卑	1801	侮	1832	麗
1647	顕	1678	奉	1709	勲	1740	虐	1771	碑	1802	炉		

第 6 水 準　　　　　　　　110字／計1942字

1833	菊	1835	芽	1837	苗	1839	藻	1841	滝	1843	渓	1845	瀬
1834	芋	1836	茎	1838	薪	1840	茂	1842	沼	1844	洞	1846	浦

1847 潟	1861 蛇	1875 爵	1889 塚	1903 韻	1917 隻	1931 恭
1848 峰	1862 巣	1876 侯	1890 藩	1904 吟	1918 斗	1932 詔
1849 峠	1863 鶏	1877 伯	1891 儒	1905 詠	1919 凸	1933 褒
1850 岬	1864 獣	1878 侍	1892 艦	1906 琴	1920 凹	1934 謄
1851 岳	1865 猿	1879 仁	1893 租	1907 宵	1921 但	1935 朕
1852 堤	1866 蚕	1880 仙	1894 帥	1908 乙	1922 且	1936 畝
1853 樹	1867 竜	1881 孔	1895 勅	1909 丙	1923 嚇	1937 翁
1854 柳	1868 姫	1882 尉	1896 遷	1910 厘	1924 隆	1938 逓
1855 桑	1869 妃	1883 吏	1897 赦	1911 壱	1925 坑	1939 塑
1856 穂	1870 嫡	1884 虜	1898 賜	1912 弐	1926 呉	1940 虞
1857 畔	1871 奴	1885 嗣	1899 謁	1913 坪	1927 艇	1941 繭
1858 暁	1872 隷	1886 陵	1900 窯	1914 斤	1928 佳	1942 璽
1859 昆	1873 后	1887 楼	1901 戯	1915 升	1929 痘	
1860 蚊	1874 騎	1888 墳	1902 婆	1916 屯	1930 曹	

第 7 水準　　194字／計2136字

1943 茨	1962 串	1981 挫	2000 熊	2019 駒	2038 旦	2057 拉
1944 栃	1963 箸	1982 痩	2001 哺	2020 呂	2039 宛	2058 乞
1945 埼	1964 丼	1983 箋	2002 牙	2021 巾	2040 隙	2059 蹴
1946 阜	1965 釜	1984 唾	2003 亀	2022 袖	2041 脇	2060 剝
1947 奈	1966 鍋	1985 咽	2004 鶴	2023 裾	2042 桁	2061 斬
1948 阪	1967 煎	1986 喉	2005 蜂	2024 籠	2043 毀	2062 俺
1949 岡	1968 膳	1987 腎	2006 虹	2025 蓋	2044 錮	2063 傲
1950 媛	1969 眉	1988 脊	2007 嵐	2026 芯	2045 勾	2064 遜
1951 畿	1970 瞳	1989 腺	2008 崖	2027 瓦	2046 賭	2065 辣
1952 鎌	1971 頬	1990 腫	2009 麓	2028 鍵	2047 醒	2066 凄
1953 弥	1972 顎	1991 骸	2010 窟	2029 枕	2048 溺	2067 貪
1954 韓	1973 拳	1992 瘍	2011 葛	2030 柵	2049 綻	2068 旺
1955 柿	1974 爪	1993 痕	2012 藤	2031 椅	2050 踪	2069 淫
1956 梨	1975 臼	1994 斑	2013 藍	2032 舷	2051 謎	2070 艶
1957 蜜	1976 肘	1995 潰	2014 堆	2033 挨	2052 蔽	2071 妖
1958 麺	1977 股	1996 椎	2015 湧	2034 拶	2053 詮	2072 貌
1959 餅	1978 膝	1997 梗	2016 沃	2035 沙	2054 匂	2073 摯
1960 餌	1979 尻	1998 鹿	2017 闇	2036 汰	2055 嗅	2074 爽
1961 酎	1980 捻	1999 虎	2018 玩	2037 頃	2056 狙	2075 璧

2076	憧	2085	頓	2094	弄	2103	羞	2112	那	2121	戚	2130	璃
2077	憬	2086	汎	2095	嘲	2104	鬱	2113	恣	2122	冥	2131	稽
2078	拭	2087	勃	2096	萎	2105	須	2114	僅	2123	侶	2132	喩
2079	貼	2088	捗	2097	叱	2106	汎	2115	苛	2124	訃	2133	彙
2080	捉	2089	采	2098	罵	2107	曖	2116	慄	2125	諧	2134	錦
2081	冶	2090	羨	2099	呪	2108	昧	2117	畏	2126	楷	2135	睦
2082	詣	2091	嫉	2100	怨	2109	瞭	2118	萎	2127	伎	2136	戴
2083	遡	2092	妬	2101	臆	2110	緻	2119	塞	2128	唄		
2084	塡	2093	惧	2102	諦	2111	刹	2120	曽	2129	瑠		

音訓索引

（*On-kun* Index）

All the reading for *kanji* entries are listed in *a-i-u-e-o* order with the corresponding *kanji* and *kanji* number.
On-readings are indicated in bold type, and *kun*-readings are in regular type.

あ				握	1257	あたたまる	温まる	839	あまえる	甘える	345
			あく	明く	106		暖まる	339	あます	余す	959
あ	亜	1818		空く	461	あたためる	温める	839	あまやかす	甘やかす	345
あい	哀	1804		開く	215		暖める	339	あまる	余る	959
	挨	2033	あくる	明くる	106	あたま	頭	166	あみ	網	1567
	愛	1079	あける	明ける	106	あたらしい	新しい	85	あむ	編む	883
	曖	2107		空ける	461	あたり	辺り	962	あめ	天	462
あい	相	391		開ける	215	あたる	当たる	402		雨	232
	藍	2013	あげる	上げる	31	**あつ**	圧	1197	あやうい	危うい	789
あいだ	間	161		挙げる	1189	あつい	厚い	848	あやしい	妖しい	2071
あう	会う	59		揚げる	1481		暑い	119		怪しい	1450
	合う	271	あご	顎	1972		熱い	866	あやしむ	怪しむ	1450
	遭う	1750	あこがれる	憧れる	2076	あつかう	扱う	1266	あやつる	操る	1485
あお	青	47	あさ	麻	1414	あつまる	集まる	224	あやぶむ	危ぶむ	789
あおい	青い	47		朝	91	あつめる	集める	224	あやまち	過ち	284
あおぐ	仰ぐ	1134	あざ	字	528	あてる	当てる	402	あやまつ	過つ	284
あか	赤	46	あさい	浅い	122		充てる	1275	あやまる	誤る	949
あかい	赤い	46	あざける	嘲る	2095		宛てる	2039		謝る	947
あかす	明かす	106	あざむく	欺く	1623	あと	後	30	あゆむ	歩む	176
	飽かす	1632	あざやか	鮮やか	916		痕	1993	あらい	荒い	1666
あかつき	暁	1858	あし	足	171		跡	1587		粗い	1560
あからむ	赤らむ	46		脚	1545	あな	穴	1122	あらう	洗う	198
	明らむ	106	あじ	味	311	あなどる	侮る	1801	あらし	嵐	2007
あからめる	赤らめる	46	あじわう	味わう	311	あに	兄	75	あらす	荒らす	1666
あかり	明かり	106	あずかる	預かる	571	あね	姉	77	あらそう	争う	361
あがる	上がる	31	あずける	預ける	571	あばく	暴く	1043	あらた	新た	85
	挙がる	1189	あせ	汗	507	あばれる	暴れる	1043	あらたまる	改まる	726
	揚がる	1481	あせる	焦る	1385	あびせる	浴びせる	1126	あらためる	改める	726
あかるい	明るい	106	あそぶ	遊ぶ	196	あびる	浴びる	1126	あらわす	表す	437
あかるむ	明るむ	106	あたい	価	425	あぶない	危ない	789		現す	578
あき	秋	98		値	426	あぶら	油	624		著す	1031
あきなう	商う	684					脂	1350	あらわれる	表れる	437
あきらか	明らか	106	あたえる	与える	713	あま	天	462		現れる	578
あきらめる	諦める	2102	あたたか	温か	839		尼	1722	ある	有る	347
あきる	飽きる	1632		暖か	339		雨	232		在る	588
あく	悪	114	あたたかい	温かい	839	あまい	甘い	345	あるく	歩く	176
				暖かい	339						

あれる	荒れる	1666	いえる	癒える	1739	いつつ	五つ	5		隠	1235
あわ	泡	1629	いかす	生かす	49	いつわる	偽る	1428		韻	1903
あわい	淡い	1401	いかる	怒る	255	いと	糸	409
あわす	合わす	271	いき	域	1072	いとなむ	営む	930

あわせる	合わせる	271	いき	粋	1069	いどむ	挑む	1268	う	右	35
	併せる	1250		息	1118	いな	否	1006		有	347
あわただしい	慌ただしい	1459	いきおい	勢い	865		稲	1233		羽	491
あわてる	慌てる	1459	いきどおる	憤る	1634	いぬ	犬	319		宇	1252
あわれ	哀れ	1804	いきる	生きる	49	いね	稲	1233		雨	232
あわれむ	哀れむ	1804	いく	育	879	いのち	命	997	うい	初	440
あん	行	58	いく	行く	58	いのる	祈る	823		憂い	1829
	安	84		逝く	1747	いばら	茨	1943	うえ	上	31
	案	305		幾	408	いま	今	27	うえる	飢える	1346
	暗	107	いくさ	戦	360	いましめる	戒める	1334		植える	678

			いけ	池	452	いまわしい	忌まわしい	1697	うお	魚	485
い	以	420	いける	生ける	49	いむ	忌む	1697	うかがう	伺う	1245
	衣	889	いこい	憩い	1287	いも	芋	1834	うかぶ	浮かぶ	820
	医	325	いこう	憩う	1287	いもうと	妹	78	うかべる	浮かべる	820
	位	417	いさぎよい	潔い	753	いや	嫌	1325	うかる	受かる	269
	囲	1062	いさむ	勇む	1154	いやしい	卑しい	1770	うかれる	浮かれる	820
	易	434	いし	石	102	いやしむ	卑しむ	1770	うく	浮く	820
	委	697	いしずえ	礎	692	いやしめる	卑しめる	1770	うけたまわる	承る	819
	依	890	いずみ	泉	840	いやす	癒やす	1739	うける	受ける	269
	為	736	いそがしい	忙しい	126	いる	入る	186		請ける	878
	胃	1105	いそぐ	急ぐ	260		居る	535	うごかす	動かす	64
	威	1333	いた	板	987		要る	424	うごく	動く	64
	畏	2117	いたい	痛い	346		射る	1015	うし	牛	483
	移	1101	いだく	抱く	1012		煎る	1967	うじ	氏	744
	異	1196	いたす	致す	725		鋳る	1601	うしなう	失う	594
	唯	1636	いただき	頂	1643	いれる	入れる	186	うしろ	後ろ	30
	尉	1882	いただく	頂く	1643	いろ	色	316	うす	臼	1975
	萎	2118	いたむ	悼む	1456	いろどる	彩る	1619	うず	渦	1498
	偉	1242		痛む	346	いわ	岩	457	うすい	薄い	799
	椅	2031		傷む	835	いわう	祝う	1018	うすまる	薄まる	799
	意	291	いためる	痛める	346	いん	引	257	うすめる	薄める	799
	違	385		傷める	835		因	406	うすらぐ	薄らぐ	799
	彙	2133	いたる	至る	1198		印	1136	うすれる	薄れる	799
	維	1297	いち	一	1		音	620	うた	唄	2128
	遺	1179		壱	1911		姻	1442		歌	200
	慰	1702	いち	市	547		咽	1985	うたい	謡	1788
	緯	1570	いちじるしい	著しい	1031		院	230	うたう	歌う	200
い	井	1064	いつ	一	1		員	395		謡う	1788
いう	言う	203		逸	1748		陰	1525	うたがう	疑う	693
いえ	家	52	いつ	五	5		淫	2069	うち	内	152
			いつくしむ	慈しむ	1778		飲	132	うつ	鬱	2104

うつ	打つ	771	うれい	愁い	1700	えらい	偉い	1242		奥	71
	討つ	946		憂い	1829	えらぶ	選ぶ	264		横	34
	撃つ	1041	うれえる	愁える	1700	えり	襟	1555	おう	生う	49
うつくしい	美しい	673		憂える	1829	える	得る	643		負う	717
うつす	写す	194	うれる	売れる	187		獲る	1408		追う	966
	映す	234		熟れる	864	えん	円	14	おうぎ	扇	1733
	移す	1101	うわ	上	31		延	689	おえる	終える	130
うったえる	訴える	1207	うわる	植わる	678		沿	1128	おお	大	87
うつる	写る	194	うん	運	304		炎	1803	おおい	多い	104
	映る	234		雲	844		怨	2100	おおいに	大いに	87
	移る	1101					宴	849	おおう	覆う	1686
うつわ	器	682	**え**				援	1270	おおきい	大きい	87
うで	腕	1342	え	会	59		媛	1950	おおせ	仰せ	1134
うとい	疎い	1826		回	162		遠	110	おおやけ	公	323
うとむ	疎む	1826		依	890		園	324	おか	丘	1202
うながす	促す	1170		恵	1077		塩	924		岡	1949
うね	畝	1936		絵	617		煙	1045	おかす	犯す	1046
うばう	奪う	1407	え	江	905		鉛	1339		侵す	1244
うぶ	産	574		重	115		猿	1865		冒す	1669
うま	馬	484		柄	989		演	616	おがむ	拝む	766
うまる	埋まる	1261		餌	1960		縁	732	おき	沖	912
うまれる	生まれる	49	えい	永	1096		艶	2070	おぎなう	補う	1001
	産まれる	574		英	155				おきる	起きる	128
うみ	海	454		泳	193	**お**			おく	屋	54
うむ	生む	49		映	234	お	汚	907		億	650
	産む	574		栄	1188		和	352		憶	651
うめ	梅	969		営	930		悪	114		臆	2101
うめる	埋める	1261		詠	1905	お	小	88	おく	奥	71
うもれる	埋もれる	1261		影	1022		尾	1723		置く	262
うやうやしい	恭しい	1931		鋭	1373		雄	1637	おくらす	遅らす	118
うやまう	敬う	478		衛	780		緒	1033	おくる	送る	206
うら	浦	1846	えがく	描く	765	おいる	老いる	737		贈る	1224
	裏	436	えき	役	609	おう	王	577	おくれる	後れる	30
うらなう	占う	1016		易	434		央	706		遅れる	118
うらむ	恨む	1452		疫	1735		凹	1920	おこす	起こす	128
うらめしい	恨めしい	1452		益	921		応	1119		興す	631
うらやましい	羨ましい	2090		液	906		押	256	おごそか	厳か	1190
うらやむ	羨む	2090		駅	56		往	520	おこたる	怠る	1698
うる	売る	187	えさ	餌	1960		欧	554	おこなう	行う	58
	得る	643	えだ	枝	972		殴	1625	おこる	怒る	255
うるおう	潤う	1509	えつ	悦	1453		旺	2068		起こる	128
うるおす	潤す	1509		越	1073		皇	579		興る	631
うるし	漆	1505		閲	1719		桜	968	おさえる	抑える	1264
うるむ	潤む	1509		謁	1899		翁	1937		押さえる	256
うるわしい	麗しい	1832	えむ	笑む	251		黄	993	おさない	幼い	1099

おさまる	収まる	828	おび	帯	1065		可	412	
	治まる	531	おびやかす	脅かす	1707		仮	1141	
	納まる	733	おびる	帯びる	1065		何	80	
	修まる	1175	おぼえる	覚える	208		花	314	
おさめる	収める	828	おぼれる	溺れる	2048		価	425	
	治める	531	おも	主	70		果	502	
	納める	733		面	438		河	1127	
	修める	1175	おもい	重い	115		佳	1928	
おしい	惜しい	1455	おもう	思う	202		苛	2115	
おしえる	教える	214	おもて	表	437		科	565	
おしむ	惜しむ	1455		面	438		架	1704	
おす	押す	256	おもむき	趣	310		家	52	
	推す	1009	おもむく	赴く	1075		夏	97	
	雄	1637	おや	親	249		荷	570	
おそい	遅い	118	およぐ	泳ぐ	193		華	1323	
おそう	襲う	1042	および	及び	1098		貨	857	
おそれ	虞	1940	およぶ	及ぶ	1098		菓	1667	
おそれる	畏れる	2117	およぼす	及ぼす	1098		過	284	
	恐れる	759	おり	折	772		渦	1498	
おそろしい	恐ろしい	759	おりる	下りる	32		嫁	599	
おそわる	教わる	214		降りる	136		暇	622	かい
おだやか	穏やか	1234	おる	折る	772		靴	995	がい
おちいる	陥る	1522		織る	882		禍	1543	
おちる	落ちる	280	おれ	俺	2062		歌	200	
おつ	乙	1908	おれる	折れる	772		寡	1660	
おっと	夫	595	おろか	愚か	1701		箇	1682	
おと	音	620	おろし	卸	918		課	669	
おとうと	弟	76	おろす	下ろす	32		稼	1232	
おどかす	脅かす	1707		卸す	918	か	日	16	
おとこ	男	67		降ろす	136		香	1705	
おとしいれる	陥れる	1522	おわる	終わる	130		蚊	1860	
おとす	落とす	280	おん	音	620		鹿	1998	
おどす	脅す	1707		怨	2100	が	牙	2002	かいこ
おとずれる	訪れる	783		恩	757		瓦	2027	かう
おどり	踊り	1383		温	839		我	1164	
おとる	劣る	1153		遠	110		画	235	
おどる	踊る	1383		穏	1234		芽	1835	かえす
	躍る	1384	おん	御	919		賀	1019	
おとろえる	衰える	1805	おんな	女	68		雅	1638	かえりみる
おどろかす	驚かす	477					餓	1347	
おどろく	驚く	477	**か**			かい	介	695	かえる
おなじ	同じ	350	か	下	32		会	59	
おに	鬼	1752		火	18		回	162	
おのおの	各	851		化	414		灰	874	
おのれ	己	632		加	295		快	656	

改	726	
戒	1334	
拐	1265	
怪	1450	
界	157	
海	454	
皆	606	
悔	1219	
械	511	
開	215	
街	371	
階	607	
絵	617	
解	293	
塊	1753	
楷	2126	
潰	1995	
壊	1038	
懐	1463	
諧	2125	
貝	719	
外	150	
劾	1614	
害	785	
涯	1497	
崖	2008	
街	371	
慨	1461	
該	1577	
蓋	2025	
概	1161	
骸	1991	
蚕	1866	
交う	504	
買う	188	
飼う	1348	
返す	184	
帰す	134	
省みる	389	
顧みる	1648	
代える	413	
返る	184	
変える	222	
帰る	134	
替える	375	

	換える	749		額	861	かたむける	傾ける	1173	かみなり	雷	843
かお	顔	573		顎	1972	かためる	固める	470	かめ	亀	2003
かおり	香り	1705	かくす	隠す	1235	かたよる	偏る	1176	かもす	醸す	1651
かおる	香る	1705	かくれる	隠れる	1235	かたらう	語らう	154	かよう	通う	204
	薫る	1710	かげ	陰	1525	かたる	語る	154	から	空	461
かかえる	抱える	1012		影	1022	かたわら	傍ら	1429		唐	1727
かかげる	掲げる	1011	がけ	崖	2008	かっ	合	271		殻	1626
かがみ	鏡	1034	かける	欠ける	659	かつ	活	517	がら	柄	989
かがやく	輝く	777		架ける	1704		括	1472	からい	辛い	344
かかり	係	447		掛ける	1477		渇	1394	からす	枯らす	1356
	掛	1477		駆ける	1611		喝	1434	からだ	体	165
かかる	係る	447		賭ける	2046		割	786	からまる	絡まる	300
	架かる	1704		懸ける	450		葛	2011	からむ	絡む	300
	掛かる	1477	かげる	陰る	1525		滑	1392	からめる	絡める	300
	懸かる	450	かご	籠	2024		褐	1556	かり	仮	1141
かかわる	関わる	446	かこう	囲う	1062		轄	1590		狩り	1514
かき	垣	1784	かこむ	囲む	1062	かつ	且つ	1922	かりる	借りる	182
	柿	1955	かさ	傘	1655		勝つ	263	かる	刈る	1612
かぎ	鍵	2028	かざ	風	465	がっ	合	271		狩る	1514
かぎる	限る	975	かさなる	重なる	115	がつ	月	17		駆る	1611
かく	各	851	かさねる	重ねる	115	かつぐ	担ぐ	1050	かるい	軽い	116
	角	716	かざる	飾る	603	かて	糧	1282	かれ	彼	1146
	画	235	かしこい	賢い	1227	かど	角	716	かれる	枯れる	1356
	拡	768	かしら	頭	166		門	445	かろやか	軽やか	116
	客	318	かす	貸す	183	かな	金	21	かわ	川	101
	革	996	かず	数	529	かなしい	悲しい	341		皮	1144
	格	852	かぜ	風	465	かなしむ	悲しむ	341		河	1127
	核	986	かせぐ	稼ぐ	1232	かなでる	奏でる	1679		革	996
	殻	1626	かぞえる	数える	529	かなめ	要	424	がわ	側	809
	郭	1773	かた	方	43	かならず	必ず	423	かわかす	乾かす	904
	覚	208		片	1143	かね	金	21	かわく	乾く	904
	較	500		形	509		鐘	1607		渇く	1394
	隔	1236		肩	1084	かねる	兼ねる	1324	かわす	交わす	504
	閣	1193		型	1318	かの	彼	1146	かわら	瓦	2027
	確	803		潟	1847	かぶ	株	973	かわる	代わる	413
	獲	1408	かたい	固い	470	かべ	壁	1029		変わる	222
	嚇	1923		堅い	1228	かま	釜	1965		替わる	375
	穫	1409		硬い	1309		窯	1900		換わる	749
かく	欠く	659		難い	526		鎌	1952	かん	干	506
	書く	181	かたき	敵	658	かまう	構う	991		甘	345
	描く	765	かたち	形	509	かまえる	構える	991		刊	1138
かぐ	嗅ぐ	2055	かたな	刀	441	かみ	上	31		甲	1816
がく	学	50	かたまり	塊	1753		神	586		汗	507
	岳	1851	かたまる	固まる	470		紙	243		缶	920
	楽	343	かたむく	傾く	1173		髪	1359		完	817

肝	1107		玩	2018		器	682	きびしい	厳しい	1190
官	540		眼	976		輝	777	きまる	決まる	277
巻	715		頑	1644		畿	1951	きみ	君	1289
看	1114		顔	573		機	334	きめる	決める	277
冠	1656	かんがえる	考える	212	き	騎	1874	きも	肝	1107
陥	1522	かんがみる	鑑みる	1608		木	20	きゃ	脚	1545
乾	904	かんばしい	芳しい	1665		生	49	きゃく	却	1616
患	1367	かんむり	冠	1656		黄	993		客	318
貫	1714				ぎ	技	369		脚	1545
勘	1757	**き**				宜	1658	ぎゃく	逆	386
寒	120					偽	1428		虐	1740
間	161	き	己	632		欺	1623	きゅう	九	9
換	749		机	38		義	493		弓	592
喚	1435		気	246		疑	693		久	1097
棺	1534		企	701		儀	936		及	1098
敢	1622		危	789		戯	1901		丘	1202
款	1624		伎	2127		犠	937		旧	1376
閑	1718		希	888		擬	1791		休	138
堪	1758		岐	1443		議	494		吸	272
感	431		汽	1491	きえる	消える	219		朽	1787
漢	527		忌	1697	きく	菊	1833		臼	1975
幹	1230		季	698	きく	利く	248		究	298
寛	1379		祈	823		効く	501		求	933
勧	1615		奇	1292		聞く	179		泣	252
関	446		紀	634		聴く	645		急	260
管	539		軌	1306	きこえる	聞こえる	179		級	410
慣	655		起	128	きざし	兆し	1269		糾	1561
監	925		帰	134	きざす	兆す	1269		宮	929
歓	1132		記	633	きざむ	刻む	1139		救	934
緩	1271		既	1162	きし	岸	456		球	935
館	330		飢	1346	きず	傷	835		給	618
還	1215		鬼	1752	きずく	築く	1056		嗅	2055
憾	1464		基	691	きせる	着せる	190		窮	1675
環	1035		規	807	きそう	競う	1020	ぎゅう	牛	483
簡	358		寄	1120	きた	北	42	きょ	去	309
観	805		亀	2003	きたえる	鍛える	1605		巨	1004
韓	1954		喜	253	きたす	来す	133		居	535
艦	1892		幾	408	きたない	汚い	907		拒	1005
鑑	1608		期	690	きたる	来る	133		拠	1213
かん	神	586	揮	776	きち	吉	893		挙	1189
がん	丸	591	貴	855	きつ	吉	893		許	667
	元	245	棋	1535		喫	752		虚	1741
	含	1290	棄	1653		詰	1576		距	1007
	岸	456	毀	2043	きぬ	絹	880	ぎょ	魚	485
	岩	457	旗	1528	きば	牙	2002		御	919

	漁	914	きり	霧	845		駆	1611	くむ	酌む	1591
きよい	清い	754	きる	切る	250	ぐ	具	720		組む	635
きょう	凶	1812		斬る	2061		惧	2093	くも	雲	844
	兄	75		着る	190		愚	1701	くもる	曇る	1281
	共	419	きれる	切れる	250	くいる	悔いる	1219	くやしい	悔しい	1219
	叫	1291	きわ	際	474	くう	空	461	くやむ	悔やむ	1219
	狂	1513	きわまる	極まる	679	くう	食う	131	くら	倉	1112
	京	233		窮まる	1675	ぐう	宮	929		蔵	1111
	供	418	きわみ	極み	679		偶	1240	くらい	位	417
	協	444	きわめる	究める	298		遇	1178		暗い	107
	況	1017		極める	679		隅	1239	くらう	食らう	131
	享	1772		窮める	1675	くき	茎	1836	くらす	暮らす	1158
	狭	560	きん	巾	2021	くさ	草	567	くらべる	比べる	276
	峡	1294		今	27	くさい	臭い	1285	くる	来る	133
	挟	1473		斤	1914	くさらす	腐らす	1730		繰る	902
	香	1705		近	109	くさり	鎖	1338	くるう	狂う	1513
	恐	759		均	1014	くさる	腐る	1730	くるおしい	狂おしい	1513
	胸	1086		金	21	くされる	腐れる	1730	くるしい	苦しい	342
	脅	1707		菌	1368	くし	串	1962	くるしむ	苦しむ	342
	恭	1931		勤	525	くじら	鯨	915	くるしめる	苦しめる	342
	強	111		筋	1059	くず	葛	2011	くるま	車	62
	教	214		琴	1906	くずす	崩す	1663	くれない	紅	1295
	経	515		禁	815	くすり	薬	315	くれる	暮れる	1158
	郷	1024		僅	2114	くずれる	崩れる	1663	くろ	黒	45
	境	1036		緊	1186	くせ	癖	1364	くろい	黒い	45
	橋	313		錦	2134	くだ	管	539	くわ	桑	1855
	興	631		謹	1582	くだく	砕く	1550	くわえる	加える	295
	矯	1549		襟	1555	くだける	砕ける	1550	くわしい	詳しい	944
	鏡	1034	ぎん	吟	1904	くださる	下さる	32	くわだてる	企てる	701
	競	1020		銀	57	くだす	下す	32	くわわる	加わる	295
	響	1023		**く**		くだる	下る	32	くん	君	1289
	驚	477				くち	口	167		訓	951
ぎょう	行	58	く	九	9	くちびる	唇	1794		勲	1709
	仰	1134		口	167	くちる	朽ちる	1787		薫	1710
	形	509		工	379	くつ	屈	349	ぐん	軍	778
	暁	1858		久	1097		掘	1259		郡	552
	業	307		区	548		窟	2010		群	489
	凝	1790		功	378	くつ	靴	995		**け**	
きょく	曲	625		句	663	くつがえす	覆す	1686			
	局	228		苦	342	くつがえる	覆る	1686	け	化	414
	極	679		供	418	くに	国	151		気	246
ぎょく	玉	575		紅	1295	くばる	配る	727		仮	1141
きよまる	清まる	754		庫	544	くび	首	393		家	52
きよめる	清める	754		宮	929	くま	熊	2000		華	1323
きらう	嫌う	1325		貢	1180	くみ	組	635		懸	450

け	毛	490		撃	1041		賢	1227		顧	1648
げ	下	32		劇	1140		謙	1581	こ	子	69
	牙	2002		激	1039		鍵	2028		小	88
	外	150	けす	消す	219		験	793		木	20
	夏	97	けずる	削る	1320		顕	1647		粉	1557
	解	293	けた	桁	2042		繭	1941		黄	993
けい	兄	75	けつ	欠	659		懸	450	ご	五	5
	刑	1052		穴	1122	げん	元	245		午	28
	系	449		血	928		幻	1814		互	1080
	形	509		決	277		玄	1276		呉	1926
	京	233		結	302		言	203		後	30
	径	1448		傑	1431		弦	1446		娯	1329
	茎	1836		潔	753		限	975		悟	1454
	計	288	げつ	月	17		原	405		期	690
	係	447	けむい	煙い	1045		現	578		御	919
	契	751	けむり	煙	1045		眼	976		碁	1828
	型	1318	けむる	煙る	1045		舷	2032		語	154
	恵	1077	けもの	獣	1864		減	430		誤	949
	経	515	ける	蹴る	2059		源	854		護	1115
	掲	1011	けわしい	険しい	790		嫌	1325	こい	恋	1078
	蛍	1676	けん	犬	319		厳	1190		濃い	627
	啓	1690		件	482		験	793	こいしい	恋しい	1078
	渓	1843		見	139				こう	口	167
	軽	116		券	714	**こ**				工	379
	敬	478		肩	1084	こ	己	632		公	323
	景	1021		研	297		戸	534		孔	1881
	継	901		県	336		古	86		勾	2045
	傾	1173		建	1055		去	309		広	113
	携	1486		軒	508		呼	197		功	378
	詣	2082		剣	791		固	470		巧	1786
	境	1036		兼	1324		拠	1213		甲	1816
	慶	1732		倹	1425		股	1977		行	58
	憬	2077		拳	1973		虎	1999		考	212
	稽	2131		険	790		故	722		好	244
	憩	1287		健	1053		枯	1356		光	464
	警	476		間	161		孤	1381		交	504
	鶏	1863		検	792		弧	1447		向	557
	競	1020		堅	1228		個	469		江	905
げい	芸	566		圏	1251		庫	544		仰	1134
	迎	1133		絹	880		虚	1741		后	1873
	鯨	915		献	1181		湖	453		孝	738
けがす	汚す	907		遣	1214		雇	1083		抗	747
けがらわしい	汚らわしい	907		嫌	1325		誇	950		攻	1040
けがれる	汚れる	907		権	804		鼓	1827		更	1076
げき	隙	2040		憲	787		錮	2044		坑	1925

	効	501		神	586	こたえ	答え	213		困	254
	幸	894		恋う	1078	こたえる	応える	1119		金	21
	肯	1403		請う	878		答える	213		昆	1859
	拘	1469	ごう	号	442	こつ	骨	1104		建	1055
	後	30		合	271		滑	1392		恨	1452
	郊	503		拷	1474	こと	言	203		根	974
	皇	579		剛	1613		事	237		婚	303
	厚	848		強	111		殊	813		混	837
	紅	1295		郷	1024		異	1196		紺	1562
	洪	1396		業	307		琴	1906		痕	1993
	荒	1666		傲	2063	ことぶき	寿	1327		献	1181
	香	1705		豪	1277	ことわる	断る	900		魂	1754
	恒	1785	こうむる	被る	1145	こな	粉	1557		墾	1798
	侯	1876	こえ	声	619	このむ	好む	244		懇	1799
	校	51		肥	1352	こばむ	拒む	1005	ごん	言	203
	高	83	こえる	肥える	1352	こぶし	拳	1973		勤	525
	降	136		越える	1073	こま	駒	2019		権	804
	航	649		超える	1074	こまか	細か	123		厳	1190
	格	852	こおり	氷	1095	こまかい	細かい	123			
	候	1174	こおる	凍る	1094	こまる	困る	254		**さ**	
	貢	1180	こがす	焦がす	1385	こむ	込む	961	さ	左	36
	耕	1782	こがれる	焦がれる	1385		混む	837		再	992
	耗	1783	こく	石	102	こめ	米	562		作	137
	黄	993		谷	458	こめる	込める	961		佐	1002
	康	1054		告	892	こもる	籠もる	2024		沙	2035
	控	1479		克	1374	こやし	肥やし	1352		茶	145
	梗	1997		国	151	こやす	肥やす	1352		査	825
	港	909		刻	1139	こよみ	暦	1720		砂	1152
	項	1222		黒	45	こらしめる	懲らしめる	1703		差	674
	硬	1309		酷	1596	こらす	凝らす	1790		唆	1433
	慌	1459		穀	1627		懲らす	1703		詐	1575
	絞	1565	ごく	極	679	こりる	懲りる	1703		鎖	1338
	喉	1986		獄	1518	こる	凝る	1790	ざ	座	175
	鉱	876	こげる	焦げる	1385	ころ	頃	2037		挫	1981
	溝	1499	こごえる	凍える	1094	ころがす	転がす	65	さい	才	739
	構	991	ここの	九	9	ころがる	転がる	65		切	250
	綱	1566	ここのつ	九つ	9	ころげる	転げる	65		西	40
	酵	1595	こころ	心	172	ころす	殺す	610		再	992
	稿	1231	こころざし	志	756	ころぶ	転ぶ	65		災	873
	興	631	こころざす	志す	756	ころも	衣	889		妻	596
	鋼	1337	こころみる	試みる	795	こわ	声	619		采	2089
	衡	1449	こころよい	快い	656	こわい	怖い	1451		砕	1550
	講	495	こし	腰	1087	こわす	壊す	1038		殺	610
	購	1210	こす	越す	1073	こわれる	壊れる	1038		財	741
こう	乞う	2058		超す	1074	こん	今	27		宰	1659

	栽	1821		索	1301	さび	寂	1380	
	細	123		策	1057	さびしい	寂しい	1380	
	祭	473		酢	1592	さびれる	寂れる	1380	
	済	516		搾	1484	さま	様	677	
	採	773		錯	1603	さます	冷ます	662	
	菜	774	さく	咲く	261		覚ます	208	
	彩	1619		割く	786	さまたげる	妨げる	784	
	斎	1781		裂く	1371	さむい	寒い	120	
	最	439	さくら	桜	968	さむらい	侍	1878	
	裁	1163	さぐる	探る	1258	さめる	冷める	662	
	歳	703	さけ	酒	144		覚める	208	
	催	1248	さげすむ	蔑む	2096	さら	皿	927	
	債	1249	さけぶ	叫ぶ	1291		更	1076	
	載	1307	さける	裂ける	1371	さる	去る	309	
	塞	2119		避ける	1365		猿	1865	
	際	474	さげる	下げる	32	さわ	沢	1395	
さい	埼	1945		提げる	767	さわぐ	騒ぐ	794	
ざい	在	588	ささえる	支える	368	さわやか	爽やか	2074	
	材	740	ささる	刺さる	1319	さわる	触る	1382	
	財	741	さす	刺す	1319		障る	1028	
	剤	1780		指す	775	さん	三	3	
	罪	1047		差す	674		山	100	
さいわい	幸い	894		挿す	1478		参	294	
さえぎる	遮る	1749	さずかる	授かる	312		桟	1532	
さか	坂	605	さずける	授ける	312		蚕	1866	
	逆	386	さそう	誘う	274		産	574	
	酒	144	さだか	定か	289		惨	1457	
さかい	境	1036	さだまる	定まる	289		散	721	
さかえる	栄える	1188	さだめる	定める	289		傘	1655	
さがす	捜す	1475	さち	幸	894		算	356	
	探す	1258	さっ	早	117		酸	1420	
さかずき	杯	983	さつ	札	984		賛	376	
さかな	魚	485		冊	1312	ざん	残	223	
さかのぼる	遡る	2083		刷	1137		惨	1457	
さからう	逆らう	386		刹	2111		斬	2061	
さかる	盛る	922		拶	2034		暫	1706	
さがる	下がる	32		殺	610				
さかん	盛ん	922		察	475		し		
さき	先	48		撮	1267	し	子	69	
	崎	1293		擦	1416		士	755	
さく	冊	1312	ざつ	雑	523		止	217	
	作	137	さと	里	1025		支	368	
	昨	621	さとす	諭す	1579		氏	744	
	削	1320	さとる	悟る	1454		四	4	じ	仕	236
	柵	2030	さばく	裁く	1163		仕	236		示	814

市	547	
矢	593	
史	705	
示	814	
司	1204	
自	63	
死	258	
糸	409	
次	660	
至	1198	
旨	1349	
私	72	
志	756	
伺	1245	
姉	77	
始	129	
使	199	
祉	896	
枝	972	
刺	1319	
肢	1355	
思	202	
施	612	
姿	661	
指	775	
紙	243	
師	967	
脂	1350	
恣	2113	
視	806	
紫	1711	
歯	702	
詞	1205	
試	795	
資	853	
詩	945	
飼	1348	
嗣	1885	
誌	524	
雌	1639	
賜	1898	
摯	2073	
諮	1580	

	渋	1400		徐	1390	証	666		醸	1651
	銃	1599	しょう	上	31	象	939	しょく	色	316
	縦	1300		小	88	粧	1284		食	131
	獣	1864		少	105	装	1370		拭	2078
しゅく	叔	1766		井	1064	焦	1385		植	678
	祝	1018		升	1915	硝	1552		殖	1540
	宿	326		生	49	掌	1677		飾	603
	淑	1767		正	407	晶	1808		触	1382
	粛	1824		召	1691	詔	1932		嘱	1437
	縮	884		匠	1715	奨	831		職	513
じゅく	塾	863		床	543	傷	835		織	882
	熟	864		声	619	照	868	じょく	辱	1795
しゅつ	出	185		抄	1465	詳	944	しら	白	44
じゅつ	述	963		肖	1811	精	877	しらべる	調べる	210
	術	370		青	47	障	1028	しり	尻	1979
しゅん	旬	664		性	421	彰	1620	しりぞく	退く	348
	春	96		姓	598	賞	711	しりぞける	退ける	348
	俊	1424		招	696	衝	1388	しる	汁	1399
	瞬	979		承	819	憧	2076		知る	143
じゅん	旬	664		松	970	償	712	しるし	印	1136
	巡	1743		昇	1280	礁	1553	しるす	記す	633
	盾	956		尚	1810	鐘	1607	しろ	白	44
	純	1068		沼	1842	じょう	上	31		代	413
	殉	1539		省	389	丈	1272		城	942
	准	1635		相	391	冗	468	しろい	白い	44
	順	952		星	463	成	377	しん	心	172
	循	1387		政	530	条	750		申	585
	準	614		昭	867	状	829		辛	344
	潤	1509		消	219	定	289		身	394
	遵	1751		笑	251	乗	135		臣	1003
しょ	処	1212		従	642	城	942		伸	1246
	初	440		将	830	浄	1495		芯	2026
	所	149		症	1363	情	654		神	586
	書	181		祥	1542	常	708		信	640
	庶	1413		称	1554	盛	922		侵	1244
	暑	119		宵	1907	剰	1321		津	1397
	署	1316		渉	505	場	335		真	242
	緒	1033		商	684	畳	1303		針	729
	諸	1032		紹	694	蒸	802		振	770
じょ	女	68		清	754	静	247		娠	1331
	如	1441		章	1027	縄	1568		浸	1496
	助	826		訟	1208	錠	1604		唇	1794
	序	953		唱	1809	嬢	1649		深	121
	叙	1617		焼	218	壌	1650		進	267
	除	958		勝	263	譲	1209		紳	1299

	森	460		推	1009	すまう	住まう	141		盛	922
	診	1361		遂	1217	すます	済ます	516		晴	281
	新	85		睡	977		澄ます	1510		婿	600
	寝	127		穂	1856	すみ	炭	875		聖	580
	慎	1220	すい	酸い	1420		隅	1239		歳	703
	震	847	ずい	随	1792		墨	1695		勢	865
	請	878		髄	1793	すみやか	速やか	383		誠	943
	審	1661	すう	枢	1530	すむ	住む	141		静	247
	親	249		崇	1664		済む	516		製	686
	薪	1838		数	529		澄む	1510		精	877
じん	人	15	すう	吸う	272	する	刷る	1137		誓	1712
	刃	1774	すえ	末	584		擦る	1416		請	878
	仁	1879	すえる	据える	1480	するどい	鋭い	1373		整	387
	尽	1726	すかす	透かす	1746	すれる	擦れる	1416		醒	2047
	迅	1744	すがた	姿	661	すわる	座る	175	せい	背	1085
	臣	1003	すき	隙	2040		据わる	1480	ぜい	税	670
	神	586	すぎ	杉	1357	すん	寸	367		説	292
	甚	1756	すぎる	過ぎる	284				せき	夕	95
	陣	1523	すく	好く	244	**せ**				石	102
	尋	1326		透く	1746					斥	1817
	腎	1987	すくう	救う	934	せ	世	156		赤	46
す			すくない	少ない	105		施	612		昔	428
			すぐれる	優れる	1168	せ	背	1085		析	985
す	子	69	すけ	助	826		瀬	1845		席	332
	主	70	すける	透ける	1746	ぜ	是	1670		隻	1917
	守	537	すこし	少し	105	せい	井	1064		脊	1988
	素	636	すごす	過ごす	284		生	49		責	638
	須	2105	すこやか	健やか	1053		世	156		寂	1380
	数	529	すじ	筋	1059		正	407		惜	1455
す	州	553	すず	鈴	1336		西	40		戚	2121
	巣	1862	すずしい	涼しい	340		成	377		跡	1587
	酢	1592	すすむ	進む	267		声	619		積	886
ず	図	329	すずむ	涼む	340		青	47		績	885
	豆	471	すすめる	進める	267		性	421		籍	1058
	事	237		勧める	1615		姓	598	せき	関	446
	頭	166		薦める	1411		制	687	せち	節	699
すい	水	19	すそ	裾	2023		征	1389	せつ	切	250
	出	185	すたる	廃る	1412		斉	1779		折	772
	吹	259	すたれる	廃れる	1412		省	389		拙	1470
	炊	1311	すでに	既に	1162		星	463		刹	2111
	垂	1322	すてる	捨てる	285		政	530		窃	1673
	帥	1894	すな	砂	1152		牲	938		殺	610
	粋	1069	すべて	全て	160		逝	1747		設	611
	衰	1805	すべる	統べる	1000		凄	2066		接	748
	酔	728		滑る	1392		情	654		雪	842
							清	754			

	節	699
	摂	1482
	説	292
ぜつ	舌	1288
	絶	734
ぜに	銭	1598
せばまる	狭まる	560
せばめる	狭める	560
せまい	狭い	560
せまる	迫る	964
せめる	攻める	1040
	責める	638
せる	競る	1020
せん	千	12
	川	101
	占	1016
	仙	1880
	先	48
	浅	122
	洗	198
	専	797
	泉	840
	宣	850
	染	908
	栓	1531
	扇	1733
	船	647
	旋	1527
	戦	360
	践	1588
	煎	1967
	腺	1989
	詮	2053
	羨	2090
	銭	1598
	箋	1983
	選	264
	線	841
	潜	1393
	遷	1896
	薦	1411
	鮮	916
	繊	1296
ぜん	全	160
	前	29

	然	401
	善	676
	禅	589
	漸	1503
	膳	1968
	繕	1572

そ

そ	阻	1519
	狙	2056
	祖	824
	素	636
	租	1893
	組	635
	措	1476
	粗	1560
	訴	1207
	疎	1826
	想	392
	塑	1939
	遡	2083
	礎	692
ぞ	曽	2120
そう	双	1763
	早	117
	争	361
	壮	1445
	走	177
	宗	816
	送	206
	相	391
	草	567
	荘	1369
	奏	1679
	倉	1112
	捜	1475
	挿	1478
	桑	1855
	窓	231
	掃	957
	巣	1862
	曹	1930
	爽	2074
	曽	2120
	葬	801

	創	1113
	装	1370
	喪	1807
	痩	1982
	想	392
	僧	1430
	総	735
	層	1725
	遭	1750
	槽	1537
	踪	2050
	操	1485
	燥	903
	霜	1689
	騒	794
	贈	1224
	藻	1839
そう	沿う	1128
	添う	1131
ぞう	造	965
	象	939
	増	429
	雑	523
	像	940
	憎	1462
	蔵	1111
	贈	1224
	臓	1108
そうろう	候	1174
そえる	添える	1131
そく	足	171
	束	382
	即	700
	則	808
	促	1170
	速	383
	息	1118
	捉	2080
	側	809
	測	810
	塞	2119
ぞく	俗	1243
	族	322
	属	1091
	続	211

	賊	1584
そこ	底	745
そこなう	損なう	396
そこねる	損ねる	396
そそぐ	注ぐ	290
そそのかす	唆す	1433
そだつ	育つ	879
そだてる	育てる	879
そつ	卒	306
	率	615
そで	袖	2022
そと	外	150
そなえる	供える	418
	備える	613
そなわる	備わる	613
その	園	324
そまる	染まる	908
そむく	背く	1085
そむける	背ける	1085
そめる	初める	440
	染める	908
そら	空	461
そらす	反らす	362
そる	反る	362
そん	存	587
	村	364
	孫	448
	尊	479
	損	396
	遜	2064
ぞん	存	587

た

た	太	124
	他	415
	多	104
	汰	2036
た	手	170
	田	103
だ	打	771
	妥	1332
	蛇	1861
	唾	1984
	惰	1460
	堕	1693

	駄	1610	たく	宅	538		奪	1407		丹	1813
たい	大	87		択	764	たっとい	尊い	479		旦	2038
	太	124		沢	1395		貴い	855		担	1050
	代	413		卓	1030	たっとぶ	尊ぶ	479		単	359
	台	532		拓	1263		貴ぶ	855		炭	875
	体	165		度	333	たて	盾	956		胆	1344
	対	363		託	1574		縦	1300		探	1258
	待	195		濯	301	たてまつる	奉る	1678		淡	1401
	退	348	たく	炊く	1311	たてる	立てる	174		短	90
	胎	1544	だく	諾	1578		建てる	1055		嘆	1436
	耐	1618		濁	1511	たとえる	例える	811		端	680
	怠	1698	だく	抱く	1012	たな	棚	1536		綻	2049
	帯	1065	たぐい	類い	563	たに	谷	458		誕	688
	泰	1680	たくみ	巧み	1786	たね	種	564		壇	1440
	袋	685	たくわえる	蓄える	743	たのしい	楽しい	343		鍛	1605
	逮	1048	たけ	丈	1272	たのしむ	楽しむ	343	だん	旦	2038
	堆	2014		竹	374	たのむ	頼む	572		団	366
	貸	183		岳	1851	たのもしい	頼もしい	572		男	67
	替	375	たしか	確か	803	たば	束	382		段	608
	隊	779	たしかめる	確かめる	803	たび	度	333		断	900
	滞	1402	たす	足す	171		旅	153		弾	590
	態	451	だす	出す	185	たべる	食べる	131		暖	339
	戴	2136	たすかる	助かる	826	たま	玉	575		談	390
だい	大	87	たすける	助ける	826		球	935		壇	1440
	内	152	たずさえる	携える	1486		弾	590			
	代	413	たずさわる	携わる	1486		霊	1688	**ち**		
	台	532	たずねる	訪ねる	783	たまご	卵	1135	ち	地	146
	弟	76		尋ねる	1326	たましい	魂	1754		池	452
	第	354	たたかう	戦う	360	だまる	黙る	869		知	143
	題	327		闘う	1328	たまわる	賜る	1898		治	531
たいら	平ら	351	ただし	但し	1921	たみ	民	536		値	426
たえる	耐える	1618	ただしい	正しい	407	ためす	試す	795		致	725
	絶える	734	ただす	正す	407	ためる	矯める	1549		恥	1366
	堪える	1758	ただちに	直ちに	220	たもつ	保つ	665		遅	118
たおす	倒す	225	たたみ	畳	1303	たやす	絶やす	734		置	262
たおれる	倒れる	225	たたむ	畳む	1303	たより	便り	227		稚	1100
たか	高	83	ただよう	漂う	1507	たよる	頼る	572		痴	1738
たかい	高い	83	たつ	達	384	たらす	垂らす	1322		質	238
たがい	互い	1080	たつ	立つ	174	たりる	足りる	171		緻	2110
たかまる	高まる	83		建つ	1055	たる	足る	171	ち	千	12
たかめる	高める	83		竜	1867	だれ	誰	81		血	928
たがやす	耕す	1782		断つ	900	たれる	垂れる	1322		乳	821
たから	宝	576		絶つ	734	たわむれる	戯れる	1901	ちいさい	小さい	88
たき	滝	1841		裁つ	1163	たわら	俵	1426	ちかい	近い	109
たきぎ	薪	1838	だつ	脱	191	たん	反	362	ちかう	誓う	1712

ちがう	違う	385		挑	1268		痛	346	つづみ	鼓	1827	
ちがえる	違える	385		鳥	486	つか	塚	1889	つつむ	包む	1013	
ちから	力	173		帳	1184	つかう	使う	199	つどう	集う	224	
ちぎる	契る	751		張	1185		遣う	1214	つとまる	務まる	388	
ちく	竹	374		釣	1335	つかえる	仕える	236		勤まる	525	
	逐	1216		彫	1358	つかす	尽かす	1726	つとめる	努める	827	
	畜	1274		眺	1548	つかまえる	捕まえる	1049		務める	388	
	蓄	743		頂	1643	つかまる	捕まる	1049		勤める	525	
	築	1056		朝	91	つかる	漬かる	1506	つな	綱	1566	
ちち	父	73		超	1074	つかれる	疲れる	275	つね	常	708	
	乳	821		貼	2079	つかわす	遣わす	1214	つの	角	716	
ちぢまる	縮まる	884		腸	1106	つき	月	17	つのる	募る	1155	
ちぢむ	縮む	884		跳	1586	つぎ	次	660	つば	唾	1984	
ちぢめる	縮める	884		徴	1148	つきる	尽きる	1726	つばさ	翼	1304	
ちぢらす	縮らす	884		調	210	つく	付く	365	つぶ	粒	1558	
ちぢれる	縮れる	884		潮	1508		突く	1121	つぶす	潰す	1995	
ちつ	秩	954		澄	1510		着く	190	つぶれる	潰れる	1995	
	窒	1674		嘲	2095		就く	514	つぼ	坪	1913	
ちゃ	茶	145		聴	645	つぐ	次ぐ	660	つま	爪	1974	
ちゃく	着	190		懲	1703		接ぐ	748		妻	596	
	嫡	1870	ちょく	直	220		継ぐ	901	つまる	詰まる	1576	
ちゅう	中	33		勅	1895	つくえ	机	38	つみ	罪	1047	
	虫	466		捗	2088	つくす	尽くす	1726	つむ	詰む	1576	
	仲	1169	ちらかす	散らかす	721	つぐなう	償う	712		摘む	1256	
	沖	912	ちらかる	散らかる	721	つくる	作る	137		積む	886	
	注	290	ちらす	散らす	721		造る	965	つむぐ	紡ぐ	1563	
	忠	758	ちる	散る	721		創る	1113	つめ	爪	1974	
	宙	1253	ちん	沈	1129	つくろう	繕う	1572	つめたい	冷たい	662	
	抽	1254		珍	1360	つける	付ける	365	つめる	詰める	1576	
	昼	92		朕	1935		着ける	190	つもる	積もる	886	
	柱	990		陳	1524		就ける	514	つや	艶	2070	
	衷	1806		賃	856		漬ける	1506	つゆ	露	846	
	酎	1961		鎮	1606	つげる	告げる	892	つよい	強い	111	
	駐	1386				つたう	伝う	278	つよまる	強まる	111	
	鋳	1601		**つ**		つたえる	伝える	278	つよめる	強める	111	
ちょ	著	1031	つ	通	204	つたない	拙い	1470	つら	面	438	
	貯	742		都	338	つたわる	伝わる	278	つらなる	連なる	299	
	緒	1033	っ	津	1397	つち	土	22	つらぬく	貫く	1714	
ちょう	丁	550	つい	対	363	つちかう	培う	1640	つらねる	連ねる	299	
	弔	1815		追	966	つつ	筒	373	つる	弦	1446	
	庁	541		椎	1996	つづく	続く	211		釣る	1335	
	兆	1269		墜	1218	つづける	続ける	211		鶴	2004	
	町	549	ついえる	費える	858	つつしむ	慎む	1220	つるぎ	剣	791	
	長	89	ついやす	費やす	858		謹む	1582	つれる	連れる	299	
	重	115	つう	通	204	つつみ	堤	1852				

ととのえる	調える	210	どんぶり	井	1964	なつける	懐ける	1463		臭う	1285
	整える	387		**な**		なな	七	7	にがい	苦い	342
となえる	唱える	1809				ななつ	七つ	7	にがす	逃がす	283
となり	隣	980	な	那	2112	ななめ	斜め	1391	にがる	苦る	342
となる	隣る	980		奈	1947	なに	何	80	にぎる	握る	1257
との	殿	1093		南	41	なの	七	7	**にく**	肉	561
どの	殿	1093		納	733	なべ	鍋	1966	にくい	憎い	1462
とばす	飛ばす	265	な	名	82	なま	生	49	にくしみ	憎しみ	1462
とびら	扉	1734		菜	774	なまける	怠ける	1698	にくむ	憎む	1462
とぶ	飛ぶ	265	**ない**	内	152	なまり	鉛	1339	にくらしい	憎らしい	1462
	跳ぶ	1586	ない	亡い	582	なみ	並	221	にげる	逃げる	283
とぼしい	乏しい	860		無い	400		波	913	にごす	濁す	1511
とまる	止まる	217	なえ	苗	1837	なみだ	涙	1081	にごる	濁る	1511
	泊まる	207	なえる	萎える	2118	なめらか	滑らか	1392	にし	西	40
	留まる	432	なおす	直す	220	なやます	悩ます	1110	にじ	虹	2006
とみ	富	629		治す	531	なやむ	悩む	1110	にしき	錦	2134
とむ	富む	629	なおる	直る	220	ならう	倣う	1247	にせ	偽	1428
とむらう	弔う	1815		治る	531		習う	201	**にち**	日	16
とめる	止める	217	なか	中	33	ならす	鳴らす	487	になう	担う	1050
	泊める	207		仲	1169		慣らす	655	にぶい	鈍い	1372
	留める	432	ながい	永い	1096	ならびに	並びに	221	にぶる	鈍る	1372
とも	友	79		長い	89	ならぶ	並ぶ	221	**にゃく**	若	125
	共	419	ながす	流す	279	ならべる	並べる	221	にやす	煮やす	1315
	供	418	なかば	半ば	159	なる	成る	377	**にゅう**	入	186
ともなう	伴う	1423	ながめる	眺める	1548		鳴る	487		乳	821
とら	虎	1999	ながれる	流れる	279	なれる	慣れる	655		柔	1310
とらえる	捕らえる	1049	なく	泣く	252	なわ	苗	1837	**にょ**	女	68
	捉える	2080		鳴く	487		縄	1568		如	1441
とらわれる	捕らわれる	1049	なぐさむ	慰む	1702	**なん**	男	67	**にょう**	女	68
とり	鳥	486	なぐさめる	慰める	1702		南	41		尿	1724
とる	取る	270	なぐる	殴る	1625		納	733	にる	似る	1172
	捕る	1049	なげかわしい	嘆かわしい	1436		軟	1308		煮る	1315
	採る	773	なげく	嘆く	1436		難	526	にわ	庭	542
	執る	1823	なげる	投げる	282	なん	何	80	にわとり	鶏	1863
	撮る	1267	なごむ	和む	352		**に**		**にん**	人	15
どろ	泥	1493	なごやか	和やか	352					任	639
とん	屯	1916	なさけ	情け	654	に	二	2		妊	1330
	団	366	なし	梨	1956		仁	1879		忍	1775
	豚	1089	なす	成す	377		尼	1722		認	668
	頓	2085	なぞ	謎	2051		弐	1912		**ぬ**	
とん	問	239	**なっ**	納	733		児	1375			
どん	貪	2067	なつ	夏	97	に	荷	570	ぬう	縫う	1571
	鈍	1372	なつかしい	懐かしい	1463	にい	新	85	ぬかす	抜かす	769
	曇	1281	なつかしむ	懐かしむ	1463	にえる	煮える	1315	ぬかる	抜かる	769
どん	井	1964	なつく	懐く	1463	におう	匂う	2054	ぬく	抜く	769

ぬぐ	脱ぐ	191	のこす	残す	223		肺	1343	はぐ	剝ぐ	2060
ぬぐう	拭う	2078	のこる	残る	223		配	727	ばく	麦	637
ぬける	抜ける	769	のせる	乗せる	135		俳	1167		博	798
ぬげる	脱げる	191		載せる	1307		敗	718		幕	1157
ぬし	主	70	のぞく	除く	958		排	1262		漠	1159
ぬすむ	盗む	268	のぞむ	望む	581		廃	1412		暴	1043
ぬの	布	887		臨む	1229		輩	1166		縛	1569
ぬま	沼	1842	のち	後	30	はい	灰	874		爆	1044
ぬる	塗る	1694	のど	喉	1986	ばい	売	187	はぐくむ	育む	879

ね

ね	音	620	ののしる	罵る	2098		倍	158	はげしい	激しい	1039
	値	426	のばす	伸ばす	1246		梅	969	はげます	励ます	832
	根	974		延ばす	689		培	1640	はげむ	励む	832
ねい	寧	1378	のびる	伸びる	1246		陪	1641	はげる	剝げる	2060
ねがう	願う	862		延びる	689		買	188	ばける	化ける	414
ねかす	寝かす	127	のべる	伸べる	1246		媒	1760	はこ	箱	1060
ねこ	猫	1410		延べる	689		賠	1642	はこぶ	運ぶ	304
ねたむ	妬む	2092		述べる	963	はいる	入る	186	はさまる	挟まる	1473
ねつ	熱	866	のぼす	上す	31	はえ	栄え	1188	はさむ	挟む	1473
ねばる	粘る	1559	のぼせる	上せる	31	はえる	生える	49	はし	端	680
ねむい	眠い	978	のぼる	上る	31		映える	234		箸	1963
ねむる	眠る	978		昇る	1280		栄える	1188		橋	313
ねらう	狙う	2056		登る	472	はか	墓	1156	はじ	恥	1366
ねる	寝る	127	のむ	飲む	132	はがす	剝がす	2060	はじまる	始まる	129
	練る	296	のる	乗る	135	ばかす	化かす	414	はじめ	初め	440
ねん	年	24		載る	1307	はがね	鋼	1337	はじめて	初めて	440
	念	1117	のろう	呪う	2099	はからう	計らう	288	はじめる	始める	129
	粘	1559				はかる	図る	329	はしら	柱	990

は

	捻	1980					計る	288	はじらう	恥じらう	1366
	然	401	は	把	1467		量る	435	はしる	走る	177
	燃	870		波	913		測る	810	はじる	恥じる	1366
ねんごろ	懇ろ	1799		派	1191		諮る	1580	はずかしい	恥ずかしい	1366
				破	1037		謀る	1761	はずかしめる	辱める	1795
				覇	1685	はがれる	剝がれる	2060	はずす	外す	150

の

の	野	404	は	刃	1774	はく	白	44	はずむ	弾む	590
のう	能	411		羽	491		伯	1877	はずれる	外れる	150
	納	733		葉	569		泊	207	はた	畑	872
	悩	1110		歯	702		迫	964		端	680
	脳	1109		端	680		拍	1255		旗	1528
	農	626	ば	馬	484		剝	2060		機	334
	濃	627		婆	1902		舶	1573	はだ	肌	1345
のがす	逃す	283		罵	2098		博	798	はだか	裸	1305
のがれる	逃れる	283	ば	場	335		薄	799	はたけ	畑	872
のき	軒	508	はい	拝	766	はく	吐く	1432	はたす	果たす	502
				杯	983		掃く	957	はたらく	働く	192
				背	1085		履く	1405	はち	八	8

	鉢	1597	はらす	晴らす	281		妃	1869	ひじ	肘	1976

	鉢	1597	はらす	晴らす	281		妃	1869	ひじ	肘	1976
はち	蜂	2005		腫らす	1990		否	1006	ひそむ	潜む	1393
ばち	罰	1317	はり	針	729		批	1051	ひたい	額	861
はっ	法	518	はる	春	96		非	707	ひたす	浸す	1496
はつ	発	286		張る	1185		彼	1146	ひだり	左	36
	鉢	1597		貼る	2079		肥	1352	ひたる	浸る	1496
	髪	1359	はれる	晴れる	281		披	1468	ひつ	匹	1203
はつ	初	440		腫れる	1990		泌	1492		必	423
ばつ	末	584	はん	凡	467		飛	265		泌	1492
	伐	1422		反	362		卑	1770		筆	355
	抜	769		半	159		疲	275	ひつじ	羊	488
	閥	1192		犯	1046		秘	1102	ひと	一	1
	罰	1317		氾	2086		被	1145		人	15
はて	果て	502		帆	1444		悲	341	ひとしい	等しい	353
はてる	果てる	502		汎	2106		費	858	ひとつ	一つ	1
はな	花	314		坂	605		扉	1734	ひとみ	瞳	1970
	華	1323		判	899		碑	1771	ひとり	独り	559
	鼻	1286		伴	1423		罷	1671	ひびく	響く	1023
はなし	話	178		阪	1948		避	1365	ひま	暇	622
はなす	放す	723		板	987	ひ	日	16	ひめ	姫	1868
	話す	178		版	1142		火	18	ひめる	秘める	1102
	離す	1008		般	648		氷	1095	ひや	冷や	662
はなつ	放つ	723		班	1541		灯	871	ひやかす	冷やかす	662
はなはだ	甚だ	1756		畔	1857	び	尾	1723	ひゃく	百	11
はなはだしい	甚だしい	1756		販	1223		美	673	びゃく	白	44
はなれる	放れる	723		飯	604		眉	1969	ひやす	冷やす	662
	離れる	1008		斑	1994		備	613	ひょう	氷	1095
はね	羽	491		搬	1487		微	1149		兵	994
はねる	跳ねる	1586		頒	1645		鼻	1286		表	437
はは	母	74		煩	1646	ひいでる	秀でる	1171		拍	1255
はば	幅	897		範	1061	ひえる	冷える	662		俵	1426
はばむ	阻む	1519		繁	1187	ひかえる	控える	1479		票	1199
はぶく	省く	389		藩	1890	ひがし	東	39		評	948
はま	浜	911	ばん	万	13	ひかり	光	464		漂	1507
はやい	早い	117		判	899	ひかる	光る	464		標	1200
	速い	383		伴	1423	ひき	匹	1203	びょう	平	351
はやし	林	459		板	987	ひきいる	率いる	615		苗	1837
はやす	生やす	49		晩	94	ひく	引く	257		秒	1151
はやまる	早まる	117		番	551		弾く	590		病	229
	速まる	383		蛮	1825	ひくい	低い	108		描	765
はやめる	早める	117		盤	1313	ひくまる	低まる	108		猫	1410
	速める	383		**ひ**		ひくめる	低める	108	ひら	平	351
はら	原	405				ひける	引ける	257	ひらく	開く	215
	腹	1088	ひ	比	276	ひざ	膝	1978	ひらける	開ける	215
はらう	払う	189		皮	1144	ひさしい	久しい	1097	ひる	干る	506

	昼	92	ぶ	分	26	ふせぐ	防ぐ	781		墳	1888
ひるがえす	翻す	760		不	422	ふせる	伏せる	1421		奮	1406
ひるがえる	翻る	760		歩	176	ふた	二	2	ぶん	分	26
ひろい	広い	113		武	1165		双	1763		文	320
ひろう	拾う	273		奉	1678		蓋	2025		聞	179
ひろがる	広がる	113		侮	1801	ふだ	札	984		へ	
ひろげる	広げる	113		部	53	ぶた	豚	1089			
ひろまる	広まる	113		無	400	ふたたび	再び	992	ベ	辺	962
ひろめる	広める	113		舞	981	ふたつ	二つ	2	へい	平	351
ひん	品	683	ふう	夫	595	ふち	縁	732		丙	1909
	浜	911		封	372	ふつ	払	189		兵	994
	貧	859		風	465		沸	1494		並	221
	賓	1662		富	629	ぶつ	仏	416		併	1250
	頻	1221	ふえ	笛	1681		物	321		柄	989
びん	便	227	ふえる	殖える	1540	ふで	筆	355		病	229
	敏	1800		増える	429	ふとい	太い	124		陛	1521
	貧	859	ふかい	深い	121	ふところ	懐	1463		閉	216
	瓶	1822	ふかす	更かす	1076	ふとる	太る	124		塀	1439
	ふ		ふかまる	深まる	121	ふな	舟	646		幣	1796
			ふかめる	深める	121		船	647		弊	1797
ふ	父	73	ふく	伏	1421	ふね	舟	646		餅	1959
	不	422		服	317		船	647		蔽	2052
	夫	595		副	898	ふまえる	踏まえる	266	べい	米	562
	付	365		復	521	ふみ	文	320	へき	壁	1029
	布	887		幅	897	ふむ	踏む	266		癖	1364
	扶	1466		福	895	ふもと	麓	2009		璧	2075
	歩	176		腹	1088	ふやす	殖やす	1540	へだたる	隔たる	1236
	府	337		複	522		増やす	429	へだてる	隔てる	1236
	怖	1451		覆	1686	ふゆ	冬	99	べつ	別	397
	附	1520	ふく	吹く	259	ふる	降る	136		蔑	2096
	阜	1946		拭く	2078		振る	770	べに	紅	1295
	風	465		噴く	1633	ふるい	古い	86	へび	蛇	1861
	負	717	ふくむ	含む	1290	ふるう	振るう	770	へらす	減らす	430
	赴	1075	ふくめる	含める	1290		震う	847	へる	経る	515
	訃	2124	ふくらむ	膨らむ	1354		奮う	1406		減る	430
	浮	820	ふくれる	膨れる	1354	ふるえる	震える	847	へん	片	1143
	符	357	ふくろ	袋	685	ふるす	古す	86		辺	962
	婦	597	ふける	老ける	737	ふれる	振れる	770		返	184
	普	427		更ける	1076		触れる	1382		変	222
	富	629	ふさ	房	1082	ふん	分	26		偏	1176
	腐	1730	ふさがる	塞がる	2119		紛	1298		遍	1177
	敷	724	ふさぐ	塞ぐ	2119		粉	1557		編	883
	賦	1585	ふし	節	699		霧	1063	べん	弁	1116
	膚	1742	ふじ	藤	2012		噴	1633		便	227
	譜	1583	ふす	伏す	1421		憤	1634		勉	140

	ほ			妄	1696	ほつ	発	286	まかす	任す	639

ほ				忘	209	ぼっ	坊	782		負かす	717
ほ	歩	176		防	781	ぼつ	没	1130	まかせる	任せる	639
	保	665		坊	782		勃	2087	まかなう	賄う	1225
	捕	1049		妨	784	ほっする	欲する	1124	まがる	曲がる	625
	哺	2001		房	1082	ほど	程	671	まき	牧	1273
	補	1001		肪	1351	ほとけ	仏	416		巻	715
	舗	1830		冒	1669	ほどこす	施す	612	まぎらす	紛らす	1298
ほ	火	18		某	1759	ほね	骨	1104	まぎらわしい	紛らわしい	1298
	帆	1444		紡	1563	ほのお	炎	1803	まぎらわす	紛らわす	1298
	穂	1856		剖	1609	ほまれ	誉れ	1713	まぎれる	紛れる	1298
ぼ	母	74		望	581	ほめる	褒める	1933	まく	幕	1157
	募	1155		貿	433	ほら	洞	1844		膜	1546
	墓	1156		棒	988	ほり	堀	1260	まく	巻く	715
	暮	1158		帽	1279	ほる	掘る	1259	まくら	枕	2029
	模	1160		傍	1429		彫る	1358	まける	負ける	717
	慕	1668		貌	2072	ほろびる	滅びる	1500	まげる	曲げる	625
	簿	1684		暴	1043	ほろぼす	滅ぼす	1500	まご	孫	448
ほう	方	43		膨	1354	ほん	反	362	まこと	誠	943
	包	1013		謀	1761		本	37	まさ	正	407
	邦	1621	ほうむる	葬る	801		奔	1819	まさる	勝る	263
	芳	1665	ほうる	放る	723		翻	760	まざる	交ざる	504
	法	518	ほお	頬	1971	ぼん	凡	467		混ざる	837
	宝	576	ほか	外	150		盆	1314	まじえる	交える	504
	放	723		他	415		煩	1646	まじる	交じる	504
	抱	1012	ほがらか	朗らか	1628					混じる	837
	泡	1629	ほく	北	42		**ま**		まじわる	交わる	504
	奉	1678	ぼく	木	20	ま	麻	1414	ます	升	1915
	封	372		目	168		摩	1415		増す	429
	胞	1630		朴	1529		磨	1731	まずしい	貧しい	859
	倣	1247		牧	1273		魔	1418	まぜる	交ぜる	504
	俸	1427		睦	2135	ま	目	168		混ぜる	837
	砲	1631		僕	1241		真	242	また	又	1762
	峰	1848		墨	1695		馬	484		股	1977
	訪	783		撲	1489		間	161	またたく	瞬く	979
	崩	1663	ほこ	矛	955	まい	毎	164	まち	町	549
	報	891	ほこる	誇る	950		米	562		街	371
	豊	628	ほころびる	綻びる	2049		妹	78	まつ	末	584
	飽	1632	ほし	星	463		枚	982		抹	1471
	褒	1933	ほしい	欲しい	1124		昧	2108	まつ	松	970
	縫	1571	ほす	干す	506		埋	1261		待つ	195
	蜂	2005	ほそい	細い	123	まい	舞	981	まったく	全く	160
ぼう	亡	582	ほそる	細る	123	まいる	参る	294	まつり	祭	473
	乏	860	ほたる	蛍	1676	まう	舞う	981	まつりごと	政	530
	忙	126	ほっ	法	518	まえ	前	29	まつる	祭る	473

まと	的	380	みずから	自ら	63		謀	1761		盟	923
まど	窓	231	みせ	店	55		霧	845		鳴	487
まどう	惑う	1071	みせる	見せる	139	む	六	6		銘	1600
まなこ	眼	976	みぞ	溝	1499	むい	六	6	めぐむ	恵む	1077
まなぶ	学ぶ	50	みたす	満たす	555	むかう	向かう	557	めぐる	巡る	1743
まぬかれる	免れる	941	みだす	乱す	932	むかえる	迎える	1133	めし	飯	604
まねく	招く	696	みだら	淫ら	2069	むかし	昔	428	めす	召す	1691
まぼろし	幻	1814	みだれる	乱れる	932	むぎ	麦	637		雌	1639
まめ	豆	471	みち	道	66	むく	向く	557	めずらしい	珍しい	1360
まもる	守る	537	みちびく	導く	480	むくいる	報いる	891	めつ	滅	1500
まゆ	眉	1969	みちる	満ちる	555	むける	向ける	557	めん	免	941
	繭	1941	みつ	密	1103	むこ	婿	600		面	438
まよう	迷う	1070		蜜	1957	むこう	向こう	557		綿	881
まる	丸	591	みつ	三つ	3	むさぼる	貪る	2067		麺	1958
まるい	丸い	591	みつぐ	貢ぐ	1180	むし	虫	466			
	円い	14	みっつ	三つ	3	むす	蒸す	802		**も**	
まるめる	丸める	591	みとめる	認める	668	むずかしい	難しい	526	も	茂	1840
まわす	回す	162	みどり	緑	731	むすぶ	結ぶ	302		模	1160
まわり	周り	558	みな	皆	606	むすめ	娘	601	も	喪	1807
まわる	回る	162	みなと	港	909	むつ	六つ	6		藻	1839
まん	万	13	みなみ	南	41	むっつ	六つ	6	もう	亡	582
	満	555	みなもと	源	854	むな	胸	1086		毛	490
	漫	652	みにくい	醜い	1755		棟	1533		妄	1696
	慢	653	みね	峰	1848	むね	旨	1349		盲	1278
			みのる	実る	672		胸	1086		耗	1783
	み		みみ	耳	169		棟	1533		望	581
み	未	583	みや	宮	929	むら	村	364		猛	1516
	味	311	みゃく	脈	1353		群	489		網	1567
	眉	1969	みやこ	都	338	むらさき	紫	1711	もうける	設ける	611
	魅	1419	みょう	名	82	むらす	蒸らす	802	もうす	申す	585
み	三	3		妙	1150	むれ	群れ	489	もうでる	詣でる	2082
	身	394		明	106	むれる	群れる	489	もえる	燃える	870
	実	672		命	997		蒸れる	802	もく	木	20
みえる	見える	139		冥	2122	むろ	室	331		目	168
みがく	磨く	1731	みる	見る	139					黙	869
みき	幹	1230		診る	1361		**め**		もぐる	潜る	1393
みぎ	右	35	みん	民	536	め	女	68	もしくは	若しくは	125
みことのり	詔	1932		眠	978		目	168	もす	燃す	870
みさお	操	1485					芽	1835	もち	餅	1959
みさき	岬	1850		**む**			雌	1639	もちいる	用いる	308
みささぎ	陵	1886	む	矛	955	めい	名	82	もつ	物	321
みじかい	短い	90		武	1165		明	106	もつ	持つ	142
みじめ	惨め	1457		務	388		命	997	もっとも	最も	439
みず	水	19		無	400		迷	1070	もっぱら	専ら	797
みずうみ	湖	453		夢	800		冥	2122	もてあそぶ	弄ぶ	2094

もと	下	32	やさしい	易しい	434		右	35	
	元	245		優しい	1168		由	623	
	本	37	やしなう	養う	675		有	347	
	基	691	やしろ	社	60		湧	2015	
もとい	基	691	やすい	安い	84		勇	1154	よ	四	4
もどす	戻す	1201	やすまる	休まる	138		幽	1820		世	156
もとめる	求める	933	やすむ	休む	138		郵	226		代	413
もどる	戻る	1201	やすめる	休める	138		悠	1699		夜	93
もの	者	148	やせる	痩せる	1982		遊	196	よい	良い	602
	物	321	やつ	八つ	8		裕	1125		宵	1907
もも	桃	971	やっつ	八つ	8		猶	1517		善い	676
もやす	燃やす	870	やど	宿	326		雄	1637	よう	用	308
もよおす	催す	1248	やとう	雇う	1083		誘	274		幼	1099
もらす	漏らす	1502	やどす	宿す	326		憂	1829		羊	488
もり	守	537	やどる	宿る	326		融	1237		妖	2071
	森	460	やなぎ	柳	1854		優	1168		要	424
もる	盛る	922	やぶる	破る	1037	ゆう	夕	95		洋	917
	漏る	1502	やぶれる	破れる	1037		結う	302		容	1123
もれる	漏れる	1502		敗れる	718	ゆえ	故	722		庸	1728
もん	文	320	やま	山	100	ゆか	床	543		葉	569
	門	445	やまい	病	229	ゆき	雪	842		陽	834
	紋	1564	やみ	闇	2017	ゆく	行く	58		揚	1481
	問	239	やむ	病む	229		逝く	1747		揺	1789
	聞	179	やめる	辞める	931	ゆさぶる	揺さぶる	1789		腰	1087
や			やわらか	柔らか	1310	ゆすぶる	揺すぶる	1789		溶	1501
や	冶	2081		軟らか	1308	ゆする	揺する	1789		様	677
	夜	93	やわらかい	軟らかい	1308	ゆずる	譲る	1209		踊	1383
	野	404		柔らかい	1310	ゆたか	豊か	628		瘍	1992
や	八	8	やわらぐ	和らぐ	352	ゆだねる	委ねる	697		養	675
	矢	593	やわらげる	和らげる	352	ゆび	指	775		窯	1900
	弥	1953	**ゆ**			ゆみ	弓	592		擁	1490
	屋	54	ゆ	由	623	ゆめ	夢	800		謡	1788
	家	52		油	624	ゆらぐ	揺らぐ	1789		曜	23
やかた	館	330		遊	196	ゆる	揺る	1789	よう	八	8
やく	厄	1721		愉	1458	ゆるい	緩い	1271		酔う	728
	役	609		喩	2132	ゆるぐ	揺るぐ	1789	よく	抑	1264
	約	381		輸	499	ゆるす	許す	667		沃	2016
	疫	1735		諭	1579	ゆるむ	緩む	1271		浴	1126
	益	921		癒	1739	ゆるめる	緩める	1271		翌	492
	訳	761	ゆ	湯	836	ゆるやか	緩やか	1271		欲	1124
	薬	315	ゆい	由	623	ゆれる	揺れる	1789		翼	1304
	躍	1384		唯	1636	ゆわえる	結わえる	302	よこ	横	34
				遺	1179	**よ**			よごす	汚す	907
やく	焼く	218	ゆう	友	79	よ	与	713	よごれる	汚れる	907
やける	焼ける	218							よし	由	623

337

よせる	寄せる	1120		履	1405		輪	498		労	443
よそおう	装う	1370		璃	2130		隣	980		弄	2094
よつ	四つ	4		離	1008		臨	1229		郎	546
よっつ	四つ	4	りき	力	173		**る**			浪	1398
よぶ	呼ぶ	197	りく	陸	833	る	流	279		朗	1628
よむ	詠む	1905	りち	律	519		留	432		廊	545
	読む	180	りつ	立	174		瑠	2129		楼	1887
よめ	嫁	599		律	519	るい	涙	1081		漏	1502
よる	因る	406		率	615		累	1302		糧	1282
	夜	93		慄	2116		塁	1692		露	846
	寄る	1120	りゃく	略	1195		類	563		籠	2024
よろこぶ	喜ぶ	253	りゅう	立	174		**れ**		ろく	六	6
よわい	弱い	112		柳	1854	れい	礼	822		緑	731
よわまる	弱まる	112		流	279		令	998		録	730
よわめる	弱める	112		留	432		冷	662		麓	2009
よわる	弱る	112		竜	1867		励	832	ろん	論	496
よん	四	4		粒	1558		戻	1201		**わ**	
	ら			隆	1924		例	811	わ	和	352
ら	拉	2057		硫	1551		鈴	1336		話	178
	裸	1305	りょ	侶	2123		零	1687	わ	我	1164
	羅	1672		旅	153		霊	1688		輪	498
らい	礼	822		虜	1884		隷	1872	わい	賄	1225
	来	133		慮	1377		齢	1404	わかい	若い	125
	雷	843	りょう	了	818		麗	1832	わかす	沸かす	1494
	頼	572		両	556	れき	歴	704	わかつ	分かつ	26
らく	落	280		良	602		暦	1720	わかる	分かる	26
	絡	300		料	240	れつ	列	812	わかれる	分かれる	26
	楽	343		涼	340		劣	1153		別れる	397
	酪	1593		猟	1515		烈	1708	わき	脇	2041
らつ	辣	2065		陵	1886		裂	1371	わく	惑	1071
らん	乱	932		量	435	れん	連	299	わく	枠	510
	卵	1135		漁	914		恋	1078		沸く	1494
	覧	1831		領	999		廉	1729		湧く	2015
	濫	1512		僚	1182		練	296	わけ	訳	761
	藍	2013		寮	1183		錬	1602	わける	分ける	26
	欄	1538		霊	1688		**ろ**		わざ	技	369
	り			療	1362	ろ	呂	2020		業	307
り	吏	1883		瞭	2109		炉	1802	わざわい	災い	873
	利	248		糧	1282		路	533	わずか	僅か	2114
	里	1025	りょく	力	173		賂	1226	わずらう	患う	1367
	理	241		緑	731		露	846		煩う	1646
	痢	1737	りん	林	459	ろう	老	737	わずらわす	煩わす	1646
	裏	436		厘	1910				わすれる	忘れる	209
				倫	497				わた	綿	881
				鈴	1336						

わたくし	私	72	わらう	笑う	251	わるい	悪い	114	
わたし	私	72	わらべ	童	1026	われ	我	1164	
わたす	渡す	205	わり	割	786	われる	割れる	786	
わたる	渡る	205	わる	割る	786	わん	湾	910	

腕	1342

字形索引
（Form Index）

Kanji are arranged under each component heading according to the number of strokes, and the *kanji* number is given. The circled number indicates the number of strokes in the *kanji* excluding the component part. The number for each component can be found in the component chart inside the back cover.

■▮	1 レフト（Left）	1-80

【2画】

1　亻

人 15
② 化 414
仏 416
仁 1879
③ 仕 236
付 365
代 413
他 415
仙 1880
④ 休 138
伝 278
件 482
任 639
仰 1134
仮 1141
仲 1169
伏 1421
伐 1422
伎 2127
⑤ 何 80
低 108
作 137
住 141
体 165
位 417
佐 1002
似 1172

伺 1245
伸 1246
伴 1423
伯 1877
但 1921
⑥ 使 199
供 418
価 425
例 811
依 890
併 1250
侮 1801
侍 1878
佳 1928
⑦ 便 227
係 447
信 640
保 665
促 1170
俗 1243
侵 1244
俊 1424
侯 1876
侶 2123
⑧ 倍 158
借 182
倒 225
値 426
個 469
停 481

倫 497
側 809
俳 1167
候 1174
修 1175
倣 1247
倹 1425
俵 1426
俸 1427
俺 2062
⑨ 健 1053
偏 1176
偶 1240
偽 1428
偵 1765
⑩ 備 613
偉 1242
傍 1429
⑪ 働 192
傷 835
傾 1173
催 1248
債 1249
僧 1430
傑 1431
傲 2063
僅 2114
⑫ 像 940
僚 1182
僕 1241

⑬ 億 650
儀 936
⑭ 儒 1891
⑮ 償 712
優 1168

2　冫

④ 次 660
⑤ 冷 662
冶 2081
⑧ 凍 1094
准 1635
凄 2066
⑭ 凝 1790

3　十

十 10
⑥ 協 444
⑩ 博 798

【3画】

4　口

口 167
② 叱 2097
③ 吸 272
叫 1291
吐 1432
④ 吹 259
吟 1904

⑤ 呼 197
味 311
呪 2099
⑥ 咲 261
咽 1985
⑦ 唆 1433
哺 2001
唄 2128
⑧ 喝 1434
唯 1636
唱 1809
唾 1984
⑨ 喫 752
喚 1435
喉 1986
喩 2132
⑩ 嘆 1436
嗅 2055
⑪ 鳴 487
⑫ 嘱 1437
噴 1633
嘲 2095
⑭ 嚇 1923

5　土

土 22
③ 地 146
④ 坂 605
坊 782
均 1014

坑 1925
⑤ 坪 1913
⑥ 城 942
垣 1784
⑦ 埋 1261
⑧ 域 1072
堀 1260
培 1640
埼 1945
堆 2014
⑨ 場 335
塔 1438
塀 1439
堪 1758
堤 1852
塚 1889
⑩ 塩 924
塊 1753
填 2084
⑪ 増 429
境 1036
⑫ 墳 1888
⑬ 壊 1038
壇 1440
壌 1650

7　女

女 68
② 奴 1871
③ 好 244
如 1441
妃 1869
④ 妨 784
妙 1150
妊 1330
妖 2071
⑤ 姉 77
妹 78
始 129
姓 598
姑 2092
⑥ 姻 1442
⑦ 娘 601
娯 1329
娠 1331
姫 1868
⑧ 婚 303
婦 597
⑨ 婿 600
媒 1760
媛 1950
⑩ 嫁 599
嫌 1325
嫉 2091
⑪ 嫡 1870

6　夕

② 外 150

⑫ 嬢 1649

8 子
子 69
① 孔 1881
⑥ 孤 1381
⑦ 孫 448

9 山
山 100
④ 岐 1443
⑤ 岬 1850
⑥ 峡 1294
峠 1849
⑦ 峰 1848
⑧ 崎 1293

10 川
川 101
⑨ 順 952

11 工
工 379
② 功 378
巧 1786
④ 攻 1040
⑨ 項 1222

12 巾
巾 2021
③ 帆 1444
⑧ 帳 1184
⑨ 幅 897
帽 1279

13 幺
① 幻 1814
② 幼 1099

14 弓
弓 592
① 引 257
⑤ 弦 1446
弥 1953
⑥ 弧 1447
⑦ 弱 112
⑧ 強 111
張 1185
⑨ 弾 590

15 彳
③ 行 58
④ 役 609
⑤ 往 520
彼 1146
征 1389
径 1448
⑥ 後 30
待 195
律 519
⑦ 徒 641
従 642
徐 1390
⑧ 術 370
得 643
⑨ 街 371
復 521
御 919
循 1387
⑩ 微 1149
⑪ 徳 644
徴 1148
⑫ 徹 1147
衝 1388
⑬ 衛 780
衡 1449

16 忄
③ 忙 126
④ 快 656
⑤ 性 421
怪 1450
怖 1451
⑥ 悔 1219
恨 1452
恒 1785
⑦ 悩 1110
悦 1453
悟 1454
⑧ 情 654
惜 1455
悼 1456
惨 1457
惧 2093
⑨ 愉 1458
慌 1459
惰 1460
⑩ 慎 1220
慨 1461
慄 2116
⑪ 慢 653
慣 655
憎 1462
⑫ 憤 1634
憧 2076
憬 2077
⑬ 憶 651
懐 1463
憾 1464

17 扌
② 払 189
打 771
③ 扱 1266
④ 投 282
技 369
抗 747
択 764
抜 769
折 772
批 1051
抑 1264
抄 1465
扶 1466
把 1467
⑤ 押 256
招 696
抵 746
拝 766
拡 768
拒 1005
抱 1012
担 1050
拠 1213
抽 1254
拍 1255
拓 1263
拐 1265
披 1468
拘 1469
拙 1470
抹 1471
拉 2057
⑥ 持 142
拾 273
指 775
挑 1268
括 1472
挟 1473
拷 1474
拶 2034
拭 2078
⑦ 振 770
捕 1049
捜 1475
挿 1478
挫 1981
挨 2033
捉 2080
捗 2088
⑧ 捨 285
授 312
接 748
描 765
採 773
掃 957
推 1009
掲 1011
探 1258
掘 1259
排 1262
措 1476
掛 1477
控 1479
据 1480
捻 1980
⑨ 換 749
提 767
揮 776
握 1257
援 1270
揚 1481
搭 1483
揺 1789
⑩ 損 396
摂 1482
搾 1484
携 1486
搬 1487
⑪ 摘 1256
⑫ 撮 1267
撤 1488
撲 1489
⑬ 操 1485
擁 1490
⑭ 擦 1416
擬 1791

18 氵
② 汁 1399
氾 2086
③ 池 452
汗 507
江 905
汚 907
汎 2106
④ 決 277
沖 912
沈 1129
没 1130
沢 1395
汽 1491
沃 2016
沙 2035
汰 2036
⑤ 泳 193
泊 207
泣 252
注 290
法 518
治 531
油 624
波 913
況 1017
河 1127
沿 1128
沁 1492
泥 1493
沸 1494
泡 1629
沼 1842
⑥ 浅 122
洗 198
海 454
活 517
洋 917
派 1191
洪 1396
津 1397
浄 1495
洞 1844
⑦ 酒 144
消 219
流 279
浮 820
浜 911
涙 1081
浴 1126
浪 1398
浸 1496
浦 1846
⑧ 深 121
涼 340
渉 505
済 516
清 754
混 837
液 906
添 1131
渇 1394
渋 1400
淡 1401
涯 1497
淑 1767
渓 1843
淫 2069
⑨ 渡 205
減 430
湖 453
満 555
測 810
湯 836
湿 838
温 839
港 909
湾 910

渦 1498		
滋 1776		
湧 2015		
⑩ 漢 527		
源 854		
漠 1159		
滑 1392		
滞 1402		
溝 1499		
減 1500		
溶 1501		
滝 1841		
溺 2048		
⑪ 演 616		
漫 652		
漁 914		
漏 1502		
漸 1503		
滴 1504		
漆 1505		
漬 1506		
漂 1507		
⑫ 潔 753		
潜 1393		
潮 1508		
潤 1509		
澄 1510		
潟 1847		
潰 1995		
⑬ 濃 627		
激 1039		
濁 1511		
⑭ 濯 301		
⑮ 濫 1512		
⑯ 瀬 1845		

19 爿

③ 壮 1445
④ 状 829
⑦ 将 830

20 犭

② 犯 1046
④ 狂 1513
⑤ 狙 2056
⑥ 独 559
　 狭 560
　 狩 1514
⑧ 猫 1410
　 猟 1515
　 猛 1516
⑨ 猶 1517
⑩ 猿 1865
⑪ 獄 1518
⑬ 獲 1408

21 阝

④ 防 781
　 阪 1948
⑤ 阻 1519
　 附 1520
⑥ 限 975
⑦ 降 136
　 院 230
　 除 958
　 陛 1521
　 陥 1522
　 陣 1523
　 陸 833
　 陳 1524
　 陰 1525
　 陶 1526
　 陪 1641
　 陵 1886
　 隆 1924
⑨ 階 607
　 隊 779
　 陽 834
　 隅 1239

随 1792
⑩ 隔 1236
　 隙 2040
⑪ 際 474
　 隣 980
　 障 1028
　 隠 1235

【4画】

22 方

方 43
④ 放 723
⑤ 施 612
⑥ 旅 153
⑦ 族 322
　 旋 1527
⑩ 旗 1528

23 日

日 16
④ 明 106
　 旺 2068
⑤ 映 234
　 昨 621
　 昭 867
　 昧 2108
⑥ 時 25
⑧ 晩 94
　 晴 281
　 暁 1858
⑨ 暗 107
　 暖 339
　 暇 622
⑬ 曖 2107
⑭ 曜 23

24 月

② 肌 1345
③ 肝 1107

肘 1976
④ 服 317
　 肪 1351
　 肥 1352
　 肢 1355
　 股 1977
⑤ 肺 1343
　 胆 1344
　 胎 1544
　 胞 1630
⑥ 胸 1086
　 胴 1341
　 脂 1350
　 脈 1353
　 朕 1935
　 脇 2041
⑦ 脱 191
　 豚 1089
　 脳 1109
　 脚 1545
⑧ 勝 263
　 腕 1342
⑨ 腰 1087
　 腹 1088
　 腸 1106
　 腺 1989
　 腫 1990
⑩ 膜 1546
⑪ 膝 1978
⑫ 膨 1354
　 膳 1968
⑬ 臆 1934
　 臆 2101
⑮ 臓 1108
⑯ 騰 1547

25 木

木 20
① 札 984
② 机 38
③ 朴 1529
　 朽 1787
③ 村 364
　 材 740
　 杉 1357
④ 林 459
　 枠 510
　 松 970
　 枝 972
　 枚 982
　 杯 983
　 析 985
　 板 987
　 枢 1530
　 枕 2029
⑤ 相 391
　 柄 989
　 柱 990
　 枯 1356
　 柳 1854
　 栃 1944
　 柿 1955
　 柵 2030
⑥ 校 51
　 格 852
　 桜 968
　 梅 969
　 桃 971
　 株 973
　 根 974
　 核 986
　 栓 1531
　 桟 1532
　 桁 2042
⑦ 械 511
　 梗 1997
⑧ 植 678
　 検 792
　 棒 988
　 棟 1533

棺 1534
棋 1535
棚 1536
椎 1996
椅 2031
⑨ 極 679
　 楼 1887
　 楷 2126
⑩ 様 677
　 構 991
　 模 1160
　 概 1161
⑪ 横 34
　 権 804
　 標 1200
　 槽 1537
⑫ 橋 313
　 機 334
　 樹 1853
⑯ 欄 1538
㉕ 鬱 2104

26 歹

② 列 812
⑥ 残 223
　 殊 813
　 殉 1539
⑧ 殖 1540

27 火

火 18
② 灯 871
④ 炊 1311
　 炉 1802
⑤ 畑 872
⑧ 焼 218
⑨ 煙 1045
　 煩 1646
⑫ 燃 870
⑬ 燥 903

⑮ 爆 1044

28 牛

牛 483
④ 物 321
　 牧 1273
⑤ 牲 938
⑥ 特 398
⑬ 犠 937

29 王

王 577
④ 玩 2018
⑤ 珍 1360
⑥ 班 1541
　 珠 1769
⑦ 理 241
　 現 578
　 球 935
⑧ 斑 1994
⑩ 瑠 2129
　 璃 2130
⑬ 環 1035

30 礻

① 礼 822
③ 社 60
④ 祈 823
　 祉 896
⑤ 神 586
　 祖 824
　 祝 1018
⑥ 祥 1542
⑦ 視 806
⑨ 禅 589
　 福 895
　 禍 1543

【5画】

31	田
	田 103
②	町 549
⑤	畔 1857
	畝 1936
⑥	略 1195

32	目
	目 168
⑤	眠 978
⑥	眼 976
	眺 1548
⑧	睡 977
	睦 2135
⑫	瞳 1970
	瞭 2109
⑬	瞬 979

33	矛
⑥	務 388

34	矢
	矢 593
③	知 143
⑦	短 90
⑫	矯 1549

35	石
	石 102
④	研 297
	砂 1152
	砕 1550
⑤	破 1037
	砲 1631
⑦	硬 1309
	硫 1551
	硝 1552
⑨	碑 1771

	磁 1777
⑩	確 803
⑫	礁 1553
⑬	礎 692

36	禾
②	私 72
	利 248
③	和 352
④	科 565
	秒 1151
⑤	秋 98
	秩 954
	秘 1102
	称 1554
	租 1893
⑥	移 1101
⑦	税 670
	程 671
⑧	稚 1100
⑨	種 564
	稿 1231
	稲 1233
	穂 1856
⑩	稼 1232
	稽 2131
⑪	積 886
	穏 1234
⑬	穫 1409

37	立
	立 174
⑨	端 680

38	牙
③	邪 1417
⑧	雅 1638

39	ネ
②	初 440

⑤	被 1145
	袖 2022
⑦	補 1001
	裕 1125
⑧	裸 1305
	褐 1556
	裾 2023
⑨	複 522
⑬	襟 1555

40	艮
②	即 700
⑤	既 1162

【6画】

41	米
	米 562
④	料 240
	粋 1069
	粉 1557
⑤	粒 1558
	粘 1559
	粗 1560
⑥	粧 1284
⑧	精 877
⑩	糖 1283
⑫	糧 1282

42	糸
	糸 409
③	約 381
	級 410
	紀 634
	紅 1295
	紏 1561
④	紙 243
	納 733
	純 1068
	紛 1298

	紡 1563
	紋 1564
⑤	細 123
	終 130
	経 515
	組 635
	紹 694
	紳 1299
	紺 1562
⑥	絡 300
	結 302
	絵 617
	給 618
	絶 734
	統 1000
	絞 1565
⑦	続 211
	絹 880
	継 901
⑧	練 296
	緑 731
	総 735
	綿 881
	緒 1033
	維 1297
	綱 1566
	網 1567
	綻 2049
⑨	縁 732
	線 841
	編 883
	締 1067
	緩 1271
	縄 1568
⑩	縦 1300
	縛 1569
	緯 1570
	縫 1571
	緻 2110
⑪	縮 884

	績 885
	繊 1296
⑫	織 882
	繕 1572
⑬	繰 902

43	耒
④	耕 1782
	耗 1783

44	耳
	耳 169
②	取 270
④	恥 1366
⑪	聴 645
⑫	職 513

45	至
	至 1198
②	到 287
④	致 725

46	舌
	舌 1288
①	乱 932
⑦	辞 931

47	舟
	舟 646
④	般 648
	航 649
⑤	船 647
	舶 1573
	舷 2032
⑦	艇 1927
⑮	艦 1892

48	虫
	虫 466
③	虹 2006

④	蚊 1860
⑤	蛇 1861
⑦	蜂 2005

49	良
③	郎 546
④	朗 1628

50	并
⑤	瓶 1822

51	自
③	帥 1894
④	師 967

52	自
④	能 411

【7画】

53	臣
	臣 1003
⑪	臨 1229

54	角
	角 716
⑥	解 293
	触 1382

55	言
	言 203
②	計 288
	訂 1206
	訃 2124
③	記 633
	討 946
	訓 951
	託 1574
④	設 611
	許 667

	訳 761
	訪 783
	訟 1208
⑤	証 666
	評 948
	詞 1205
	訴 1207
	診 1361
	詐 1575
	詠 1905
	詔 1932
⑥	話 178
	試 795
	誠 943
	詳 944
	詩 945
	誇 950
	詰 1576
	該 1577
	詮 2053
	詣 2082
⑦	語 154
	読 180
	誘 274
	説 292
	誌 524
	認 668
	誤 949
⑧	誰 81
	調 210
	談 390
	論 496
	課 669
	誕 688
	請 878
	諸 1032
	諾 1578
	謁 1899
⑨	論 1579
	諮 1580

謀 1761
謡 1788
諦 2102
諧 2125
⑩ 講 495
謝 947
謙 1581
謹 1582
謎 2051
⑫ 識 512
譜 1583
⑬ 議 494
護 1115
譲 1209

| 56 | 谷 |
谷 458
④ 欲 1124

| 57 | 豆 |
豆 471
⑨ 頭 166

| 58 | 豸 |
⑦ 貌 2072

| 59 | 貝 |
貝 719
② 則 808
③ 財 741
④ 敗 718
販 1223

⑤ 貯 742
貼 2079
⑥ 賄 1225
賂 1226
賊 1584
⑧ 賦 1585
賠 1642
賜 1898
⑨ 賭 2046
⑩ 購 1210
⑪ 贈 1224

| 60 | 足 |
足 171
⑤ 距 1007
⑥ 路 533
跳 1586
跡 1587
践 1588
⑦ 踊 1383
⑧ 踏 266
踪 2050
⑫ 蹴 2059
⑭ 躍 1384

| 61 | 身 |
身 394
③ 射 1015

| 62 | 車 |
車 62
② 軌 1306

③ 軒 508
④ 転 65
軟 1308
⑤ 軽 116
軸 1589
⑥ 較 500
⑧ 輪 498
⑨ 輸 499
⑩ 轄 1590

| 63 | 酉 |
③ 配 727
酌 1591
酎 1961
④ 酔 728
⑤ 酢 1592
⑥ 酪 1593
酬 1594
⑦ 酸 1420
酵 1595
酷 1596
⑨ 醒 2047
⑩ 醜 1755
⑬ 醸 1651

| 64 | 釆 |
④ 釈 763

| 65 | 里 |
里 1025
④ 野 404

| 66 | 君 |
君 1289
③ 郡 552
⑥ 群 489

【8画】
| 67 | 金 |
金 21
② 針 729
③ 釣 1335
④ 鈍 1372
⑤ 鉄 147
鉱 876
鈴 1336
鉛 1339
鉢 1597
⑥ 銀 57
銅 1340
銭 1598
銃 1599
銘 1600
⑦ 鋭 1373
鋳 1601
⑧ 録 730
鋼 1337
錬 1602
錯 1603
錠 1604
錮 2044
錦 2134

⑨ 鍛 1605
鍋 1966
鍵 2028
⑩ 鎖 1338
鎮 1606
鎌 1952
⑪ 鏡 1034
⑫ 鐘 1607
⑮ 鑑 1608

| 68 | 青 |
青 47
⑥ 静 247

| 69 | 食 |
食 131
② 飢 1346
④ 飲 132
⑤ 飾 603
飼 1348
飽 1632
⑦ 餓 1347
⑧ 館 330

| 70 | 幸 |
幸 894
③ 執 1823
④ 報 891

| 71 | 卓 |
③ 乾 904

④ 朝 91
⑤ 幹 1230
⑩ 韓 1954

| 72 | 京 |
④ 就 514

【9画】
| 73 | 革 |
革 996
④ 靴 995

| 74 | 音 |
音 620
⑩ 韻 1903

| 75 | 食 |
⑥ 餅 1959
餌 1960

【10画】
| 76 | 馬 |
馬 484
④ 駅 56
駄 1610
駆 1611
⑤ 駐 1386
駒 2019
⑧ 験 793
騒 794

騎 1874

| 77 | 骨 |
骨 1104
⑥ 骸 1991
⑨ 髄 1793

| 78 | 竟 |
⑩ 競 1020

【11画】
| 79 | 魚 |
魚 485
⑥ 鮮 916
⑧ 鯨 915

| 80 | 隹 |
② 勧 1615
④ 歓 1132
⑦ 観 805

---

② ライト （Right）　81-189

【1画】
| 81 | し |
③ 孔 1881
④ 礼 822

札 984
⑥ 乱 932
⑦ 乳 821

【2画】
| 82 | 几 |
④ 机 38
肌 1345

⑤ 処 1212
⑧ 飢 1346

| 83 | 刀 |
② 切 250

| 84 | 刂 |
② 刈 1612
③ 刊 1138
④ 列 812

刑 1052
⑤ 利 248
別 397
判 899
⑥ 到 287

制 687
刷 1137
刻 1139
刺 1319
刹 2111

⑦	則 808
	削 1320
⑧	剣 791
	剖 1609
	剛 1613
	剤 1780
	剝 2060
⑨	副 898
	剰 1321
⑩	割 786
	創 1113
⑬	劇 1140

85 力

	力 441
③	功 378
	幼 1099
⑤	助 826
	励 832
⑥	効 501
	劾 1614
⑦	勅 1895
	勃 2087
⑨	動 64
	勘 1757
⑩	勤 525
⑪	勧 1615

86 匕

②	比 276
	化 414
③	北 42
⑩	靴 995

87 十

③	汁 1399
⑦	計 288
⑧	針 729

88 卩

④	印 1136
⑤	即 700
	却 1616
⑥	卸 918

89 厶

②	仏 416
③	払 189
⑤	私 72

90 又

	又 1762
②	収 828
	双 1763
⑥	取 270
	叔 1766
⑦	叙 1617

91 丁

	丁 550
③	打 771
④	灯 871
⑤	町 549
⑦	訂 1206

【3画】

92 口

②	加 295
⑤	知 143
	和 352

93 寸

	寸 367
②	付 365
④	対 363
	村 364
⑥	封 372

	耐 1618
⑦	討 946
	射 1015
⑧	尉 1882

94 己

	己 632
③	妃 1869
⑥	紀 634
	記 633
	配 727

95 干

	干 506
③	汗 507
④	肝 1107
⑦	軒 508

96 彡

④	形 509
⑧	彫 1358
	彩 1619
⑪	彰 1620
⑫	影 1022
⑬	膨 1354

97 阝

④	邦 1621
	那 2112
⑤	邸 1238
	邪 1417
⑥	郊 503
	郎 546
⑦	郡 552
	郭 1773
⑧	部 53
	郵 226
	都 338
	郷 1024

98 亍

③	行 58
⑧	術 370
⑨	街 371
⑫	衝 1388
⑬	衛 780
	衡 1449

99 扌

	才 739
④	材 740
⑦	財 741

100 及

	及 1098
③	吸 272
	扱 1266
⑥	級 410

101 也

②	他 415
③	地 146
	池 452

102 勹

⑤	的 380
⑥	約 381
⑦	酌 1591
⑧	釣 1335

【4画】

103 戈

②	成 377
	伐 1422
③	我 1164
	戒 1334
⑤	威 1333
⑦	械 511

	戚 2121
⑧	減 430
⑨	戦 360
⑪	戯 1901

104 支

	支 368
③	技 369
	岐 1443
④	枝 972
	肢 1355
⑨	鼓 1827

105 攵

③	改 726
	攻 1040
④	放 723
	枚 982
	牧 1273
⑤	政 530
	故 722
⑥	致 725
	敏 1800
⑦	教 214
	敗 718
	救 934
	赦 1897
⑧	敬 478
	散 721
	敢 1622
⑨	数 529
⑪	敵 658
	敷 724

106 斗

	斗 1918
⑤	科 565
⑥	料 240
⑦	斜 1391

107 斤

	斤 1914
③	折 772
④	祈 823
	析 985
⑦	所 149
	断 900
	斬 2061
⑨	新 85
⑩	漸 1503

108 方

	方 43
③	防 781
	坊 782
	妨 784
④	肪 1351
	紡 1563
	訪 783

109 月

	月 17
④	明 106
⑥	朗 1628
⑧	朝 91
	期 690

110 欠

	欠 659
②	次 660
④	欧 554
	炊 1311
⑦	欲 1124
	軟 1308
⑧	欺 1623
	款 1624
⑩	歌 200
⑪	歓 1132

111 殳

③	投 282
	役 609
④	殴 1625
⑤	段 608
⑥	殺 610
⑦	設 611
	殻 1626
⑨	殿 1093
	毀 2043
⑩	穀 1627

112 犬

	犬 319
③	状 829
⑧	献 1181
⑩	獄 1518
⑫	獣 1864

113 卆

④	枠 510
	砕 1550
⑥	粋 1069
⑦	酔 728

114 分

	分 26
⑥	紛 1298
	粉 1557

115 亢

③	抗 747
	坑 1925
⑥	航 649

116 反

	反 362
②	仮 1141
③	坂 605

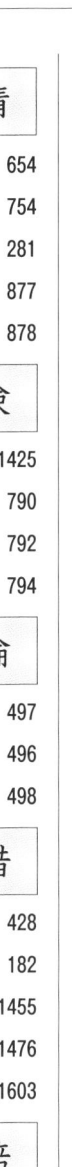

■□　③ トップ（Top）　190-248

【2画】

一 192
① 亡 582
② 六 6
　方 43
　文 320
③ 市 547
　玄 1276
④ 交 504
　衣 889
　充 1275
　妄 1696
⑤ 忘 209
⑥ 夜 93
　京 233
　卒 306
　育 879
　盲 1278
　享 1772
　斉 1779
⑦ 変 222
　帝 1066
　亭 1652
　哀 1804
⑧ 高 83
　恋 1078
　畜 1274
　衰 1805
⑨ 産 574
　率 615
　商 684
　斎 1781
⑩ 蛮 1825
⑪ 裏 436
　棄 1653
⑫ 豪 1277
⑬ 褒 1933

193 八
② 今 27
　介 695
③ 令 998
④ 会 59
　全 160
　企 701
⑤ 余 959
　含 1290
⑥ 金 21
　食 131
　命 997
　念 1117
　舎 1654
⑧ 倉 1112
⑩ 傘 1655

194 八
　八 8
② 分 26
　父 73
　公 323
⑤ 谷 458
⑦ 盆 1314
⑧ 釜 1965
⑨ 貧 859

195 冖
② 冗 468
③ 写 194
⑦ 軍 778
　冠 1656
⑧ 冥 2122

196 十
① 土 22
② 支 368
③ 古 86
⑤ 克 1374

⑥ 直 220
　南 41
⑧ 真 242
　索 1301
⑩ 喪 1807

197 ム
③ 台 532
　弁 1116
⑥ 参 294
⑦ 怠 1698

198 丷
④ 羊 488
⑤ 弟 76
⑥ 並 221
⑦ 前 29
　首 393
　美 673
⑧ 差 674
　益 921
　兼 1324
⑩ 着 190
　普 427
　尊 479
　善 676
⑪ 義 493
　慈 1778
⑬ 養 675

199 卜
① 上 31
③ 占 1016
⑥ 卓 1030
⑦ 点 399
　貞 1764

200 マ
② 予 403
③ 矛 955

⑦ 勇 1154
　柔 1310

201 ク
④ 色 316
　争 361
　危 789
⑤ 角 716
⑥ 免 941
　負 717
⑦ 魚 485
　亀 2003
⑩ 象 939

【3画】

202 口
② 兄 75
　号 442
④ 足 171
　呈 1657
　呉 1926
　呂 2020
⑥ 品 683
⑦ 員 395

203 土
② 去 309
③ 寺 328
④ 赤 46
　走 177
⑤ 幸 894

204 士
　士 755
③ 吉 893
④ 売 187
　声 619
　志 756
　壱 1911

205 夂
② 冬 99
③ 各 851
④ 条 750

206 大
　大 87
① 太 124
⑤ 奇 1292
　奔 1819
　奈 1947
⑪ 奪 1407
⑬ 奮 1406

207 宀
③ 安 84
　字 528
　守 537
　宅 538
　宇 1252
　宛 2039
④ 完 817
⑤ 定 289
　官 540
　宝 576
　実 672
　宗 816
　宙 1253
　宜 1658
⑥ 客 318
　室 331
　宣 850
⑦ 家 52
　案 305
　害 785
　宴 849
　宮 929
　容 1123
　宰 1659

　宵 1907
⑧ 宿 326
　密 1103
　寄 1120
　寂 1380
　寒 120
　富 629
⑩ 寝 127
　寛 1379
　塞 2119
⑪ 察 475
　寧 1378
　寡 1660
　蜜 1957
⑫ 寮 1183
　審 1661
　賓 1662
⑬ 憲 787

208 ⺌
③ 当 402
　光 464
④ 肖 1811
⑤ 尚 1810
⑦ 党 710
⑧ 常 708
　堂 709
⑨ 掌 1677
⑫ 賞 711

209 ⺍
④ 労 443
⑤ 学 50
⑥ 単 359
　栄 1188
⑦ 挙 1189
⑧ 蛍 1676
　巣 1862
⑨ 覚 208
　営 930

⑩ 誉 1713
⑭ 厳 1190

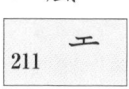
210 山
⑤ 岸 456
　岩 457
⑥ 炭 875
⑧ 崩 1663
　崇 1664
　崖 2008
⑨ 嵐 2007

211 工
⑦ 貢 1180

212 艹
　芝 568
　芋 1834
④ 花 314
　芸 566
　芳 1665
　芯 2026
⑤ 若 125
　英 155
　苦 342
　芽 1835
　茎 1836
　苗 1837
　茂 1840
　苛 2115
⑥ 茶 145
　草 567
　荘 1369
　荒 1666
　茨 1943
⑦ 荷 570
　華 1323
　菜 774
⑧ 著 1031
　菌 1368

菓 1667
菊 1833
萎 2118
⑨ 落 280
葉 569
葬 801
募 1155
葛 2011
⑩ 蓄 743
夢 800
蒸 802
墓 1156
幕 1157
蓋 2025
⑪ 暮 1158
慕 1668
蔑 2096
⑫ 蔵 1111
蔽 2052
⑬ 薬 315
薄 799
薦 1411
薫 1710
薪 1838
⑮ 藩 1890
繭 1941
藤 2012
藍 2013
⑯ 藻 1839

亡 213

亡 582
③ 妄 1696
④ 忘 209
⑤ 盲 1278

【4画】

日 214

① 旦 2038

② 早 117
④ 易 434
昇 1280
昆 1859
⑤ 星 463
冒 1669
是 1670
⑧ 暑 119
量 435
最 439
景 1021
⑪ 晶 1808
暴 1043
⑫ 曇 1281

木 215

⑤ 査 825
⑧ 森 460

止 216

止 217
④ 歩 176
肯 1403
⑧ 歯 702
⑨ 歳 703

火 217

④ 炎 1803

王 218

⑧ 琴 1906

⺰ 219

② 考 212
老 737
③ 孝 738
④ 者 148

⺜ 220

⑦ 貫 1714

爪 221

爪 1974
③ 妥 1332
④ 受 269
采 2089
⑨ 愛 1079
⑬ 爵 1875

圭 222

③ 麦 637
④ 青 47
表 437
毒 788
⑥ 素 636
⑦ 責 638

玄 223

② 充 1275
育 879
⑨ 棄 1653

【5画】

甘 224

④ 甚 1756

田 225

② 男 67
里 1025
④ 界 157
思 202
胃 1105
畏 2117
⑥ 異 1196
累 1302
⑦ 畳 1303
塁 1692

癶 226

④ 発 286
⑦ 登 472

禾 227

② 秀 1171
委 697
季 698
④ 香 1705

穴 228

穴 1122
③ 究 298
空 461
突 1121
④ 窃 1673
窓 231
室 1674
窟 2010
⑩ 窮 1675
窯 1900

立 229

② 辛 344
音 620
⑤ 竜 1867
産 574
章 1027
童 1026
⑧ 意 291

四 230

⑦ 買 188
⑧ 置 262
罪 1047
署 1316
⑨ 罰 1317
⑩ 罷 1671
罵 2098

⑭ 羅 1672

夫 231

奉 1678
④ 奏 1679
⑤ 泰 1680

⺍ 232

⑤ 党 710
常 708
堂 709
⑦ 掌 1677
⑩ 賞 711

⺌ 233

② 労 443
③ 学 50
栄 1188
⑥ 蛍 1676
⑦ 覚 208
営 930

羊 235

③ 美 673
差 674
⑤ 羞 2103
着 190
善 676
⑦ 義 493
羨 2090
⑨ 養 675

羽 236

⑤ 習 201
翌 492
⑪ 翼 1304

自 237

自 63
③ 臭 1285
息 1118
⑧ 鼻 1286

血 238

血 928
⑥ 衆 1194

西 239

③ 要 424
⑤ 票 1199
⑫ 覆 1686

篆 1983
⑨ 箱 1060
範 1061
箸 1963
⑩ 築 1056
篤 1683
⑫ 簡 358
⑬ 簿 1684
⑭ 籍 1058
⑯ 籠 2024

⑬ 覇 1685

曲 240

曲 625
⑦ 農 626
豊 628

亦 241

③ 変 222
④ 恋 1078
⑤ 蛮 1825

关 242

② 券 714
③ 巻 715

【7画】

辰 243

③ 唇 1794
辱 1795

采 244

⑤ 番 551

【8画】

隹 245

② 隻 1917
④ 集 224
焦 1385

⻗ 246

雨 232
④ 雪 842
雲 844
零 1063
⑤ 電 61
雷 843
霊 1687

竹 234

竹 374
④ 笑 251
第 354
符 357
笛 1681
⑥ 答 213
等 353
筆 355
筒 373
策 1057
筋 1059
⑦ 節 699
⑧ 算 356
管 539
箇 1682

⑥ 需 681
⑦ 震 847
　 霊 1688

⑨ 霜 1689
⑪ 霧 845
⑬ 露 846

247　非
④ 悲 341

⑦ 輩 1166

248　無
④ 無 400

⑦ 舞 981

■▫ 　4　ボ ト ム（Bottom）　249-299

【2画】

249　儿
② 元 245
③ 兄 75
④ 先 48
　 光 464
　 充 1275
⑤ 見 139
　 売 187
　 克 1374
　 児 1375
⑥ 免 941
⑧ 党 710
⑪ 寛 1379
⑮ 覧 1831

250　八
② 六 6
③ 穴 1122
④ 共 419
⑤ 貝 719
　 兵 994
　 呉 1926
⑥ 典 630
　 具 720
⑦ 貞 1764
⑧ 真 242
⑨ 黄 993
　 異 1196
⑭ 興 631
⑮ 翼 1304

251　力
　 力 173
④ 劣 1153
⑤ 男 67
　 労 443
　 努 827
⑦ 勇 1154
⑩ 募 1155
⑪ 勢 865

252　十
⑤ 辛 344
⑥ 卒 306
　 卓 1030
　 阜 1946
⑦ 草 567
　 卑 1770
⑧ 宰 1659
⑨ 率 615
　 章 1027
⑪ 準 614

【3画】

253　口
② 右 35
　 古 86
　 石 102
　 台 532
　 占 1016
　 司 1204
　 召 1691
③ 名 82
　 合 271
　 各 851
　 吉 893
　 舌 1288
　 后 1873
④ 言 203
　 谷 458
　 告 892
　 否 1006
　 君 1289
　 含 1290
⑤ 岩 457
　 舎 1654
⑦ 哲 1010
　 容 1123
　 唇 1794
⑧ 啓 1690
⑨ 喜 253
　 善 676
　 営 930

254　土
② 圧 1197
③ 至 1198
⑥ 型 1318
⑧ 基 691
　 堂 709
⑨ 堅 1228
　 塁 1692
　 堕 1693
⑩ 墓 1156
　 塗 1694
　 塑 1939
⑪ 塾 863
　 墨 1695
⑫ 墜 1218
⑬ 壁 1029
　 墾 1798

255　夂
④ 麦 637
⑥ 変 222
⑦ 夏 97
⑩ 愛 1079
⑫ 憂 1829

256　夕
　 夕 95
③ 多 104
⑩ 夢 800

257　大
② 央 706
⑤ 突 1121
⑥ 美 673
　 契 751
　 臭 1285
⑨ 奥 71
⑩ 奨 831

258　女
③ 妄 1696
④ 妥 1332
⑤ 妻 596
　 委 697
⑥ 要 424
　 姿 661
⑦ 宴 849

⑧ 婆 1902

259　子
③ 字 528
④ 孝 738
⑤ 学 50
　 季 698
　 享 1772

260　寸
③ 寺 328
　 守 537
④ 寿 1327
⑥ 専 797
⑨ 尊 479
　 尋 1326
⑪ 奪 1407
⑫ 導 480

261　山
③ 缶 920
⑤ 岳 1851
⑦ 島 455
⑧ 密 1103

262　巾
② 市 547
　 布 887
④ 希 888
⑥ 帝 1066
⑦ 帯 1065
⑧ 常 708
⑩ 幕 1157
⑫ 幣 1796

263　廾
② 弁 1116
④ 弄 2094
⑨ 葬 801
⑪ 算 356
　 鼻 1286
⑫ 弊 1797

264　小
⑥ 県 336

【4画】

265　心
　 心 172
③ 忘 209
　 志 756
　 忌 1697
　 忍 1775
　 芯 2026
④ 忠 758
　 念 1117
⑤ 思 202
　 怒 255
　 急 260
　 怠 1698
　 怨 2100
⑥ 恩 757
　 恐 759
　 恵 1077
　 恋 1078
　 息 1118
　 恣 2113

⑦ 悪 114
　 窓 231
　 患 1367
　 悠 1699
⑧ 悲 341
　 惑 1071
⑨ 意 291
　 想 392
　 感 431
　 愁 1700
　 愚 1701
　 慈 1778
⑩ 態 451
⑪ 慰 1702
⑫ 憲 787
　 憩 1287
⑬ 懇 1799
⑭ 懲 1703
⑯ 懸 450

266　小
⑥ 恭 1931
⑩ 慕 1668

267　手
　 手 170
⑥ 挙 1189
　 拳 1973
⑧ 掌 1677
⑪ 撃 1041
　 摯 2073

268　日
① 白 44

② 百 11
旨 1349
④ 者 148
昔 428
⑤ 春 96
⑥ 書 181
⑦ 曹 1930
曽 2120
⑧ 替 375
普 427
⑩ 暮 1158
暦 1720
⑪ 暫 1706

269 月
③ 肖 1811
④ 青 47
育 879
肩 1084
肯 1403
⑤ 背 1085
胃 1105
⑥ 骨 1104
脅 1707
脊 1988
⑨ 腎 1987

270 木
② 未 583
末 584
③ 来 133
条 750
④ 果 502
⑤ 染 908
栄 1188
柔 1310
架 1704
某 1759
⑥ 案 305
桑 1855
⑦ 菜 774
巣 1862
梨 1956
⑧ 葉 569
⑨ 業 307
楽 343
棄 1653
彙 2133
⑫ 薬 315
築 1056

271 水
⑤ 泉 840

272 火
③ 災 873
④ 炎 1803

273 灬
⑤ 点 399
為 736
⑥ 馬 484
烈 1708
⑦ 黒 45
鳥 486
⑧ 無 400
然 401
煮 1315
焦 1385
⑨ 蒸 802
照 868
煎 1967
⑩ 熊 2000
⑪ 熟 864
熱 866
黙 869
勲 1709
⑫ 薫 1710

274 王
① 主 70
玉 575
③ 呈 1657
⑤ 皇 579
⑦ 望 581
聖 580
⑬ 璧 2075

275 友
友 79
⑩ 髪 1359

【5画】

276 田
② 苗 1837
⑤ 留 432
畜 1274
⑦ 番 551
富 629
⑧ 雷 843
⑩ 繊 1951
⑪ 奮 1406

277 白
① 百 11
④ 皆 606
⑥ 習 201

278 皿
皿 927

① 血 928
④ 盆 1314
⑤ 益 921
⑥ 盗 268
盛 922
⑧ 盟 923
⑩ 監 925
盤 1313

279 目
③ 盲 1278
④ 省 389
首 393
看 1114
冒 1669
眉 1969
⑦ 着 190
⑧ 督 926

280 石
⑧ 碁 1828

281 示
示 814
③ 宗 816
祭 473
票 1199
禁 815
⑨ 察 475

282 立
⑥ 翌 492

283 正
正 407
⑪ 整 387

【6画】

284 糸
① 系 449
④ 素 636
索 1301
⑤ 累 1302
⑥ 紫 1711
⑨ 緊 1186
⑩ 繁 1187

285 羽
④ 翁 1937

286 虫
④ 蚕 1866
⑤ 蛍 1676
蛮 1825
⑧ 蜜 1957

287 衣
衣 889
④ 表 437
⑤ 袋 685
⑥ 装 1370
裂 1371
⑧ 製 686
⑯ 襲 1042

【7画】

288 見
⑤ 覚 208
⑩ 覧 1831

289 言
⑥ 誉 1713
⑦ 誓 1712
⑫ 警 476

290 豆
⑤ 登 472
⑥ 豊 628

291 豕
⑤ 象 939
⑦ 豪 1277

292 貝
② 負 717
貞 1764
員 395
③ 貢 1180
④ 責 638
貨 857
貧 859
貫 1714
貪 2067
⑤ 貸 183
買 188
貿 433
貴 855
費 858
賀 1019
⑥ 資 853
賃 856
⑧ 質 238
賛 376
賞 711
⑨ 賢 1227

293 車
② 軍 778
⑧ 輩 1166

294 辰
⑥ 農 626
⑧ 震 847

295 里
⑤ 量 435
童 1026

【9画】

296 音
⑪ 響 1023

297 食
⑧ 養 675

【10画】

298 馬
⑫ 驚 477

【11画】

299 鹿
鹿 1998
⑧ 麗 1832
麓 2009

■ ⑤ トップ・レフト （Top & Left） 300-307

【2画】

300 厂
② 反 362 ／ 厄 1721
③ 圧 1197
④ 灰 874
⑦ 厚 848 ／ 厘 1910
⑧ 原 405
⑫ 歴 704 ／ 暦 1720

301 ナ
② 友 79
③ 右 35 ／ 左 36

布 887
④ 有 347 ／ 存 587 ／ 在 588

【3画】

302 尸
① 尺 762
② 尼 1722 ／ 尻 1979
③ 尽 1726
④ 局 228 ／ 尾 1723 ／ 尿 1724
⑤ 屈 349 ／ 居 535
⑥ 屋 54
⑦ 展 1092
⑨ 属 1091
⑪ 層 1725
⑫ 履 1405

303 广
② 広 113 ／ 庁 541
④ 床 543 ／ 序 953
⑤ 店 55 ／ 府 337 ／ 底 745
⑥ 度 333
⑦ 座 175 ／ 席 332 ／ 庭 542 ／ 庫 544 ／ 唐 1727
⑧ 康 1054 ／ 庶 1413 ／ 麻 1414 ／ 庸 1728 ／ 鹿 1998
⑨ 廊 545 ／ 廃 1412
⑩ 廉 1729
⑪ 腐 1730
⑫ 慶 1732

【4画】

304 戸
戸 534
③ 戻 1201
④ 房 1082 ／ 肩 1084
⑥ 扇 1733
⑧ 雇 1083 ／ 扉 1734

【5画】

305 疒
④ 疫 1735
⑤ 病 229 ／ 疲 275
症 1363 ／ 疾 1736
⑥ 痕 1993
⑦ 痛 346 ／ 痢 1737 ／ 痘 1929 ／ 痩 1982
⑧ 痴 1738
⑨ 瘍 1992
⑫ 療 1362
⑬ 癖 1364 ／ 癒 1739

【6画】

306 虍
② 虎 1999
③ 虐 1740
⑤ 虚 1741
⑦ 虜 1884 ／ 虞 1940
⑨ 慮 1377 ／ 虜 1742

【11画】

307 麻
麻 1414
④ 摩 1415
⑤ 磨 1731
⑩ 魔 1418

■ ⑥ レフト・ボトム （Left & Bottom） 308-315

【3画】

308 夂
④ 廷 1211
⑤ 延 689
⑥ 建 1055

309 辶
② 込 961 ／ 辺 962
③ 巡 1743 ／ 迅 1744
④ 近 109 ／ 返 184
迎 1133
⑤ 述 963 ／ 迫 964 ／ 迭 1745
⑥ 送 206 ／ 逃 283 ／ 退 348 ／ 逆 386 ／ 追 966 ／ 迷 1070
⑦ 通 204 ／ 連 299 ／ 速 383 ／ 途 960
造 965 ／ 逐 1216 ／ 透 1746 ／ 逝 1747 ／ 逼 1938
⑧ 週 163 ／ 進 267 ／ 逮 1048 ／ 逸 1748
⑨ 道 66 ／ 遅 118 ／ 遊 196 ／ 過 284 ／ 運 304
達 384 ／ 遍 1177 ／ 遇 1178 ／ 遂 1217
⑩ 遠 110 ／ 違 385 ／ 遣 1214
⑪ 適 657 ／ 遮 1749 ／ 遭 1750
⑫ 選 264 ／ 遺 1179 ／ 遵 1751 ／ 遷 1896
⑬ 還 1215 ／ 避 1365

【4画】

310 辶
⑩ 遜 2064 ／ 溯 2083

【7画】

311 走
走 177
② 赴 1075
③ 起 128
⑤ 越 1073 ／ 超 1074
⑧ 趣 310

312 麦
麦 637
⑨ 麺 1958

【8画】

313 免
免 941
② 勉 140

【9画】

314 是
是 1670
⑨ 題 327

【10画】

315 鬼
鬼 1752
⑤ 魅 1419

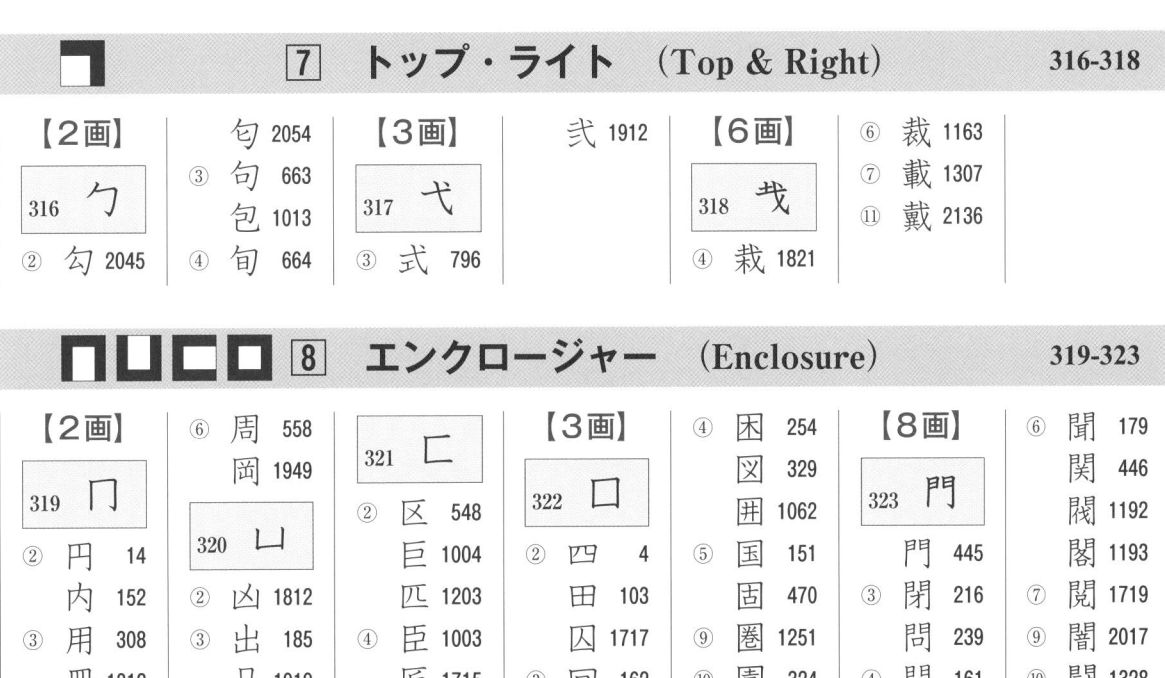

⑦ トップ・ライト （Top & Right）　316-318

【2画】　316 ク
② 勾 2045　句 2054　③ 句 663　包 1013　④ 旬 664

【3画】　317 弋
③ 式 796　弐 1912

【6画】　318 戈
④ 栽 1821　⑥ 裁 1163　⑦ 載 1307　⑪ 戴 2136

⑧ エンクロージャー （Enclosure）　319-323

【2画】　319 冂
② 円 14　内 152　③ 用 308　冊 1312　④ 同 350　肉 561　⑥ 周 558　岡 1949

320 凵
② 凶 1812　③ 出 185　凸 1919　凹 1920　⑥ 画 235

321 匸
② 区 548　巨 1004　匹 1203　④ 臣 1003　匠 1715　⑤ 医 325　⑧ 匿 1716

【3画】　322 囗
② 四 4　田 103　囚 1717　③ 回 162　団 366　因 406　④ 困 254　図 329　囲 1062　⑤ 国 151　固 470　⑨ 圏 1251　⑩ 園 324

【8画】　323 門
門 445　③ 閉 216　問 239　④ 間 161　開 215　閑 1718　⑥ 聞 179　関 446　閥 1192　閣 1193　⑦ 閲 1719　⑨ 闇 2017　⑩ 闘 1328

⑨ ソリッド （Solid）

【1画】
一 1　乙 1908

【2画】
七 7　八 8　九 9　十 10　人 15　力 173　入 186　刀 441　了 818　又 1762

【3画】
上 31　女 68　子 69　大 87　小 88　夕 95　山 100　川 101　口 167　寸 367　工 379　凡 467　干 506　丸 591　弓 592　己 632　与 713　才 739　久 1097　及 1098　丈 1272　刃 1774　巾 2021

【4画】
日 16　月 17　火 18　水 19　木 20　中 33　少 105　止 217　犬 319　牛 483　王 577　夫 595　欠 659　氏 744　井 1064　片 1143　肌 1345　丹 1813　弔 1815　斤 1914　斗 1918　牙 2002

【5画】
本 37　生 49　母 74　世 156　半 159　目 168　立 174　甘 345　以 420　必 423　民 536　申 585　由 623　史 705　皿 927　氷 1095　永 1096　皮 1144　旧 1376　甲 1816　且 1922　井 1964

【6画】
自 63　耳 169　竹 374　糸 409　虫 466　羽 491　州 553　米 562　良 602　曲 625　舟 646　求 933　卵 1135　兆 1269　串 1962　臼 1975

【7画】
車 62　束 382　身 394

【8画】
東 39　長 89　事 237　非 707　承 819　武 1165

【9画】
昼 92

【10画】
鬼 1752

【11画】
粛 1824　爽 2074

【12画】
幾 408

【15画】
器 682

語彙索引
（Vocabulary Index）

All the vocabulary contained in this book is listed in *a-i-u-e-o* order with the corresponding *kanji* number under which they appear.

くまもとけん［熊本県］ 2000	くんとう［薫陶］ 1526	けいとう［傾倒］ 1173	けつあつ［血圧］ 928
くみあわせ［組み合わせ／組合せ］ 635	ぐんばつ［軍閥］ 1192	げいにく［鯨肉］ 915	けついん［欠員］ 659
くみたてる［組み立てる］ 635	ぐんび［軍備］ 613	けいば［競馬］ 1020	けつえき［血液］ 928
くみちょう［組長］ 635	くんよみ［訓読み］ 951	けいばつ［刑罰］ 1052	けつえきじゅんかん［血液循環］ 1387
くみん［区民］ 548	くんりん［君臨］ 1289	けいはんしんちほう［京阪神地方］ 233	けっか［結果］ 502
くも［雲］ 844	くんれん［訓練］ 296, 951	けいひ［経費］ 858	けっかく［結核］ 986
くもつ［供物］ 418		けいび［警備］ 476	けっかん［血管］ 928
くもり［曇り］ 1281	**け**	けいふ［系譜］ 1583	けっかん［欠陥］ 1522
くもる［曇る］ 1281	〜け［〜家］ 52	けいぶ［軽侮］ 1801	げっきゅう［月給］ 618
ぐもん［愚問］ 1701	け［毛］ 490	けいべつ［軽蔑］ 2096	けっきょく［結局］ 228
くやしい［悔しい］ 1219	けい［刑］ 1052	けいぼ［敬慕］ 1668	けっきんとどけ［欠勤届］ 1090
くやむ［悔やむ］ 1219	けいい［敬意］ 478	けいほう［警報］ 476	けつごう［結合］ 302
くら［蔵］ 1111	けいい［経緯］ 1570	けいほう［刑法］ 1052	けっこん［結婚］ 302, 303
くら［倉］ 1112	けいえい［経営］ 930	けいむしょ［刑務所］ 1052	けっこん［血痕］ 1993
くらい［暗い］ 107	けいえいしゃ［経営者］ 930	けいもう［啓蒙］ 1690	けっこんいわい［結婚祝い］ 1018
くらい［位］ 417	けいえん［敬遠］ 478	けいやく［契約］ 751	
くらす［暮らす］ 1158	けいおうぎじゅくだいがく［慶應義塾大学］ 863, 1732	けいゆ［経由］ 515	けっこんしき［結婚式］ 796
くらべる［比べる］ 276	けいかい［警戒］ 1334	げいゆ［鯨油］ 915	けっさい［決済］ 516
くらやみ［暗闇］ 2017	けいがいか［形骸化］ 1991	けいようし［形容詞］ 1123	けっさく［傑作］ 1431
くり［庫裏］ 544	けいかく［計画］ 235, 288	けいらん［鶏卵］ 1863	けっして［決して］ 277
くりかえす［繰り返す］ 902	けいかん［警官］ 476	けいり［経理］ 515	けつじょ［欠如］ 1441
くる［来る］ 133	けいき［契機］ 751	けいりか［経理課］ 669	けっしょう［結晶］ 1808
くるう［狂う］ 1513	けいき［景気］ 1021	けいりゅう［渓流］ 1843	けっしん［決心］ 277
くるおしい［狂おしい］ 1513	けいぐ［敬具］ 478	けいりん［競輪］ 498	けっせき［欠席］ 332, 659
くるしい［苦しい］ 342	けいけん［経験］ 515, 793	けいれき［経歴］ 515, 704	けっせきとどけ［欠席届］ 1090
くるしむ［苦しむ］ 342	けいこ［稽古］ 2131	けいれつこがいしゃ［系列子会社］ 449	けっそく［結束］ 382
くるしめる［苦しめる］ 342	けいご［敬語］ 478	けいろうのひ［敬老の日］ 478	けつだん［決断］ 900
くるま［車］ 62	けいこう［傾向］ 1173	けうな［希有な］ 347	けってい［決定］ 277, 289
くれない［紅］ 1295	げいごう［迎合］ 1133	げか［外科］ 150, 565	けっていてきな［決定的な］ 277
くれる［暮れる］ 1158	けいこうぎょう［軽工業］ 116	けがす［汚す］ 907	けっぱく［潔白］ 753
くろ［黒］ 45	けいこうとう［蛍光灯］ 1676	けがれた［汚れた］ 907	げっぷ［月賦］ 1585
くろい［黒い］ 45	けいこうとりょう［蛍光塗料］ 1676	けがわ［毛皮］ 1144	けつぶつ［傑物］ 1431
くろう［苦労］ 342		げかん［下巻］ 715	けっぺきな［潔癖な］ 1364
ぐろう［愚弄］ 2094	けいこく［渓谷］ 458, 1843	げき［劇］ 1140	けつぼう［欠乏］ 860
くろうと［玄人］ 15, 1276	けいこく［警告］ 476	げきじょう［劇場］ 1140	げつまつ［月末］ 584
くろじ［黒字］ 45	けいさい［掲載］ 1011, 1307	げきぞう［激増］ 1039	げつようび［月曜日］ 17
くわ［桑］ 1855	けいざい［経済］ 515, 516	げきつい［撃墜］ 1218	けつれつ［決裂］ 1371
くわえる［加える］ 295	けいさつ［警察］ 475, 476	げきてきな［劇的な］ 1140	けつろん［結論］ 302, 496
くわしい［詳しい］ 944	けいさつしょ［警察署］ 1316	げきど［激怒］ 255	けねん［懸念］ 450
くわだて［企て］ 701	けいさつちょう［警察庁］ 541	げきどう［激動］ 1039	けはい［気配］ 246
くわだてる［企てる］ 701	けいさん［計算］ 356	げきやく［劇薬］ 1140	けびょう［仮病］ 1141
くわばたけ［桑畑］ 1855	けいじ［掲示］ 814, 1011	げきりゅう［激流］ 1039	げひんな［下品な］ 683
くわわる［加わる］ 295	けいじ［刑事］ 1052	げこ［下戸］ 534	げぼく［下僕］ 1241
ぐん［郡］ 552	けいじ［慶事］ 1732	けさ［今朝］ 27, 91	けむい［煙い］ 1045
ぐん［軍］ 778	けいしき［形式］ 796	げさく［戯作］ 1901	けむし［毛虫］ 466
ぐんか［軍靴］ 995	けいしちょう［警視庁］ 476, 541	げざん［下山］ 100	けむり［煙］ 1045
くんこう［勲功］ 1709	けいじどうしゃ［軽自動車］ 116	げし［夏至］ 97, 1198	けもの［獣］ 1864
ぐんこくしゅぎ［軍国主義］ 778	けいじばん［掲示板］ 814, 1011	けしき［景色］ 316, 1021	げり［下痢］ 1737
くんしゅ［君主］ 1289	けいしゃ［傾斜］ 1173	けしゴム［消しゴム］ 219	ける［蹴る］ 2059
ぐんしゅう［群集］ 489	げいじゅつ［芸術］ 566	げしゃ［下車］ 32	けわしい［険しい］ 790
ぐんしゅう［群衆］ 489	けいしょう［軽傷］ 835	げしゅく［下宿］ 326	けん［県］ 336
ぐんしゅうしんり［群集心理］ 489	けいしょう［警鐘］ 1607	げじゅん［下旬］ 664	〜けん［〜県］ 336
	けいしょく［軽食］ 116	けしょう［化粧］ 414, 1284	けん［件］ 482
ぐんしゅく［軍縮］ 884	けいぞく［継続］ 211, 901	けしょうしつ［化粧室］ 1284	〜けん［〜軒］ 508
ぐんじゅさんぎょう［軍需産業］ 681	けいそつな［軽率な］ 116, 615	けしょうひん［化粧品］ 1284	けん［剣］ 791
	けいだい［境内］ 152, 1036	けす［消す］ 219	〜けん〜［〜兼〜］ 1324
ぐんじゅひん［軍需品］ 681	けいたいでんわ［携帯電話］ 1486	げすい［下水］ 32	〜げん［〜軒］ 508
くんしょう［勲章］ 1709		げすいこう［下水溝］ 1499	げん［験］ 793
ぐんじん［軍人］ 778	けいちょう［慶弔］ 1815	けずる［削る］ 1320	げん［弦］ 1446
くんせい［薫製］ 1710	けいてき［警笛］ 1681	けた［桁］ 2042	けんあくな［険悪な］ 790
ぐんそう［軍曹］ 1930	けいと［毛糸］ 490	げだつ［解脱］ 293	けんあん［懸案］ 450
ぐんたい［軍隊］ 778, 779	けいど［経度］ 515	けたはずれ［桁外れ］ 2042	げんあん［原案］ 405
	けいとう［系統］ 449		けんい［権威］ 1333

し

そくざに [即座に]	700	そんけい [尊敬]	478, 479
そくじに [即時に]	700	そんげん [尊厳]	1190
そくしん [促進]	1170	そんざい [存在]	587, 588
ぞくす(る) [属す(る)]	1091	そんしつ [損失]	396
ぞくせい [属性]	1091	そんしょく(が)ない [遜色(が)ない]	2064
そくせいさいばい [促成栽培]	1170	ぞんじる [存じる]	587
そくせき [足跡]	1587	そんだいな [尊大な]	479
ぞくぞくと [続々と]	211	そんちょう [村長]	364
そくたつ [速達]	384	そんちょう [尊重]	479
そくてい [測定]	810	そんとく [損得]	643
そくど [速度]	333, 383	そんみん [村民]	364
そくばく [束縛]	1569	**た**	
そくめん [側面]	809	た [田]	103
そくりょく [速力]	383	たい [隊]	779
そげき [狙撃]	2056	だい [台]	532
そこ [底]	745	～だい [～台]	532
そこなう [損なう]	396	だい～ [第～]	354
そこね [底値]	745	だい～か [第～課]	669
そし [阻止]	1519	だい～かん [第～巻]	715
そしき [組織]	635, 882	だい～しょう [第～章]	1027
そしつ [素質]	636	だい～じょう [第～条]	750
そしょう [訴訟]	1207, 1208	たいい [大尉]	1882
そぜい [租税]	1893	たいいく [体育]	879
そせん [祖先]	824	だいいちに [第一に]	354
そぞう [塑像]	1939	だいいちにんしゃ [第一人者]	
そそぐ [注ぐ]	290		354
そそのかす [唆す]	1433	たいいん [退院]	230, 348
そだいゴミ [粗大ゴミ]	1560	たいいんれき [太陰暦]	1720
そだつ [育つ]	879	だいえいていこく [大英帝国]	
そだてる [育てる]	879		155
そち [措置]	1476	たいおん [体温]	839
そっきょう [即興]	631, 700	だいおんじょう [大音声]	619
そつぎょう [卒業]	306, 307	たいかい [大会]	59
そつぎょうしき [卒業式]	796	たいがい [大概]	1161
そつぎょうせい [卒業生]	306	たいかく [体格]	165
そっきん [側近]	809	たいがく [退学]	348
そっちょくな [率直な]	220, 615	だいがく [大学]	50, 87
そで [袖]	2022	だいがくいん [大学院]	230
そと [外]	150	たいかこうぞう [耐火構造]	
そとぼり [外堀]	1260		1618
そなえる [供える]	418	たいがん [対岸]	456
そなえる [備える]	613	たいかんしき [戴冠式]	2136
そのあと [その後]	30	だいかんみんこく [大韓民国]	
そのご [その後]	30		1954
そのた [その他]	415	たいき [大気]	246
そのほか [その他]	415	たいきおせん [大気汚染]	
そふ [祖父]	824		907, 908
そぼ [祖母]	824	だいきぎょう [大企業]	701
そぼくな [素朴な]	1529	たいきけん [大気圏]	1251
そまつな [粗末な]	1560	だいぎし [代議士]	755
そむく [背く]	1085	だいきぼな [大規模な]	1160
そむける [背ける]	1085	たいきゃく [退却]	348, 1616
そめる [染める]	908	たいきゅうせい [耐久性]	1618
そやな [粗野な]	1560	たいきん [大金]	87
そよかぜ [そよ風]	465	だいきん [代金]	413
そら [空]	461	だいく [大工]	379
そらす [反らす]	362	たいぐう [待遇]	1178
そる [反る]	362	たいくつな [退屈な]	348, 349
そろうな [疎漏な]	1502	たいけい [体系]	449
そん [損]	396	たいけん [体験]	793
そんがい [損害]	785	たいこ [太鼓]	1827
そんがいばいしょう [損害賠償]	712, 1642	たいこう [大綱]	1566
たいこく [大国]	87, 151	たいはん [大半]	159
だいこくばしら [大黒柱]	990	だいひょうてきな [代表的な]	437
だいこん [大根]	974	たいふう [台風]	532
たいさ [大佐]	1002	だいぶつ [大仏]	416
たいざい [滞在]	1402	だいぶぶん [大部分]	53
だいざい [題材]	740	たいへいよう [太平洋]	917
たいさく [対策]	1057	たいへんな [大変な]	222
だいさんしゃ [第三者]	148, 354	たいほ [逮捕]	1048, 1049
たいし [大使]	199	たいほう [大砲]	1631
たいじ [胎児]	1544	たいぼく [大木]	20
たいした [大した]	87	たいほじょう [逮捕状]	1048
たいして [大して]	87	だいほん [台本]	532
だいじな [大事な]	237	たいま [大麻]	1414
たいしゃ [大赦]	1897	たいまん [怠慢]	653, 1698
だいじゃ [大蛇]	1861	だいみょう [大名]	82
たいしゃく [貸借]	182, 183	だいめい [題名]	327
たいじゅう [体重]	115	たいよう [太陽]	124, 834
たいしゅうぶんか [大衆文化]	1194	たいようけい [太陽系]	449
たいしょ [対処]	1212	たいようれき [太陽暦]	1720
たいしょう [対象]	939	たいらな [平らな]	351
たいしょう [大小]	87, 88	だいり [代理]	413
たいしょう [代償]	712	たいりく [大陸]	833
たいしょうてきに [対照的に]	868	たいりつ [対立]	363
だいじょうぶ [大丈夫]	87, 1272	たいりょうせいさん [大量生産]	435
だいじょうぶっきょう [大乗仏教]	135	たいりょうの [大量の]	435
だいじん [大臣]	1003	たいりょく [体力]	165, 173
たいしんこうぞう [耐震構造]	1618	たいわ [対話]	363
だいず [大豆]	87, 471	たいわん [台湾]	910
だいすきな [大好きな]	244	たうえ [田植え]	678
たいせい [大勢]	865	だえき [唾液]	906, 1984
たいせいよう [大西洋]	917	たえず [絶えず]	734
たいせき [退席]	348	たえる [絶える]	734
たいせき [体積]	886	たえる [耐える]	1618
たいせき [堆積]	2014	たえる [堪える]	1758
たいせつな [大切な]	250	たおす [倒す]	225
たいぜんと [泰然と]	1680	たおれる [倒れる]	225
たいそう [体操]	1485	たか [多寡]	1660
たいそう [大層]	1725	たかい [高い]	83
だいそつ(しゃ) [大卒(者)]	306	だかい [打開]	771
だいたい [大体]	165	だがし [駄菓子]	1610
だいたいエネルギー [代替エネルギー]	375	たかまる [高まる]	83
たいだな [怠惰な]	1460, 1698	たがやす [耕す]	1782
たいだん [対談]	390	たから [宝]	576
だいたんな [大胆な]	1344	たからもの [宝物]	576
たいちょう [隊長]	779	たき [滝]	1841
だいちょう [大腸]	1106	たきぎ [薪]	1838
たいてい [大抵]	746	たきぎのう [薪能]	1838
たいど [態度]	451	たきつぼ [滝壺]	1841
だいとうりょう [大統領]	999, 1000	たきにわたる [多岐にわたる]	1443
だいどころ [台所]	149, 532	だきょう [妥協]	1332
だいにじ(せかい)たいせん [第二次(世界)大戦]	360	たく [炊く]	1311
たいねつガラス [耐熱ガラス]	1618	だく [抱く]	1012
たいのう [滞納]	1402	たぐい [類い]	563
たいはいてきな [退廃的な]	1412	たぐいまれな [類いまれな]	563
たいばつ [体罰]	1317	たくえつした [卓越した]	1030
		だくおん [濁音]	1511
		たくじしょ [託児所]	1574
		たくす [託す]	1574
		たくせん [託宣]	1574
		たくち [宅地]	538
		たくはいびん [宅配便]	538

字形構成素チャート (Component Chart)

① レフト（Left）

2 亻1	冫2	忄3	**3** 口4	土5	夕6	女7	孑8	山9	川10	工11
巾12	幺13	弓14	彳15	忄16	扌17	氵18	斗19	犭20	阝21	**4** 方22 日23
月24	木25	歹26	火27	牛28	王29	礻30	**5** 田31	目32	矛33	矢34 石35
禾36	立37	牙38	衤39	艮40	**6** 米41	糸42	耒43	耳44	至45	舌46 舟47
虫48	良49	并50	臼51	肖52	**7** 臣53	角54	言55	谷56	豆57	豸58 貝59
足60	身61	車62	酉63	釆64	里65	君66	**8** 金67	青68	食69	幸70 卓71
京72	**9** 革73	音74	倉75	**10** 馬76	骨77	竟78	**11** 魚79	雀80		

② ライト（Right）

1 し81	**2** 几82	刀83	刂84	力85	匕86	十87	卩88	厶89	又90	丁91
3 口92	寸93	己94	干95	彡96	阝97	亍98	才99	及100	也101	勹102
4 戈103	支104	夂105	斗106	斤107	方108	月109	欠110	殳111	犬112	卆113 分114
亢115	反116	尺117	少118	艮119	区120	**5** 生121	田122	白123	皮124	召125 合126
台127	圣128	令129	包130	主131	司132	乍133	且134	申135	由136	**6** 羊137 羽138
聿139	舌140	艮141	色142	虫143	寺144	各145	交146	毎147	戋148	朱149 兆150
7 見151	谷152	豕153	辛154	辰155	里156	兌157	余158	甫159	束160	疋161
8 長162	隶163	隹164	青165	僉166	侖167	昔168	音169	直170	非171	帚172
9 頁173	扁174	俞175	軍176	単177	易178	复179	**10** 韋180	鬼181	冓182	
11 鳥183	曽184	責185	商186	**13** 義187	蔓188	梟189				

③ トップ（Top）

1 一190	丿191	**2** 亠192	人193	八194	冖195	十196	厶197	丷198	卜199	マ200
ク201	**3** 口202	土203	士204	夂205	六206	宀207	屮208	⺍209	山210	亐211 艹212
亡213	**4** 日214	木215	止216	火217	王218	耂219	毋220	⺌221	圭222	去223